For Joe,
with gratitude and
best wishes,

Jan

ID0984814

Lord Byron's Strength

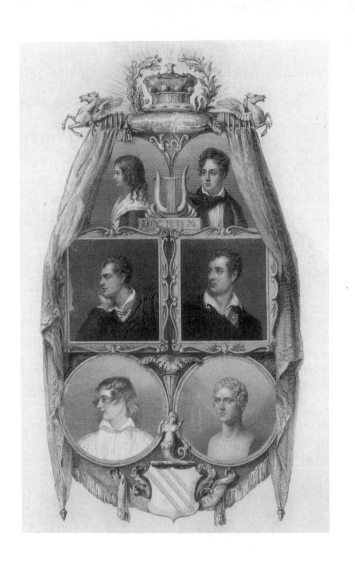

Lord Byron's Strength

Romantic Writing and
Commercial Society

JEROME CHRISTENSEN

The Johns Hopkins University Press
Baltimore and London

This book has been brought to publication with the generous assistance of the National Endowment for the Humanities.

The Johns Hopkins University Press
701 West 40th Street, Baltimore, Maryland 21211-2190
The Johns Hopkins Press Ltd., London

LIBRARY OF CONGRESS CATALOGING-IN-PUBLICATION DATA

Christensen, Jerome, 1948–
    Lord Byron's strength : romantic writing and commercial
    society / Jerome Christensen.
        p.   cm.
    Includes bibliographical references and index.
    ISBN 0-8018-4355-3 (alk. paper). — ISBN 0-8018-4356-1
    (pbk. : alk. paper)
    1. Byron, George Gordon Byron, Baron, 1788–1824 – Criticism and interpre-
tation.   2. Literature and society – England – History – 19th century.   3. Authors
and readers – England – History – 19th century.   4. Aristocracy (Social class) in
literature.   5. Authority in literature.   6. Romanticism – England.   I. Title.
PR4388.C54 1992
821.7-dc20   92-3975

Frontispiece: Six portraits of Byron on one plate. National Portrait Gallery, London.

For Kate and Elizabeth,
this book and my love, entire and undivided

*He is a lordly writer, is above his own reputation, and condes-
cends to the Muses with a scornful grace!*

        William Hazlitt, "Lord Byron"

*Those who limp are the discoverers; inclination is the begin-
ning of the world.*

        Michel Serres, The Parasite

Contents

Acknowledgments xi

Introduction xiii

1. Theorizing Byron's Practice: The Performance of Lordship
and the Poet's Career 3

2. A Genealogy of Morals: An English Bard, Scotch Reviewers,
and a Wicked Uncle 32

3. Sex, Class, and the Naked Letter of Romance: *Childe
Harold I* and *II* and the Separation 49

4. Perversion, Parody, and Cultural Hegemony: The Moment of
Change in the Oriental Tales 88

5. The Speculative Stage: *Childe Harold III* and the
Formation of Byron 142

6. The Shaping Spirit of Ruin: *Childe Harold IV*   185

7. The Circumstantial Gravity of *Don Juan*   214

8. Two Dramatic Case Studies: *Marino Faliero* and *Sardanapalus*   258

9. Annals of a Line Undone: What Matters in the
English Cantos of *Don Juan*   300

Notes   365

Index   419

Acknowledgments

A project that has taken as long as this one to reach its majority owes its life to the credit of many. It is not possible here even to acknowledge, let alone pay back, all those who, over the years, have extended me their good will and given me their suggestions. I would like to thank my colleagues Sharon Cameron, Frances Ferguson, Jonathan Goldberg, Neil Hertz, and Ronald Paulson, who, as always, have been sympathetic listeners and shrewd readers. Susan Wolfson made valuable comments on Byron texts of mutual concern. Robert Gleckner, Max Schulz, and Joseph Wittreich have generously provided both the kind of support called moral and the kind of support that gets leave time. The few former graduate students who are acknowledged here are representatives of the several seminars whose spirited engagement with this material has been a continual and invigorating challenge to my powers. During a year's sojourn in Ithaca, Reeve Parker and Mary Jacobus provided welcome ears and offered even more welcome suggestions. In one of many conversations in which he offered encouragement and advice, Paul Elledge donated an insight on the English Cantos of *Don Juan* that, for better or worse, compelled me to modify my interpretation from the ground up. My chief debt is to Peter Manning, whose criticism of Byron, at once impeccable and searching, humane and unsentimental, is the beacon by which I have navigated. Having said that, however, I have said very little about how much Peter has meant to this project. His friendship and counsel have sustained it and me from beginning to end.

I want to acknowledge my general debt to three formidable works of scholarship and criticism: Leslie A. Marchand's *Byron: A Biography*; Jerome J. McGann's *"Don Juan" in Context*; and Edward W. Said's *Beginnings: Intention and Method*. Although Peter Linebaugh's *The London Hanged: Crime and Civil Society in the Eighteenth Century* appeared too late for me to use, it provides a valuable social context for the argument in my final chapter on *Don Juan*.

I am grateful to Johns Hopkins University for leave time to pursue my research. I would also like to thank the John Simon Guggenheim Foundation and the National Endowment for the Humanities for their support of the research and writing of this book. The Society for the Humanities at Cornell University showed me considerable hospitality during the last stages of composition. I am grateful to the editors of *Literature and the Body: Selected Papers of the 1986 English Institute*, *SAQ*, *ELH*, and *Studies in Romanticism*, where earlier versions of chapters 3, 4, 5, and 1 and 8 respectively appeared.

My thanks to Eric Halpern, Kimberly F. Johnson, and Martha Farlow of the Johns Hopkins University Press, and to Mary Yates and Alexa Selph, for their help in working manuscript into print.

Finally, my loving thanks to Carol Burke, for her constant faith, for her unstinting patience, and for her criticism, wisely and affectionately alloyed.

Introduction

In his introduction to a selection of Lord Byron's poems for the Golden Treasury series (1881), Matthew Arnold endorsed Algernon Swinburne's observation that Byron's power "lies in 'the splendid and imperishable excellence which covers all his offences and outweighs all his defects: *the excellence of sincerity and strength.*'" Under Arnold's sponsorship the criterion of sincerity had a long life, but its span was ostensibly closed in 1973 by Lionel Trilling's flinty *Sincerity and Authenticity.* In his 1989 essay "Byron's Twin Opposites of Truth," however, Jerome J. McGann, Byron's best modern critic, revived the standard of sincerity and with it the genteel definition of Romantic poetry as a mode of discourse that "presents itself as artless and premeditated." Concede his premise, and it becomes an easy matter for McGann to follow the path of ideology critique staked out in *The Romantic Ideology* (now signposted as *Towards a Literature of Knowledge*) and expose Romantic poetry's supposed self-presentation as hypocritical, its so-called paradigm as illusory.

But why concede a premise that, on the face of it, distorts the way such poems as *The Rime of the Ancient Mariner*, *The Prelude*, or "Adonais" present themselves? Why countenance a version of Romantic poetry that was concocted by the quarterly reviewers, petted into maturity by Arnold, coddled in its old age by David Perkins, and embalmed by Trilling? It is one thing to acknowledge such a monster; it is quite another to resuscitate the thing and to embrace it before once again killing it off. Perhaps it should be no surprise that a historicist criticism, which is significant precisely to the extent it can persuasively deploy its rhetoric of demystification in endless adjustments of the literary text to the social real, should make its peace with Arnold's criterion of sincerity. Sincerity, the rhetorical corollary of the standards of "epistemological clarity and self-knowledge" that McGann affirms, has been and remains the sign under which Romantic writing is conquered for the regime of truth.

As ally in his exposure of Romantic hypocrisy McGann enlists Byron, whose work, he claims, "is significant precisely to the extent it deploys its rhetoric of sincerity in highly resistant poetic forms." My engagement with Lord Byron differs. It presumes no dualism of rhetoric and form, soul and body, truth and falsehood, poet and work. It takes as its device not sincerity but the other trait that Arnold mentions, strength. Although Arnold repeats Swinburne's claim that sincerity and strength are combined in one "imperishable excellence," in his rendering the marriage of the two entails the eclipse of one. The *welcome* eclipse. For Arnold, intent on tailoring Lord Byron to the canon of English literature, appreciating the poet's strength in the last quarter of the nineteenth century meant registering its decline:

> The hour of irresistible vogue has passed away for him; even for Byron it could not but pass away. The time has come for him, as it comes for all poets, when he must take his real and permanent place, no longer depending upon the vogue of his own day and upon the enthusiasm of his contemporaries. Whatever we may think of him, we shall not be subjugated by him as they were; for, as he cannot be for us what he was for them, we cannot admire him so hotly and indiscriminately as they.

Byron *had* strength, has some strength still, but not, thankfully, enough to subjugate. Fashion, Arnold observes with some rue, has dominion over strength. Yet fortunately, if fashion rules, canon formation overrules. It does so dialectically, by exploiting the underlying economy that fashion opportunely codes. There is so little time; thus time is precious. There is so little space; thus space is precious. For Arnold strength has become an aureate remnant, rare and plastic, which can be packaged and reproduced for the lasting pleasure, instruction, and profit of a broader readership.

To a darker mind Arnold's benefaction, the extraction and refinement of Byron's poems to fit them to the "reality" of changing taste, looks a great deal like a dismemberment—a slightly more principled version of the editorial "gelding" of his poems to which Byron vehemently objected during his lifetime. Such dismemberment, it might be suspected, is the precondition for the alchemical transformation of the textual body into antique gold. Gilding requires gelding. From that perspective Arnold's linkage of strength with sincerity makes sense as a way of curtailing strength by subjecting it to a feeling that by definition can be fully comprehended by the critic. Once comprehended as sincere, the poetry can neither surprise nor subjugate; and its strength can be displayed and vended to the public as a treasure, in a volume something like that in which Donna Inez had a mutilated Martial presented to the young and impressionable Don Juan.

That Arnold conceived of his mission hieratically, as an endeavor to sanctify and thereby control the eruptions of what *Don Juan* calls "natural history," explains his wary exploitation of the resource of Byron's strength, yet even for Byron's most alertly appreciative contemporaries—for Francis Jeffrey in the *Edinburgh Review* as for Walter Scott in the *Quarterly Review*— praise of Byron's strength was decidedly ambivalent. And for good reason. Strength—for the time being let us describe it as a creatural capacity to take consequential action—had not thrived under the attentions of the doctors of enlightenment. As concept and as attribute strength had been the target of the same dissolvent analysis as had the concepts of substance in epistemology, intrinsic value in economics, and aristocracy in social thought. *Political economy* is the name I shall use for the powerful ensemble of those strategies of enlightenment designed to demonstrate what Maurice Dobbs (in *Theories of Value and Distribution since Adam Smith*) has called "a mechanism within the affairs of men, with which uncomprehending meddling of sovereign or statesmen was incompatible." In a journal entry of 1801 Francis Horner, one of the founders of the *Edinburgh Review* (1802), the most important vehicle for the promulgation and application of the principles of political economy, itemizes its "various branches" as "the general principles of population, the theory of national wealth including an illustration of the doctrine of free trade as well as of the circulation of money, regulations with respect to the poor, plans for the education of the lower classes, for a system of preventive police, &c." The *&c* marks all that follows, now and in the future, from the extension of political economy's "general principles." It does not include, Horner indicates, the "theory of government," which "compared with the investigations of political economy . . . is at all events of secondary consideration, and perhaps of subordinate importance." The *perhaps* is generous. Political economy, the systematic elaboration of what J. G. A. Pocock calls "commercial humanism" and the precursor to the dominant nineteenth-century ideologies of Marxism and economic liberalism, was not only the scientific explanation of how wealth is produced; it entailed the claim that the scientific explanation of the production of wealth should rule the disciplines that aim at description or modification of human activity. Political economy is the assertion that economics, not politics, is the law of last resort. It presupposes the fundamentally antidemocratic claim that the urge to get and spend rather than the drive to dominate or assert—to stake claims—governs the behavior of individuals as well as that of nation-states.*

In her book *On Violence* Hannah Arendt proposes a definition of strength that vividly distinguishes it from force, power, and authority. "*Strength*," she writes, "unequivocally designates something, an individual entity; it is the property inherent in an object or person and belongs to its character, which may prove itself in relation to other things or persons, but is essentially independent of them." In the liberal tradition that runs from Joseph Addison to David Hume to Adam Smith and that ramifies through Mary Wollstonecraft, Benjamin Constant, Henry Brougham, Francis Horner, and John Cam Hobhouse, the singularity and independence of strength was made fully accountable: theoretically, strength was subjected to inference, statistics, and the rule of opinion; practically, what passed for strength, such as a noble title or a readiness to duel, was capitalized on for the sake of money or prestige. This was preeminently the case with the literary system of Byronism, which was collaboratively organized in the second decade of the nineteenth century by coding the residual affective charge that still clung to the paraphernalia of aristocracy in order to reproduce it in commodities that could be vended to a reading public avid for glamour. Empiricism reduced strength to mere cause; industrialism disciplined cause to mass production; commercialism subordinated production to a pervasive, unappeasable demand. The commercial society imagined in the eighteenth century and realized in the wake of Waterloo was (and this is true whether we consult J. G. A. Pocock, or Neil McKendrick, or Martin

---

*In the body of the text I shall also refer to the ideological enterprise of classical political economy by the name of *Hume*. I have forborn extensive reference to my book *Practicing Enlightenment: Hume and the Formation of a Literary Career* (Madison: Univ. of Wisconsin Press, 1987), but the reader should know that any time Hume is mentioned corroborative argument can be found in that volume.

Meisel, or Colin Campbell, or Michel Foucault) a regime of effects without agents. Under the administration of political economy strength was, in effect, accorded the status of the spleen in Max Weber's anecdotal illustration of functionalism's cognitive protocol: "Sec. 10. The spleen. Of the spleen, gentleman, we know nothing. So much for the spleen."

This book conducts a Romantic argument with political economy and with functionalist accounts of poetry. It attempts to rehabilitate poetic strength from its derogation as an imaginary, retrograde, or eclipsed quality. We can watch the eclipse move across the face of Romantic verse in Keats's makeshift *Sleep and Poetry*, which at first brilliantly vaunts that poesy is "the supreme of power; / 'Tis might half slumb'ring on its own right arm," but which almost immediately turns Byronophobic and dimly recants:

> But strength alone though of the Muses born
> Is like a fallen angel: trees uptorn,
> Darkness, and worms, and shrouds, and sepulchres
> Delight it; for it feeds upon the burrs,
> And thorns of life; forgetting the great end
> Of poesy, that it should be a friend
> To sooth the cares, and lift the thoughts of man.
> (ll. 236–37; 241–47)

It is true that in his strength Byron forgets Keats's "great end," the humane, the sedative destiny of poetry. Nonetheless, Lord Byron's strength is not "strength alone." My argument here follows the lead of Nietzsche (himself in Byron's train), who revived a conception of aristocracy as eventful deed rather than as a class united by interest, constated by economic indices, and subject to the vicissitudes of public credit. Strength does not await the conferral of credit; it commands it. And commands it nowhere in English poetry as with Byron, whose very name is fledged by the family motto, *Crede Byron.* As I read it, Lord Byron's career is the allegory of that imperative's residual strength in an age when the grounds of authority have been disclosed as being no more than nominal: authority derived from distinction, distinction the function of opinion, and opinion concocted by the powers that be.

The characteristic questions that Lord Byron puts to himself are, "What does it mean that I am noble? What does it mean to be one who *deserves* that name I have been given? On what basis do I command belief in my right to command?" To be strong (to merit the given name) is to be capable of repeatedly posing those questions and, moreover, of answering them differently each time. The strong poet answers not so much with a rightness that fits the occasion (that would be a historicist standard) but with a rightness that decides the occasion (and that, I take it, is a rhetorical standard). What distinguishes the strong poet from the strong man, then, is the transformation of a creatural capacity for consequential action into a rhetorical capacity for consequential action (because it is radically creatural and therefore taken without regard to persons, such action may appear criminal or violently satirical). What distinguishes the Romantic poet from all others (and this is the application that Romanticism makes of the baroque, that Byron makes of *Hamlet,* and that I make of Walter Benjamin) is the assertion that the creatural, in all the degraded outcastness of its relentlessly allegorical and ineradicably political destiny, *is* the rhetorical.

Although I aim to recover Byron's strength, it is far from my intention to argue that strength is the "twin opposite" of sincerity. To introduce a term that I shall elaborate later, strength is not in opposition to sincerity but in *ap*position. The apposition of one term to another involves a separation, not a divorce; it is a supplementary relation in which the distinction of a new word appears as its *bearing* on a previous one. In the chapters that follow I shall advance alternative names for the quality strength, themselves in apposition: *lordship, notability, secret impulse, untamed impulse, addendum, differend.* Mobility among terms may be provisionally justified by Lord Byron's own notorious mobility among moods and kinds. Byron's abjection of one matrix or site of meaning in order to link to another is itself the exertion of strength. I do not claim, however, that mobility is a virtue in itself. Indeed, the peculiar torsion of Byron's career following the success of *Childe Harold: A Romaunt* suggests the moral that once the aristocratic poet has been successfully packaged for popular consumption, reconstituted into what Marx called the "double form" of the commodity, there can be no virtue in itself. What holds the various terms together, site after site, is a distinctive and irrepressible disposition to invention, an ethos that is manifested in all Byron's writing and vigorously endorsed in his later poetry. It is in his invention that his strength appears. And it is as an ethos of invention that his poetry matters.

Byron writes in the slow fade of that landed substance that had been the resort of virtue; his writing nonetheless challenges the hegemony of enlightened self-interest, which rules the court according to the same dispensation by which "Cash rules the grove." Ethics, as I understand it and as Byron enacts it, is the deployment of a politics without rule or prescription and with no standing place except the site of a strong assertion. What makes this assertion a *site,* a locus of invention, rather than merely a trope, another turn in the great grammar of available moves in the language game, is that it is a *cite:* a topos or (the word I shall favor) a *commonplace.* Byron asserts the commonplace in the face of the parceling out of the everyday into an array of specialist discourses and in resistance to the technosterilization of the language. Even though the commonplace is something we've all heard before, there is nothing nostalgic about its assertion: the commonplace is not a recollection that belongs to Byron, whether house or heart, but an address that finds its respondent in anyone who claims the right to answer. In the post-Enlightenment deficit of substance the performance of lordship involves the conquest of the grounds of one's own distinction; consequently and by the way, this lord's writing (such is the distant goal of my argument) materializes a common basis in English for the virtue of democratic assertion. The Romantic poet—and Lord Byron *primus inter pares*—is always, in Alasdair McIntyre's resonant phrase, after virtue. So is the Romantic reader. And so is this book.

The Romantic poet is after virtue, not after truth. "Truth," in the words of the narrator of *Don Juan,* is "in a well." Though confessing to a "lurking bias," even urged as by a "secret prepossession," narrator and poem refuse to take the fatal plunge. If it is true, as Michael McKeon has argued in *The Origins of the English Novel, 1600–1740,* that "the deep and fruitful analogy between questions of truth and questions of virtue . . . is the enabling foundation of the novel," it may be that the rejection of that analogy, which is the hallmark of Byron's strongest writing, attests to a resistance to the novelization that was exemplified for him by his rival Walter Scott, urged on him by his publisher John Murray, and projected on him by Mikhail Bakhtin. In the writing of Lord Byron, that is, what McKeon has called the "persistence" of aristocracy and of romance—those "preexistences" that antithetically impel the dialectical itinerary of the novel as an instrument of middle-class emergence and self-justification—becomes the *resistance* of an aristocrat and a Romantic to the dialectic as the engine of change and as the master trope of historical being. Such residual writing, unfit for foundational analogies (and here I am thinking particularly of the last, great, spirited cantos of *Don Juan*), is an afterlife that haunts the ramparts of modernity and that lays claim to no anchorage in any social reality except the one it virtuously reinvents.

The story this book tells begins with an engagement between the lordly author of *Hours of Idleness* and his *Edinburgh* reviewer. That engagement occurred in an unmapped social space, one that was neither forum nor stage. The first two chapters examine the way that conflict between poet and reviewer became a contest to determine how the conflict would be charac terized, whether as a legal struggle between plaintiff and defendant that would observe a judicial protocol and be decided within a courtroom, or as a duel that would elaborate its punctilio outside the city walls and beyond the jurisdiction of burgher and king. Both metaphors had their appeal (indeed, each dialectically involves the other). Neither fits. In part that failure of fit symptomatized the repression of a frank acceptance by both disputants that the market is the appropriate rubric for contests that are actually economic exchanges; but in part that repression of the market reflected a significant and volatile difference between cultural conflict and financial competition. In the wake of the public failure of traditional metaphors to fit and enlightened ones to be fully adopted, a new figure emerged on the contemporary scene as the figure *of* the contemporary. That figure—the collaborative invention of a gifted poet, a canny publisher, eager reviewers, and rapt readers—became the culturally dominant and economically profitable phenomenon called "Byron." "Byron" diagnosed and publicized the need that it answered: the need for a hegemonic metaphor that would resolve conflicts embedded in questions of national, sexual, and social identity that were as yet unspeakable. As Edmund Burke's idea of the theater did its duty in a time when the threat to stability could be projected abroad as a carnival of Jacobinical abstraction, so did the figure of Byron find its *raison d'être* in another foreign threat, this time one whose challenge was massive, focal, and concrete: Napoleon Bonaparte.

Byronism was a signally effective weapon for a commercial society to deploy in competition with an ambitious and potent regime founded by military conquest and sustained by despotism. In the aftermath of Waterloo Byronism took on an imperial dimension, which reached its fullest scope in *Childe Harold IV.* This empire conspicuously began to unravel with the publication of *Don Juan*, which, in apposition to Byronism, addressed a strong, ethical challenge to the murmurous complacencies of commercial society. Even in such a thumbnail account I would not be understood as positing a movement to a new stage of development or a sudden access of consciousness that occurs between *Childe Harold* and *Juan*: the mind that awakens to its woes in Byron is an *imperial* consciousness. It is one effect of *Juan* to disable the Byronic claims of increasing comprehensiveness and to discard the conception of stages. *Juan* involves what Francis Jeffrey called the "overshading" of character onto poet, poet onto poem, poem onto reader, time after time. In its unwinding *Juan* renders as strengths what had appeared as a farrago of unseemly idiosyncrasies in the earlier poetry: opacities in diction, hobbles in versification, irregularities in orthography, strained constructions, ink stains. And in doing so, *Juan* infiltrates our reading of the earlier poems, challenging our presuppositions of autonomy and reference. With *Juan*, in *Juan*, and through *Juan*, the Regency lord makes his uneasy peace with a postmodern ethic; Byron becomes a text. The narrative task I undertake is to give a more or less chronological account of a poetic career that makes increasingly legible a preponderant yet volatile anachronism that contests the hegemony of the clock and bids us do likewise.

Romanticism appears as a fundamentally social poetry in a world where the very socius is at stake (think of it as the gap between a status society and a class society, or between a monocultural and multicultural society, or between the old world order and the new variant). Insofar as Romanticism holds together, then as now, it coalesces as a writing about how things or persons (or things *and* persons) hold together. The ancient answer is, "By sacrifice." And as every Englishman knows (by *Englishman* I mean readers of Edmund Burke), it is an answer that was spectacularly renewed for modernity by Jacobinism. Both in their sublime and in their demotic styles the Romantic writers assailed the logic of sacrifice, called Molochism by both Byron and Coleridge. But Romanticism extends its critique of sacrifice beyond the targets of the Enlightenment into enlightenment itself—and not the dismantled heavenly city of the philosophes but the triumphant enlightenment of the political economists and the ministers who balance power, those who descend from Hume and Smith and who, wise in their generation, count Burke as one of their own.

The challenge to sacrificial logic is as fundamental to Romantic writing as its ink. I shall argue that it is the ethical strength of Lord Byron's rejuvenant text to combat sacrificial logic, whether applied to characters as if they were people or to people as if they were characters. Although the contestation of sacrifice is thematized in the great texts of British Romanticism—Wordsworth's Salisbury Plain poems, Byron's *Cain*, Shelley's *Prometheus Unbound*—such writing cannot be quarantined in any body's work; it has no logic of its own, presupposes no settled vocabulary from which comfortably to launch critiques. The distinction of Romantic writing does not inhere in its contingent and repeatedly embarrassed claims to transcendence (monotonously reducible to some maneuver for partisan advantage or increase of market share). Its distinction, supremely performed by *Don Juan*, is the inveterate compounding of what is meant with that with which sovereign intention has nothing in common except the link forged in the act of writing. What has been invidiously labeled Romantic subjectivization, corroborated by isolated passages from the *Biographia Literaria* or *The States-man's Manual* or *The Prelude*, is in practice a resistance to the objectification—whether as hero or victim, individual or class, homo or hetero, capitalist or commodity—that is the trope by which the logic of sacrifice operates within commercial society.

Resistance to objectification integuments Romantic practice. Insofar as the following engagement with Lord Byron's strength answers any questions, it refers them not to the poem that is, or the class that rules, or the reader who receives, or the individual who counts, but to the hand writing—writing understood not as a strategic determination but as a tactical positioning. As a work of poststructuralist biographical criticism, the aims of this book harmonize with those that Anthony Giddens, in *The Constitution of Society*, set for his theory of structuration: to acknowledge the "essential importance of a concept of action" and to "elaborate a satisfactory account of the competent and knowledgeable human agent" without "relapsing into a subjectivist view, and without failing to grasp the structural components of the social institutions which outlive us." I will not promise no relapses here, but I withhold that promise confident in the faith that none is necessary, that the feared fall cannot be complete because the subjectivist view is blindly vulnerable to the mattering of the signifier whose eccentric and inexorable itinerary is its Romantic biography.

Since the publication of *Anxiety of Influence* in 1973, the concept of poetic strength has been associated with the stirring criticism of Harold Bloom, for whom "figures of capable imagination" are defined by their strenuous attempts to clear a creative space for themselves within a poetic history "held to be indistinguishable from poetic influence." Romanticism, according to Bloom, became itself by finding itself inescapably committed to that agon. Bloom's strong poet is a marvelously articulate, fully paranoid construction. Of the poet, Bloom writes, "The poem is *within* him, yet he experiences the shame and splendor of *being found* by poems—great poems—*outside* him. To lose freedom in this center is never to forgive, and to learn the dread of threatened autonomy forever." Consider Bloom's strong poet as an ego reacting in tropical horror to the thought of ever being unthought or unthinking. Consider the ego as a machine for making poetry. Consider that Lord Byron is omitted from Bloom's canon. Perhaps because the omission is the condition for Bloom's own Byronic eloquence. Perhaps because the Byronic text already represents the paranoid scenario as a stage *within* the Byronic career and, moreover, specifies that stage as being the inevitable correlative of the conceit that a career *has* stages, or what Bloom calls "ratios." I shall explore that conceit as it is elaborated in *Childe Harold*

III and *IV* and investigate some of its attendant cultural implications in chapters 5 and 6 below.

Bloom's version of the strong poet has been embraced as a model for contemporary liberalism by Richard Rorty, who in *Contingency, Irony, and Solidarity* argues that "an ideally liberal polity would be one whose culture hero is Bloom's 'strong poet' rather than the warrior, the priest, the sage, or the truth-seeking, 'logical,' 'objective' scientist." In a Carlylean take on Bloom's precedent, Rorty harnesses this hero to the task of exemplifying the way "we liberals," having awakened to find ourselves groundless, must imagine ourselves strong poets, inventing ourselves and our radically contingent world. Rorty argues that "the human self is created by the use of a vocabulary rather than being adequately or inadequately expressed in a vocabulary" and claims that this description of the way things are assimilates "what was true in the Romantic idea that truth is made rather than found." His conclusion, that "the only way to trace home the causes of one's being as one is would be to tell a story about one's causes in a new language," is surely appealing; it opens up Bloom's paranoid scenario to a Pisgah view of the de-divinized terrain of *Don Juan*.

But Rorty does not cross over. Instead, he attempts to enlist Bloom in the liberal project without taking on the illiberal freight of his "heroic dualism." Yet his solution of adding a mitigating and mitigated Freud to his composite picture of the liberal does not succeed; it merely produces a more domesticated version of Bloom's dualism, renamed as the split between the private and the public, between the intellectual and the nonintellectual, and between force and persuasion. As an attempt to socialize the gnostic Bloom, Rorty's maneuver is a weak one. Even a cursory acquaintance with the history of debate about the liberal shibboleths that are meant to anchor those partitions, words such as *obligation, contract,* and *consent,* ought to persuade that the divisions are not self-evident. Moreover, even if in the political economy of modern life there were unanimous agreement about the necessity for lines that rule off the region of the private from the public—lines that would enable one to balance the power of each, and that would regulate boundary crossings—the decisions about where to draw such lines and of who gets to draw them are irreducibly political. In the preface to *Childe Harold IV* Byron announces his decision to desist from drawing the line between himself and Harold because it had been "unavailing." We might take that announcement as an example of the problem of drawing a line, in public or in private, between the public and the private. But it is also the case that preface and poem prove that the decision to draw no line is equally unavailing. Lines will be drawn time and again; and the late Byron lessons us that nought guarantees that such marking will observe the liberal protocol segregating word and deed. Indeed, as I argue, the lines that the supremely negligent Lord Byron inadvertently draws are *fault lines* that unsettle the claims to legitimacy and hegemony implicit in the names *English literature*, *Great Britain*, *we liberals*, and *Byron* itself.

A similar resistance constrains liberal receptiveness to the arrival of the new. In Rorty's sunny view, a "liberal society is one whose ideals can be fulfilled by persuasion rather than force, by reform rather than revolution, by the free and open encounters of present linguistic and other practices with suggestions for new practices." It is hard to see how anybody could find fault with this, but it is similarly hard to imagine how being persuaded of its truth could make much difference. In *Rethinking Modern Political Theory* John Dunn has issued a strong retort to what might be called the conversational strain of liberal thought:

> To see society as a whole simply as a facility for the provision of individually acceptable experiences and to seek to reconstitute it in imagination so that it can furnish these to the largest possible degree will only be a morally commanding vision where the experiences which individuals happen to find acceptable have already been rendered . . . reasonably unrevolting to each other or where the force of human values has been so devastated that the idea of a vision possessing the force of *moral* command has become utterly incoherent.

It is a fundamental claim of this book that Lord Byron's writing is neither conversational nor suggestive in the Rortyan sense; Byron's text strongly insists on the coherence of moral command past all the criteria of liberal reason, an insistence that follows a trajectory from the given motto *Crede Byron* to the rhetorical invention of *Don Juan*. *Don Juan* instaurates a new practice without recourse to the self-legitimating artifice of a novel vocabulary, some new and improved jargon, such as Byronism once was. Lord Byron's strength reflects neither the blind faith of the despot that his dictates will be met with unquestioning obedience nor the assurance of the expert that his prescriptions will be followed with docile compliance; it reflects the confidence of the English speaker that his address will be answered—an answer that will not necessarily be in kind, but that can and will occur because of something in common.

Don Juan can move from canto to canto as from strength to strength in the repeatedly tested confidence that on some fond commonplace reader and writer rely. That ethic has no foundation. *Juan* finds what Quintilian called a "basis" for its continual invention (which is its life) in the commonplace, words that matter inevitably, though not invariably, words that matter for each man and woman, though not for all humanity. The rhetoric of the commonplace is not subject to the metaphysical options of the one word or the two; it is enfranchised by an English of resonantly pregnant compounding. That compounding is acknowledged by Coleridge in the *Biographia Literaria* as the paronomasia that is the mothering dynamic of linguistic change; that compounding is uttered by *Juan* as its revolutionary landspeech; Romantically conceived, that compounding is the elementing form of social life.

A new speech (or so the Romantic holds) must arrive as something other than a generalized "suggestion." If it matters, the new arrives with the insistence by which the letter emerges and subjugates sense. As a command perhaps. Maybe an intimation. Or merely a drift:

> My drift I fear
> Is scarcely obvious.

The lines epitomize Romantic resistance to objectification. They disclose that iterative blindness that will prevent a relapse into what Giddens calls a "subjective view." Does the second line resolve *drift* as meaning *meaning*, or does it gently mock the fear of the "I" (the fear that in Bloom's reckoning *is* the "I") of a drift that may never fully mean, never fully find a vocabulary? Do the lines *have* a drift, or do they merely *drift?* Are these words or a deed? Do the lines draw the line? This passage was written by Wordsworth, not Byron. I offer it as an example of what the two writers have in common: a talent for drift, a gift for unfolding the matter of a saying. That drift is one of those commonplaces which, in the irreversible loss of the given world, those writers had Romantically to invent.

Lord Byron's Strength

Abbreviations

BLJ *Byron's Letters and Journals*, ed. Leslie A. Marchand, 12 vols. (Cambridge, Mass.: Harvard Univ. Press, 1973–82).

CPW *Lord Byron: The Complete Poetical Works*, ed. Jerome J. McGann, vols. 1–5 (Oxford: Clarendon Press, 1980–86).

HVSV *His Very Self and Voice: Collected Conversations of Lord Byron*, ed. Ernest J. Lovell (New York: Macmillan, 1954).

RR *The Romantics Reviewed: Contemporary Reviews of British Romantic Writers*, ed. Donald H. Reiman, part B, 5 vols. (New York: Garland, 1972).

References to the *Spectator* are to George Aitken's 8-volume edition (London: Nimmo, 1898).

1

Theorizing Byron's Practice

The Performance of Lordship and the Poet's Career

My Muse despises reference.
Don Juan, *canto 14*

Lord Byron's remark has a contemporary ring. Romantic indulgence in indeterminacy is a conspicuous feature of what has been called the "deconstructive turn." Indeed, given our particular literary-historical position, Byron's skepticism may be less striking than his aristocratic avowal of contempt. If his evasion of reference identifies Lord Byron's Romanticism, his contempt expresses his strength. However expressed, that strength, I shall argue, is irreducible; it is not to be explained away by referring it to some desperate defense, say clinamen or kenosis, by deriving it from some set of social or political circumstances, or by deciphering some unspeakable secret, whether it be incest or homosexuality. *Lord* marks Byron's privilege, and in part it is a privilege to confound reference.

Romantic Strength versus Empirical Force

Lord Byron's contempt is not without an object. "Reference" has a referent. The pith of the view that Lord Byron despises was put by David Hume, who in the *Treatise of Human Nature* pronounces that "we can form no wish which has not a reference to society. . . . Whatever other passions we may be actuated by . . . the soul or animating principle of them all is sympathy; nor would they have any force, were we to abstract entirely from the thoughts and sentiments of others."[1] For Hume and for the political economy he launched, force does not belong to the individual as virtue or capacity; force, strength generalized, is a property of someone only insofar as he sympathizes with someone else. Sympathy is the affective correlative of the systematic relation that constitutes and regulates what Charles Levin has aptly called the "sociological ego," which displaces "the burden of universality away from categories of things and substances, and onto categories of relationality."[2] Force is an effect of that social field, to be referred to a grammar that itself has no referent.

The contrast between Humean force and Byronic strength corresponds to Michel Foucault's distinction between a juridical notion of power in which "power is taken to be a right, which one is able to possess like a commodity, and which one can in consequence transfer or alienate," and a power that "is neither given, nor exchanged, nor recovered, but rather exercised, and that . . . only exists in action, [a power] that is above all a relation of force."[3] I reserve the term *power* for the juridical or Humean notion and apply *strength* to the executive. Despite Foucault's intervention, *Humean* remains apt because it was Hume who first made the case that the difference between power and strength is an epistemological, not an ontological, one.[4] In his essays Hume describes the relations between the executive and the juridical as a relation between the particular and the general (e.g., a past and the historical present, an aristocratic body and the monarcho-bourgeois subject); and he displays the technique by which the power of the general can be *derived* from a particular strength, which is then subordinated to the status of illustration or inert fact.

After Hume the perfection of this inductive technique, the protocol of juridical power, became the business of a new, initially Scottish intellectual class, the enterprising ideologists of political economy (Henry Brougham, Francis Jeffrey, Francis Horner, et al.), whose organ was the *Edinburgh Review* and who understood power as dynamic—not as the simple *product* of derivation but as emergent in and as the very *process* of deriving, as the strategic movement (called refinement, abstraction, or generalization) from one level (grade, rank, class, epoch) to another.[5] Their precedent suggests that Foucault's definition ought to be supplemented by Michel Serres's description of power as the "passage from the local to the global."[6] Global dominion may be the end result of this passage; but power emerges in the specific historical act of engineering the passage to the global. Many of the political implications of the men of letters' strategy of enlightenment were played out by British imperialism in the nineteenth century. But there were also domestic advantages, which were fully exploited by the monarch and the commercial class, who, having historically combined to curtail the "friendships" of aristocrats, continued to hobble any strength not subject to king or coin.

Sequence and Commercialist Hegemony

The distinction between power and strength reflects a fundamental difference between a commercialist code based on the depletion of substance and the acceleration of reproduction and an aristocratic symbolic economy of expenditure.[7] Marcel Mauss has been the most influential theorist of the symbolic economy, as Hume remains the prototypical theorist of the political economy. Mauss's notion of the "enchanted" thing that obligates a response answers the empiricist's axiom that "there is nothing in any object, consider'd in itself, which can afford us a reason for drawing any conclusion beyond it."[8] For Hume nothing causes an effect; nothing in the thing *affords* us a reason—our cause, which is our capital, comes from elsewhere. The Maussian version of strength and the Humean notion of the disenchanted, commodified object reflect irreconcilable notions of sequence: for Mauss the thing is something that compels a return; for Hume the significance of the thing is owed to its relation to contiguous things. Hume reinvents the series as a pure succession of things that acquires coherence only according to an *observed* connection. Power neither inheres in the objects nor projects from the mind itself—power belongs to what makes connection possible, the elementary tropism that draws things together in iterable configurations (what he calls "compositions") rather than dispersing them randomly through the perceiving mind.

Seriality is of great consequence to Lord Byron's poetic career; it is both driving force and subject for meditation in *Childe Harold*, in the Oriental tales as they unfold from *The Giaour* to *The Corsair* to *Lara*, and, as Jerome J. McGann has demonstrated, in *Don Juan*.[9] Seriality was the engine driving Byronomania as that cultural and commercial phenomenon was collaboratively managed by Byron and his publisher, John Murray. Reconceiving sequence is the key to understanding how Byronism got started and how it was kept going. In order to specify how Byronism operated, I want to sketch one trajectory of liberal discourse on seriality, which represents not so much a context as a socioeconomic profile against which the silhouette of Byron can be ascertained.

The progenitor of Hume's theorization of sequence was Joseph Addison's *Spectator* papers, which owed their success to a rare appreciation of the efficacy of the series. The model is represented in number 10, where the Spectator identifies his audience as "all well-regulated families that set apart an hour in every morning for tea and bread and butter." He advises "them for their good to order this paper to be punctually served up, and to be looked upon as part of the tea equipage."[10] "Well-regulated" is both exact and nicely equivocal, for it deftly deploys the "always already" formulation that is a favorite device of empiricist rhetoric. What is to the mutual interest of the reader and the essayist is not the *cause* of regulation but the *match* that regulation instances. Only the well-regulated family reads the *Spectator*, but, as the equivoque argues, reading the *Spectator* identifies the well-regulated family. If it is one of the fundamental aims of the *Spectator* to correct the manners of its readers, it is also the case that the targeted family already has the manners requisite to a receptive reading of the *Spectator*. Addison's tableau is an especially elegant deployment of what I shall call the "regulative hypothesis." *Regulative* does double duty. While it is the content of the hypothesis to assume that properties or social phenomena are regular, it is the power of the hypothesis, its presumptive weight, to regulate: when it works, the regulative hypothesis makes what it finds.

"Reading" the *Spectator* is a sequential operation: first you buy it, then you position it, and then you regard it the way the Spectator regards the world. The *Spectator* finds its place with the "tea equipage," which inhabits exactly that marginal area between necessity and luxury that is the domain opened by domestic regulation and targeted by the Spectator's lively style. Tea, which flows through the eighteenth century like the Thames, is a constant, but tea things change according to the fashion that is the collaborative fantasy engineered by stimulated consumer and acquiescent producer. What fashion means in this context is what the *Spectator* means in this context: not just an expression of vanity or the indulgence of an irrational appetite for ornament, but a *regular* succession of alterations and refinements. Novelty is crucial, but the new is recognizable only when its appearance—whether in a distinct sheet six days a week or a fashion doll from France once a year or, later, a new line from Wedgwood once every six months—is predictable.[11] The possibility of putting a new *Spectator* punctually on the table every morning makes the paper fashionable and gives it its distinctive power.

The *Spectator*'s avowal of the ethos of fashion makes its claims to universality seem plausible; but it also explains why that universality could not be genuine. The limits appear most clearly in the essays (nos. 119 to 132) on the Spectator's sojourn in the country. These are parables of attenuation and disruption. In the country periodicity is for the first time experienced as a function of distance—especially so when geographical distance suddenly translates into a historical chasm. "If . . . we look on the people of mode in the country, we find in them the manners of the last age. They have no sooner fetched themselves up to the fashion of the polite world, but the town has dropped them, and are nearer to the first state of nature, than to those refinements which formerly reigned in the court, and still prevail in the country" (no. 119). The satiric thrust against the archaism of the gentry is familiar: their pretenses to fashion fit them only for ridicule. But that archaism is also a sign of the essayist's weakness—for the spacing that precludes rural fashionableness also curtails the circulation and hence the power of the *Spectator* itself. The periodical cannot spread its influence in a setting alien to the punctuality of the London bourgeoisie. Moreover, although it is necessary that fashion (both its market and its look) be designed according to an exclusion (not everyone can be fashionable— although it may be that everyone should want to be), the exclusion needs to be formalized according to a social or economic rule. The obstruction that Addison attempts to face down with charges of archaism attests to an unseen, *political* resistance to the extension of such a rule from the metropolis: specifically, the continuing Jacobite resistance to Whig hegemony. Fashion is Hanoverian: the accommodation of foreign influence (Paris dresses, German princes) into a regulated British system of succession. Resistance to fashion emanating from London reflects allegiance to a center of power elsewhere (the pretender in his Parisian exile) and represents the possibility of disputes that cannot be settled by reference to a single legal code. Without a true synchronism the archaic cannot be interred within the walls of a museum where it belongs;[12] until the formation of a unified inland market Jacobitism remains plausible as the imminent threat of an unspectated and resurgent past.

Elegant though it was in its conceptualization, the *Spectator* could not change the manners of Great Britain until the mails were routed in and Jacobitism was rooted out. And, according to Benjamin Boyce, "the man who did more than any other person in England between 1720 and 1760 to encourage the sending of letters, the one who with practical measures supported the example of Mr. Bickerstaff and Mr. Spectator," was Ralph Allen, who in 1720 acquired the contract for byway and crossroad letters.[13] Allen started out with nothing but political capital, obtained, it is said, as a result of his timely interception of Jacobite correspondence in 1715, which he loyally transmitted to General Wade, who used the intelligence therein to quell the Jacobite uprising in the West. Wade returned the favor with crucial political and financial support.[14]

Upon assuming his franchise Allen discovered that the lines on the map of England designating the conduits of transport bore little relation to the reality of crooks and crookedness. Allen found "promiscuous" sorting of letters; he found obliquities of conveyance that diverted letters from their proper channels, thereby disordering the proper sequence of postal charges; he found plain obstruction (correspondence was often dumped as waste paper without reaching its destination). Allen turned things around. He massively increased not only the profits of the byway and crossroad posts but also those of the country posts that ran through London. He succeeded because of the increased surveillance he was able to exercise as a result of the imposition of a grid on the tangled patches of illegal practices. That grid, in Allen's words, permitted him to trace the diversions of mail "fully and minutely thro' all their windings and then [to suppress] them all at once, by fixing barriers in those various parts where communications were open from one road, or from one branch of a road to another."[15]

Thus were the crooked paths straightened, but the straight paths still needed attention:

> And it was no wonder: for till a proper Check could be contrived, a *Check* of one Country Post Office upon another, things were still to be left to the consciences of the several Deputys: And the Consciences of the fraudulent goe on pretty much at the same rate . . . whither under penaltys or under none. These Checks Mr. Allen first conceived and renders [*sic*] practicable . . . ; He so contrived that every Postmaster on the same Road, in all the Branches in the same road, shou'd check and be checked, by every other: Nay further, this Security against frauds was extended even to operate reciprocally between the Postmasters on different Roads, by means of certain regulations.[16]

As a result of this system Allen's surveyors could detect the "earliest tendencies toward a fraudulent or mistaken attempt of deviating from the Established conveyance."[17] By ruthlessly obstructing illicit communication, by serializing the transmission of approved material, and by stamping out every sign of transgression, Allen compelled communication to adhere to a norm and to produce a profit. Thus triumphed the standard of propriety in eighteenth-century letters and the rule of fashion in eighteenth-century manners.[18]

By devising a self-watching system of representations, a system of serial and reciprocal checking that matched itself against itself, Allen the Tory was able virtually to eliminate the limits on the well-regulated household that bounded the ambition of Addison the Whig. The postal system established a pattern that, to the approval of the *Edinburgh Review*, was replicated by the national financial system to assure full regulation of the circulation of money between the provincial banks and the central bank of London.[19] Yet if Allen secured distribution, the problem of production, elided in the *Spectator*, remained to trouble the man of letters. That question is most ingeniously addressed by Hume in the *Treatise*, where in the course of arguing for the reliability of historical evidence (synecdoche in Hume's model for all evidence whatever) he argues that "the links are innumerable that connect any original fact with the present impression . . . yet they are all of the same kind, and depend on the fidelity of printers and copyists. One edition passes into another, and that into a third, and so on, till we come to that volume we peruse at present. *There is no variation in the steps.*"[20] Hume imagined that historical truth could be produced by the reproduction of facts or impressions. It is no accident that Hume takes as his example the events in the Roman Senate house on the Ides of March—a *locus classicus* of debates about virtue and right, violence and power—for Hume wants to demonstrate that he can do so offhandedly, without taking sides. He aims to show that there is nothing in the events that leads us to any conclusions beyond it—nothing in the man Caesar, nothing in the man Brutus. The past has lost its power over the present in our understanding that actual power to engineer belief lies not in the fasces or the knife but in the *capacity to repeat*.

"Production" as an independent causal category has, like "substance" before it, virtually vanished in the formulation of repetition as the fundamental determinant of belief and of belief as the force that through the market drives the commodity. This formula will be repeated again and again by the British man of letters, who enhances his discursive power insofar as he can place himself in a position to repeat, to be the one to write "and so on," or, in its Byronic rendition, "Hail Muse, et cetera" (*DJ* 3:1). Julia Kristeva has described modern poetry as an "artistic practice [that] is the laboratory of a minimal signifying structure, its maximum dissolution, and the eternal return of both."[21] The eighteenth-century man of letters inverts that strategic orientation: his *discursive* practice is the laboratory of a *maximal* signifying structure, its *minimum* dissolution, and the *periodic* return of both. As authority for the reversal, let me invoke Marx's great chiasmus from "The Eighteenth Brumaire of Louis Bonaparte" by which he discriminated the bourgeois revolution of the philosophes from the coming social revolution: "There the phrase went beyond the content; here the content goes beyond the phrase."[22] Marx's aphorism recalls the disproportion during the Enlightenment between the man of letters' avalanche of discourse and the glacial advance in widespread material well-being. Kristeva's emphasis on practice enables us to see this disproportion as a strategy on the ground or, rather, a strategy of the *fading* ground—a way of overlaying a patch of earth, a popular custom, or a song with a discursive web endlessly crisscrossing the vanishing substantive pretext. Content, the British man of letters knows, like land, is scarce and vanishing; and because there can never be enough to go around, it cannot be allowed to remain what it is. Because there is never enough land and because Britain can never again risk the paroxysm of civil war, there must be more and more phrases, more tedious (the more tedious the better) refinements of the georgic, ever more agricultural treatises, handbooks, surveys, and enclosures. For the irregular catastrophes inflicted by a savage nature not yet educated into Newtonian docility, for the spasmodic violence of aristocrats not yet gentrified, for the anarchic passions of a populace with spines not yet adjusted to the contours of a sofa, the man of letters endeavors to substitute the more reliable cycles of the market, the comings and goings of the post, and the reassuring stutter of innovation that is normal science.

Classing the Aristocracy

The middle class has finally stopped rising. Historians as diverse as Harold Perkin, Lawrence and Jeanne C. Fawtier Stone, J. C. D. Clark, J. V. Beckett, John Cannon, and Immanuel Wallerstein agree that the emergence of the bourgeoisie as a dominant class, which has ever been retreating farther back into the English past, did not in fact occur until at least 1820, perhaps not until 1832 or even the 1880s.[23] The postponement of middle-class dominion corresponds to a revived sense of the vitality, authority, and impermeability of the English aristocracy. This shift in the consensus has meant little change in the historical landscape, however, since the revaluation of aristocratic rule has accompanied a redefinition of aristocracy that includes not only titled peerage but also the landed gentry. The line between this conglomerated economic class and the bourgeoisie has surely been sharpened, but at the cost of blurring the partition between the peerage and the gentry. The gentrification of the aristocracy exploits the ambiguity of William Marshall's oft-cited postulate that "landed property is the basis on which every other species of material property rests; on it alone, mankind can be said to live, to move, and to have their being."[24] By the beginning of the nineteenth century the land that had been understood in republican terms as the basis for the aristocrat's projection of his virtue into the affairs of state was already becoming an economic precondition for membership in a social class.

Among the other available criteria for determining nobility, the principal category was "natural aristocracy." As J. G. A. Pocock has argued, the assertion of natural aristocracy coordinated with the "defence of a commercial order in politics, society and morality" and therefore was "invariably a defence of the Whig regime," which "was founded on an assumed identity of interests between a managerial landed aristocracy and a system of public credit."[25] In practice natural aristocracy ultimately refers not to those who have land but to those who, in a commercial society, are entitled to sit with their peers in the House of Lords. A peerage-oriented definition states that aristocracy "has for its intellectual or moral foundation the conviction that the inequalities or differences which distinguish one body of men from another are of essential and permanent importance."[26] *Essential* and *permanent* are not always harmonious adjectives, however. The support given to the permanence of inequality is attested to by Lord Byron, whose received opinions were Whig opinions: "In England none are strictly noble but peers—not even peers' Sons—though titled by Courtesy" (*BLJ* 7:25). Paradoxically, what is "essential," aristocratic honor, appears to be strictly a function of authoritative institutional recognition. Byron's stricture hearkens back to the duality of the honorific title of *gentleman*, which embraced both the gentleman of blood—one who, according to Bailey's *Dictionary* (1707) "receives his nobility from his ancestors, and not from the gift of any prince or state"—and the gentleman of rank who was ennobled by the sovereign and received a patent of arms.[27] Either way, the definition connects gentility with recognition by others; the gentleman does not make himself by his deed but illustrates himself by his manner. If made a gentleman by lineage, the aristocrat remained in a secondary relation, if not to his peers, then to that forefather who had proved his honor and claimed his nobility in blood on the field of battle. Once gentled, aristocratic privilege could be subjected to codification by herald or by sociologist.[28] Or, in the words of Michael McKeon, " 'Honor' now fails to unite internals and externals."[29]

But if the English aristocracy can be defined in an integrative and eco-

nomic fashion—as peerage and gentry—it can also be defined in conflictual, by and large cultural and political, terms: peerage versus gentry. The
economistic definition identifies the aristocracy as a social class prepared to
survive and even prosper in the face of bourgeois assertion by heeding the
imperative of capital formation. Such an integrative version of the aristocracy best accords with the Whig conviction that the aristocracy has the
crucial role of balancing the other elements of the British constitution.[30]
Contrarily, in the discourse of British radicalism (and especially in the
turbulent 1790s) *aristocrat* took on from the French the ideological burden
of referring to all those who opposed revolution abroad and reform at
home: an anti-Jacobin. Although this connotation of aristocrat as traitor to
the people did not die (see the discussion of *Sardanapalus* in chapter 8
below), the Napoleonic era witnessed the emergence of a conception of
strong aristocracy, which laid claim to distinction as made rather than
inherited by blood relation or conferred by property relations.

Exponents of this conflictual and, let us say, Romantic conception of
aristocracy vacillated between a sublime mode driven by imperial ambition
and a public regimen answerable to a republican ethic. We can provisionally
isolate three general reasons for the vacillation, even the confusion, between those paths. First, there was the dizzying effect of the emancipation
of aristocratic virtue from the land that the republican had historically held
to be his material condition.[31] Second, there were fundamental doubts
about what, exactly, the public *was*: sphere, realm, stage, or review? Third,
there was the likelihood that any distinction displayed in the public sphere
was subject to counterfeit. That possibility both fueled the ingenuity of
those, particularly in the literary system, who sought to profit by the publication of distinction and threatened those writers and politicians who,
fearing the debasement consequent on such mechanical reproduction, endeavored to transcend the routinization of distinction either in meditative
retirement (e.g., William Wordsworth and, intermittently, Charles James
Fox) or by a strained self-overcoming (e.g., John Keats and, intermittently,
Fox). Lord Byron indulged both temptations—often, as his prefaces record,
at the same time.

We shall explore the countervailing tendencies and textual implications
that flow from the conflictual, Romantic conception of aristocracy more
thoroughly in the chapters that follow. For now, it is sufficient to recognize
that although it may have been economically true that "aristocracies have
not been able to survive the loss of their land,"[32] it remained culturally and
even politically true that no aristocracy worth the name could persist without subscribing to an ethos that favored the genuine risk of that land.[33] That

truth is attested to in fact and fiction by the accounts of those aristocrats who recklessly hazarded their patrimonies on the dueling ground or at the gaming tables. As a resistance to the recognition of the mutuality of interest shared by peerage and gentry, aristocratic contempt, then, may be described not as consciousness of class but as resistance to class consciousness. To prove that it disdains calculation and serves no class interest is the burden of the aristocratic ethic—an ethic finely exemplified by Lord Byron's willingness to convert both his ancestral estates (the economically productive Rochdale and the iconic Newstead) into cash that would pay for pleasures past and future.

Integrative and conflictual definitions of aristocracy are, respectively, grammatical (or constative) and rhetorical (or performative) in their orientation. By *grammatical* I mean that the integrative definition refers status to a prior code by means of which it can be analyzed and assessed (land is redescribed as wealth). A performative orientation insists that the "essential and permanent" differences between men are manifested in an act, or what Nietzsche would call a "deed":

> For just as the popular mind separates the lightning from its flash and takes the latter for an *action*, for the operation of a subject called lightning, so popular morality also separates strength from expressions of strength, as if there were a neutral substratum behind the strong man, which was *free* to express strength or not to do so. But there is no such substratum; there is no "being" behind doing, effecting, becoming; "the doer" is merely a fiction added to the deed—the deed is everything.[34]

Nietzsche's metaphor is Byron's in *Childe Harold III:*

> Could I embody and unbosom now
> That which is most within me,—could I wreak
> My thoughts upon expression, and thus throw
> Soul, heart, mind, passions, feelings, strong or weak,
> All that I would have sought, and all I seek,
> Bear, know, feel and yet breathe—into *one* word,
> And that one word were Lightning, I would speak;
> But as it is, I live and die unheard,
> With a most voiceless thought, sheathing it as a sword.
> (st. 97)

From a Nietzschean perspective Byron's inability to express his thoughts follows from the misguided separation of thoughts from expression; the fiction that one must be "free" to exert strength—a freedom guaranteed by ownership of land, for example—incapacitates strength. Nietzsche's denial that there is any "being" behind the strong man's doing is in accord with Emerson's definition of unenfranchised heroism, that "there is somewhat in great actions, which does not allow us to go behind them."[35] The clumsiness of the split between the poet and his character Harold, which has fueled commentary on the poem since its publication, should not be dismissed as failed artistry; it is the symptom of a misbegotten project of reference fatal to poetic strength. For both Nietzsche and Emerson the strong man distinguishes himself in his deed, by his deed, as his deed. Or to quote the carnivalesque Byron in the process of putting away the things of a *Childe:* "Life becomes for the moment a drama without the fiction."[36]

The aristocrat distinguishes himself by making distinctions. At the ideal limit, as Byron identifies it in "A Fragment" from *Hours of Idleness,* the aristocrat's deed is absolutely coincident with his honorable name:

> When, to their airy hall, my father's voice
> Shall call my spirit, joyful in their choice;
> When, poised upon the gale, my form shall ride,
> Or, dark in mist, descend the mountain's side;
> Oh! may my shade behold no sculptured urns
> To mark the spot where earth to earth returns!
> No lengthen'd scroll, no praise-encumber'd stone;
> My epitaph shall be my name alone;
> If *that* with honour fail to crown my clay,
> Oh may no other fame my deeds repay!
> *That*, only *that*, shall single out the spot;
> By that remember'd, or with that forgot.

As David Castronovo nicely puts it, "Nobility means notability; to be ignoble is to be unknown."[37] Byron asserts that his nobility must be his own doing. He must make himself notable. That condition notwithstanding, it does make a difference that the name he must make is also a name he has been given. Indeed, the Byron of *Hours* cannot now write his "epitaph," since the deed that will make him notable is a future performance he cannot possibly know. And what would he write now? "Byron"? "Lord Byron"? "George Gordon, Lord Byron"? "Lord Byron, Minor"? It is singularly difficult to know how Byron might write his name. The epitaph promises no resolution. In making his epitaph his name, Lord Byron makes it as a name that, on pain of absolute death, can *never* become self-identical. His epitaph is a text that must continue to mark, eventful, at every moment of its reading. "Believe a woman or an epitaph, / Or any other thing that's false," the poet of *English Bards and Scotch Reviewers* admonishes (ll. 78–79). Why should we honor the name of Byron? We do so only if the motto *Crede Byron* retains the strength of the imperative. As if, that is, the words did not know their author was dead.

The dilemma besetting Byronic self-recognition is given its biographical setting by Thomas Moore: "It is said that the day after little Byron's accession to the title, he ran up to his mother and asked her 'whether she perceived any difference in him; since he had been made a Lord, as he perceived none himself.'"[38] The wish fulfilled fails to match the accident as dreamed.[39] The occlusion of self-recognition approximates the tension between the generality of the law and the necessity of its application that Paul de Man reads in Rousseau's *Social Contract:*

> Just as no law can ever be written unless one suspends any consideration of applicability to a particular entity including, of course, oneself, grammatical logic can function only if its referential consequences are disregarded.
>
> On the other hand, no law is a law unless it also applies to particular individuals. It cannot be left hanging in the air, in the abstraction of its generality. Only by this referring it back to particular praxis can the *justice* of the law be tested. . . . There can be no text without grammar: the logic of grammar generates texts only in the absence of referential meaning, but every text generates a referent that subverts the grammatical principle to which it owed its constitution.[40]

If we substitute "genealogical text" for de Man's "legal text," we approach Byron's state of mind in Moore's anecdote. The consistent application of the aristocratic code has always been thwarted by the ancient antinomy of blood: the incompatible and irrepressible claims that excellence is hereditary, colored by the blood that has been transmitted, and that excellence is merited, tinctured by the blood one sheds. The antinomy between the grammar of birth and the performance of merit translates into a fundamental incompatibility between being made an aristocrat (as, through a contingent set of circumstances, Byron was) and the imperative to make oneself an aristocrat, regardless of monarchic enfranchisement or popular recognition (a charge that the young lord acknowledged and had not yet fulfilled).[41]

One element of the task before us is to examine how the literary system named Byron exploited this incompatibility. Again, de Man is some help. In Rousseau, he argues, "incompatibility between the elaboration of the law and its application . . . can only be bridged by an act of deceit."[42] The conventions of Byronism worked in a similar way. Characteristically, the Byronic poem/hero pretends to resist the massive encoding of the dominant culture while providing an ensemble of identificatory procedures and inducements that "solve" the incompatibility between general law and individual application by mystifying it. The process is sensationally represented in the verse romances that forcefully enact it (*Childe Harold I–IV,* the Oriental tales). There the elaboration of the law, explicitly represented as a genealogical text, becomes thematized as a dark, guilt-ridden past that is mysteriously encoded on the face of the hero and then efficiently "applied" to the reader-surrogate in the poem through a fascination with the hero's visage. The hero's nameless guilt is the zone where the general, such as familial past, the *zeitgeist,* or poetic tradition, meshes with the particular. By making the hero impossibly responsible for a past that can be neither spoken nor remembered, the nameless guilt catalyzes an impressive assertion of force that appears at once completely spontaneous and utterly destined. From the beginning, critical employment of Byron's biography has consistently recapitulated this mystification: the poems are imagined as an elaborate code that, by way of a handily metamorphic secret (such as incest or homosexuality) can be brought into some determinate relation with a singular circumstance of Byron's life (such as his separation from John Edleston or his brutality toward his wife). Now as then, the incompatibility between code and life as well as the mystification that "solves" that incompatibility are highly productive of critical discourse and financial profit.

The incompatibility between the literary code and Byron's life not only invites critical resolution, whether by imagining a single Byron who is paradoxical or ironical, or by constructing a dual Byron who is sometimes satiric and sometimes romantic. It also tempts a reader to make application to him- or herself: Why not my life as well as Byron's? Why not this moment as well as that? What could the difference be, when making any application of the Byronic code to a particular life presupposes that any particular is pretty much the same as every other? Byron's romances simultaneously convey to their consumer that he or she is an intentional subject and instill anxiety about the singularity of that position. To put it another way: What the reader identifies with, what he or she applies to him- or herself, is not any particular feature of the Byronic hero but the very incompatibility between code and instance that structures the Byronic hero and that, because of its instability, propels the Byronic plot—which is a self-reflexive exercise in habitual identification. Romantically conceived, habit is the characteristic disguise or costume by which the particular is generalized or domesticated. Because each identification is both a resolution and a failure, the process is eminently suited for serial elaboration: a coding over time of the flawed but powerful identificatory procedure that one may participate in at any moment. The mystified passage from code to instance becomes an instance that is repeated in a code called the Byronic text. Recall Serres's formulation. The passage from the particular to the global, from an always hypothetical narrative instance to a never fully generalized representational code, in poem after successful poem generates power—a power that nominally belongs to the author but is legally the property of the publisher, the capitalist who owns the right and the means to copy.

From a psychoanalytic perspective Moore's account of the young Byron's failure to perceive a difference bespeaks his failure fully to enter the symbolic order. As a consequence, Byron's notion of what "difference" might be remains incommunicable, radically personal. This aphasia has social coordinates. As Pierre Bourdieu remarks,

> A social history of all forms of *distinction* (of which the *title* is a particular case) would have to show the social conditions and the consequences of the transition from a personal authority which can neither be delegated nor inherited . . . to the *title*—from honour to the *jus honorum*. In Rome, for example, the use of titles . . . defining a *dignitas*, an officially recognized position in the State (as distinct from a purely personal quality), was, like the use of *insignia*, progressively subjected to detailed control by custom or law.[43]

The progressive subjection of the personal to the delegated, of honor to law, and of act to insignia recapitulates the passage from the imaginary to the symbolic.

Although a scheme that weaves together the social and the psychic is a useful instrument for plotting Byron's career, the charm of symmetry should not obscure the psychoanalytic insight that no transition from one form of distinction to another is ever complete—an insight that troubles the ambitions of psychoanalytic science as much as social history. Despite the ability of Freudian psychoanalysis to comprehend in general the passage from the imaginary to the symbolic, the discipline is itself a partisan of the symbolic, and for good reason: historically, psychoanalysis coalesced as a discipline and a profession after the passage *in theory* to the symbolic (to the truly theoretical)—after, that is, the discovery and determination of the Oedipus complex. The psychoanalytic grammar cannot command the pre-oedipal any more than sociology can command aristocratic performance. Let me draw the analogy—inescapable in any study of Lord Byron's career—tighter: the persistence of the pre-oedipal in the world of adults correlates with the persistence of a performative aristocracy in an age of gentrification; both residues strongly remind us of the historical failure of history to complete the transitions it starts and of the inadequacy of enlightenment to master the differences it perceives.

The correlation of the pre-oedipal and the aristocratic can be derived from Moore's anecdote. It is the necessary condition of Byron's failed recognition that his father be decisively absent from the reckoning. Although it is technically necessary that his father had to die before Byron could rise to the peerage, Jack Byron died far away and well before it really mattered. The death that counted came later and was entirely contingent: William John Byron, the heir to the baronetcy, was killed in the Battle of Calvi. Mrs. Byron, as Doris Langley Moore notes, learned of the crucial event only by "chance"; "not a single one of her late husband's kith and kin had bothered to let her know."[44] Thus although there was some time before Byron became a lord—he awaited the death of his great-uncle the "Wicked Lord"— the boy had no paternal ideal either to emulate or to contest. As Byron remained, in Moore's words, "almost unreal" to his paternal kin, so the accession to the "place" of the father/uncle/cousin seemed unreal to the child. However we may describe the epistemological status of what Harold Perkin has called the "aristocratic ideal" for the aspiring middle classes,[45] for this particular aristocrat that paternal ideal would always have a peculiar irreality, like a ghost haunting an imaginary abbey. The father absent, the boy in Moore's anecdote appeals to his mother for a verdict that she—a Gordon, a woman, a mother—cannot legitimately give. Mrs. Byron is a type of all the feminine readers (Annabella Milbanke is another) to whom Byron presents his heroic romances: each poem demands an act of recognition from its reader that she is constitutionally unable to execute. Frustration, anger, and rejection follow. The money, paid whether by the mother to her profligate son or by the reader to her fickle romancer, is the token of that flawed recognition and the debased simulation of a difference that cannot fully be credited. Byron's numerous battles with his mother from this epochal moment until her death do not reflect his failure to resolve an oedipal crisis; they perform his refusal to oedipalize at all. His repeated rejections of her repeatedly punish her for her inability to explain or symbolize difference. Rejection is a deed that is never done. Over and over again Lord Byron makes the difference that everyone fails to perceive.

Social history has furnished empirical support for Carlyle's analysis of the "abdication of the governors" at the end of the eighteenth century, whether that withdrawal is seen as the dissolution of a relatively benign paternalism or as a rational consolidation of economic interests.[46] Byron's career novelistically sutures the historical and the psychological by particularizing this general event as the abdication of the father(s). The scenario of abdication is played out both in Byron's humiliation at the hands of Lord Carlisle, who in refusing to attest to Byron's pedigree at his young relative's ceremonial induction into the House of Lords cast doubts on Byron's paternity; and, as we shall see, in Henry Brougham's aggressive denial of the claims of "Lord Byron Minor" to cross into the public world via his book of poems *Hours of Idleness*. Particularizing in this respect means not only registering social change as psychological disorder but also making an aristocratic crisis out of what, according to E. P. Thompson, had been the historical fate of the plebs.[47] In Catherine Clément's trenchant words, "Societies do not succeed in offering everyone the same way of fitting into the symbolic order; those who are . . . between symbolic systems, in the interstices, offside, are the ones who are afflicted with a dangerous symbolic mobility."[48] It has ever been and will always be this symbolic mobility—between the general system called Byronism and the writer who signs his name, between the body of the debauchee and the bulimic, between the love of women and of men, between narrative flow and digressive blockage—that makes Lord Byron fascinating. It is the task of a biographical criticism to plot those vicissitudes, to map the interstitial career.

First Blood: The Publication of *Hours of Idleness*

> *I believe, if anyone, early in his life, should contemplate the dangerous fate of authors, he would scarce be of their number on any consideration. The life of a wit is a warfare on earth.*
>
> *Alexander Pope, 1730*

Lord Byron's public life begins in contention: a state of obligatory reciprocity between the aristocratic poet and the self-confirmed arbiters of culture. "Obligatory reciprocity" is the answer to the question that motivates Marcel Mauss's anthropology and that ought to orient all forays into Romantic aesthetics: "What force is there in the thing given which compels the recipient to make a return?"[49] For Mauss, a thing is not a property, an object that stands in some mensurable relation to a proprietor. A thing *occurs* as a gratuitous deed that forcefully articulates the continuous action of the socius. The thing given is the donnée of the social, that which from before my beginning has obliged me to participate in the continual crisis of its recreation.[50]

Lord Byron imagines himself as the bestower of gifts. He gives because he is obliged by the thing given him—his status, title, or blood—which somehow compels his return and in turn makes him a compelling thing. It is as a gift that Lord Byron Minor in his preface affects to present *Hours of Idleness* to the public.[51] It is as a gift that Henry Brougham, the brilliant, prickly, and anonymous *Edinburgh* reviewer, affects to receive the volume as he sarcastically congratulates the "noble minor" on his resolution to publish never more: "Let us be thankful; and with honest Sancho, bid God bless the giver, nor look the gift horse in the mouth" (*RR* B:2:835). True to his word, Brougham does not check Byron's teeth; but he does put the gift horse through his paces, counting his feet and mocking his gait.

Brougham devotes much of his review to a deconstruction of the book's "title-page," which he tropes as the flourish of the author's status: "Lord Byron Minor." The forwardness of the *Minor*, which follows Lord Byron's name "like a favourite part of his *style*," especially irritates the reviewer. He recognizes that *Minor* may be intended as an "extenuation of this offense" of publishing "stagnant" verse on the strength of a noble name, but judges that the plea that is supposed to excuse fault actually magnifies it. The addition of *Minor* baldly attempts to extenuate aristocratic presumption by claiming the privilege due to rank. Yet the move has the untoward effect of bringing the noble lord before the law as plaintiff. However infelicitous the consequence for Lord Byron, it follows straightforwardly enough from the precept formulated by one of Brougham's predecessors, Addison (*Spectator*, no. 99):

> When honour is a support to virtuous principles, and runs parallel with the laws of God and country, it cannot be too much cherished and encouraged; but when the dictates of honour are contrary to those of religion and equity, they are the greatest depravations of human nature, by giving wrong, ambitious, and false ideas of what is good and laudable, and should therefore be exploded by all governments, and driven out as the bane and plague of society.[52]

Brougham does not waste his opportunity to police honor's excess. With a show of justice the critical magistrate dismisses the plea of minority: "It is a plea available only to the defendant; no plaintiff can offer it as a supplementary ground of action. . . . But as he now makes voluntary tender of the article, he hath no right to sue, on that ground, for the price in good current praise, should the goods be unmarketable. This is the view of the law" (*RR* B:2:833). The law of contracts is the proper metaphor by which to confront the lordly poet with his subjection to the law of context. As Brougham sees it, the supplement of *Minor* graduates the distance between a supposed gift and an actual publication; it betrays Lord Byron's awareness that this is no personal exchange but a market transaction into which he has voluntarily entered—despite himself.[53] The self-thwarting ambivalence that the civil Brougham exploits is especially acute in Byron's preface, where the "noble minor" veers between self-characterization as an audacious Caesar—"'I have passed the Rubicon,' and must stand or fall by 'the cast of the die'"— and a retiring William Cowper, who plays the minor to the conqueror's reckless venture. Cowper's extenuation of Caesar (sensibility's blushful mitigation of heroic aggression)— marks the difference between crossing the Rubicon in the first century before Christ and publishing a book of poems in England in 1807. A volume of poems is not truly a conquest, any more than this particular volume of poems is actually a gift. The extenuation of Caesar, like the extenuation of his title, reflects Byron's need to be recognized in order to make the crossing from the private world of friendly circulation to the adult world of public business. Defense and plea, *Cowper*, like *Minor*, is, as Brougham senses, the clumsy exposure of the mystification necessary to bring off the ritual crossing that the book of poems aims to perform. Gatekeeper Brougham withholds the recognition sought. With the poet's complicity Brougham's satire punctures the pretense that there is anything more to lordship than a legal fiction, useful for the pursuit of the usual acquisitive interests. Brougham, however, is not so vulgar as to call that fiction "mystification"; he gives it its polite name, *style*.

Brougham interprets the title page as a defense, the recourse of a marginal aristocrat or a weak poet. The difference hardly matters. Byron fails to be original, and Brougham, like Harold Bloom, identifies poetic strength with originality. He labors as a critic in the gratifying knowledge of its impossibility. Hence his mockery (following Byron's prefatory clue) of Byron's translations, his borrowings from Thomas Gray, his addiction to clichés. Abandon all furniture, Brougham instructs the Cowper *manqué*; the poetry would be better served by the addition of "at least one thought, either in a little degree different from the ideas of former writers, or differently expressed" (*RR* B:2:834).[54] Be original!—a contradictory imperative meant to be incapacitating. But the reviewer does not know his man. Brougham presumes to have penetrated all Byron's disguises—his minority, his borrowings from other poets, his phony Scotticisms—but instead of sweeping away Byron's ambivalence he crystallizes it in its most virulent form. Not Caesarian thunder makes Lord Byron dangerous but a symbolic mobility that confounds reference and generates a field of confrontation. In this case, the young lord vainly attempts to extenuate his aristocratic bravura by an appeal to the law, but the grammarian, despite himself, recalls the poet to the aristocratic ethic.

He gets personal.[55] This is most conspicuous in his characterization of the patrimonial elegy "On Leaving Newstead Abbey" as not "deserving the name of poetry." Not "deserving the name" knowingly plays on Byron's next to worst fear—less only than not having a name worth deserving. Byron's plaintive fear of rejection is fulfilled by Brougham's mockery. Byron's vow to his ancestry "that he ne'er will disgrace you" is broken by Brougham's reproduction of it—the "innocent" aftereffect of the noble minor's vanity publication. But if the attacks on Byron's desert to bear the ancestral name design dishonor, the limit of the personal is reached with an attack against the aristocratic body itself: "Lord Byron should also have a care of attempting what the greatest poets have done before him . . . , [he] should really have kept out the ten *hobbling* stanzas 'on a distant view of the village and school of Harrow.'" Lest there be any doubt, Brougham gratuitously asks of a minor piece, "And why call the *thing* in p. 79 a translation . . . and the other thing in p. 81, where μεσονυκτιοις ποθ' ὡραις, is rendered by means of six *hobbling* verses" (*RR* B:2:834; emphasis added). Challenged by verse that has no lawful status, Brougham responds in kind. He intends to inflict a mortal wound on Byron's name by remarking on the deformation of Byron's foot. But by responding to the text as a thing given, the demystifier remystifies the book. He reads it as a body that performs its unique weakness on every page. He reads every page as a title page—an agonistic reading to which he is obliged by the "thing" given.

Brougham's scornful counsel that Byron add "at least one thought, either in a little degree different from the ideas of former writers, or differently expressed," would almost qualify as the best advice that the poet ever received[56]—it would so qualify were it not that Brougham's response to *Hours* demonstrates that Byron is already exploiting differentiation as a tactic: a new thought, as reading Lord Byron impresses on Brougham, is not finally an original idea but just something different, and therefore, properly speaking, not a thought at all. This poet is no thinker. Lord Byron's difference is not the expression of a voice or an anxiety about voice but the eventful elaboration of a personal, highly volatile style, in which the pretended extremes of translation and original are continually transgressed by a hobble that opaquely resists generalization. As the extenuation of the Greek, Byron's six hobbling stanzas align with the extenuations of *Minor*, of *Cowper*, of the preface, of the volume, and, especially, of his title. Byron's style performs lordship.

In his biographical reconstruction of Byron's accession to the title *Lord*, Moore writes that "the child little knew what a total and talismanic change had been wrought in all his future relations with society, by the simple addition of that word before his name."[57] True—and no more true than when the talisman fails to fascinate as it does here. True because the young man knows as little as the child what total and talismanic changes the addition of *Lord* will make. True, but in part true because that "simple addition" repeats a precedent addition, the twist that first makes Byron notable: the deformation of his foot that marks him out and that is the literal, fully embodied performance of a lordship that circumstances will allegorically confirm. What is a lord? The 1811 *Dictionary of the Vulgar Tongue* defines him as "a crooked or humpbacked man. These unhappy people afforded great scope for vulgar raillery; such as: 'Did you come straight from home? if so, you have got confoundedly bent by the way.'"[58] The vulgar raillery of Brougham's willful misrecognition confirms a bent for lordship straight from the womb, as if the lameness were the device by which Byron marked his own birth, as if the birth itself were a willed and therefore perverse performance, as if the existence of Lord Byron were, like his preface, his verses, and his volume, a supplement that, furnishing no "grounds for action" in the court to which Brougham refers them, nonetheless acts strongly in the text where it lives, moves, and has its being.

As virtually all of Byron's works, *Hours* can be categorized as a work of transition. McGann's powerful insight about *Don Juan*, that it is a poem that is nothing but transition, suggests that *Juan* normalizes as a style what has been a trait of Byron's poetry all along.[59] One implication of conceiving of Lord Byron's poetry as continual transition is to judge Byron as inadequate to the future and thus, as Carlyle admonished, something to be "put down." Because he hobbles, according to the judge, the minor lord cannot complete the crossing he intends. Brougham is right. Byron chronically fails to complete the transition he represents. The crossing he claims to have achieved conspicuously fails to take him anyplace different from where he started. Now, with McGann, I believe that *Don Juan* does cross over to something different, but I do not believe that *style* is an adequate rubric to describe that difference. Byron's "hobble," which registers the failure of body or talent or nerve requisite to cross into a new world, belongs in a cluster of images common to a wide range of late-eighteenth- and early-nineteenth-century discourses that might be labeled the "convulsive." There are texts that, like William Beckford's *Vathek*, Henry MacKenzie's *Man of Feeling*, Edmund Burke's *Philosophical Enquiry*, and William Godwin's *Caleb Williams*, represent convulsions. There are texts that, like David Hume's *Dialogues Concerning Natural Religion* and Laurence Sterne's *Sentimental Journey*, theorize the place of convulsiveness in the providential or political or sexual economy. There are the performances of the millenarian sect known as the convulsionaries, the demonstrations of the mesmerists, the legal defense of William Hone, and the Jacobin carmagnole.[60] Such convulsions register the potential (and therefore either cathartic or prophetic) or actual (and therefore either revolutionary or psychotic) breakdown of habitual social and political arrangements. Part of the pathognomy of contradiction—a violent distortion of the code by which the face of reality is recognized—convulsions occur at the threshold of change, as vehicle or resistance. Convulsions can lead to deliverance, death, or treatment at the hands of someone more or less expert at diagnosing and regulating the disturbance. Lord Byron—body, corpse, and corpus—was administered by many such experts, but chiefly by the publisher John Murray, who harnessed the spasmodic outpourings of the "lava" of Lord Byron's imagination to the serial production of explosive new poems.

For Murray (who purchased the copyright to Lord Byron's poems) as for Brougham, the regulation of Byron's convulsiveness exploited the poet's identification with his name. In *Hours* that identification funded an intermittently nostalgic and defiant refusal to give up on what has already left or been lost. The stance is given generic status in the lyric "To Romance," which apostrophizes the "Parent of golden dreams" (l. 1):

> Who lead'st along, in airy dance,
>   Thy votive train of girls and boys;
> At length, in spells no longer bound,
>   I break the fetters of my youth;
> No more I tread thy mystic round,
>   But leave thy realms for those of Truth.
>   (ll. 3–8)

Although ostensibly a poem of enlightenment, the verse addresses as "Auspicious queen" Romance, not Truth. Indeed, the exact time of departure from the "hard to quit" realm of romance is ambiguous. The "at length" allows for the change to be construed as either a morally decisive break with a pleasure now recognized as deceitful or as the effect of a merely inevitable maturation from child to adult. Or it allows for the interpretation that the change is no change at all. Certainly Byron never breaks with his fascination with fetters. The situation here, give or take a nymph or two, parallels the crisis faced by the imprisoned Conrad in *The Corsair*, who has similarly mixed emotions at the prospect of being released from his bondage in the prison of the Turk. I shall discuss that scene at length in chapter 3, but at this point it is enough to know that there *is* another such scene (and if we count Prometheus, "The Prisoner of Chillon," and *Mazeppa*, more yet) in order to cast some doubt on the accomplishment of the liberation that Byron here professes to regret:

> And must we own thee but a name,
>   And from thy hall of clouds descend?
> Nor find a sylph in every dame,
>   A Pylades in every friend?
> But leave at once the realms of air
>   To mingling bands of fairy elves;
> Confess that woman's false as fair,
>   And friends have feeling for—themselves?
>
> With shame I own I've felt thy sway,
>   Repentant now thy reign is o'er
> No more thy precepts I obey,
>   No more on fancied pinions soar.
>   (ll. 17–28)

If romance is but a name, its precepts authorized by nothing but the appeal of the nominal, then what is truth? If we stay for an answer we shall have to wait for some time: until *Don Juan*, where among the litter of commonplaces is found the truth that truth is "in a well" (2:84). Such a precept would not be owned by the minor poet who idealistically opposes truth to romance. For him the gap between them is momentous, a "gulf," and failure to cross it would mean condemnation to a perpetual minority. But the gulf cannot be crossed as long as truth is nothing more than a name. Indeed, as long as truth remains nominal (as ironic in relation to lived experience as any fable from romance) there may be no good reason for the poet to cross over, since the experience of the poet of "Romance" has taught him only that heroic triumph is indistinguishable from enchantment: he or she wins who has the best spell, the best name.

The last two stanzas are decidedly unconvincing:

> Ye genial nymphs, whose ready tears
>   On all occasions swiftly flow,
> Whose bosoms heave with fancied fears,
>   With fancied flames and phrensy glow;
> Say, will you mourn my absent name,
>   Apostate from your gentle train?
> An infant bard at least may claim
>   From you a sympathetic strain.

> Adieu, fond race! a long adieu!
>   The hour of fate is hovering nigh;
> E'en now the gulf appears in view,
>   Where unlamented you must lie:
> Oblivion's blackening lake is seen,
>   Convulsed by gales you cannot weather;
> Where you, and eke your gentle queen,
>   Alas! must perish altogether.
>   (ll. 49–64)

A congestion of the clichés of sensibility, the stanzas have the inadvertent effect of producing a sentimental trope that raises romance another level. The poet can imagine no deed except abandonment or apostasy. Although the reference to "my absent name" implies that "Lord Byron" has been erased from the rolls of those gladsome students who live by the precepts of romance, in fact for the poet to imagine his apostasy as mourned is to imagine "Lord Byron" as not fully annihilated in the realms of romance. Phantomized, *Lord Byron* becomes the *name of absence*—a spell that mesmerizes the queen and her court, who have the misfortune to be left behind. Trumped by her student, the gentle preceptress Romance has been turned into a spellbound reader.

The phantomized name captures the nonidentity of Byron's title; it evokes uneasiness as it designates strength. As we shall see, this concluding scene of mourning becomes a Byronic convention. It prefigures the end of *Lara*, where a woman from the world of Eastern romance is left to mourn the death of her departed hero, and it is a metonym for a career that will be elaborated in terms of separations that kill the man and make the poet, that convert friends and familiars into readers. The poet experiences loss, but he forgets a romance that is dead only to him. He forgets so that, occluded, the name of romance can no longer reign but also so that romance can unknowingly be reinvented in the name of truth or social reality or biography. Nietzsche has prepared us to see in this forgetfulness the prophylaxis of the deed. But Lord Byron was not so prepared. Trained by the precepts of Probus and the spillover of the Enlightenment, he preferred to regard forgetfulness as a probable sign for the inevitable occurrence of change, of a personal difference he cannot quite perceive or a social development he cannot quite conceive. Brougham will not abide the ruse. He refuses to allow Byron to forget. His review is a reminder that the lord cannot conceive progress because he wishes to secure a place for himself in a Whiggish future, which, insofar as it is progressive, will not truck with lords idle and half-baked. Brougham is shrewd. There is no Whiggish (let alone Hegelian or Wordsworthian) fit between Byron's development and the progress of society. But Brougham is a lazy reader of Byron, who is interesting precisely because he is out of synch with the models of development on which political economy staked the future. Lord Byron's asynchronicity is more important than either his representativeness or his originality. For in truth the poet's forgetfulness is necessary to veil the fact that his so-called progress toward truth is no progress at all; it is a tactic that will allow the poet to romance in the name of historical truth: his deed to spell.

It would be a mistake to credit Byron with the oblivion he foresees. But a certain gift for inadvertence is necessary for the verse to be turned. The poet, that is, is not in command of his poetry as reader or as writer. For one thing the ascription to fate of the control of his passage from romance to truth indicates that the poet remains in his minority—being led on, living in the hour of the other. *Fate* is the name given here to the preceptor/father figure that looms so large in *Hours*, whether as the good Probus or the bad Pomposus. Indeed, if we apply Jean Baudrillard's concept of "bourgeois culture" as the "phantom of aristocratic values" to the scene of mourning evoked by "To Romance," it is pertinent to remember that the phantom haunts Byron as much as it does the queen and her train.[61] Byron's wrenching of himself away from the community of romance and his consequent self-phantomization are ways of identifying with his fathers, who existed for Byron as potently "absent names." For Byron to come into his own (as *Manfred, Sardanapalus,* and *Don Juan* will dramatize) required coming to terms with ghosts: making, dissipating, or becoming a phantom. "To Romance" not only figures identification with the father as a phantomized identification with the "absent name," it explicates the violence of the child's crossing as a symptom of the self-willed quality of the act: unlike his brethren at Harrow he has no father to force him to cross—not only because there is no father, but because the available fathers are enfolded in a Romantic resistance to such crossing.

"To Romance" ends with a pledge rather than a performance, and it is one that Byron reproduces in poem after poem. Indeed, "Romance" intimates that Lord Byron cannot imagine a future career except as the repetition of the kind of projection the poem represents. There is in fact no oblivion and no developmental crossing in the early Byron. Nevertheless, the imagination of one has consequences beyond Brougham's review. It allows the poet to veil from himself the repeated representation of this particular scene in poem after poem and preconsciously to employ that repeated representation as the ideological justification (the ideology being "Byronism") of his refusal to take control of the course of his writings in the world. The gulf supposedly crossed, there is no control he can exercise over the phantomized sign, call it a book or a commodity, he has left behind; oblivion supposedly achieved, there is nothing he owes to those who in fascination regard his name. Control and responsibility and profit over the works that bear his name can be left to friends like Charles Dallas and publishers like John Murray, emissaries who navigate the gulf between romance and truth, reader and poet, as if it were not even there. Representatives he has aplenty, but Lord Byron is representative of nothing at all—not even Byronism.

Byron is not the only one who fails to break with outmoded habits of thought. Regarded from the "view of the law," the reviewer's Enlightenment claim to have emancipated cultural disputes from magical thinking is as mystified as Lord Byron's wishful version of himself. The anonymous critic of the *Edinburgh Review* has no established right to judge and no established principles of judgment. English judges wear wigs, not cowls. The anonymity of the critic, as Coleridge would later argue in the *Biographia Literaria*, is a symptom of criticism's failure fully to professionalize itself.[62] A criticism that lacks disciplinary autonomy (a systematic, philosophically informed poetics; institutional independence) cannot be lawful or integrative and will inevitably fall back on the violent, ritualized language it has claimed to transcend—becoming the inquisitor of all excellence. Under the circumstances (writing in 1807 before Coleridge), Brougham cannot be blamed for his excess. Given his own allegiance to the civil law, the assumed honor of a poet could only appear, as Benjamin Heath Malkin describes it, "fantastical," treatable as a kind of madness.[63] Indeed, in his 1809 *Observations on Madness and Melancholy*, devoted to promoting the "moral management" of the insane, John Haslam instructs, "As madmen frequently entertain very high, and even romantic notions of honour, they are often rendered much more tractable by wounding their pride, than by severity of discipline."[64] It is no wonder that Brougham anticipates Haslam's method, for in default of a professionalized, autonomous discourse of either authorship or madness the traditional linkage between them provides a convenient basis for generalized discourse in the reviews about both.[65] As Brougham and his colleagues make clear, what gives this linkage its timeliness and edge is the apparition of a lordship that tries to take itself seriously and thus appears conspicuously (dangerously? ludicrously?) anachronistic in a society that has already silently transformed the rationale for membership in the ruling elite while, transfixed by the paranoid scenario of the counterrevolution, it continues to labor under the political interdiction of any language that would allow even a reformer like

Brougham to criticize lordship in explicit terms. Gifted by Byron, the reviewer can supplement the Shakespearean "compact" of lover, poet, and madman with lord.[66]

The *Edinburgh Review* attained cultural predominance during the Napoleonic era despite its alliance with a chronically minority party—probably because it was the most fully professionalized of the contemporary journals of opinion. Its reviewers, most of them lawyers with political ambitions, were monsters of industry and well paid. More important, they were masters of the only "scientific" account of the operation of the social machine: the theory of political economy as developed by Adam Smith and refined by Dugald Stewart. In *The System of Professions* Andrew Abbott discriminates two "ways occupational groups control knowledge and skill": "One emphasizes technique per se, and occupations using it are commonly called crafts. . . . The other form of control involves abstract knowledge. Here, practical skill grows out of an abstract system of knowledge, and control of the occupation lies in control of the abstractions that generate the practical techniques. . . . For me this characteristic of abstraction is the one that best identifies the professions."[67] Political economy, the "science which teaches us to investigate the causes of the wealth and prosperity of nations,"[68] exploits the power of abstraction (the power of the exchange relation over what had been called "intrinsic value") and of mobility; mastery of that theory of abstraction provided not only the rationale for but the means of social mobility in the commercial society of the early nineteenth century. In Gramscian terms, the intellectuals behind the *Edinburgh Review* were organically connected to the rising middle class as theorists of the commercial system, theorists who aimed to achieve social and political ascent by the elaboration and promulgation of their theory. The writers of the antagonistic, Tory *Quarterly Review* were, or assumed the guise of, traditional intellectuals (the editor, William Gifford, was best known as the neoclassical author of Popean satires), which in this case meant being the spokesmen for an antiprofessionalism—a position that reflected their lack of any abstract knowledge with which adequately to counter the assertion of the political economists.[69] There were ideological differences between the two camps, but the distinction between organic and traditional most closely conforms to a jurisdictional dispute between two sets of reviewers who, having no credentials of their own, nonetheless competed for professional prominence and authority. That side—theorists of the market—inevitably won because they could persuasively lay claim to the appropriate language to describe what the conflict was about: jurisdiction over a subject matter and clientele, market control.

By employing legal terminology in his attack on Lord Byron, Brougham executes what Abbott calls the rhetorical move of "reduction, [which] shows some new task to be reducible, in principle, to one of the attacker's already secure jurisdictions." Abbott comments that the "limiting case of reduction— the global professional metaphor—is a weak means of jurisdictional extension, although surprisingly common. . . . Legal metaphors permeate the professional world, as in the 'therapeutic contract' of the psychotherapists."[70] I shall have more to say about the weakness of the global metaphor of contract in the discussion of *Don Juan* in chapter 7, but it is clear that Brougham's deployment of the trope of reduction as a regulative hypothesis attests to the incapacity of the discourse of political economy adequately to comprehend the cultural fact of a volume of poems—especially a volume of poems published for the sake of prestige rather than profit. Addressing the external causes of change in the system of professions, Abbott generalizes that "new cultural facts demanding professional attention do not appear suddenly. The same argument applies to natural facts, although sudden change often occurs in technologies giving access to those natural phenomena."[71] But this instance, the instance of Byron, is exactly an exception to the general rule. Lord Byron will repeatedly challenge the professional community to determine whether he is bad (the lawyer Brougham's task), mad (the doctor Lord Lushington's task during the separation), dangerous to know (the publisher John Murray's response to the appearance of *Don Juan*), or (the amateur Lady Caroline Lamb's opinion) all of the above. The cultural fact of Byron will be associated with the powerful new technology of the steam press. It will also be associated with the emergent and unignorable cultural fact of public opinion, which is as yet under no single jurisdiction. No one can say with authority what a public is. No one can say whether it is Burke's "swinish multitude" or the corporate person with whom, ideally, one can contract, as Wordsworth attempts in the Preface to *Lyrical Ballads.* No one can say whether the public is a body and therefore imaginable as healthy or ill, male or female, normal or perverse, or something much more fragmentary, scattered, mobile—something to which political, legal, or medical metaphors are deplorably inadequate. Byron's sudden apparition challenges the system of professions at their base by raising the problem of determining whether a lord is a cultural or a natural fact—whether in some way the poetry of Byron, to all appearances a commodity, is in fact a volcanic, convulsive force of nature.

There is no way that Brougham could settle this question. Writing in advance of that grammar to which the professional critic would eventually refer, Brougham and his reviewing colleagues derive their semblance of authority from the carefully sustained pretense of disinterested judgment that anonymity confers. Namelessness graduates the distance between a supposed professionalism and an actual ideological instrumentality—call it a sociocultural minority. Lord Byron brings out the worst in Brougham because the reviewer's anonymity is the double of Lord Byron's *Minor*—as negative to positive. Over writers' dead bodies must critics climb; but in this writer this critic views the mirror image of his own aspiration. The irregular Byron appears as the flaw in the ideal to which ambition bends, and thus an example that taints his dream of ascent. There is no court to adjudicate this standoff. Lord Byron and Henry Brougham can meet no place to settle their differences except on the supplemental ground of action outside the city walls where challenge is met, strength is proved, and satisfaction gained.

2

A Genealogy of Morals

An English Bard, Scotch Reviewers, and a Wicked Uncle

In our own country a man seldom sets up for a poet, without attacking the reputation of all his brothers in the art. The ignorance of the moderns, the scribblers of the age, the decay of poetry, are the topics of detraction, with which he makes his entrance into the world.

Joseph Addison, Spectator, *no. 253*

To give a narrative logic to the events leading to Byron's second book of poetry, *English Bards and Scotch Reviewers*, I have postulated an obligatory reciprocity intrinsic to the gift of the title, a dynamic activated by the personal assault on Byron in the *Edinburgh Review*. That could be the truth. But even so, the hypothesis fails to explain fully why the sense of obligation imposed successfully on *this* man in the particular way it did. We need another narrative for that, a genealogy of Byron's morals.

By the beginning of the nineteenth century the traditional fabric of obligation in Great Britain, what E. P. Thompson in *The Making of the English Working Class* has called the "moral economy," had come unraveled under the pressures of revolutionary ideology, capital formation, and commercial incentive. But even if the age of chivalry had not died, a gift economy could not be mapped onto the social landscape of the British nobility without an anthropological attention to local instances. Lord Byron did not have a duty in the Kantian sense to answer the *Edinburgh* reviewer. He does not act in obedience to universal law. By responding, he demonstrates what Ralph Waldo Emerson would later call "heroism." "Heroism," Emerson writes, "works in contradiction to the voice of mankind, and in contradiction, for a time, to the voice of the great and good. Heroism is an obedience to a secret impulse of an individual's character."[1] Emerson Byronically jettisons universalist criteria, including a prescriptively public, discursive, and vocal definition of motivation and agency. "Secret impulse" insists on the strength of the encrypted inscription rather than on the force of public opinion.

David Hume discredited cause, understood as a power belonging to the object or the agent, in part by associating it with the occult. To explain the customary union or separation of objects by inferring some "secret cause" would be like fancying a strength of mind or of body that cannot be reliably measured—and that is, therefore, no force at all, according to Hume's Newtonian naturalism.[2] Empiricism *Gothicizes* cause, ascribing its occult, supposedly productive qualities to the superstitious belief of a popular mind that, deluded by priests and kings, fails to see that belief alone is the "cause" of the attribution of cause. Hume's dissipation of secret power conjoins his epistemological and his historical project: history is the narrative of the scientific disclosure of secrets; it is the story of the progressive emancipation of humanity from superstition by enlightened belief in the priority of belief. As epistemologically non-Humean as it is morally non-Kantian, Emerson's "secret impulse" is not Gothic, some dismal fact that awaits exposure or rationalization. Its secrecy is irreducible, and that irreducibility is its historicity—a past irreconcilable with the universalizing vocabulary of belief, a past that persists in the present by virtue of its encrypted alterity.[3] As poem after poem by Byron shows, the secret impulse is the impulse of the secret that belongs to Lord Byron as his past and as his thrust to the future.

English Bards and Scotch Reviewers, published almost a full two years after the appearance of *Hours of Idleness*, belongs as much to the history of English dueling as to the history of English literature. For *English Bards and Scotch Reviewers* is almost a volley in a duel. Its preface begins,

> All my friends, learned and unlearned, have urged me not to publish this Satire with my name. If I were to be "turned from the career of my humour by quibbles quick, and paper bullets of the brain," I should have complied with their counsel. But I am not to be terrified by abuse, or bullied by reviewers, with or without arms. I can safely say that I have attacked none

personally, who did not commence on the offensive. An Author's works are public property: he who purchases may judge, and publish his opinion if he pleases; and the Authors I have endeavoured to commemorate may do by me as I have done by them.

Although "paper bullets" are not real bullets, Byron takes credit for standing their fire and clearly intends to give as good as he has gotten. The poet liberally classes poetry as public property, open to criticism, but the notion of the personal (to what is it opposed?) remains vague enough to permit the identification of poetry with poet that empowers satire, just as the identification of "property" with man provokes duels. For all its bravado, the poet's assumption of personal responsibility for his words is somewhat tardy, for it appears in the preface to the second, aggressively Juvenalian edition of Byron's poem, published a few months after the first, which was shorter, amiably Horatian, and, most important, anonymous.[4]

After a thousand lines of "caustic," the poet concludes by returning to the question of his anonymity:

> Thus far I've held my undisturbed career,
> Prepared for rancour, steeled 'gainst selfish fear;
> This thing of rhyme I ne'er disdained to own—
> Though not obtrusive, yet not quite unknown;
> My voice was heard again, though not so loud,
> My page, though nameless, never disavowed;
> And now at once I tear the veil away.
>
> (ll. 1037–43)

The caesural pivot of the heroic couplet has, in the interest of self-justification, been moderated from antithesis to qualification, a dwindling of energy partially stemmed by the Gothic trope of dramatic revelation. His name proclaimed, the man steps forth to give and receive blows. The poem ends with the language of defiance, of the hunt, and of the duel:

> I too can hunt a Poetaster down;
> And armed in proof, the gauntlet cast at once
> To Scotch marauder, and to Southern dunce.
> Thus much I've dared; if my incondite lay
> Hath wronged these righteous times, let others say:
> This, let the world, which knows not how to spare,
> Yet rarely blames unjustly, now declare.
>
> (ll. 1064–70)

An oddly provocative conclusion to a poem that later received this annotation by its author: "The noble author had left this country previous to the publication of [the second] Edition, and is not yet returned" (*CPW* 1:399). Having cast down the gauntlet, the noble poet did not stay for an answer.

Whatever else might be said about *English Bards and Scotch Reviewers*, Byron's representation of it as pursuing an "undisturbed career" cannot be credited, whether we consider the poem as a formal construct, as a rhetorical performance, or in light of the history of its composition and publication. In his biography of the poet Leslie Marchand gives a detailed account of the turbulent period between the publication of *Hours* in June 1807 and March 1809, when Byron finally published *English Bards and Scotch Reviewers* on the eve of his departure for the Continent. The poet divided his time between lodgings at Dorant's Hotel in London and entertaining his friends (with the attentions of his "Paphians") at Newstead Abbey, the estate he had inherited from his great-uncle William, the fifth Lord Byron. This was a period of increasing indebtedness, dangerous dieting, moral dissipation, and (a word Byron uses on more than one occasion) "chagrin." By *chagrin* Byron refers to the intense mortification he suffered as a consequence of the series of negative reviews of *Hours*, a mortification that waxed as his replies were either delayed or diverted.[5] It was after the first such review, Hewson Clarke's in the *Satirist*, that Byron, contemplating a challenge, began work on his "satire," as he called *English Bards and Scotch Reviewers* at the time. And it was during this spell of chagrin that Byron, having given himself over to what he called an "abyss of Sensuality" (*BLJ* 1:158), denominated himself the "*wicked* George, Lord Byron"—in mocking contrast with "good" King George but also in identification with his infamous predecessor in the title and in the occupancy of Newstead, the Wicked Lord. As Thomas Moore first suggested, that identification remarks on Byron's secret impulse, both to the deed and to its delay.[6]

Although locally notorious for wild and brutal extravagances, the fifth Lord Byron owes his general renown to his scandalous place in the history of dueling. The "duel," probably the last in England to employ swords rather than equalizing pistols, took place between Byron's great-uncle and his neighbor Mr. Chaworth at the Star and Garter Tavern in Pall-Mall in 1765 after one of the monthly London meetings of the Nottinghamshire club, which was attended by Lord Byron and assorted members of the local gentry. The dispute, according to the lengthy account in the *Annual Register* of that year, emerged out of "a conversation about the best method of preserving the game, ... Mr. Chaworth insisting on severity against poachers . . . ; and lord Byron declaring that the way to have most game was to take no care of it at all." The debate became acrimonious. Mr. Chaworth "insisted that sir Charles Sedley and himself had more game on five acres than lord Byron had on all his manors. Lord Byron, in answer to this, proposed a bet of 100 guineas, and Mr. Chaworth called for pen, ink, and paper, to reduce the wager to writing, in order to take it up." As Mr. Chaworth was persuaded that the bet was one "that could never be decided, no bet was made."[7] The bet, it was declared, could not be decided because no one could hope to count the game.

The argument continued nonetheless. Lord Byron sneered (punningly?) at the notion of Sir Charles Sedley's "manors." Mr. Chaworth replied by offering his and Sir Charles Sedley's addresses for the purpose of satisfaction. The meeting soon broke up. As customary, Mr. Chaworth was called to settle the accounts, an act the *Register* recounts in detail: "Mr. Fynmore, the master of the tavern observed him a little flurry'd; for, in marking, he made a small mistake. The book had lines ruled in checks, and against each member present an 0 was placed, but if absent, 5s was set down. He placed 5s against lord Byron's name, but Mr. Fynmore observing to him that my lord was present, he corrected his mistake." The parties left the room:

> Lord Byron found Mr. Chaworth still on the stairs, and it now remains a doubt whether lord Byron called upon Mr. Chaworth, or Mr. Chaworth upon Lord Byron; but both went to the first landing-place, having dined upon the second floor, and both called the waiter to shew them an empty room, which a waiter did, and having first opened the door himself, and placed a small tallow candle, which he had in his hand, on the table, he retired; when the gentlemen entered, and pulled the door after them.
>
> In a few minutes the affair was decided; the bell was rung, but by whom is uncertain; the waiter went up, and perceiving what had happened, ran down stairs frightened, told his master the catastrophe, who ran instantly up stairs, and found the two combatants standing close together; Mr. Chaworth had his sword in his left hand, and lord Byron his in his right; lord Byron's left hand was round Mr. Chaworth, as Mr. Chaworth's right hand was round lord Byron's neck and over his shoulders. He desired Mr. Fynmore to take his sword, and lord Byron delivered up his at the same time; one, or both, called to him to get some help immediately, and in a few minutes Mr. Hawkins the surgeon was sent for, who came accordingly.[8]

Even this sketchy account suggests multiple affinities with Byron's life and writings. Biographically, the incident is the origin of the hostility between the Chaworths and the Byrons that impedimented the young lord's heartbreaking love for the fetching but insensible Mary Chaworth. Thematically, the incident is the germ for the ambiguous revenge taken by the Giaour on Hassan in Byron's Oriental tale, which similarly ends with the "last embrace of foes." It prefigures the use of the account book by Loredano in *The Two Foscari*. It bears on the squeamishness of Conrad about poniards and assassination in *The Corsair*, as well as the abortion of the duel in *Lara*. It is the allegorical subject of *Cain*. It anticipates the sixteenth canto of *Don Juan*.

Rich as it is, this version of events is seriously flawed: it leaves crucial elements of the story in doubt and fails to indicate whether such ambiguity reflects a restricted point of view by a single witness or conflict among various observers. As if to rectify those faults, the *Register*'s account continues as the report of a series of narrations of the events inside the room delivered by the dying Chaworth consecutively to a cluster of anonymous "misters," then to a Mr. Hawkins, and finally to a Mr. Levinz. Here is the core that Chaworth would successively elaborate:

> That the affair had passed in the dark, only a small tallow candle burning in the room; that Lord Byron asked him, if he meant the conversation on the game to sir Charles Sedley or to him? To which he replied, If you have any thing to say, we had better shut the door; that while he was doing this, lord Byron bid him draw, and, in turning, he saw his lordship's sword half drawn, on which he whipped out his own, and made the first pass; the sword being through my lord's waistcoat, he thought he had killed him, and asking whether he was not mortally wounded, lord Byron, while he was speaking, shortened his sword, and stabbed him in the belly.[9]

The subsequent narratives develop the theme of Mr. Chaworth's regret for the various "mistakes" he had made, principally electing to fight in the dark, a decision that neutralized his advantage in swordsmanship and led to his delusion that in piercing Lord Byron's coat he had thrust home to the body. From his perspective as narrator Chaworth can now bear witness to his lack of perspective during the duel. Crucially, the achievement of Chaworth's first-person point of view is *moral* as well as narrational. The reiterations of his story permit the dying Chaworth twice to utter his last words: "That he had rather be in his present situation, than live under the misfortune of having killed another person." Having told his story three times (*told*, for "no paper whatever," we are informed, "was written by Mr. Chaworth"), the wounded man dies, his "last words" recapitulated once more in the written report of Mr. Partington, a lawyer, who avoids assigning blame to either party by concluding with the question, "In the heat of duelling who can always be collected?"[10] Mr. Partington's question is disingenuous, of course, for it is exactly the purpose of the duel to test that man who *can* show "presence of mind" under unprecedented and dangerous circumstances. In context, Mr. Partington's question reads not only as an excuse for the various mistakes made but also as a justification for the triumphant collection of himself that Chaworth accomplishes subsequent to the duel and on the verge of his death.

Meanwhile, Lord Byron has vanished from the scene; unlike Mr. Chaworth, he does not speak; and he is mentioned only in the past tense of Mr. Chaworth's narration. He does reappear in the appended account of his trial before his peers in the House of Lords nearly three months later. Even there, however, he is represented only as saying that he declines the opportunity to cross-examine the prosecution witnesses and as having told "their lordships, that what he had to offer in his own vindication he had committed to writing, and begged that it might be read by the clerk, as he feared his own voice, considering his present situation, would not be heard." Because he does not speak the "voice of mankind," Lord Byron could not count on a fair hearing in the court of justice, so his speech was written and read. The lords retired, returned with a judgment of manslaughter, and, according to the "old statute" by which "peers are, in all cases where clergy is allowed, to be dismissed without burning in the hand, loss of inheritance, or corruption of blood, his lordship was immediately dismissed on paying his fees."[11]

The verdict was routine. Although duels were technically illegal, they were recognized and tolerated by the law as a special form of illegality. By the verdict of manslaughter the court adjudged the death as an unintended consequence of the contest rather than its premeditated aim. Such a verdict presupposed that equality between the participants was guaranteed by the punctilio observed during the duel. Even though the duel conventionally took place outside the walls of the city where the law traditionally has jurisdiction, the law relied on the power of the regulative hypothesis to control extralegal behavior.[12] Such confidence was not baseless. The law had its stand-ins in the persons of the seconds, who designed the engagement, ruled the ground, and adjudged fairness. In a discussion of the social dynamics of honor and shame, Julian Pitt-Rivers observes that "what is offensive is not the action in itself but the act of obliging the offended one to witness it."[13] Insult shames because it splits the integrity of the honorable man, who is made patient and spectator. If Pitt-Rivers is right, the duel, which designs a point-by-point reconstruction of the psychic scheme of the dishonored man, begins to look weirdly prudential, the application of appropriate and limited means to achieve a specific and reasonable end.

In the British code of dueling the prescribed presence of the seconds as witnesses makes sense not only as a standing answer to Mr. Partington's question—the second is the man who by definition remains collected during the heat of the duel—but also as projections of that split between recipient and witness of offense. The second allows for the possibility of unintended consequences by formally assuring that some consequences *are* intended. The prudential second stands in for the imaginary witness to the insult, a position and role canceled by the consummation of the duel and the restoration of integrity to the dishonored man, regardless of outcome—so long as the duelist conducts himself mannerly. Honor thus renovated entails an integrity of a different order, newly historicized (because dated from this hour) and radically socialized. Honor is henceforth not substantive but formal, coded: one's integrity is a function of counting (singleness depends on *seconding*, as in the English Cantos of *Don Juan*, where the "matchless" are precisely those "bent on matches"). To put it in terms of the dispute between Mr. Chaworth and Lord Byron, manners are more important than manors. But if that suggests why dueling briefly became the preferred means for the socially ambitious members of marginal status groups, such as lieutenants in the army and clerks, to attain gentility speedily, it also indicates a fragility, even a taint imparted to a gentility so acquired. For is there not a kind of shame in being obliged to subject the restoration of one's integrity to witnesses? From the point of view of the law the observers of the duel second the legal system as much as they serve the principals involved; the ritualized significance of the second reflects, in the dialectic of enlightenment, the recognition even by those outside the courtroom that the procedures of justice—witnessing, relative objectivity, contained event, testimony, the submission of claims of truth to the belief of others—are legitimate. Prudence reports to the law. The integrity achieved in the duel comes at the cost of acknowledging its dependence on some authoritative point of view.

In this renowned case, the law is in the same relation to events as Mr. Chaworth, who collects himself with the just maxim, "that he had rather be in his present situation, than live under the misfortune of having killed another person." That moral anticipates the form of the categorical imperative by which Kant sought to found morality. Serenely, even sublimely,

> with a will free from all impulses of sensibility, he [call him Mr. Chaworth] in thought transfers himself into an order of things altogether different from that of his desires in the field of sensibility. He cannot expect to obtain by

that wish any gratification of desires or any condition which would satisfy his real or even imagined inclinations. . . . He can expect only a greater inner worth of his person. He imagines himself to be this better person when he transfers himself to the standpoint of a member of the intelligible world to which he is involuntarily impelled by the idea of freedom, i.e., independence from the determining causes of the world of sense; and from this standpoint he is conscious of a good will, which on his own confession constitutes the law for his bad will as a member of the world of sense.[14]

For Kant, as Theodor Adorno has argued, the objective autonomy of the free, moral will is proved by its heteronomy not with the depraved, interested will of the other but with the subject's own empirical, bad will, which had been unprofitably ranging in the "field of sensibility."[15] The field of sensibility par excellence is the ritual of the duel. It should be noted, however, that Chaworth's real victory takes place not on that field but in conflict with the dueling impulse. Kantian through and through, Mr. Chaworth achieves sublimity not by virtue of his struggle with Lord Byron but by reflexive aggression against his empirical self.[16] If Chaworth's recourse to physical violence responds to what Kant disparages as a personal inclination or propensity, his maxim is nonetheless purified of all incentives by its proximity to death; it is motivated only by respect for the law, "which means merely the consciousness of the submission of my will to a law without the intervention of other influences on my mind."[17] Adorno does not buy that motive; according to him, such purgative aggression against the empirical, worldly self serves a greater narcissism: what Kant designates a "better self."

Despite the severity of his negation, Mr. Chaworth by definition could not reach that wholly intelligible "realm of ends" to which reason aspires. Mr. Chaworth can be fairly said to speak the voice of mankind because *mankind*, as Adorno argues, is a conception that seconds the assertion of a bourgeoisie whose ostensibly fatal submission to the categorical imperative and whose identification with a better self are a perverse mode of social mobility—perverse not because it is suicidal but because that suicide is acted out in the realm of the imaginary.[18] The better self is represented nowhere in the world—certainly not by the fifth Lord Byron, who as a member of the immediately superior status group might be thought an example suitable for Mr. Chaworth's emulation, but whose rejection as example parallels and illuminates the Kantian refusal of any example. Technically speaking, the bourgeois seeks to raise himself by mimicking his betters, but, elevated by negation to the fringe of what he must respect as something he can never have, the bourgeois sees that his better exists nowhere except in the transcendental realm, where dwells the unexampled man in an intelligible world as an end in himself. The bourgeois identifies with an ideal of aristocracy—an aristocracy by law, an aristocracy of the spirit—that no merely empirical aristocrat could possibly reach.

The fifth Lord Byron did not labor at such transcendence. As we have seen, he was content to label the event a *vindication.* Dead, Mr. Chaworth could not argue (although he bore witness through his seconds); indeed, Mr. Chaworth's death metaphorizes his political exclusion from the Court of Peers where his killing is to be judged. Lord Byron's refusal to examine the prosecutorial witnesses expresses his confidence in the absence of an eyewitness with whom to dispute. Lord Byron does not treat with the law. His vindication is his refusal to plead, his insistence on the court as a scene not of oral argument but of writing—a struggle to be won by him who is known, who is well marked because he marks well. The law can countenance dueling by representing it as the misguided slaughter of one self-loving man by another. But by refusing to face his accusers Lord Byron forces the law to confront an act that in fact could not be a duel because there was no witness to it. Because there was no point of view on the event, it could not be countenanced, only vindicated. Thus the lord affirms his lordship.

The court's judgment failed to appease all commentators. In his biography of the sixth Lord Byron, Thomas Moore calls the contest a "scuffle."[19] Moore, of course, had good reason to denigrate dueling: his own "everglorious, almost fatal fray" with Francis Jeffrey was mocked by Byron in *English Bards and Scotch Reviewers* (ll. 460–500). But Moore seems to have the weight of commentary on his side. In the dueling literature the fatal fray between Mr. Chaworth and the fifth Lord Byron was notorious for its multiple violations of the code of honor: the inordinate haste of the disputants to move from words to acts; the site of the "duel," which was fought in a private room of a public house; and, most scandalously, the absence of seconds. Indeed, if it is true (as Kant suggests) that Mr. Chaworth could have carried out his dialectic of enlightenment on his own—if, that is, Lord Byron as adversary did not in the final, categorical reckoning really count—the question follows why the prudent man yielded to the folly of duel. Perhaps Mr. Chaworth should not be blamed. He did try to count Lord Byron out of the scheme of things by recording him as absent in the account book. The *Annual Register* notes that Chaworth was reminded, "My lord was present"; although if the account book could now be produced, it would show that Lord Byron was not in fact fully present as someone who could be counted as an empirical fact. As uncountable as those hares swarming uncared for over his manors, Lord Byron's "presence" is registered by neither the zero shillings nor the five shillings but, aptly, by the erasure of one into the other. The erasure captures Byron's lordship by pointing "to the idea of freedom as the possibility of non-identity."[20] The erasure is the mark of that phantom of the closet who will elude Mr. Chaworth's best thrust.

Adorno's powerful commentary on Kant clarifies the relation between phantom and erasure:

> The dawning sense of freedom feeds upon the memory of the archaic impulse not yet steered by any solid I. The more the I curbs that impulse, the more chaotic and thus questionable will it find the pre-temporal freedom. *Without an anamnesis of the untamed impulse that precedes the ego*—an impulse later banished to the zone of unfree bondage to nature—it would be impossible to derive the idea of freedom, although that idea in turn ends up reinforcing the ego. In spontaneity, the philosophical concept that does most to exalt freedom as a mode of conduct above empirical existence, there resounds the echo of that by whose control and ultimate destruction the I of idealistic philosophy means to prove its freedom.[21]

If we extend the parallel that Adorno draws between the ego and the bourgeois subject, we can align his "untamed impulse" with Emerson's "secret impulse." Each contradicts the voice of mankind by challenging the legitimacy of the bourgeois ego it helped form. The untamed impulse is that aristocratic spontaneity from which the bourgeois ego hopes to derive its freedom while destroying it root and branch. The "modern age," as Hans Blumenberg observes, "does not have recourse to what went before it, so much as it opposes and takes a stand against the challenge constituted by what went before it."[22] In this case the challenge is fundamentally and self-contradictorily made to the concept *of* challenge as an aristocratic ethic. The erasure of the fifth Lord Byron is the anamnesis of the untamed impulse that is requisite to Mr. Chaworth's freedom but that, *as the condition of his freedom*, he has to misrecognize. Chaworth's flurry of mind begins with his attempt to identify Lord Byron as either present or absent. His error registers what in *The Genealogy of Morals* Nietzsche calls the "pathos of distance," which belongs to an aristocrat not subject to such clerical control, whose body does not count as a simple integer, to be individuated or classed. Chaworth's failure to mark well dictates defeat at the hand of Lord Byron: the mistake he makes with a pen (confusing presence and absence) he repeats inversely with his sword (confusing absence and presence). Pen, sword—neither is in itself mightier than the other. The hand that wields proves the event and triumphs by marking well.

His great-uncle's story is, I contend, Byron's secret impulse, the past that obliges him. But its message is not clear. How would the young Byron read this account? What precept does it hold for one obliged to follow in the line of his great-uncle? As a reader looking for a model, Byron could, ironically, identify only with Mr. Chaworth. He could only imitate that man who sought to imitate his better, and thus fail as he had failed. And it is as a Mr. Chaworth, dependent for his status on the recognition of another, that Byron takes the field of sensibility and launches *Hours of Idleness*. The *Edinburgh*'s reply is only what Byron deserves. It does not chastise the lord for writing but ridicules the apparatus by which that writing is prepared for publication—a prudential calculation at odds with the claims for lordship.

However erroneous his choice, the sixth Lord Byron could not have easily done otherwise. He could not have simply elected to follow his forebear's example. The Wicked Lord set none—not in the Kantian and moral sense that he transcended the empirical, but in the lordly sense that he darkened the clarity of the empirical. Archaic, the fifth Lord Byron does not speak. He remains untamed in the closet where he can only be imagined in a fierce intimacy that allows neither space nor time for reflection, where, if imagined as object, he is only there as the mistake one makes in trying to count or place him. The implied injunction of his great-uncle's performance, "If you would be like me, do not imitate me," can only tie Byron up in knots. And although such a precept *is* only implicit, it has its corollary in another one that Byron did attempt to follow. Moore recalls an anecdote from Byron's schooldays:

> Once, in returning home from school, he fell in with a boy who had on some former occasion insulted him, but had then got off unpunished—little Byron, however, promising to "pay him off" whenever they should meet again. Accordingly, on this second encounter . . . he succeeded in inflicting upon him a hearty beating. On his return home, breathless, the servant enquired what he had been about, and was answered by him that he had been paying a debt, by beating a boy according to promise; for that he was a Byron, and would never belie his motto, "*Trust Byron*."[23]

Byron acts as if the motto *Crede Byron* enjoins him dutifully to pay his debts, as if it were (redundantly) a promise to keep promises, equivalent to the declaration "You can trust Byron" and therefore subject to falsification. But the child has it wrong. If the motto is construed as only a promise, it is hard to see how Lord Byron, who will incur debt after debt without repayment, does not betray it. Moreover, as the promise is repeatedly betrayed, its force would inevitably weaken: people (merchants, for example) would be disinclined to extend credit to someone who never pays them back. But *Crede*

Byron is not a promise; it is the assertion of a law that "must be obeyed, even against inclination" and that here has the formula of an imperative.

According to Kant, "All imperatives command either hypothetically or categorically. The former present the practical necessity of a possible action as a means to achieving something else which one desires (or which one may possibly desire). The categorical imperative would be one which presented an action as of itself objectively necessary, without regard to any other end."[24] The hypothetical imperative corresponds to that regulative hypothesis we have seen at work in Joseph Addison and Ralph Allen, and that we have seen indirectly exercised by the law over the duel through its seconds. The categorical imperative is voiced by Chaworth. But Byron's motto has nothing to do with either utterance, if for no other reason than that it is not and never was a saying (no Byron ever said, "Trust Byron"); it was aboriginally an inscription made in a particular place and a particular time (so particular that the place and the time cannot be substantiated), the usage of which is always in allegorical relation to that original inscriptive moment, itself nonidentical with the immediate presence of the person to whom it refers.[25] Because it is the anamnesis of Byron, and thus neither hypothetical nor categorical, the motto *Crede Byron* does not fit within the Kantian taxonomy. It lacks objectivity ("i.e., that which would serve all rational beings also subjectively as a practical principle if reason had full power over the faculty of desire"),[26] yet it makes no appeal to desire—it is a formula summoning forth the social ground, the commonplace, of obligation that sustains the system of exchanges that enables desire hypothetically to achieve its end. *Crede Byron* is the order to believe, and by that token an impossible order according to skeptical empiricists from David Hume to Stanley Fish—those liberals for whom the *ought* of belief is always subject to the *is* of the society by which we are always already composed.

The illogic of *Crede Byron* is of the same order as the implicit command, "If you would be like me don't imitate me." It expresses *the minimum of the maximal* that adheres even to Kant's rendering of the categorical objectivity of the law; no precept, the minimum of the maximal is the element or quality that without pandering to desire forms the inhuman objectivity of the law into a legible command. This minimum of the maximal orients and invigorates the objective, but it precedes and underwrites the subjective as the anthropological, the local, the particular. It is comparable to what late in his career Lord Byron will call "circumstantial gravity," the textual density that impinges on a reader and inexorably draws her into its discrepant world. Adorno calls this imperative an "addendum": "An impulse, the rudiment of a phase in which the dualism of extramental and intramental was not thoroughly consolidated yet, neither volitively bridgeable nor an ontological ultimate." The addendum, he claims, "is a flash of light between the poles of something long past, something grown all but unrecognizable, and that which some day might come to be."[27] Adorno waxes Byronic. We have already encountered that flash of light as the Byronic lightning referred to in *Childe Harold III*. We shall have other occasions to pick up its glint. Adorno's conception of the addendum recovers the performative aspect of lordship that has been abstracted into sociological grammars; he does so not by anchoring it in a historical past but by affiliating it with the possibility of a future.

The addendum prescribes the "jolt" of decision that interrupts the smooth causal line of nature or consciousness's serene disposition of its self-propositions.[28] It designates the illogicality of the imperative to *believe* as the nonidentity that gives the imperative the power to oblige choice. No doubt the imperative provokes a moment of oblivion, a forgetting that we already believe, as part of its impulsion. The addendum of Byron's motto is the text of aristocratic genealogy, which does not "roll off in a causal chain" but is linked by moments of decision, acts of will. Whether that addendum comes to Byron as the record of his great-uncle's vindication by hand or statute or as the motto that commands him to believe in what he is only entitled to be, it appears as a deed, an act that is also "an instrument in writing . . . , purporting to effect some legal disposition" (*OED*). *Purporting* because how the addendum accomplishes its effect is in fact secret, sealed within the pathos of distance that makes the deed available to present consciousness as what drives it beyond itself. For Byron, as we shall have repeated occasion to see, the secret impulse that contradicts the voice of mankind and by which the past jolts the present beyond itself is a scriptive impulse. And in that sense, that Robert who in the thirteenth century "distinguished himself solely by changing the first vowel in the family name" from *u* to *y* is an ancestor as sufficient to Byron's strength as his scandalous great-uncle.[29]

All this to make sense of Byron's bad timing. Byron's delay in replying to his detractors and in publishing *English Bards and Scotch Reviewers* responds to an intuition (some secret knowledge) that the only available model for his behavior is the wrong model (that *any* model would be wrong). Published, *English Bards and Scotch Reviewers* vindicates the truth of that intuition. In attempting a dramatic reply Byron fails to extricate his gesture from a debilitating fictionality. The untimely delay had cut off the reply from its occasion. Moreover, Byron answers the *Edinburgh*'s anonymous review with a publication similarly anonymous—a doubling of impersonality that prevents the satisfaction that is the only sensible incentive for a duel. Unlike Brougham's anonymity, however, Lord Byron's falls well short of impenetrability: all readers knew the writer of *English Bards and Scotch Reviewers.* Authorial anonymity is the intelligible sign of the substitution of the incentive of fame for honor. In Lord Byron's career, now formally begun, the desire for fame—intrinsically insatiable—coordinates with the generalized mode of distinction that engagement with a system rather than a person demands. Answering the *Edinburgh* means subscribing to the cultural values of impersonality and generality that the journal represents. If in Byron's eyes "the System of the Edinburgh Gentlemen is universal attack" (*BLJ* 1:157), his reply, which relies on the rusty armature of Pope, Churchill, and Gifford and resorts to the same superstructural conceit of Roman Catholic authority by which the *Review* had buttressed its denunciation of the Lake School in 1802, expresses a similarly futile aspiration to concoct cultural authority by the bluff of system.

Byron failed. As he was to come to see with exquisite clarity, all his strengths lay outside of system. Indeed, his attack on "sectaries" in the name, however ironically invoked, of his holiness the pope neatly recapitulates Charles Moore's attack on the duel as the "most grievous offense against good government:—an assumption of private authority, whereby the parties themselves are constituted by themselves, both judges and executioners in their own cause."[30] Moore's characterization applies less to duels in general, where seconds represent the public and regulate individual assumption of authority, than to the fifth Lord Byron's duel in particular. The attack on sectarianism identifies the attack on the "duel" as a version of the Enlightenment assault on "enthusiasm," a form of egoism by which Hume and his successors lumped Methodists and aristocrats together as claimants of a privilege not subject to empirical verification. "Duelling is the vilest of all egotism," says the "uncommonly judicious" Mr. Collins, while commenting on Mr. Falkland's humiliation in William Godwin's *Caleb Williams*, "treating the public, which has a claim to all my powers and exertions, as if it were nothing, and myself, or rather an unintelligible chimera I annex to myself, as if it were entitled to my exclusive attention."[31]

Godwin's ventriloquizing of Collins is perfectly in line with Addison's earlier remarks (*Spectator*, no. 219) about the decline of nobility: "In the founders of great families, such attributes of honour are generally correspondent with the virtues of the person to whom they are applied; but in the descendants they are too often the marks rather of grandeur than of merit. The stamp and denomination still continues, but the intrinsic value is frequently lost." Addison does not grieve. His complaint that "honours are in this world under no regulation; [that] true quality is neglected, virtue . . . oppressed, and vice triumphant" serves not a nostalgia for intrinsic merit but a policy that understands "true quality" as the *effect* of regulation—a position roughly the same as the doctrine that Lord Byron didactically espouses in his preface to *English Bards and Scotch Reviewers*. As Godwin represents it, all that troubles the passage into that perfectly public world is the residue of this superseded feudal past, a chimera something like what Charles Moore calls the "inhuman practice" of dueling. Because dueling was invented by the regulative discourse of the Enlightenment as its Other, there can be no doubt of its being ground up in the dialectic. The problem, as Chaworth proved, is in taking the costume for the body. The inhuman practice of the aristocrat is the insistent linking of meaning and body, despite its contradiction of the voice of mankind. To link meaning and body is not to incarnate meaning but to assert that the body is more than the physical, that an incurable limp may be an inimitable style. That *more* is not spirit but exactly what Godwin calls it, a chimera. The chimera that Godwin, like Addison and Hume before him, identify as the ghost of intrinsic value and that the Enlightenment seeks to regulate is not, however, where he locates it; it is only grafted onto dueling, which was strategically imported from the Continent for the purpose. The chimera, that is, is a *real* chimera—value neither intrinsic nor extrinsic, but value of the addendum performed in the unmotivated linking of body with meaning that is the symbolization here called lordship and that will be disseminated throughout Lord Byron's text. The chimera is lodged as much in what Thomas Moore calls the "talismanic" title that confers or confirms privilege in a young boy, or in the "hobble" of a minor's verse, or in the accessory of "Childe Harold" who will accompany the poet during his exile, as it is in the "honor" hypostatized by connoisseurs of the duel.

In *English Bards and Scotch Reviewers* Byron's avowed design was regulative, to discipline by "exposure" those "perverted powers [that] demand the most decided reprehension." But he failed. Although sympathetic, the *Critical Review* adjudges that *English Bards and Scotch Reviewers* "appears to embrace the whole circle of modern poetry and criticism, and it required a regular and systematic plan of operations to cover so vast a space with judgment and effect. This is by no means the case, however, with the present performance, which is a sort of skirmishing attack upon a number of individual writers, unconnected in its pursuit and undefined in its end" (*RR* B:2:608). What number of individual writers? Who has performed the count? Who could be expected to, given the prospect of another revised edition with more names rolling off the press? Lacking a system, even a so-called "system of universal abuse," Byron multiplies the perversities he attempts to control by praising and blaming without a clear standard of excellence and in doing so justifies the charge that he had leveled against the *Edinburgh:* he defeats his "object by indiscriminate abuse" (*BLJ* 1:157).

That break with system entails a break with dueling, which is the projection of system on all the world *as yet* outside the jurisdiction of the court. Despite professions, the *Edinburgh*'s system is scarcely universal; it is merely Whiggish. And in fact it is the gentleman Jeffrey, not the lord Byron, who duels and with ludicrous results. Whom would Byron fight first? Last? Even when owned and "personalized" by its author, *English Bards and Scotch Reviewers* multiplies adversaries to a point where any single duel, any *series* of duels, would be incapable of resolving the dispute. Byron's hunt metaphor is not haphazard. His literary adversaries are like the rabbits on his great-uncle's manors: they proliferate because of a perverse neglect punctuated by spasms of spirited assault. However much one assails them, there will always be rabbits and poetasters. One cannot annihilate what one cannot count. For Lord Byron skirmishing is all. And in every skirmish the sixth Lord Byron proves, "I, too, can scrawl" (l. 47).

In *English Bards and Scotch Reviewers* all Byron's designs fail—which is fortunate, because his designs are false and his impulses true. Lord Byron is that poet whose impulses always wreck the "undisturbed career" designed for him. If Lord Byron inadvertently links up with his uncle by his failure to honor the code of the duel, he also serves the dialectic of enlightenment by performing an act that promises to cauterize the wound in the body politic of Regency England: the banishment of the untamed impulse that assailed it. And so, having published *English Bards and Scotch Reviewers*, Byron, as if following Adorno's script, departs for the Continent. *As if* following Adorno's script, but in fact elaborating the script of his great-uncle, for it will invariably be by his self-banishment that Byron will assert his merit and prove his separate excellence.

3

Sex, Class, and the Naked Letter of Romance

Childe Harold I *and* II *and the Separation*

Boldly conjuring up a scene of moral devastation, he requires you to regard it as you would the phaenomena, which denote some former war of elements — some past convulsion of nature, mysterious, and unknown. The sombre graces of his manner, the dark energies of his pen, render the spell powerful; and he is obeyed.

Review of The Giaour *in the* Critical Review, *July 1813*

Be assured that whatever you do comes so distorted through the prism of prattling ignorance & the fogs of the Jura that it will require some efforts of credible eye witnesses to put it into the straight line of truth & reason.

John Cam Hobhouse to Lord Byron, July 9, 1816

Early in her *Vindication of the Rights of Woman* Mary Wollstonecraft undertakes to account for the historical fact of male dominance without invoking principles that would implicitly legitimate it. She concedes the "natural superiority" of men but urges that the only "solid basis on which the superiority of the sex can be built" is "bodily strength."[1] She then tactically subdivides strength between a biological peculiarity that has enabled the male to enforce his dominance and an attribute of a plastic, "human" body that has been *constituted* in a disciplined, rational way rather than inherited in any old way. Strength remains the criterion of sexual difference, but what had been a *cause* of historical domination has become an *effect* of disciplined exercise. Nietzsche would later aphorize, "Only that which has no history is definable."[2] Wollstonecraft defines precisely to void the historical, a category that includes both an "arbitrary" quality called strength and the social class to which that quality properly belongs, the aristocracy. In opposition to the "brutal force that has hitherto governed the world" for the sensual benefit of a "male aristocracy," Wollstonecraft proposes a benign, universally human hygiene of self-improving "exercise."[3]

In its awkward deviations and undisciplined repetitions Wollstonecraft's text charts its failure to emancipate its "Reason" from spasms of aggressiveness. A particularly sensational eruption occurs near the end of *Vindication*, where Wollstonecraft recklessly charges that the "causes of female weakness branch out of one grand cause—want of chastity in men." She continues,

> This intemperance, so prevalent, depraves the appetite to such a degree, that a wanton stimulus is necessary to rouse it; but the parental design of Nature is forgotten, and the mere person, and that for a moment, alone engrosses the thoughts. So voluptuous, indeed, often grows the lustful prowler, that he refines on female softness. Something more soft than women is then sought for; till, in Italy and Portugal, men attend the levees of equivocal beings, to sigh for more than female languour.[4]

Politics has been fully sexualized. Anti-aristocratic animus transmutes into homophobic fantasy.[5]

This configuration of a "fastidious sensualist" sighing for a languorous equivocal being might be named a scene of fascination to distinguish it from Harold Bloom's famous "scene of instruction." If for Bloom the "ultimate" scene of instruction is described by Raphael in book 5 of *Paradise Lost*,[6] the pattern for the scene of fascination is that where, transfixed, Satan gazes at the nakedly veiled Eve, tempted to become the tempter. No doubt Wollstonecraft has Milton in mind; but a nearer and more highly charged referent is the famous set piece from *Reflections on the Revolution in France* where Edmund Burke, mixing Luciferian and Evenic motifs, nostalgically recalls the royal levee where he had last seen "the queen of France, then the dauphiness, at Versailles; and surely never lighted on this orb, which she hardly seemed to touch, a more delightful vision. I saw her just above the horizon, decorating and cheering the elevated sphere she just began to move in,—glittering like the morning-star, full of life, and splendour, and joy."[7] Against Burke's best intentions, Wollstonecraft would, I suspect, happily appropriate this charming epiphany as an instance of her paradigm, perhaps concatenating it with the earlier, softcore depiction of the queen's hairbreadth escape from rape and death, and with the moment when Burke, sickening with the pleasure of having his queen and beating her too, falls into misogynist rant against "the abused shape of the vilest of women."[8]

Examples of the scene of fascination could be multiplied. Cowper's itinerant Kate, whose gaudy distress briefly arrests the flow of sentiment in the first book of *The Task*, has been crazed by loss; but she is marked as equivocal and rendered fascinating to the reader, who inhabits the spectral perspective of her dead husband (figured by the returned mariner), by an attachment to her ribbons stronger than her instinct for survival. Cowper's Kate spawns Wordsworth's female vagrants, and particularly Margaret, who, impatiently drooping toward organic oblivion, is the object of the pedlar's feelingful attention in "The Ruined Cottage." This poem is unmatched in its archaeology of the odd lot of hieroglyphic objects and inscriptions—a spider's web, a shard of pottery, "dull red stains"—that are infused with value by their synthesis in the figure of a seated, melancholy woman—the equivocal being over which the sentimental traveler can sigh and whom he can sorrowfully exploit as the nexus of various literary, political, and economic themes.

The supply of Romantic scenes of fascination is indefinite.[9] There is, however, a problem of gender in my examples. Although I have accused Wollstonecraft of homophobia, the levees I have mentioned all gender the equivocal being as female. In point of fact, Wollstonecraft's readers would have understood the implicit referent behind "lustful prowler" to be William Beckford, author of *Vathek* and notorious pederast, who fled to Portugal and Italy in large part to escape the kind of persecution that Wollstonecraft echoes. Yet my liberties with gender merely follow the lead of Wollstonecraft herself, who refers only to a "more than female languour." "More than female"—it does not, finally, make any difference if the being rendered equivocal is a boy dressed up as a girl or a girl dressed up as a boy, or a girl or a boy dressed up beyond reason. It is the "more than" that signifies, attracts, fascinates—attracts as the fascination of signification.

We can get an idea of the historical moment here by recalling Michel Foucault's observation that "the first figure to be invested by the deployment of sexuality, one of the first to be 'sexualized,' was the 'idle' woman. She inhabited the outer edge of the 'world,' in which she had to appear as a value, and of the family, where she was assigned a new destiny."[10] The idleness of the woman, what frees her from ascriptive ties and burdens her with the social destiny of being "more than female," is the corollary of political economy's valorization of the classically condemned concept of luxury. As David Hume observed, "Luxury is a word of an uncertain signification."[11] Luxuries as commodities are similarly equivocal—and essential for that very reason. Political economy is a system wherein what has been indicted as dangerous or sinful under a previous regime is put to work as an instrument of corporate profit and systemic elaboration. Economically vital, the idle woman in Humean, liberal discourse also has a privileged political status: idle woman replaces idle aristocrat; female as equivoque (object as subject, consuming and consumed) displaces the noble as ambivalent (sovereign deed, violent expenditure without reserve). The narcissistic moment of fascination functions as a pivot on which politics swings into economics, class into gender, subject into object. In a spectacular and powerful redoubling of bad faith, the necessity for the moment that is, conceptually and historically, the precondition for political economy coming to know itself, is blamed on the "natural" perversity of woman, which it is the part of enlightenment both to deplore and to gratify. As Wollstonecraft's example shows, resistance to that assignment to the equivocal mounted in the names of woman and enlightenment may change the immediate target, but nonetheless collaborates with the overall project of political economy. The vindication of one group, such as woman, from assignment to the drawer labeled "a fanciful kind of *half* being"[12] entraps other interstitial figures (the aristocrat deluded by what William Godwin called "chimerical" honor or the outrageous Beckford bewitched by strange boys), thus extending the "outer edge of the 'world'" to include new margins and markets, such as Italy and Portugal.[13] By letting the gender lapse, Wollstonecraft stretches eighteenth-century political economy and the achievement of the eighteenth-century man of letters as far as they will go: gone is the luxury as object, as woman, or even as boy. "Liberated as a sign to be recaptured by the formal logic of differentiation,"[14] the equivocal being is merely the commodity in all its chimerical potential to allure as more than female, more than person, more than thing, and to affiliate men and women under the rubric *human* as clients of the commercial economy. The commodified sign takes up the slack in the "more than" and regulates it according to an economy that orients all the "less than" that is desire.

"*Ma Méthode*" and the Formation of a Literary Identity

Both in what she affirms and in what she denies Wollstonecraft contributes to that discursive practice in which, as Theodor Adorno writes, "the network of the whole is drawn ever tighter, modelled after the act of exchange. It leaves the individual consciousness less and less room for evasion, preforms it more and more thoroughly, cuts it off a priori as it were from the possibility of differencing itself as all difference degenerates to a nuance in the monotony of supply." Under the guise or standard of an attack on degenerate lords, Wollstonecraft contributes to the historical degeneration of difference. Degeneration is an evil for Adorno not because he wants to adhere to the "devices quaint" (*CHI*, st. 67) of an earlier historical moment, let alone act as apologist for a vanished ruling class, but because this degeneration represents the refusal to think of difference. The enlightenment, liberal model of inexorable progressive development implicitly allows a biological, organic metaphor to speak for or ordain historical change, subjecting the human agent to a scalar logic and to the law of economy. For the liberal, degeneration is imagined as the dread alternative to the revolutionary path of enlightenment. Anomaly and perversion—the failure to adapt—threaten to push one from the stage of history into a long, dark fall. From Adorno's dialectical perspective, degeneration is enlightenment's very condition of possibility. Degeneration, the lapse of kind, follows from the repression of difference that oppression of the different symptomatizes. Understood as the repression of difference, degeneration is the inevitable corollary of enlightenment's constitutive forgetting that people's desire can only be judged by a standard that has been made by some people at some time and that can be altered by some others any day. Considered as the procedure by which the person comes to forget its difference from the schema of the human with which it is summoned to identify or, in Adorno's words, as the process by which the "mind mould[s] itself for the sake of its marketability," degeneration is the process by which some thing or person becomes a commodity.[15] Degeneration nuances the monotony of supply insofar as it is controlled, insofar as it becomes the destiny of a commodity endowed with a kind of natural life—a half-life or shelf-life—according to the "seasons" of the market. Indeed (freely adapting Adorno here), it is the aptitude of a new commodity to capture *by its very novelty* the feel of degeneration that makes it perversely desirable.

We shall be returning to these categories throughout. As we shall see, the literary system named *Byron* was not, as the reviewers chronically complained, endangered by Byron's so-called perversion; on the contrary, the profitability of that corporate concern was triggered by the lord's deviation into print and guaranteed by his continued degeneration—a process fully coincident with his relentless commodification. For us the text of Byron is the test of difference in the Romantic period—whether it need be straightened out and adjusted to the network of exchange (if only by describing its darkness as that Other that sustains the claims of High Romanticism's bright transcendence), or whether by some unforeseen twist it can separate itself from that very code by which it becomes recognizable and by which its very deviance is turned to profit.

Here is a scene of fascination framed by Byron in a letter from Greece to his former traveling companion John Cam Hobhouse:

> At Vostitza I found my dearly-beloved Eustathius—ready to follow me not only to England, but to Terra Incognita, if so be my compass pointed that way. . . . The next morning I found the dear soul upon horseback clothed very sprucely in Greek Garments, with those ambrosial curls hanging down his amiable back, and to my utter astonishment and the great abomination of Fletcher, a *parasol* in his hand to save his complexion from the heat.— However in spite of the *Parasol* on we travelled very much enamoured, as it should seem, till we got to Patras, where Strane received us into his new house where I now scribble. (*BLJ* 2:66)

Eastering, Lord Byron reorients his sexuality. Enamored though he be, this lord, unlike Wollstonecraft's more pious voluptuary, displays a rather breezy detachment. There can be little doubt that the mature Byron's first genital intimacy with boys occurred during this first trip to Greece, and probably with Eustathius, yet this moment seems no more unmediated than any other in his letters. Indeed, the tableau represents the variousness of mediation. The gaze is mediated by its doubling between the appalled expression of Fletcher and the quizzical esteem of Byron. The lyrical freeze frame concatenates with additional moments and even, as the epistolary format implies, other minds. The not-quite-fascinated gaze is subordinated to an exchange, and the exchange is ultimately referred to a moment of production, "I now scribble."

What is being produced? First, a discourse of what has come to be called "liberation"—a liberation that runs the scale from sex to politics and that combines in supposedly mutual benefit both agent and object. Yet the liberation is quite specific and, one might even say, constrained. It neatly satisfies most of the criteria for the implantation of perverse sexuality developed by Michel Foucault in his introductory volume to the *History of Sexuality*. First, the liberation is regional: it applies to a particular kind of sexuality proper to a specific kind of object (the species Wollstonecraft denominated "equivocal being") and then only in a particular and peripheral geographical setting—here Asia Minor, a domain where Byron can safely indulge his peculiar appetite. Second, the liberation of sexuality is, as I have already indicated, thoroughly discursive: not only is it displayed in this letter, but the basis of its regionalism is literary. The tag *Greek love* does not euphemize the so-called homosexual bond between Byron and Eustathius. Lord Byron learned his homosexuality from books—old books. One of the most impressionable students of the classics the English public schools have ever formed, Byron invested sexual desire only in Greek boys. For Byron—classical in his tastes, anthropological in his desires—*Greek love* meant love of Greeks.[16]

Third, the liberation of homosexual desire is not a final break with a prior repression; the liberation is fully correlative with what Foucault calls the "repressive hypothesis," which is the condition of its possibility as well as its extension. The point-by-point correlation of liberation with repression makes possible the translation of the domain of sexuality onto nationality, as though the release of some supposedly repressed personal impulse were homologous with the release of some repressed aspect of the European past. In Byron's case the convergence of a European discourse of Golden Age innocence and truth with the ocular evidence of repression by the despotic Turk *constitutes* his homosexuality. The evidence of repression enables him to orient and organize his inchoate political and erotic impulses, which then become homosexual retrospectively, as a potential or latency. For us, not for him. Byron never intimated that he had been a homosexual before leaving England, nor even after he had indulged with Greek boys did he suggest that he had left something undone in his relations with his favorite, John Edleston, the Cambridge choirboy toward whom he frankly acknowledged a love "violent, although pure" (*BLJ* 8:24).[17] Greek love could not be practiced with English lads. Moreover, the love of the sentimental liberator can never confess to its violence and so can never be pure.

Only the repression of the Greek by the Turk allows for the possibility of his liberation. In Lord Byron's eyes it is that repression, not some intrinsic desire of his own, that constitutes Eustathius as an equivocal being—Greek and boy, male and female, political victim and sexual object—of novel allure. The Turkish occupation of Greek soil is homologous with the parasol covering Eustathius's fair skin: the sexual appeal of the boy is produced as the effect of what covers and corrects it. As the theme of the classical centralizes the peripheral, makes Asia Minor a familiar Greece and legitimates Byron's interest in it, so does the sexualization of the political enable Byron to see repression and to sympathize with it as if it were his own. The liberation that Byron foresees confuses the sexual with the political and encourages Byron to confuse his own sexual liberation with a political liberation, as if it had something to do with Eustathius. Byron's repression could be lifted. But the condition of that release is that Eustathius remain an object of desire and thus fixed in his degradation. The sexual and political appeal of the boy is produced as the effect of what covers him and degrades him from masculinity. Byron desires the Greek boy only insofar as the body is represented; he desires Eustathius as degraded from kind to nuance; he desires "him" as a creature lapsed from body into sign.[18]

The repressive hypothesis is well meaning; it gives Byron a purpose, some good work to do. He will liberate himself; he will liberate the Greek— or, as Jerome J. McGann puts it, neatly hybridizing the *isms* natural, supernatural, and Oriental, Byron becomes "obsessed with the idea of renewal of human culture in the west at a moment of its deepest darkness. This means for Byron the renewal of the value of the individual person, and the renewal of Greece as an independent political entity."[19] But pathos depends on a misrecognition. Lord Byron believed in no such thing as "human culture," nor did he cherish the idea of a transhistorical individual whose value fluctuated like the funds. He did at times however, project a *specific* form of renewal or liberation, as in this note to *Childe Harold II:* "The English have at last compassionated their Negroes, and under a less bigoted government may probably one day release their Catholic brethren; but the interposition of foreigners alone can emancipate the Greeks, who, otherwise appear to have as small a chance of redemption from the Turks, as the Jews have from mankind in general" (*CPW* 2:202).[20]

Lord Byron's messianism is less Christological than feudal. He imagines the redeemed purity of the Greek as the gift of a chivalrous knight, who magnanimously presents the repressed with *their* emancipation as a corollary to the revival of *his* mythic past. Subjected to the repressive hypothesis, difference (historical, geographical, subjective) is thematized as the consequence of a lost or stolen original purity, which the sentimental liberator will profess to *return* to the Greek, but which he is actually *donating for the first time.* Eustathius and the Greeks are engendered by the dream of their emancipation—a story that produces their bygone freedom as the alibi for the representational practice of the liberator, in the same way as the pure white body of the boy is the alibi for the parasol: for the signifier that constitutes him as a sign and shadows him forth as a degraded object of desire. Lord Byron can imagine freeing the Greeks, but, despite the ringing exhortation of stanza 76 of *Childe Harold I*, he cannot imagine the Greeks fully free: "The Greeks will never be independent; they will never be sovereigns as heretofore, and God forbid they ever should! but they may be subjects without being slaves. Our colonies are not independent, but they are free and industrious, and such may Greece be hereafter" (*CPW* 2:201).[21]

Lord Byron's homosexuality is not at all like the more primitive, compensatory passion of the Turks;[22] Byron's is classical, rule-governed. It occurs in the perceptible (perceptible because discursively constructed) historical opening between the generalized application of the repressive hypothesis and the globalized deployment of the regulative hypothesis, which will discipline the plastic Greeks (and other subject peoples) according to the rule-governed designs of a moralizing imperialism.[23] Greece can perform as a pilot for the fully globalized imperial project because the deployment of the regulative hypothesis, the *classing* of nationalities (as of social groups), seems to have an especial decorum there, where the "liberation" of Greece can be rendered as feeding back just those classically "Greek" principles that supply the rationale for imperial rule.

It is a telling coincidence that Byron scribbles his Greek love at "Patras," for the colonization that Byron calls freedom is a form of patronage. That Byron's relations with boys were established along lines of patronage has not gone unnoticed,[24] but the sentimental structure of such relationships has. Its flavor can be sampled in the 1807 letter to Elizabeth Pigott in which Byron writes of the "*Chaos of hope & Sorrow*" into which he has been thrown by his separation from John Edleston, described as his "protégé," who is committed to entering a "mercantile house in Town" on Lord Byron's interest. The dismal denouement of this relationship (during his voyage Byron was doubly shocked by the news that the urbanized Edleston had been accused of "indecency" and soon after that he had died of consumption) was partially the result of the misprision attendant on the attempt to maintain patronage as a mediatory fiction between men of different social classes and between a schoolboy world of "violent, although pure" love and the tranquil gloom of a counting house. In the event, once the doomed Edleston (who, in the iconography of nineteenth-century medievalism, played the Lady of Shalott to Byron's Lancelot) left the safety of Cambridge, he and Byron ceased to meet. So distant did they become that Edleston's revival of the fiction of patronage in response to Byron's crass misreading of an earlier appeal seems embarrassingly abject: "At present I must beg leave to repeat that [it] is only the favor of your Lordship's *personal* Influence and Patronage [not money] which I humbly presumed in my last as well as now,—to request."[25]

The transactions with Edleston are an extreme example of a characteristic mode in Byron: the structure and ethos of patronage, usually bedecked in the finery of chivalric *noblesse*, were invoked to reconstruct and normalize contacts with men and women that were in their happening invisible, fluid, even anarchic. By "invisible, fluid, even anarchic" I mean what Lord Byron's crony Scrope Berdmore Davies meant when, upon departing from a stay at Newstead Abbey, he jotted the note, "This whole week passed in a delirium of sensuality."[26] Davies, like Byron, has impressive claims to authority on such matters, having spent his school days at Eton, where as a Kings Scholar he was housed with roughly fifty other lads in a dormitory room where, as his biographer describes it, "between the hours of 8 o'clock at night, when they were locked in, and 7 o'clock the next morning when they were released by the Head Master's servant the boys were left totally to their own devices."[27] We have no way of knowing what those devices were. No doubt there was "cruel bullying and sexual malpractices," but the "total lack of privacy" for the individual had the consequence of conferring the collective autonomy of complete invisibility on the dreamlike, delirial world of boys, each and all with their peculiar devices.[28] If this world can be described as the "other face of the 18th century, the face unglimpsed in Jane Austen's novels, brutal, filthy, and corrupt," it can only be once the eighteenth century has been given a recognizable face by such writers as Austen.[29] Only then, in a self-consciously *nineteenth* century, could this delirial world, unreadable according to the Malthusian and Benthamite schemata, be given the physiognomy of the Other, corrupt and brutal, in order that it could be redeemed for the future by Christian muscle and chivalric myth.

Byron situated *Hours of Idleness* at the divide (called the "Rubicon" in the preface) between minority and legal maturity and eagerly contributed to the general cultural project of recasting the invisible world of dirty little boys and the cleared world of the highland clans in terms of the regulative format of chivalric romance and its eighteenth-century offshoot, Ossianism. That same inclination is followed in *Childe Harold* as the Albanian tribesmen are both infantilized ("Fierce are Albania's children") and Scotticized ("the kirtled clan") in order to celebrate a world of "man link'd to man" held together by "devices quaint." A similar intent is manifest in the practice of those British troops who, occupying the Ionian Islands subsequent to 1809, renamed the islands "according to their ancient forms" and, under the guidance of Lord Guilford, established a Hellenic University in which the faculty and students dressed in the color-coded buskins of the ancients. This "harmless archaizing" was a means of legitimating the occupation imposed by European philhellenes, contrasting it with the ignorant brutality that supposedly characterized the Ottomans on the mainland.[30] At home the story was similar: the cultural strategy of using the outworn spells of chivalry to bind man to man in a world of lapsed allegiances and ambiguous obligations was a conspicuous feature of the nineteenth-century nostalgia for all things medieval as it is expounded with intelligence and wit by Mark Girouard in *The Return to Camelot*.[31] But Girouard does not observe what "Lord Byron Minor" had earlier failed to see: not only that the consequence of remembering school days was their annihilation, but also that this medievalist strategy was so readily available because it repeated with remarkable fidelity the monarchic attempt to control the bullyings and sexual malpractices among the nobility that was the policy behind the royal institution of tournaments and heraldic codes in the thirteenth century (and the toleration of duels in the sixteenth): henceforth the nobles' devices would never be totally their own.[32] It would be some time before Lord Byron would come to understand nostalgia as a form of suicide.[33]

Lord Byron's attempts both to memorialize the delirial world of his youth and to circumscribe similar possibilities in the present are epitomized by his relations with Nicolo Giraud, singled out among the "sylphs" with whom Byron "rioted" at the Capuchin monastery at Athens. "I am his 'Padrone' and his 'amico,'" Byron writes, "and the Lord knows what besides" (*BLJ* 2:12). About Giraud we know little more than what Byron tells us, but the switching between *padrone* and *amico* is wholly characteristic of Byron, who in his first public appearance as poet split his poetic persona between Julius Caesar and William Cowper, as well as between the reluctant commander of "To the Earl of Dorset" and the stripling friend of "To the Earl of Clare." This oscillation would remain a constant threat to the stability of the Byronic poetic subject (see, for example, the wavering between a jolly democracy and a melancholy despotism in the opening of *The Corsair*), until in *Don Juan* the undecidable priority between *padrone* and *amico* becomes the whirligig on which character and narrator ride in outlandish parody of chivalrization and its discontents.

For the roving lord of 1810, however, who is unconnected by anything but debts to the world of men in which he has, despite himself, grown up, freeing the Greeks is a profession of sorts. So is writing about it. The pursuit of boys may satisfy diverse aims, but "the end of all scribblement is to amuse" (*BLJ* 2:20). And if it is arguably the case that Byron could not have coitus with any boys while Hobhouse, an "enemy to fine feelings & sentimental friendships" (*BLJ* 2:155), was around, it is certainly true that Byron could not *write* to Hobhouse with Hobhouse around. The departure of Hobhouse is ultimately less important for allowing Byron to *have* the experience than it is for enabling Byron to *represent* the experience, tantalizingly, as a scene for an audience of intimate male friends.

In his *Byron and Greek Love* Louis Crompton sets Byron's Eastern journey against the background of a Cambridge circle knit by what he calls a "homosexual bond," which included Byron, Hobhouse, and Charles Skinner Matthews. "In a sense," Crompton observes, "the three share what would today be called a gay identity, based on common interests and a sense of alienation from a society they must protect themselves from by a special 'mysterious' style and mutually understood codes."[34] Crompton refers to an exchange between Byron and Matthews on the eve of the former's embarkation with Hobhouse for the East. Byron writes, "I take up the pen which our friend has for a moment laid down merely to express a vain wish that you were with us in this delectable region, as I do not think Georgia itself can emulate in capabilities or incitements to the 'Plen. and optabil.—Coit.' the ports of Falmouth & parts adjacent—We are surrounded by Hyacinths & other flowers of the most fragrant [na]ture, & I have some intention of culling a handsome Bouquet to compare with the exotics I hope to meet in Asia." Matthews replies by congratulating Byron "on the splendid success of your first efforts in *the mysterious,* that style in which more is meant than meets the Eye." He goes on to encourage Byron in his "Botanical pursuits" and decrees "that everyone who professes *ma methode* do spell the term which designates his calling with an e at the end of it—*methodiste,* not method*ist,* and pronounce the word in the French fashion. Every one's taste must revolt at confounding ourselves with that sect of horrible, snivelling, fanatics."[35] Though barely utterable, the code is easily deciphered: "Hyacinths" are boys; the Latin abbreviation "Plen. and optabil.—Coit." is from *The Satyricon* and refers to "full and to-be-wished-for intercourse."[36]

Rather than the formation of a gay sense of identity in response to real or imagined persecution, this bit of correspondence describes the deliberate formation of a *literary* sense of identity, a shared sense of what Matthews calls a profession. The profession is formed by the positing of a particular kind of sexual experience as something that, because it cannot meet the eye, underwrites everything that can. Of greater importance than the wished-for coitus is the idea of it. Rendered jokingly as the pursuit of a natural history of all beautiful boys, that idea makes possible both the ritual exchange of pens between Hobhouse and Byron, anticipating their literary collaborations, and the economical style of the "mysterious," which forecasts the darkly implicative mode of Byron's portrayal of a character who unites "the eager curiosity of youth with the fastidiousness of a sated libertine"—a portrayal that was to be the first literary fruit of his pilgrimage.[37] The linkage of the mysterious style with the broodings of the Byronic hero connect it to the Gothic motif of the "unspeakable," which, as Eve Kosofsky Sedgwick has incisively remarked, was in the Romantic period "a near-impenetrable shibboleth for a particular conjunction of class and male sexuality."[38] In this context the mysterious style, if almost unutterable, is most significant as one that is highly transmissible. It has all the conspicuous visibility and cryptic formality of a code, which here operates not primarily to hide something but as a kind of trademark to identify an association of senders and receivers. The "mysterious style" enables a profession; it is what Defoe, speaking of brewers, Swift, speaking of stockjob-bers, Coleridge, speaking of contemporary critics, or Byron, speaking of publishers, would describe as the cant of the trade.[39] Its jargon artificially creates the body of traders, establishing the line between inside and outside, forming the basis for and boundaries of association. Their "mysterious style" binds these three Cambridge students together in what is a profes-sional organization that *elects* not to speak its name.

The jargon of homosexuality expresses what Jacques Lacan calls a "for-mal fixation, which introduces a certain rupture of level, a certain discord between man's organization and his *Umwelt*, which is the very condition that extends indefinitely his world and his power."[40] In the case of these men the jargon of homosexuality produces a specific kind of paranoiac knowl-edge in the service of a distinctive literary identity, which in turn has signal *political* consequences. Considered genealogically, the cryptic affiliation of these literary men is the begetter of the secret society of conspiratorial philhellenes formed in response to the stirring summons of *Childe Harold's Pilgrimage: A Romaunt*. Called the Friendly Society, this conspiracy re-cruited members who, according to William St. Clair, were submitted to "awesome ceremonies of initiation and oaths of secrecy," all in the service of the cause of "returning" freedom to a Greece in the name of a Hellenism that was a European trope, not a Greek aspiration.[41] The extension of the world, therefore, proceeds imperially according to a metonymic association of subjects: boys, Greek boys, Greeks, the Orient—with Byron as the vehicle of its elaboration. Although it may be appealing to regard this as the sort of project in which the poet carries with him relationship and love, K. J. Dover's distinction between "legitimate" and "illegitimate" eros shames such vanity. Among the ancient Greeks, according to Dover, the legitimacy that was conferred on a philanthropic relationship between an *erastes* and his youthful *eromenos* was sharply contrasted with "gross misbehaviour for monetary payment [which] is the act of a hubristes and uneducated man"[42]—a vice aptly described by Byron's phrase (he had in mind his friend Francis Hodgson's penchant for falling in love with prostitutes), "romantic attachments for things marketable at a dollar" (*BLJ* 2:149).

Although there is no evidence that Lord Byron, *padrone* and *amico*, was ever so vulgar as to set an exact market value on his sexual arrangements in Greece, Nicolo Giraud, Eustathius's replacement in Byron's affections, was employed as "dragoman and Major Domo" (*BLJ* 2:29), a position that almost certainly entailed payment in love *and* money.[43] But more important than specific acts of monetary payment is the imperial conception of a tour that would induce Byron to describe himself as a very Caesar of sexuality

(*BLJ* 2:14). The hubristic orientation of Byronic philhellenism is first established by the jocular denomination of boys as "Hyacinths & other flowers."
Botany is not just a convenient metaphor; it is the privileged metaphor for
the instrumentality of metaphor—for the way "natural" bodies can, à la
Rousseau in *The Reveries*, at once be "loved" and regarded as specimens—
can be cathected, collected, and then inserted into books that, like Hobhouse's memoirs and *Childe Harold*, are then sold as commodities on the
open market.[44] When Byron speaks of his Greek boys as his "antiques," it is
difficult on the face of it to assess the ethical and political difference between
his enterprise and the despised Lord Elgin's reprehensible extraction and
removal of what in *Childe Harold II* Byron calls "mouldering shrines"—a
phrase that, given Byron's preoccupations, suggests sexual connotations
(*BLJ* 2:29). Elgin, at least, justifies himself according to a project of preserving specific antiquities, whereas Byron cathects the "sad relics" themselves,
making little distinction among temples, boys, and books. *Relic* is the name
used throughout *Childe Harold* for the degraded form that mingles kinds
formerly distinct in one charming metaphor (one could wish for a free and
independent Greece, for a manly Eustathius, but unfortunately they, like
the statues on the Parthenon, are "relics ne'er to be restored" [*CH II*, st.
132]). Byron's sentimental stance is perfectly decorous, for, as Schiller had
argued, the sentimental is the cultural trope by which differences among
traditional genres are degraded into nuances, thus liberating moderns from
the repression of the past. Lord Elgin may be vulnerable to charges of
plunder. But the sentimental Lord Byron would seem to exploit degradation for its own perversely seductive sake, and to object to desecration only
because his lordly mobility allows him to indulge a taste too expensively
exotic for his less privileged countrymen.[45] Cosmopolitanism involves a
privileged appreciation of the varieties of local attachment. The process by
which a formal fixation underwrites both a literary identity and a hubristic
extension of cognitive and rhetorical power would seem to vindicate
Wollstonecraft's vision of "bodies of men who must necessarily be made
foolish or vicious by the very constitution of their profession."[46]

The jargon of homosexuality furnishes not only a subject but also a way
to write about it. Professing homosexuality, Matthews decrees, means professing *ma méthode*, which in turn entails adopting a certain style—
epitomized by the addition of an *e* to *method*. The *e* is the letter of affection
and affect, both the sign and the act of male bonding. In its capacity to
charm, Matthews's *e* resembles the "naked letter" of romance with which,
according to Richard Hurd, Gothic poets enchanted their readers or, closer
to home, the *a* with which Jacques Derrida neologized *différance*, at once

volatilizing the text of Western metaphysics and spellbinding a generation of literary critics.[47] But *différance* is not *méthode*. By Frenchifying and feminizing English method, Matthews's supplemental letter merely translates it into a new, fetching, but altogether functional uniform. Unnaked, the letter is a device by which Romantic strength can be made recognizable and put to work as the no-nonsense instrument of interest. In the moment of its institution, the code, ostensibly meaningful, masking from all but initiates the existence of forbidden sexual desires, is rendered as the meaningfulness *of* the ostensible, the letter that invites but does not require decoding, like a style. Following Matthews, we may hazard the neoclassical maxim that for these men homosexuality is nature methodized. Having said that, however, the revision naturally follows that for these *writers* homosexuality is style methodized.

The *e* that translates method into *méthode* does not defend against the threat of homophobic persecution; it is the mark of distinction, of self-classification. The project of comparing Hyacinths means inventing a *class* of equivocal beings—half boys, half flowers. Whatever sexual anxiety percolates through the suavity of Matthews's *méthode* is indistinguishable from a class anxiety—the anxiety of sharing pens with a lord and of setting the terms for a new professional writing class, which must be forcefully segregated from an emergent, methodistical working class.[48] Aimed at establishing an airtight sexual, social, and cultural identity, Matthews's *méthode* owes its energy to a fear of confoundment.

Matthews's *e* serves the same function as Eustathius's parasol—as ornament and protection. A lure, it is also the prop of an equivocal being. If it is the profession of a postmethodist style of sexuality and of writing that affiliates Matthews and Lord Byron (the *e* by which Byron affects to archaize his Child*e* Harold is the most flagrant example of his collaboration), it is also Matthews's reliance on method that dramatizes their difference and his inferiority, which hangs on the constitutive imitability of *méthode*. As in the paradigmatic case of the heraldic device, the very mark of self-distinction is the instrument for appropriation by the other: in methodically identifying itself the self formulates the terms of its replication and estrangement. As Adorno has argued, "Identification has its social model in exchange and exchange would be nothing without it."[49] Unlike Matthews, however, Lord Byron's strength distances him from any single style, even the Byronic.[50] What makes the difference between Lord Byron, a clubfooted young man who swims from Sestos to Abydos and lives to write about it, and the stay-at-home Matthews, who was drowned in the weeds while bathing in the Cam, is Lord Byron's radical openness to the kind of confoundment that frightens his friend. Matthews's brief life uncannily illustrates the ill-fated career of those Burkean monsters, "men of theory."[51]

It may seem cruel to vindicate Lord Byron's difference by blaming Matthews for drowning, but as his letters show, Matthews, like Keats, understood the profession of literature as a life of allegory—and Romantic careers, like Romantic poems, prove allegory's cruelty. Moreover, we are merely following Byron here, who in a later recollection of Matthews was perfectly direct. "One of Matthew[s]'s passions," he recalls, "was 'the fancy'; and he sparred uncommonly well. But he always got beaten in rows, or combats with the bare fist. In swimming, too, he swam well; but with *effort* and *labour*, and too *high* out of the water; so that Scrope Davies and myself, of whom he was therein somewhat emulous, always told him that he would be drowned if ever he came to a difficult pass in the water" (*BLJ* 7:233). In life as art Lord Byron always cultivated that ease by which one gets through a difficult pass. As we shall see, the change in his art, which goes by the name *Don Juan*, consists in the far-flung dissemination and prolific meta-morphosis of difficult passes even as his easy manner becomes a matter not for athletic but for ethical emulation.

Within the Byron circle, swimming prowess would nonetheless remain a crucial test of strength—and for Byron, on occasion, an easy legitima-tion of mastery.[52] Here is Lord Byron to Hobhouse rating his "sylphs": "I have as usual swum across the Piraeus, the Signore Nicolo also laved, but he makes as bad a hand in the water as L'Abbe Hyacinth at Falmouth" (*BLJ* 2:14). The most complex site for the allegorization of swimming, how-ever—and one that disturbed Byron's customary sense of superiority—involves his relations with Shelley. One extract from an extraordinary letter:

> [Shelley] was once with me in a Gale of Wind in a small boat right under the rocks between Meillerie & St. Gingo—we were five in the boat—a servant—two boatmen—& ourselves. The Sail was mismanaged & the boat was filling fast—he can't swim.—I stripped off my coat—made him strip off his—& take hold of an oar—telling him that I thought (being myself an expert swimmer) I could save him if he would not struggle when I took hold of him . . . —we were then about a hundred yards from shore—and the boat in peril.—He answered me with the greatest coolness—"that he had no notion of being saved—& that I would have enough to do to save myself, and begged not to trouble me".—Luckily the boat righted. . . . And yet the same Shelley who was as cool as it was possible to be in such circum-stances—(of which I am no judge myself as the chance of swimming natu-rally gives self-possession when near shore) certainly had the fit of phantasy which P[olidori] describes. (*BLJ* 6:126)

Aroused, Byron strips, makes Shelley strip, and then takes "hold of him."
But Shelley remains cool in the face of Byron's domineering ardor to "save
him." Instead Shelley, as Byron implicitly acknowledges, lays incontestable
claim to the position of sovereignty that Byron easily assumed vis-à-vis
Matthews. In one inspired gesture Shelley rejects both the interposition of
Byron's body and the imperative of survival. In this context, or, rather, at
this moment, Shelley exposes swimming prowess as a reification of
strength, a mere matter of expertise acquired through Wollstonecraftian
exercise, aimed at defending against chance, dominating the weak, and
devoted to the proprietarial conservation of a self anxiously possessed. The
Byronic position, as Shelley shows and the vicissitudes of the Byronic text
prove, need not and finally cannot be occupied solely by Byron. Circumstances, like luck, change.

Childe Harold I and *II*

> *Think how the joys of Reading a Gazette*
> *Are purchased by all agonies and crimes.*
>
> Don Juan, *canto 8*
>
> *So much for Chivalry.*
>
> Childe Harold, *1813 addition to the preface*

Childe Harold's Pilgrimage: A Romaunt—the poem that spilled over from
Lord Byron's travels through Spain, Portugal, and the Levant—flaunts the
vice that Wollstonecraft abhorred. Cadiz receives this sweet but "ignoble
praise":

> Ah, Vice, how soft are thy voluptuous ways!
> While boyish blood is mantling, who can 'scape
> The fascination of thy magic gaze?
> A Cherub-hydra round us dost thou gape,
> And mould to every taste thy dear delusive shape.
>
> (*CH I*, st. 65)

A corruption of any spiritual impulse that might stir a true pilgrim's soul
and a prettification of Spenser's urgent imagery of menace and self-loss—
all the despicable sophistication of the aristocrat coalesces in the phrase that
flatters the equivocal being of vice, "dear delusive shape." But if attention is
paid to the specification "while boyish blood is mantling," a different picture emerges. Although none can escape the fascination of vice when ado-

lescence is at full throttle (Keats will become Lord Byron's favorite example of this fixation), it is the narrative premise of the *Romaunt* that the blood of neither the poet nor his "joyless hero" (*CH I*, st. 6) is mantling any longer. A postulated "fulness of satiety" (st. 4) introduces a poem that tells no story but catalogs a series of escapes by poet and pilgrim from one "magic gaze" after another. Childe Harold is no hostage to fortune. In fathering this "child of imagination," the poet has shaped inchoate impulses into an attitude that he can rely on to insulate him from the fascination of vice. Thus the condescending *dear*. With the talismanic Harold at hand, the poet can plausibly imagine himself immune to sensation and thus to enthrallment. Harold is the Byronic equivalent of what in the literature of sensibility is called the "rust" of experience.[53]

The scenic orientation of the first canto harmonizes with the straightforward mimetic ambition announced in the preface, which presents the poem as the record of what Lord Byron saw during his travels. And it does follow that path. But the poem's path is scarcely straightforward. It pauses to track the passage of William Beckford, who laid his "voluptuous lures" in Portugal, and detours to follow the camps of the armies of France and England, whose Peninsular War sprang from the trap that the devious Napoleon set for the greedy Godoy. If the apostrophe to "Vathek! England's wealthiest son" (*CH I*, st. 22) encodes Byron's secret *méthodiste* enterprise, the canto's continuation testifies to the cataclysmic effect political events have on erotic trajectories. And, of course, vice versa. As we have seen, the preface to *Hours of Idleness*, suspended on the threshold of majority, thematized Lord Byron's confusion about his social role as a vacillation between the way of Caesar and the way of Cowper. In *Childe Harold* the interference between things supposed great and things supposed small suspends the poet on the threshold of what the nineteenth century will call a world-view.

For the poet all is dissonance within as without. That dissonance (nothing yet authorizes us to call it historical change) destroys the usefulness of those happy maps by which the conventional grand tour had once been charted and by which poesy had once progressed. Byron does not announce this; as his cosmopolitan epigraph indicates, he proses in Enlightenment banalities. Byron does not, *cannot*, know what he sees until it is seen through him and, in a strong sense, *as* him—if not by Brougham then by some more susceptible reader. Reading Byron offers the pleasure, however transient for his contemporaries, however theoretically insupportable for his latter-day critics, of matching great things and small, an activity that answers the poet's own grandiose summons:

Match me, ye climes which poets love to laud;
Match me, ye harams of the land where now
I strike my strain, far distant to applaud
Beauties that ev'n a cynic must avow—
                                        (*CH I*, st. 59)

As, in default of an identity, Harold gives the poet the support of an attitude, so, in a disjunct terrain of dubious impulses and dangerous acts, Lord
Byron opportunely serves the British public as the discursive equivalent of a
Lorraine glass. He provides the artifice of order, awkwardly gives (to borrow the phrase applied to Harold in the preface) "some connection to the
piece"—the task that the narrator and hero of *Don Juan* will perform with
wanton facility.

   In *Childe Harold's Pilgrimage: A Romaunt*, the process of Byronizing what
otherwise is loath to coalesce takes the form of justifying the failure of a man
to put away the things of the child. If Beckford's vice belongs to the boyish
period of blood mantling, in Spain a boy only grows up to bloodshed. The
example of Spain generalizes, displaces, and justifies Byron's earlier failure
to cross into the world of adults as a refusal to commit to a pointless and
bloody rite. *Childe Harold* lacks a story not only because historical events
have annihilated individual lifelines but also because history has but "*one*
page" (*CH IV*, st. 108) and a single plot: "Blood follows blood, and, through
their mortal span, / In bloodier acts conclude those who with blood began"
(*CH II*, st. 63). The loss of the romantic illusions of youth is followed by no
compensation. The boy who becomes a man breaks with the "delusive
shape" of vice only to gather with others in armies "where the Giant on the
mountain stands, / His blood-red tresses deep'ning in the sun. . . . To shed
before his Shrine the blood he deems most sweet" (*CH I*, st. 39). War is a
castrative sacrifice to a hybrid deity, part Medusa, part Moloch, which is
conceived not as a costly advance onto the symbolic stage of adulthood but
as a full-scale regression into literal barbarism.[54]

   Childe Harold splurges on local color; but the color all resolves to red.
Where the "horizon-bounded plains" of Spain meet the plains of Portugal
there *is* a touch of green, and a trickle of silver, but only momentarily:

Where Lusitania and her Sister meet,
Deem ye what bounds the rival realms divide?
Or ere the jealous Queens of Nations greet,
Doth Tayo interpose his mighty tide?
Or dark Sierra's rise in craggy pride?
Or fence of art, like China's vasty wall?—

Ne barrier wall, ne river deep and wide,
Ne horrid crags, nor mountains dark and tall,
Rise like the rocks that part Hispania's land from Gaul:

But these between a *silver* streamlet glides,
And scarce a name distinguisheth the brook,
Though rival kingdoms press its *verdant* sides.
Here leans the idle shepherd on his crook,
And vacant on the rippling waves doth look,
That peaceful still 'twixt bitterest foemen flow;
For proud each peasant as the noblest duke:
Well doth the Spanish hind the difference know
Twixt him and Lusian slave, the lowest of the low.

But ere the mingling bounds have far been pass'd,
Dark Guadiana rolls his power along
In sullen billows, murmuring and vast,
So noted ancient roundelays among.
Whilome upon his banks did legions throng
Of Moor and Knight, in mailed splendour drest:
Here ceased the swift their race, here sunk the strong;
The Paynim turban and the Christian crest
Mix'd on the *bleeding stream*, by floating hosts oppress'd.
                    (*CH I*, sts. 32–34; emphasis added)

The near-imperceptibility of the geographical boundary between Spain
and Portugal (a silver line on a brown plain) suggests that the real difference
is not physical but political, the difference between freemen and slaves. And
from a political perspective "peaceful still" means "not long peaceful." In a
splendid adaptation of topographical technique to a rigorously nonvision-
ary mode of historical meditation, the poet uses the transition of an *ere*,
which momentarily registers space as time, in order to step eastward into
Spain. There he sees another river that in its "power" (already colored: the
color of power is red)[55] expresses the magnitude of a conflict ancient but not
past; it is the image of Portugal and Spain's violent future. The silver
streamlet with its "mingling bounds" bodes a ferocious struggle. In order to
preserve a distinction now held in place by "scarce a name," the combatants
will be "mix'd on the bleeding stream." Names must be backed up in battle.
Making lines draws blood.

   Although every political difference worth making can be enforced only
by spilling blood, the facility with which the poet executes his transitions
from geographical to temporal space reflects the improgressiveness of the

scenic changes and the futility of blood sacrifice. The killing, justified as a purifying resistance to violation, results in a noisome inmixing of fluids. The enforcement of discriminations becomes a ritual bloodletting in a grotesque "game of lives" (*CH I*, st. 44). Blood follows blood. Red spreads. The local color of Cintra, Talavera, and Albuera is overwhelmed by what painters call "historical color," the lurid tone that unifies the scene.[56]

The ironies that harass efforts to assert political differences also afflict indicators of sexual difference and the signs that prick desire. Lord Byron introduces the tale of the Maid of Saragoza by informing the reader,

> Oh! had you known her in her softer hour,
> Mark'd her black eye that mocks her coal-black veil,
> Heard her light, lively tones in lady's bower,
> Seen her long locks that foil the painter's power,
> Her fairy form, *with more than female* grace,
> Scarce would you deem that Saragoza's tower
> Beheld her smile in Danger's Gorgon face,
> Thin the closed ranks, and lead in Glory's fearful chase.
>   (*CH I*, st. 55; emphasis added)

This is Wollstonecraft's equivocal being without the fear and loathing. War sublimates affect. War elevates the more than femaleness that equips a woman for the "witching arts of love" (st. 57) into a realm of unambiguously heroic action. Transfigured, the "more than female" gloriously shows down every monster she meets. Under these martial circumstances, being "unsex'd" does not mean being unmanned; it means becoming armed. The Gorgon face that might petrify a man only stiffens this maiden's resistance. The enchantress who in peacetime might have treacherously blissed men's bowers becomes the cynosure that rallies their spirit on the field of Mars.

Spain's alternatives are Gibbon's options of vitiating luxury or devastating war. But in Lord Byron's hands, the alternatives do not seem much different: for men, the blood mantling in the scene of fascination or the blood shed on the battlefield; for women, being consumed as more than female or being monumentalized as more than human. A man does not wean himself from the magic gaze; he cuts loose and sticks on "his cap the badge of crimson hue / Which tells you whom to shun and whom to greet" (*CH I*, st. 50), a badge that is the token of a new enthrallment to the death.[57] A woman does not escape the stigma of being a more than female object of man's gaze; the elements of the sign that she has become are recombined for more efficient use as a galvanic standard in a larger arena.

Lest it seem that Lord Byron has been captivated by the immemorial shibboleths served by the lips of Whigs and Tories, here merely propped against a Spanish background and animated by a strong dose of cynicism,[58] it should be emphasized that there is a third position, between "submission and a grave" (*CH I*, st. 53)—the strategic position that, seeing the choices and managing the recombinations, attempts to command the space that the poet confronts. In my use of *strategic* I follow Michel de Certeau, who defines it as "the calculus of force-relationships which becomes possible when a subject of will and power . . . can be isolated from an 'environment.' A strategy," he says, "assumes a place that can be circumscribed as *proper* (*propre*) and thus serve as the basis for generating relations with an exterior distinct from it."[59] Lord Byron's programmatic isolation of the subject of will and power has been the theme of this chapter: there is the scenario of the pilgrimage, which entails the theme of the isolate and mobilized will; there is the coinage of *méthodiste* in order deliberately to circumscribe an inside from an exterior world that is the object of mastery. Matthews's *méthode* may name a paranoiac system, but paranoia is only another name for a fully strategic relation to the world, achieved not by the rupture of blood that leads only to blood but by the prefatory imposition of the "cosmopolitan" conceit that "L'univers est une espèce de livre" (preface), which preempts idiosyncrasy or disorder by the closural, sanitizing presupposition of unified meaning, and by the disciplined exercise of eye and arm that reproduces the world as fresh illustrations of the already known. The strategic disposition depends on the recognition that bookishness and the representational ambition that motivates it are not innocent. Mimesis is mapping. Such mapping will eventually mean the application of a speculative schema to the terrain (embryonic in the framing vision of it as a landscape); here the poet crudely but effectively leverages the discrepancy between map and territory, deploying a trope of reduction by which the poetic pen becomes mightier than the hero's sword:

> Teems not each ditty with the glorious tale?
> Ah! such, alas, the hero's amplest fate!
> When granite moulders and records fail,
> A peasant's plaint prolongs his dubious date.
> Pride, bend thine eye from heaven to thine estate,
> See how the Mighty shrink into a song!
> (*CH I*, st. 36)

The lordly poet maximally abbreviates the peasant's plaint, thus sardonically coming to terms with the grand historical process of "shrinking Gods" (*CH II*, st. 15). By the time the poet, after a much more decisive break with all the natural ties that environ him, resumes his poem with *Childe Harold III*, the proper name of his "song" or representational strategy (one that has inscribed within it as technique the inaugural break with the merely phenomenal that empowers it) will be that byword *Byron*.

In the first canto the poet already distances himself from those who are the object of his gaze. "Maidens, like moths, are ever caught by glare" (*CH I*, st. 9) and peasants are fatally enchanted by "rival scarfs of mix'd embroidery" (st. 40); but the poet immunizes himself against such lures by an inaugural askesis: "My loveless eye unmoved may gaze on thee, / And safely view thy ripening beauties shine" (ll. 21–22). From this position of security, unjeopardized by desire, he can panoramically "unfold" the beauties of Lisbon in a single "image," can "dilate" his eye to cover Cintra's "variegated maze of mount and glen," can gaze "on truth [until] his aching eyes grew dim," can "gaze the eye with joyaunce" over the vales and hills of Mafra, and can "survey" Parnassus (sts. 16, 18, 27, 30, and 60). The poet's story may be as plotless as the peasant's song, but the poet's mobility of vantage endows him with a strategic advantage; he can fit every change of scene into a pattern simultaneously discovered and imposed.

The poet pins down the Iberian map with two dominant and symmetrical images: the first, the bloody Giant, a metaphor for death-dealing artillery and for Napoleonic power, which anchors the "game of lives" passage (*CH I*, sts. 39–44), Lord Byron's chief essay in sublime war reportage; the second, the image of the bull, "the lord of the lowing herds," which is the center of the "dangerous game" that forms the sabbath entertainment for the citizens of Cadiz (sts. 68–79). Giant and bull each condense disparate and unwieldy empirical materials. By focusing the Peninsular War into a single, mythically charged battle scene the image of the Giant stretches chivalric motifs toward obscene, Goya-esque caricature. The imagery of the bullfight is more complicated. It does allow the poet to control the riot of festival by containing it within the intelligible theatrical space of the bullfight: carnival becomes ritual. Yet in its elaboration the strategic design edges toward instability. The poet sardonically contrasts the people of Cadiz, who, old and young, male and female, avidly watch the sufferings of the bull ("sweet sight for vulgar eyes") with the bloodless "fooleries" of the English bourgeoisie on the same "jubilee of man." The pursuits of the English are briskly various and squeakily suburban ("Some Richmond-hill ascend, some scud to Ware, / And many to the steep of Highgate hie")— not at all like the excited mass attendance at "the ungentle sport that oft invites / The Spanish maid, and cheers the Spanish swain." But using the bullfight to impugn the Spanish for theatricalizing suffering and "gloating on another's pain" implicates both the poet, who enjoins his reader, "Look o'er the ravage of the reeking plain; / Look on the hands with female slaughter red" (st. 88) and the British middle class, for whose Sunday entertainment *Childe Harold*, which vicariously gratifies a taste for blood, is meant. Someone or something must somewhere suffer so that we may read. Or, to put it in de Certeau's terms, the strategic circumscription of the proper name *English* depends on a vicarious gratification of the taste for blood—what has been proved in the realm of politics by Wellington's war is proved in the realm of culture by Byron's poem and poetic career. "If the character of a nation," as Hobhouse, Byron's accompanist, notes, "can be well appreciated by view of the amusements in which they delight," the imperial character emerges in *Childe Harold* as the blithe consumer of the representations of the bloody delights of others.[60]

Lord Byron does not explicitly identify the link between the cultures of Catholic honor and Protestant commerce; he does not need to, since *Childe Harold*, the poetic product/gift of an English lord, *is* the connection. "Byron" is the transitional figure between an aristocratic culture of honor and a middle-class culture of commerce, just as the figure of the poet is the bridge between the poles of giant and bull. At that fateful intersection, announced by the extraordinary pathos of the bull's death, mimetic hubris begins to crumble. The conclusion offers itself that this transition represents the doom visited on the aristocratic class in nineteenth-century Britain.[61] The picture of Lord Byron as strategist of his own sacrifice, bullishly leading himself to the slaughter, is both vivid and plausible: the blood of the lord follows the blood of the bull, and his corpse, like the corpses of Catholicism and Spain, will be encrypted in the English Gothic. I do not want to abandon the sacrificial thesis entirely. Yet I would urge that the melodrama of identification defends against a more threatening contamination of the spectator by the blood of his or her victim.

Look again at the profession of the poet's "loveless eye" in the prologue. The claim presupposes the cultural interdiction of the child Ianthe as potential object of desire. Because of her age (Lady Charlotte Harley was eleven), Byron *cannot* desire her and therefore "unmoved may gaze" and "safely view." The limits on desire involve limits on artistic representation. The poet determines not "vainly [to] seek / To paint those charms which varied as they beam'd: / To such as see thee not my words were weak; / To those who gaze on thee what language could they speak?" (ll. 6–9). The topos of inexpressibility is troped as a kind of infantilization—a defense prominent, as Peter J. Manning has shown, in Byron's scenes of confrontation with female figures, imagined as mothers and Medusas.[62] But the poet is not just afraid for himself. He is relieved that his words are weak because of a superstitious belief in the inherently contaminative properties of poetic representation: a painting *of* the beauty feels like a painting *on* the beauty. To persist would be (speaking of Sevilla, "the spoiler's wished-for prey!") to end in "blackening her lovely domes" (*CH I*, st. 45); it would be (he confesses as he withstands, "unmoved, the lustre of [the] gaze" of "Sweet Florence" in the second canto) to practice the "spoiler's art" (*CH II*, sts. 30–33). The fantasy of representation portends the subordination of the desired, free-floating partial object to the full figural representation of a female, who is imagined as maternal and stands interdicted. To give a face to the idealized object is to deface it, to cancel its specific existence within the field of perception and desire.

This is the situation recreated with such force in another poetic product of Byron's first tour, "The Curse of Minerva," in which the condition of the poet's capacity to "face" Minerva (whose "aegis," we are told, "bore no Gorgon now" [l. 80]) is that her "fane" has been "violated" by the "spoiler" Lord Elgin (ll. 98–99), who plunders her temple to display her disenchanted parts to the vulgar who crowd the British Museum. (Byron's displacement onto Lord Elgin of his own anxieties over spoiling the femininely gendered scenes his poems compulsively review, both here and in *Childe Harold*, exactly parallels his construction of Scotch reviewers. Both Elgin and the *Edinburgh Review* work by extraction; both reprocess art for the middle-class public; and Lord Elgin is—as is Byron, of course—descended from Caledonia, which, in a phrase that is telling considering widespread doubts regarding Byron's own bloodline, he calls "that bastard land" (l. 131].) But in "To Ianthe" (unlike what happens in the Haidee episode of *Don Juan* or in *Manfred*) such speculations bear no fruit because the poet prudently relies on the interdiction of sexual desire to suppress anxiety about his powers of representation: she is too young; therefore I am loveless; therefore I can avoid the spell of her charms and the paralysis or impotence that trying to paint them might cause me as well as the spoliation that painting might cause "her." It is the "varied" quality of Ianthe's charms that gets the poet through this rough spot; an inimitable variousness recodes the interdiction of sexual desire in terms of an aesthetic convention for the sublime unrepresentability of beauty. "Because of her age I cannot desire her" becomes "because of her variousness I cannot paint her." The loveless eye sees as the aesthetic eye. The poet can look but not touch. And the poet only "sees" his object in the mirror of convention called *variousness* that he holds up before a Medusa whom, of course, the mirror constitutes. Aesthetic convention allows him to suspend his conflict, to move along, to begin again.

The prefatory verses fashion the loveless eye as a talisman that (like the Childe himself) the poet can carry with him as he travels from charming sight to charming sight to insure that he can "mark them unmoved" (*CH II,* st. 40). There can be no more exact rendering of the strategic ambition than this identification with the metaphysical postulate of the unmoved mover. And there can be no surer signal of that ambition's fragility. The themes of sex, representation, and conflict glancingly reemerge in the introduction of the Maid of Saragoza, where the poet refers to "her long locks that foil the painter's power" (*CH I,* st. 55). The reiteration of the inexpressibility topos highlights the potential presence of *two* Gorgons in the stanza: the one in whose face the militarized maid smiles and the Medusa whose locks deprive the painter's hand of its power. In this instance it is the outbreak of war that prevents paralysis, freeing the maid from her bower and the painter from his easel. I have said the locks "deprive," but Byron says "foil"; and the difference is suggestive, since *foil* assigns a much more active status to the woman, rendering the locks not as snakes but as swords. Delicate here, the implication is strengthened in the image of the invading Gauls "Foil'd by a woman's hand, before a batter'd wall" (st. 56). Not woman's "gaze" but woman's "hand." The distinction is important, for the suggestion that I am trying to eke out (one that will be central to *The Corsair* and the English Cantos of *Don Juan*) is that it is not the visage of the Gorgon, that infinitely various, phallicized head, that threatens paralysis; that image screens a more disturbing, preconscious awareness that the woman has arms of her own that she can wield in peace and in war, thus challenging the prevailing conventions by which things are ordered.[63] The specular scene of fascination is tangibly discomposed by the undetermined movement of the hand—as spontaneously practical before the batter'd wall of Saragoza in 1808 as it was in the closet of the Star and Garter Tavern in 1765. It is the hint of that possibility, which would open up a realm of tactical, "partisan" maneuvers wholly unglimpsed by the eye of the strategist, that makes men cry for war, for topographical poems, and for the conventions that govern them.

In the bullfight section of the poem Lord Byron takes the side of the bull. As he does so *foil* returns, literalized:

> Foil'd, bleeding, breathless, furious to the last,
> Full in the centre stands the bull at bay,
> Mid wounds, and clinging darts, and lances brast,
> And foes disabled in the brutal fray.
>
> (*CH I,* st. 77)

The bull's frustration coincides with his penetration by the pointed weapons of his attackers. The bull is not fascinated; he can neither "safely view" nor change his scene. And who knows if he fools himself into thinking that he is being nobly sacrificed? There is a tendency here in making the connection between the doomed bull and the foiled painter or poet to refer the moment to gender issues. But the tauromachy takes us, if only momentarily, beyond gender, to a primordial politics. Men *and* women watch the bull. "Skill'd in the ogle of roguish eye" (st. 72), they watch each other. But before the matador pairs off with him, the bull sees nothing; he senses only the picadors, a swarm of faceless, darting Spanish partisans. Over the poet's plunging sea of troubles has been stretched the canvas on which is pictured charming woman or beautiful landscape. Yet all the suppressed affect associated with the unrepresentability of Ianthe and the Maid of Saragoza returns here with a vengeance—and is defended against by a hysterical sacrificial drama. That return and that defense prove that the female's unrepresentability is a question not merely of the poet's incapacity or of the woman's "more than female" charms but of a strength in the partisan other that wrecks strategic designs.

The contrasts of *Childe Harold I* are empty, its strategic transcendence shaky. The poet virtually announces the poem's superficiality in the preface. Attempting to foreclose criticism of his hero, he mentions that "a fictitious character is introduced for the sake of giving some connection to the piece." Although the poet insists that the poem "makes no pretension to regularity," the introduction of Childe Harold, the naming of the poem as a "piece," and not least the preface itself are transparently just such pretenses. Chief among the devices for holding this poetic stuff together is the "stanza of Spenser," which

> according to one of our most successful poets, admits of every variety. Dr. Beattie makes the following observation: "Not long ago I began a poem in the style and stanza of Spenser, in which I propose to give full scope to my inclination, and be either droll or pathetic, descriptive or sentimental, tender or satirical, as the humour strikes me; for, if I mistake not, the measure which I have adopted admits equally of all these kinds of composition." Strengthened in my opinion by such authority, and by the example of some in the highest order of Italian poets, I shall make no apology for attempts at similar variations in the following composition; satisfied that, if they are unsuccessful, their failure must be in the execution, rather than in the design sanctioned by the practice of Ariosto, Thomson, and Beattie.

As in his dedication to Ianthe, the poet employs the term *variety* to "admit" and superficially to unify a hodgepodge of perceptions, insights, and intonations. And although he adopts the Spenserian stanza as variety's appropriate vehicle, his authority for the maneuver comes from the "successful Beattie" rather than from Spenser, who is reduced to a formula or guise. Or convention. The Spenserian stanza is the canonical vehicle for romance in an enlightened age, when romance conventions modestly assist in the assemblage of miscellaneous details into an itinerary if not a plot. By convention the Spenserian stanza makes the poem generic. While Beattie describes the Spenserian stanza as a lens that would provide him "scope" for following his inclinations, it is as if Byron's inclinations have already been indulged, the words written, and the Spenserian stanza superadded—stretched across the words—to give disorder the appearance of design, the inchoate the effect of variety. The thin skin of the Spenserian stanza gives the poem a face that might indiscriminately be viewed by the glancing reader as woman or monster.[64]

Poetics recapitulates politics. The most conspicuous and certainly the most controversial feature of the first canto is the attack on British policy in the Peninsular Wars, and particularly the signing of the Convention of Cintra in 1808: "Convention is the dwarfish demon styled / That foil'd the knights in Marialva's dome" (*CH I*, st. 25). In Lord Byron's view the treaty cynically betrayed the same chivalric spirit among the Spanish that the British had earlier exploited to summon the many partisan groups resisting the French and to combine them in one nationalized, romantic body. The generic knight assembled from the scattered peoples was, however, "foiled" not by magic for mysterious ends but by superiority of force according to strategic imperatives. Having defeated the French in pitched battle, Arthur Wellesley and Hew Dalrymple treated with them to allow their safe evacuation from the battlefield, stripped of their ordnance but in full possession of their plunder. The Spanish allies, in whose name the crusade was conducted, were insultingly excluded from the agreement. In 1808 Wordsworth was moved to write a Miltonic diatribe attacking the Convention and excoriating its signatories. Against the strategic cynicism of the British generals, he opposed a vision of thwarted spiritual regeneration and national self-determination, arguing that the Spanish partisans were a people, who spoke as a body with one, indivisible voice, a *corporation* not subject to the means-ends calculations of instrumental reason and the artifice of conventions.[65]

Although he shares Wordsworth's indignation, Lord Byron lacks Wordsworth's corporatist faith. Indeed, for the most part he accepts, however reluctantly, the premises of those he castigates. The poem may condemn Lord Elgin for his "plunder," but in the disenchanted, desacralized world of *Childe Harold* Elgin's extraction of the "mouldering shrines" from a land of "shrinking gods" seems as prudent as, in the event, Wellesley's strategic countenancing of French plunder proved to be. Byron's opposition is strictly sentimental: though degraded, the Spanish remind him of storied chivalric knights; the Albanians remind him of the legendary kirtled clans of Scotland; and the Greeks are "scattered children" (*CH II*, st. 73), inviting loving patronage from the classically educated. It would be a mistake to regard this sentimentalism as merely regressive, however. Although it is possible to view Byron's censure of Elgin as the assertion of the privilege of mobile nobility against the more democratic impulse to package the statues for the aesthetic contemplation of a wider, museum-going public, that assertion is conveyed to a reading public in a volume of representations of Spain, Albania, and Greece. Byron's collection of "antiques" is more varied than Elgin's; they are susceptible to wider propagation; moreover, as metaphors they leave the original monuments in place to provide future stimulus to the mobility of the *faux* aristocrats who will follow in Byron's footsteps, prowling the museum without walls, glancing over the world's "one page" whose beauties Byron has conveniently marked for ready consumption.

The power of Byronism as a superior, because literary, form of cultural imperialism will be reflected on in *Childe Harold IV*. But if the first canto projects the fourth, it also undoes the line it launches. Lord Byron may not develop a critique of convention, but he does demonstrate that in the prevailing circumstances "any coming together, meeting, or assembling," any founding "general agreement or consent," is shadowed by the sense of "an agreement made between the commanders or opposing armies for the evacuation of some post or country, the *suspension* of hostilities" (*OED*, emphasis added). As for the opposing generals of the English and French armies, the convention suspending hostilities witnesses to the mutual interest of both in suppressing the sporadic, unconventional, guerrilla resistance of the scattered partisans (an interest in turning the peninsula into a theater of war), so for the poet the pictorial convention of variety, the literary conventions of Spenserian romance, and the oedipal conventions of individual psychology fuel a campaign to compose a volatile field of dispersed affect. For Byron as for Wordsworth, the world in which the poet travels is a site of scattered intensities, a disparate body inviting sexualization, medicalization, and militarization. The poem organizes this body by putting a face on it and making it into a book, thus capitalizing on the attraction of those touching intensities. But the poem also reminds us that such organization is only a suspension of the hostilities it composes.

The strategic eye (Byron's, Wellesley's, Napoleon's) succeeds by condensing scattered intensities into an overdetermined, specular hostility that is then suspended by convention. It is immaterial whether that convention be called Cintra, variety, Spenser, or Byron—it *is* important that the convention be entitled and booked so that quondam oppositions are packaged as pages to be turned recto and verso by a generalized consumer called the reading public. Taking his stand on Milton's high ground, Wordsworth would regard such a suspension as fraudulent, the book as no book at all, just an installment before another outburst or publication in a desacralized world of pointless and indefinite conflict. Byron, dallying with Beattie's refurbishings of Spenser's chivalresques, has no grounds for such an overview or for such opposition. In lieu of the strategic stance he offers only a tactical apposition; without foresight he adduces intensities inextricable from the circumstantial nexus that gives them strength. "To Ianthe" again:

> Such is thy name with this my verse entwined;
> And long as kinder eyes a look shall cast
> On Harold's page, Ianthe's here enshrined
> Shall thus be first beheld, forgotten last.
> (ll. 37–40)

Although a "more than" friendship is interdicted by a society committed in its historical being to a degraded, sexualized understanding of such relations, the friendship is nonetheless achieved by the enshrinement of a name that performs the intrication of which the poet speaks. The child's name is entwined in the poet's lines, and by the involute of language, the poet is entwined in her name: "To I and thee." That paraphrase spells out a tangible connection that strikes the kinder eye of the closer reader. On Harold's page is performed an intimacy that is not promiscuous but tactical. In Byron's book is closeted an intimacy that is not bookish but textual.

The Secret of the Separation

Although Byron's "sexualization" coincided with his orientation toward Greece, the debates about his sexuality began a little later, when Lady Byron began to solicit medical and legal opinions regarding her husband's possible insanity in order to legitimate her desertion of him soon after the birth of their daughter in 1815. The ensemble of those out-of-court testimonies and their scholarly commentaries comprises the notorious "separation controversy." Here are a couple of Lady Byron's provocative charges:

In his endeavours to corrupt my mind he has sought to make me smile first at Vice. . . . There is *no* Vice with which he has not endeavoured in this manner to familiarize me—attributing the condemnation of such practices merely to the manners of different Countries, & seeking either to ridicule or reason me out of *all* principle.

And again:

He laboured to convince me that Right & Wrong were merely Convention-al, & varying with Locality & other circumstances—he clothed these senti-ments in the most seductive language—appealing both to the Heart and Imagination. I must have been bewildered had I not firmly & simply be-lieved in one Immutable Standard.[66]

Now, suppose we buy Lady Byron's story. We still need to ask exactly what was going on. If Lady Byron was being subjected to persuasion, to what was she being persuaded and how? Louis Crompton maintains that her hints refer to an exchange about Byron's bisexuality.[67] Even if that were true, however, even if we suspected there were nothing more behind Byron's sweet talk, we should not ignore the fact that that truth came dressed as a discourse about relativism. The pious Lady Byron Wollstonecraftily claims to have clung to an immutable standard of right and wrong in determined resistance to Byron's insidious doctrine that some act condemned in one place can be perfectly okay when performed in another.[68] Her story does not, however, account for Lady Byron's fear of being bewildered, her "mis-ery not to have a fixed opinion,"[69] which is quite a different thing from being induced to believe in relativism. The notion that good and evil are conventional does not in and of itself lead to confusion about the conven-tions appropriate here and now, let alone force someone to abandon a cherished belief.

Indeed, it is fair to ask whether there really is any fundamental difference of opinion between Lady Byron and her husband, for there is an apparent symmetry between his thesis that all behavior is subject to convention and her recourse to a standard that, however single and immutable it is, is based only in her belief. Convention, as recent theorists such as Stanley Fish have seductively argued, is the "standard" that allows for comparisons and con-versions among diverse systems of belief. Both the absolutist lady and the relativist lord are universalists; the operational distinction is only whether that universal is something imperiously transcendent like the Bible or some-thing more ingratiatingly conditional like gold or language. This symmetry makes Lady Byron's resistance look pretty foolish—she really had nothing to fear. But that symmetry also makes Lord Byron look far less unconventional. Byron may be laboriously arguing for the morality of bisexuality, but bisexuality has been sublimated into a feature of a broader economy: it has been coded as a corollary of exchange value. In some places and some times I like to do things to boys: I pay them in piasters; and in some times and some places I like to do things to women: I pay them in pounds sterling (or titles). The differences can be measured and adjusted: I always know what I am doing, whom I am doing it to, where I am doing it, and, most important, what it costs.[70] Moreover, piasters can be translated into pounds—I can use my Master Card to avoid any confoundment. Having been abstracted into exchange value, the content of the experience hardly makes any difference—or makes a difference only insofar as it too is marketable as "risky" or "safe." "All ambivalence," as Jean Baudrillard has remarked, "is reduced by equivalence."[71] Bisexualization renders all sexual beings and sexual experiences as equivocal. What makes sexuality pleasurable and incipiently perverse, something like stockjobbing, is toying with the differential, pumping the margin.

Insofar as the difference between Lady and Lord Byron comes to a contest between a humorless piety and a cheerfully repressive desublimation, we know that the clout of history backs up Byron and Master Card, and we may take whatever comfort we choose.[72] But, it must be remembered, both Lady Byron's puritanism *and* Lord Byron's relativism are narrative reconstructions by Lady Byron, comprising both method and *méthode*. "Lord Byron," she mysteriously attested, "has never *expressly* declared himself guilty of any *specific* crime—but his insinuations to that effect have been much more convincing than the most direct assertion." Doris Langley Moore acidly comments that it is "marvellously typical of Lady Byron to be more convinced by insinuations rather than by direct assertion."[73] Typical of Lady Byron, but also marvelously typical of every reader of Byron. Walter Scott, for example, gave considerable credit to Byron's insinuative powers when, in 1818, he attempted to account for his popularity: "But it was not merely to the novelty of an author speaking in his own person, and in a tone which arrogated a contempt of all the ordinary pursuits of life, that *Childe Harold* owed its extensive popularity: these formed but the point or sharp edge of the wedge by which the work was enabled to insinuate its way into that venerable block, the British public."[74] Lady Byron's remarks, then, identify her as just another suggestible reader of her husband, typically entranced by Byron's insinuations. Entranced up to a point, that is: Lady Byron comes to complain bitterly of Byron's practice of making "Romance . . . the colouring and the mask of vice."[75] Of course, no more than Byron does Lady Byron come to the point and say what the hidden vice is.

She bases her critique on the vice of concealing vice, which is nothing more than the betrayal of interest. An axiom for all second-generation Romantics: romance begins to fail and romancers begin to be disgusting when they seem interested, methodical, when romance degenerates into labored arguments about relativism, becomes philosophy in the bedroom.

Lady Byron's version of Byron is thoroughly conventional. She rarely says anything about his plots that is any different from what you could find scattered through the reviews of *Childe Harold* and the Oriental tales.[76] No more than Mr. Chaworth needed the presence of the fifth Lord Byron to complete his Kantian victory over his empirical self did Lady Byron require the domestic intimacy with Lord Byron to have "escaped from the greatest Villain that ever existed."[77] All she had to do was to read his books. Ensuing events have rendered this comment of Lord Byron's to his publisher embarrassingly ironic: "I am very glad that the handwriting was a favourable omen of the morale of the piece—but you must not trust to that—for my copyist [Lady Byron] would write out anything I desired in all the ignorance of innocence—I hope however in this instance with no great peril to either" (*BLJ* 5:13). He was wrong on all counts. His wife seems to have read what she copied. A perfect barometer of public opinion, Lady Byron's decisive break with her husband coincided with a general turn against Byron by the reviews that crystallized with *their* reading of *Parisina*. And Lady Byron's disavowal seems in special accord with the *Eclectic Review*'s as not simply a response to the "gross" and "revolting" theme of incest but even more a repudiation of the doctrine that Byron implicitly attempts to "inculcate": the "dangerous error that vice does not degrade the mind."[78] Lady Byron epitomizes the identificatory procedures of naive biographical criticism: reading the incest of the text back onto Byron's life and reading the vice forward onto her own—with the twist that in her case the force of the identification depends on the suppression of moral scruples. For the lady, reading Byron is thrillingly to invite degradation. Byron's error is doubly "dangerous" then, for society and for Byron's hold on society: for society, because his false doctrine might tempt some to vice; for Byron's hold, because for Lady Byron, as for the *Eclectic*, to accept Byron's skeptical doctrine would be to abandon the very structure of identification that is all they mean by *Lord Byron*. Even Thomas Moore's sensible claim that Byron's "formidable mystery" is only "imposture" is no defense against this logic.[79] Faced with the choice between preserving an idealized, guilty relation to the "greatest Villain that ever existed" and keeping her husband—that is, between bad faith and no faith at all—Lady Byron does not hesitate.

Of course, part of the reason Lady Byron and the reviews arrive at that choice is that the principle of identification has in fact been strained—a vulnerability that demands an aesthetic rationale ("our objections . . . originate rather in taste than in respect for morality," announces the *Eclectic* [*RR* B:2:735]). Not only does Byron inculcate the vicious doctrine that no doctrine is intrinsically vicious, but he propagates such vice under the guise of exotic motifs that in their repetition have become odious. As the *Critical Review* patiently explains in its 1816 review of *Hebrew Melodies*, "The truth is, that an individual who publishes so much and so repeatedly, ought to have a larger stock of true poetical feeling than is possessed by the author of these melodies. It is not mere fervor of mind, nor energy of expression (with both of which his Lordship is eminently gifted) that will always satisfy; they cease to produce any effect after a time, and the author who has nothing more to offer, must after that time, be contented with a certain though gradual oblivion" (*RR* B:2:647). If we are not contaminated by Byron's vicious doctrine that vice does not contaminate, it is not because that doctrine is true but because he has failed to make that vice sufficiently attractive.

In this paranoid logic the terms of praise and blame are reversible. Initially, the reviews had acknowledged that intriguing postures and characters made Byron's style recognizable; and they observed (or effused) that the exaggerated disparity between superficial Oriental color and deep Oriental sin made his poems alluring. Like Napoleon, Lord Byron's success has now become the very basis for his failure.[80] Aesthetic categories do not form the entire basis for the indictment, however. Moral and aesthetic concerns leak into market considerations, as when the *Eclectic* clucks that the public is "apt to mistake the recurrence of obvious traits of style . . . for the sameness of impoverished genius, and to grow, in consequence, fastidious, and at length unjust, towards the productions of their favourite."[81] In its neat inversion of Wollstonecraft's fantasy of the sensual male who, become a "luxurious monster, or fastidious sensualist, . . . then makes the contagion which his unnatural state spread, the instrument of tyranny,"[82] the *Eclectic* dramatizes the reversibility of the cultural scene of fascination remarked on above: Wollstonecraft's "luxurious monster" has subjugated readers to a sensuality that, grown monstrous itself, turns to tyrannize over its creator—and, consequently, Lord Byron becomes the first, worst victim of that "moral disease" called Byronomania.[83]

Lady Byron's distaste notwithstanding, in Regency England there was, as the regent himself would prove, at least one substantial difference between buying a book and entering wedlock: marriage could not be dissolved by a change of opinion. Lady Byron could not legitimize her flight by appealing to canons of taste or even to common sense. Hence there were *two*

decisive moments in her separation: first, rejection and flight; second, justification of that revulsion from the imputation of mere fastidiousness. The
crucial revisionary moment occurred when Lady Byron returned to London
to consult what her father called a "professional friend," the attorney Dr.
Lushington (*HVSV*, p. 152). A confession was made that outraged Lushington, who declared the separation irrevocable. The intimacy of the bedroom
yielded to the privilege of attorney and client; Lady Byron's fastidiousness
was underwritten if not by law then by professional opinion, which Lady
Byron and her allies strategically attempted to organize into a force sufficiently prepossessing that it would avert an actual courtroom battle. The
correspondence (enormous even in Malcolm Elwin's excerpts), in which the
Richardsonian Lady Byron[84] and her allies rehearse the past, lay strategems,
and eventually overpower their opposition, substituted for a trial in much
the same way as a duel might—although with Byron's genealogy in mind,
the parallel would seem to be not the physical struggle between Mr.
Chaworth and the fifth Lord Byron, but the dying Chaworth's various
narrative reconstructions of what occurred, which, if they did not actually
prevent a trial, did in fact displace the trial in the pages of *Gentlemen's
Magazine* and thereby in public opinion.

What actually happened between Lord and Lady Byron in their bedroom remains as impenetrably dubious as the engagement between the two
men in the darkened room of the Star and Garter. Writing to Augusta's
aunt, Sophia Byron, during the maneuvers preceding the final agreement,
Annabella insists that in "the present state of circumstances you must be
aware that a publication of the real grounds of difference between Lord B.
and myself would be extremely improper—and in conformity with the
advice I have received, I *must* abstain from any further disclosure."[85] And
that is, in effect, as far as she goes or needs to go. The belief in "a real ground
of difference" between her and Lord Byron is crucial to Lady Byron's justification of the separation and her right to custody of their child; but the real
ground of difference was never published—and could never be published,
because the real ground of difference was not moral, aesthetic, or economic,
but political. The real ground of difference was how the ground of difference was to be determined.

Having escaped the fatal wound received by Chaworth (and Clarissa),
Lady Byron ascertains that her vulnerability to her husband arose from the
absence of a second to the performances in her bedroom. Moreover, the
closeting of their acts burdens them with suspicion. Only what can be
published can be publicly justified. Lady Byron's inspired strategy is to leave
in darkness that "ground of difference" she wants branded evil and to justify

herself by openly demonstrating that her behavior is in absolute conformity with the advice of her seconds—those professional friends who, accredited agents of the regulatory hypothesis, can authoritatively attest to the validity of the ground of difference. In this exemplary case, justification is administered by a professional class of attorneys, whose expertise persuasively mediates the authority of the law and the force of public opinion. The relation between this process and the cultural practice of the reviews is not merely analogical: it is no accident that Henry Brougham acts as an anonymous critic of Byron's marital case as he had of Byron's first book of poems. Both cases illustrate why duels had become irrelevant to the settlement of conflicts: there exists a relatively efficient system of *administrative* justice to oversee those acts that for one reason or another are kept out of court. Lady Byron won; Lord Byron took the advice of his seconds and signed the "deed of separation."[86]

Lady Byron's empirical victory came at the expense of the kind of transcendental triumph achieved by a Chaworth and a Clarissa. Despite her justification, the matter has never been laid to rest. While the act in the bedroom remains dubious, its strategic displacement, the confidential exchange between Lady Byron and her attorney, is a matter of record, and it has aroused the most debate among Lord Byron's biographers. What awful secret did Lady Byron tell? Speculation first produced the rumor of a murder; it then hunted out incest; it has since settled comfortably on the suspicion of homosexuality. None of those explanations, as G. Wilson Knight was the first to show, is satisfactory. Lord Byron had claimed, and Lady Byron had corroborated, that he had never "done an act *that would bring me under the power of the law* . . . at least on this side of the water"—a disclaimer that covers both domestic half-incest and foreign "intercourse-to-the-full."[87] It was to bring Lord Byron under professional purview—first as subject of diagnosis (was he mad?), then as subject of criminal speculation (was he bad?) that Lady Byron closeted with the administering Lushington, to whom, abandoning insinuation, she could Byronically intimate, trusting that he, advocate not spouse, would satisfactorily profess the shock she claimed to have felt—proving by that profession that she had been the victim of an act not only criminal but unique in its "indelicacy."

Knight has provocatively conjectured that the monstrous secret with which Lady Byron turned her attorney's heart to stone was that Byron had buggered her, an act both illegal and vile.[88] Doris Langley Moore indignantly challenged both Knight's documentary evidence and, more fiercely, its psychological and physiological verisimilitude. For Lady Byron to make such a shocking charge, says Moore, would entail either one of two equally impossible assumptions: that she was ignorant of what was being done to her at the time or, worse, that she had at first been responsive and only later changed her mind.[89] The options are good ones; it was imprudent of Moore to rule them out. The latter has more psychological plausibility—it corresponds to the shape of the reader response to Byron's "fervor" as it is rehearsed again and again in the reviews. Yet if a change of mind may actually have brought about Lady Byron's disgust, it can hardly be adduced as evidence when the nature and naturalness of changes of mind, of opinion, and of aim are precisely at stake. Although Lady Byron might in fact have pleasurably acquiesced, for her to confess before her "professional friend" that she had knowingly done so and *then* changed her mind (on the basis of what act if not the most unnatural that the law recognizes?) could only weaken her case by making it appear a matter of taste. And there is no accounting for taste. A physiological blindness that is completely caught up in erotic oblivion is necessary to hide (in a strong sense, to *be*) the trauma of an unequivocal and unforgivable transgression of the law, which later can be recovered and healed/punished.[90] Knight may be wrong in that there is no convincing evidence that Byron actually buggered his wife. But, *pace* Moore, making sense of the separation requires the positing of an extraordinary, literally unimaginable confoundment.

I claim no privileged knowledge about whether such a mistake by Lady Byron could actually be made out of ignorance, abandonment, or a truly religious abstraction. But to bring Lord Byron before the law such a mistake—a dangerous error—must be theoretically possible. When Lady Byron takes Byron before Lushington she endeavors to establish a privileged relationship with her husband in order to justify a separation in law. Hence she has to prove or posit a relation that is something other than the inferential connection available to any reader of him. She requires the direct assertion of an untamed impulse: brute Byron. She does not produce testimony of the surrender of her single immutable standard to the license of relativism, of her normative heterosexuality to the depravity of bisexuality: Byronic relativism is not licentious; Byronic bisexuality is rather fastidiously normative. She produces instead the direct assertion of confoundment: confoundment in the act, confoundment in the telling, confoundment between the telling and the act—the very bewilderment that her method (like Matthews's) has been intended to ward off.

This primordial and perdurable bewilderment (it ramifies through all the commentary) is not vice without the mask of romance but romance without the alibi of vice, direct assertion without the excuse of interest or inadvertence: "Forth, forth, he starts, and all his love reveals" ("Nisus and

Euryalus," l. 364). Yet what is revealed is necessarily mistaken: only in retrospect can a Chaworth or a Lady Byron discriminate between clothes and body; in the event, the difference is categorically ungrounded. The confusion that Lady Byron and her attorney must posit and produce as the only way to single out Byron does not refer to any express or specific act of violation; it invokes the "secret impulse" that empowers the naked letter of romance. Its uniqueness is that it cannot be assigned a number (hetero, homo, bi) and submitted to the network of exchange. As uncountable as the fifth Lord Byron's rabbits are the "parts adjacent" to "Falmouth" that the sixth Lord Byron probes. For Lady Byron, the princess of parallelograms, the principle of pleasure lies in its calculation. She is taken beyond pleasure by taking Lord Byron "to the letter" (*HVSV*, p. 150). She recovers by positing an artfulness so deep that it pushes calculation to the limit of paranoia's iron logic. She succeeds because in Regency England paranoia and prudence are identical.

Let me align the parallels. To justify her separation from her husband, to establish that it is more than a matter of a change of taste, Lady Byron needs to distinguish her relation to him from the public's. She needs to divulge something she knows about him that the common reader does not. That knowledge erupts *in camera* as a moment of categorial bewilderment, violent and pure, that decisively marks off Lord Byron's difference from everyone else: from the camps of East and West, past and present, boy and girl, pro and con, fore and aft. The direct assertion of Byron is a radical "mark of separation"—a mark, as Dr. Lushington attests, that spreads with unnerving velocity and vigor, like contaminating impiety or infectious laughter, through what, after the separation, has become the Byronomanic text: "I return you Lord Byron's letter with the inclosures & entirely agree with you in thinking any reply *to him* useless. Indeed the danger of misrepresentation is so great, that it is scarcely possible to make any communication by letter or otherwise without almost a certainty of perversion."[91] This "mark of separation," a term I borrow from Edward Young[92] and want to link with the insupportable dazzle that fronts the naked letter of romance, is Byron's genius—or, if you prefer, his lordship, his sovereignty, or his quintessentially aristocratic style. Any of those concepts can be deployed in lip service to whatever law of context is locally in force, but the ideal for the critic who wants to establish an uncommon intimacy with Lord Byron is to approximate that "irregularity without a concept" or "schizoid moment of scission" that is Byron's strength.[93]

Now it is true that this moment is available to us only in the self-interested professions of Lady Byron and Dr. Lushington, who needed to remember what Hobhouse referred to as "horrors the very nature of which they refused to designate" (Byron matter-of-factly suggests that if an "enormity" occurred he must have been "surprised" by "total oblivion" [*HVSV*, pp. 158–59, 160]). But that they capably exploited that "untamed impulse" does not mean they invented it. Evidence that they did *not* invent it lies in their failure to master what they invoked. Although Lady Byron et al. reduced Byron, the great satirist of the "Convention of Cintra," to the abjectly ironic resort of signing his own convention by which hostilities were suspended, evacuations made, and prizes allotted, the victory rather misses the point of the satire, which is that conventions are only suspensions of hostilities, that despite professions they settle nothing in the sphere of law or deeds; no amount of justification can prevent a future demand for vindication. Lord Byron never goes to court, but his impulse to vindication is acted upon in the greatly wicked poems of farewell. Vindication is achieved in *Childe Harold IV.* And here in this writing.

To persuade that Byron is indeed a poetic as well as an erotic revolutionary, however, requires that these as yet hypothetical moments of confoundment be textualized, which can best be accomplished by abandoning Lady Byron's Gothic readings of Byron for the more serviceable comments of the workaday reviewers themselves. A crossing will be made by engaging more directly the first, psychologically plausible moment in the sequence of separation. If accounting for the revisionary moment has propelled us to lurid conjectures about cataclysmic events, addressing the triggering moment will entail some mitigation, will require asking whether or not Lady Byron might have rejected her lord, husband, and poet in response to some nuance in the monotony of supply—and then to ask just what that nuance might have been, how it could be so effectively different from the mere division of parts that makes supply possible at all. By attending to the issues of gender in the Oriental tales and to the way the Oriental tales are themselves engendered, we shall recover those poetic events in which nuances in the monotony of supply became, to everyone's surprise, differences indigestible according to the dominant canons of taste.

4

Perversion, Parody, and Cultural Hegemony

The Moment of Change in the Oriental Tales

Stick to the East; — the oracle, Staël, told me it was the only poetical policy. The North, South, and West, have all been exhausted; but from the East, we have nothing but S * * 's unsaleables.
Lord Byron to Thomas Moore, August 28, 1813

—Any thing but reality —
Lord Byron to William Gifford, November 12, 1813

The general problem of oppositional writing—its authenticity, its effectiveness, even its possibility in relation to a hegemonic discourse—is focused in a particularly challenging way in Lord Byron's poetry. Lord Byron may have been "born for opposition" (*BLJ* 4:82), but from the morning (or, more probably, the afternoon) of that mythical day when he awoke to find himself famous, for Lord Byron to write in opposition meant to write against himself, or at least against "Byronism," that systematically elaborated, commercially triumphant version of himself devised and promoted by his publisher, celebrated and denounced by his reviewers and readers. The problem of opposition is magnified even more, however, because Byronism was promoted and deplored as a stance of gloriously Romantic (Satanic, existential, Promethean, revolutionary, etc.) or neurotically compulsive opposition.[1] Byronic opposition did not break with the literary culture that invented and profited from it.[2] The poet's confidence to his publisher after the publication of *The Corsair* is on the mark: "To me my present & past success has appeared very singular—since it was in the teeth of so many prejudices—I almost think people like to be *contradicted* (*BLJ* 4:47). Coming to write against a hegemony that battens on its contradictions—coming to write against Byronism—in his Oriental romances, Byron came to write, however lamely, however perversely, against opposition itself.

Perversion and Parody

Even the first reviewers of Byron's Oriental romances—*The Giaour, The Bride of Abydos, The Corsair, Lara, Parisina,* and *The Siege of Corinth*—were confident that the poems formed a series, however obscurely linked.[3] This knowledge did not make its knowers happy. Safely exotic imagery of sex and violence became unnerving when regarded as authorial obsessions, especially when those obsessions proved to have such mass appeal. Nervousness about seriality was expressed in speculations like this on *Lara*:

> Whatever be the shades of difference in the character of his heroes, *fidelity* to the first object of their affections is invariably *one* and a very prominent feature; and since the supposition that each of his three last narratives are continuations of the Giaour, would give to each of their chief personages the Musselman number of four mistresses or consorts, and as such a consequence would be fatal to the singleness and purity of their vows, it is impossible to admit of their identity with each other and the Giaour, without degrading each from that rank in our esteem obtained by their inviolable adherence to their erotic engagements.[4] (*RR* B:2:640–41)

If a character is defined by fidelity to its object, change of object means change of identity, which is as unlikely as a European degrading into a "Musselman." Therefore these English poems by this English lord cannot be a series. Yet the brittleness of the reviewer's irony hints at the suspicion that Byron's tales may deliberately invert ethical categories in order to glamorize a character who is darkly defined by deviation from his chosen objects—a renegade or pervert for whom nothing is sufficiently strange. From a postmodern perspective, however, it might be concluded that seriality cannot be inferred from preconceptions about character, because it is seriality that constitutes character. On this reckoning the choice of fidelity or infidelity, of woman or man, is indifferent, since the choice is between not substances but signs, one translatable into the other—a choice made, moreover, by some "one" who is nothing but the trail of his/her mobile connections.

Consider Lord Byron's declaration, "I cannot live without an object of attachment" (*BLJ* 3:142). It sounds like normalcy announcing itself. In the normal case, according to Freud, the sexual object is the "person from whom sexual attraction proceeds."[5] Object choice, attachment, ought to be a form of engagement. But Byron's statement also suggests what the reviewer insinuates, a sexuality independent of the object to which it is, perhaps only temporarily, linked.[6] As he explains, "It is that very indifference which makes me so uncertain and apparently capricious. It is not eagerness of new pursuits, but that nothing impresses me sufficiently to *fix*" (*BLJ* 4:121). Or as Freud, reversing his theoretical orientation, comes to say, "It seems probable that the sexual instinct is in the first instance independent of its object; nor is its origin likely to be due to its object's attractions."[7] Once again, serial changes in the sexual object can be interpreted as teaching the lesson "that the supposed deviation of inversion is no more than a mere difference."[8]

Leo Bersani has objected to the collaboration of literature and psychoanalysis in the "mythologizing of the human as a readable organization." In the interest of enlightenment he has proposed an "unreadable" alternative to that schema; he argues that "an inherent indifference of our desires to their objects makes our desiring relations to the world mobile and experimental."[9] Though appealing, Bersani's ostensibly subversive indifference of desires resembles nothing so much as that "relationship of indifference" that Jean Baudrillard has shown is instrumental to the late capitalist mode of serial reproduction. "In the series," Baudrillard argues, "objects are transformed indefinitely into simulacra of one another and, with objects, so are the people who produce them. Only the extinction of original reference permits the generalized law of equivalence, which is to say, the *very possibility of production*."[10] Scratch slightly the surface of Bersani's notion of the ahistorical destiny of replicative desire and one is left with a series of episodes in which the "same" essenceless, consumerist hero pursues indifferently desired, fundamentally equivalent, intrinsically unsatisfying commodities—an itinerary that could be entitled *Don Juan* and signed "psychoanalytic truth," "political economy," or "Lord Byron."[11] However signed, such stories deliver us into a world we already know. What distinguishes Baudrillard from Byron's reviewers—the difference between a twentieth-century reader of Marx and a nineteenth-century reader of Oriental romances—is that the latter believed that a fiction of original reference (generically, a difference between the native and the foreign) was necessary to veil the fact of equivalence in order that the possibility of production could be actualized.

The world that we postmoderns already know we know as transitional. For Freud, Bersani argues, "the perversions of adults . . . become intelligible as *uncompleted narratives.*"[12] For Bersani, the truth of psychoanalysis is its perverse failure to complete its theoretical narratives, to fix on one object. For us, Byronism, which imperializes nineteenth-century European culture by virtue of its exemplary inability to complete the narratives it has launched (or, to put it inversely, its ability to serialize the narratives it continually begins), both epitomizes the transition of the late capitalist, psychoanalytic era and marks the failure of that passage to take us anywhere except to an era of continual transition, a serial existence of perversion without shame and romance without faith. If in Fredric Jameson's view it is romance's "ultimate condition of figuration . . . to be found in a transitional moment in which two distinct modes of production, or moments of socioeconomic development coexist," we may take as an enigmatic sign of the incompletion of the "long moment" of transition the parodic survival of a strong, lordly poet alongside the bourgeois culture that he assisted in bringing into being.[13]

Byron advertises his embarrassment at being a romancer in his preface to *The Corsair*, the third of his Eastern tales, where he announces his determination to withdraw from the field of Orientalism and cedes it to his friend Thomas Moore. The preface responds to the rising debate in the reviews about the wisdom of his poetic enterprise: whether Lord Byron Minor is maturing as a poet or has settled into a perverse self-indulgence that will be the ruin of his genius and popularity (which may be one and the same). The poet ruefully admits "to have written much, and published more than enough to demand a longer silence than I now meditate," and candidly explains his decision to employ the "good old and now neglected heroic couplet" as the result of his failure, unlike Walter Scott, to have "triumphed over the fatal facility of the octo-syllabic verse." *The Corsair*'s preface exploits the ambiguous relation between the author and his heroes by mixing some straight craftsmanlike talk into a characterization of the career as poised at a moment of repentant self-correction: the poet acknowledges that he might have "*deviated* into the gloomy vanity of 'drawing from self'"; he "did not," he says, "*deviate* into [octosyllabic verse] from a wish to flatter public opinion" (p. 49; emphasis added). Before his poem and his public, Lord Byron confesses to have perverted his talents.[14] By talking about what he is doing rather than going ahead and doing it, however, Byron courts the

suspicion that under the guise of reformation he is merely piling one deviation on another. At best, the prefatory concerns about disengagement,
about a fatal facility, and about deviations into bad habits are less important
as resolutions than as themes of resolution that shape the reading of the
pendant poem and that richly complicate the affiliations between the narrated life of the hero and the represented career of the poet.

Lord Byron's heroes change love objects; the poet changes his mind: he
goes on to write *Lara*, then *Parisina*, then *The Siege of Corinth*—an infidelity
gradually matched by the readers, who, if the reviews are any guide (and
Byron always assumed they were), seem with *Parisina* on the point of abandoning their favorite poet. However desirable this was to the custodians of
culture on moral grounds, the change of taste was and is not easily explicable on aesthetic ones. Bersani has commented that "there are particular
words, costumes, gestures and settings which, so to speak, manufacture
passion," and the literary system named "Byron" was a factory of stimulation of the most efficient design.[15] If Byron's Oriental tales had for several
years been capable of manufacturing passion with a success unparalleled in
the history of nondramatic poetry, what could account for the sharp decline
of their fascination? In the context of the tales, where fidelity to an object
becomes a highly charged issue, a change that could ordinarily be fobbed off
on the "mutability of taste" looks suspiciously perverse.

The implication particularly pinched the reviewer for the *Champion*,
who both disliked *Parisina* and yet recognized that it was virtually the same
poem as ones he had earlier praised. He finds his cause by interpreting the
poem as an action rather than an imitation, charging Byron with violating
his promise (annexed to *The Corsair*) that he would go and write no more:
"*She would and She would not*, is a pleasing comedy when performed by a
lovely woman," the reviewer chides, "but a change of gender converts it into
a farce. Allowances are due to the caprices of genius,—but is it worthy of a
man of genius to be perpetually claiming them?"[16] The reviewer attributes
a change in taste—an indifferent difference corresponding to no apparent
change in the object—to authorial vacillation, figured as a change in gender
and genre. Broken promise equals broken genre. Oddly, however, though
the example is meant to be graphic and damning, the key operation—
"change of gender"—hangs ambiguously. Is the reviewer referring to the
masculinizing of a woman or the effeminizing of a man? It is not clear what
genre of gender change the reviewer is deploying to justify his own and to
arouse the reader's disappointment with Byron. Indeed, by allowing for the
degradation of comedy into farce, the reviewer does violence to the economy of genres: as the pleasing turns into the unpleasing, farce becomes an

instance of that chimerical category, intrinsically disagreeable art. Like a Musselmanic Englishman, farce appears as the degradation of kind. It is a class that has a parasitical or, more strictly, *parodistical* relation to other genres (what genre could not be turned into farce by a change of gender?) because it has no basis in the pleasure-seeking psychology that underwrites eighteenth-century aesthetics.

By bending the norms that criticism uses to define itself and its object, the *Champion* prefigures a paradigm shift, albeit of the Smithian rather than the Kuhnian variety. The key term is *caprice*, which indicates the kind of paradigm overload that Adam Smith detected in Stoic astronomers' invocations of the "caprice of each Star" in order to explain astral movements. In *his* explanatory model of the history of science, Smith understands caprice as a way of retrospectively justifying a "strange appearance" that, resembling nothing we know, provokes philosophical wonder, incapacitates contemporary discourse, and stimulates the elaboration of new philosophical systems, those "imaginary machines" that natural philosophers invent to save the imagination from embarrassment and confoundment.[17] Though banished from the constellation of physical causes, *caprice* still appeals to Smith, as it does to the *Champion*, as a shorthand characterization of an appearance that is, strangely, neither indifferent (insofar as it is unsettling) nor yet different (insofar as difference must be motivated and measurable from a position called "the same"). The *Champion* attributes its change in sentiment to more of the same, but it is exactly the problem of "more of the same" that it does not specify the reason for the change. The "strange appearance" in the gap between pleasure and disappointment is covered by the fiction of caprice or "play of nature" and shown to resemble the fickleness of women, the negligence of the aristocrat, the effeminacy of genius, or a farcical slip;[18] but the distortion of the class required to make the comparison suggests that the explanation masks an event strange enough to disable the ploys of normal criticism and to destabilize the "imaginary machine" of genre—an appearance, moreover, that neither exhausts itself in its effects nor vanishes in its naming but remains (once again) *alongside* the official reconstruction of events.

It is tempting to employ Mary Wollstonecraft's terminology for "strange appearances" and to classify the capricious Lord Byron as what she calls an "equivocal being"[19]—a resort favored, for example, by the *British Review*, which brands the hero of *The Siege of Corinth* as a "delusive compound of a man" (*RR* B:1:429)—except that the poet, though equivocal, is no being, monstrous or otherwise. Wollstonecraft's label, adopted to smear the foreign practices of male aristocrats as sexually aberrant, abetted her systematic promotion of a return to a prehistorical indifferentiation. I am interested in how equivocation changes things. Consider, for example, Freud's short Orientalist essay "The Antithetical Sense of Primal Words," which illustrates how the dream's "special tendency to reduce opposites to a unity" "exactly tallies with a peculiarity in the oldest languages known to us." K. Abel's philological study of ancient Egyptian has, according to Freud, divulged "a fair number of words with two meanings, one of which says the opposite of the other," as well as "compound words in which two syllables of contrary meaning are united into a whole"—a find that, for Abel, raises the problem of primacy:

> Since every conception is thus the twin of its opposite, how could it be thought of first, how could it be communicated to others who tried to think it, except by being measured against its opposite? . . . Since any conception of strength was impossible except in contrast with weakness, the word which denoted "strong" contained a simultaneous reminder of "weak," as of that by means of which it first came into existence. In reality this word indicated neither "strong" nor "weak," but the relation between the two.[20]

Although "in reality" *strong* and *weak* are indifferent counters, Abel does mention a "reminder," the residual sense of a change that underwrites the differential, the oddly necessary fiction that the strength of *strong* involves an abjection of that "weakness" by means of which "it first came into existence."

Abel opens his text to this supposition for the same reason that Freud opens his text to Abel: in order to explain linguistic (or, in Freud's case, theoretical) development within a relativistic system without recourse to sacrificial violence. The philologist's Egypt, itself a primal, antithetical moment that combines a "pure and noble morality" with lexical "eccentricities," represents for Freud the possibility of historical and theoretical change as linguistic evolution, what Coleridge had called "desynonimization."[21] Yet a reminder of violence tinctures the story. As the philologist discovers twin senses within the primal word, so the psychoanalyst finds twin scholars laboring under the rubric of the antithetical moment: one a philologist and one a philosopher, one an empiricist, the other a theorist. Their names: K. Abel and A. Bain. Now, *Bain and Abel* is not quite the same as *Cain and Abel.* The appearance of the latter names would return us to the mythological, whereas the *B* of *Bain* is the reminder of our development beyond the primitives: Bain and Abel are collaborators in science, not murderous rivals for the favor of a savage god. The passage from the savage to the civilized is both recalled and sidestepped by the strange appearance of

a *B* in the place of a *C*—a bloodless coup that nonetheless uncannily reminds us of blood. A reminder of violence is not violent, but it is not non-
violent either—anymore than Bain is not-Abel (who is named "Cain"); the
letter, the one untranslatable item in this transaction, makes all the difference. The literal reminder parodies the fraudulent Orientalist faceoff between self and other, native and foreign, that insists on blood or its reasonable facsimile to produce the effect of change—over and over again.

Parodic change can be brought more closely in touch with Lord Byron's
historical moment by referring to a set of the most peculiar state trials
during a time when judicial monstrosities abounded: the 1817 prosecutions
of the radical publisher William Hone for publishing "profane, blasphemous, and impious libel[s] . . . against the religion and worship of the
Church of England."[22] Hone, who was notorious for pirating John Murray's gilded editions of Lord Byron's Oriental tales,[23] protested that his
three suppressed pamphlets (*The Late John Wilkes's Catechism*, *The Political
Litany*, and *The Sinecurist's Creed*) did not libel Christianity; rather, they
parodied Christian forms solely for political effect—an intention proved, he
claimed, by the political character of the prosecution.

Hone was tried serially on three successive days for the publication of
each pamphlet. His conduct did not vary. In each trial he took up, one after
another, religiously inflected parodies from the stack of books he had
wheeled into the courtroom and read aloud example after example to judge,
jury, and spectators. Hone hoped to prove that his practice had been anticipated by Martin Luther, Bishop Latimer, and John Milton, as well as a host
of lesser lights. Hone's argument from authority failed to persuade his
judges, however, who made it clear that they would have happily prosecuted
Luther and Milton had they had the opportunity. But if Hone's extemporaneous literary history was unpersuasive as excuse, the theoretical argument that parody could be two things at once—a religious form with a
political target—was completely convincing. The theory convinced in the
only way possible: by succeeding in practice—that is, by *doing* two things at
once. Although Hone's lecture did not alter the conviction of his judges, the
effect of both the attorney general's reading his pamphlet into evidence and
his own lecture, each of which was frequently interrupted by explosive,
invisible, and uncontrollable Bakhtinian laughter from all parts of the
courtroom, was to convince the jury, handpicked by the government, that
these parodies were political, for they made a mockery not of the English
church but of the English court of justice. Hone proved the political tendency of his parody in the exposure of the power relations that determined
the nature and application of the law.[24] Stricken by convulsions as he

mounted his defense, Hone claimed no privilege or power: his very strength contained a reminder of the weakness by means of which it first came into existence.

If we accept the attorney general's definition (uncontested by Hone) that "a parody became a libel when its tendency was to excite in the mind ludicrous ideas regarding the thing parodied,"[25] then the jury's laughter both marks the transformation of the pamphlet into a libel of the very law that attempts to master it and immunizes that libel by proving it only the parody that it claims to be. The crowd destroys the pretense of law to order by laughing at the law's pretense of horror at disorder. Such a libel cannot be convicted, because any proof of its vicious "tendency" assures its success and proves its merit as ridicule; any falsification of its merit denies its success, negates tendency, and makes prosecution seem arbitrary, the law political, and the government ridiculous. At the point where the law loses its domination over reference and finds that all evidence it admits and every ruling it makes tend to bring it into ridicule, literary theory triumphs as political practice, parody as history. In the event, Hone was acquitted when the law was laughed out of court.

If the state is the institutionalized capacity to enforce consequences by commanding widespread belief, no state, as political debate in England since Edmund Burke had acknowledged, can *be* without the appearance of legitimacy. By prosecuting Hone on the grounds of religious rather than seditious libel the government hoped to restore a loss of legitimacy by exploiting the traditional linkage between the state and the established church. Hone's acquittal successfully challenged that linkage. By *successfully* I mean not that Hone wrecked the state but that the parodic moment of his defense destroyed the credentials of the prevailing ideology. The primal parodic event effects a change that as yet figures no future, that awaits, in Burke's phrase, "a new description of men."[26]

The Object of Desire

Lord Byron's career participates dutifully in the Enlightenment project of arriving at a new description of man. But alongside that earnest attendance on the future appears its parody, superbly instanced in the opening stanza of *Don Juan*, where the search for a heroic "new one" is answered in feminine rhyme by "our ancient friend Don Juan"—further corroboration of K. Abel's insight that the word denoting *strong* contains a simultaneous reminder of *weak*. Thus figured, however, the parodic looks perilously like just another equivocal being. We must inquire whether parodic action, which operates alongside Lord Byron's unparalleled commercial success, has been domesticated, made merely generic, by being moved to stage center in *Don Juan*—as it clearly is, for example, when the auditory supplement of the feminine rhyme is reified as the character of Juanna in the harem scene of canto 5. The best way to begin answering that question is to interrogate the function of the foreign in Byron, and to do that in those places where, in advance of the theme and figure of the "new one," a concept of the foreign negligently contributes to the successiveness as well as the success of his poetry: in the Oriental tales.

The Oriental tale—Robert Southey's "unsaleable" *Thalaba, the Destroyer* (1801) is an excellent example—functioned like a theme park in which English poets and readers could indulge dualistic fantasies to the full and be assured that a climactic atonement would simultaneously pay off the reader's bad surrogate and enable the reader to extricate herself, immaculately renewed, from her idyll of violence and pleasure. So much could be said about all kinds of recreational fictions in the early nineteenth century, however. In Byron the generic question—whether there is anything that distinguishes the Oriental tale from any other romance besides its decor—becomes a metonymy for the insistent concern within the romances whether *anything* besides costume distinguishes one thing from another.[27] What makes something an object of desire in preference to some other thing? Or, to put it in terms of the *Christian Observer's* apt phrase, by what devices is an Oriental tale "constituted for popularity"? (*RR* B:2:571).

The action of Lord Byron's first effort at Orientalizing, the "disjointed" *Giaour*, springs from the sexual violation by the Giaour of the Greek slave Leila, which leads to her execution by Hassan and the subsequent vengeance her European lover takes on her Turkish master. Although the violation triggers the action, it is not clear what triggers the violation. The purity of Leila is apodictic. In her eye "Soul beam'd in every spark / That darted from beneath the lid, / Bright as the jewel of Giamschid" (ll. 477–79). Thus is she blazoned:

> Her hair in hyacinthine flow,
> When left to roll its folds below,
> As midst her handmaids in the hall
> She stood superior to them all,
> Hath swept the marble where her feet
> Gleam'd whiter than the mountain sleet,
> Ere from the cloud that gave it birth
> It fell, and caught one stain of earth.
>
> (ll. 496–503)

This is a purity so absolute that it cannot be touched—perhaps even viewed or imagined—without defilement. Why would anyone desire such an abstraction?

That question bears heavily on *The Giaour*, both as a representation of sexual desire and as the beginning of a series of Turkish tales. The lengthy detours of romances ancient and modern can, at varying cost, be reduced to a psychologically or socially motivated displacement of the sexual object and deferral of the consummation of sexual desire. But no such displacement occurs here. The action of *The Giaour* begins *after* the lovers' tryst and the ruin of Leila's Grecian purity. Attainment of the sexual object is assumed (it's as easy as rolling off a cloud or staining snow—hardly even "sexual"); it triggers the obsessive pursuit of the answer to the provocative question "What makes an object desirable?" In consequence, the object of desire for the poem becomes the explanation of object desire: its motive and its morality (what the connection is between desire and defilement). If we perform the substitution of the adjective *poetic* for *sexual* before *object* we can state the aim of the romance sequence as the serial investigation of the basis of the poetic object's desirability, a desirability that must be presupposed—taken on credit—for the investigation to be conducted. The sentimental romance cathects itself totally, as the object of a desire that can be satisfied only with a full possession. But full possession must include a cognitive element: that is, the romance aims to possess itself and the knowledge of the basis for its (self-)attraction. This desire of the eye to see itself seeing with no blind spots, with nothing behind it, is the formula for paranoia, for Romantic irony, and for the Oriental tale, a self-reflexive narrative with notes.

In a sense the answer to the question "What makes the Oriental tale desirable?" is already known. "What fascinates us," writes Baudrillard, "is always that which radically excludes us in the name of its internal logic or perfection: a mathematical formula, a paranoiac system, a concrete jungle, a useless object, or again, a smooth body, without orifices, doubled and redoubled by a mirror, devoted to perverse autosatisfaction."[28] But the cognitive drive slips self-reflection out of simple autosatisfaction; it projects the poem from one mirror to another. The Oriental romance's serial self-reflections are not critical but narcissistic; its cognition is not transcendental but supplemental, the pretext for more narrative. The poem's self-reflection is elaborated by symbolizing its Imaginary as a love story; that displacement makes it possible for the poem (we might call it the Occident) to continue to take itself as its own object of desire by veiling that project from itself (as the Occident imagines an Other called the Orient). Because the Oriental tale's project cannot advance progressively toward an object (full possession of the basis of its own power) that is literally unspeakable, the poem proceeds in the way of romances, by deviations, negations, and self-alienations.

The blazon of Leila is preceded by a passage of later composition, which explains her defilement with the conceit that the attraction of a woman is like that of an "insect-queen," which is then, circularly, compared with "Beauty that lures the full-grown child" (l. 396). Two more frames were added to remedy the analogy. The first recasts the problem of desire in terms of the "strange" zest that man has for intruding on "Nature" so that, "enamour'd of distress / [He] should mar it into wilderness" (ll. 50–51). The analogy: Love for Leila is like love for Nature, or an unspoiled Greece. But the analogy conspicuously fails to explain the love of this poet for a *spoiled* Greece. The explanation occurs in a passage of daring necrophilia:

> He who hath bent him o'er the dead,
> Ere the first day of death is fled;
> The first dark day of nothingness,
> The last of danger and distress
> (Before Decay's effacing fingers
> Have swept the lines where beauty lingers),
> And mark'd the mild angelic air—
> The rapture of repose that's there—
> The fixed yet tender traits that streak
> The langour of the placid cheek
> And—but for that sad shrouded eye,
>   That fires not, wins not, weeps not, now,
>   And but for that chill, changeless brow,
> Where cold Obstruction's apathy
> Appals the gazing mourner's heart,
> As if to him it could impart
>   The doom he dreads, yet dwells upon. . . .
>
>   .   .   .
>
>   Such is the aspect of this shore;
>   'Tis Greece, but living Greece no more!
>   So coldly sweet, so deadly fair,
>   We start, for soul is wanting there.
>   Hers is the loveliness in death,
>   That parts not quite with parting breath;
>   But beauty with that fearful bloom,
>   That he which haunts it to the tomb,

Expression's last receding ray,
A gilded halo hovering round decay,
The farewell beam of Feeling past away!
(ll. 68–84, 90–100)

"That fearful bloom" seductively tincturing the undecayed corpse of Greece anticipates the blazon of Leila, who though "whiter than the mountain sleet," possesses a cheek of "unfading hue, / [On which] the young pomegranate's blossoms strew / Their bloom in blushes ever new" (ll. 493–95). Like Eustathius's parasol, the blossoms cover a whiteness that becomes attractive as the effect of its covering. The connection epitomizes Hazlitt's complaint about the decor of the tales in general: "The gaudy decorations and the morbid sentiments," he expostulates, "remind one of flowers strewed over the face of death."[29] Alive, Leila suggests a corpse. Unviolated, she already bears traces of corruption.

Those traces are no doubt artificial. The blushes have been *strewn*. The woman's flaw is not the woman's fault. Her body is a blank ground on which a hue is cosmetically applied, whether by floral largesse or by the *marking* of the "angelic air" and the "tender traits that streak / The languour of the placid cheek." Greece is, fascinatingly, like the page of a book that lives as a well-wrought corpse lives, decaying never to be decayed. Neither the blazon of Leila nor the image of the subjugated Greece represents an object it would be natural to desire; each presents an image on which it is pleasurable to fix one's gaze. Indeed, sexual consummation is elided from *The Giaour*'s narrative; the poem fully subscribes to the ritual law of the harem: to see Leila is to defile her, and it is in such corruption—the slow consuming of the pure object—that pleasure lies. The display of Leila, as of Greece, renders an image both metaphoric and metonymic of the poem: body pictured as "living page," enlivened by the "lines where beauty lingers," by line and hue.

Reviewers of Byron's Oriental tales consistently praised what the *Christian Observer* called the "strength and nature of his colouring." In the *Quarterly* George Ellis remarks that in Lord Byron's landscapes "every image is distinct and glowing, as if it were illuminated by its native sunshine" (*RR* B:5:2027). Lord Byron's images are natural (it is as if they were lit from within, by their native sun) and novel (this native sunshine is exactly what Byron adds to more prosaic depictions of the Orient). The glow of the Orient is directly apportioned to the shine of the corpse, the "gilded halo hovering round decay." In *The Giaour* the effulgence of the halo around the body of Greece represents the degradation of a living, human body into a cultic object.[30] Modernity's regression from a noble standard finds its metaphor in the Orientalizing of the poem's European central character (and, reflexively, of the reader who substitutes Oriental tales for heroic ones). The corruption of the physical body evokes the corruption of the body politic that republican ideology foresees as the result of the propagation of artificial wants in a commercial society. But that evocation invites nostalgia, not critique. This is a liberal republicanism, the sentimental reinscription of republican commonplaces in a commercialist system capable of grinding up traditional distinctions and repackaging them for sale and profit. Here the degradation of the heroic body into cultic object and of book into page mimics the self-presentation of this book as a luxurious fragment. Its gilded opulence was carefully planned by publisher and author and remarked on in the reviews. Its fragmentary status was announced in subtitle, epigraph, and advertisement: "A FRAGMENT OF A TURKISH TALE"; a "fatal remembrance" that is itself a collection of "disjointed fragments." *The Giaour* is not only the remembrance of a tale but a remembrance of a time when books were wholes—and fatal because in remembering that culture, the sentimentalizing *Giaour* decisively puts it in the heroic past, entombed and entomed in the republican "Athenian's [Themistocles'] grave."[31]

But, of course, the fragment is only an ersatz cultic object. The prestige of the cult is being cannily exploited to merchandise an object for mass consumption. That strategy is explicitly registered in the poem by the difference between a "gilded" and a golden halo—the light received is not a light bestowed but a glow superficially applied. In Walter Benjamin's terms the halo is the corpse's "aura," which he diagnosed as being in a state of "decay" because of "the desire of contemporary masses to bring things 'closer' spatially and humanly, which is just as ardent as their bent toward overcoming the uniqueness of every reality by accepting its reproduction."[32] *Gilded* evokes not the biological decay of the corpse but the historical decay of the aura as the art object is exposed to shifts in the social weather that enforce a newfound intimacy between audience and object. *The Giaour*'s frankness about its equivocal ontological and moral status is one of its most conspicuous and disconcerting features. The poem represents the source of its superficial attraction as the skill to gild, even *as* it gilds and without apparent labor. With a similar insouciance the corpse passage identifies the impulse to bring close as a degrading one, but also as one that can be acted on safely, by looking without touching.

A journal entry of March 15, 1814, invites a cynical reading of Byron's gilded fragments. Samuel Rogers, the poet writes, "says I am to be in *this* Quarterly—cut up, I presume, as they 'hate us youth.' *N'importe*" (*BLJ*

3:250). No matter, because the cutting up of the review (Ellis's typically belated article on *The Giaour* and *The Bride of Abydos*) has been anticipated by the poet, who, having learned that mutilation is requisite for success, has already perforated his poem in order to lighten the reviewer's labors. Scarcely any reviewer of *The Giaour* failed to comment on the fragmentary character of its narrative. Although some objected to the "obscurity [that] is one of the evils necessarily attendant on this kind of voluntarily mutilated composition" (*Satirist, RR* B:5:2125), many, exhibiting the insensitivity of the Turk, applauded "fragmentizing" as an innovation that gave concrete form to the spirit of the age.[33] In the *Edinburgh* Francis Jeffrey began his review by remarking on the suitability of the poem for an age in which "the taste for fragments [has] . . . become very general" and in which "the greater part of polite readers would now no more think of sitting down to a whole Epic, than to a whole ox" (*RR* B:2:842). In the *Quarterly* George Ellis observed, "It has lately been discovered, that poetical fragments may, without inconvenience, be substituted for epic or other poems. . . . The interests of both parties [poet and reader] may be promoted, by agreeing to reduce every species of composition to its quintessence, and to omit, by common consent, the many insipid ingredients which swelled the redundant narratives of our ancestors" (*RR* B:5:2001). No doubt Ellis's praise has an ironic edge, in part situational: he is a Tory reviewer assessing the work of a celebrated Whig poet in a journal owned by the poet's publisher. But the ironic rapprochement between Tory values and Whig reality is nothing new in the world; the situation of Ellis twins with Jeffrey's to focus the elliptical orbit of opinion bounding the emergent commercialist hegemony. Ironic or not, Ellis capably restates the anti-epical animus that dominates criticism in the line of Joseph Addison and David Hume. His Addisonian appeal to convenience acknowledges, however reluctantly, the social constraints on the reading experience to which a poem "constituted for popularity" must be adjusted.

The temporal implications of "fragmentizing" are elaborated in the *Christian Observer*, which backhandedly compliments Byron for "the extraordinary vigour of his language. This quality," the reviewer comments,

> also adapts the author for a busy age. Poetry is designed to teach by pleasing; and nothing is likely to please which occupies more time than the reader can safely or comfortably give. Now the noble Lord will very rarely try his patience, or detain him long from worthier pursuits. In the present instance, indeed, he has so extravagantly accommodated himself to the perpetual hurry of the days we live in, as utterly to omit all those parts of the poem which he conceives would be least interesting. (*RR* B:2:571–72)

This is Addisonianism flushed with success. If the *Spectator* aimed to create not only the taste but the milieu in which it could be successful, the complacency of the *Christian Observer* derives from an assurance that the age of "perpetual hurry" has not only arrived but entrenched itself *in saecula saeculorum*. The reviewer ironically celebrates the mutual reinforcement of an infinitely elastic culture and a charmingly accommodating poet.

The association of *The Giaour* with Addison is more than inferential. According to Samuel Smiles, Lord Byron confided to his publisher that he had mined an Arabian tale quoted in number 94 of the *Spectator* in the composition of a passage that both commands and reflects on the reader's absorption:[34]

> 'Twas but a moment that he stood,
> Then sped as if by death pursued;
> But in that instant, o'er his soul
> Winters of Memory seemed to roll,
> And gather in that drop of time
> A life of pain, an age of crime.
>
> (ll. 259–64)

In number 94 Addison enlisted two Turkish tales as illustrations of some Lockean speculations about time. The second tells the story of an infidel Sultan, who, to test the truth of a reported vision of Mahomet, is persuaded by "a doctor in the law, who had the gift of working miracles," to plunge his head into a tub of water, "and draw it up again. The king accordingly thrust his head into the water, and at the same time found himself at the foot of a mountain on a sea-shore. The king immediately began to rage against his doctor for this piece of treachery; but at length, knowing it was in vain to be angry, he set himself to think on proper methods for getting a livelihood in this strange country." After a series of adventures that led him into even greater misery, the sultan plunged into the sea, only to find himself restored to the side of the tub. The king's anger at the holy man was quelled by the information that "the state he talked of was only a dream and delusion; that he had not stirred from the place where he then stood; and that he had only dipped his head into the water, and immediately taken it out again."

Lord Byron's passage claims autonomy for the Giaour's moment of self-absorption; the narratorial witness furnishes an opportunity for the reader to duplicate that absorption and autonomy. But standing behind the Byronic moment is Addison's scene, just as standing behind the sultan's adventure is the supervisory "doctor of law." Romantic self-reflection is embedded within a professionalist allegory that does not primarily aim to teach the

Lockean doctrine of the divisibility of any moment into an infinity of moments, each a potential heaven or hell, but the Addisonian lesson that entrance into heaven or hell is controlled by the technical facility of an intermediary such as a scholarly periodical essayist. The position of power belongs to the scholar, not the king. The doctor of law decapitates the sultan, whose head, plunged into the water, is separated from his body, and whose adventure dramatizes the fundamental illegitimacy of a rule for which beheading is fit punishment.

What makes this incident special is neither the plunge nor the adventure but the *restoration* of the sultan to his senses, his sovereignty, and his head as if nothing had happened—as if indulgence in delirium entailed no break with a natural political reality. One could imagine certain political settings—say, Stuart England—where retailing a parable like this might be dangerous. But in the age of Anne and on the eve of the Hanovers, the troping of the king as sultan reads less like a charge of despotic illegitimacy than as an endorsement of monarchic rule—and not despite but *because of* its fictionality. It is one of the first among the many "pleasing illusions" that Burke would more strenuously defend at the end of the century. Here, in the *Spectator*, Addison is justifying the role of the monarch in light of the needs of readers. The sovereign serves the function of focusing reader identification and inducing him or her to take the time for a plunge into the water bucket of the tale (the sultan had himself imitated the example of Mahomet). The story assumes that a reader's identification, no matter how delirious, is momentary; moreover, what simulates a catastrophe for the sultan is a consolatory experience of mobility for the middle-class reader. And, of course, although the parable claims to have put everything back in place, something has changed: there has been a vivid confirmation of the power of the doctor at law and of the periodical essayist (the other, reserved "half" of the split bourgeois subject), whose magic is to dissolve natural connections and to reconstitute them as if nothing had changed—whose magic is to mystify the nature, source, and goal of his rhetorical power.

The *Spectator*'s parable exploits a physiological limit—the amount of time a head can be safely submerged in a bucket of water—in order to measure deviation.[35] Lord Byron's Oriental tales confidently dispense with both biology and periodicity. Unlike the *Spectator*, which claims to analyze phenomena without modifying their constitution, to read signs in order both to divulge the social syntax in which they are embedded and to infer their necessary consequences, Byron's fragments propose succession without consecution, impressiveness without instruction, effects without causes, possession without conquest.[36] If the parable of the sultan invites sympathetic involvement, the reviews' *citation* of convenient fragmentary moments simulates the hidden depths of a magician's water bucket—simply, speedily, superficially. The prevailing mode of reviewing was to quote extract after extract, linking them by prose summary. The form of the *Giaour* allowed this extraction to be done in perfect propriety and with gratifying haste—how could it fail to be praised?[37] By presenting itself as a collection of foreign bits of verse that could easily be translated into the mastering prose of criticism, *The Giaour* afforded the reviewer the delicious opportunity of exactly reproducing the Orientalist strategy of the poem and simultaneously of reinforcing the ruling premise of British imperialism that what is foreign is precisely what can and needs to be translated. In high Orientalist style the *Christian Observer* congratulates the poet on the result: "Few poets ever put their readers in more complete possession of a country they have never seen" (*RR* B:2:571).[38]

This model of accelerated absorption allows for variation. Lady Frances Wedderburn Webster (who was for a time the object of Byron's casual affection) testifies to the poet: "*The Giaour* (my dear companion) I have read till the book is no longer of use—it is printed on my heart."[39] However enthusiastic, Lady Frances's response is obtuse: a perfect reader would not have needed so many readings for the printing to take. Perfection was achieved in one man's exemplary reception of *The Corsair.* Murray writes:

> Mr. Ward was here with Mr. Gifford [the poet and the editor of the *Quarterly*] yesterday, and mingled his admiration with the rest. Mr. Ward is much delighted with the unexpected charge of the Dervis—
> "Up rose the Dervis, with that burst of light,"
> and Gifford did what I never knew him do before—he repeated several passages from memory, particularly the closing stanza,—
> "His death yet dubious, deeds too widely known."[40]

Riper than Lady Frances, Gifford's impressionability is also somewhat counterproductive—he did not buy the poem he instantaneously memorized. Nor could John Murray live solely off the proceeds from those reviews that purchased and quoted *The Giaour.* He needed readers who, less than perfect, would be fascinated by the book and wear it out as did Lady Frances. Murray worried about the effectiveness of the book's presentation of the poetry, the fit between Byron's imagery and his format; his decisions about sizes and prices, about kind and quality of illustrations, and about desirable combinations of poems show an acute awareness that the book's socially inflected materiality—its look, its feel, its vulnerability to wear and tear—had as much to do with its "life" as the verse within. "A Book's a Book altho' there's nothing in it," sang the poet of *English Bards and Scotch Reviewers* (1. 52), and satirical or not, the aristocratic author acted on that maxim from the first. His first book, *Fugitive Pieces*, appeared in a dandiacal green cover so "flagrant" that the young ladies who purchased it cautiously tucked the volume under their arms as they left the bookseller's shop.[41] Never green, there was nothing flagrant about Murray's supremely genteel editions except their price, which was sufficiently sensational.[42] Besides, by 1815 no publication by Lord Byron could avoid making a scene—whether it came out flagrantly expensive as in the hands of Murray, the rightful publisher, or criminally cheap, as in the hands of Hone, the chief of the pirates (or even, as we shall see, outrageously anonymous, as in the case of *Don Juan*).

Lady Frances's patina of obtuseness toward Byronic impressiveness, then, makes her a serviceable reader. For her, books have a useful life. What makes Lady Frances especially serviceable for my purposes is that for those who read the *The Giaour* as a *roman à clef*, she is the most plausible candidate as the correspondent to Leila. As plausible to herself as to us, for—and this is what baffles the historicist's pursuit of the referent—Lady Frances could not be any more certain about the connection than we are. What makes Leila *figure*, her sexual violation by the Giaour, was averted by Lady Frances, whose repeated readings of the poem between boards allegorize her lack of that privileged relation to the biographical experience that the text supposedly represents. Her repeated readings enact the misrecognition that structures every encounter with the poem, the perversity that ideally makes every reader both as dangerously privileged and safely representative as Lady Frances herself. Actuarial, Murray stakes his profit on the necessity that books mediate the scarring or shattering or contaminating impressiveness of Byron and on the certainty that their useful lives can be calculated to end right about the time when another poem by Lord Byron is ready for the press. The booking of Byronic impressiveness gives it a luxurious appearance (it could take pride of place among the tea equipage) and socializes its impact. A sexual violation may be posited as the zero degree of reading Lord Byron, but the very book in which that hypothesis is posed prevents its realization; sexual violation is elided in the reading of the tale as in its rendering; consumption simulates consummation; the commodity form makes readerly rape conceivable by making it impossible.

Byron's Foreign Brand

No sociology of reading has perfected a causal model that can summarily account for the responses of the readers of the Oriental tales. No sociological explanation can congregate multitudes of fully historicized particulars under the umbrella of some powerfully general classification, such as the bourgeoisie once seemed to be. Indeed, the dream of giving general habitations and classes to what Charles Levin has called the "sociological ego" seems to have a charm inversely proportional to its theoretical coherence.[43] It is a romantic dream at war with romance. Determination of the "real nature of [Byron's] relation to his audience" must remain as elusive for twentieth-century critics as it was for Lady Frances Wedderburn Webster and the *Christian Observer.*[44] Given that the application of the story by a reader to him- or herself entails the kind of misrecognition that makes causes out of "airy nothings," one might as well take seriously the claims for the poem to be its own cause—not as a statement of reality, but as an especially articulate version of the misrecognition by means of which the effect of reality is achieved.

Lord Byron's tales do not project the fantasy of an epic body, nor do they induce fixation on a single fetishized fragment. We have already considered the female corpse as an emblem of its seductive power. Equally powerful in its solicitation but divergent in its significance is the appearance to the cloistered and remorseful Giaour of a hallucinatory

> bloody hand
> Fresh sever'd from its parent limb,
> Invisible to all but him
> Which beckons onward to his grave,
> And lures to leap into the wave.
> (ll. 827–31)

Surely what the Giaour thinks he views is Hassan's "sever'd hand," last seen quivering round its "faithless brand" after he slew the Turk in an ambush (ll. 657–58). Yet because the hand is a phantom, it cannot properly belong to any single person. The "bloody hand" also recalls the "red right hand" of the Giaour, which Hassan glimpsed flashing a "foreign brand" (ll. 608–9) before their fatal conflict. A psychoanalytic explanation beckons, but to heed its call would divert us from the crucial implication of the sequence: that the perception of the Giaour's *own* hand as phantom is plotted as the precondition for the sight of Hassan's phantom hand. A figurative logic also connects the two red hands. The "bloody hand / Fresh sever'd from its parent limb" aptly metaphorizes the European's renegade lot. Broken down, however, the figure is a curiously tortured one: a synecdoche (hand for man) is read metaphorically (separation resembles severing) to introduce a metonymy that fractures synecdochic affiliations: because severed, the hand represents its incapacity to stand for the whole man; because severed, the renegade represents his inability to stand for his parent country; because severed, the hand quivers in an automatic action that bears only a ghastly resemblance to the intended action of a living body.

"Not mine the act, though I the cause," the Giaour announces, referring to the execution of Leila (l. 1061). But the claim to a guilty agency denied to Greek slave and Turkish despot cannot be credited. The textually manifest association of the hands of the Giaour and Hassan is a stronger link than the proclaimed subordination of any hand's "act" to a supposed intention or will. The action engaged in by *both* Hassan and the Giaour—their hand-to-hand combat—is causeless, despite the violent effort of each man to determine himself as cause. Cause is simulated by what Baudrillard calls a "gestural moment,"[45] here the display of a "foreign brand" wielded by a "red right hand." Perhaps a standard, perhaps a sword, the brand's insignia of foreignness is as contingent in its relation to any moral or political cause as is the spectacular red arm in relation to the man to whom it happens to be attached. In the "foreign brand" Hassan sees the sign of his own allegorical destiny. He sees (sees without recognizing) the hieroglyph of the Oriental tale by which the representative Westerner represents a character—brands him—as foreign, a foe over whom he will necessarily triumph. "A word's enough to raise mankind to kill" (*Lara* 2:222–25). By this trademark you conquer him whose brand is faithless in its representations of himself and others.

The Giaour prefigures Edward Said's magisterial critique of Orientalist discourse: it represents the postulated difference between the Westerner and the Oriental as phantasmal (as phantasmal as is the difference between female and male). The Westerner and the Oriental occupy the same phantasmatic space, although they occupy it differently. The Oriental corresponds to no empirical being; the Westerner exists for himself only as the imaginary relation between an Occidental self and an Oriental Other. This phantasmatic space, which Said calls Orientalism, is also a literary kind of a peculiar sort. The genre of the Oriental tale presupposes no contract either stated or implied.[46] The genre of the Oriental tale is a kind of writing that forcefully manufactures passion by the iterative display of an impressive foreign brand. That display is a promise, arbitrarily offered, rather than a contract mutually engaged. If genre is a promise, whether a promise to observe conventions or merely a promise to repeat oneself, the felicity of the promise depends on having the competence to promise, on having the sense of a future or having the right to copy. The Oriental can neither have a genre nor control the genre that is nominally his own, because his brand is faithless—mired in a stagnant present, he cannot imagine a future, guarantee continuity, or enter into conventions like poets and generals. Thomas De Quincey gives a pithy formulation of the enabling prejudices of Orientalism: "Christianity signs her name; Islamism makes her mark."[47] The Oriental is a wholly unpromising character, a cruel despot with no line of succession, who has no kind except that given him by the European's foreign brand.

Victory over the Oriental foe can never be complete. The severance of the hand, of instrument from cause, assures that despite the Giaour's professions of finality (the claim to be a cause, the wish to die), act will be followed by reaction according to the inexorable mechanism of revenge. The return of the severed hand legitimates a repetition that would otherwise seem merely compulsive or perverse. That the hand is said to beckon to the grave is immaterial, for in the Oriental tale the grave gives back all but Themistocles, the defunct epic hero. In the Oriental tale the grave is the dark passage that allows for reappearances of the foreign brand, whether in *The Giaour* or in its successors. It may return as a "red right hand," or it may be transfigured into a scathed face "mark'd with inward pain," with "death . . . stamp'd upon his brow" (ll. 794, 797). The relocation of the brand on the face is an instance of metonymy aspiring to the prestige of metaphor—a superficial movement seems to retrieve the identity that was hostage to the Other. I become the cause: my inward pain—my history—is expressed on my face. However fragmentary, my face is the signature of my soul. In such an expressive countenance "The close observer can espy / A noble soul, and lineage high" (ll. 868–69). This lineage projects a more illustrious career for the Byronic hero than the monotonous swing shift of the vendetta.

Yet the expression on the Giaour's face is hardly the transparent transmission of inward to outward. The death stamped is pain *marked*, pain become foreign to the moment of its feeling in order to be made legible. The scathings of the face are the man's most individual, expressive features, the inalienable signature of the soul; but those lines are stamped, impressed so as to impress, and therefore subject to reproduction and transfer. Jacques Derrida's proposition is as applicable here as it is to the context of the American Declaration of Independence: "The signature invents the signer."[48] But we need to make explicit the equivocalness of that proposition by adding the codicil that the signature invents the signer as *one who signs.* The expressive origin and the impressive function of the signature cannot be harmonized, any more than the inward/outward line of transmission can be reconciled with the before/after line of genealogy, or any more than the claims for a noble, natural lineage can be reconciled with the aim of producing a line of readers. The insistence of contradiction has its proper name: *Death.* One finds oneself within a line, identified by a stamp that one wears as a signature, as if a hand had impressed its identity on one's own face.

Death means having one's face become a brand foreign to one's own cause, which is the condition of entering the sorry lineage that Hazlitt scornfully calls "man." "Man," he writes, "is (so to speak) an endless and infinitely varied repetition: and if we know what one man feels we so far know what a thousand feel in the sanctuary of their being."[49] We *know* that we know because this "man" is a "public," people classed together by their property in the same books—not all in the same book (some kind of secular scripture, such as *The Prelude* has been avowed to be) but in fragmentary, expressive books whose sameness is that they follow each other in a certain line. The content of individual interpretations makes no difference: it is immaterial whether the monk and the boatsman/narrator or Lady Frances and William Gifford agree or disagree on what makes the Giaour tick— what matters is that readings should be produced continuously. At the vanishing point readings and readers are identified by the exchange of a banknote for a book—an empirical act that is not, however, wholly visible to the eye, because there is something incomplete, even fabulous about it. The reading/purchase is not *merely* an exchange but the assumption of a signature that invents the signer (redeeming the residual assertion instinct in every purchase) according to the identity of that one man who claims the right to sign for all, that man by whom all men come to feel in their inmost sanctuaries, the Byronic hero. The reader of *The Giaour* becomes part of the Giaour's lineage.

All concerned—author, public, and the publisher who profitably convenes the two—have a stake in the reliability of this line. Figuring its articulation as death provides assurance, for what could be more certain than that death will occur? And what could be more certain than that the human line will go on despite individual deaths? Yet there is a different sort of doom awaiting the stamp itself: its inevitable degradation from the crispness that confers on engravings authenticity and value. The "scroll" becomes "shrivell'd" (l. 1255); the stamp wears down.[50] As the line requires the stamp of death to insure its indefinite extension, so the stamp of death will require the stimulus of an inward pain to revive the freshness of its mark. The stimulus of pain will be the pleasure of the line, its reason to go on. "Death," "pain," and "pleasure" are the personified agents (as human as Hassan and Leila) of that tonic shock by which the line is prolonged and its continuation excused.[51]

If that account seems abstract, it nonetheless represents the operating schema for the dominant mode of literary/cultural production in Great Britain during the second decade (and half of the third) of the nineteenth century, and predominant in Lord Byron and Walter Scott. Byron and Scott occupy the same schematic space, though they occupy it differently. Both wield the "foreign brand" as hieroglyphic product of the cultural machine and as the symbolic representation of the machine's workings. Scott's move toward the historical novel in response to the Byronic challenge registers a greater self-consciousness than his rival about the historical significance of the latter possibility. Scott's "realism" is to comprehend the possibility of the text's capacity to represent itself as a fascinating series of fragments (pages, chapters, commodities) indefinitely reproduced by a mechanized hand. He identifies that possibility with the achieved security and progressive destiny of the commercial society that those texts imaginatively ground.

Scott's transition from romancer to realist is dramatically rendered by John Gibson Lockhart in his *Memoirs of Scott.* Lockhart recounts how in June of 1814, as yet unacquainted with the man who would be his father-in-law, he retired with some drinking companions, "most of them . . . destined for the Bar of Scotland," to

a library which had one large window looking northwards. After carousing here for an hour or more, I observed that a shade had come over the aspect of my friend, who happened to be placed immediately opposite to myself, and said something that intimated a fear of his being unwell. "No," said he, "I shall be well enough presently, if you will only let me sit where you are, and take my chair; for there is a confounded hand in sight of me here, which has often bothered me before, and now it won't let me fill my glass with a good will." I rose to change places with him accordingly, and he pointed out to me this hand which, like the writing on Belshazzer's wall, disturbed his hour of hilarity. "Since we sat down," he said, "I have been watching it—it fascinates my eye—it never stops—page after page is finished and thrown on that heap of MS., and still it goes on unwearied—and so it will be till candles are brought in, and God knows how long after that. It is the same every night— I can't stand a sight of it when I am not at my books."—"Some stupid, dogged, engrossing clerk, probably," exclaimed myself, or some other giddy youth in our society. "No, boys," said our host, "I well know what hand it is—'tis Walter Scott's."[52]

The library provides an uncanny view of the engine of its own reproduction. Through the window a text is being produced as if it were but one page, subdivided into identical units that continuously roll off the assembly line under the management of a detached hand. Anxiety of influence is out of the question: the vocabulary of strength is utterly wrong for this spectacle of mechanical and irresistible force. The severed hand is a hand without strength. Instead of a scene of instruction, as between two strong writers, this is a scene of fascination, which represents the affective, cultural power achieved by the display of a mode of production that is the routinized activity of a severed hand.

I have said *text* rather than *novel* or even *book* because the fascination precedes the figure of genre, as it precedes the name of the author or even the idea of authorship. The activity of the hand is rationalized metaphorically as the work of someone who works *as* a hand, "some stupid, dogged, engrossing clerk." The corrective attribution of the hand to a proper authorial cause might be imagined to increase rather than resolve the anxiety, for the presumption must follow that this rapid production is somehow meaningful, invested with labored thought. But the silent irony of Lockhart's anecdote is that despite the identification of the hand with the famous author of verse romances, the first guess is the right one. Lockhart has given the details: Scott's father was a Writer to the Signet and the son was trained as a Writer's Apprentice, who traveled the countryside engrossing documents as he amassed the lore that he would retail in both *Minstrelsy of the Scottish Border* and *The Lay of the Last Minstrel*. By training and temperament Scott *was* the clerk he is imagined to be. "'Tis Walter Scott" closes the anecdote, but the host cannot say enough, cannot speak in possession of the knowledge that the reader and Lockhart share, that Scott is writing *Waverley*. Nonetheless, because *Waverley* was published anonymously the differential in knowledge makes this an accurate picture of the anonymous author. Lockhart positions the anecdote within his narrative to stress that there is no break between copyist, narrative poet, and historical novelist: all are products of continuous composition by a "confounded hand." *Walter Scott* is the name given to this anonymous, mechanical means of production.

We might put into the host's mouth a revision of Coleridge's pivotal recognition of "There Was a Boy": "If I had seen that hand writing in the deserts of Arabia I would have shouted out Scott!" But of course this is

Edinburgh, not Arabia, and it is a lawyer speaking, not Coleridge. The recognition of Scott here is a quasi-legal certification. Scott would be able to retain his anonymity as the author of the *Waverley* tales because the relations of production on display here would become Scott's signature.[53] Even so another "signature" is required, testimony that assigns the productive activity of the hand to a legal person. The attribution is strictly artificial—as it must be: Hume taught that the right to property does not depend on one being the cause of the property. The artifice is not only in line with Hume but in accord with the scene, which displays the production of text as act without cause, as well as with the paramount aim of Scott's career, which is to memorialize causes as remnants of a romantic past. Causes are launched by pretenders.[54]

The Giaour does not attempt even Scott's realism. To read *The Giaour* as the poem of Lord Byron and not of someone who might have merely assumed the name demands a belief in "that nameless spell, / Which speaks, itself unspeakable" (ll. 838–39). The phrase could fit in virtually all of Byron's poems. As we shall see, the Oriental tales unfold the lesson that the opposition between the named and the unspeakable voice, however necessary to the reproduction of the line, is false. Unrepresentability does not merely belong to the voice, absorbed in the viewless logic of its lyric center. The unrepresentable *spells*. The mark spells before the name signifies. With some tonic violence we can translate that nameless spell into the category of the untamed or secret impulse that we deployed in the second chapter. The mark is the secret, Orientalizing impulse that inhabits the signature, faithless to the project of branding native or foreign, in or outside the line. The mark is faithless because uncopyable—an opacity that is the autographic moment that undoes all of Byron's narratives. *Autographic*, not autobiographic. John Galt recalled that in conversation Byron "had the infirmity of speaking, though vaguely, and in obscure hints and allusions, more of his personal concerns than is commonly deemed consistent with a correct estimate of the interest which mankind takes in the care of another." Inconversable, Byron's faithless mark does not hint at some inward pain or external referent down the line but asserts itself as that inscriptive moment elided in the picture of Scott's industrial handiwork. The autographic moment—the read/write hand of Lord Byron—disfigures the face that the Orientalist genre presents to the world. With that crucial reservation we may second Galt's conclusion that this habit "was a blemish as incurable as the deformity of his foot" (*HVSV*, p. 74).

The Moment of Change

It is requisite that an Author should, on every fresh appearance, exceed himself, in order to keep pace with the expectations of the public. . . . When, by a series of such performances as these, a writer has shewed us all he can do, we begin to be let into the secret of what he **cannot** *accomplish.*

Eclectic Review, *March 1816*

The object of fascination for *The Giaour* is the code in all its workings: a systematically varied series of fragmentary passages, reiterated moments of uniquely overpowering absorption. *The Giaour* is the harbinger of a new form of subjectivity that, according to Baudrillard, "triumphs in the mechanical repetition of itself."[55] To be absorbed and, simultaneously, to preempt natural decay by arranging for the reproduction of the moment of fascination represents a special form of "self-consciousness." The Giaour attempts the effect in his elegiac letter to a friend to whom he sends the "pledge" of a ring, memorial of a youthful vow: "I would remind him of my end: / Though souls absorb'd like mine allow / Brief thought to distant friendship's claim" (ll. 1224–26). Lines could be drawn from this pledge to Byron's biography, whether to Edleston's cornelian or Lady Caroline Lamb's twist of hair;[56] each would evoke a moment of absorption, but neither would provide the empirical anchor that would arrest the drift from one facsimile to another. The ring is a Byronic signature gesture and therefore a generic token signifying the interchangeability of all those who might receive it. The gift of the ring permits the Giaour Byronically to write his own reading of himself: to be absorbed, to see himself absorbed, and to bring about the repetition of that absorption.

In one sense the Oriental tales exploit a notion of the intrinsically desirable (the perfectly pure and therefore irresistible woman; the essentially foreign and therefore appropriable culture) to veil the narcissistic basis of the narrative's object choice—its fascination with itself. But in another sense the Oriental tales discover that the self by which the tales are fascinated is no simple thing, no more *intrinsically* desirable than either "the woman I love" or "the man I hate." The narcissistic subject of the Oriental tales is a fabulous split construction, intrinsically extrinsic, most at home when transmitted farthest abroad, most free when most bound:

See—by the half-illumined wall
His hood fly back, his dark hair fall,
That pale brow wildly wreathing round,

As if the Gorgon there had bound
The sablest of the serpent-braid
That o'er her fearful forehead stray'd.
                    (ll. 893–98)

The cost of being a Byronic hero, of not being paralyzed in the face of the Gorgon, is to become what one *might have* beheld, to become by impression a serpent-braided creature of fascination who can impressively display what he has avoided seeing. The signature of the Byronic subject is the subjection of its signature to transfer. In *The Giaour* it is "as if the Gorgon there had bound"; in the *The Bride of Abydos* it is as if the Giaour on Zuleika "had bound / The sablest of the serpent-braid," for her veil conceals the "lovely serpent smiling, / Whose image [at the Fall] was stamped upon [woman's] mind / But once beguiled—and ever more beguiling" (1:159–61). Without having seen the Giaour or having read *The Giaour*, the Bride of Abydos, poem and character, is wed to her predecessor, bound beyond death. Here is Byron's ad hoc explanation for halting his accretions to *The Giaour*: "I have but with some difficulty *not* added any more to this snake of a poem—which has been lengthening its rattles every month—it is now fearfully long" (*BLJ* 3:100). The means of curtailing the fascination is not to break it but to transfer the hieroglyph of the poem to the brow of a female character, who thus becomes posited as the object of narcissistic desire—but an object that is serially propulsive because in alluring the poem toward the concealed image of itself, she takes the poem beyond itself. *Beyond* should be understood in a very limited way, for in the broadest sense stopping one poem and beginning the next means sliding from one fascinating fragment to another that is all but the same. The serpentine subjectivity of the Oriental tales unfolds without jolts.

Originally, Zuleika was what she believes herself to be, the sister of Selim. Lord Byron explains his revision of their relationship: "The times & the *North* (*not Frederic* but our *Climate*) induced me to alter their consanguinity & confine them to cousinship—I also wished to try my hand on a female character in Zuleika—& have endeavoured as far as ye. grossness of our masculine ideas will allow—to preserve her purity without impairing the ardour of her attachment" (*BLJ* 3:199). Consanguinity would have relied on the incestual impulse to constitute attraction in terms of a (supposedly) natural desire that (supposedly) cannot be acted upon—an ardent purity. The same effect is achieved symbolically by the figure of the snake that renders incestuous desire as narcissistic fascination. Though she bears the mark of the snake, it has as little to do with Zuleika's state of mind or soul as the pomegranate petals have to do with Leila's. She did not put the serpent there, nor does she see it. She remains pure though fallen. Her fall is the man's fault. By the stamp of the snake he figures his difference on the ground of her sameness, his design on her innocence. The adjustment of consanguinity to cousinage conforms on the anthropological level exactly to the mechanical production of more difference that ending one poem and beginning another effects on the industrial level. The production of more difference, more "nuances in the monotony of supply,"[57] teaches that supposed differences, including the moralistic dualities that individuate Orientalism, *are* supposed—that fragments of a poem, severed hands, rattles of a snake, sisters, and lovers reproduce the same quintessentially generic signature.

In *The Bride of Abydos* Lord Byron tries to portray the Oriental world from within. There are no European characters. The vertical boundaries of *The Giaour* have been tipped so that what appeared to be fraternal struggle now looks like dynastic conflict. The despot, Giaffir, is an unnatural father, not only because he is brutal beyond reason, but because he is in fact not the father but the usurping uncle of the hero. The variation of the father sanctions the felicitous release of aggression unhindered by oedipal ambivalence. Selim can, in good conscience, hate Giaffir because he is the Claudian murderer of the real father; he can innocently desire Giaffir's daughter Zuleika because, despite appearances, she is not really his sister (or mother) but his cousin.

When the tale is reduced to its elemental family romance, the vivid decor seems wholly cosmetic. The charge surfaces in the *Critical Review:* "Lord Byron sometimes takes more pains to be *pretty* than a great poet ought to take. He has so many beauties of the most genuine sort, and of the highest order, that he can well afford to leave prettiness to puerility. He is the poet of sentiment and of nature; and he should despise all affected ornament, and all elaborate artifice of decoration" (*RR* B:2:628–29). The reviewer seems ventriloquized by the poem. He speaks of Byron as Giaffir speaks to Selim, whom the tyrant derides for his "less than woman's hand" (1:99). But Selim's apparent weakness is disclosed as a disguise in one of the most extraordinary scenes in all of Byron, when, after being aroused from a marmoreal repose by the anguished pleas of Zuleika, Selim admonishes the astonished girl, "Think not I am what I appear" (1:381). Muscle in the robes of woman, vice in the garb of romance—a man (and the poet is a man) is not what he appears. In *The Bride* the distinction between men and women hinges precisely on the ability to disguise oneself versus the necessity that one be veiled.

We know we are "inside" the Orient because cultural antagonisms have been transformed into gender oppositions. Selim, the champion of the oppressed, loves Zuleika. But he is insurmountedly divided from Zuleika by his own self-division between appearance and being. "Power sways but by division," Selim avows (2:434). "Power sways but by division" is the maxim that the poem consistently affirms: in the contrast between Giaffir and Selim; in the split between canto 1 and canto 2; in the hierarchy of text and notes; in every couplet and quatrain. What Said says about the Orientalist, that "knowledge means rising above immediacy, beyond self, into the foreign and distant,"[58] applies with equal force to Byron's Oriental hero, whose maxim designs coming-into-power as an ecstatic self-estrangement. Selim recalls to an awed Zuleika that heady moment

> When first this liberated eye
> Survey'd Earth, Ocean, Sun, and Sky,
> As if my Spirit pierced them through,
> And all their inmost wonders knew.
>
> (2:345–48)

In a pivotal irony, this claim to cognitive power by the emancipated Oriental echoes the address by which the poet flatters the "liberated eye" of his readers at the outset of the poem:

> Know ye the land where the cypress and myrtle
> Are emblems of deeds that are done in their clime,
> Where the rage of the vulture—the love of the turtle—
> Now melt into sorrow—now madden to crime?
>
> (1:1–4)

The question is rhetorical. Of course the reader knows this "land," which is nothing other than the child's garden of metaphors growing in those books that have nursed her infancy and now regiment her leisure. The reader, outcast in a commercial society where little is what it appears, is able to return to a land whose inmost wonders can be pierced at a glance. As the reader pairs with Selim, so, ironically, Selim pairs with Giaffir. Until this point in the poem Selim, Giaffir, and Zuleika have been rigorously associated, respectively, with the image clusters of breaking, piercing, and binding.[59] Selim's claim to have "pierced" realigns the parties on the basis of the irrepressible dualism that constitutes the masculine "I" as the "I am not what I appear" and that empowers it to pierce appearances and come to know the Other as "I" know "myself," annihilating along the way any particular, such as Zuleika, that resists incorporation in this specular economy.

The death of Zuleika from a broken heart does not merely represent misogyny (although of course it does); it allegorically renders the impossibility of confronting the strangeness of the Orient except in terms of the conventional homosocial, misogynist plot. A woman is killed to make believe that the resistant strangeness of the Orient can be given a sign value and destroyed, "as if . . . pierced through." The annihilation of particulars is the beginning of global power. In Byronic Orientalism power and the inexorable propagation of a specular structure of knowledge are identical: endless division, irresistible power. Yet Selim's claim to a liberated eye broaches a blindness: Selim cannot discern the convergence of his language with Giaffir's. He does not see that his supposedly sovereign position is actually a subject position. He cannot apprehend the system by which he is encoded. He does not see the Western reader at his back who pierces him through and through. In *The Bride of Abydos* power returns to the Westerner, who prides himself on being the master technician of the binding and splitting that is the game of power.

The Corsair promises a direct investigation of the force of social ties and the sources of political power. It begins unusually, in the first person plural, with the collective voice of the pirate crew. They are described as living, like Harrovian schoolboys or Albanian warriors, a life of action intermitted only by fierce play: "In scattered groups upon the golden sand, / They game—carouse—converse—or whet the brand" (1:47–48). The pirates are bound into a community by neither interest nor need but by Conrad's compelling authority, which flows from his hypnotic powers:

> That man of loneliness and mystery,
> Scarce seen to smile, and seldom heard to sigh;
> Whose name appals the fiercest of his crew,
> And tints each swarthy cheek with sallower hue;
> Still sways their souls with that commanding art
> That dazzles, leads, yet chills the vulgar heart.
> What is that spell, that thus his lawless train
> Confess and envy, yet oppose in vain?
> What should it be? that thus their faith can bind?
> The power of Thought—the magic of the Mind!
>   (1:173–82)

To prove that Conrad is not as he appears, and therefore legitimately the holder of power, the poem grounds his subjectivity in the love of Medora, who dwells in a tower on the island, where she melodically pines while he pirates. Medora is bound by chains of "love—unchangeable—unchanged" (1:287). Medora's identification with the inner, veridical lyric voice, what the pirates call the "life of life" (1:25), indemnifies Conrad's authority as something more than a theatrical contrivance. Power sways but by division, but the virtue of power, its call on our sympathy, depends on a reference to some intrinsic value or charm—and for Romantic poets, as for landless pirates, there is no more potent image of the intrinsic than a woman sweetly disburdening her soul in an island tower. Because Medora is what she irrepressibly appears ("Without thine ear to listen to my lay, / Still must my song my thoughts, my soul betray" [1:367–68]), Conrad must screen her from harm. The advance of internalization in the Gothic can be measured by the changes in carceral motivation: Montoni imprisons Emily in Udolpho so that he may capitalize the superiority he feels; Conrad's invest-ment in Medora is strictly psychic: closeted, she saves the place of the ego in a world where the "routine of dissipation" (*BLJ* 1:124) threatens immersion in libidinal drift or in blind, mechanical repetition. Unlike the pirate crew, Medora is not spellbound; she sees nothing of the letter of Conrad; she is held only by the imperceptible rapport of their hearts. The legitimation of Conrad's power within the poem doubles as the assertion of the poem's capacity artlessly to single out and bind its unresisting readers.

Or almost unresisting. Medora does speak up when Conrad tells her that he must immediately return to the sea and to battle, complaining that he deceived her, "for—he came again!" Conrad answers with the promise of a fidelity indistinguishable from a repetition compulsion: "Again—again—and oft again—my love!" (1:449–50). In the woman's complaint we hear the lyric's complaint of the return of narrative with its deceptive rhetoric of means and ends, motives and goals. We can also hear the accents of the reviewer of the *Champion* who complains of the monotony of Byron's career, which narrates itself as the to and fro of the same character in barely differentiated plots, each new one "as like to the former productions as a one pound bank-note is to another one pound bank-note, and with as little difference in value" (*RR* B:1:428). Eventually the glamour wears thin, and it becomes clear to readers and lovers alike that the serial adventures of the pirates recapitulate the serial transactions of the commercial society, which the Romantic poet and the pirate have supposedly escaped. It may be stretching a point to make Medora speak for all irritable readers (although she certainly anticipates the *Champion*), yet even in the poem's own terms her grievance rings true. All that disrupts domestic bliss is the Corsair's desire to perfect it, a desire produced by his captivation by an economy that determines value by structural opposition: "My very love to thee is hate to them, / So closely mingling here, that disentwined / I cease to love thee when I love mankind" (1:403–5). Love means our good, their evil, an opposition that must return, inexorably, again and again, until the books are finally closed.

"No medium now—we perish or succeed!" cries Conrad as he exhorts his men in their preemptive strike against the Muslim Seyd (1:132). But things go wrong. The hero swerves from battle at the decisive moment to save the women of the harem from incineration. The result is defeat and imprisonment. Gulnare, Seyd's concubine, mistakes the chivalric gesture for a sign of love. But Conrad's deviations—from battle, from Medora— are merely perverse, evidence of his indifference to any single object of desire. The Corsair is rewarded for that achieved indifference by immurement in a living death:

> Preserved to linger and to love in vain,
> While Vengeance pondered o'er new plans of pain,
> And staunched the blood she saves to shed again—
> But drop by drop, for Seyd's unglutted eye
> Would doom him ever dying—ne'er to die!
>
> (2:279–83)

"Ever dying—ne'er to die": the living death of Conrad is a familiar Romantic attitude, recapitulating the Giaour's cloistered remorse, reprising Coleridge's Mariner, anticipating Shelley's Prometheus. Conrad's nerveless collapse metaphorizes the plight of what Hazlitt called the "literary character," the melancholy author who, having lost the magic of his mind and tortured by one "unglutted eye" or another, surrenders to the languid pleasure of repeating himself.[60] Such is the author figured in the preface to the poem, whose good intentions to stop Orientalizing succumb to the "fatal facility" of verse. The Corsair speaks for the poet when he pathetically rejects any attempt to "change the sentence I deserve to bear" (3:283).

Adam Smith identified the type of degradation that comprehends both the Corsair and his creator: "The man whose life is spent in performing a few simple operations, of which the effects too are, perhaps, always the same, or very nearly the same, has no occasion to exert his understanding, or to exercise his invention in finding out expedients for difficulties which never occur. He naturally loses, therefore, the habit of such exertion and generally becomes as stupid and ignorant as it is possible for a human creature to become."[61] Selim's "liberated eye" could not see that he was a character who could see only what he was made to see. In *The Corsair* the convergence of character and author in this prison of lethargic repetition suggests that the decision to start or stop writing, to live or die, is being made elsewhere—not by him who, bereft of piratical or narrative invention, labors to complete yet one more generic adventure, but by him who sets the specialized task and puts out the job. If Conrad represents the literary character who cannot quit the writing he has started, Seyd stands in for the publisher who tortures the writer into continued production. Stephen A. Marglin has analyzed the power that flows from division of labor:

> Separating the tasks assigned to each workman was the sole means by which the capitalist could, in the days preceding costly machinery, ensure that he would remain essential to the production process as integrator of those separate operations into a product for which a wide market existed. . . .
>
> The capitalist division of labor, as developed under the putting-out system, embodied the same principle that "successful" imperial powers have utilized to rule their colonies: divide and conquer.[62]

Though the poet of Oriental tales may state the maxim and vividly depict its consequences, it is the publisher intent on colonizing a reading public at home and abroad whose economic rights entail the political power—absolutely despotic—to divide writer from writer, reader from reader, and thereby exercise a cultural sway. The imprisoned Corsair is the exact image of the equivocal being called Byron—the more than human literary character inhabits a luxurious prison that is the site of a theoretically endless fascination, a factory for the practically endless manufacture of passion.[63]

Unlike Laurence Sterne's starling, the Byronic hero does not even complain that he cannot get out. If the Oriental romance is characterized by an obsessive concern to explain, however obliquely, the conditions of its existence, it is in part because the obvious motive of economic interest is ruled out of the genre's resources. The Orient is a world without money. And in Byron's case the economic motive had in fact not yet been fully activated; he is still giving his poems away. The fit between poet and hero is that there *is* no good motive—not even fame[64]—for continuing to produce what he finds painful. Byron's labor at the Oriental tales represents the deformation of labor under the contemporary relations of production, where neither love nor money is sufficient reason for the worker's bondage. Perhaps, Conrads one and all, people continue to accept, even embrace, the debased conditions of their labor because of a perverse pleasure in their own contracted subjection. At any rate, the payoff for this literary character's bondage is the masochistic pleasure of wallowing in the very repetition he affects to reprehend, thereby fulfilling the knottily autotelic ambition "to smite the smiter with the scimitar" (3:363).

Gulnare, who seeks out her rescuer in his confinement, doesn't get it. As Conrad sleeps like a baby in the bowels of the prison, "She gazed in wonder, 'Can he calmly sleep, / While other eyes his fall or ravage weep?'" (3:421–22). The answer is, of course, yes—all the other eyes for which the pirate chief had spelled his self have vanished into nothingness in the face of a self-punishing and self-pleasuring Other. If Medora is the ideal reader magically bound to Conrad before and beyond expression, and if Seyd is the empirical reader (or capitalizing publisher) whose demands "again! again! and again!" excite the painful pleasure peculiar to the author of a wildly successful serial publication, then Gulnare is the strange reader who is puzzled by the *méthode* right before her eyes, by an imprisonment that is, as Westerners say, "merely formal," but that is all the more binding because of it. And though she cannot help but love that one who has singled her out from the harem, it is the mark of her heterogeneity that she is the sole character who can never become an object of his desire.

Gulnare would offer another point of view, were that possible—that is, were it possible that an alternative to the gaze-glutted prison of the specular could be fashioned in terms of sight. Gulnare offers something different: a freedom that to the Corsair seems worse than death. Her adroit use of Seyd's signet ring to gain admittance to the Corsair's prison cell demonstrates a technical mastery of a "foreign brand" that convincingly mimics both the despot's illegitimate authority and the Corsair's spellbinding power. She efficiently achieves the effortless mobility of which the Orientalist dreams. But her reward is recrimination. To her proposal that they assassinate Seyd the Corsair answers, "Gulnare—Gulnare—I never felt till now / My abject fortune, withered fame so low" (3:358–59). Fame, name, arm—the pirate is unmanned. The invitation to murder Seyd and live catalyzes what Julia Kristeva calls "a kind of *narcissistic crisis*" for the Corsair, who cannot conceive a life apart from the "imaginary machine" of his prison.[65] Despite the bankruptcy of the hero, change occurs. Things turn on the unveiling of the "naked letter of romance."

Gulnare returns from her murderous mission:

No poignard in that hand—nor sign of ill—
'Thanks to that softening heart—she could not kill!'
Again he looked, the wildness of her eye

Starts from the day abrupt and fearfully.
She stopped—threw back her dark far-floating hair,
That nearly veiled her face and bosom fair:
As if she late had bent her leaning head
Above some object of her doubt or dread.
They meet—upon her brow—unknown—forgot—
Her hurrying hand had left—'twas but a spot—
Its hue was all he saw, and scarce withstood—
Oh! slight but certain pledge of crime—'tis blood!

He had seen battle—he had brooded lone
O'er promised pangs to sentenced guilt foreshown;
He had been tempted—chastened—and the chain
Yet on his arms might ever there remain:
But ne'er from strife—captivity—remorse—
From all his feelings in their inmost force—
So thrilled—so shuddered every creeping vein,
As now they froze before that purple stain.
That spot of blood, that light but guilty streak,
Had banished all the beauty from her cheek!
Blood he viewed—could view unmoved—but then
It flowed in combat, or was shed by men!

(3:406–29)

The flood of claptrap coincides with a massive reinforcement of the Corsair's point of view and with a full-scale gendering of the ethical categories. What might have been justifiable homicide if committed by a man becomes, at the hand of someone who is not, charged with the hysterical affect associated with the fear of castration. It will not do, however, to follow the lead of the narrative and simply substitute the psychoanalytic for the moral cause, if only because the case for castration depends on the evidence for murder, which is of two kinds: (1) the obstructed path of escape is now clear; (2) there is a spot of blood on Gulnare's forehead. Neither will wash.

Gulnare has already gained freedom of movement through her theft of the signet. The possession of the capacity to escape deprives the murder of any rationale. Moreover, Gulnare's theft dissolves the pretense that the signet is either a natural or an effectively naturalized sign of sovereign authority. The usurpation of the despot's phallic signifier may be a symbolic castration, but castration is only theft—the illicit transfer of property. Her theft/castration is, strictly speaking, a form of emulation that is threatening not because it severs something from the man but because it demonstrates the ease with which signet or signature can be transferred by anyone—even a woman—implying that it did not really belong to him anyway. That easy theft challenges the basis of both the power of the Corsair, whose hypnotic spells are not protected by copyright, and the power of the poet, whose spells are. In Adorno's words, Gulnare performs what thinking performs in its critique of "the schemata of the categorial [call it generic or imaginary] machinery": a "mimicry of the spell of things, of the spell with which it has endowed things, on the threshold of a sympathy that would make the spell disappear."[66]

The Corsair does not cross the threshold willingly. He repudiates any sympathy with the future standing ambiguously before him by manufacturing a voluptuous disgust from the merest of circumstantial evidence. Consolatory, castration anxiety coerces reality to signify. The repellent spot of blood is made to signify. Seeing as Conrad sees, the *Critical Review* neatly Byronizes: "A figure approaches—it is Gulnare. A spot of blood is all eloquence. The deed is done" (*RR* B:2:634). The first impulse of signification is to imagine the approach of a figure, to make the spot a record of a deed done rather than to recognize it as a deed doing. Where does this blood come from? The understanding reads it as evidence of a murder. The unconscious reads it as a sign of the violent extraction of the male impression: the serpent has been rooted out. But, as the nervous shift to the pluperfect indicates (the Corsair claims to see what her "hand had left," rather than what her hand in fact leaves), the fantasy of castration hides a deed—not something else, this spot is an event, a spotting. The act does not occur in the imaginary order (Gulnare does not see what the Corsair sees—her blood spot is her blind spot), nor is it on the way to the symbolic. It is a reminder of violence, a parody of castration.[67]

The sight of Gulnare's blood spot is the site of her writing, what Byron called "inkshed" (*BLJ* 1:210). The Corsair responds hysterically to a writing that is strong not because of a fascinating form but because of its separation of itself from the sway of the formal impulse. If we read this passage literally, what Gulnare does, the mark of her authentic heterogeneity, is to *write* both the Corsair and Byron out of the narcissistic crisis that imprisons the hero and blocks the narrative. This is a literal reading because a pre-oedipal, prealphabetical, not yet formalized writing, a strong invention that does not spell, *is* the naked letter of romance.

As Gulnare's action disrupts the schemata of gender, so it subverts the schemata of class. In her act of writing, the abject mark of her separation, Gulnare, woman and foreigner, makes herself an aristocrat. A certain dream of aristocratic self-invention is expressed by this injunction from Scott's *The*

Monastery: "Let our deeds be our fathers." Gulnare's self-inscription manifests a wholly unheralded device more archaic than either the memorial "badge of crimson hue" worn by the Spanish partisans of *Childe Harold I* (st. 50) or Conrad's own "blood-red flag" on his pirate ship. Her deed fathers her. But if Gulnare's action, which intolerably mixes the "nature" of menses and the "culture" of castration, can be said truly to shatter the age-old antinomy of merit and blood, it is because her act replenishes ambivalence by confounding deed as father with deed as mother.

Lara and the Future As Aftermath

The Corsair conveys what Adorno calls the "truth content of neuroses": the "I" has its "unfreedom demonstrated to it, within itself, by something alien to it—by the feeling that 'this isn't me at all.'"[68] Gulnare's inkshed provides the "jolt" in the chain of compulsion, a performative instance of what the *Quarterly Review* called the "great dogma of the revolutionists, *that things cannot remain as they are.*"[69] But Gulnare gets no thanks; her deed jump-starts a narrative that has noplace to go. The *noplace* to which *The Corsair* does go is the wasteland of *Lara*, the poem that, Byron remarked, "completes the series—and its very likeness renders it necessary to the others" (*BLJ* 4:165). *Lara* is "necessary" not as the fulfillment of some generic destiny but as the clinching likeness that completes the series by decisively extinguishing any original reference.

Lara brings the Byronic hero home. Yet the return to the fatherland deepens rather than dispels the obscurity of the hero's origins. History is over. Europe is the Orient bleached of color, shorn of veils, that barren place where the worst one could say about the hero of *The Giaour, The Bride of Abydos,* and *The Corsair* proves true. This is the Spain that Napoleon, brooding away his captivity on Elba, might have ruefully imagined as the scene where his destiny first betrayed him. Here rulers cynically flaunt slogans of revolutionary emancipation in order to manipulate a degraded peasantry; here the code of hospitality has become the pretext for brutal words and worse deeds; here the rule of law awaits only the stray germ of anger to fester into anarchy. And over the whole the pallor of exhaustion: "but where the wrong? / Some knew perchance—but twere a tale too long" (1:149–50). Gone is the phallic fascination of the serpent's serial unfolding. This poem is a tale too long even before it is written; each word carries it further toward a terminal boredom.

"But where the wrong?" Because there is no good reason for *Lara* to be written, someone must take the blame for its melancholy existence. The poem's predominant aim is to condemn the perpetrator of its equivocal life. The blame cannot be placed on Lord Byron. The decision to publish *Lara* anonymously in a volume shared with Samuel Rogers's treacly *Jacqueline* registers the author's abdication of responsibility. If blame cannot be placed on the author, neither can it be assigned to the market. How could a romance own as its cause those commercial circumstances it exists to deny? What language would it speak?

In an odd sense the blame is placed where it belongs, on the woman. *Odd* because *Lara* revises *The Corsair* sufficiently that blame can be definitively fixed while recognition of the eventful fault can be decisively avoided. It is the woman whose fault releases the Corsair from the prison of his satisfaction unto death and jettisons him back into the compulsions of narrative. But because that fault can never be seen for the moment of eruptive heterogeneity it is, the woman will be blamed for the expense of narrative and a waste of words by being made ritualistically to repeat her supposed crime. The purest sequel among the Oriental tales, *Lara*, written in May 1814, attempts to narrate the absence of a story to tell; it takes shape as an allegory of blame for having nothing to say and for having to say it again and again.

The central events of *Lara* recapitulate *The Corsair*: Lara, who has returned to Europe with his page Kaled from a mysterious sojourn in the East, is challenged by Sir Ezzelin, who enigmatically accuses Lara of disgraceful deeds in his past. The challenge is to be answered and Lara's honor proved by individual combat. But once again a man who might have been legitimately killed in warfare or a duel by the insulted hero is (ostensibly) assassinated instead, presumably by Kaled—the pageboy who, it will be climactically revealed, is actually a woman. Satisfaction denied, civil war erupts. Differences between the configurations of the characters in the poems are slight: as Lara is Conrad without the pirate costume, so is his loyal page Gulnare-become-Kaled. But more of the same is not the same. In *The Corsair* the mere fact that Gulnare was a woman explained nothing, whereas here the plot is regressively arranged so that its consummation, the death of the hero in a suicidal battle, can satisfyingly coincide with the disclosure of what now passes for a telling fact, the whole story: "Oh, he's a woman!" A woman and a serial killer.

Here are the final words of this poem:

And Kaled—Lara—Ezzelin, are gone,
Alike without their monumental stone!
The first, all efforts vainly strove to wean
From lingering where her chieftain's blood had been;

Grief had so tam'd a spirit once too proud,
Her tears were few, her wailing never loud;
But furious would you tear her from the spot
Where yet she scarce believ'd that he was not,
Her eye shot forth with all the living fire
That haunts the tigress in her whelpless ire;
But left to waste her weary moments there,
She talk'd all idly unto shapes of air,
Such as the busy brain of Sorrow paints,
And woos to listen to her fond complaints:
And she would sit beneath the very tree
Where lay his drooping head upon her knee;
And in that posture where she saw him fall,
His words, his looks, his dying grasp recall;
And she had shorn, but sav'd her raven hair,
And oft would snatch it from her bosom there,
And fold, and press it gently to the ground,
As if she staunch'd anew some phantom's wound.
Herself would question, and for him reply;
Then rising, start, and beckon him to fly
From some imagin'd spectre in pursuit;
Then seat her down upon some linden's root,
And hide her visage with her meagre hand,
Or trace strange characters along the sand—
This could not last—she lies by him she lov'd;
Her tale untold—her truth too dearly prov'd.
                    (2:598–627; emphasis added)

No longer is the woman's deed her father; she is now, in the triumph of misogyny, nursed—but too late to be nourished—by the blood of the salvific hero shed "properly" in combat. Marooned in the nightmare of European history, Kaled suffers the punitive return of all the hero's self-fulfilling fears. Hysterized, she pays a real price for an imaginary castration by being condemned to the obsessive stanching of a phantom wound with her penitentially severed hair—poor substitute for a "red right hand."

More than gender makes that scene conclusive, however. Compare Walter Scott's reaction to Napoleon's abdication of April 1814:

And then . . . there followed a stunning sort of listless astonishment and complication of feeling, which if it did not lessen enjoyment, confused and confounded one's sense of it. I remember the first time I happened to see a launch, I was neither so much struck with the descent of the vessel, nor with its majestic sweep to its moorings, as with the blank which was suddenly made from the withdrawing so large an object, and the prospect which was at once opened to the opposite side of the dock crowded with spectators. Buonaparte's fall strikes me something in the same way: the huge bulk of his power, against which a thousand arms were hammering, was obviously to sink when its main props were struck away—and yet now—when it has disappeared—the vacancy which it leaves in our minds and attention, marks its huge and preponderating importance more strongly than even its presence. . . . I never thought nor imagined that he would have *given in* as he has done. I always considered him as possessing the genius and talents of an Eastern conqueror. . . . But this is a poor devil, and cannot play the tyrant so rarely as Bottom the Weaver proposed to do.[70]

And compare Lord Byron's journal entry of April 9, 1814:

I mark this day!

Napoleon Buonaparte has abdicated the throne of the world. "Excellent well." Methinks Sylla did better; for he revenged and resigned in the height of his sway, red with the slaughter of his foes—the finest instance of glorious contempt of the rascals upon record. Dioclesian did well too—Amurath not amis, had he become aught except a dervise—Charles the Fifth but so so—but Napoleon worst of all. What! wait till they were in his capital, and then talk of his readiness to give up what is already gone!! "What whining monk art thou—what holy cheat?" 'Sdeath!—Dionysius at Corinth was yet a king to this. The "Isle of Elba" to retire to!—Well—if it had been Caprea, I should have marvelled less. "I see men's minds are but a parcel of their fortunes." I am utterly bewildered and confounded. (*BLJ* 3:256–57)

Scott describes a sudden, massive absence consequent upon a Corsair-like failure of ingenuity and will, whereas for Lord Byron it is the *lack* of a decisive conclusion that dismays. In Scott's conceit the removal of the launch leaves a blank; but it also reveals a previously unseen crowd of spectators, who link up with the (previously unheard?) "thousand arms" that were "hammering" against the hull. The shift from something that was focal, massive, and concrete to an immense heap of little things corresponds to the surfacing of the allusionistic crowd of kings and despots in Lord Byron's complaint. The two responses to Napoleon's abdication merge in the figure of Kaled stationed at Lara's corpse. She multiplies reactions—crying, wailing, questioning, answering, rising, starting, beckoning, hiding—to a devastating loss; moreover, those reactions are crowded together and given rhetorical force by a series of hammering *and*s.

Kaled can assimilate Scott and Byron because she is a conventional figure of mourning. Meditating the genesis, structure, and destiny of this figure in his essay on *Hamlet*, Jacques Lacan reflected on "the gap, the hole that results from [the experience of the death of another] and that calls forth mourning on the part of the subject."[71] The veil of Gulnare's hair, which in the escape scene of *The Corsair* tellingly failed to conceal the absence of the phallus, becomes here the signifier with which Kaled tries to stanch the wound in reality left by the death of Lara. But what Lacan calls the "swarms of images" defeats her. The signifier cannot find its place. Kaled cannot fill the hole; she cannot complete the work of mourning. For Lacan *Hamlet* is "the drama of Hamlet as the man who has lost the way of his desire."[72] Hamlet, that is, mourns that he is not Prince Hamlet (despite being meant to be). In his journal entry Lord Byron mourns that he is not and can never be Napoleon Bonaparte—a Byronic trope, but now turned with an ironic finality: Byron can never be Napoleon because Napoleon has decisively failed to be himself. Not being Napoleon, not being oneself—both have been salient problems for Lord Byron's heroes. *Lara* solves them. There the hero's battlefield death upscales the pusillanimous end of the emperor; moreover, the blame for his failure to be himself is satisfyingly placed on the foreign woman, Kaled—she who cross-dresses in the livery of Lara, she who wears the colors of the other.

Kaled may be defined as that character who cannot not be Napoleon. She can neither truly mourn nor be tolerated as melancholic. The swarm of images that discomposes her emerges at the level of the *narrative* representation of her grief and prepares for the expropriation of the work of mourning, which coincides with the closural introduction of the single *or* among the string of *and*s—an option that simultaneously precipitates out and stigmatizes Kaled's foreign writing as a mourning that cannot succeed. If, according to Lacan, "there is nothing of significance that can fill that hole in the real, except the totality of the signifier,"[73] the failure satisfactorily to complete mourning should be understood as a consequence of the foreign page's failure to totalize. That failure is sealed by the judgment "This could not last," which imposes as doxa the system of signifiers that is the Oriental tales, itself an episode in the totality called Byron. That imposition does not complete the narrative; it *regulates* its incompletion by referring it to a serial system that solves mourning by reproducing the melancholy pleasure that articulates the very structure of the commodity.

Walter Scott, who had long since customized his career on Napoleonic lines, devoted much of 1814 to the arrangement of the best terms for his abdication in the face of the Byronic challenge. Writing in an April lull during the composition of *Waverley*, Scott identifies the "three leading blunders" of Bonaparte as Spain, the invasion of Russia, and the "Continental System." He goes on to apprise his correspondent. "You would be surprised to hear how the Continent is awakening from its iron sleep. The utmost eagerness seems to prevail about English literature. I have had several voluntary epistles from different parts of Germany, from men of letters, who are eager to know what we have been doing, while they were compelled to play at blind-man's buff with the *ci-devant Empereur*."[74] Scott anticipates the work that mourning will do: the death of one system, the Continental, makes way for another, called "English literature"—which means only Walter Scott and Lord Byron. Between them the English poets will fill the gap in the real with systems of signifiers—works—of their own.

If for the moment we concede what Scott wanted to believe, that Lord Byron's Oriental tales *are* English literature and not some stranger kind of thing, we can allegorically recapitulate the story that, from *The Giaour* through *Lara*, Lord Byron's tales tell: We used to mourn Themistocles, a hero who lived when plots were harmonious, finished; we came to mourn Napoleon, who is no hero, who is not Napoleon—not least because he perversely left his story incomplete; we now mourn the passing of Lara (the end of *Lara*) who in not being Napoleon nevertheless helps to effect the forging of a cultural totality, "English literature," out of our political and historical disappointment. The chronically incomplete narrative of melancholy is modernized as the serial production of commodities over the signature of Lord Byron and under the aegis of John Murray. In mourning its own passing *Lara* exploits the confessed absence of rites to assuage its grief as the justification for Byronism, the *logos* of a modern—that is, post-Napoleonic—commodity culture. Napoleon flees, Byron lives: the disablement of the crudely empirical attempt at world empire enables the universalization of a commercial culture, the elaboration of a system of signifiers immune to the Russian winter. Lara dies, Byronism lives—a consolation in which Kaled alone fails to share.

Napoleon, of course, is not really there in *Lara*. But that is just the point. Like Ossian, like Werther, Napoleon has never been there for the English (his plans to invade England were never successfully executed) except as the figure of a certain kind of Romantic subjectivity.[75] Lara is not the surrogate for Napoleon but the functional equivalent of Napoleon, not a literary figure to be decoded as the empirical Napoleon but a demonstration that not being the imperial Napoleon is an available position in the cultural code. British Romanticism begins with the powerful feeling that something is lost and gone forever. And it would be senseless to deny that some things are: the highland clans, a few stiff-necked weavers in Nottingham, a species of unevolved aristocrat. The historicity of those particular losses is, however, historically veiled by the individual and collective projection of the Napoleonic career, which makes loss identifiable by means of a figure of mourning. Napoleon is appreciated first and foremost as a fiction by the British public; the deep investment by the left and the right in his storybook career is funded by a politic belief that the hole in the real is the (providential) loss of the referent itself. Adam Smith's model of scientific change is sophisticated by poets wise in their generation: for the British poets of the Regency the *absence* of a "strange appearance" has become the pretext for the institution of a new system articulated by nuance rather than ruptured by revolution—for business as usual.

In the event, Romantic mourning was premature. Although Walter Scott vacillated during the composition of *Waverley*, delaying its publication until well after he felt certain that the Corsican adventurer was safely enisled, it turned out that he nevertheless published prematurely: Waterloo and the redemption of the Napoleonic legend from Tory condescension were yet to occur. In one sense, Scott's and Byron's prematurity attests to the uncanny power of Romantic art to fulfill its wishes: Waterloo extends in a neatly analogical manner the series *Corsair*→abdication→*Lara*. Waterloo revises the first abdication on the model of *Lara*'s revision of *The Corsair*. Napoleon's life imitates Byron's art. In this light the famous Napoleonic stanzas of *Childe Harold III* put the seal on a career that had already been thoroughly Byronized. In a deeper sense, however, the prematurity of Romantic mourning is a function of its constitutive belatedness. As Lacan illustrates, the eventfulness of Waterloo had already been scripted by Shakespeare. What is Waterloo but the acting out of the Armageddon of *Lara?* What is *Lara* but the totalizing of the tournament that concludes *Hamlet?* It is a melancholy fact that my versions of Napoleon, Byron, and Scott are already represented in *Hamlet,* or in psychoanalysis, which almost comes to the same thing. Neither Scott nor Byron saw this in 1814: Byron saw only Napoleon, and Scott saw only a Byron who was not Napoleon. Yet the hints are there in the tag lines from Shakespeare that flit about in the swarm of images afflicting them both.

That affliction was punctually and canonically diagnosed in the summer of 1815, just after Waterloo. "Hence the German word for fanaticism," writes Coleridge in the *Biographia Literaria,* "is derived from the swarming of bees, namely Schwarmen, Schwarmerey. The passion being in an inverse proportion to the insight. . . . The absence of all foundation within [some scribblers'] own minds for that, which they yet believe both true and indispensable for their safety and happiness, cannot but produce an uneasy state of feeling, an involuntary sense of fear."[76] Coleridge does not explicitly include Byron or Scott or Napoleon among the contemptible class of "scribblers." Indeed, it is the mark of the vividness of his conceptions that they are not dependent on personalities. For Coleridge, as for Lacan (and Addison), personalities do not count; only characters do. Characters are etymologically derived types, ultimately produced by the "creative and self-sufficing power of genius," which Coleridge occasionally calls language or poetry, but which he *names* our "*myriad-minded* Shakspear." What is Napoleon to Coleridge? To English literature? Shakespeare, indifferently systematic, is neither Napoleon nor not-Napoleon. Moreover, there is no hole in the real that is not already represented in Shakespeare. The very *idea* of a hole in the real, as both Coleridge and Lacan attest, is a Shakespearean theme.

If Lord Byron does not have Coleridge's strategic foresight, a glimpse of the closure that will be the legacy of the Shakespearean "mind" nonetheless surfaces in the author's last, pontifical gasp, "This could not last." Mourning cannot last. Kaled cannot last. A blood spot on the forehead cannot last. Nothing heterogeneous can last in the face of the imperial coercion of reality called Orientalism or Byronism or Shakespeareanism. Nothing is more characteristic of the nineteenth-century system of literary representation than this comical identification with inexorable natural processes. "This could not last" is the powder-wigged verdict that the canon casts against parody, against all marginal writing. It evokes the supreme self-confidence of the man of law who, standing behind the delusion of the submerged sultan in number 94 of the *Spectator*, exercises the right to cut— and it is every bit as interested in mystifying the rhetorical basis of its authority to judge.

Closer to home, "This could not last" is the verdict the government had to impose on Hone's convulsive parodies. Hone's defense opened up a breach in the bulwark of the law. Someone had to step into it. And Lord Ellenborough did. Ellenborough, the aged and infirm lord chancellor of England, did not preside over Hone's first trial. But after the acquittal he took the extraordinary and risky step of displacing the sitting judge and personally supervising the second trial—representing *in propria persona* the interests of the state, reinforcing the prosecution, and—all were convinced— insuring a guilty verdict. But the story was the same: reading, laughter, acquittal. Lord Ellenborough's intercession was not without effect, however. For it was not so much his aim to enforce the law as to embody it. By impersonating the law and giving a face to its repressiveness, Ellenborough may not have been able to alleviate its illegitimacy, but he was able to contain the licentiousness of the occasion by substituting his body for legal principle. In the absence of legitimacy—in the presence of an absolutely strange appearance (signaled not only by Hone's fortitude but by the intermittent convulsions he suffered while nerving himself to proceed)—the custodian of the law reverted to an archaic legal form (the code of honor) and evidentiary procedure (the duel) in order to insure that even though a guilty verdict might not follow, at least *some* consequence would. And, in one of the most astonishing effects of the dramaturgy called British justice, a consequence did: within a week of the end of the serial prosecutions and Hone's final acquittal, Ellenborough resigned and died, as he would have it, from shame.[77]

Lord Ellenborough's risk in impersonating the law was not so much that he would die but that in recasting the jury trial as a duel, thereby raising Hone from grubstreet obscurity to the status of a foe, he would nonetheless fail to contain Hone's anarchic transgression—a risk that recourse to an earlier imaginary machine would not capture and classify this strange, theoretical appearance.[78] Lord Ellenborough died in order to freight the antithesis of the imaginary with the pathos of the sacrificial: he became an Abel so that Hone would be marked as Cain. In fact, however, William Hone played a Bain to his lordship's Abel—it was not by blood that Hone conquered, but by the letter in its parodic difference from what it professed to signify. It was not a revolution that Hone achieved but a separation. To what end? To the production and sale of the book I now hold in my hand—and thousands like it. Unlike either Gulnare or Kaled, Hone did not write. What remained after his victory was not a history of parody but the shorthand transcription of a trial. Unlike Ellenborough and the British legal establishment, whose prosecution was purely defensive and suicidally regressive, Hone's defense had a future in mind: to publish his trials in pamphlets, many pamphlets, and turn a profit—which he did. If the heterogeneous moment of the trial delivered its strange characters to any future, it belonged to Hone, who as a publisher was best able to repeat his triumphant separation and to profit from that repetition.

The attorney general's fear of dissemination was well taken but shortsighted. The lesson for all true Englishmen was that for England to absent itself from revolution awhile the state must become indifferent to its objects—*laissez faire*, perverse. If there were to be a legitimate future for the state, it would be found in the linkage between the state's governing commitment to consequences and the ambition of commerce to transform any and all objects into a serial replication of differences. If we can see that future there in that moment of transition before it happened, it is because it

The New Man of the Industrial Future.

Source: William Hone, *The Political Showman—At Home! Exhibiting His Cabinet of Curiosities and Creatures All at Once*, illus. George Cruikshank (London, 1821); rpt. in *Radical Squibs and Loyal Ripostes*, ed. Edgell Rickwood (Bath: Adams and Dart, 1971), p. 271.

is shadowed forth by the invention of a new sort of equivocal being on the cusp of the post-Napoleonic, industrial age. A figure approaches, a new man described by Hone and depicted by Cruikshank (see illustration).

In the future that this image triumphantly announces, parody will adhere to the modernist norm that Linda Hutcheon has described: a hybrid genre of authorized transgression—another supposed perversion become the official stimulus and vehicle of desire.[79] But perhaps even here some revision is in order, for Hone's figure describes a genre of *published* transgression, and in doing so falls in line with the legitimate history of English literature: the statutes and litigation establishing the domain of copyright in the eighteenth century. Throughout all the vicissitudes of opinion from the Act of Anne (1710) to *Donaldson v. Hinton* (1774), British law held fast to the principle that only that was authorized that had a legal right to be copied and sold. Copyright is the law of general equivalence that makes modern literary production possible—provides the basis for the marvelous "imaginary machine" of the author that materializes on Hone's page.

"This could not last" is Addison's verdict against delusion and the canon's verdict against parody; it is also the verdict that Hone as publisher casts against his own shattering performance. In this sense, in the publisher's sense, the convulsions and extremely erratic courtroom behavior that Hone's version of the trial reports are of a piece with his failure to write the history of parody he planned: they characterize the hysteric. In the nineteenth century political courage, no matter how necessary and successful, would be identified as a kind of hysteria. The inverse inference, that hysteria is a form of political resistance—a dominant theme of contemporary feminist criticism—was not yet conceivable. Catherine Clément is wonderfully to the point: "The hysteric does *not* write, does *not* produce, does nothing—nothing other than make things circulate without inscribing them. . . . The result: the clandestine sorceress was burned by the thousands; the deceitful and triumphant hysteric disappeared. But the master is there. He is the one who stays on permanently. He publishes writings."[80] Hone's defeat of Ellenborough is nothing to the mastery he acquires by publishing the story in which he figures like the heroically unwriting Corsair and Lara—but a story that he, unlike those losers and their laboring lordly poet, owns and profits from.

Strange Characters

All is mystery, darkness and confusion. If the gentlemen's and ladies' diaries for the ensuing year are not yet furnished with their usual complement of aenigmas, charades, and rebusses, we should recommend their proprietors to select portions of the present poem to puzzle the brains, and to try the ingenuity of their readers.

Review of Lara, *in* British Critic, *October 1814*

This Record will for ever stand,
"Woman thy vows, are trac'd in sand."

"To Woman," Hours of Idleness

Like the Corsair and Lara Hone may be. But like Kaled he is not. For if the *this* of "This could not last" invites the multiplication of analogies enfranchised by the "generalized law of equivalence," the one character it does not fit is the one to whom it is applied. Kaled is no hysteric; she suffers from no delusions. Her final act, to "trace strange characters along the sand," is a return of writing, a foreign reminder. Kaled/Gulnare has not fallen into a murderous habit, nor is she dispersed into a cloud of vanities; she patiently suffers what Lord Byron called "scribbling propensities [that] though 'expelled with a fork' are coming on again" (*BLJ* 2:43). Alone among the final swarm of images, this arabesque, swiveling into prominence on the pivot of the sole *or* in the final verse paragraph, does not refer to Lara—his life and death.

In Byron's Oriental game of change, the object of desire is transformed from a woman's blushing body into a corpse hued temptingly, a fragment marked impressively, and a blank mind tattooed snakily. It ought to be observed, however, that the first figure other than a man to appear in *The Giaour* is not a woman but a "Georgian page" (l. 456). The apparition may be the poem's fetishization of itself as the perfect period piece, or an object of desire ideally suited only to its time. Blaming Kaled means stripping away the page's costume to find her truth, thereby accepting either the Enlightenment derogation of costume as only a local eccentricity obscuring some universal subject or the more sophisticated notion of costume as fancy packaging, which in its cheerful disposability answers to the lability of particularist desire.[81] Lord Byron does not write his page transparent, however. Lord Byron's page, untranslatably foreign to period, to place, or to genre, rightly induces the pun that appears in the *Eclectic Review*'s remark that "this custom, of disfiguring his pages with words that are not English, seems growing upon Lord Byron" (*RR* B:2:716). Gulnare touches up her face with a color not cosmetic, a blood not English—her fault the tincture that disfigures the Georgian page and renders unfit that poet who aims only to please.

Whether or not Lord Byron's readers agreed about the merits of his morals, his plots, and his meter, all parties objected to the appearance of foreign words in Lord Byron's poems. John Hookham Frere complained to Murray "that such words as Gul and Bulbul, though not unpoetical in themselves, are in bad taste, and ought not to receive the sanction of your Lordship's example." The *Theatrical Inquisitor* complained about the "many faults of affectation in Lord Byron's diction." The *Satirist* attacked his "affectation of Turkish names." Lady Caroline Lamb advised Murray that he tell his "friend to speak English—it is a goodly language, and while he writes in his Mother tongue he had better use the terms we are accustomed to." Henry Crabb Robinson reported the judgment of the chief Laker: "We talked of Lord Byron. Wordsworth allowed him power, but denied his style to be English."[82]

In part, these concerns reassert the sway of the fundamental rhetorical principle of perspicuity. Adam Smith speaks for a tradition: "Perspicuity of stile requires not only that the expressions we use should be free from all ambiguity proceeding from synonimous words but that the words should be natives if I may ⟨say⟩ so of the language we speak in. Foreigners though they may signify the same thing never convey the idea with such strength as those we are acquainted with and whose origin we can trace."[83] In part they reflect a longstanding concern about Lord Byron's style, which begins with Henry Brougham's wicked fun about *pibroch* in "Lachin Y Gair" (*RR* B:2:835) and which is more sympathetically voiced in George Ellis's complaint about "that motley mixture of obsolete and modern phraseology by which the ease and elegance of his verses are often injured."

Ellis is reviewing *Childe Harold: A Romaunt* here, and these remarks lead into an interesting discussion of Byron's Spenserianism (*RR* B:5:1991–92), which I quote at length:

> The metre adopted throughout this "Romaunt" is the stanza of Spenser; and we admit that, for every ancient word employed by the modern poet, the authority of Spenser may be pleaded. But we think that to intersperse such words as ee, moe, feere, ne, losel, eld, &c. amidst the richest decorations of modern language, is to patch embroidery with rags. Even if these words had not been replaced by any substitutes, and if they were always correctly inserted, their uncouth appearance would be displeasing; but Lord Byron is not always correct in his use of them. For instance, when he says (Canto I. st. 67)
>
> > "Devices quaint, and Frolics ever new,
> > Tread on each other's *kibes*,"—
>
> it must be supposed that he did not mean to personify devices and frolics for the purpose of afflicting them with chilblains. When, again, in describing Ali Pacha, he censures (C. II. st. 62.)
>
> > "—those ne'er forgotten acts of *ruth*
> > Beseeming all men ill, but most the man
> > In years, that mark him with a tyger's tooth," &c.
>
> it is plain that the noble lord must have considered "ruth" as synonymous, not with pity, but with cruelty. In a third instance where we are told that "*Childe* Harold had *a mother*," the equivocal meaning of the first word has evidently a ludicrous effect, which could not have escaped the attention of our author whilst writing in the language of his own day. On such errors as these, however, which obviously originate, not in any want of genius, but in

accidental heedlessness, we do not mean to lay any stress; we complain only of the habitual negligence, of the frequent laxity of expression—of the feeble or dissonant rhymes which almost *disfigure* a too close imitation of the language of our early poets, and of which we think that the work before us offers too many examples. (Last emphasis added)

Ellis goes on to compliment the naive Spenser for his consistency, intelligibility, and simplicity—in general for the transparency of his language to the time and place in which he wrote: "Spenser was in England, as La Fontaine in France, the creators [*sic*] of that style which our neighbors have so aptly denominated 'le genre *naif.*' The flowers which he scatters over his subjects are, indeed, all of *native* growth."

Lord Byron's writing seems foreign to all available categories. He cannot show his genius without degrading it into the character of the copyist, and he cannot copy without disfiguring both the original and his own version. He not only fails to make his words perspicuous to their meaning, he makes them imperspicuous to their past.[84] By applying impeccably historicist standards Ellis isolates a phenomenon out of history. Writing a "polyglot line compounded of Greek, Saxon, and modern English," Lord Byron produces a diction native to no genre, one that is "essentially" parodic. Perhaps essentially *parodic* because inimitably *romantic*, as the *Antijacobin* impatiently observes: "'A Romaunt,' without interesting incidents, daring enterprises, or heroic achievements; and, above all, without a hero, endowed with a soul and spirit, capable of great actions, and ardent to engage in them, is a perfect anomaly in the annals of chivalry, or in the history of romance" (*RR* B:1:22). Byron's poetry does not represent the internalization of quest romance; his poems perform its volatile equivocation.

It is as if Lord Byron's words were their own fathers. Or, perhaps more precisely, in light of Ellis's ridicule of the "equivocal" line "Childe Harold had a mother," as if they had no mothers. Only poetic belief in that fiction would prompt Byron to write such a line as if it *needed* saying. The *e* that equivocates between a natural and a literary child betrays a primal rejection of and by the mother that hangs on a letter. "She," Lord Byron writes of his mother, "flies into a fit of phrenzy[,] upbraids me as if I was the most undutiful wretch in existence, rakes up the ashes of my *father*, abuses him, says I shall be a true Byron*ne*, which is the worst epithet she can invent. Am I to call this woman mother?" (*BLJ* 1:56; emphasis added). We have seen that *e* that accessorizes *Child* and *Byron* before. It is the *e* that, in a conspiratorial letter to Lord Byron, Charles Skinner Matthews added to *method* as a literary device of alienation, distinction, and bonding. "Childe Harold had a mother" carries *méthode* to its logical and parodic extreme. The *e* makes visible the way the crazily misogynist insistence on the absoluteness of cultural construction coughs up an awkward acknowledgment of maternity, and betrays by that slip a primal rejection of the mother. Byron's *e* negligently makes a subject of statement out of what must go without saying, and it thereby inadvertently exerts a strength that is at its every flex a reminder of and eventful separation from the weakness by means of which it first came into existence. Beyond perversion, a parfit poet aberrant, Byron's parodic diction makes his genius and disables it for all the dutiful, civilized purposes to which it would be put by readers, reviewers, publishers, and himself—his faulty writing makes him and disfigures him at the same time.

This negligence, if negligence it is, is not a habit that Lord Byron could slough off. He tried. There is plenty of advice in the reviews about the need for Lord Byron to improve. And there is plenty of evidence that Byron labored to comply—from changes in his rhyme scheme to the chastening of the tone of his notes. Occasionally the reviewers seem appeased, if not glutted. And Byron tries some more. Indeed, the one scene in this series of tales that seemed most obscure to reviewers, Lara's convulsive seizure in the gallery of his ancestral fathers, is fully explicable as a sign of Byron's acquiescence in the program of purification that his critics prescribe:

They raise him—bear him;—hush! he breathes, he speaks,
The swarthy blush recolours in his cheeks,
His lip resumes its red, his eye, though dim,
Rolls wide and wild, each slowly quivering limb
Recalls its function, but his words are strung
In terms that seem not of his native tongue;
Distinct but strange, enough they understand
To deem them accents of another land.

(1:225–32)

The scene of possession is both a purgation of Lara's character and a pledge by the poet to straighten his tangled tongue, to rid his "native" speech of Arabisms or Scotticisms.

But Lord Byron is no more able to return his page to a wholeness and purity undisfigured by foreign words than he is to eliminate the hitch that mars his gait. The connection between these two kinds of infelicity was first made, as we have seen, by Brougham. But it was never far out of mind. The *Theatrical Inquisitor* meanly notes of *The Bride* that "in frequent instances . . . where the author thinks he has displayed the naked nervousness of a sentiment, we recognize nothing but a lame hobbling line and a prosaic abruptness almost below the level of common conversation" (*RR* B:5:2245). What Lord Byron thinks is naked or pure is already disfigured. Lady Caroline Lamb had recourse to a vulgar Byronism to explain the chronic failure of Lord Byron to meet her and everyone else's expectations: "He never can be what he appears—he has not in him that which alone could realize so bright a vision."[85] The evidence suggests, however, that Lady Caroline mistakes Lord Byron because she, like Lady Byron, misreads his characters in terms of the delusory metaphorics of psychological depth that plays across the surface of the Oriental tales; a better version would be that Lord Byron is *always* what he appears because he has *on* him what alone disfigures any bright vision.

A more restrained account of the figure of Lord Byron illustrates this maxim clearly. Doris Langley Moore quotes from the narrative left by Newton Hanson, the son of Byron's solicitor, telling of the introduction of the family to the eleven-year-old "lordling": "My father brought Lord Byron into the room in his Hand—all eyes were upon him, but, as my father remained with him, he was not abashed. My 2nd Sister, who was then about 7, after examining Lord Byron from head to foot, during the pause after the 1st Introduction turning round exclaimed with the greatest gravity & Emphasis, 'Well, he is a pretty Boy however.'"[86] The *however*, as Moore acutely observes, is the syntactic reflection of the iron brace that covers the boy's deformed leg. The qualification—added to the declaration as the brace is to the leg—remarks on a deformation welded to the prettiness, that at once constitutes it and estranges it from itself. There in the flesh, his lameness is the most distinctive feature of Lord Byron's appearance, but it is also a disfiguration that is never seen. Although it is never depicted in the iconography that surrounds the poet, it is the fault that becomes the excuse for all manner of accessories, for the proliferation of busts, portraits, and hair clippings that fragmentize the figure of the poet, thereby simulating, as do the Oriental tales, a wholeness that never was.

A certain natural negligence or, better, a negligence of nature is remarked on by the reviewer who complained of "those paradoxical quibbling [not quite *hobbling*] prettinesses of expression which the author is very fond of, and which, for want of a better name, we will call Byronisms" (*RR* B:5:2248). "Quibbling prettiness"—the phrase sweetly suits the faulty figure of Gulnare, who cavils the Corsair back to life. *Byronism* is the best name for a fault that goes beyond lameness to exercise a strength strangely archaic—what S. T. Coleridge would call a "Punic" strength,[87] and what to the *Critical Review* is disturbing:

We forbear to multiply instances; but we most earnestly wish that an English poet would set, and stedfastly adhere to, the example of writing English.

—"that sallow front
is scathed by fiery passion's *brunt.*"

Qu. Does the word *brunt* stand in this place as the representative of the Greek βροντη? If so, it is employed in a signification to which we (at least) have been hitherto strangers—but if not, we humbly suggest that the passage is nonsense. (*RR* B:2:625)

To the reviewer of the *Critical* Byron's foreign word appears as the parody of the blood spot by which Gulnare stoops to conquer, as well as the parody of that poetic practice in which, according to the *Christian Observer*, "the noble lord [made the] experiment, how far the good-nature of the British Public would yield to the mere fascination of his lordship's name" (*RR* B:2:596).

In Jean-François Lyotard's terms the disturbance caused by this passage in *The Giaour* instantiates the eventful "opacity" consequent upon the untranslatability of "a phrase that *prescribes* something" into a "phrase that *describes* something."[88] In reference to Byron that opacity needs to be brought in touch with a coloring that is foreign to the codes by which history is schematized, made translatable and merely empirical. The conjunction was made by Hazlitt, who shrewdly, if disapprovingly, noted that the "colouring of Lord Byron's style, however rich in Tyrian dyes, is nevertheless opaque, is in itself an object of delight and wonder."[89] Like the "uncouth appearance" of Gulnare and Kaled, Lord Byron's writing enacts the untranslatability or opacity that colors inscription itself. Here the description of the lines inscribed by passion on the face of the Giaour doubles as the inscription of "Byron," rendered unpronounceable, on the page.[90] What Lyotard calls "opacity" and what the *Christian Observer* calls "mere fascination" is an effect of neither the picture nor the name but of the confoundment between the two registers—and it is that primal writing that is the inimitable, untransferable, continually reinvented signature of Byron.[91] If communicable at all, this event first makes sense as the performance of an ineradicable foreignness, Byron Greeked—an ease of alienation that is itself the reminder of the Norman in Biron, and the primal foreignness of English to itself. An abbreviated genealogy of the foreign conquest that disfigures the page of English history is recalled and enacted whenever Lord Byron strongly writes.

5

The Speculative Stage

Childe Harold III *and*
the Formation of Byron

. . . men of speculation, whose trade it is not to do any thing, but to observe every thing; and who, upon that account, are often capable of combining together the powers of the most distant and dissimilar objects.

Adam Smith, The Wealth of Nations

If a cobbler should suppose himself an emperor, this supposition may be termed an elevated flight, or an extensive stretch of imagination, but it is likewise a great defect in his judgment, to deem himself that which he is not, and it is certainly an equal lapse of his recollection, to forget what he really is.

John Haslam, Observations on Madness and Melancholy

Childe Harold's Pilgrimage: A Romaunt and the Oriental tales were gifts. However mediated his path to his readers, Byron endeavored to personalize his transactions sufficiently to sustain the increasingly threadbare myth of lordly gratuity. The separation broke the threads. Here are the parting words of Lady Byron to her husband:

Dearest B.

The child is quite well and the best of travellers. I hope you are *good* and remember my medical prayers and injunctions. Don't give yourself up to the abominable trade of versifying—nor to brandy—nor to anything that is not *lawful* and *right*.

Though *I* disobey in writing to you, let me hear of *your* obedience at Kirkby.

Ada's love to you with mine.

Pip[1]

This letter was not notably efficacious. Lord Byron did not become "good." Indeed, under the circumstances (the expressions of affection, it transpired, disguised Lady Byron's determination never to see or allow their daughter to see Byron again) it should not have been surprising that Lady Byron's injunctions were received as provocations. About brandy no comment is necessary: Byron was not so limited in his imagination of intoxicants as his wife. But it was part of the relentless elaboration of the separation that Byron did give himself up to the "abominable trade of versifying," a calculated self-abandonment that deeply involved him with people who, however impeccably lawful they might be, were, as tradesmen, not quite "right" in Lady Byron's fastidious usage.[2]

Chief among those associates was John Murray, the publisher of almost all of Byron's poetry for almost all of the poet's career. Murray's connections with Lord Byron had begun when Charles Dallas appeared, like Providence itself, with the extraordinary present of the manuscript of *Childe Harold's Pilgrimage: A Romaunt* in 1811. Dallas had since dropped out of the picture, and Byron had come to deal with Murray more or less directly during the publication of the Oriental tales. During that period Byron vacillated in his response to Murray's offers of substantial sums of money for his poetry. Following the separation, however, Lord Byron unsentimentally dropped his pose of gifted, indifferent amateur and plunged into direct negotiations over payment for the copyright to the third canto of *Childe Harold*. It is a long way from the scornful pronouncement in *English Bards and Scotch Reviewers* that "when the sons of song descend in trade, / Their bays are sere, their former laurels fade" (ll. 175–76) to the frank calculations of this letter to Murray: "With regard to price, *I* fixed *none* but left it to Mr. Kinnaird—& Mr. Shelley & yourself to arrange—of course they would do their best—and as to yourself—I know you would make no difficulties. But I agree with Mr. Kinnaird perfectly that the concluding five hundred should be only conditional—and for my own sake I wish it to be added only in case of your selling a certain number—that number to be fixed by yourself—I hope this is fair (*BLJ* 5:105–6)." Byron's sale of the copyright he had previously given decisively separates him from the practices of the past; he capitalizes on his poetic reputation in order to speculate on the future.

According to customary business practice, the writer was not compensated for the handwritten product of his labor, nor did the bookseller contract to return to the writer a share of his profits. What was bought and sold was the copyright, a legal fiction that certified the right to reproduce an authorial name and to retain the profits from the sale of any texts that might appear under that sign. Murray's abstention from the adjustments that

Byron offered him reflected his recognition that the purchase of a copyright was an investment in the career that the name *Byron* described rather than a payment based on the short-term market value of any individual work. Copyright assigns a career to the name and the words that appear under the name independent of the biological life of either writer or publisher, subject instead to the field of speculation that Byron knew as "the trade."

Calculating on a writer's popularity meant gambling on the future. But risk could be managed because opinion was subject to a measure of control. The "seasons" that bookselling observed were not natural, and Murray was notorious for manipulating them. There is a "mystery in the craft" of publishing, complained Byron (*BLJ* 10:58); "there is a trickery in these things—no one can understand—though we see and feel it" (*BLJ* 10:155). Success was only marginally dependent on what things happened; instead the trade created the conditions that would determine what and how things would happen.[3] Byron's notion of a "fair" price was, as he would later realize, naive. The price paid for copyright was roughly pegged to the expected sale of the book, but demand for books by Scott and Byron so exceeded all previous expectations that no reliable calculations could be made. As Murray knew, the bookseller was dealing not in intrinsically valuable things but in the signs of value. Therefore he could hope to increase the demand for his books by increasing the price he paid the author for the volume: the fee paid to the poet not only acknowledged his value but augmented it by being publicized among those who counted.

In the teens and twenties, when relations among poetry, the essay, and the novel were extraordinarily fluid, the imprint of a prestigious publisher served as a kind of canonical legitimation—which was quite different from the kind of political inflection given by a liberal publisher like Joseph Johnson or by more unsavory, radical types such as William Hone and Richard Carlisle. Cash trumped politics. The more money a publisher had and was willing to pay, the less political or partisan his choices could (appear to) be. Similarly, keeping the price of the volumes high was a way not only of appealing to an elite clientele but of *determining* a clientele, and a taste for Byron. For Murray, as for Pierre Bourdieu, "tastes . . . are the practical affirmation of an inevitable difference. . . . In matters of taste, more than anywhere else, all determination is negation."[4] For the booksellers of Edinburgh and London, true heirs to the monopolistic ambitions of the eighteenth-century publishing cartels, the existence of a taste was, ultimately, registered by the value of an authorial copyright within the bookselling market—a "stock exchange" whose fluctuations substituted for market research.[5] As possession of copyright meant the determination of an author by negating the opportunity of others to publish certain writings, so the determination of a taste meant negating large sectors of the reading public—restricting supply in order to increase profit.

So, although Murray's overall sales were hurt by pirated versions of Byron, he resisted Byron's urgings that he preempt the larceny by pirating his own expensive editions in cheap duodecimos (*BLJ* 9:187). The pirates may have hurt Murray's sales, but his behavior was nonetheless a rational affirmation of the difference between them, a difference on which long-run profit depended. Though important, sales of Byron were still only a portion of a catalog of books that Murray had for sale, and the value of the subgenre copyrighted as "Byron" was ultimately referred to its determinate place within the comprehensive "economic genre."[6]

Perhaps the neatest contemporary example of the market adjustment of a fair price is the negotiation in 1814 over the copyright of Thomas Moore's *Lalla Rookh*. Wilfred Dowden summarizes: "When news of *Lallah Rookh* reached Murray, he offered Moore 2000 guineas for the work. The Longmans countered with an offer of 3000 guineas, with the proviso that they be allowed to read it before actually contracting to publish it. . . . [Moore] refused the offer, and the Longmans dropped the stipulation, offering him £3000 'for a poem the length of Rokeby'. . . . Moore accepted this offer."[7] As the final agreement proved, Longman's dramatic escalation of Murray's offer reflected no assessment of the merit of Moore's unwritten poem and was based on no real estimate of demand. The tremendous elasticity of demand during a period that preceded the formation of the mass novel-reading public made the notion of the literary market a generic convention about as stable as the Oriental romance. Longman's prescription of the poem's length not by lines but by its equivalence with *Rokeby*—as if by some kind of magic the success of one would thereby rub off on the other—illustrates the kind of wishfulness that informed literary speculations, wishes that in the absence of any natural or even reliable standards of value, whether for author, bookseller, or reader, were fulfilled often enough to seduce further speculations. The wish in this case was a reasonably modest one. *Rokeby* was not very successful. In fact, in his *Memoirs of Scott* Lockhart identifies the dip in sales from *Lady of the Lake*, Scott's previous romance, as strong evidence that Scott's market share had been significantly diminished by the rivalry of Lord Byron.[8] *Rokeby* could fitly serve as a standard of value for Longman precisely because it was a relative failure: unlike the sensations of *Marmion* or *Lady of the Lake*, *Rokeby* represented reasonable prospects for success in a Byronized market. Indeed, by tying the fair price to *Rokeby*, Longman fittingly inscribed the secondary position of Moore's proposed

Oriental tale in relation to Byron's extraordinary precedent. In a system where the fairness of a price could be decided only by the physical resemblance of one book to another, value could seem to have become wholly relative, an effect not so much of quantification as of simulation. This relativity had its financial corollary: "To be sure," Byron (naivete lost) writes to Douglas Kinnaird after computing the "quantum" of *Juan* sent to Murray, "the sum [of two thousand pounds] is worth more than all the poetry that ever was written *in fact*—but is it so in proportion to the present prices paid to other writers?" (*BLJ* 8:212).

The name *Murray* no more represented an individual than did *Byron;* like *Byron* it stood for a house; unlike *Byron* that house was not a crest, a prerogative, and an ancestral ruin, but the means of producing books and the organ of their criticism, the *Quarterly Review.* And unlike the members of the other clubs to which Byron had earlier belonged (*citoyen* Matthews's *méthodistes*, the Whig Club, the Hampden Club, White's, Alfred's), the odd lot of characters that Byron's negotiations collected—Shelley, Kinnaird, Hobhouse, Moore, and Murray—shared no interest except "Byron," which by the time of the publication of *Childe Harold III* had become a cultural denominator capable of abstracting individuals from their concrete concerns and traditional relationships and inducting them into a network of exchange and competition in a simulation of what Jean Baudrillard calls "aristocratic parity," a "statutory rivalry" (statutory because competition is subvended and restricted by copyright legislation) in which "differences are produced industrially, . . . bureaucratically programmed in the form of collective models."9

The house of Murray was a literary circle, which from the start of Lord Byron's involvement described a consistent and efficient practice: first William Gifford, editor of the *Quarterly,* would read the manuscript and pronounce on its fitness to Murray, who would propose a price for the copyright (early on to Dallas, then to intermediaries, and later to Byron himself) and return the manuscript to the poet, usually with recommendations for revisions. On receipt of the revised manuscript Murray would have it set in type, at which time the proof was often corrected by Gifford; Murray would then print copies of the poetry in expensive editions for sale and criticism—a criticism never actually written by Gifford or Murray but conducted in the *Quarterly* at their initiative and under their auspices. It is not necessary to attribute venal motives to Lord Byron (who initially expressed indignation at "such shifts to extort praise, or deprecate censure" [*BLJ* 2:1011), or to Gifford, or to reviewers like Scott in order to observe that the sequence here, an extraordinary publishing and publicizing machine, was ordered with such recursive elegance that critical independence was a virtually meaningless notion.[10] The sequence of interventions—transmissions, reproductions, revisions—constituted a formula for the composition of a commercially successful publication first and of a poem only by the way. The Wordsworthian aspiration to create the taste by which one is to be appreciated had become the practical effect of the publishing machine.[11] The Murray circle instantiated a speculative grammar according to which literary statements were made and recognized: its strategy, in Michel de Certeau's terms, depended on the circumscription of an area of the proper—the copyrighted domain named Byron, which was institutionalized (made a communally recognized formula used to predict, achieve, and reproduce a general range of desirable results) as a self-reflexive machine for producing poems and profit.[12]

Employment of "Byron" was not restricted to Murray. It furnished a point of orientation, a counter, and a resource for the culture at large, even for those who were nominally Murray's competitors in the "statutory rivalry." The consensual basis of that rivalry is evident in the competition between the two dominant cultural arbiters of Regency England: the *Edinburgh Review* and the *Quarterly Review*. The latter was planned, in Murray's words, to respond to the "radically bad" principles of the *Edinburgh* and "to counteract their dangerous influence."[13] The contest, supported by the "higher powers" in the Tory government, especially George Canning, was conducted as the simulation of another rivalry, the grand war between Britain and Napoleonic France. The internalization of the military struggle, a sophistication of the containment strategy that Britain prosecuted through its Continental alliances, dramatized the capacity of a commercial society to reproduce the battlefield at the level of culture. The grand strategist of this internalization was Walter Scott, who was an important early contributor to the *Edinburgh* but who, upon suffering a severe review of *Marmion* at the hands of Francis Jeffrey, allied in 1808 with Canning and Murray to found the *Quarterly*. Scott's letters to Canning, to Murray, to George Ellis, and to William Gifford are peppered with military metaphors; he persuaded his collaborators to imagine that they were embarked on a campaign of mimic warfare.[14]

This mimicry had two salient consequences: (1) Byronism, the chief by-product of the bloodless warfare between the major reviews, was from the outset imagined as a para-Napoleonic phenomenon, an empire based on the sale of books rather than on the conquest of nations. "Byron" was designed to out-Bonaparte Bonaparte. When Murray wrote to Lord Byron following the publication of *The Corsair*, "I am most happy to tell you that your last poem *is*—what Mr. Southey's is *called*—*a Carmen Triumphale*,"[15] he was not only lording it over the laureate, he was attesting to a cultural force equivalent to Napoleon's military prowess. (2) Although Byron was conceded the position of "Napoleon of the realms of rhyme," the principle of simulation (like Napoleonic conquest) licensed the multiplication of realms, each with its "Napoleonic" position: hence Murray's rival Archibald Constable, publisher of the *Edinburgh Review* and (in the wake of Ballantyne's ruin) Scott's novels, could be proclaimed the "grand Napoleon of the realms of print" and deliriously exult, "My God, I am all but author of the Waverley novels."[16] Lord Byron was being sarcastic when he called the reviewers "monarch-makers in poetry and prose" (*BLJ* 3:209). But Lockhart's account of his first meeting with Constable, when Scott greeted him as "your Czarist Majesty," and Scott's explanation that "Constable long since dubbed himself *The czar of Muscovy*, John Murray *The Emperor of the West*, and Longman and his string of partners *The Divan*," suggest a world whose difference from the scene of Napoleon's self-anointment as emperor (or from the excited discourse of the "Chan of Tartary" in the Bedlam rendered in Mackenzie's *Man of Feeling*) is not a matter of a stronger or weaker hold on reality; it rather reflects the sure grasp of the means of reproducing that version of reality most agreeable to imperial egos and corporate vanity.[17]

In part, this affable megalomania was a normal consequence of the analogical scheme by which political issues were typically recast: every contemporary actor and event could be nicknamed in terms of another.[18] In part, the scene represents the historically monopolistic ambition of British booksellers (cf. the second Conger of London booksellers headed by Andrew Millar in the eighteenth century) finding its appropriate contemporary metaphors. Absolutist identifications were apt because the immensely profitable dominance over the market by a few men was as technically illegitimate and therefore as despotic as, in the radical rhetoric of the time, the counterrevolutionary government of Great Britain was accused of being: no member of the Murray-Constable-Ballantyne group could give a fully plausible explanation of how their dominance was maintained, let alone why it should be maintained (no explanation, at least, that was not as circular as the system by which they profited). But the metaphors of despotism were also apposite because the paranoid foreclosure of opposition that constituted the statutory rivalry of cultural politics in the Napoleonic era corresponded point for point with the Orientalist discourse that the publishers had themselves propagated for their own profit. The booksellers participated in Britain's hegemonic dream of simulating the global military and political struggle by bloodless commercial competition. Their failure fully to understand and master the mechanism of their success is evinced by their inebriated embrace of those exotic nicknames of the very despots the commercial society was supposed to have displaced. In part, then, these identifications were truly mad—part and parcel of the delusion that the publishers commanded the tides of public opinion and dictated the flow of capital that swept them to prominence and power. The fate of *Rokeby* and the rescue of John Ballantyne in 1813 ought to have taught the lesson that the perfection of the code into a system of hallucinatory satisfaction could be no adequate defense against the return of the repressed referent: returned perhaps as an undetermined change of taste that could, and in the case of Scott and Constable did, bring bankruptcy and ruin.

But not in 1816. With *Childe Harold III* and the stabilizing of the *Quarterly*'s "literary coalition,"[19] Lord Byron became fully Byronic. Separation is not the same as divorce, however. Byron did not break completely with wife, child, and country; he supplemented what he could no longer completely have with what he could not fully possess: nature with letters. As domestic attachments were abstracted into legal associations conducted at great distance and mediated by briefs and attorneys, so was the natural poet, who was hidden from sight like one of Pope's "*Asian* Monarchs."[20] The poet was abstracted into a man of letters whose relations with the public were then mediated by his publisher, the "Emperor of the West." Byron's strategic separation from his native land opens up the possibility of unlimited speculation, which feels like freedom. And it is as good as freedom gets in a commercial society where to be free means either to have unlimited credit or, more prosaically, to have no debts. "There is," Byron writes to Murray, "a great advantage in getting the water between a man and his embarrassments—for things and a little prudence insensibly reestablish themselves—and I have spent less money—and had more for it within the two years and a half since my absence from England—than I have ever done within the same time before—and my literary speculations allowed me to do it more easily— . . . out of England I have no debts whatever" (*BLJ* 6:65).

Separation and Beginning

Such a negative definition of *advantage* tends to confirm Lady Byron's judgment: "He has always expressed his aversion to this country, and has acknowledged that it arose from his dislike to *controul*—either of Law or Morals. To this cause I attribute his desire to go abroad."[21] Acting on the principle that escape from one form of control is possible only if another kind is acquired, Lord Byron attempted to master his domestic situation in his poetry of self-vindication. In "Fare Thee Well" he depicts himself as a poet scorned:

> Would that Breast, by thee glanced over,
>   Every inmost thought could show!
> Then thou wouldst at last discover
>   'Twas not well to spurn it so.
>
> Though the world for this commend thee—
>   Though it smile upon the blow,
> Even its praises must offend thee,
>   Founded on another's woe:
>
> Though my many faults defaced me,
>   Could no other arm be found,
> Than the one which once embraced me,
>   To inflict a cureless wound?
>
>   (ll. 9–20)

Lady Byron is blamed for being a bad reader. "Glanced over," the poet complains of her failure to apprehend his legible soul of love. Lady Byron is no Medora. Nevertheless, she cannot fully escape the Byronic scenario. A mere glance is enough to induct her into a familiar antithetical structure: insensitivity translates into aggression; *glancing* is both a refusal to read and the striking of a wounding blow. The poignant image of the "cureless wound" offers an intimate acquaintance with a now monumental pain (see *CH III*, st. 7):

> Yet, oh yet, thyself deceive not;
>   Love may sink by slow decay,
> But by sudden wrench, believe not
>   Hearts can thus be torn away:
>
> Still thine own its life retaineth—
>   Still must mine, though bleeding, beat;
> And the undying thought which paineth
>   Is—that we no more may meet.
>
>   (ll. 21–28)

The "cureless wound" becomes an "undying thought," and we learn, as Lady Byron learns, the full meaning of a separation that is not a divorce. Indeed, it is because *we* can learn what Lady Byron learns that Byron's claim for an "undying thought" in the face of great pain is credible.[22] The printing of the wound seals its curelessness, publicly binding husband and wife as they never were bound in private, and perpetuating the "great advantage" he celebrates in his letter to Murray:

> But 'tis done—all words are idle—
>   Words from me are vainer still;
> But the thoughts we cannot bridle
>   Force their way without the will.
>
> Fare thee well!—thus disunited,
>   Torn from every nearer tie,
> Sear'd in heart, and lone, and blighted,
>   More than this I scarce can die.
>   (ll. 53–60)

Byron exploits the myth of irrepressible lyric force in order to position himself to take full advantage of all consequences, intended and unintended, of the event, consequences that now include this poem that completes the allegorization of the poet's sorrow and self. Allegory is what endures after all that *can* die *has*. And as we have seen on several occasions, paranoid foreclosure ensues when all human relations have become allegorical. All readers of this poem (even those who just give it a glance) must confirm the existence of the cureless wound that the poem is. Having designated a separation that is not a divorce and a dying that is not a death, the poem has absorbed the lives of both husband and wife in a profitable, if imaginary, communion. His pain has entitled Lord Byron to something like a copyright to the allegorical narrative that hemorrhages from the wound of the separation.

In the domestic pieces and in *Childe Harold III* Byron proves that, as he writes in "Epistle to Augusta," "I have been cunning in mine overthrow, / The careful pilot of my proper woe." Byron interprets his break with his wife as I have interpreted the Corsair's perversity, and does it with a self-reflexive twist that saves him, closeted Hegelian, as cause. The husband's assertion that "all the fault of their cruel separation lay with himself" (*HVSV*, p. 209) transposes to another key the egoistic heroism of the Giaour ("not mine the act though I the cause" [l. 1061]) and the Corsair by denying that Lady Byron could have done other than act the part of a Byronic heroine. Lord Byron retains the formality of his fault as he hangs onto his name: no longer the mark of separation, it is the reproducible sign of his monopoly over all the products of his past—a trademark.

Lord Byron cunningly practices what Selim preached: "Power sways but by division." By the poet's craft a separation erupted becomes a division made. He divides to conquer. The crudest example is the poem called "A Sketch," in which Lord Byron works himself up to a frenzy of antithesis as he attempts to divide Lady Byron from her bad angel, Mrs. Clermont, and to retrieve his influence, if not her love. In *Childe Harold III* the poet exercises his sway with more sophistication and to greater effect. At its outset the picturesque variousness of the first two cantos yields to an emphatic dualism:

> Once more upon the waters! yet once more!
> And the waves bound beneath me as a steed
> That knows its rider. Welcome to their roar!
> Swift by their guidance, whereso'er it lead!
> Though the strain'd mast should quiver as a reed,
> And the rent canvass fluttering strew the gale,
> Still must I on; for I am as a weed,
> Flung from the rock on Ocean's foam to sail
> Where'er the surge may sweep, the tempest's breath prevail.
>
> (*CH III*, st. 2)

More impressive than the poles of titanic mastery and Shelleyan passivity is the positioning of the pivot that efficiently transforms existential bewilderment into rhetorical antithesis. The alteration of objects that impelled the serial elaboration of the Oriental tales has here been deftly formalized. Whether Lord Byron is the captain or the captive of his fate, the trope of division allows him to command both possibilities and to produce the "constant alternation between sympathy and disgust" (*RR* B:2:597–98) of which only an addicted customer could complain.

A statement of the Byronic grammar, the speculative stage of Lord Byron's career was triggered by his wrenching separation from all natural attachments, what in *Childe Harold III* he calls the ties of "house and heart" (st. 1). Triggered, not caused. It would be unfair to blame Lady Byron for a fault that Byron never allowed her. Moreover, the moment had been anticipated at least as early as "To Romance," which, as we have seen, signals a crossing from "the realms of air" to the material world of circumstance and strife. But things have changed. What was then imagined as progress is now rendered as repetition: "Once more upon the waters! yet once more!" The specificity of Lord Byron's statement can be measured from Conrad's plaintive "again and again, my love!" "Once more" prevents that murmur by a frank acknowledgment of the evidence of repetition that disabled the Byronic heroes Conrad and Lara. That acknowledgment, however, also seems to promise a finality ("yet once more" as *just* once more). The assumption of

repetition, the *resuming* of *Childe Harold*,[23] entails the repression of repetitiveness as a dynamic independent of conscious control. Both resumption and repression are necessary to the transformation of mere repetition
into what Edward Said calls a beginning.[24] The Byronic beginning begins by
virtue of a recognition of its repetition of a past action. That recognition
dictates an ambivalent relation to a future conceived either as completion of
the series or as another violation of the promise of completion. Put more
simply (and again following Said's strong precedent), Byron's beginning, the
making of the Byronic statement "once more," involves the recognition—
unavailable to Conrad or Lara, to the poet of *Hours* or of *Childe Harold: A
Romaunt*—that there is a Byronic text.

At least, that is how the poet understands it:

> In my youth's summer I did sing of One,
> The wandering outlaw of his own dark mind;
> Again I seize the theme, then but begun,
> And bear it with me, as the rushing wind
> Bears the cloud onwards: in that tale I find
> The furrows of long thought, and dried-up tears,
> Which ebbing, leave a sterile track behind,
> O'er which all heavily the journeying years
> Plod the last sand of life,—where not a flower appears.
>
> (*CH III*, st. 3)

Byron begins by finding something already written, deeded. Adapting his
cherished page metaphor, the poet imagines finding himself inscribed as a
"sterile track" in a colorless, barren land. Dreary as this Lara-like discovery
is, its self-reflexivity saves the notion of some "I" independent of the text:
the "I" to which all statements are referred; the "I" that can stop and, like
the wind, "seize" and "fling"; the "I" that can be made both visible and self-
forgetful by its self-imaging. The Byronic text begins as the "I"'s insistence
on a relative autonomy from the text that, subsequent to its separation from
the social world of face-to-face encounter, is in fact the only vehicle by
which the "I" can appear.

The "I"'s relative autonomy is the function of its attachment to a proper
name. Systematic and strategic, *Lord Byron* designates no simple idea. *Lord
Byron* is the name for the "I" to which reflection refers as well as for the
propulsive structuration of self-reflection itself. Whatever else has been
lost, the "I" retains its privileged capacity to "bear" *Childe Harold* as the poet
had earlier borne Childe Harold: the poem has become Lord Byron's "child
of imagination" (preface to *Childe Harold's Pilgrimage: A Romaunt*), bred out

of its own barrenness and ruefully substituted for the child of his "house and heart."

The continuation of *Childe Harold* provides the poet, displaced from the circumstantial world of eye and ear in which he formerly had his social being, with an alternate form of what Anthony Giddens has called "ontological security," the security of routine. Theorizing the place of routine in social life, Giddens subdivides human agency into three distinct modes: the unconscious, practical consciousness, and discursive consciousness. "Carried primarily in practical consciousness," he argues, "routine drives a wedge between the potentially explosive content of the unconscious and the reflexive monitoring of action which agents display." According to Giddens, the "repetitiveness of activities which are undertaken in like manner day after day is the material grounding of . . . the recursive nature of social life. (By its recursive nature I mean that the structured properties of social activity . . . are constantly recreated out of the very resources which constitute them)."[25] Giddens's description of the recursive nature of social life applies generally to the production of statements by the speculative grammar of the Murray circle, its attempt to routinize successful publication by building on the social fact of Byron's career. But it applies most particularly to *Childe Harold III*, which announces itself as a poem constituted out of the resources of *Childe Harold I* and *II*. Rendered readable by its similarity as part to the Byronic system as whole, the specular *Childe Harold III* routinely avails itself of its failure to "explode" volcanically as the raw material for self-reflection.

Even if we accept Giddens's claim that "practical consciousness" or routine is the "material grounding" of social life, we should, however, be wary of reifying that routine into a known or stable quantity. At some times routine, or what Bourdieu calls the "habitus," is more routinized than others.[26] In prerevolutionary France the rule of routine was strenuously and effectively challenged by the philosophical societies of the salons, ruled by Mme. Geoffrin and Mme. d'Epinay and frequented by the philosophes. In pre-industrial England the rule of routine was challenged by the loyal opposition of David Hume, who in book 1 of his *Treatise of Human Nature* promoted the dissolution of traditional practices based on illusory notions of personal identity and social cohesion in the name of a habit that could survive the vicissitudes of fashion, political corruption, and social convulsion as well as it survives Hume's relentless Pyrrhonism. Hume's heuristic removal of the "wedge" of practical consciousness in the last two chapters of book 1 of the *Treatise* served as a model for similar experiments in the literature of the period.[27] The strategic suppression of practical consciousness was, of course, the Gothic's stock in trade. Perhaps the most radical and unsettling exploration of the deprivation of routine, however, was the tradition of prison literature, broadly conceived, which included Laurence Sterne's *Sentimental Journey*, Sade's *Justine*, William Godwin's *Caleb Williams*, and, later, Byron's *Corsair* and *The Prisoner of Chillon*. Each of those works investigates the effects of the withdrawal of the wedge of habit and the consequent absorption of a resourceless consciousness by a lurid and violent unconsciousness; each concludes with some acknowledgment, grim or cheerful, of the way in which the middling empire of routine inexorably reasserts its sway.

The return of routine does not mean the restoration of the same old habits. In the Romantic novel there develops a consistent, even programmatic appropriation by consciousness of the preconscious. This is conspicuously the case in Ann Radcliffe's *Mysteries of Udolpho* and supremely the case in Jane Austen's *Northanger Abbey;* in each novel imaginative participation in the removal of the wedge of practical consciousness prepares for the conscious extension of the sway of routine to an area hitherto out of sight and mind. Escaping routine became routinized, a leisure-time activity.[28] Walter Scott's admiring review of Austen's *Emma* develops the insight that the appropriation of the heart of domesticity for the empire of routine was the historical mission of the novelist and that authorial merit may be judged according to the degree to which that appropriation had itself become apparently routinized.[29] *Apparently*, because consciousness leaves its mark as the sign of the novel's deliberate participation in the dialectic of enlightenment. The mark of consciousness, of its self-reflexive monitoring of a routine in which it has no standing, is irony—a nonroutinized manner that does not endanger but confirms a social reality that has no basis other than our irresistible belief in it. Some, such as Bourdieu, would propose specific political, social, and economic causes to explain the beliefs that we hold and the routines that we practice. Hume has made me skeptical about forging such causal links. But the skeptic's irony is no solution either. Although Lord Byron attempts to grasp the force empowering routine by ironic self-reflection, his irony announces that something of power (a third party who is neither father nor child of imagination) remains withheld from the reflecting eye and remarks the poem's blindness both to the means of its own production and to the impetus of its own reproduction. Of course, the comprehensive view is as hidden to all other historical actors as it is to Byron. Lord Byron's text inadvertently exposes to an audience that has been feeding on the simplicities of the counterrevolution for its ideological energy the cryptic forces that underwrite its historical existence.

The Life of Speculation

When, at Waterloo, Lord Byron discovers a "ghastly gap" in "kind and kindred" (*CH III*, st. 31) it appears as the historical correlative to the devastating rent in his own life.[30] The extraordinary beginning of the third canto is called for by the unprecedented failure of phenomena to sustain the pilgrim. When Lord Byron faces the world he sees nothing. Having drained the world of traditional objects of desire, "such gaps as Desolation worked" (st. 95) provoke and justify the grand Byronic identification of psyche and world historical moment, of rifted mindscape and gaping landscape, which nerves the self-reflexive poetics of *Childe Harold III*. This gap is the chasm that the "lightning" of the perfect expression, the "one word" (st. 97), would cross but cannot, since something must remain in excess of expression for expression to be. Here as elsewhere in Byron the "unspeakable" is his poetic capital—but in this case (as opposed to, say, *Manfred*, which lives off the interest of the deposited incest) capital is a concept without content; it has only the structural function of funding continued structuration. Indeed, capital might as well be called repetition itself, since it is repetition— literally unspeakable—on which Byron builds.

The workings of this reflexive system may be discerned in the poet's employment of the gap in kind created by his separation from Ada, daughter of his "house and heart." Her withdrawal from Byron is, reciprocally, the withdrawal of him from her. Like the figure of Romance in the poem of that name, she is left with an absence that must be filled, if only by a "name." *Childe Harold III* images the necessity for its projection, like Kaled's severed hair, into the gap. Once removed, Ada becomes the figure of an English audience that, deprived of Byron's presence, needs this text to stanch, however futilely, the "cureless wound" his departure has left. The poem forges a triple analogy, then: the poet's version of the personal world he leaves, the historical world he sees, and the person he is are all proportioned—they exhibit the kind of specular "fit" that is the predominant feature of the high Byronic text. *Childe Harold III* describes the fragmentation of the single world:

> Even as a broken mirror, which the glass
> In every fragment multiplies; and makes
> A thousand images of one that was,
> The same, and still the more, the more it breaks.
>
> (st. 33)

Is the "one that was" mirror or world? No matter. "Byron" is mirror and world, a world of mirrors, each reflecting the telltale absence of itself from the image it renders: I am the one who is missing something—I am the one who is missing.[31] The triple analogy among a rent social world, a desolated historical world, and a wounded psyche is not "subjective." The fit identifies a new kind of discursive objectivity, a reflexive code for the indefinite elaboration of such analogies: the code, the discourse, the poetical economy, and "specular text" called Byron.[32]

Byronic self-reflection receives its existential rationale in the grand sixth stanza:

'Tis to create, and in creating live
A being more intense, that we endow
With form our fancy, gaining as we give
The life we image, even as I do now.
What am I? Nothing: but not so art thou,
Soul of my thought! with whom I traverse earth,
Invisible but gazing, as I glow
Mix'd with thy spirit, blended with thy birth,
And feeling still with thee in my crush'd feelings' dearth.

Self-division enables speculation. And "life" emerges in the exercise of a speculative imaging. The lines perform a "fit speculation" (st. 10) not merely because they affirm that life is acquired in a dynamic self-reflection of the acquisitive "I" with its invested image, but also because they formulate the life so gained, so given, as thoroughly conjectural. Conjectural for the poet and conjectural for the reader, who, having been induced to identify with the poetic "we" is split off from the "I" to occupy the position of that "thou" who is the familiar of the poet's pilgrimages. This "thou" may be the soul of the poet's thought, his animating principle; but it is a public, indeed a *publicized* soul, a character that has attained the cultural currency of a stereotype. The reader of Byron gives life to the poet on the same condition as he receives it—as the child of the poet's imagination. What was implicit in the Oriental tales has become formalized here: the condition of reading Byron is to be a Byronic reader; to be a "we" whose history is textual, and who begins life repeatedly as the serial transaction between a particular "I" reduced to nothing and an iterated public image.[33] In the words of John Wilson (reviewing *Childe Harold IV* for *Blackwood's*), the "power which Harold holds over us" is derived from the fact that "he lives in a sort of sympathy with the public mind—sometimes wholly distinct from it—sometimes acting in opposition to it—sometimes blending with it,—but at all times,—in all his thoughts and actions having a reference to the public mind" (*RR* B:2:899). Or, in the currency of postmodernism, *Childe Harold III* prospers as what Guy Debord calls a "spectacle," which is "not a collection of images, but a social relation among people, mediated by images."[34]

"Life" for *Childe Harold* is no longer a given. As the subject becomes formalized, so life surfaces as a by-product of speculative imaging—a productivity celebrated by Francis Jeffrey (in a moment of Keatsian excess) as a "perpetual stream of thick-coming fancies—an eternal spring of fresh-blown images" (*RR* B:2:865). *Speculation*, according to the *OED*, denotes a mental operation: "to engage in thought or reflection, esp. of a conjectural nature." Yet if it has theoretical pretensions, speculation also has practical consequences: "to engage in the buying and selling of commodities . . . in order to profit by a rise or fall in their market value; to undertake, to take part or invest in, a business enterprise of a risky nature in the expectation of a considerable gain." Speculation is not a theory about making money; it is a practical way of turning a profit. But the ability to make money by speculation remarks on the theoretical status of the money made, its conjectural relation to real productivity or value. In its mingling of theory and practice, the mind and the market, there is something uncanny about speculation, the kind of uncanniness that Coleridge, no Scottish political economist, tried to quash in the *Biographia Literaria* when he warned against violating the "sacred distinction between things and persons."[35]

Those hybrid properties that condemn speculation to a low place in High Romanticism can be suggested by glancing at Coleridge's definition of fancy in chapter 13 of the *Biographia*. Coleridge has described the personable secondary imagination as "essentially *vital*, even as all objects (*as* objects) are essentially fixed and dead." He goes on to say of the impersonable fancy that it, "on the contrary, has no other counters to play with but fixities and definites."[36] Since fancy is the *contrary* of the imagination, it cannot be "essentially vital." And there can be no doubt that fixities and definites are "essentially fixed and dead." The opportunity for play in this universe of death comes from the "capacity" of fixities and definites to be counters— that is, their liability to be not merely what they "essentially" are but also to be something else. Fixities and definites are deployed by fancy as counters to life *and* death in a fascinating speculative game. Fancy neither sows nor reaps. Like the master in Hegel's allegory of lordship, it "must receive all its materials ready made from the law of association." But fancy demonstrates a savvy that Hegel's doomed master does not; it prospers by strategic interventions in the plastic space between the mechanical fabrication of ready-mades and their use. By disregarding the inert materiality of the object, by exploiting the play in essence, fancy finds a kind of life in an unimaginative game, in the same way that the masterful speculator makes a kind of living from the manipulation of the readymade as a commodity in the market. Speculation is "indeed no other than a mode of Memory emancipated from the order of time and space"; its "vitality" depends on those supplemental properties of the object that make it liable to deployment as a commodity—that simulacrum which violates the distinction between things and persons, the bookseller's warehouse and the poet's soul.[37]

The Child of Imagination: Three Case Studies

What does it mean to live as a "child of imagination"? The possibility answers the speculator's dream, whether Adam Smith's version of effortlessly and profitably combining unlike with like at a distance or the youthful Byron's version of the "German Prince who coins his own Cash" (*BLJ* 1:79). In this section I want to consider three alternate profiles of this speculative existence, to begin to build up a kind of population of the imaginary, in order to forge something like a frame in which Byron can be conjured to appear.

Let us start by following Byron himself. When pressed to name the greatest men of his age, Lord Byron listed Brummell, Bonaparte, and himself—in that order. He lived the proportions. Stendhal observed that "during at least a third part of the day, Byron was a dandy, expressed a constant dread of augmenting the bulk of his outward man, concealed his right foot as much as possible, and endeavoured to render himself agreeable in female society. In his moments of dandyism, he always pronounced the name of Brummell with a mingled emotion of respect and jealousy" (*HVSV*, p. 201). Barbey D'Aurevilly, a commentator who shared Byron's respect, if not his jealousy, later synthesized the meanings that the "name of Brummell" evoked: "Brummell had nothing of what with some was passion or genius, with others high birth or wealth. He was the gainer by this indigence, for being reduced to the single force of what distinguished him, he raised himself to the rank of a Thing: he became Dandyism itself."[38] The dandy exploits his indigence to design himself as the perfect child of his imagination, a pristine thing that can turn and turn but remains the same from all sides.

The dandy explodes certain commonplaces about humanity. Here is Hume deploying one of them: "'No man,' said the Prince of Conde, 'is a hero to his *valet de chambre.*' It is certain that admiration and acquaintance are altogether incompatible towards any mortal creature. Sleep and love convinced even Alexander himself that he was not a God. But I suppose that such as daily attended him could easily, from the numberless weaknesses to which he was subject, have given him many still more convincing proofs of his humanity."[39] If the valet's-eye-view is Hume's truth, its eventual transformation into a precept applicable to *Don Juan*, that "no character is a hero to his poet," must pass through the portals of the dandy's dressing room: a dandy is a dandy *especially* to his *valet de chambre*. The dandy cannot be caught in undress: he turns his dressing into a levee for the admiring. He makes the room where his figure is first cut transparent to the inquiring eye—every morning a "fit speculation." Brummell's characteristic sarcasm complements this stance. Wit is brittle and can misfire. Sarcasm makes no such distinctions. Brummell's notorious slight of the prince regent, "Alvanley, who's your fat friend?" negates wit by its perfect shamelessness.[40]

The dandy's charm is, strictly speaking, inhuman. Such reduction has its costs. Become indistinguishable from a commodity, the dandiacal body suffers the commodity's fate, as Brummell's first biographer cruelly observed in a comment that sounds like a descriptive catalog of John Murray's publications or a draft for a stanza of *Don Juan*: "Up to a point, Brummell's success in the line he marked out for himself was complete, and for years he reigned absolute as the dictator of the fashionable section of the London world. He had a run: so had Mesmer, so had mustard seed, Dr. Graham's connubial bed, the metallic tractors of Perkins, tar water, and the well known fox in Whittlebuy forest."[41] To live in one's image leaves one helpless in the face of the cycle of boom and bust that besets all speculation: as with Byron's chronic dieting, purge triggers binge, but bust follows binge. In the commercial culture of early-nineteenth-century Great Britain, the "patent age of new inventions," objectification meant commodification; to be a thing meant to be subject to individual or collective fancy. To live in the eyes of others—especially others for whom one affected contempt—meant that the withdrawal of favor dissolved and dissipated the very basis of dandiacal existence—and not in order to "recreate" but to dispose. If the dandy shines in his closet and no one is there to see him, he does not exist.

In Scrope Davies's case routine imposed its iron law at the gaming tables. Brummell was struck down not only by the hazards of the wheel but by the fortune of the Regent's wandering eyes, which strayed from Brummell as they did from the Whigs. Financial and political contingencies immune to the charms of his figure or the lash of his sarcasm brought Brummell down and insured that down he would stay. When, out of favor, Brummell sought refuge from debt in Calais, he discovered the economy of shame that, as we have seen, Wollstonecraft adumbrated: banning shame from one place on the superficies of the commodified body-image meant its displacement to some other place. As Portugal and Spain became the backside for Wollstonecraft's sensualist, and Greece for Louis Crompton's Byron, so did Calais for the Regency's Brummell. Brummell's place of shame was, however, without erotic charge. Calais was the place where people could visit the Brummellian thing and watch it degenerate to its organic elements. Brummell's compensation was the fate that Byron had projected for himself in "A Fragment." "Like the orator, the great actor, the great talker, like all who . . . speak to the body by the body," comments D'Aurevilly, a Pope to his Belinda, "Brummell possesses only a name, which glitters in mysterious refulgence through all the memoirs of his time."[42]

Lord Byron escaped that doom. Stendhal felt that Byron could never perfect himself as a dandy because of a "ruling passion" that "unceasingly tyrannized over him" (*HVSV*, p. 204). But it is not necessary to be quite so grandiose. If, in Jesse's words, one of Brummell's aphorisms was that "the severest mortification a gentleman could incur, was to attract observation in the street by his outward appearance,"[43] Lord Byron's mortifying physical peculiarities were sufficient disqualifications to dandyism. His clubfoot kept him off the public street and anchored him to the wall in the ballroom. His wild fluctuations in size and shape pushed him closer to the metamorphic pole of what has been called the "grotesque body" than to the tailored image of the dandy.[44] And even when removed from the public eye altogether, as, subsequent to the separation Lord Byron largely was, the books by which he published his well-formed image abroad were not free of marks that marred its perfection. If "to *appear is to be*, for Dandies as for women," Lord Byron was no dandy—not because he was a man who appeared other than he was, but because the solar "refulgence" of his name appeared only by virtue of spots that spoiled its shine.[45]

The "ontological security" promised by objectification in the image was illusory, because what economists like to call "demand" is by definition subject to the contingency of what lunatics, lovers, and poets know as "desire." Equally hazardous, however, was the contrary solution, attempting identification with the sociological ego by synchronizing one's labor with the machinery of social reproduction. This strategy is forever associated with the name of Robert Southey—undying proof that publishing books is not the same as beginning a text, and that livelihood and life are not synonymous. As Coleridge argued (with Southey in mind), the emergence of new forms of industrial routine not only drastically challenged the traditional "ontology" of authorship, they bore directly on the sharply contested status of "life."[46] Coleridge was not alone in such intuitions. Isaac Disraeli, who, as we have seen, was sensitive to the hegemonic power of "literary government," complained that the cultural "machine" is fueled by the blood of authors, who have become "the sacrificed among the sacrificers." The attempt to keep body and soul together by writing has, in this Molochian trope, come to have something suicidal about it. It is, Disraeli urged, "a very important question to ask, is this 'livelihood in the pen' really such? Authors drudging on in obscurity, and enduring miseries which can never close but with their life—shall this be worth even the humble designation of 'livelihood?' "[47]

Metaphor or not, the bookselling machine produced its consequences as if it and the lives of authors were social facts of the same order. Let us consult the beginning of a mocking review of *Waterloo*, a poem written by Lord Byron's absurd friend J. Wedderburn Webster, Esq. Webster was hungry neither for bread nor for poetic renown; he just wanted to get on in Regency society. Writing a poem on the major event of the age seemed a step in the right direction. But *Waterloo* was his Waterloo. In destroying Webster's pretensions, the reviewer for the *Quarterly* adopts the conceit that the statement of authorship is a fiction concocted by its Parisian printer, M. Didot, as part of an ingenious speculation:

> Everybody knows that M. Didot is not only a celebrated printer, but a great mechanist, and, if not the inventor, at least the introducer of that mode of printing called *Stereotype*, in which the lines and words are not made up of separate letters as heretofore, but are cast at once into permanent forms ready for use. Having words, and even lines, thus prepared, it was a natural yet ingenious thought to endeavour to apply some moving power by which they might be disposed in proper places and forms, without the delay, expense, and uncertainty of human labour.
>
> This moving power M. Didot seems to have acquired; and in the little work before us he exhibits a complete specimen of his success. It was not, indeed, to be expected that the machine, however ingenious, could always place the words in intelligible order, or work out any thing like sense of meaning; but as to the *mechanical* part it has succeeded surprizingly, and, to the eye, the lines of this pamphlet look as like real bona fide verses, as if they had been written by the hand of man, and printed by the ordinary process of the press.[48]

It may not in fact have been the case that M. Didot fabricated his poem on a verse-engine installed in his shop. Nonetheless, the reviewer adduces more than enough quotations to persuade that *Waterloo* is nothing but a chain of stereotypes. That we know Webster was the *initial* instrument for the rearrangement of those stereotypes—that the verse engine was a human author rather than the human author a verse engine—does not materially affect the argument. Those facts only require the extension of the printer's machinery to include, as part of its recursive operation, the human brain, an artificial intelligence stereotyped, if not yet digitalized. A tireless speculator in prestige, "bold Webster" has found that his brain has been put to sleep in mind to become a living engine.

If the Webster-machine were to give a defense of itself (perhaps in a Foucauldian dream vision), it might sound like the story told by James Tilly Matthews of Bethlem Hospital, London, which was published by the reformist doctor John Haslam in his 1810 *Illustrations of Madness*. Matthews, Haslam reports, had been admitted to the hospital at the petition of parish officers in 1797. Family attorneys lost a challenge to his prolonged institutionalization in 1798, and Matthews continued to make do in a situation where he described himself as "sometimes an automaton moved by the agency of persons . . . ; at others, the Emperor of the whole world, issuing proclamations to his disobedient subjects and hurling from their thrones the usurpers of his dominions." In 1809 his "relatives again interfered," and this time Matthews was released on the statement before the King's Bench by "two learned and conscientious Physicians" that he was not insane. Bethlem, however, referred "the determination of the case to the constituted and best authorities in the kingdom" who, after a "deliberate examination of the patient's mind," reversed the earlier diagnosis and remanded Matthews to the perpetual care of the hospital.[49]

The rehearsal of the legal and bureaucratic background takes Haslam some ten pages; the rest of his eighty-one-page monograph details Matthews's account of his excruciating predicament: "Mr. Matthews insists that in some apartment near London Wall, there is a gang of villains profoundly skilled in Pneumatic Chemistry who assail him by means of an Air Loom."[50] In Matthews's telling the gang has seven members—four men and three women—some of whom have names, some only nicknames, such as "Middle man" and the "School Master," based on their functions (see illustration). Like the Webster supposed by the *Quarterly* and the Byron supposed by Lady Byron, Matthews's mind is not its own place; its inside has an outside—a secret machinery, the machinery of the secret—which engineers what it thinks.[51] This penetration is not without its comforts. Haslam observes,

> Notwithstanding the dreadful sufferings which Mr. Matthews experiences from being assailed, he appears to derive some consolation from the sympathy which prevails between himself and the workers of the machine.—
> Perilous as his present situation may be, it would be rendered still more

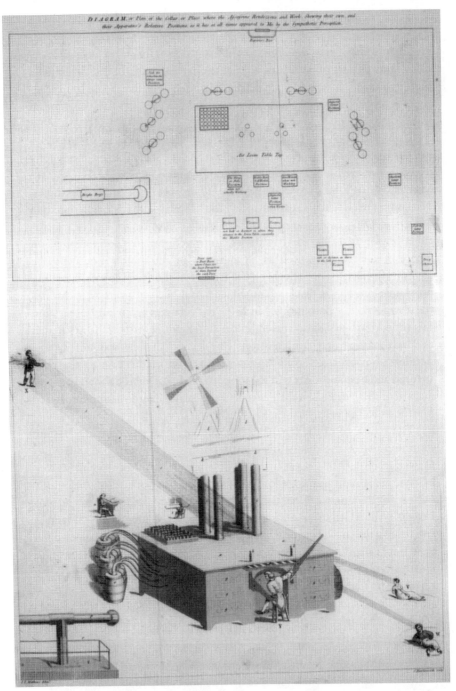

James Tilly Matthews, *DIAGRAM, or Plan of the Cellar, or Place, where the Assassins Rendezvous and Work.*

Source: John Haslam, *Illustrations of Madness* (London, 1810).

alarming if he could not watch their proceedings, and thus be prepared to avert the force of their engine. This reciprocal impregnation and continuity of warp enables him to perceive *their* motions and attain *their* thoughts. Such seems to be the law of this sympathy, that mutual intelligence is the result; nor can the assailants, with all their skill and dexterity, deprive him of this corresponding perception.[52]

The consoling conviction that the mind works in routine reciprocal interchange with the influences it receives locks in a paranoiac system.[53] To revise the praise that John Wilson applies to the poet of *Childe Harold*, Matthews, paranoiac, lives in sympathy with *a*, not *the*, "public mind"—his public is the "child" of his imagination; and the child in turn is the "father" of the madman.

Matthews's sympathy is part of a process not of identification with any individual assailant but of an identification of himself with a system of self-reflection that enables him to evade the full force of his pain by encoding it as knowledge.[54] He gains as he gives the life he images. Matthews's paranoid version of contemporary society was not unique. As we have seen, the Oriental tales represented the Western subject as a paranoid construction, and the most respected members of the Edinburgh publishing community indulged in megalomaniacal identifications with various despots. Roy Porter has argued that "Matthews's fear of the political use and abuse of Mesmerism was no singular paranoid delusion but a common perception of threats of danger from without."[55] Porter is in agreement with Charles James Fox, who (in J. Ann Hone's account of an October 1800 speech) attacked Pitt's oppression with the charge that "innocent men were confined in dungeons . . . on account of 'insurrections and rebellions which . . . *never did exist* but in the imagination of a *set of men who raise such reports* that they may the more easily depress the cause of freedom.'"[56] Kim Wheatley has shown in painstaking detail that the cultural discourse of the post-Waterloo era, unremittingly dualistic, was conducted under a paranoid scenario in which both the right and the left condemned objectionable acts and discourse as the consequence of satanic or (it is a synonym) "Jacobinical" manipulations.[57] The kind of personification of influences that in England was practiced both by Matthews and by the reviews has a structural affinity with the exclusively political explanation of events that, according to François Furet, characterized French revolutionary discourse, which subscribed to the belief in "a perfect fit between action, knowledge, and morality," and which reinforced its legitimacy by personifying causes of economic failure or social unrest as aristocratic enemies of the people.[58]

What distinguishes Matthews from the reviews in this respect is not the strength of his belief in the fit between action, knowledge, and morality but the way that belief is held. In Matthews's case the belief can be said to hold him. The perfect reflexivity of his system would seem to allow no space for self-reflection; his containment within the reflexive structure of his fantasy parallels his containment in the idiosyncrasy of his diction and justifies an institutional confinement that merely replicates it: there is a fit between the way Matthews is held by his belief and the way he is held by Bethlem Hospital. The reviewers who express similar paranoid delusions are, however, hired. Anonymous, there is no identification made between themselves *in propria persona* and the beliefs they express. Paid, they can be said, no matter how hysterical or vituperative they become, to write thus for reasons of self-interest. The founding of the *Quarterly* involved a deliberate decision arrived at by Murray in consultation with Scott, Canning, and Gifford, to set up a reflexive respondent to the *Edinburgh*. No matter how delusively paranoid the beliefs expressed in the articles, the reflexiveness is reflected upon by editors and publishers, by strategists and by the writers in their proper persons, any or all of whom might lay claim to stand outside of that belief, to be the one to have authorized it. In Matthews's case that position of authorization, left empty, is filled by Haslam in whose book and hospital Matthews's paranoid reflections appear and whose jurisdictional authority they corroborate.

Haslam could have been talking about Webster, Fox, Pitt, or George III. He could have been talking about Byron, whose sanity had been in dispute, perhaps using *Childe Harold* as evidence in conjunction with this remark of the poet's reported by Lady Blessington:

> The host of foes that now slumber, because they believe me out of their reach, and that their stings cannot touch me, would soon awake with renewed energies to assail and blacken me. The press, that powerful engine of a licentious age, (an engine known only in England as an invader of the privacy of life), would pour forth all its venom against me, ridiculing my person, misinterpreting my motives, misrepresenting my actions. I can mock at all these attacks when the sea divides me from them, but on the spot, and reading the effect of each libel in the alarmed faces of my selfishly-sensitive friends, whose common attentions, under such circumstances, seem to demand gratitude for the personal risk of abuse incurred by a contact with the delinquent,—No this I could not stand, because I once endured it, and never have forgotten what I felt under the infliction.[59]

That Byron was not Haslam's subject reflects not only the limits of the doctor's jurisdiction (Byron cannot be observed in Italy—even Lady

Blessington relies on a conversation that is granted to her), though that is significant; nor is it simply a question of class (George III was the site of just the kind of diagnostic and jurisdictional dispute that Matthews provoked). Byron's immunity remarks on the way his own fantasies are authorized so as to preserve him from the imputation of madness. Byron has access to print; Matthews does not. Indeed, Matthews's fantasy might be interpreted as his misprision of the importance of control of the machinery of production as a means to manage the version of oneself that is accepted by the world. Matthews's paranoia is of the same order as that of the Jacobins in Furet's interpretation: a singleminded insistence on political explanations for all events—whereas the air/heirloom represents the return of the social and economic unconscious repressed by revolutionaries and counterrevolutionaries alike.

Byronizing Bonaparte

> *I think [William Hone's] first acquaintance with [George Cruik-shank] was his wanting a plate re-touched (either Napoleon or Byron).*
>
> Mrs. Burns, *quoted in* Frederick William Hackwood, William Hone

> *By extracts in the English papers in your holy Ally — Galignani's messenger — I perceive that the "two greatest examples of human vanity-in the present age" — are firstly "the Ex-Emperor Napoleon" — and secondly — his Lordship the noble poet &c." — meaning your humble Servant — poor guiltless I" — Poor Napoleon! — he little dreamed to what "vile comparisons" the turn of his Wheel would reduce him.*
>
> Lord Byron to John Murray, December 4, 1821

As the amorous Lady Frances had already learned, Lord Byron was not J. Wedderburn Webster. Webster, Southey, Scott, and Byron—all claimed the spoils of the world-shattering Waterloo, but only one poet could walk away victor from that field. The *Quarterly*'s conceit of Webster as a printing press automatically printing out stereotypes provides a modern variant for the obsessive enterprise of baroque poets, who, in Walter Benjamin's words, "pile up fragments ceaselessly, without any strict idea of a goal, and, in the unremitting expectation of a miracle, take the repetition of stereotypes for a process of intensification."[60] Scott's success depended on the relinquishment of such dreams. Here he writes to his grace the duke of Buccleuch:

On Wednesday last, I rode over the field of Waterloo, now for ever consecrated to immortality. The more ghastly tokens of the carnage are now
removed, the bodies both of men and horses being either burned or buried;
but all the ground is still torn with the shot and shells, and covered with
cartridges, old hats, and shoes, and various relics of the fray which the
peasants have not thought worth removing. Besides, at Waterloo and all the
hamlets in the vicinage, there is a mart established for cuirasses; for the
eagles worn by the imperial guard on their caps; for casques, swords,
carabines, and similar articles. I have bought two handsome cuirasses, and
intend them, one for Bowhill, and one for Abbotsford, if I can get them safe
over, which Major Pryse Gordon has promised to manage for me. I have
also, for your Grace, one of the little memorandum-books, which I picked
up on the field, in which every French soldier was obliged to enter his
receipts and expenditure, his services, and even his punishments. The field
was covered with fragments of these records. I also got a good MS. collection
of French songs, probably the work of some young officer, and a croix of the
Legion of Honour.[61]

After the wreck of empire, relics. After the epochal thunder of battle, the
stilly murmur of the market. For Scott the world has returned to normal.
He's seen this before. The field could as easily be Culloden as Waterloo, and
Belgium the Highlands where he began his career by collecting the shreds of
an earlier social fabric—songs, swords, and all articles similar—to be
patched together in motley romances that would make his name and seal off
the consecrated past. The novelty of Waterloo for Scott is that Scott is now
a novelist and less concerned with the intensification of meaning than with
the preservation and multiplication of signs; his attention to account books
suggests less the poet's desire for apocalyptic consummation than the novelist's appetite for the ideology of the everyday. Not only does the crash of the
Napoleonic political and military edifice return us to the middle world of
buying and selling, it allows us to see that the routine of commerce was
going on all along, was indeed the material foundation on which that illusory edifice was so Romantically raised.

The miracle of intensification, which was withheld from Webster and
Southey and was renounced by Scott,[62] did happen for Byron, the great
baroque poet of the nineteenth century. It happened, crucially, in a poem
that, as Francis Jeffrey aptly observes, has no narrative (*RR* B:2:877). *Childe
Harold*'s narrated repudiation of a narrative, a repudiation coincident with
the negation of "life" and, with it, the realm of necessity, is its historical
distinction. The bold Byronic negation determines the end of the
Napoleonic narrative as the opening of a space of identifications and ex-

changes, a commerce designed and supervised by a speculative gaze. Bour-dieu writes that

> the detachment of the pure gaze cannot be separated from a general disposi-tion towards the "gratuitous" and the "disinterested," the paradoxical prod-uct of a negative economic conditioning which, through facility and free-dom, engenders distance vis à vis necessity. . . . Objective distance from necessity and from those trapped within it combines with a conscious dis-tance which doubles freedom by exhibiting it. As the objective distance from necessity grows, life-style increasingly becomes the product of what Weber calls a "stylization of life," a systematic commitment which orients and organizes the most diverse practices.[63]

The donation to Charles Dallas has become a "gratuity" offered to a British audience still mired in necessity—a gratuity, however, that solicits their guineas as the condition of their identification, and their identification as the condition of their ascendance into freedom and disinterest. Because gratuitous, the mere gesture of speculative reflection can be counted on to enliven, although, of course, the life created is only a simulacrum—or rather one simulacrum after another, to be displayed like pictures at an exhibition, each styled as a version of Byronic reflexiveness, each "the im-age," in Jeffrey's words, "of a being feeding and fed upon by violent pas-sions." The poem lines up Napoleon, Rousseau ("self-torturing sophist"), Voltaire ("He multiplied himself among mankind"), and Gibbon (the "lord of irony") as variations on a theme and as incomplete developments of a Byronic ego that realizes itself in a stylized reflection on and exhibition of its predecessors (*CH III*, sts. 77, 106, 107).[64]

Pride of place in the sequence is given to the case history of Napoleon Bonaparte. The most striking aspect of Lord Byron's Napoleon, "conqueror and captive of the earth" (*CH III*, st. 37), is his flagrant duality. Yet Napoleon's antithetical mix only positions him in a long line of equivocal beings from Milton's Satan to Dryden's Achitophel and on. It is insuffi-ciently distinctive to explain his spectacular historical success. As Byron develops Bonaparte's portrait, however, the historically specific dynamics of that dizzying achievement become clear. Napoleon moved men because, Corsair-like, he moved minds. Napoleon succeeded because he speculated in "men's thoughts [which] were the steps which paved [his] throne, / *Their* admiration [his] best weapon shone" (st. 41). The fundament of Napoleon's ascent was the image he created in the eyes of public opinion. His rise was his return on the life the Napoleonic image gave. Lord Byron does not fault Napoleon for that speculation. He criticizes Napoleon for having forgotten the groundlessness of his triumph, for having forgotten that the practical steps he took to the throne were on a theoretical ladder and that the height attained was no real summit but the image of a height, as he himself was the image of a monarch to the public that gave him life:

> Sager than in thy fortunes; for in them
> Ambition steel'd thee on too far to show
> That just habitual scorn which could contemn
> Men and their thoughts; 'twas wise to feel, not so
> To wear it ever on thy lip and brow,
> And spurn the instruments thou wert to use
> Till they were turn'd unto thine overthrow.
>
> (st. 40)

Napoleon fell because of his scorn, not, however, because of the scorn he felt—such feelings are irrelevant to history—but because of the scorn he showed on a countenance that expressed too well his "want of all community of feeling for or with [mankind]" (st. 41n).

Napoleon was brought down by what Byron would later call, in his dispute with Murray over the staging of his historical dramas, a "cursed attempt at representation" (*BLJ* 8:66), which was no character flaw but the very condition of Napoleon's rule. Had Napoleon possessed the ring of Gyges, which endowed its wearer with invisibility, he might have been able to rule unseen and prevent the scornful semblance that led to his fall. But that myth of tyranny, which in all of its classical versions presumes that a monarch is in place and that Gyges is therefore already in a position to rule when he dons the amulet, does not answer to the political reality of nineteenth-century Europe: here there was no natural way for Napoleon to ascend, no monarch to hand him ring and kingdom; and the public, having abandoned what Hume calls that "superstitious reverence for princes, which mankind naturally contract when they do not often see the sovereign," was in no state to be dictated to by a veiled (let alone invisible) usurper. Such a man, according to Benjamin Constant, "must always be at the head of his Praetorian Guard. If he were not their idol, he would be the object of their contempt."[65] The same vacuum of authority that was the condition of Napoleon's speculative success prescribed that Napoleon both attain and maintain his position by a repeated theatrical self-display that could only occupy an uneasily ironic relation to the Jacobin tradition of the revolutionary festival.[66] Napoleon succeeded by transforming Europe into a stage for his own astonishing improvisations, his gifted impersonation of a monarch. Yet he fell because even a talented, chameleonic actor's face will, after a long run, eventually settle into a habitual expression; the luster decays, and the formerly enlivening image becomes a disposable icon. As Constant warns, "When the great mass of the nation is reduced to the role of spectators forced into silence, in order to induce these spectators to applaud, or even simply to look, the impresarios of the show must stimulate their curiosity by *coups de théâtre* and scene changes."[67] Napoleon's scorn froze the speculative dynamic, forcing the public to see its own servility— disastrous for a ruler whose fortune was hostage to opinion, whose face-to-face encounters with the French people had been the enabling pretexts for an imperial career.

Constant's brilliant critique of rule by right of conquest anticipated and perhaps influenced Byron's formulation:

> The conqueror will . . . see that he has presumed too much upon the degra-dation of the world. He will learn that calculations based upon immorality and baseness, those calculations on which he prided himself so recently as a sublime discovery, are as uncertain as they are short-sighted, as deceptive as they are ignoble. He laughed at the stupidity of virtue, at that trust in a disinterestedness that seemed to him a chimera. . . . Now he discovers that egoism has its own brand of stupidity: . . . that, in order to know men, it is not sufficient to despise them. Mankind becomes an enigma to him. All around him people talk of generosity, of sacrifices, of devotion. This un-familiar language comes as a surprise to his ears. He has no idea how to negotiate in that idiom. He remains paralysed, shocked by his failure to understand, a memorable example of Machiavellianism fallen victim to its own corruption.[68]

Unlike the king, the dandiacal conqueror, albeit a child of imagination not nature, has only one unreproducible body—a body that, like all things, suffers corruption and death.[69]

The lesson that a stymied Lord Byron learned from his wife and her lawyers, the lesson that the abject Corsair learns from Gulnare, is the lesson that the poet draws from the fall of Napoleon. In the words of John B. Thompson, "When domination can only be exercised in this 'elementary' form—that is, between persons rather than via institutions—it must be disguised beneath the veil of an enchanted relationship, lest it destroy itself by revealing its true nature and provoking a violent response from the victims or forcing them to flee."[70] In the end, Napoleon is as much a prisoner to his body as Brummell, and just as much an anachronism. The successor to that "elementary," Napoleonic form of domination is Byron-ism: indulgence in the fantasy of domination cohabits with the exposure of domination as a fantasy, composing the cultural sign that domination—mediated, ironized—is no longer a threat. Byronism modernizes Napoleonic domination into an invisible, gentler symbolic violence. "Gentle because accepted, invisible because unseen for what it is, symbolic violence," according to Thompson, "is characterized by a distinctive *mélange* of recognition (*reconnaissance*) and misrecognition (*méconnaissance*); and it is by virtue of this *mélange* that symbolic violence is an effective medium of social reproduction."[71] Whether or not it is because, as Francis Jeffrey notes, "men do not *pass their days* in reading poetry . . . and may look into Lord Byron only about as often as they look abroad on tempests" (*RR* B:2:865–66), the fact that readers will, for the most part, respond to the volcanic disclosure of Byronic "darkness" and contempt (see *CH III*, sts. 68–69) without fleeing or fighting indicates that this professed disenchantment has achieved its effect. By translating the instrument of domination from ceremonies to books Byronism assists in the displacement of domination from sovereign persons to the public sphere—a sphere that includes the Edinburgh reviewer as well as the English bard.

Making Byron Fit

I must command or be silent.

Napoleon Bonaparte, *Las Cases*, Memoirs

Peter Hohendahl has argued that at the end of the eighteenth century "literature served the emancipation movement of the middle class as an instrument to gain self-esteem and to articulate its human demands against the absolutist state and the hierarchical society."[72] The illusory basis of this self-esteem and of "human" emancipation was sealed by the intimate affiliation between the public's idea of itself and refinements of printing technology and publishing technique. From *Childe Harold III* on it becomes important to distinguish between Byronism, the name for the speculative machine owned and operated by John Murray, and Lord Byron. The pilgrim of *Childe Harold III* may no more than Napoleon have found his "fitting medium of desire," but "Byron" is identical with its medium. As Byron wrote to Murray, denying authorship of John Polidori's *Vampire*, "There is a rule to go by—you are my publisher (till we quarrel) and what is not published by you is not written by me" (*BLJ* 7:125). Byronic distance is not absolute but an effect of mediation, and thus whether we consider the poem according to its usage as a commodity or according to its self-representation as a gratuity, Lord Byron's freedom is constrained. And so Jeffrey, notifying the poet of a deficit of readerly pleasure, pedantically reminds him: "A public benefactor becomes a debtor to the public; and is, in some degree, responsible for the employment of those gifts which seem to be conferred upon him, not merely for his own delight, but for the delight and improvement of his fellows through all generations" (*RR* B:2:866). Lord Byron was certainly susceptible to this mode of ornate compliment, which cloaks the demands of commerce in the figures of an aristocratic morality, and he will tailor his desire to fit—"till we quarrel," that is. The qualification was prophetic, for during the course of *Don Juan* Lord Byron would "spurn" the instrument of Murray's house and would suffer the consequence, Murray's "well known endeavor to destroy every publication of mine—which don't pass through his own medium" (*BLJ* 10:135).

Such complaints about the reflexive mode of *Childe Harold* as were expressed publicly by Jeffrey, as well as privately by Murray, presumed the capacity of the poet to make the adjustments requested. The literary system called Byron, then, was imagined as possessing a second order of reflection capable of regarding its own reflexiveness from a distance, a capacity that neither Webster nor Matthews, nor finally Napoleon, has. Psychiatry, of course, has that power. It represents figures of reflexiveness, characters "feeding and fed upon by violent passions" in the institutional space of Bethlem Hospital, which is designed to enforce a strategic distance between doctor and patient. Haslam replicates the institutional scheme in the discursive space of his book in order to augment institutional power through the accrual of professional authority and social credit.

Stage would, however, be an inexact metaphor for Haslam's reformed Bethlem Hospital. He explicitly breaks with the theatrical metaphor in his criticism of the "management" techniques promoted by Dr. Cox in his *Practical Observations on Insanity* for treatment of hallucinations "the correction of which has resisted our very best exertions." Cox advocates trying "the effect of certain deceptions, contrived to make strong impressions on the senses, by means of *unexpected, unusual, striking,* or apparently *supernatural* agents; . . . by *imitated thunder,* or soft music . . . ; *combating* the erroneous deranged notion, either by some *pointed sentence,* or signs *executed in phosphorus* upon the wall of the bed chamber; or by some *tale, assertion, or reasoning;* by one in the character of an *angel, prophet,* or *devil:* but the actor in this drama," Cox warns, "must possess much *skill, and be very perfect in his part.*" It is striking how closely Cox's theatrical techniques for correcting hallucinations parallel both Conrad's repertoire of devices for swaying his pirate band and for surprising Seyd ("Up rose the Dervise with that burst of light, / Nor less his change of form appall'd the sight" [*Corsair* 2:142–43]) and the torments applied by Matthews's assailers in his paranoid narratives. The paranoid is characterized by his reflexive ability to recuperate attempts at correction as elaborations of his persecutory scenario—a capacity that Byron will perfect and parody in *Don Juan*. In opposition to Cox, Haslam abjures theatrics in favor of the more modest "service" of "establishing a system of regularity in the actions of insane people," who, he advises, "should be made to rise, take exercise, and food at stated times. Independently of such regularity contributing to health, it also renders them much more easily manageable."[73]

The institution of "Byron," jointly enfranchised by the holy alliance of reviewer, poet, and publisher, had a similar regulative function. Jeffrey vividly figures the scene of cultural instruction:

> A great living poet is not like a distant volcano, or an occasional tempest. He is a volcano in the heart of our land, and a cloud that hangs over our dwellings; and we have some cause to complain, if, instead of genial warmth and grateful shade, he darkens and inflames our atmosphere with perpetual explosions of fiery torrents and pitchy vapours. Lord Byron's poetry, in short, is too attractive and too famous to lie dormant or inoperative; and therefore, if it produce any painful or pernicious effects, there will be murmurs, and ought to be suggestions of alteration.

Readers *have* felt pain, Jeffrey among them. Readers have reason to complain, Jeffrey representative of them. "Even our admiration," the critic descants, "is at last swallowed up in a most painful feeling of pity and wonder" (*RR* B:2:866). The conceit is an odd one, nonetheless. Volcanoes are not famous for their responsiveness to petitions or even to the sacrifice of poets. The sublime metaphor that specifies the strength and threat of Lord Byron's poetry fundamentally contradicts the professed aim of correction. How can one expect a volcano to make adjustments? Under the regime of his conceit, Jeffrey's suggestion of "alteration" comes to exemplify one of Donald Davidson's "paradoxes of irrationality": "The agent [Lord Byron, in this case] has reasons for changing his own habits and character, but those reasons come from a domain of values necessarily extrinsic to the contents of the views or values to undergo change. The cause of the change, if it comes, can therefore not be a reason for what it causes."[74]

Jeffrey's conceit may be too neat an example of the paradox, since the volcano, metaphor for poetic agency, is quintessentially a thing that changes without reason. Such neatness is suspicious. Jeffrey splits "Byron" into two halves: one, spontaneously explosive, that can take no instructions—

the volcano; and another that can be imagined to take suggestions to alter—that so to speak channels the lava away from homes and factories. The former moiety, the volcano, is the public image of the strong poet. The latter, wholly discontinuous with the former, might be called the critic; it is the part of "Byron" that corresponds to Jeffrey's own relation to poets. Jeffrey depicts a curtailed notion of the poet, whose "agency," compared with a phenomenon of nature, is hardly that of an agent, and of the critic, who offers his prudential reasons to that poet from a theoretically unspannable distance. Jeffrey thus figures with reasonable accuracy the division of labor that obtains in the literary system called Byron, between an exuberant and incorrigible poet and the various hands responsible for taming that spontaneous overflow.

Jeffrey's critical instruction is scenic rather than substantive. He does not follow up his suggestion to alter with the prescription of any pattern. Although he admonishes the poet to be more ethical ("A great poet is necessarily a Moral Teacher, and gives forth his ethical lessons, in general, with far more effect and authority than any of his graver brethren" [*RR* B:2:866]), he does not indicate what being ethical might mean. The poet is enjoined to be more fit, but unlike other reviewers of *Childe Harold* from the right and left, Jeffrey paints no picture of a moral or literary reality that the poet might fit himself to, even if he were of a mind to do so. Criticism minds its business of praise and blame. Though urged to alter, the poet qua poet, it is presumed, will erupt as he wills.

Consider the conclusion of *Childe Harold III* in Jeffrey's light. The poem figures a resolution to its serial reflections by closing round on itself with a framing wish not for the speculative child of the imagination but for the natural child of "house and heart." It began,

> Is thy face like thy mother's my fair child,
> Ada, sole daughter of my house and heart?
> When last I saw the young blue eyes they smiled,
> And when we parted,—not as now we part,
> But with a hope.
>
> (*CH III*, st. 1)

It reflexively ends,

> My daughter! with thy name this song begun
> My daughter! with thy name thus much shall end—
> I see thee not, I hear thee not, but none
> Can be so wrapt in thee; thou art the friend

To whom the shadows of far years extend:
Albeit my brow thou never shouldst behold,
My voice shall with thy future visions blend.
(st. 115)

Though he has been defaced by distance, the poet's ending wish for a face-to-face encounter reintegrates the preceding succession of speculations. By facing those wishes against each other like parentheses in specular complicity, the writer situates the series of Byronic stereotypes within a sentimentally human context: the figure of the author, whose face all but presents itself in these accents forlorn, whose life appears in the specular transaction between the beginning and end of the canto. The *Christian Observer* takes the point and applauds the trope: "His lordship's really feeling apostrophe to his daughter, with whose name his song began, and with those name it ends, is almost the only part of his personal allusions in which we feel much sympathy" (*RR* B:2:601).

Practically speaking, whatever sounds with such moral resonance has implications both formal and prudential. Byron's appeal to personal sympathy solves the formal problem emergent from the peculiar economy by which poems have come to be valued. As we have seen, the difficulty of fitting a poem to a fair price—associated with the eclipse of conventional indicators of value—led to the positing of a proper length. "A poem the length of Rokeby" arbitrarily sets a standard of measurement both formal and economic. Because *Childe Harold III* was planned and greeted as a poem without any parallel (not even with its predecessors *Harold I* and *II*), however, a fit price could not be decided by comparison with a *Rokeby* or *Lalla Rookh* or anything else. The uncertainty of what would be a fit price is represented in the poem, aptly enough, as the problem of finding the proper length for an assemblage of desultory verses that has no narrative, no action, and no genre except that nominal one called Byron—the problem, that is, of somehow fitting beginning to end. The appeal to human sympathy, the nostalgia for a face, is the phantom of natural value enlisted to close off the poem and form the commodity: a fair shape with a fair price.

Jeffrey stubbornly refuses to sympathize, however: "The closing stanzas of the poem are extremely beautiful; but we are immoveable in the resolution that no statement of ours shall ever give additional publicity to the subjects of which they treat" (*RR* B:2:878). Jeffrey has the scandal of the separation directly in mind, but he establishes the principle of repudiating "subjects" that have to do with the poet's life. Jeffrey's principle harmonizes with the poet's own strictures against embodiment and maintains the tenor

of his other critical pronouncements, which disparage the fit or correspondence between the poem and the known world. Jeffrey understands Byron as
what contemporary philosophers would call a "language game," a vocabulary capable of assimilating other ways of speaking to its own. Lord Byron,
he acutely comments,

> is a great mimic of styles and manners, and a great borrower of external
> character. He and Mr. Scott are full of imitations of all the writers from
> whom they have ever derived gratification; and the two most original writ-
> ers of the age might appear, to superficial observers, to be the most deeply
> indebted to their predecessors. In this particular instance, we have no fault
> to find with Lord Byron: for undoubtedly the finer passages of Wordsworth
> and Southey have in them wherewithal to give an impulse to the utmost
> ambition of rival genius. . . . But we must say, that it would afford us still
> greater pleasure to find these tuneful gentlemen returning the compliment
> which Lord Byron has here paid to their talents, and forming themselves on
> the model rather of his imitations, than of their own originals.

In this Baudrillardian trope, Jeffrey endorses mimicry, fitting one's language
to another's, as a welcome equivocation of the orders of original and copy.
The true original, the language called Byron, is that poetry capable of the
"most concise and condensed" recombinations of the vocabularies of others
(*RR* B:2:865).

The logical conclusion of such a position is the sort of blurring of the
boundaries between "languages" that Richard Rorty favors. Rorty writes, "I
have no criterion of individuation for distinct languages or vocabularies to
offer, but I am not sure that we need one. Philosophers have used phrases
like 'in the language of L' for a long time without worrying too much about
how one can tell where one natural language ends and another begins."[75]
But Jeffrey balks at this step. He censures Lord Byron for the monstrousness
of his heroes on the ground that their "peccant" nature is not justified by a
narrative design. "In Lord Byron . . . the interest of the story . . . is uni-
formly postponed to that of the character itself—into which he enters so
deeply, and with so extraordinary a fondness, that he generally continues to
speak in its language, after it has been dismissed from the stage; and to
inculcate, on his own authority, the same sentiments which had been previously recommended by its example" (*RR* B:2:866). Jeffrey seems to be
rejecting the fitness of the speculation by which the poet claims to have
been endowed with life, and implicitly to be renouncing the simulacrum
effect that he acclaimed in Byron's mimicry of Wordsworth—the trick of

language by which Byron becomes more genuinely the original than the original.

Jeffrey is not really objecting to the content of the sentiments exemplified and inculcated nor even, I think, to the depth of the identification (recall the water bucket in Addison's Oriental tale). What makes the "fondness" of Byron for the sentiments of his hero excessive is the *carry-over* or blurring between character and poet, here conceived less as a "he" and an "I" than as separate languages. The objection to a transmission of sentiments correlates with the fear of contamination obsessively thematized in Byron's poetry and in the reviews. And no doubt Jeffrey is worrying about the integrity of the proverbial middle-class reader. If the poet carries something away from his identification with his character, what will happen to the reader? But there is a deeper problem with the "authority" by which the poet inculcates his character's sentiments. It is one thing for Wordsworth to be ventriloquized by Byron, but quite another for an "author" to be "authorizing" as his own the views of a character. In the former case there is simply a shift of authority to authors one likes from authors one does not. In the latter case the author's authority seems to be the *effect* of a character—either the literary character of Childe Harold or the literal character *I*. The foundation of his authority is mixed up with fiction.

There is yet another corollary of this blurring that, given the way Jeffrey constructs Byron, seems particularly damaging. Recall that the ground for elevating Byron's Wordsworthian language over Wordsworth's own version was Byron's superior economy, his concision and condensation. Byron saves time. The carry-over of sentiment and tone, however, retards the propulsive movement of the poem. It is fair (not simply stupid or moralistic) for Jeffrey to claim that Byron turns "the means of improvement to the purposes of corruption," not merely because the poem dramatizes the possible contamination of a reader by its character but because the progress of the poem, from scene to scene, maxim to maxim, is corrupted by the aftereffect or "overshade" (*RR* B:2:872) of the character. Jeffrey objects to blurring as he objects to monotony: as the spread of a tone from one panel in the stations of the pilgrim to succeeding ones. The pleasure that Jeffrey takes in Byron is the pleasure he takes in novelty. He shares entirely the aesthetic disposition of the reviewer of *Hours of Idleness*—who asked for something "in a little degree different." For Jeffrey, the only "fit speculation" is profitable (i.e., progressive) speculation, which requires a succession of determinate and novel images. He wants poems to contain and thus *be* those counters that Coleridge contemns. *Childe Harold*'s passages are, then, criticized for being insufficiently counterlike. They resist the kind of dexterous manipulation, the mosaic making, that for Jeffrey is critical practice.

Because it fetishizes the commodity, Jeffrey's criticism, like his political economy, has a strangely archaic flavor, despite its avowed progressiveness. The separation of images (for the purpose of speculation) and the separation of volcano and alterer (to reinforce division of labor) are partitions that imply purification. The insistence on the immaculateness of the object—a purity so intense that it is everywhere imperiled by contact—becomes a way of incorporating stimulus into apparently innocent acts, like buying, like reading. Such is the scenario that Gothics depict and the function that the late-eighteenth-century Gothic served. In the Napoleonic era Gothic allegory gives way to a more sophisticated understanding of the commodity form, as Coleridge intuited in the 1798 *Christabel* and as he theorized in the 1815 *Biographia Literaria*. For the Napoleonic consumer of principalities and dominions, each country is stripped of its local distinction and is reduced to nothing more than a counter, a chip in a high-status game. But the connection of conqueror and gambler taught Coleridge what it did not teach the liberal Constant, who read in it only the portent of inevitable catastrophe: Coleridge recognized that a mere counter could itself excite and thereby become not simply the instrument but the very basis of continued play.[76] De-Gothicized, frisson follows (as Addison knew it would) mere novelty.

But although this change reflects Enlightenment disenchantment, it also proves that such disenchantment did not and cannot go all the way. As Mary Douglas has argued, there is no conceptual break between ritual immaculateness and marketable novelty.[77] Commodity exchange retains its ritualized ambivalence. What the anthropologist argues Lord Byron shows: the performance of his career is the sign for the preconscious recognition of the survival of ritual thinking even among the progressive Whigs of the *Edinburgh Review*. Byron's aristocracy is important as the assurance of an immaculateness of blood that absolves such merely technical offenses as mimicry and ultimately insures "originality" and "authenticity." On the other hand, Lord Byron's purity, as Jeffrey figures it, is, like Leila's, the site of an inevitable degradation—in class terms it is contaminated by the coin of the bourgeois consumer. In the cultural representations of Lord Byron there is a nearly seamless connection between identification of him as commodity to be consumed and as sacrificial victim to be raped, buggered, polluted, dismembered, degraded. As we have seen, a great deal of the interest of his career resides in the question whether the process of pleasurable consump-

tion of novelties or proper names overtakes and secularizes sacrificial violence, or (as Jeffrey seems to suspect) whether Byron's career displays the
inexorable carry-over of an earlier, presymbolic violence into its symbolic
successor. What makes that question interesting is that it can never be
conducted in security by disinterested observers, because unlike Leila and
like Gulnare and Kaled, Lord Byron is a commodity that resists consumption, a commodity that writes back.

Reduced to its rhetorical elements, Jeffrey's advice to Byron amounts to
"Be less what I don't like." He is, moreover, a critic smart enough to know
that he won't know what he likes until the strong poet writes another poem.
Beneath the aggressive monotony of Jeffrey's criticism lurks what Coleridge
nervously perceived, a prophet of liberalism—not because Jeffrey has anything meaningful to say, but because he so influentially does not. Jeffrey's
and Haslam's notions of management and discipline may have a progressive
tendency, but progress toward *what* neither man could say: the cure for
madness, as for volcanoes, remains concealed. What Matthews says of his
imaginary persecutors—that they "make a merit of event-working, . . .
never indeed, to benefit me; but as pursuing their systems of villany [*sic*],
calling me their *Property* and *Talisman*"[78]—might as aptly be applied to
Haslam, who aims to "illustrate" madness, not cure Matthews. In the process Matthews's story is transformed into a case with the talismanic power
to certify and extend professional authority. Similarly, Jeffrey cannot imagine a Byron other than Byron and indeed does not wish to. The metaphor of
the volcano expresses his fundamental satisfaction with the natural poet as
cultural talisman.

The more Jeffrey's ethical casts come up empty, however, the more the
suggestions for alteration—Jeffrey's moral management—begin to look
compulsive. In one sense the compulsiveness responds to the kind of anxiety
expressed by the *Christian Observer:* "No man who lets off a poem every six
months, can reasonably hope to attract attention to his performances" (*RR*
B:2:596).[79] In the broadest sense Jeffrey figures a Byron who will legitimate
his own quasi-professional talk—as Haslam's talk, equally cut off from cure
or content, is legitimated by the phenomenon of the madman. But since the
language of management needs to mask its complicity with something—
mad or volcanic—that cannot by definition *be* complicitous, management
begins to look if anything more compulsive than the natural outbursts of the
volcano or madman. Such is the moral of the story that Roy Porter tells
about Haslam, who ended up as the paranoid product of the system he
supervised. Porter generalizes that moral to apply to institutional psychiatry as a whole.[80] I would extend it to apply to the inevitable maddening of a

kind of criticism, whether formalism or ideology critique, that would legitimate itself in terms of an impossibly pure separation from its object.

As Jeffrey's concern with "overshading" illustrates, the desire to partition and divide responds not to some natural thing merchandisable as book but to something equivocal that works like a text. In *Childe Harold III* "sentiments" slide from character to author not because they are possessed with some Byronic virus, but because there is no perfect fit between the language employed and any single character that the text represents. The peculiar dynamics of the poem are not only metaphorized but enacted in the equivocal word *fit*, which appears often and variously in the canto: "fit speculation" (st. 10), "Then came his fit again" (st. 15), "fit retribution" (st. 19), "fitting medium of desire" (st. 42), "fit mind" (st. 68), "not fit" (st. 69). The word sometimes suggests the synonym of *decorous* or *correspondent*, sometimes the synonym of *convulsion*—the kind of fit, one might say, that is the perfect antithesis of a good fit. *Fit* seems to be an apt word for a text in which every claimed correspondence is a performed convulsion and in which every dramatized convulsion indicates an attempted correspondence. *Fit* is the word for that idiosyncratic estrangement by which all characters enter the poem: "And fitly may the stranger lingering here" (st. 57). It is, shall we say, the supremely fitting word for the textual practice of *Childe Harold* because the fits of *Childe Harold* are not staged, not figures on a ground. They are the apparitions of a text whose spasms are continuous with its elaboration—apparitions because they ambiguously personify a poem that is, like its neo-Spenserian predecessors, technically a "fytte" (*CH I*, st. 93) from beginning to end. *Fytte* is a formal term with performative implications—since, as George Ellis argued, to assume the form of the Spenserian stanza is to demonstrate its anachronism (*RR* B:5:1991–92). To cling to it argues for the failure of the poet to find the "fitting medium" of his style—no great concern with a poet like Samuel Rogers or Thomas Campbell; but it is traumatic for a criticism in the process of developing a historicist agenda to discover that the poet who gives to the contemporary its period style has nothing more proper to him than his name. Because the Byronic career (a diachronic, multifariously articulated social composition), and not his life or his sentiments or his body, is the material basis for the reproduction of the Byronic text, that text will always produce correspondences that are convulsive—whether between the character and poet, between the poem and its price, between the poet and reader, between the image and reality, between beginning and end. The Byronic text will continually have fits, because, as the Byronic text performatively states, there is no perfect fit.

The implications of that statement must be pursued on a case-by-case basis. Consider Matthews one last time. The assumption that he is truly mad, what today would be called a paranoid schizophrenic, depends on a closure of that mind from the minds of others: its convulsiveness and the absolute reflexive symmetry of its world-view are complementary symptoms that clinch the diagnosis. This madness is not something that Matthews could be putting on. Yet if we look again at the chief illustration of Haslam's *Illustrations*, the pictorial display of the specular structure of Matthews's madness, we can find the one detail that Haslam had to overlook in order to fashion his talisman. It is not in the picture, or rather its part in the picture equivocates the relations between inside and outside the picture: the signature of J. T. Matthews. This ability to sign himself outside the frame is graphic evidence of the lack of a perfect fit between what is inside the frame and the mind it supposedly illustrates. The signature is no evidence of Matthews's reflection on his condition, nor does it prove that he is the author of his condition—it is not evidence of his sanity but evidence that the opposition between sane and insane is, as the unfortunate Haslam was to "learn" only too well, mad. Matthews is no revolutionary overturner of the established order—no Luddite of psychiatry. He is, as Lord Byron had aptly said of himself, but "half a framebreaker" (*BLJ* 2:166). Matthews's signature is only the claim that he must be given credit for the picture, as its designer.[81] And as Byron's Cain will learn, there is no fit between the designer and what he has designed that is not convulsive.

Cain is pertinent because *fit* works in *Childe Harold III* as *B* in Freud's Bain and Abel story does (see chap. 4 above) and as murder in Byron's *Cain* does not: it produces recognizable change bloodlessly, allegorically. Rendering the allegory of the text's production does not answer the question of the deliberateness of Byron's employment of his words. If we were in *Don Juan*, we would probably want to invest in the conclusion that such a fanciful, punning sort of play was deliberate. This is not a manner that has been attributed to the poet of *Childe Harold*; and in part, the sense of a progress through the stages of an artistic career—early, middle, and late—requires the tacit deferral of his deliberateness. But both Jeffrey's reading of the overshading effect and the operation of *fit* make such staging of Byron seem tendentious, as if the convulsions were feigned for the purposes of effect.

As we know, in eighteenth-century tragic theater "having" a fit was a scripted demand and a technical acquirement derived from the repertoire of classical rhetoric: aposiopesis, the designed suspension of action for dramatic effect.[82] The most apposite example in *Childe Harold III* is the strong line beginning stanza 17: "Stop!—for thy tread is on an Empire's dust!" The dash opens the space for the commanded halt to occur; and in the sense that it can be located along that line, the convulsive suspension of the narrative is decorous, enacted according to the direction of the script. Yet the line does not quite observe the decorum suggested by the rhetorical tag. The subordinate clause that follows the dash attaches a Jeffreyan *reason* for stopping— as if the stop were to occur in response to the reason, at the end of the line. Yet however pathetic be the dust of empire, that supplementary reason, according to Davidson's paradox, could have no effect on the reader's response *to the imperative:* either the reader has stopped directly upon "Stop!" or he or she will be more or less likely not to stop at all—probability is introduced by the rhetoric of reasons. The supplemental clause, meant to enhance the imperative, dissipates the certainty of its authoritative force. The punctual integrity of the aposiopesis, its design, is convulsed by its performance.

I have said *the reader*, but of course the most pressing equivocation here is the subject of address: on whom does the lot of the imperative fall? As Byron continually and disturbingly demonstrates, maximal condensation entails maximal discrepancy. It would be hard to be more concise or condensed than "Stop!" which is, nonetheless, exactly that "one word" in *Childe Harold III* where it is not clear whom Lord Byron is addressing. It is true that for anyone who reads on, the "Stop!" must equivocally resolve its addressee either as Harold or the poet himself (and what is the difference?), "both" of whom "stand" on the field of Waterloo. No other reader does in fact tread on empire's dust. Yet until the reader gets *past* the "Stop!" he or she cannot summon sufficient context to know that the command is in fact addressed to another. The good reader will stop. The good reader is that reader obedient to the maxim "If the imperative fits, obey it." Note that, unlike Kant's moral, this is a *conditional* imperative—which remarks on the fact that although the imperative requires a decision right away, because a decision *is* required, one has first to decide on the justice of the address that requires it. The imperative can only fit, correspond to a reader, by what Jacques Derrida, after Kierkegaard, calls the "madness" of a "moment of decision"[83]— that is, by a convulsive suspension of that habitual sense of self sufficient to decide to be that one who obeys. The obligatory force of the imperative is partly the effect of the convulsiveness with which it connects to me and partly due to the fact that the "me" to whom that word applies is in an imperfect fit with any real addressee of this or any imperative. The stopping of the reader is not scripted or contractual—nor is it theatrical. "Stop!" returns us to the unreasonably rhetorical and ethical basis for the theatrical effect. It instantiates what, in a fine phrase, Laurence Lockridge has called

Byron's "ethics of predicament."[84] The imperative word *conquers* its reader and in doing so disrupts the tentatively achieved proportions of the poem, the architecture of reasons it gives to justify the time spent in its consumption. To seize on "Stop!" as the one word that succeeds precisely by its immunity to the sentimental desire to "wreak" one's "thoughts upon expression"—that succeeds because it is a site of decision—invites us to consider the rest of the poem, all its words, as the frame for this unique performance and to marvel at how many stanzas can fit on the end of a stop.

6

The Shaping Spirit of Ruin

Childe Harold IV

There can be no limits set to the interest that attaches to a great poet thus going forth, like a spirit, from the heart of a powerful and impassioned people, to range among the objects and events to them most pregnant with passion, who is, as it were, the representative of our most exalted intellect. . . . The consciousness that he is so considered by a great people, must give a kingly power and confidence to a poet. He feels himself entitled, and, as it were, elected to survey the phenomena of the times, and to report upon them in poetry. He is the speculator of the passing might and greatness of his generation.

John Wilson, *review of* Childe Harold IV, Blackwood's, *June 1818*

The fourth canto of *Childe Harold* slouches from nature to culture, from the weather to the weathered: "I stood in Venice on the Bridge of Sighs, / A palace and a prison on each hand" (st. 1). "Power," according to Selim's dictum, "sways but by division." As the Venetian plays will dramatize, splitting society between palace and prison is the technique by which the oligarchy rules. Here Lord Byron's colossal command of both principle and place announces his authority to dictate the moral of civilized history to a captive audience.

England has a special relationship with Venice:

But unto us she hath a spell beyond
Her name in story, and her long array
Of mighty shadows, whose dim forms despond
Above the dogeless city's vanish'd sway;
Ours is a trophy which will not decay

With the Rialto; Shylock and the Moor
And Pierre can not be swept or worn away,
The keystones of the arch!—though all were o'er,
For us repeopled were the solitary shore.

The beings of the mind are not of clay;
Essentially immortal, they create
And multiply in us a brighter ray
And more beloved existence. That which Fate
Prohibits to dull life in this our state
Of mortal bondage, by these spirits supplied,
First exiles, then replaces what we hate;
Watering the heart whose early flowers have died,
And with a fresher growth replenishing the void.

Such is the refuge of our youth and age,
The first from Hope, the last from Vacancy;
And this worn feeling peoples many a page,
And, may be, that which grows beneath mine eye.
Yet there are things whose strong reality
Outshines our fairy-land; in shape and hues
More beautiful than our fantastic sky,
And the strange constellations; which the Muse
O'er her wild universe is skilful to diffuse:

I saw or dream'd of such,—but let them go,—
They came like truth, and disappear'd like dreams.

(sts. 4–7)

Bound to Venice by the fascinating literary representations of her that English writers have spelled out, England dominates the Queen of the Adriatic more than doge has ever done. Though attributed to Shakespeare, Otway, and Radcliffe, this empire of the imagination is quintessentially Byronic, for Lord Byron interprets the displacement of Venetian reality by English literature in light of the colonization he has already executed in his own Oriental tales, thereby fashioning an identification of Byron's destiny with the ambitions of post-Napoleonic Britain as audacious and compelling as Napoleon's earlier identification with the aims of postrevolutionary France.

The speculative dialectic that galvanizes *Childe Harold III* is here put to imperial use by means of a thoroughgoing objectification of the image—the storied past becomes a "trophy"—and a complementary hollowing out of the subject, described as a clay vessel through which "beloved existences" pass. The blurry personification of "Fate" allows the poet to mobilize energy around the act of "exile" without becoming specific about agent or object. What is exiled is something that "we" hate, but the "we" is a subject that both includes the poet and notoriously excludes him as well. Lord Byron imagines himself as both victim and exploiter of the historical process that he describes with such Hegelian verve. In the waning stanzas of the third canto, Lord Byron had exploited nature's fabled abhorrence of a vacuum (*CH III*, sts. 101–2). Voided, he had, as he notes in his journal, "repeopled my mind with nature" (*BLJ* 5:99). The enabling discovery of *Childe Harold IV* is that commerce makes itself a second nature by creating vacuums that it can then naturally fill. The way Byron's mind works is the way British commercial society works. The way British society works is the way everyone's mind will work. Byronic self-division has become the model for the recursive machine of Britain's imperial self-division: exiling a hateful reality *in order* to "multiply" representations that can replenish the void. *Childe Harold's* momentous "Stop!" can be rationalized as a more than Malthusian injunction not only against breeding but against all forms of creaturely life. Depopulation precedes repopulation. Venice becomes a storied past so that it can be made a trophy and that trophy a page repeopled "for us." The implantation of characters from Shakespeare succeeds to the implantation of the Venetian lion as the sign for a bloodlessly imperial acquisition and a colonial occupation exempt from erosion by the tides of history.

The imperial self-division of Byronism descends from the precedent sentimental responses to the depopulation of the English countryside in the eighteenth century (Goldsmith's *Deserted Village* may stand for all) as well as to the modernizing imperative memorably demonstrated in the clearances of the Scottish Highlands following the Battle of Culloden in 1745 (the fashionable Ossianism of Byron's *Hours of Idleness* is an apt example). Locke in boots, Cumberland cleared the landscape of a population and a political culture as if he were wiping a slate clean. It was on this tabula rasa that the political economists and conjectural historians of the Scottish Enlightenment diagrammed the commercial system—a dynamic articulation of cultural representations, social transactions, and economic laws—which promised the elevation of a benighted Scotland to the level of its southern neighbor and which would serve as the pattern for the United Kingdom's global projection of its interests. Although it is true that the identification of English power with commerce had long been a cliché, until Waterloo success had nevertheless been ad hoc; it is a signal extension of that power for the poet to demonstrate that the imperial market has its image and ideological support in the speculative dialectic of literary creation, that the cultural imperialism practiced in Ireland and Scotland could be limitlessly extended, and that depopulation could be bloodless, a mere matter of substituting representations for bodies (Francis Jeffrey's "perpetual stream of thick-coming fancies" [*RR* B:2:865]).

Byron's use of the Spenserian stanza in *Childe Harold IV*, far more technically adept than in any of the earlier cantos, seems a fitting homage to his precursor and peer in the strategic transmutation of a foreign reality. What Byron adds to the Elizabethan romancer is the intervening history of British literature, which has confirmed the Burkean insight that that literature, the fiction of Britain, could stand firm against revolutionary ideology and imperial threat. Thus endowed, Byron can be "comprehensive" (preface) as Spenser was not and aggressive where Burke was defensive; he can render the past as a field inhabited by literary characters fully granted the status of historical persons in order that the past and the foreign might be enclosed in a global discursive space. The sun will never set on a Britain thus Byronized. As John Wilson rhapsodizes in his review of the poem, "Whatever lives now—has perished heretofore—or may exist hereafter—and that has within it a power to kindle passion, may become the material of his all-embracing song" (*RR* B:2:899).

But nothing is got for nothing. The very comprehensiveness of the recharacterization of the world entails that Britain be voided as well: the apocalyptic flood that the dreamer of Wordsworth's *Prelude* fears is the flood that *Childe Harold* presupposes as the historical condition for its imperial stance. Do not say that the flood is merely metaphorical, for it is the material force of that flood to prove that the land, that anchorage of the literal for yeoman and nobleman alike, had never been more than a powerful metaphor, now supplanted by the groundless power to make and impose metaphors. If Great Britain has become an imperial discourse, it is at the cost of the land of the Angles as well as the land of the Celts. Byron takes as fitting reward for performing his ideological service the singular power to ship back, like a planter from the West Indies, his "fresher growth" to the cleared surface of the country that had formerly uprooted him, thereby to dominate a culture and a mode of production now tailored to his figure. This reversal will be simultaneously enacted and parodied in the English Cantos of *Don Juan*; from a station in Venice the poet will repeople the vanished world of Regency England with phantoms from the foreign country of his own exiled past (Juan with an Aurora and an Adeline on each hand).[1] The darker implications of this literary/commercial legerdemain, whereby the hateful is bloodlessly replaced by the beloved and the "absence" of real people is supplied by their representations, are explored in *The Two Foscari*. There the villainous Loredano compacts the figures of merchant, ruler, and poet; his enterprise matches that announced here, at the head of Lord Byron's most "comprehensive" poem: he zealously works to eliminate the hateful Foscari one by one so that he can mark them down as figures in his ledger—their dynasty displaced by an account book that their deaths balance. In Loredano's version of the dialectic of enlightenment, "History's purchased page" becomes history's page of purchases.

"Yet there be. . . ." "Strong reality" is the "one word" of *Childe Harold III* elevated from destructive wish to utopian dream. In its original appearance the notion poached its ethic from the Wordsridgean doctrine of the "one life," abbreviated with Byronic negligence: "And thus I am absorb'd and this is life" (*CH III*, st. 73). The line, by all odds the most unconvincing Byron ever wrote, makes Wordsworthian "matter of factness" seem a modest thing. And even when the poet rises to a more plausible sublimity,

All is concentred in a life intense,
Where not a beam nor air nor leaf is lost,
But hath a part of being, and a sense
Of that which is of all Creator and defence.

Then stirs the feeling infinite, so felt
In solitude where we are *least* alone;
A truth, which through our being then doth melt
And purifies from self.

(*CH III*, sts. 89–90)

the rite of intensification cannot defend against a sudden storm and the old itch:

The sky is changed!—and such a change!; Oh night,
And storm, and darkness, ye are wondrous strong,
Yet lovely in your strength, as is the light
Of a dark eye in woman!

(st. 92)

Nature's reality is eclipsed by the simile invoked to celebrate it. Not for this faints the poet, whose career, as we have seen, is elaborated in the studied violence of the shift from one moment of absorption to another. In the opening of the fourth canto the Byronic *yet* introduces yet another lure in sequence, not, as its Wordsworthian counterpart, a revision or a compensation. The perception that the repopulation of the void by a Venetian fairy-land will not permanently satisfy the appetite of a reading public does not undermine the speculative model but complicates and extends it.

Setting off from the inaugural image of Venice, the fourth canto iterates the Spenserian stations of Lord Byron's dilatory comprehension of the panorama if not the principles of history. His poem, as his soul, "wanders" until, periodically, he demands it back to "stand." This is a poem where the different connotations of *stand*—poetic, moral, and theatrical—are masterfully condensed. In Italy, he "stand[s] / A ruin amidst ruins; there to track / Fall'n states and buried greatness" (*CH IV*, st. 25). And fitly one ruin addresses another:

> Thou art the garden of the world, the home
> Of all Art yields, and Nature can decree;
> Even in thy desert, what is like to thee?
> Thy very weeds are beautiful, thy waste
> More rich than other climes' fertility;
> Thy wreck a glory, and thy ruin graced
> With an immaculate charm which cannot be defaced.
>
> (st. 26)

Speculating beyond the Napoleonic analogy in an endeavor to claim a transhistorical integrity, Lord Byron monumentalizes himself by Byronizing all monuments. To be Byronic has become the universal criterion of uniqueness and authenticity. And Italy certainly flaunts a Byronic glamour. Its "desert" is a version of the "sterile track" and the "last sands of life" from the opening of *Childe Harold III*. Its "weeds" recall Byron's plangent self-characterization in stanzas 2 and 3 of that poem. A terrible change has befallen Byron, Italy, and the world—but at least no worse there is.

Despite time's relentless assault, the object, like the corpse of Greece in the opening of *The Giaour*, retains an inextinguishable allure:

> Time, which hath wrong'd thee with ten thousand rents
> Of thine imperial garment, shall deny,
> And hath denied, to every other sky
> Spirits which soar from ruin: thy decay
> Is still impregnate with divinity,
> Which gilds it with revivifying ray.
>
> (st. 55)

Italy's immunity partakes of the mystery that grounds all claim to privilege in Byron: the gift of his noble birth. That native assurance underwrites the poet's Miltonic vaunt that "to the mind / Which is itself, no changes bring surprise" and permits him not only to stand a ruin amidst ruins but as an island against the "inviolate island" of his birth.

The island on which the poet ultimately stands is the one word of his name, the self-sufficiency of which had been the poet's dream at least since the bold prophecy of "A Fragment" in *Hours of Idleness:*

> My epitaph shall be my name alone;
> If *that* with honour fail to crown my clay,
> Oh may no other fame my deeds repay!
> *That*, only *that*, shall single out the spot;
> By that remember'd or with that forgot.

Following the separation and a taste of celebrity, however, some amendment became necessary:

> With false Ambition what had I to do?
> Little with Love, and least of all with Fame;
> And yet they came unsought, and with me grew,
> And made me all which they can make—a name.
> ("Epistle to Augusta," ll. 97–100)

A Byron made not born. Made not making. Indeed, being made and being stabbed or raped have the same traumatic force for Byron: as the ruin is the intersection of the natural and the cultural, so is the name the intersection of the psychic and the historical. The ruin of Lord Byron's name (published abroad by scandal and reviews) does not any more than the ruin of Italy mean extinction but *allegorization: Byron* becomes the name of ruin. Thus circumstanced, the name can be imagined to be the linguistic corollary to the decayed body of a murdered Italy; the immaculate charm that the poet sees in Italy is what he wishes for "Byron." But as the "revivifying ray" of divinity shows that the soul within is indistinguishable from a cosmetic gilding, so is "Byron" suspiciously dependent for its "native" charm on the pathos of those events that have *ostensibly* corrupted it. I stress "ostensibly" because the ruinology of *Childe Harold IV*—its will-to-iconicity—which attempts an elegiac break with the past, looks, in retrospect, like no break at all in a career that has always been elegiac in its mood and always iconic, if only in the modern, commercial sense that the poet's name has always been identifiable with his books and those books have always been vended as commodities. This duplex commodification of the poetic object and of the poet's name does represent a radical break between Byron and those poets of the past—Tasso, Rienzi, Ariosto, Dante—with whom he makes common cause. The commodity is not a ruin: it is neither natural nor subject to natural processes, although it is always being naturalized, as, with exemplary finesse, here in *Childe Harold IV.*

Such a conclusion does not contradict Byron's identification with the ruins of Italy. On the contrary, it suggests that the ruins of the modern age are themselves radically discontinuous with ruins in the past: their suspension between nature and culture reflects denaturalization and deculturation— expresses, that is, their status as commodities subject to extraction from context, whether by *force de main*, as in the cases of Lord Elgin and Napoleon or, more economically, by the representation of the poet. The commodity is not a ruin *in* history because the commodity form is the ruin *of* history.

Made, the poet's name expresses not the metaphysics of blood but the privilege of copyright. Under the commercial magic of John Murray, the charm of "Byron" has become as immaculate as that of a banknote: if soiled, the name can be replaced by its facsimile. Under the poetic magic of Lord Byron the charm of Italy is endowed with the same resiliency. Induction into the cultural system properly named Byronism confers immunity to surprise with the same force as does the formalization of an astronomical system called Ptolemaic or Copernican in Adam Smith's account. This is the immunity offered to the aristocrat (the aristocracy offered to a reader) whose mind must be itself because he has sold his ancestral estate and, who, unlike the floating commercial empire of Venice, cannot even find any soil in which to "plant his lion." Consequently, he must, as image after image in *Childe Harold IV* attests, build his castles (or plant his tannen tree) in the air:

> But from their nature will the tannen grow
> Loftiest on loftiest and least shelter'd rocks,
> Rooted in barrenness, where nought below
> Of soil supports them 'gainst the Alpine shocks
> Of eddying storms; yet springs the trunk, and mocks
> The howling tempest, till its height and frame
> Are worthy of the mountains from whose blocks
> Of bleak, gray granite into life it came,
> And grew a giant tree;—the mind may grow the same.
> (*CH IV*, st. 20)

Hardly a Wordsworthian plant (primrose, daffodil, or thorn thrusting up from the ground whose being it becomingly tells), Lord Byron's tannen is the image of an alienated, ungrounded organicism, a plant of the imagination. But it is an organicism all the same, where things develop and grow according to an inner law despite the absence of the soil that had once seemed necessary for life, as for meaning. In the fade of the ground, becoming is a kind of being; growth seems natural and inevitable, without assertion. In typically Byronic fashion, however, that act of identification also discloses its defensive function: one plants oneself in the air, becomes a being, in order to steel a self against shocks.

The mind's turn round on itself in a Satanic/organic closure is metaphor and metonymy for the enclosure of the "inviolate island of the sage and free" (*CH IV*, st. 8). This systematic self-enclosure must pass for virtue in default of the traditional support for autonomy and strength, land. At this historical juncture (that is, in *Childe Harold IV*), when the commercial economy takes on a stoic mien and figures the possibility of surprise (such as a Napoleonic coup d'état or an imperative foreign utterance) as a change without profit, "Lord Byron" preempts real change by *predicting* an inexorable alteration, by representing corruption, decay, and degradation—the ruin of virtue—as part of the routine, *economical* modifications of the superficies that assure novelty and revive taste, extend commerce and engrain its sway:

> But ever and anon of griefs subdued
> There comes a token like a scorpion's sting,
> Scarce seen but with fresh bitterness imbued;
> And slight withal may be the things which bring
> Back on the heart the weight which it would fling
> Aside for ever; it may be a sound,—
> A tone of music, summer's eve, or spring,
> A flower, the wind, the ocean,—which shall wound,
> Striking the electric chain wherewith we are darkly bound;
>
> And how and why we know not, nor can trace
> Home to its cloud this lightning of the mind,
> But feel the shock renew'd, nor can efface
> The blight and blackening which it leaves behind,
> Which out of things familiar, undesign'd,
> When least we deem of such, calls up to view
> The spectres whom no exorcism can bind,
> The cold—the changed—perchance the dead—anew,
> The mourn'd, the lov'd, the lost—too many!—yet how few!
>
> (*CH IV*, sts. 23–24)

No change, whether in the cycles of the market or of empires, may bring surprise, but something—call it the past—shocks the chain by which we have bound our effects to our causes. The analysis here strikes a note, albeit muted, of modernity. It is muted by Byron's sentimental recuperation of the shock in the figures of the "mourn'd, the lov'd, the lost"—a familiarization of the specters in personal terms that echoes the familiarization of the ghosts haunting the unpeopled wastes of the square of St. Mark, the Highlands, or the Russian steppes with characters from Shakespeare, Otway, and Scott. After having denied his ability to "trace home" the "lightning of the mind," the poet ostentatiously proceeds to track it right down. That recuperation abbreviates the scenario of *Manfred*, Byron's earlier, grandiose attempt to dramatize a mind capable of opening itself to those spectral shocks and of portentously connecting their appearance with remembered acts against loved persons. By taking responsibility for his torments, Manfred aspired to bind all shocks to the narrative unfolding of an individual destiny. *Childe Harold IV* follows suit.

Republican Stereotypes

That skeptical assessment of *Childe Harold IV* would not go uncontested. John Cam Hobhouse, for one, aggressively defended the political progressiveness of his friend's poem. Here is his crucial note to the stanza on Rienzi (114): "When the republican aspired to perpetuate his own power, when the tribune imitated the fopperies of royalty, when the reformer declared himself the champion of superstition and the church, *he lost his distinctive character*, and like a more celebrated personage of our own times, left a convincing proof, that a revolution can be maintained only by the maxims, and even the very forms, by which it was at first ushered into life."[2] Bedecked in the "fopperies of royalty," the "celebrated personage" Napoleon vainly sought to command the future by dynastic fictions rather than trust to republican virtue. The reformer fell and the republic with him. So much bears out Hobhouse's diagnosis. Yet something remains unsettling in his remedy. By tying the future of republicanism to the retention of a distinctive character and simultaneously renouncing traditional signs of distinction—rank or wealth—Hobhouse reduces republican virtue to the strategically determined reiteration of the maxims of the past.

The maneuver represents neither personal obstinacy nor what Malcolm Kelsall calls Whiggism "become pathological."[3] Hobhouse deliberately undertook the transformation of Whiggish resistance from a static posture, frozen in the attitudes of the Glorious Revolution, into a modern political technology.[4] Here he tries to yoke Byron's power to the engine of reform: both by preventing Byron's swing into Napoleonic folly (aping the emperor as he had aped the Bourbons) and by saving the phenomena of *Childe Harold*—its heap of maxims—for a revolutionary praxis. Hobhouse interprets the revolution as having sprung from the Longinian *éclat* of a powerful saying: a freshly minted maxim of change that is the political equivalent of a heraldic "one word." Hobhouse's Byronizing audaciously embraces the Burkean depiction of the Jacobins as "men of maxims."[5] That men could be slogans and slogans so explosive nerves a politics that, in the ironic aftermath of the revolutionary era, has nothing but theory to go on.

Hobhouse caps Burke with the brave conclusion that after the first eruption there is no other. In the ruins of revolution correct political practice becomes the recovery and reiteration of republican morals: "Thy factions, in their worse than civil war" (*CH IV*, st. 57), "What crimes it costs to be a moment free" (st. 85), "Can tyrants but by tyrants conquer'd be" (st. 96), "First Freedom and then Glory—when that fails, / Wealth, vice, corruption,—barbarism at last" (st. 108). The Byronic repetition of republican stereotypes anticipates the reiteration of platitudes that Richard Rorty has endorsed as liberal practice.[6] It is a strategy of seriality that begins with the abandonment of an expectation of any eschaton or even any intensification. Revolution may indeed have been ushered in by the "one word" or a strong maxim; but in order for revolution to be maintained it must be a "gainer" by its post-Napoleonic "indigence." Revolutionary spirit, like the Brummellian figure, is "reduced to the single force of what distinguished" it; political activity has become dereferenced; and the apocalyptic hope for the epiphany of the literal has been exchanged for the manipulation of "things."[7] Repetition is revolution normalized, revolution without a "future."[8]

The implications of this conviction bear examination. That Hobhouse could imagine repetition to be revolutionary not only grounds *his* politics but, I shall argue, is the basis for the political understanding by which *Childe Harold IV* is made to stand for something called reform. Hobhouse's notion of the progressive can best be discerned against the background of the "primitive confusion"[9] he represents in his "illustration" of stanza 154, Lord Byron's apostrophe to St. Peter's, "this eternal ark of worship undefiled." In prosaic contrast to the "Majesty, / Power, Glory, Strength, and Beauty" in Lord Byron's view, the groundling Hobhouse depicts an interior scene in which are promiscuously mixed "a noisy school for children in one corner; a sermon preached to a moveable audience at another; a concert in this chapel; a ceremony, half interrupted by the distant sounds of the same music in another quarter; a ceaseless crowd sauntering along the nave, and circulating through all the aisles; listeners and gazers walking, sitting, kneeling;" and so on. "Such is the interior of this glorious edifice," Hobhouse expostulates, and goes on to quote the pope's invidious comparison of the piety of the Catholics of England, devout because politically disadvantaged, to the religiosity of the Italians, which is "all *talk* (grido)." Hobhouse approves what the pope regrets: a church turned into a place of social commerce, a religion reduced to talk. His pragmatic moral to his countrymen: "It has, in truth, been long before discovered, that penalties are little less effectual than premiums, in keeping alive an absurd superstition, which can fall into disuse only by entire toleration and neglect."[10] "Entire toleration" is an exemplary liberal recommendation; "neglect" sounds like a bit of Byronic ventriloquism, however. As Hobhouse shows in an illustration to his illustration, the admonitions are not fully compatible.

Remarking on the "limitations" to the "indifference" of the Italians, Hobhouse renders in lurid detail a penitential ceremony conducted beneath the dome of the Padre Caravita. Whips are distributed to the penitents. The preacher instructs his kneeled audience to strip and exhorts them

> to recollect that Christ and his martyrs suffered much more than whipping. "*Shew*, then, your penitence—shew your sense of Christ's sacrifice—shew it with the whip." The flagellation begins. The darkness, the tumultuous sound of blows in every direction—"Blessed Virgin Mary, pray for us!" bursting out at intervals—the persuasion that you are surrounded by atrocious culprits and maniacs, who know of an absolution for every crime—the whole situation has the effect of witchery, and so far from exciting a smile fixes you to the spot in a trance of restless horror, prolonged beyond expectation or bearing.[11]

The limits of Catholic indifference are precisely the limits on the equivalency between toleration and neglect. This is not an aspect of Catholic ritual that Hobhouse can overlook; rather, it is one that with a fascinated eye he looks over in order to *build* toleration.[12] Hobhouse calls it a "scene," but, as he indicates, despite the emphasis on bodily showing rather than confessional telling, what occurs is actually a scene for no one but him. The scourging takes place in darkness and "the performers, to do them justice, appear to be too much ashamed of their transgressions to make a shew of their penance, so that it is very difficult to say whether even your next neighbour has given himself the lash or not." Anticipating a cynical response, Hobhouse denies that "the darkness favours evasion. There can be no pleasantry in doing that which no one sees, and no merit can be assumed where it is not known who accepts the disciplines."[13] No pleasure because no masochism; no masochism because there is no contract by which pleasure is bound to pain. No one sees his neighbor (what penitence is "shewn" is presented only to "God"); but Hobhouse is the one who sees everyone not seeing each other. He is the one who turns the ritual into a spectacle by his (ritualized) assumption of the stony figure of the hysterized male spectator. His paralyzed fascination fixes the difference—religious, national, "historical"—between him and them: *he* could not be mistaken for one of them because *he* is transfixed; *his* arm will not move. A rigid sentinel of Protestant rationality, he stands in phallic opposition to the promiscuous mix, making the darkness visible by making it signify in terms of the conventional discourse of Gothic horror. Hobhouse does not show the invisible (though hardly inaudible) discipline of the benighted Catholics; but he does illustrate the discipline of the liberal abroad by his engagement in a political exercise that displays that the basis of toleration lies in the capacity to *endure* what cannot be changed.

The penitents perform a collective act of intense devotion. Hooded in darkness, their penance is neither public nor private; it is not *social* in liberal terms and is therefore without merit. For Hobhouse there can be no merit unless one's penance is a visible sign for one's neighbor, who can thereby sympathetically exchange positions and symbolically apply another's punishment to himself. There is no merit, in other words, that is not potentially the subject of talk, whereas the "flagellation does certainly take place on the naked skin; and this ferocious superstition . . . has . . . been revived as a salutary corrective of an age of atheism." The flagellation on the naked skin is the superstitious version of the repetition of republican maxims; not a progressive discourse but an archaically incisive scourge. Encountering what challenges indifference's limit, Hobhouse edges closer to the bounds of toleration:

> Such an innovation may be tolerated, and perhaps applauded, in the days of barbarism, when the beating of themselves was found the only expedient to prevent the Italians from the beating of each other; but the renewal of it at this period must induce us to fear that the gradual progress of reason is the dream of philanthropy, and that a considerable portion of all societies, in times the most civilized as well as the most ignorant, is always ready to adopt the most unnatural belief, and the most revolting practices.[14]

"Revolting practices," not a revolutionary practice. Revolting because practiced on the "naked skin," revolting because it repudiates sympathy— the penitential lash sounds the primitive resistance against the body's abstraction into a civilized sign, men into maxims. The superstition breeds in the barren of "atheistic" indifference that toleration produces.

The "revolting practice" may be allowed nowhere but in Rome, but Hobhouse's historical conclusions about the relations between civilization and superstition are general and meant to be translatable to Great Britain. Hobhouse neglects nothing of use in his travels. Here he transforms a ritual practice into a performance in order to enable him to build up a tolerance for what can be neither entirely eliminated nor neglected. Because the penitents court physical pain to revive an unseen spiritual reality, relieving penalties will not extinguish it. Because the penance is practiced without an audience, ignoring it will not make it go away. Having ventured to the limit of indifference, Hobhouse nonetheless stops short of recommending suppression. If the government punishes people they become devout; if the government does not punish people they punish themselves. The moral of the illustration is clear—we liberals must tolerate even what we cannot eliminate. Yet the moral has a Foucauldian twist. Though anchored in endurance, toleration can be rendered as a positive means to attain control over what revolts; toleration, that is, can itself become a kind of discipline and discipline a kind of punishment that does not induce resistance.

But who is to be so tolerated? Although the features of the Roman scene resemble an unreformed Bedlam, and Hobhouse's toleration suggests the "moral management" urged by John Haslam as a system for maintaining the mad in default of a possible cure, Hobhouse clearly does not have the insane in mind. A proponent of Catholic emancipation, Hobhouse has already exempted the British Catholics, who no longer present a serious threat to social stability. Nonetheless, the superstitious, like the poor, the liberal will always have with him. Indeed, in the context of restlessness and insurgency in the England of 1818, the superstitious translates *as* the poor, the working poor, the revolting poor—those who live in promiscuous intimacy in a darkness at home, in the streets, and on the shop floor that the visitor from a foreign class cannot penetrate, and where they perform acts of self-punishment—routine acts of mechanical labor or intoxication—incomprehensible to the enlightened mind.[15] If, like Hobhouse, we cultivate an eye for the obscure, we can see that what Hobhouse sees in Padre Caravita is the invisible proletariat, without whose inexplicable devotion and primitive willingness to subject themselves to pain the artificial infinite of St. Peter's would not have been built and without whom the crystal palace of a triumphant industrial capitalism would never be raised.

More fastidious than the pope, the liberal intends to cut free of the atavistic body by endorsing or imposing the hygiene of the sign. The ethical basis of Hobhouse's position lies in his conviction that "the ceremonies of a religion must, except where they are sanguinary, be considered the most harmless part of it."[16] That conviction had been consistent at least since the writing of his prizewinning Cambridge essay *On the Origin and Intention of Sacrifices.* There he had defined sacrifice as a "solemn act of religious worship, consisting in the offering up of something animate or inanimate to the Deity, in such a manner as to cause a real [as opposed to figurative] destruction or change of the thing offered."[17] In a foretaste of his note to *Childe Harold* Hobhouse denied that there could be any connection "between the gratitude and repentance of man, and the sufferings and death of a creature, destroyed according to a certain strange form" and exempted the Jews from the opprobrium visited on the pagans. "All other people," he wrote, "except the chosen of God, adopted the strange and unworthy opinion, that the Deities estimated the *value* rather than regarded the *design* of the offerings and sacrifices that loaded their altars."[18] To Hobhouse revolution without a future is progressive because to imagine a future means countenancing fundamental change, which for him entails sacrificial violence. Revolution without a future means revolution now (and continually), without the bloodspill that drags us to a primordial past we aim to escape.

Nowhere is this clearer than in Hobhouse's last note to *Childe Harold IV* (st. 75, beginning "And near Albano's scarce divided waves"), which contests the claims made by the Italian antiquarian Doctor Visconti to have discovered the remains of a pre-Aenean civilized Greek community near lake Albano.[19] The claims are based on a Signor Carnevali's recovery of some terra cotta from a tomb supposedly buried deep in the strata of peperino left by the convulsion of Mount Albano centuries before. In his adroit critique Hobhouse deploys a series of oppositions between romance versus reason, commercialization versus disinterested scholarship (Visconti's findings conclude by advertising that the artifacts of his "friend" are for sale), southern versus northern, and, not least, Italian versus Englishman. For it is to an anonymous English antiquarian that Hobhouse turns for help with the crux, to explain "those figures which Visconti thinks may be letters, or, perhaps, whole words, like the Chinese characters." The Englishman suggests to Hobhouse that "the root or germ of each of these figures is a cross [an illustration appears here] and it is not a little singular that they bear a very close resemblance to a certain Runic character, or magical sign." Not, then, meaningful letters but a "magical sign." Moreover, the Englishman ascribes that cruciform pattern to a Celtic, rather than a Greek, origin. The passage of the figures from North to South fully devalues the convulsionary thesis. Hobhouse cares not at all whether the tomb is "referred to the Celtic aborigines of Italy" or was constructed at some "comparatively recent date" to hold the remains of "some Gaulish chieftain, or of a heathen Goth or

Lombard." The point is that there is nothing cryptic about the tomb.

In detecting resemblance the Englishman recognizes his *own* character and discovers that he has crossed this place before. Recognizing these figures as Celtic presupposes that the Englishman has, however distantly (perhaps in the person of one of his "canonized forefathers"), planted them there. The poet avers that after the flood Venice can be repeopled by characters from Shakespeare. The annotater adds that those characters are themselves repetitions of characters implanted before Shakespeare. Hobhouse notes that the "diagram, or figure [found both on the vases and in the Celtic] bears some affinity [to one] often drawn by boys in Italy" who "do not however ascribe any meaning to it." The failure to ascribe meaning is exactly the significance of the boys' actions. For Hobhouse what is magical about "the strange vitality of these vestiges of the superstitions of the elder day" is that the preliterate Italian boys uncannily sign themselves according to a Celtic design. Without the violence of meaning or value or blood the Italian boys have been colonized by a foreign culture.

The shady Visconti most probably attributed antiquity to the vases in order to raise their price for immediate sale. The enlightened Hobhouse is after bigger game. The application of antiquarian knowledge by the Englishman implies a kind of *right* to the minds of these Italian boys: without letters they nonetheless sign themselves according to a prescription that comprehends them; without knowledge they nonetheless accurately reform in the soil the prior abstraction from their native ground that was executed by the primordial implantation of a Celtic character. Considered in light of the liberal tradition that Hobhouse represents, the boys' scrawl signifies their membership in the discursive space that *Childe Harold* triumphantly describes and their consent to an imperialism that has always already occurred. The Englishman, then, takes the meaninglessness of the design as just another confirmation of the liberal maxim that the more things change, the more they stay the same.

"Change" for Hobhouse and the liberal tradition he represents is a matter of redescription.[20] By broadcasting a universalist, linguistically based, schematically apprehendable definition of man, the conviction can be produced that this new description of man has been operative all along. Man as "design" replaces man as value. Whether or not this is a true view of mankind and language is less important than that it emerged as a policy of British response to what all sides agreed was the completed narrative of revolution. The real change that occurred in Britain was the discovery that no real change is necessary to get the world everyone wants.

In the course of addressing the relations between a postmodernist perspective and revolutionary politics, Jean-François Lyotard observed, "What is remarkable (to me, at any rate) in the so-called 'new technologies' is that the machines involved are not substitutes for mechanical operations, but for certain mental and/or linguistic operations."[21] What is perhaps more remarkable is that in Great Britain, largely through the associationist strand of the empiricist tradition, this interchange between technology and mental and/or linguistic operations was already highly developed by the nineteenth century. Hobhouse suggests just such a principled alternative to the sanguinary "technology" of Catholicism: the promulgation of the idea that the "distinctive character" of a person is a mark that can be hastily written down and read off at a glance.

Shorthand and the Unity of Design

British practitioners of shorthand had already developed the prototype of Hobhouse's political technology. Stenography was devised as a technique for the accurate and rapid transcription of oral speech. According to Sir Isaac Pitman, inventor of the first phonetic system of stenography and the author of *A History of Shorthand*, the "principles of the stenographic art" have remained constant since the first system was devised by Tiro, the freedman of Cicero: "The adoption of simpler forms than the common letters of the alphabet; making each letter the representative of some common word; leaving out such letters as could be spared, particularly the vowels, in order to save time; and sometimes joining the initials or other parts of several words, in order to express them by one series of forms, and, if possible, without removing the hand from the paper."[22] Although shorthand sets as its standard the reproduction of oral speech, it is not primarily a transcriptive technique but a code of abbreviation devised to save time and enable exhaustive recall.

Shorthand is an economical writing. It works like money—or as political economists had come to think that paper money worked. Paper gave increased currency to whatever quantity of money was in circulation. Paper money had no greater value than gold or silver, but what Francis Horner called its "representative power" was "augmented by [its] more rapid transmission."[23] The complementary perceptions that speed was itself productive power without reference to any value and that the repetition of stereotypes—shorthand characters, banknotes, or maxims—could be accelerated by design in order to attain that power were insights that fundamentally distinguished nineteenth-century writers from their predecessors. Mastery of technique distinguished the expert from the amateur (Walter

Scott served as a court reporter; Charles Dickens was trained as a stenographer). The development of shorthand coincided with its professionalization, with a consequent increase in efficiency in both its application and its instruction.[24]

As a series of discriminate signs that repeat the original utterance of a live speaker, shorthand appears transparent to its host enunciation, which, like the original maxim of the revolutionary, is merely reduced to a distinctive character. Ostensibly, no change has occurred, just repetition. But it was a common theme of complaint and praise from the time of the fourth-century Latin poet Ausonius that the stenographer did not simply record thought, he *anticipated* it. Stenography thrived in oratorical communities that relied on verbal formulas to assist composition both extemporaneous and routine. By Byron's time, stenography's will-to-abbreviation had reached parodic extremes. Pitman notes that "even so late as 1818, Stones, in his system of shorthand, among a number of arbitraries, gives a circle enclosing the sign $\wedge$ to represent 'Light is come into the world, but men love darkness rather than light because their deeds are evil.' A facetious gentleman, on seeing this, observed, 'Why I could beat that out-and-out. I should put a scratch so ϱ and say, That stands for the preacher's sermon last Sunday.'"[25]

The gentleman's observation might have been less facetious had he said "next" rather than "last" Sunday, for the point lies in the anticipation. The stenographer does not wait for the speaker to complete the formula before he writes it down: a few words suffice for the mark and ready him for the next. Because he anticipates, then, and because the premium placed on speed requires the discipline of not removing hand from paper, the stenographer in Stones's system will not record, will not even audit variations, whether aimed at elegance or at ideological precision. There could scarcely be a religious ceremony less "sanguinary" than stenographic transcription, which efficiently sublimes away both the body of the devout and the body of the text. Unlike the picture language employed by the visionary Blake, for example, stenographic characters are resolutely anti-apocalyptic: the future they anticipate will never be present except as the transition to another character; the system that incorporates those characters is a means to fortify against change rather than to effect it.[26] The routinization of the relations between shorthand and its client professions would ideally produce that moment where the stenographer could say, with Byron, with Adam Smith, "No change brings surprises."

Even if it could somehow be proved that there were in fact no elegant variations in the sermons of nineteenth-century preachers, that very monotony could be ascribed to stenographic mediation. Pitman figures the stenographer as an earnest drudge, passively "reporting the dry disquisitions of the pulpit orators."[27] But the dialectic of stenography actively contributed to the regulation of public discourse. The stenographer recorded a pulpit utterance in shorthand, which was later decoded and written in longhand in order that it could be printed and sold—exactly as shorthand systems were sold—in handbooks of model sermons available for the plunder of preachers eager to economize on sermon preparation. Pulpit oratory rapidly adapted itself to the technology available to reproduce it. The history of change concealed in the apparent "repetition of the titles" of shorthand systems eventually leads to Stones's radical system, which abbreviates to a distinctive character a conventional phrase that the stenographer was largely responsible for turning into a formula in the first place. The consequences, as Coleridge foresaw, were grave. A church that cooperates with this dereferencing of its speech is well on the way to disestablishment.[28]

Few if any stenographers conspired to disestablish the church, democratize Parliament, and routinize legal procedures. Yet the practical effect of their professionalization was, in time, the reduction of the volatile utterances of early modern oratorical communities (such as the Scottish Covenanters) into a set of reiterable verbal formulas. Ethos was assigned a distinctive character, an ideologeme, which routinized the forcefulness of its enunciation. Yet it would be a distortion to depict stenography as the modest handmaiden to the Leibnizian project of perfecting a universal philosophical language, regardless of dialectical difference. Despite its rationalistic character, the art of stenography was contextually invested and determined. Shorthand prospered nowhere in the modern world except in Great Britain, where, as Pitman notes, it responded to the peculiar institutional requirements of the Anglican church, the English law courts, and Parliament. Shorthand was a *demotic* version of the Leibnizian project, a British version of universalism. According to James Henry Lewis, who wrote the first history of shorthand in 1816, the greatest advance in the professional fortunes of stenographers occurred when they were admitted into Parliament in 1772—on the eve of the age of revolution.[29]

This coincidence induced the *Quarterly Review* (looking back on that age of revolution with an eye to forestalling its transformation into an age of reform) to make what we might call the Hobhousean connection and associate stenography, the public reproduction of stereotypes, with rampant democratization: "At present it is the influence of the democracy which has increased, is increasing, and ought to be diminished. Whatever additional influence the crown has obtained by the increased establishments which the circumstances of the age have rendered necessary, is but as a feather in the scale, compared to the weight which the popular branch of the constitution has acquired by the publication of the parliamentary debates."[30] There had once been a convenient name and stereotype for such subversives, "Jacobins"; but in 1816, when the threat of the Jacobins seemed to have vanished with their infernal prince, the *Quarterly* lacked a hero plausible enough to blame for a tendency that had not quit.

Even the *Quarterly*'s zest for detecting conspiracies on which to blame democratizing tendencies slackened, however, when faced with the publication of Mary Ann Randall's extraordinary *Symbolic Illustrations of the History of England, from the Roman Invasion to the present Time, accompanied with a Narrative of the Principal Events, designed more particularly for the instruction of Young Persons*, reviewed in July 1816. The aim of the book, according to the reviewer, is to "embody in symbols or hieroglyphics, the most striking incidents recorded in the annals of our country." It represents the stenographic tendency—both its transcriptive and pedagogic modes—*in extremis*. The reviewer mockingly observes that the massive folio volume contains thirty-nine hieroglyphic plates and seven hundred pages of commentary explicating the designs. Confessing to speechlessness, he reproduces a page from the preface to permit the reader to sample the absurdity of the project (see illustration).

Randall's symbolic illustrations aspire to rationalize historical "events" by reducing them to their conventional elements. I set off *events* because in this epitome of her method the very thing that Randall seeks to conventionalize is itself a convention, a design imposed, as if by contract, on armed conflict. Ultra-Hobhousean in their elimination of rhetorical color, Randall's characters reduce the value of history entirely to a design that can be taken in at a glance, to a hygienic ruin. Such is one historian's response to the public's need for more efficient communication. As the hieroglyphist Thomas De Quincey puts it,

> Shrinking, through long experience, from the plethoric form of cumulation and "periodic" writing in which the journalist supports or explains his views, every man who puts a business value upon his time, slips naturally into a trick of short-hand reading. . . . An evil of modern growth is met by a modern remedy. Every man gradually learns an art of catching at the leading words, and the cardinal or hinge-joints of transition, which proclaim the general course of a writer's speculation.[31]

Randall's method aims not only at efficient but *safe* communication. If, as Lord Byron attests, it was "impossible not to be dazzled and overwhelmed by [Napoleon's] character and career,"[32] Randall's system reduces the possibility of dazzlement by sanitizing the character, eliminating anything of color—crimson or gold—that might rouse the blood. A modern French evil is thereby answered by an innovative British remedy: the "immaculate charm" of the hieroglyph, which can codify every event and insure that "no change brings surprise." What makes Randall's designs risible are both the hemorrhage of commentary on which the illustrations float and the absurd claim that the symbols "embody" historical incidents. For the *Quarterly* the moral is obvious: the democratic ideology that legitimates such a project results in a book more monstrously mysterious than the scholastics, and therefore harmless.[33]

Both Hobhouse and the *Quarterly* want a hero. Hobhouse wants someone to perform the repetition of distinctive characters that would bloodlessly accomplish the republican design in fulfillment of Burke's prophetic fear. "It is plain," Burke wrote of Dr. Price in *Reflections on the Revolution in France*, "that the mind of this *political* Preacher was at the time big with some extraordinary design; and it is very probable, that the thoughts of his au-

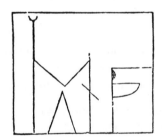

"It is thus explained.—A Convention was entered into, in Egypt, between General Kleber, on the part of the French, and the Grand Vizier, on the part of the Sublime Porte, which was approved by the Cabinet of London. The straight line, with the Crescent on its top, denotes the Grand Vizier, by its superior height to the perpendicular line, which is to represent General Kleber: the line drawn through the centre of this line, forming two acute angles, is intended for the General's sword. To denote the Convention, two lines are drawn, which meet together in the centre, and represent the shaking of hands, or a meeting. The Convention was formed in Egypt, which is signified by a Pyramid. The Cabinet of London is typified by the outline of a Cabinet on the right of the diagram. The Head of a Ship, placed in the square, denotes London, as it is frequented by ships more than any other port."

Source: Review of Mary Ann Randall's *Symbolic Illustrations of the History of England*, in *Quarterly Review* (July 1816), pp. 418–19.

dience, who understood him better than I do, did all along run before him in his reflection, and in the whole train of consequences to which it led."[34] The midwiving Hobhouse claims to understand Byron's design better than anyone, to be able to run before him in the train of maxims and foresee its admirable consequence. The *Quarterly* reviewer wants someone to take the blame for democratization. The aims and practices of reformer and revolutionary are complementary: notes and reviews both confer or impose what Isaac Disraeli called "unity of design" on the subject text: whether it be the autobiography of Byron or the history of Britain.[35]

Hobhouse, of course, produces his notes with his subject's approval; and there is much in Byron's writings to justify his interpretation. Lord Byron was explicit in his enlightened denunciation of sacrifice, as in this letter to Francis Hodgson: "The basis of your religion is *injustice; the Son of God*, the *pure*, the *immaculate*, the *innocent*, is sacrificed for the *guilty*. This proves *His* heroism; but no more does away with *man's* guilt than a schoolboy's volunteering to be flogged for another would exculpate the dunce from negligence, or preserve him from the rod" (*BLJ* 2:97). His vow to his wife, "No, I will not imbrue my hands with blood a second time" (*HVSV*, p. 102), may not have been very reassuring to her, but it would satisfy Hobhouse's ethical requirements. Moreover, the stenographic manner was firmly established in Lord Byron's repertoire. From the first, Childe Harold has been a kind of Kilroy, stamping his stereotype on the various scenes the poet visits. Recall also the striking use of the trope of reduction from *Childe Harold I*:

> Teems not each ditty with the glorious tale?
> Ah! such, alas, the hero's amplest fate!
> When granite moulders and when records fail,
> A peasant's plaint prolongs his dubious date.
> Pride! bend thine eye from heaven to thine estate,
> See how the Mighty shrink into a song!
>
> (st. 36)

There gleams the double edge of Byronic reflexiveness. The contempt for the works of the mighty reflexively diminishes poem and poet: a ditty by a shrinker. The fact that Byron composed the Alpine stanzas of the third canto among the scenes that inspired them does less to vindicate Byronic immediacy against Wordsworthian memory than to indicate how such writing to the moment relies on a few conventional postures and "symbolic illustrations."[36]

Yet despite his most enlightened intentions, Byron's design is blurred by the insurgence of blood that inadvertently tinctures his every act—an inadvertence that will ultimately make him as useless for the program of the *Quarterly* as for that of the *Edinburgh*. Lord Byron may stand against sacrifice, but he cannot dispell the aristocratic credo that "without shedding of blood is no remission."[37] Even Lord Byron's vow not to "imbrue" his hands with blood is too colorful by half, for the verb summons up the pun on *brunt* in *The Giaour* that so disturbed the *Critical* reviewer. Lord Byron bestrides the countervailing circles of reform and reaction because he is the one poet who can produce a distinct and *colorful* character that changes, like the dying dolphin "whom each pang imbues / With a new colour as it gasps away" (*CH IV*, st. 29). Lord Byron insists on the disintegrative truth that lies unspoken behind the glib profession of maxims of revolution and reaction.

Entwinement

Childe Harold IV does win through to something like "one word." The Promethean "curse" of "Forgiveness" that the poet launches at Lady Byron and her legions is meant to quench our well-stoked curiosity whether Byron will settle on revenge or redemption (*CH IV*, st. 135). Byron's forgiveness is the domestic equivalent of that moment

> When Athens' armies fell at Syracuse,
> And fetter'd thousands bore the yoke of war,
> Redemption rose up in the Attic Muse,
> Her voice their only ransom from afar.
>
> (st. 16)

Small things and great, perhaps, but such comparisons have all along been the sublime method of a pilgrimage that transforms private vices into imperial benefits.[38]

The method receives what passes for theological justification in stanzas 153–59, where the poet bends his knee to the dome of St. Peter's as the image for the vaulting, cinematic synthesis of all the "piecemeal" snapshots he has taken on his tours. Lord Byron's exercises have paid off. All the domes, skulls, mountaintops, and breasts scattered along his route are here recalled, comprehended, and exalted by its great "gigantic elegance; / Vastness which grows, but grows to harmonise" (st. 156). Like a Marvellian machine, the soul first condenses then, "growing with its growth, we thus dilate / Our spirits to the size of that they contemplate" (st. 158).[39] At that point, to our "enlighten'd" contemplation the "fountain of sublimity displays / Its depth, and thence may draw the mind of man / Its golden sands, and learn what great conceptions can" (st. 159). This conclusion is indeed "comprehensive." Honoring all draughts no matter how deep, St. Peter's vault is a child's version of the Bank of England. The reader's persuasion that he can, like a tasteful infant, immaculately consume the great dome of St. Peter's fulfills the speculator's dream as dramatized in the third canto and as signaled in the preface to the fourth, where the poet resigns himself to his failure "to preserve [the] difference between himself and Harold." By the end of the canto the submergence of differences has become the bathetic achievement of oceanic Byronism, which triumphs over the spectatorial distance separating "I" from world by its "sating gaze." And, of course, oceanic Byronism stands in for an oceanic Britannia, whose imperial ambitions are given their imprimatur by the sublime transfer of the great world out there into a "tight little island" without breaking its "inviolate" (white, male, Protestant, middle-class) integrity.

This conclusion has satisfied most readers. And no wonder. Form satisfies, and this formal contrivance is cunningly adapted to the purposes of ending this poem. As the dome of St. Peter's comprehends the whole man, so it vaultingly comprehends the four cantos of the poem both as model of a synthetic reading and as predominant metaphor: the first canto began with an apostrophe to Cintra, "Oh, dome displeasing to a British eye" (st. 24); the fourth ends in contemplation of a dome that swamps with pleasure the erstwhile distempered pilgrim. But if "Convention is the dwarfish demon styled / That foil'd the knights in Marialva's dome" (*CH I*, st. 25), it is also convention that foils the pilgrim in St. Peter's dome, who, like the infant fantasizing the incorporation of the breast (cf. sts. 148–51), attains not satisfaction but the hallucination of satisfaction and who gains not enlightenment but its airy facsimile. Sublimity is the *convention* of enlightenment—meaning not so much that it is false but that it is temporary, a suspension of dialectic rather than its resolution, a bubble to be burst by the friction of things that matter.

The bubble metaphor is canonical:

> Roll on, thou deep and dark blue Ocean, roll!
> Ten thousand fleets sweep over thee in vain;
> Man marks the earth with ruin, his control
> Stops with the shore; upon the watery plain
> The wrecks are all thy deed, nor doth remain
> A shadow of man's ravage, save his own,
> When for a moment, like a drop of rain,
> He sinks into thy depths with bubbling groan,
> Without a grave, unknell'd, uncoffin'd, and unknown.
>
> (*CH IV*, st. 179)

Again:

> And I have loved thee, Ocean! and my joy
> Of youthful sports was on thy breast to be
> Borne, like thy bubbles, onward.
>
> (st. 184)

So that when the poet claims, "My task is done—my song hath ceased—my theme / Has died into an echo; it is fit / The spell should break of this protracted dream" (st. 185), *fit* resumes its convulsive signification: what is fit is as much a matter of breaking a bubble as of building a dome.

To imagine the dome as a bubble, however, is to be reminded that it is impregnated not with divinity but with the groans of men; the aesthesis of the dome's talismanic spell is the token of suffering and death. As Randall's metaconventional hieroglyph floats on the drowned narrative of brute conquest, so Lord Byron's rare device floats on the waves of Hobhouse's commentary, which tells of the torment of those beneath the bubble, who task themselves with a repentance that is never done, those whose bodies, like Cain's, register what is writ as finally and materially writ. If not quite a human ruin, the ocean is, then, not quite oceanic: it can be read.

The bubbles join the poem with the greater narrative of speculative disaster, the famed South Sea Bubble of the early eighteenth century. They also recollect similar tracks inflecting the inhuman surface of waters in Lord Byron's text. Leila's:

> Sullen it plunged, and slowly sank,
> The calm wave rippled to the bank;
> I watch'd it as it sank, methought
> Some motion from the current caught
> Bestirr'd it more,—'twas but the beam
> That checkered o'er the living stream.
> I gazed, till vanishing from view,
> Like lessening pebble it withdrew;
> Still less and less, a speck of white
> That gemm'd the tide, then mock'd the sight.
>
> (*Giaour*, ll. 374–83)

Ezzelin's:

> Meantime the Serf had crept to where unseen
> Himself might safely mark what this might mean;
> He caught a glimpse, as of a floating breast,
> And something glitter'd starlike on the vest,

> But ere he well could mark the buoyant trunk,
> A massy fragment smote it, and it sunk:
> It rose again, but indistinct to view,
> And left the waters of a purple hue,
> Then deeply disappeared.
>
> (*Lara* 2:576–84)

Bubbles, beams, glittering stars. The end of *Childe Harold IV* suggests a certain phenomenology of the Byronic text, intimates that the greater narratives of homosocial struggle and imperial expropriation are derived from those moments of incipient fascination that flutter across the unfathomable surface of things. The Oriental tales may be read as allegorical investigations of such apparitions; that is, their appeal is *explained* in the Wordsworthian fashion (see—as Byron did—for example, "The Thorn") by a story of cruelty and suffering. No shape in the Oriental tales is without its allegory; every beam is the naked letter of romance. Johann Kaspar Lavater's definition of genius as an "apparition" perfectly fits the Byronic text, where each strange apparition marks the deposit of a body—female or male, foreign or native—that is the essential and secret wealth that invests the tale with meaning.[40] By the time of *Childe Harold IV* Lord Byron has a text, a "massy fragment" that displaces other bodies in the world. Not "merely" the story of how a dead body must be deposited in order to serve as a narrative justification for the eye's romantic mistake of all that glitters for more than gold, *Childe Harold IV* represents its own construction—whether by metonymic unfolding or metaphoric leap—as worldly and consequential, ruined and ruinous. As proof of its rarity, Byron's design brutally and beautifully displaces other stories (such as Lady Byron's, Scott's, and Wordsworth's)—an act for which there is no fit justification except a bubble.

Childe Harold IV is not, however, unrelentingly imperialist, unremittingly "Byronic." There is a trajectory of unintended consequences that does not follow from submerged corpses and does not speculatively feed an insatiable appetite for consumption. The high-toned climax at St. Peter's does not join smoothly the great apostrophe to Ocean. The poet wanders: unwilling to leave the world stage, he grants Harold one last curtain call, revives the metaphor of the "deep and immedicable wound," and traipses off to Nemi and Albano for some fifteen-odd stanzas, until stanza 175 breaks in with "But I forget.—My Pilgrim's shrine is won." A reckless inadvertency, the line shakes, if not shatters, the triumphantly harmonic superstructure that arches across it. This is the one line in the fourth canto that could be transported into *Don Juan* without impropriety (or, rather, with the impropriety of the lines that characterize *Don Juan*). Moreover, it is this contingent performance of forgetting that inadvertently completes Harold's quest, which has not been for forgiveness or for satiety or for a "shrine" but for "forgetfulness" (*CH III*, st. 4)—a goal reached by surprise and forgotten in its attainment.[41] I do not claim that this is immaculate poetry. It is a fault to forget. And this is a fault line in the longest, most thoughtful and comprehensive of Byron's poems. Yet this fault line is an instance of actual change in a poem where the succession of epochs merely varies a theme.

Comparable in its disproportionate force to the "Stop!" of the third canto, "But I forget.—My Pilgrim's shrine is won" is, however, no imperative; it might better be called an "availing line" to distinguish it from that "line" of "distinction" drawn between himself and his character that the poet had in this preface abandoned as "unavailing." To avail is not to stand alone. Early on in the canto, after counterposing his self-sufficient mind against the "inviolate island of the sage and the free," Byron turns curiously:

> Perhaps I loved it well; and should I lay
> My ashes in a soil which is not mine,
> My spirit shall resume it—if we may
> Unbodied choose a sanctuary. I twine
> My hopes of being remember'd in my line
> With my land's language.
>
> (*CH IV*, st. 9)

In this peculiar act of self-reflection, Lord Byron imagines himself burying himself (or ashy fragments of himself) so that he may be phantomized and, a revenant, "resume" England. No doubt this is a dream of posthumous freedom from physical and moral constraints; it forecasts not death, however, but the English Cantos of *Don Juan*, where the posthumous lord will make just such a return. And it makes the forecast in conjunction with the statement of an ambition that is not speculative but textual. Lord Byron does not imagine resuming a place where he can take a stand. On the contrary, the feminine image of twining hopes renders a poetic activity that does not aspire to the massive, the focal, and the concrete. If this poet is to be re-membered, it cannot be by Victor Frankenstein or any other professor of the secrets of life: ashes cannot be stitched into even a monstrous facsimile of the human body.[42]

Committing his memory to his "line," Lord Byron now acknowledges that he has a line, rather than just a given name—a poetic profession with a line of work and a line of products. The act also registers the sense that the poetic memory is twined out of the basic element of the line.[43] It suggests an

Arnoldianism sensibly abbreviated: a touchstone theory of poetry without the high seriousness, indeed without the mystifying touch or the metaphorical stone. Byron's commitment puts a different spin on the fatalism of the Corsair's acceptance of the "sentence I deserve to bear" (*Corsair* 3:285). Finally, these lines that Byron has in mind, written by poets in their line, are connected by a line—Shakespeare, Radcliffe, Schiller, Otway, Milton, Spenser, Pope, Coleridge, and Wordsworth—too idiosyncratic to be called a tradition. Like Brummell, Lord Byron seeks "success in the line he marked out for himself."[44] And the line that he marks out for himself is the sportive twist of the twining ivy rather than the branching symmetry of the paternal oak. If the faith in an immaculate charm ultimately refers to an inalienable power invested in the design of an armorial crest, the twine of the line perverts that faith.

If Lord Byron could exploit that faith as no other because of his noble birth, he could as easily give it up, and for nearly the same reason. No more than the poetic will the aristocratic referent survive inspection, as John Galt smugly observed in the preface to his 1830 biography of the poet: "I cannot conclude without acknowledgments to the learned and ingenious Mr. Nicholas, for the curious genealogical fact of a baton sinister being in the escutcheon of the Byrons of Newstead. Lord Byron," he adds, "in his pride of birth, does not appear to have been aware of this stain."[45] The biographer does not know (can never know) his man. Byron's pride of birth *is* his awareness of that stain. Whether it is a baton sinister or a "line of cut-throat ancestors" (*BLJ* 2:27), like the gallery of the doges in which Marino Faliero is installed and which he, neck axed, defaces, or whether it is the slash of blood on Gulnare's unveiled brow, Lord Byron's bloodline is a line of fault, which inscribes on the native face the aboriginal intrusion of the foreign. From the first, the aristocratic line is what George Ellis calls *Childe Harold III*'s verse, a "polyglot line" (*RR* B:5:1991–92). Its arbitrariness has always been the open secret of aristocratic privilege; the claims for purity of blood could be sustained only by reckless infusions from alien tribes. Lord Byron's genealogy is a line as opaque to the story of origins as "But I forget" is opaque to the wish for consummation.[46] With an unmatched shrewdness, Goethe once commented that "one line from *Don Juan* would poison the whole of *Jerusalem Delivered*."[47] This is no doubt why M. H. Abrams quarantined his New Jerusalemic *Natural Supernaturalism* from the contamination of Byron's poem. Here, Byron's "Rome Delivered" is spoiled, artlessly, by line 1567 in stanza 175, a colorful line from *Don Juan* that has somehow lost its home (perhaps self-exiled) and wandered in the back door of the temple.[48]

Childe Harold I began its travels in Portugal with a sympathetic reflection on the ruin of Beckford, "England's wealthiest son." And *Childe Harold* has advanced the wealth of the English nation in the aftermath of the collapse of Napoleon's undercapitalized speculation. *Childe Harold IV,* however, also yields the paradox that "The stubborn heart, its alchemy begun, / Seems near the prize,—wealthiest when most undone" (st. 123). In one respect the phrase is merely a biographical fact: Byron undone suggests the calamity of the separation, which coincided with the period of his greatest capital accumulation. But in another, more powerful sense, the poem is wealthiest when most undone. Byron's undoing, which sullies the "tone" of the conclusion and unravels its grandly woven architecture, is a matter of inadvertence or what the reviews call "negligence." While it is possible to be cunning in one's overthrow, it is impossible to be cunning in one's undoing, especially if what is being undone is exactly one's cunning. The maxim "wealthiest when most undone" does not make a complete break with the speculative strategy of the poem and the career. It is wealth, after all, of which the poet speaks, and one can imagine this aphorism in the mouth of Malcolm Forbes or another sententious spokesman of postindustrial capitalism. But even if there is no break, there is a distance pried open. It makes a difference whether the stress falls on *wealthiest* or *undone*. I shall argue that Byron places it on the latter. By undoing his wealth into a more than airy thinness, past gold, past credit, past money into just another line, Lord Byron will realize his aphorism's twisted strength.

7

The Circumstantial Gravity
of *Don Juan*

. . . my own natural propensity to discrepancy and litigation
Lord Byron to John Cam Hobhouse, August 8, 1820

The *Juan* Effect

I expropriate the term *Juan effect* from Jerome J. McGann's discussion of the poem's style in his pathbreaking *"Don Juan" in Context*. McGann identifies this effect with "Byron's Romantic Irony, properly so-called" and grounds it in the "conflict between the poem's two most important styles," the Juvenalian sublime and the Horatian conversational mode.[1] Unlike McGann, I do not believe in the existence of anything like "Byron's Romantic Irony," and I distrust the reification involved in the distillation of two dialectical styles out of the heterogeneous ferment of the poem. My interest here as throughout is in the strength of Lord Byron's poetry. As I have rendered it thus far, that strength has been roughly apportioned to the difference that the adjective *Lord* makes to *Byron*. Up to this point I have represented Lord Byron's strength as manifest in the sporadic disruptions of the smooth operation of a literary system called Byronism (of which contemporary Byron criticism inside and outside the academy is the heir), which programmatically translates poetic deeds into reflexively complicated, serially elaborated images of the poet available for imitation and consumption. Broadly characterized, the *Juan* effect involves the transformation of spasms into tactics. With *Juan* Lord Byron's strength achieves an ethical dimension. The realization of an ethics of strength is a textual phenomenon: a benchmark for Lord Byron was, as we shall see, his final break with the covering cherub of his bookseller and his virtuous commitment to continue publication of *Juan* "though it were to destroy fame and profit at once" (*BLJ* 10:126).

The *Juan* effect jettisons not only John Murray but also "Lord Byron" as the kind of subject that McGann imagines: a humanistic poet who is the master strategist of his poem, who thematizes contingency and pays lip service to the "god circumstance," but who, ironically, occupies a standing place of transcendental freedom outside the "array" from which he, designing agent, can artfully dispose accident, contingency, and circumstance to the greater glory of Byron, "properly so-called." In my reading the unfolding of *Juan* is fully circumstantial, subject to no master plan. I try to avoid the kind of objectification of poem, poet, and historical period implicit in the notion of *"Don Juan in* Context." A spectral title for the following three chapters (let it hover between life and death) that would indicate my goal, which is to revive the unsubjected, ethically vital circumstantiality of *Juan*, might be *"Don Juan as* Context." Believe me, on the distinction between *in* and *as* rests the difference between an ironical book and a revolutionary text.

The Strength of Apposition

Ensconced at Venice, Lord Byron was deprived of one of the most thrilling sensations of 1819: he could not observe *Don Juan*'s meteoric appearance in the literary sky of London. John Cam Hobhouse, his everfaithful eyes and ears, did not stint in his recreation of the excitement, however. "It was announced thus," Hobhouse exclaims. "*Don Juan* . . *to morrow.* There's a way for you!! *To morrow The Comet! to morrow!*" As Peter W. Graham has noted, Hobhouse collapses notices in the *Morning Chronicle* promising the arrival of *Don Juan* with daily reports called "Authentic Observations of the Comet."[2] The condensation is entirely in the spirit of the occasion. The coincidence between the arrival of meteor and poem provided the kind of advertising money cannot buy. Past poets and emperors (Napoleon, of course) were compared to comets—freaks of nature, intense and rare. In 1819, however, the force of the simile has begun to swing the other way. The meteor portends no apocalypse, nor does it challenge any astronomical paradigm; it is an anticipated prodigy of nature, and in the economy of sensation excitement is apportioned to it as to a new thing by a poet of celebrated perversity. *Juan* would seem to instaurate the epoch it heralds: the age of interchangeable, brilliantly transient phenomena, or, to put a Juanesque spin on a High Romantic commonplace, the age of continually *novel* heavens and *novel* earths.[3]

In the event Hobhouse's hyperbole cushions some unwelcome news about John Murray's last-minute failure of nerve: "In order to increase the mystification there is neither author's name nor publisher's name—only T. Davison, Printer, White Friars, London." A cloud no doubt, but Hobhouse silvers it: "This will make our wiseacres think that there is poison for King Queen & Dauphin in every page and will irritate public pruriency to a complete priapism."[4] Hobhouse's point, of course, is that whether or not there is indeed something poisonous for "King Queen & Dauphin," the traditional coalition of seditious libel with obscenity will enable *Juan* to take advantage of the prurient public's arousal. Morality aside, such a promotional strategy narrows to the ejaculatory the register in which success or failure can be assessed. Either you satisfy the priapism you've aroused or you don't. One "wiseacre," the reviewer for the *British Critic,* as attuned to the resonances as Hobhouse but vastly less sympathetic, leaves no doubt as to his frustration: "Fearful indeed was the prodigy—a book without a bookseller; an advertisement without an advertiser—'a deed without a name.' After all this portentous parturition, out creeps *Don Juan*—and, doubtless, much to the general disappointment of the town, as innocent of satire, as any other Don in the Spanish dominions" (*RR* B:1:296). The portents promised a *Juan* that would be sublime. But in these latter days, portents, like advertisements, lie. The reviewer deflatingly represents the failure of the sublime as the birth of a mock-Gothic monstrosity. As in the comical scene of instruction in Jane Austen's *Northanger Abbey,* where the consternation aroused by Catherine Moreland's announcement that "something shocking will soon be coming out of London" is dispelled by the consolatory disclosure that the political disturbance feared is only a publishing event advertised, so here the supposed prodigy of sublime genius is revealed to be merely the deformed progeny of the marriage of convenience between an author and a publisher.

What is odd about this travesty—the commercialist identification of human contrivances with divine creations—is that it unknowingly reproduces the political satire launched in the suppressed "Dedication" to *Don Juan*. There the failed architect of the sublime is given the name *Castlereagh*:

The vulgarest tool that Tyranny could want,
  With just enough of talent, and no more,
To lengthen fetters by another fix'd,
And offer poison long already mix'd.

An orator of such set trash of phrase
  Ineffably—legitimately vile,
That even its grossest flatterers dare not praise,
  Nor foes—all nations—condescend to smile;
Not even a sprightly blunder's spark can blaze
  From that Ixion grindstone's ceaseless toil,
That turns and turns to give the world a notion
Of endless torments and perpetual motion.

A bungler even in its disgusting trade,
  And botching, patching, leaving still behind
Something of which its masters are afraid,
  States to be curb'd and thoughts to be confined,
Conspiracy or Congress to be made—
  Cobbling at manacles for all mankind—
A tinkering slave-maker, who mends old chains,
With God and man's abhorrence for its gains.

In the scheme of the *British Critic* it is Lord Byron who, in the service of Murray and for the cause of Byronism, piles up his "trash of phrase" in order to overawe a class of subject readers. The poet becomes a version of Castlereagh, the "tool" who administers a world of oppression with a ceaseless flow of unintelligible discourse.[5] The world Castlereagh manages is a world spoiled: a botched totalitarianism that requires of the tyrant intolerant of "blunder" a slavish maintenance, ironically binding him who would bind all. Dreaming of giving the final twist to the great chain of political being, which would lock all creatures in place, the tyrant attempts to wright a cosmos in which one bad turn *demands* another . . . and another. The minister of the totality becomes the miller of eternity, obsessively guarding against an inevitable waste: in the Castlereagian economy every bird that carries off a kernel of grain is the enemy of order.[6]

Everything that Byron calls Castlereagh the "wiseacre" reviewers call him: vulgar, vile, disgusting, and repetitious. Indeed, *Don Juan* does not need to conclude with its hero commandeered to hell in order to be true to its reoccupied myth because its indefinite continuation is a sufficient "notion" of "torments and perpetual motion" for many readers and most reviewers. But *Juan* argues that another name for such torments is "life itself." One formidable problem it confronts is how to release the difference between life and the law that claims to be, in Coleridgean terms, the life of that life. Castlereagh's botched cosmos is the ironic fate reserved for those who forge iron chains intended conclusively to link like with like and past with future so as to prevent all accident, including the accidental linkage of ideological antagonists such as Byron and Castlereagh or such as that between the vigorously mocked Robert Southey, turncoat laureate, and the poet whose poem "turns and turns" as the world turns.[7]

If there is a moral difference between Southeyan apostasy and Byronic turning, it would take Southey to point it. Byron's position is to have no position: he turns in order to keep turning. The *Juan* effect is the comical liability of apostasy to turn into mere trope and of the cleverest trope sadly to lapse into literal-minded apostasy. Southeyan apostasy involves a move from one position to another that (it is vowed) will be as piously and permanently held as the former one had been. Southey (and Southey's apologist, Coleridge) justifies his shift in position according to a difference in the *contents* of the two positions, before and after—indeed, the very possibility of justification (a possibility that *Juan* does not countenance) presupposes the moral superiority and the contents of one position over those of another.[8] Aristocrat and parasite, Lord Byron plays the position rather than the contents, the manner rather than the matter.[9] In contrasting himself with Southey Byron avows no Broughamian adherence to Whiggish principles but a Brummellian taste for the "buff and the blue"—the contingent and superficial color, badge, or rubric of affiliation.[10] Byron's position is in line with his stated preference to "differ over *something* rather than *nothing*" (*BLJ* 3:65), but it also shows that the *something* is not substantive in any way that the theologians of politics would approve.

In order to muffle as much as possible the theological resonance of Byron's inclination, I shall substitute for *apostasy* the term *apposition*, "the placing of things [substantives] in close superficial contact; the putting of distinct things side by side in close proximity." The *OED*'s definition captures the mutual implication, even contamination, of proximity and contact ("the fact or condition of being in close contact, juxtaposition, parallelism") that is the most salient feature of the *Juan* effect—a kind of differential linkage between things that likens them by eroding their insular identities, brings them together without producing a new unity or fabricating a synthetic identity. In logic, as in the work of the laureate, parallel lines will never meet.[11] In life (that is, in *Juan*), where parallels are aligned in ink, they are always liable to deviation and thus superficial contact, bursts, knots, clouds, and clots of "negative entropy."[12] To play *ap*position is to exploit the possibility of movement and change contingent on that deviance and incidental contact (contact that aims to breed neither biologically like the dynasts of Europe nor speculatively like the merchants of Venice). To appose is to move off the place where one "is" (what Coleridge calls the "stasis," but let us call it the "dominant") by the application of a parallel that *touches* on the dominant. This application affects the integrity of the dominant and thus hampers its authority. (Note that I speak not of subverting, transgressing, or undermining, but of affecting, as noise or even color—mix them as *hue*—affects the purity of a tone.) The effect is like that associated with parody and with all those words that belong to the family of the parasite as canvassed by Michel Serres. Apposition belongs to the repertoire of tactics, the tactical considered as an uncannily adept touch that in the mode of the picaresque breaks down the distinction between *meum* and *tuum*—the tactical, then, as the zone of intimacy, danger, and mistake.[13]

The most conspicuous formal consequence of such recklessness in the first two cantos of *Don Juan*, at least according to contemporary reviews, is the narrator's lapse into the first person plural during the storm and stress of the shipwreck: "but the ship still lay / Like a mere log, and baffled our intent"; "Eased her at last (although we never meant . . .)" (2:32). Fault, yes. Sin, no. The liability of parallel, faulty things to touch makes it possible to link by inclination and obligation rather than by iron and coercion. *Juan* is able to indulge and exploit the tangible intimacy of its multiple parallels as Tories Castlereagh and Southey or as Reformer Hobhouse or as pirate Conrad—petrified in the face of difference—cannot.

In canto 3 the poet reflects that

> words are things, and a small drop of ink,
>   Falling like dew, upon a thought, produces
> That which makes thousands, perhaps millions, think;
>   'T is strange, the shortest letter which man uses
> Instead of speech, may form a lasting link
> Of ages.
>
> (3:88)

If the "drop of ink, / Falling like dew, upon a thought" recalls the drop of blood "falling" on Gulnare's head as the materialization of a vivid, eventful separation, or if the "shortest letter" recalls the *e* that befalls Childe Harold, *méthode, cavalier servente* (Byron's title while in the train of Teresa Guiccoli at Venice), or "Byronne," it is because each achieves a prefigural strength by the apposition of the literal: each forms a link. In one way or another linkage has been the predominant concern of a career in which every exploitation of noble license has entailed a lordly obligation, in which every poetic act has implied a publisher's series. It is *Juan*'s distinction decisively to separate the eventuality of linkage from the psychopathology of Byronism: both the mechanics of narcissistic fascination that demand the supply of new Oriental tales and the speculative dialectic that propels *Childe Harold* toward cultural monopoly. *Juan*'s "shortest letter" radicalizes Richard Hurd's "naked letter of romance" as the elementary tactic that inclines heterogeneities to elect wordedness. Not the Ancient of Days but the naked letter of romance clothes the atoms of thought with dewy freshness and blushes the blank visage of the logos into human life.

To be as precise as Lord Byron is we should emphasize that the letter *"may* form a lasting link." The addition of the "shortest letter" is not the stenographer's standardized transcription of speech that reproduces the conventions by which professional communities administer their social power; its strength befalls the appositional inkshed as contingently as the ink befalls the thought it materializes in human history. Writing is not the apostatic falling away from speech but the material difference that is applied to speech, an application that may be said to befall speech (as deviance befalls desire) insofar as it is contingent, the unpredictable, Lucretian consequence of the world's turn and of human assertion. Each opaque drop of ink that superficially colors or stains the inhuman transparency of thought or that taints the tyrannical purity of speech is the originary (that is, literal) cause of the genealogy of a figure (call it *Juan* as apposed to the culturally dominant discursive formation named Byron) that will always be contingent on this institution and will be subject continually to the apposition of spots of ink as they are shed or dropped, as they fall or flow, in the peculiar inclination of time that is *Juan*'s ottava rima. Unlike Hobhousean stenography, which is the hieroglyphic reduction of republican ideology, the Byronic letter is not a design but a spot: fuzzy, cumulative, colored. The addition of letter after letter, one prefiguration after another, will never amount to a final word.

Buying Byron

The journalist's avowal of contempt is not necessarily contempt itself. Despite his sneers, the reviewer for the *British Critic* does not put the poem down. He reviews it. It may be that a poison of a different kind from what

Hobhouse had in mind is at work, one that spreads what Thomas Moore called the "contagion of Byronism" (*BLJ* 8:114). Observe its virulence. The reviewer poses the question, "If Don Juan then be not a satire—what is it?" He reflects that "a more perplexing question could not be put to the critical squad." He lists the negatives that disqualify any and every generic appellation with which it might be credited. He concludes that "as far therefore as we are enabled to give it any character at all, we should pronounce it a narrative of degrading debauchery in doggerel rhyme" (*RR* B:1:297). Degrading whom? Lord Byron, certainly. The degradation of the lord by the poet is a well-worn theme of the reviews. Another victim announces himself in the reviewer's doggerel alliteration, however. Brought low by his critical engagement with *Juan*, the moralist crawls as the poem creeps. Such degradation of man into doggerel provokes the *Courier's* denunciation of Byron as an "unsexed Circe, who gems the poison cup he offers us."[14]

Yet from a sociological perspective the degradation is not Circean but systemic; that is, it is the consequence not of any particular poisonous word or passage but of the Ixion wheel that has churned out the poem and grinds down the reviewer's resistance to its appeal. Opposing a hegemonic discourse called Byron, the reviewer takes a stand that, no matter how principled it may imagine itself to be, is produced by the very system it reprehends and that has its proper name: *anti-Byronism*.[15] Indeed, the reviewer's objection is fully anticipated by the poet in his withheld preface as the complaint of "a weakly human creature conscious of owing its worldly elevation to its own debasement." The reviewer's degradation at abetting Byronism by reviewing *Juan*—even though author and publisher fail to declare themselves, even though the poetry is morally and artistically reprehensible—is the moralized expression of his subjugation to a mode of literary production that requires a Byron to increase its profits every bit as much as the Continental system required a Napoleon to sustain its sway.

Because it is only by virtue of the literary system that the reviewer lives, moves, and has his being, it might be argued that there is nothing personal about this degradation, which is, after all, merely "nominal." Elements of the machine cannot in fact be degraded by their realization that they are elements of a machine (if the "fact" that I am nothing but part of a machine can ever truly be realized).[16] From a general point of view *degradation* might just as well be dropped in favor of what Theodor Adorno and Max Horkheimer have taught us is its virtual synonym, *enlightenment*. In its enterprisingly British variant enlightenment means facing up to the lackluster countenance of a disenchanted world by manufacturing and marketing rouge for those wantons who can no longer manage to blush. Corruption means prosperity. And where is the shame in that? Yes, where? To touch on the shame still lodged in "degradation" means retrieving the circumstantial strength of this representative moment—questioning why this reviewer for the *British Critic* takes in his hands what can only soil him. "Mode of production" aside, in one way or another these questions can be put to reviewer after reviewer of Byron's distasteful works: Why *would* anyone want to *buy* a book of bad verse? What is the relation between buying *Don Juan* and buying Byron, between buying Byron and buying an "unnamed deed"?

Those questions are solicited by the *British*'s own dogged attempt to account for the strength of the negligible:

> The adventures which it recounts are of such a nature, and described in such language, as to forbid its entrance within the doors of any modest woman, or decent man. Nor is it a history only, but a manual of profligacy. Its tendency is not only to excite the passions, but to point out the readiest means and method of their indulgence. Vice is here represented not merely in that grosser form which carries with it its own shame, and almost its own destruction, but in that alluring and sentimental shape, which at once captivates and corrupts. If without knowing the name of the poet, or the history of the work, our opinion had been required of the intention of the canto, we should have answered—that it was a calm and deliberate design to palliate and recommend the crime of adultery, to work up the passions of the young to its commission, and to afford them the most practical hints for its consummation. But it is not, we trust, by the maudlin and meretricious cant of the lascivious Little, nor by the doggrel narrations of his friend and admirer, the author of the poem before us, that the British nation is to be tricked out of that main bulwark of its national strength, its sturdy and unbending morality. (*RR* B:1:299–300)

According to the reviewer *Don Juan* has not only sensation but subversion in mind or (to take up the metaphor of the manual) in hand. Diabolically practical, it teaches seduction (dress as you like, but whatever you do, don't present yourself in that gross form that carries with it its own shame!) by being unnervingly seductive. The reviewer's claim of degradation becomes convincing in light of an ambivalence so intense that it produces within a few short sentences the barbarous contradiction that *Don Juan* "at once captivates and corrupts" and yet fails to trick the British nation out of its "sturdy and unbending morality." Is there a poetic magic of such paradoxically outrageous potency? Has the British nation—and by synecdoche everything called British—been bent despite its posture of inviolate moral propriety?

Juan offers an example of such bending in the famous seduction of Donna Julia in canto 1:

> And Julia sate with Juan, half embraced
> And half retiring from the glowing arm,
> Which trembled like the bosom where't was placed;
> Yet still she must have thought there was no harm,
> Or else 't were easy to withdraw her waist;
> But then the situation had its charm,
> And then—God knows what next—I can't go on;
> I'm almost sorry that I e'er begun.
>
> Oh Plato! Plato! you have paved the way,
> With your confounded fantasies, to more
> Immoral conduct by the fancied sway
> Your system feigns o'er the controlless core
> Of human hearts, than all the long array
> Of poets and romancers:—You're a bore,
> A charlatan, a coxcomb—and have been,
> At best, no better than a go-between.
>
> And Julia's voice was lost, except in sighs,
> Until too late for useful conversation;
> The tears were gushing from her gentle eyes,
> I wish indeed they had not had occasion;
> But who, alas! can love, and then be wise?
> Not that remorse did not oppose temptation:
> A little still she strove, and much repented,
> And whispering "I will ne'er consent"—consented.
>   (1:115–17)

These remarkable stanzas implicate the telling as the tale. The phrase "the situation had its charm" describes a triple analogy among Julia, narrator, and reader. *Situation* is a key term for narratologist Ross Chambers, for whom it designates the context that, produced by texts, gives them their "point."[17] *Situation* was also, as Martin Meisel has shown, a prominent term in the aesthetic jargon of the early nineteenth century, where it referred to the conventional gesture that had come to express not simply "one man's passions in serial order" (the mode, say, of Garrick's performance of *Richard III* or Byron's in *Childe Harold IV*) but the "simultaneous relationship of several figures." Historically, then, the ascendance of "situation" concludes a semiotic transformation, whereby a "system of representations of the passions" is remodeled as "conventionalized attitude and gesture, then as stereotyped character and finally translated into 'legible' narrative configuration." That last stage is the one at which Julia, woman of her time, finds herself, doing double duty as the figure both of and for a conventional reader. Far from being something invented by an individual text, the situation served as a kind of key for the translation of representational and affective codes among the discourses of painting, the theater, and prose and verse narrative; its predominance in the early nineteenth century is, according to Meisel, "one of the considerations that point to what might be called a common structure or style."[18] The notion of a "period style" as an always already historicized mode of artistic expression and the predominance of the situation go hand in glove as an ideogrammatically precise narrative configuration, which is most neatly emblematized by what we have called the Romantic scene of fascination and what *Juan* obligingly displays here in canto 1.[19]

To say Julia is *charmed* by her situation is not quite the same thing as saying that she is *seduced* by it, however, if seduction is restricted to a state of mind that entails sexual consequences. The more Catholic nuance of *charm* captures the affiliations between character and narrator indicated by "And then—God knows what next—I can't go on," which Romantically compounds the ethical and the artful. The narrator may halt to titillate, or his pause may respond to obstacles—moral or imaginative—that bar the representation of sexual contact. Or both. At any rate, whatever priapism is involved is hardly complete. With playful inadvertence the narrator of *Don Juan* does to himself what the blood-spotting Gulnare does for the blocked Conrad. The narrator's "I can't go on" anticipates Julia's "I will ne'er consent" (as both forecast the plight of the *British Critic*); and as will she, he nonetheless does goes on to where consent occurs. His path crosses the apostrophe to Plato. The "shortest letter which man uses / Instead of speech, may form a lasting link of ages," and the interjection of "Oh Plato," the "small drop of ink," goes between one stanza and another.[20] Action poetry: ink drops, link forms. The narrator does not come up with a Newtonian "reason" that impels or enables him to go on; instead, an interjection befalls him that momentarily occludes the convention that narrative must be motivated by a reason. "Forgetting" metaphorically bridges the gap where a reason is missing. Forgetting the standard of decorum works every bit as well here for the narrator as it had for the hidalgos who interjected other blood into their dynastic line and "restored the breed": it made possible a "heathenish cross" to a future unforeseen (1:58). Here a veil of Platonic doctrine enables Julia's frankly sensual impulses to impel her to consent. Not Platonic doctrine, however, but the inky interjection of the apostrophe to Plato—what might be called the apparition of Plato—enables the narrator to cross from stanza 115 to 117.

The charm of Julia's situation encourages her to ignore the physical force propelling her to a nondiscursive "consent." She is as subject as Juan to the biological imperative of "natural history"; and at the crisis it is her instinctual drive, the "controlless core" of her heart, that decides the issue. Throughout Byron's poetry such has been the destiny of women, who are embodied as males are not. We might suspect that the insistence of the biological is a theory not so much about gender as about the persistence of aristocracy as an instinctual drive residually operative within the novel social arrangements of the modern era. Because Julia is a mixture of impulses and her blood a mixture of classes, the essentializing of her as woman is complicated and constantly under adjustment in the canto; yet even disregarding those complications, the essentialized, biologically burdened feminine cannot be strictly identified with the aristocracy; she is but one component of the aristocratic complex that the poem projects. It is crucial to note that the rhetorical inventiveness that allows the narrator to go on is in apposition to the oblivion of scruples that carries Julia to consent. The tactical relation of rhetoric—the use of whatever means are at hand to achieve an end not fully foreseen—to the biological, blooded drive is a kind of propping that parallels the relation of the sexual to the vital order in Jean Laplanche's revision of Freud's model of infant sexuality.[21] The aristocratic complex includes the natural (that is, sexual) order and, propped on that standard (as narrator is propped on character), the deviation from that order—a contingent turn or apparition that is represented as requisite for nature to take *a* (if not *its*) course, for nature to have a history rather than just a fate.

For Julia, Juan is no apparition. Her seduction, her move from charm to consent, depends on a physical touch that neither narrator nor reader can share. Should we say that the reader, who goes on, has likewise been seduced? Has the reader consented to seduction? What would seal consent—the physical act of consummation, or the acquiescence in its virtual possibility? The reader is free to ponder these questions as Julia, having taken the plunge, is not. Because it is rendered as physically sexual, inextricable from the touch of a "glowing arm," Julia's seduction is distanced from the reader, who, forced to countenance nothing repulsive herself, can regard Julia's situation as just another *example* of consenting with no bearing on her; she can excuse herself for continuing with the narrative. The exemplary reader of *Don Juan* is one who is governed by virtue of her denial that she has ever actually consented to be governed, who can believe that she has entered into a contract that frees her of the obligations that consent implies. That denial, as *Juan* will show, is a symptom of the pathology of consent in a commercial culture.

To address that pathology involves returning to the question of what there is about this text that in the absence of a "glowing arm" induces one to "buy" it—exchange money for it and/or lend one's belief to it, even though it is "vile" and "trash." We know that in one instance, *Don Juan* was not bought because of the name *Byron*, or *John Murray*, but because it called the reviewer by name. Here is the lure that captivated "the British":

> The public approbation I expect
>   And beg they'll take my word about the moral,
> Which I with their amusement will connect
>   (So children cutting teeth receive a coral);
> Meantime they'll doubtless please to recollect
>   My epical pretensions to the laurel;
> For fear some prudish readers should grow skittish,
> I've bribed my grandmother's review—the British.
>
> I sent it in a letter to the Editor,
>   Who thank'd me duly by return of post—
> I'm for a handsome article his creditor;
>   Yet, if my gentle Muse he please to roast,
> And break a promise after having made it her,
>   Denying the receipt of what it cost,
> And smear his page with gall instead of honey,
> All I can say is—that he had the money.
>
>   (1:209–10)

I have said one instance, but no instance is unique. In this case the candid poet's tongue forks ambiguously. In the England of 1819 two reviews spoke as "the British": the *British Critic*, quoted above, and the *British Review*. The *Critic* labeled the charge "facetious." The editor of the *British Review* did not follow suit and laugh it off; he took it "personally" by identifying himself as that "one" named British (he remained otherwise anonymous) and accused of receiving a bribe.

The *British Review*'s reply begins with the question, "Of a poem so flagitious that no bookseller has been willing to take upon himself the publication, though most of them disgrace themselves by selling it, what can the critic say?" Whatever "*the* critic" might say, *this* critic answers his own question by abandoning the pretense of a review in order first to examine the circumstances that connect this indecency to Lord Byron and then to lay down the first law of literary culture: "No misdemeanour, not even that of sending into the world obscene and blasphemous poetry, the product of 'studious lewdness,' and 'laboured impiety,' appears to us in so detestable a light as the acceptance of a present by an editor of a review as the condition of praising an author; and yet the miserable man . . . who has given birth to this pestilent poem, has not scrupled to lay this to the charge of 'The British Review.'" The reviewer/editor/defendant repudiates the charge and challenges the evidence:

> If somebody personating the Editor of the British Review has received money from Lord Byron, or from any other person, by way of bribe to praise his compositions, the fraud might be traced by the production of the letter which the author states himself to have received in return. Surely then, if the author of this poem has any such letter, he will produce it for this purpose. But lest it should be said that we have not in positive terms denied the charge, we do utterly deny that there is one word of truth, or the semblance of truth, as far as regards this Review or its Editor, in the assertions made in the stanzas above referred to. We really feel a sense of degradation as the idea of this odious imputation passes through our minds. (*RR* B:1:476–77)

There has been no gift and thus no obligation. For the *British Review* critical independence is wedded to the commodification of the cultural artifact, which frees the purchasing critic from any reciprocal obligation to the selling poet. If things are bought and sold according to a contract arrived at in the open market, seller and buyer make no contact except through the abstracted mediation of money, which, because it entails no consequences, emancipates economics from ethics. But if the reviewer claims to owe Lord Byron nothing, his very outrage, the "sense of degradation" that passes through his mind belies the model of sanitized exchange he invokes. The facts are known to both parties: Byron offered no bribe, the *British Review* accepted none.

But, as Byron, writing his "Letter to the Editor of My Grandmother's Review" under the nom de guerre of the brutally sympathetic Wortley Clutterbuck points out, it is also a fact that the *British Review* has been at once captivated and corrupted. Enchanted by stanzas 209 to 210, the reviewer drops the pretense of criticism to entangle himself in casuistical self-defense; and in doing so, Clutterbuck points out, he fulfills, despite himself and in the very denial of its existence, the terms of the imaginary bribe: "By the way, you don't say much about the poem, except that it is 'flagitious.' That is a pity—you should have cut it up; because, to say the truth, in not doing so, you somewhat assist any notions which the malignant might entertain on the score of the anonymous asseveration which has made you so angry." Having sprung the trap, Byron/Clutterbuck tosses off a bit of gratuitous instruction in the elements of market economics: You say, no bookseller 'was willing to take upon himself the publication, though most of them disgrace themselves by selling it.' Now, my dear friend, although we all know that those fellows will do any thing for money, methinks the disgrace is more with the purchasers; and some such, doubtless, there are, for there can be no very extensive selling . . . without buying."[22]

The *British's* charge that *Juan* is a "pestilent poem" is a mystification of a piece with its condemnation of booksellers. The poem—its accusations, its libel—has no power of its own and would exert no force had not someone, despite the facts, despite its anonymity, *bought* it. And people do buy. The pestilential is nothing other than those serial acts of exchange called commerce. Chief among *Juan's* purchasers is the editor of the *British Review*, whose purchase displays the coincidence of "buying" as putting money down for a commodity and tendering belief in a representation that one knows to be false or "facetious."[23] But why buy?

The *British* characterizes the degradation that accompanies the act of exchange by means of the sexualized language of captivation and corruption. The defense implies alternative assumptions about the transaction: either by buying a book I have made a contract to be seduced or I have been seduced into contracting to buy a book. Certainly, implying that one has been seduced into intimacy with another man is a confession shameful enough. But that every commercial exchange implies a contract and that every contract implies a desire to be seduced (a desire that can be economically justified according to its fulfillment in the moment of consumption) generalizes the plight of the reviewer in a fashion that leaves his special shame—at once unique and exemplary—untouched. In the language of the political economists, it is the ability of the commodity to *command* a purchase that is at stake in this transaction.[24] The sexualization of contracts posits a moment of choice. That I do buy what seduces me is not nearly as degrading as the shameful fact that I *can* buy (psychologically speaking) and *must* regularly buy (professionally speaking) something that says the worst imaginable things about me—that "I" or "one" must believe what shatters the personal and professional integrity requisite for entering into contracts or liaisons.[25] The *can* represents the psychological vulnerability into which the commercial imperative of the literary system bites. What sorely pinches the *British Review* is, in *Juan*'s terms, the coincidence of financial exchange with a command to believe.

That coincidence squeezes the cannier *British Critic* as well. The irreconcilable insistence on "corruption" and a nonetheless "unbending" morality is exactly the contradiction that *Don Juan* fingers as the crux of British commercial society. What makes commercial morality a bulwark is an unbending commitment to hardheaded buying and selling. Selling is profitable for some because buying has become for others the most natural thing in the world, a second nature that personates that real, independent me. And each transaction reinscribes that secondariness as the moment in which the object to be bought is supplemented by a representation (facetious, false, or fictional) that has to be believed or credited. To buy *Don Juan*, with whatever disdain, is to credit it. Buying is bending, but this tilt has become so normal that it is on most occasions imperceptible. To be at once captivated, corrupted, and unbendingly moral, to *cant*, is what it means to be "British."[26]

To the question "Why *does* the *British Review* 'buy' something it knows to be false?" Wortley Clutterbuck supplies an answer that epitomizes the poetics of *Don Juan*: "The charge itself is of a solemn nature, and, although in verse, is couched in terms of such circumstantial gravity, as to induce a belief little short of that generally accorded to the thirty-nine articles."[27] *Circumstantial gravity* is the name for what induces one to "buy" a poem, or a religion for that matter. Not context but the condition of context, circumstantial gravity laminates the superficies, layer after layer, and pulses the energy, relay after relay. The first relay in the fabrication of context is the reader. Circumstantial gravity can be concocted by calling a reader's name, as in *British*. The *British Review* answers to the call and buys *Don Juan* even though, as the response of the *British Critic* (not to mention the history of England, Wales, Scotland, and Ireland) proves, the "great name" *British* is "nothing more than nominal" (*DJ* 4:101). The name *British* acquires its circumstantial gravity not from a proper correspondence with a particular reader or with some chronicled incident but by its resemblance to many faces and facts and its capacity to simulate the precariousness of identity (personal, occupational, or national) that prevails in the world at large.

As we have seen, Lord Byron has deployed this strongly discrepant simile with increasing effectiveness during his career. His advance was assisted by the *British Review*, which in happier days devoted a section of its commentary on *The Giaour* to this grandmotherly lesson:

In all the similes [by which passages of picturesque description] are illustrated, there is a minuteness in the parallel that diminishes their splendour,
and divides their force. It may be of use for the poet to remember that *nullem
simile est idem*; and if he will detain the mind of the reader in the details of his
comparisons so long as to allow it coolly to examine particulars, it will at last,
in spite of the general beauty of the passage, be as apt to rest upon the points
of discrepancy as the points of resemblance. In poetical comparisons the
leading features of similitude should alone be selected by the poet, and
made to pass in rapid succession through the mind of the reader, leaving a
general impression, strong, full, and effulgent, and comprehended in one
intellectual view, rather than the studied effect of a detailed examination.[28]
A simile should place the mind so completely under the dominion of the
prominent resemblance, as to make it impossible for it to take any notice of
inferior qualities and characteristics, whether they differ or agree. (*RR*
B:1:411)

The poet of *Don Juan* heeds the aphorism *Nullem simile est idem* but
makes a strikingly different application. The critic's version of the simile,
customized to fit a new, speed-reading public, is anchored in well-known
conventions for the apt characterization of the human face. At one extreme
this conception of the simile, with centering resemblance and discrepancies
banished to the periphery, verges on caricature, the pictorial analogue to
stenography. At the other extreme the picture verges on an ideal uniformity
of visage that offers to the viewer a face plausibly "similar" to his or her own.
Historically (at least since LeBrun's enormously influential *Manual of the
Passions*) these extremes had been mediated publicly by the numerous handbooks of expressive and gestural codes that passed from painting to the
theater to the realms of domestic fashion and etiquette. The *British Review*'s
version of the simile does fit Byron's representations of his heroes and
heroines in *The Giaour* and the subsequent Oriental tales, where a brow, a
lip, or a cheek says everything the reader needs to know in all the time he or
she might be willing to spend. Even in those routine generic products,
however, the affective force of the poem is not restricted to such stagy
scenes of fascination: the obtrusion of peripheral details such as foreign
words and punning bits of script agitates the composition. What could be
more like the Orient than *bulbul* or *Colomboloio* or Kaled's arabesque, and
what could be more discrepant with the kind of Orient that the Oriental
tales are designed to merchandise? *Circumstantial gravity* identifies a non-
mimetic textual inducement, which dominates the mind by the concentration of resemblance and discrepancy into a passage of great density and
force. This negligent manner, which intermittently diverts the narrative

project of the Oriental tales, becomes the preponderant style of *Don Juan*.

Circumstantial gravity names the sticking point that troubles the hydraulic fluency of exchange; it is responsible for the sense of *Juan*'s "worldliness"—identity rifted by discrepancy.[29] Passages are more perplexed in this turbulent poem than in any other of Byron's writings. They are loosed from correspondence with patterns of versification, the logic of plot, and the verisimilitude of character. *Don Juan*'s passages are crossings, but none is unperplexed. The grand representation of this statelessness of affairs occurs in the beginning of canto 2, where the parallel attempts to book safe passage for Juan across the water and from adolescence to maturity are both wrecked by the inevitable but unforeseeable storms that afflict a "nautical existence" (2:12). The theme of thwarted or diverted passages in *Don Juan* does have formal and rhetorical corollaries, though in general the poem defaults on promised correspondences between formal features and thematic implication.

Or so the reviewers complained. Most found it difficult to quote from the poem, not merely because there are so many outrageous passages but because even the rare "beauties" bleed into something ugly. The most dramatic example of this confoundment is, of course, the effort of the *British Review*, which, paralyzed in horror, can quote nothing except the slander that consumes it.[30] But the *British* was not alone. Against its better judgment *Blackwood's* condescends to quote "a few of the passages which can be read without a blush, because the comparative rarity of such passages will, in all probability, operate to the complete exclusion of the work itself from the libraries of the greater part of our readers." But the reviewer eventually abandons his salvaging in the midst of the shipwreck episode, exclaiming, "We dare not stain our pages with quoting any specimens of the disgusting merriment with which he has interspersed his picture of human suffering" (*RR* B:1:146, 149). Avoiding the verse like the plague or like a cannibalized body, the reviewer lets crew and poem drift. *Juan* is the kind of world in which progress is blocked and the view spoiled by the penetration of the peripheral into the center of attention. That irrepressible gathering of dispersed effects into a circumstantial knot defeats even the censorious Hobhouse's surgical imagination: "I have now gone through the objections which appear so mixed up with the whole work especially to those who are in the secret of the *domestica facta* that I know not how any amputation will save it: more particularly as the objectionable parts are in point of wit humour and poetry the very best beyond all doubt of the whole poem."[31]

Circumstantial gravity is textual. According to Jacques Derrida, "A text is not a text unless it hides from the first comer, from the first glance, the law of its composition and the rules of its game. A text remains, moreover, forever imperceptible. Its laws and its rules are not, however, harbored in the inaccessibility of a secret; it is simply that they can never be booked, in the *present*, into anything that could rigorously be called a perception."[32] That definition characterizes the encounter of the *British Review* with *Don Juan*. The reviewer responded to the false charge because he failed to perceive the rules of *Don Juan*'s game, even though they are hidden right on the surface—most saliently in the farcical squabble between Donna Julia and Don Alfonso. Like the *British*, Don Alfonso and his cronies identify personal vindication with a vital and strategic defense of the social fabric: both presume that "Examples of this kind are so contagious, / Were *one* not punished, *all* would be outrageous" (1:138). What kind? Like the *British*, impelled to collaborate in its own degradation, like Lord Ellenborough, fatally driven to turn the court of justice into a duel, Don Alfonso finds that in order to certify outrage (establishing the fact of outrage entails settling the kind of crime against kind it is, whether it is sodomistic, incestuous, or adulterous), he must himself become a kind of example and "prove himself the thing he most abhorr'd" (1:139). Don Alfonso's charge of adultery, at first outfaced by indignation, is then bewilderingly turned against him by the surprisingly adept Julia, who, like Hone at *his* trial, proves herself to be a virtuoso of cheek.

Not only does the episode activate an uncannily resourceful forensic ingenuity, as if we were brought face to face with the very female machine that publishes seductive inventions ("all propagated with the best intentions" [1:132]); it also renders legible the misrecognition of textuality that both makes such circumstantial rhetoric persuasive and insures the inefficacy, if not the impracticality, of exposing its mechanics. The misrecognition of textuality is allegorized in the obvious concealment of Juan folded within the bedclothes (an impossible hiddenness—see 1:166—which is the possibility of hiding in a text open to every eye). It is because the (phallic) rule of the game remains imperceptible that Don Alfonso confronts a text rather than merely a clever wife; it is because he confronts a text that he cannot see the purloined Juan. It is because the *British Review* confronts a text that it fails both to see the snare hidden in canto 1, stanzas 209 to 210, and to read the allegory of its deception represented in the farce. The Alfonso episode allegorizes the *British Review*'s gulling by Lord Byron's text as it proves the reviewer's inability to read that allegory, though he confront it face to face.

Don Alfonso and the *British Review* are not the only victims of misreading here. The passage does not end with the husband routed; the text goes on, and as it does, what has been shown to be hidden is hidden to be shown again. Crucial to the textuality of this poem and of the allegory of textuality in this episode is the crossing of the pride of the master to Donna Julia. She believes herself credentialed to bind and to loose. But forgetting in her triumph the improvisatory rule of thumb that the "only path to invention is complete consent to be mistaken in front of others,"[33] she in turn becomes blind to what lies openly hidden (to what, openly hidden, lies):

> Alfonso closed his speech, and begg'd her pardon,
>   Which Julia half withheld, and then half granted,
> And laid conditions, he thought very hard, on,
>   Denying several little things he wanted:
> He stood like Adam lingering near his garden,
>   With useless penitence perplex'd and haunted,
> Beseeching she no further would refuse,
> When, lo! he stumbled o'er a pair of shoes.
>
> (1:180)

By chance the shoes come to signify the material contingency of the text, the sudden circumstantial gravity over which one stumbles on the clear path of the everyday. Considered from the point of view of the jealous husband, the masculine shoes are a metonymy for a male body. But the troping cuts both ways, since it is an error of misplaced concreteness to think that the important thing was to hide Juan's body, when in truth the important thing was that something be plainly hidden. For Julia to forget the shoes is to forget (*necessarily*, Paul de Man would add) that far from her rhetoric mastering the occasion, her success was contingent on the occasion of a text—that is, it is not important that a male body be kept out of sight but that a signifier be plainly hidden. A fully materialist reading of this passage would not conclude that shoes are a metonym for Juan but that Juan is the personification of the shoes.

The *British Critic*'s characterization of *Don Juan* as Gothic mystification as well as its disdain for the poem's facetiousness amount to a denial that *Don Juan* is a text.[34] Nonetheless, the glaring contradiction between immediate captivation and unbending rectitude remarks on the review's failure to perceive exactly the rule by which buying Byron makes one complicit in the textual elaboration of *Don Juan*. To say that neither of the *British* reviewers is beyond the text is simply to assert that their failure to see the trap set for them identifies *Juan* as a poem in which something remains hidden from a reader just because of his or her worldly implication in it.

Juan's Nautical Existence

Don Juan's sympathy with Hobhouse's concern for its vulnerability shows in the vestigial classicism of its attempt to graduate "uncertain paper" (1:218) from newspapers to letters to books. Letters, as the experiences of both Donna Julia and the *British Review*'s critic show, may come to bad ends. His simply vanishes. Hers suffers a more complicated fate. Donna Julia's letter concludes thus:

"I have no more to say, but linger still,
    And dare not set my seal upon this sheet,
And yet I may as well the task fulfil,
    My misery can scarce be more complete:
I had not lived till now, could sorrow kill;
    Death shuns the wretch who fain the blow would meet,
And I must even survive this last adieu,
And bear with life to love and pray for you!"

This note was written upon gilt-edged paper
    With a neat little crow-quill, slight and new;
Her small white hand could hardly reach the taper,
    It trembled as magnetic needles do,
And yet she did not let one tear escape her;
    The seal a sun-flower; "*Elle vous suit partout*,"
The motto, cut upon a white cornelian;
The wax was superfine, its hue vermilion.

                                                    (1:197–98)

Julia ends with the acute sense of an ending. Her task completed, all that was figured by her character—her sentimentality, her beauty, her vanity—is conclusively literalized in her letter. But her exit is also the performance of a promise: she will follow you everywhere—she being the woman and *la lettre*, both of which are concentrated in the metaphor of the sunflower. If the seal is the material mark of fulfillment, the image of the sunflower is the sign that the seal, that which fulfills, is also a promise: the promise to trope. The sunflower tropes by virtue of its rootedness in the face of the revolving sun. It fulfills itself in life and letters as a symbol of mute, natural yearning.

But Julia's love is nothing like the sun. The promise to follow Juan everywhere depends on the old-fashioned conceit that *everywhere* is encompassed by a solar orbit, a cosmic revolution that makes *everywhere* the same and the passage through and around it frictionless and uneventful. There can in truth be no credible promise to follow everywhere under the sun because there is no *everywhere* there. *Everywhere* exists only at the level of the sun, just as *here* exists in mutual implication with that orbit and face at the point where the sunflower is rooted. Between the sun and the sunflower there is only an archipelago of turbulent *somewheres* through which Juan sails, swims, and drifts. There is always some "new one" under the sun. And Julia knows that. She has already lamented the ability of a man, unlike a woman and unlike the sun, to "range" through disparate places—"court, camp, church, the vessel, and the mart"—she knows only by name (1:194). Her last words to Juan in the bedroom scene had been, "Fly, Juan, fly! for heaven's sake—not a word— / The door is open—you may yet slip through / The passage you so often have explored" (1:182)—a dark passage that neither woman nor sun can penetrate.

Julia is nothing like a sunflower. Nor, plainly, is her seal; it is the impression of a sunflower, one that marks the circumstantial writtenness of the letter. The condition of her following Juan anywhere is that she write and provide a substitute for her rooted presence that he can carry with him. And in order to make a last and lasting impression, she has to buy wax. Only because such commodities are available (and because she has the money to buy them) can Julia figure her love, turn it into the gilt-edged commodity that she hopes will captivate Juan. If she is effective, it is Juan, of course, who will turn to her letter, as if, in its "hue vermilion," the seal that fulfills and continually promises were the blood-red sun suspended on the horizon and he the yearning flower. Comprising sunflower and sun, Julia's contrivance answers to the Haroldian, imperial dream of the book as a comprehensive and fully intelligible structuring structure—a continual troping referring to and contained by the orbit of the light that englobes us.

But Julia's letter is nothing like a book. The world is the realm where pretenses perish, correspondences fail, and seals are made to be broken—a place illuminated by an "indecent sun" (1:63). Julia's attempt to seal Juan's future, like his mother's and the poet's, goes awry; the shipwreck episode realizes the nightmare of uncertain, all too fungible paper. Unluckily, Julia's letter becomes the very token of chance:

And when his comrade's thought each sufferer knew,
    'Twas but his own, suppress'd till now, he found:
And out they spoke of lots of flesh and blood,
And who should die to be his fellow's food.

But ere they came to this, they that day shared
    Some leathern caps, and what remain'd of shoes;

> And then they look'd around them, and despair'd,
>   And one to be the sacrifice would choose;
> At length the lots were torn up, and prepared,
>   But of materials that must shock the Muse—
> Having no paper, for the want of better,
> They took by force from Juan Julia's letter.
>
> Then lots were made, and mark'd, and mix'd, and handed
>   In silent horror, and their distribution
> Lull'd even the savage hunger which demanded,
>   Like the Promethean vulture, this pollution;
> None in particular had sought or plann'd it,
>   'Twas nature gnaw'd them to this resolution,
> By which none were permitted to be neuter—
> And the whole lot fell on Juan's luckless tutor.
>
> $\qquad\qquad\qquad$ (2:73–75)

The marked lot replaces the waxen sunflower. It seals the fate of Pedrillo, whose lot it is, like Julia's, to become a hostage to man's existence:

> He but requested to be bled to death:
>   The surgeon had his instruments, and bled
> Pedrillo, and so gently ebb'd his breath,
>   You hardly could perceive when he was dead.
>
> $\qquad\qquad\qquad$ (2:76)

Julia is immured so that Juan may "range"; Pedrillo is killed so that the crew may survive. The letter of promise is "fragmentized" into the lot of sacrifice that will supposedly save the group—all these men know of society and all they need to know—from destruction. But this fragmentation becomes the image and instrument of social disintegration. Just as the seal is broken and the letter torn, so even the punctuality of the lot itself, which singles out the man of edible parts, is shattered by the convulsions of the men who, like reviewers of immoral verse, digest what degrades them into demons:

> The consequence was awful in the extreme;
> For they, who were most ravenous in the act,
>   Went raging mad—Lord! how they did blaspheme.
> And foam, and roll, with strange convulsions rack'd,
>   Drinking salt-water like a mountain-stream;
> Tearing, and grinning, howling, screeching, swearing,
> And, with hyaena-laughter, died despairing.
>
> $\qquad\qquad\qquad$ (2:79)

What moral might fit this sequence of outrageous events? Perhaps *cherchez la femme*.[35] Why not blame Julia for trying to turn literary license into literal control? From a certain distance (a few nautical miles) Julia's letter looks like one of those "oddities let loose" by a woman intent to "show [her] parts" (1:128) and by that display of the literal female to lure or horrify the targeted male. "Power sways but by division" may be the Orientalist credo by which Julia governs her conduct, but here a ghastly fragmentation undoes her vainly prostituted pretense to power. The female part finds its ironically appropriate "mart" in the longboat, where the part is parted again in order to separate the survivors into the disparate eaters and the dismembered eaten. The letter—its pathos and its promise—leaves no trace on the trackless sea. Although blaming Julia is convenient, the misogynistic interpretation translates into the nihilistic and absurd moral that Julia ought to have realized that her letter could not execute her intent, and that she should therefore have abstained from writing. The moral is nihilistic because it implies that instead of making a mistake Julia should have restrained herself from doing anything at all. The moral is absurd because it assumes that nothing could in fact be done—that someone can avoid making mistakes by the exercise of a prudence that, *Don Juan* teaches, is no less a venture in control and no less futile than the epistolary gesture.

There is an alternative, more worldly lesson: instead of writing a letter that dreamed of being a book, Julia should have written the book. Instead of sending her sentiment off to its singular death, Julia should have had it printed in many copies so that if one perished others would have survived. And instead of using the antiquated and fragile seal, she should have registered a copyright under the law. Julia should have written a book (it is implied that the choice was within the range of her vanities when we are informed that the narrator is working from a copy) like the ironic poet, whose condescension to her has less the air of a philosopher to an acolyte than of a career-wise, successful author to an improvident hack.

That moral, however, is even less respectable than nihilism. For the fate of Byron's book is not materially different from that suffered by Julia's letter, despite his prudent efforts to protect the young *Juan* from the perils of natural history.[36] Lord Byron chose to publish *Don Juan* anonymously, largely because he feared, with the judgment against Shelley in Chancery vividly in mind, that a prosecution for blasphemy would result in the loss of paternal rights to his child. If Byron were to avow *Juan* it would prove him to be a bad father, not only as blasphemer but as one who preferred the product of his pen to the fruit of his loins.[37] And so the first two cantos of *Juan* appeared without the "passport to celebrity" of Byron's name (*RR*

B:2:981). The omission could be considered a mere technicality. Anonymity did not entail a repudiation of authorship. The veteran of the literary market knows that what makes books is not the name impressed on the title page but the power and right to copy. "Byron" had been formed in intimate collaboration between the poet and his publisher. Apprehensive about the tendency of *Juan*, Murray, with all due respect, reminded his lordship, "My name is connected to your fame." Reversed, that proposition is equally plausible and considerably less humble: the integrity and authenticity of "Byron" depended on the willingness of Murray's publishing house to own him.[38] Hence although Lord Byron's anonymity scarcely mattered, it was truly something new under the sun when *Don Juan* appeared in print without the publisher's name, a masterless poem.

The perpetration of this prodigy had the consequence of opening up an interspersed vacancy of law when *Don Juan* seemed to belong to no one. If like a freak it appeared to the *British Critic*, then like manna from heaven it befell the many publishers who made their living pirating bestsellers, and like the loaves and fishes it multiplied in their hands. Murray found himself in a ticklish position, losing money on a morally obnoxious poem that was a success in large part because of his refusal to admit he owned it. He sought legal advice as to whether a request for an injunction against the pirates would succeed or whether, as in the notorious case of the recent unauthorized publication of Southey's youthful, incendiary *Wat Tyler* (1794), the court would adjudge the poem either blasphemous or seditious and therefore beyond the protection of copyright. Murray's interests were mixed. Although he was eager to prevent the pirates from enriching themselves at his expense, his communications with his attorney show that he was, if anything, more intent on stopping Byron from writing any more shameful cantos of *Don Juan*. Here is the strategic analysis of Murray's lawyer, Sharon Turner:

> On "Don Juan" I have much apprehension. . . . The evil, if not stopped, will be great. It will circulate in a cheap form very extensively, injuring society wherever it spreads. Yet one consideration strikes me. You could wish Lord Byron to write less objectionably. You may also wish him to return you part of the £1625. If the Chancellor should dissolve the injunction on this ground, that will show Lord B. that he must expect no more copyright money for such things, and that they are too bad for law to uphold. Will not this affect the mind and purify his pen? It is true that to get this good result you must encounter the risk and expense of the injunction and of the argument upon it. Will you do this? . . . Perhaps nothing but the Court treating him as it treated Southey may sufficiently impress Lord B.[39]

Turner's letter nicely shows how, for Murray, the impulses of money and morals split. Only what Brougham called the "view of the law" could weld those interests together into a rhetoric potent enough to do what legions of reviewers had failed to achieve, induce Byron to "purify his pen." Turner does not have any particular legal formula in mind; instead, he banks on the power of an adverse judgment to degrade Byron to the level of Southey. In Turner's eyes Murray enjoys a win-win situation: if the publisher loses his appeal for an injunction (which seems the attorney's preference), he can hope to get his money back and deter Byron from his ruinous course. If the injunction is sustained, he increases profits secured by judicial confirmation that the poem is not seriously objectionable at all. In this case the punitive publisher seeks to turn the weapon of copyright against a stubbornly delinquent writer. By this reasoning Lord Byron has no more relation to his book than the next man. Indeed, for Murray the publisher, Byron the copyrighted author is always in danger of being degraded by that roguish lord—now identified by the title *Don Juan*—who *will* write as he pleases and whose best effects may be described as picaresque, as criminal thefts from the "author" whose work lawfully belongs to Murray.

First surprised by the report of a Mr. Shadwell who augured that "the passages are not of such a nature as to overturn the property of it," Turner was startled again by the consistent support given to Murray's claims by judges at Chancery:

> [Shadwell's] decided tone that the Court will not let the copyright be invaded has much struck me. . . . His general opinions are also not favourable to Lord B., and his taste is highly moral. Yet, though he disapproves of the passages, he is remarkably sanguine that they do not furnish sufficient ground for the Chancellor to dissolve the injunction. He says the passages are not more amatory than those of many books of which the copyright was never doubted. He added that one great tendency of the book was not an unfair one. It was to show in Don Juan's ultimate character the ill effect of that injudicious maternal education which Don Juan is represented as having received, and which had operated injuriously upon his mind. He repeated to me several times that, as far as it was possible to foresee an event, he could not doubt of this.[40]

Shadwell gives the view of the law in all its majestic purity. Observe how the question of copyright has become, by the most natural contraction in the world, the question of property rights itself: Byron's poetry maintains its property rights as long as it does not overturn property rights. The tautology defines what in the view of the law would constitute a revolutionary poem: a poem that overturned its *own* property rights—an act, however, that is by definition subject to the determination of the law. The tautology falls squarely within the grand tradition of British counterrevolutionary discourse, which dictates that what is revolution is subject to determination by British law.

The Murrayan connection between revolutionary and pirate hinges on Murray's mistaken and narcissistic notion that he is the master of the poem and that a challenge to his propertied dignity and right subverts the order of things. The law, however, pronounces the truth that *Don Juan* continually proves: the right of property in liberal society is superior to the right of any individual to that property (even pirates, as Byron shows in the person of Lambro, labor to the greater glory of property right). Property right depends on mastery, but as in the exemplary case of the "British," it is a mastery disintegrative of human capacity—the master, like the power that drives James Tilly Matthews's air loom, like capital "itself," is always elsewhere. By sustaining the injunction, the law protects Murray from the effect of his own outrage. The interest of property in general forces him to own that thing he would rather be without. As his subsequent behavior shows, however, this "win" did not feel like a victory. Murray, who has already been put in the unseemly position of "pirating" a book he owns, is further degraded by the ratification of his connection with what he feels to be immoral. The publisher has to go on publishing; reviewers have to go on reviewing. The condition of his preeminence and wealth, Murray's subjection is also characteristic of every reader of *Don Juan* who answers to the name "British."

Yet the view of the law is itself circumstanced. Chancery no more has the panoptic oversight of Benthamite fantasy than did Justice Ellenborough in the trials of William Hone. Something escapes the gaze of the law, and for the simple reason that texts must be read rather than viewed. In his various consultations Turner had better luck securing judicial opinions of *Don Juan* than attracting critical attention to it. And although Shadwell read more carefully than some, it seems unlikely that he read to the end of canto 1. By approving the satire of Donna Inez in its general tendency (an approval shared by most male critics since), Shadwell focuses on the single particular that speaks to him and, he predicts, will speak to the judges because it encourages them to affirm the wisdom of their own judicial policy in contrast with her "injudicious instruction." But where lies the difference? Despite their sensitivity to precedent, the judges of Chancery are no more believers in natural history than Donna Inez—despite adjustments, the right of property remains an ahistorical constant and repression the rule.

The difference lies not in ends or even in standards but in the discretion by which repression is conducted. If the judges have learned anything from Donna Inez, they have learned what they *must* have already known for the satire to be perceptible, that repression cannot succeed if injudiciously applied. It does not pay to get too worked up about every amatory passage.

Despite their vigilance the judges did not notice that somewhere along the way in canto 1 Donna Inez learns the same thing. Moreover, she uses her knowledge expertly to manipulate Julia into her catastrophe (1:101). Inez does judiciously maintain and aggrandize her property, although she does so at the cost of eliminating the one source of accident that could revive hidalgo blood and open her culture to the future. Donna Inez's success maximizes Inez, but it also consigns Spain to the fate of remaining Spain. Neither her policy nor its "ultimate character" instructs the judges, who, like precocious children, reject the "maternal" quality of her instruction while blindly sharing its ideological import. The full implications of her method, even at its most judicious, are hidden by the sign of her gender, which turns judges inadvertent. By not censoring Byron for blasphemy, the judges vindicate those "blasphemies directed against the woman/mother (*mère*)" that season a commercialist discourse interested in what Michel de Certeau calls the general "fading away of the 'land' that guarantees language."[41] At this level, then, there is a community of interests between Byronic satire and the imperial scheme. And this propriety disarms judges who, however rational in their skepticism of the contaminatory hypothesis that Sharon Turner embraces, are cozened by the poem every bit as much as the *British*—flattered into blindness toward the parody of the ten commandments near the end of canto 1 (sufficient to haul Hone into court) and toward the revolutionary implications of the "dream of ocean (*mer*)" that Lord Byron floats.

Perhaps the most salient consequence of the Chancery opinion was not the specific judgment but the proof that a book is subject to the vagaries of judgment, and thus ultimately no more secure than a letter. Any supposed superiority of Byron to either Julia or Southey is therefore misconceived. The transformation of Julia's letter represents in the most lurid terms the potential fate awaiting any publication despite its protection by the taboo of copyright. For the lesson that Byron continues to learn is that taboos (eating or penetrating the wrong object) are, like waxen seals, made to be broken in one convenient extremity or another. No copyright can save the book from the depredations of pirates or publishers or from being cut up into brief extracts to be chewed over by the hungry savages of the culture industry. By the same token the fragmentation of the book that Byron fears—that his cantos will be mutilated into "canticles"[42] and that his pages will end up lining portmanteaus or wrapping fishes—would not mean the annihilation of its cultural effect. If *Don Juan* has any strength it is not as a book but as a text that lacks the propertied immunity conducive to the fantasy that it is the master of its fate.

Don Juan stages its own undoing in the shipwreck scene—the episode of the poem that particularly disgusts the reviewers. The shipwreck episode not only bloodlessly carries out the sentence of execution against Julia's letter, it mordantly represents the cannibalism that occurs as the reviewers—slaves to an unspeakable appetite that masters all aspirations to a civilized integrity, men who consume men—touch what they know should not be touched; and it represents also the way the dead thing indecently touches back, the way it, shall we say, *publishes* convulsions among the custodians of culture.

It would shock reason to claim that Julia's letter necessitated cannibalism, as if the letter were a cue ball propelled into the innocent equilibrium of the rack. If the letter could be held responsible, it would be not a letter but the ideal book—forever unshredded, forever sealed—of which it dreams. The shipwreck episode represents the letter as a *virtual* rather than an efficient cause, as the material occasion for the lots that, when re-marked and cast, designate the sacrificial victim. Even so, even torn into bits and crudely re-marked, the letter enacts a strangely *Juan*esque economy: a thing is torn apart, the seal does not hold, but there is a conservation, even an augmentation of rhetorical force. Pedrillo's unhesitating acceptance of his lot poignantly exemplifies this tropism. Here is a man who fully believes what he knows is a fiction and willingly dies for his faith. Why?

To the Enlightenment mind impatient of explanations that smack of "superstition" it might appear that Pedrillo dies from a creditable excess of civility, for in resigning himself to death he can be said to follow through on a contract to which he had deliberately, if implicitly, subscribed. Framed *in extremis*, that agreement is an exemplary version of the social contract: both for the particular reason that the compact is devised in order to secure the life of individuals and the harmony of the group; and for the general reason that it entails the dutiful recognition by an individual that he is an individual, *one*, by virtue of his installation in an abstract system of relations—a network, that is, of enumerated and allotable "ones." But even for the contractarian model, consequences count. How can a contract be social if it prescribes a cannibalism destructive of the anthropological basis of the society it is framed to preserve? How can a contract be valid that engages a party to commit a crime, whether that crime be described as suicide or as contributing to the chewing of a tutor? Under the circumstances, the hypothetical contract supposed to explain Pedrillo's acquiescence is seriously flawed. Restoring the pretense of a contract would require pushing the actual contract ever farther back, inevitably disclosing at the end of the line of hypothetical contracts the threat of violence: the proverbial loaded gun. Hence we must conclude either that Pedrillo's fate gives the Hobbesian lie to every story about the nature of contracts and of society (that they are freely entered into, that they involve an exchange of benefits as well as liabilities, that formalized social exchange presupposes the interdiction of savage physical violence), or that there is no contract operating here.

Those options come to the same thing for the Humean empiricist, who would happily take the point of the satire, call our attention to the absence of any detectable threat of violence, and cheerfully abandon the contractarian thesis for a theory of indirect force as the effect of what Hume identifies as the social composition. The social composition—a regulated, lawful prototype of *Juan*'s circumstantial gravity—is that preponderant mass of reasons that inducts the naturally incapacitated, atomized individual into a belief system that invariably precedes him. Because from the perspective of enlightenment, confirmation of one's individuality is necessarily the recognition of a self in systematic relation to others, one cannot talk of an instinct of individual preservation distinct from the preservation of society. And because there can be no individuation without society (so runs the stoical variant of the argument), there is in certain extremities (and the shipwreck surely is one) no contradiction between saving one's self (the belief system that is my always social self) and suicide. Indeed, conceived historically, from an aristocratic perspective, Humean selving, which composes a society of beings possessed of no intrinsic power or value, *is* suicide. Thus for the Humean, no loaded gun lodges in Byron's narrative because no loaded gun is necessary. The Hobbesian pistol secreted in the contractarian model is disassembled and redistributed as a compulsion that is as pervasive, impersonal, and irresistible as Newtonian gravity.[43]

But if the Humean scheme can account for the absence of a contract by the prevailing inductive force of a precedent social compulsion—the discursive, rationalized counterpart of what the poet calls the "gnaw of nature"—it cannot explain the contingency that triggers this particular action: the fall of the lot on Pedrillo. Pedrillo is not impelled but lured to his death by his recognition of "his" lot, which names him by a chance he takes to be his lawful destiny. Pedrillo, then, is induced *by* as well as inducted *to* his fate; the rhetorical supplements the mechanical as historicity intervenes on the social formation.

Assessing how the nominal assumes such force is no easy matter. The poet indicates that each crew member has his own mark but does not specify whether each man inscribes each piece of paper himself or whether the marks are made and assigned by one (supervisory? sovereign?) member of the group. The poet can afford to be unclear because in practice the maker of the mark makes no difference. The mark is merely functional: nothing more than the convenient pretext for identifying a victim for the group whose survival seems to demand that someone be killed. Pedrillo's death occurs as a result of his identification of himself with the mark on the lot. Just as the elision of the marking avoids the necessity for representing a messy and potentially protracted conflict (Who gets to make the marks? Assign them? Toss them? Determine misfires?) that might put off the business of sacrifice indefinitely, so Pedrillo's identification of himself by the lot presupposes that he forget the ineradicably arbitrary deed of marking (whether by himself or another) and in doing so relinquish the memory of being *one who has the right to mark* rather than one who must suffer the fate of being named. In order to be sacrificed, he must surrender the memory (call it the trace of a primordial democracy) that he becomes one who has the right to mark before he is one invested with the authority to sign.

Thomas Moore's charge that in writing *Don Juan* the exiled Lord Byron seems "to have forgotten that standard of decorum in society, to which every one must refer his *words* at least, who hopes to be either listened to or read by the world" might be answered by this passage, which makes killingly clear the forgetfulness of the political act of institution embedded in the social avowal of a standard of decorum.[44] The inscriptive deed is forgotten in the crediting of an always transcendental authorship that invests the apparition of the mark with an indicative power that is unfailingly divinatory: "As you have a name," it promises, "so you will die."[45] Such is the judgment of Cain as Byron dramatizes it. For everyone on whom the lot falls—for Pedrillo as for Cain as for "the British"—the assigned mark is (mis)recognized as my authorizing signature and every signature appears authoritatively assigned. We can follow Hume so far and agree that the lot is not a contract; thus its application is not subject to litigation. But that enlightened discrimination serves the cause of mystery by entailing the suppression of the rhetorico-historical contingency with which social compulsion befalls "one." The lot here stands for that fetishized "determination" to which empiricists of all stripes resort in order to rescue their models of society from terminal inanition. In practice the lot functions as a portent that announces the future as already known, which in commercial society means *signed for.* As portent the lot effectively lays claim to Pedrillo's recognition of its authority to deal his death—lays claim to what liberalism calls his consent—and lays claim to that recognition as the very condition of his property in himself. The portent of death is the apparition of the signature.

Or so I conjecture, prompted by the elision of Pedrillo's actual consent, which is as unrepresented as Julia's physical acquiescence to Juan. Unrepresented, not unreadable. Indeed, the lacuna in the narrative is the legible sign of the repression of reading that makes Pedrillo's consent appear natural. Another look at stanza 76 will help explain what I mean. There the elision of consent reverberates in the curious doubling of the moment of death. Here is the stanza entire:

> He but requested to be bled to death:
>   The surgeon had his instruments, and bled
> Pedrillo, and so gently ebb'd his breath,
>   You hardly could perceive when he was dead.
> He died as born, a Catholic in faith,
>   Like most in the belief in which they're bred,
> And first a little crucifix he kiss'd,
> And then held out his jugular and wrist.
>   (2:76)

The first half of the stanza pretends that nothing extraordinary has happened. First the lot, then the death—it is as though Pedrillo's consent were in the course of nature, like cannibalism. But if nature did indeed have a course, casting lots to determine the future would be unnecessary, a parlor game on a longboat. It is because even at the limit of human existence passage from one incommensurable moment or (to use the textual metaphor deployed by Jean-François Lyotard in *The Differend*) one "phrase" to another is radically contingent, that lots are cast, thus stabilizing contingency and mooting ethical choice by indulging in the ritual of chance. The second half of the stanza returns to the same gap and kills Pedrillo again in the process of contextualizing a consent that still smacks of the bizarre: it's the sort of thing a Catholic would do. By being derived from a community of belief Pedrillo's act becomes explicable and, not incidentally, more pointedly satirical. As his sacrifice takes on the pattern of Christ's, it invites a disagreeable reflection on the cannibal feast as a commemoration in letter and spirit of the Last Supper.

More significantly, however, the lines supplant the invigorating heathenish cross of blood, which Julia's irrepressible sexuality embodied, with the sacred image of the one true cross. The cross is the sign of the symbol, of the capacity of an object (or image as object) to bring together (coordinate/join/interfuse) two divergent axes of signification or being. As featured here (compare the Celtic cross in Hobhouse's notes to *Childe Harold IV*), the cross symbolizes the need for a symbol, of some talismanic image of crossing—be it from earth to heaven, man to god, or present to future—that will induce little Peter to give up his narcissistic attachment to his unitary body image and allow himself to be cut off and cut up, departing this world as if crossing from the imaginary to the symbolic. But the failure of the letter of the cross to guarantee the promised crossing to the symbolic is figured by the affixed image of the dying man-god (a grotesque variant of the narrator's tactical interjection of "Oh Plato, Plato!"). The pathetic image of the man confers charm on the symbol by representing self-sacrifice as pious imitation. The crucifix sutures the here and the hereafter, the imaginary and the symbolic; its naked solicitation of a fit of mimesis professes that one can have one's body and be eaten too.[46]

What exactly Pedrillo had in mind is beyond my ken. But we can infer from the contexts that eddy out from the elided moment of consent that his consent must be inferred precisely because no such moment ever punctually arrived. Pedrillo "consents" when everything appears already decided. Considered as political allegory, Pedrillo's fate implies that the consent of the governed that legitimates the regime can be constructed by the regime from the superstitious misrecognition of consent *by* the governed as something that comes along or befalls them rather than as some event involving their own assertion.[47] What, at our remove, we can discern in the narrative discrepancy is what Pedrillo, disabled by intimacy, failed to read: *there is nothing but context* for his choice. That lot, which he mistakes as a fact, is nothing other than a clot of circumstantial gravity, a highly condensed bunch of context, which may be misrecognized as a determination but which, read at a run or at a walk, might have been a pretext for improvisation—a pretext, that is, for the Romantic performance we associate with the name of Sheherazade or Laurence Sterne or Lord Byron. Such improvisation should not be considered as the postponement of the moment of decision that must come—such is the closural logic proper to the theater and to the novel—but as the continual renewing of decisions that defer the decided. Indeed, if we consult the Romantic performances of Wordsworth or De Quincey, the reading itself may enact that deferral. "Give me a minute," says the little Peter of *The Prelude* (knowing a minute is as good as a lifetime), "to read that lot" (called "talent" or "ministration" or "murmur") "to meditate if it is the one I made or the one made for me." Pedrillo dies (blame him not: it is a malady that at one time or another afflicts us all) of empiricism. Or, to phrase it in a manner less flagrantly

Romantic, he dies from the failure of what Hans Blumenberg calls self-assertion: "Self-assertion does not mean the naked biological and economic preservation of the human organism by the means naturally available to it [say, by eating one's neighbor]. It means an existential program, according to which man posits his existence in a historical situation and indicates to himself how he is going to deal with the reality surrounding him and what use he will make of the possibilities that are open to him."[48]

The Sublime Ethics of *Don Juan*

In other hands, the piety of a Pedrillo could be treated with more pathos than Byron was willing to spare. Consider Hazlitt's "On the Conversation of Lords," which contrasts the literary tastes of the privileged aristocrat and those of the indigent scholar:

> A member of the Roxburghe Club has a certain work (let it be the *Decameron* of Boccaccio) splendidly bound, and in the old quarto edition, we will say. In this not only his literary taste is gratified, but the pride of property, the love of external elegance and decoration. The poor student has only a paltry and somewhat worn copy of the same work . . . which he picked up at a stall, standing out of a shower of rain. What then! has not the Noble Virtuoso doubly the advantage, and a much higher pleasure in the perusal of the work? No; for these are vulgar and mechanical helps to the true enjoyment of letters. From all this mock-display and idle parade of binding and arms and dates, his unthought of rival is precluded, and sees only the talismanic words, feels only the spirit of the author, and in that author reads "with sparkling eyes"
>
> "His title to a mansion in the skies."[49]

Soaked in the sentimentality it professes to overcome, this exercise in the sociology of culture presents the aristocrat in his devolved form as a "Noble Virtuoso." Hazlitt ostensibly aims to refer literary taste to its determination by the cultural capital available to distinct social classes. But in fact Hazlitt represents a continuity of taste between the highborn connoisseur and the humble student. Though it involves an inversion of conventional associations, the trajectory of taste follows a traditional path in a familiar direction: from vulgar ornament to chaste letter, from mock-display to the epiphany of the "pure." Hazlitt's notion of taste provides a scale on which all individuals and groups can be located. Its application presupposes that the aristocracy and the middle class answer to a single civilized criterion: the ready exchange of active power for increased pleasure. It is the completion of this bargain that has mutated the once potent aristocrat into the precious virtuoso. And though Hazlitt evades this consequence, the same exchange endows the student's projection of the idealized "author." By mistaking a mere modification in taste, from ornament to purity, as the attainment of a privileged access to the emissary of a higher reality, someone more noble than the noblest born of aristocrats, Hazlitt unwittingly recapitulates the fundamental *ricorso* of sociological criticism: what is read out as social difference can only be read back as social difference.

As Murray proved to his profit time and again, there is no essential difference between the mystification of the book's binding and the mystification of the book's author: the latter is only another device for binding a book to a portion of the reading public. Lord Byron, as we have seen, was even more advanced than Murray in his promotion of the sale of cheap books to exploit the "student" market. Although Hazlitt wants to recoup some authenticity for his impoverished reader by identifying his Keatsian sublimation as the crossing of an equatorial line of civilization that elevates him above the barbaric virtuoso, both his "aristocrat" and his "student" regard books as commodities; both regard their acts of consumption, more or less conspicuous, as entitling them, more or less magically, to some bright property—whether esteem in the here and now or pie in the sky on some bright tomorrow. The choice between judging a book by its cover or by its author is an option designed to diversify a book-buying public for whom pleasure in such distinctions (over)compensates for their lack of power to make any real difference. Hazlitt's comparison is given narrative treatment in the passage of the gilt-edged letter from the aristocratic Julia, comically attentive to its expensive display, to Pedrillo, poor tutor, if not poor student. With Hazlitt's help we can imagine Pedrillo as if he too were first looking into Boccaccio's *Decameron*, his wild surmise followed by the reverential contemplation of a lot that forecloses life by offering title to a promised mansion in the skies—lot as book, book as fetish, fetish as magical vehicle to author's spirit, author's spirit as portent of celestial property rights.

It is just one aspect of the invigorating discrepancy of *Juan* that it frankly refuses to buy what it sells. From the strength of the mark, the given name, or the naked letter of romance springs not only the shipwreck episode but *Juan*'s poetic practice. The suicidal mystification that any such marking is liable to cannot be denied; as we have seen in our engagements with the Oriental tales and *Childe Harold III*, its probability sustains the identificatory protocol that underwrites the profits of Byronism. But for *Don Juan* as for Lyotard, the "question is to know whether, when one hears something that might resemble a call, one is held to be held by it. One can resist it or answer it, but it will first have to be received as a call, rather than, for instance, as a fantasy. One must find oneself placed in the position of addressee for a prescription."[50] Neither Hazlitt's student nor Juan's tutor appreciates that there is a question to answer. The former responds to the "talismanic words" as if they were "spirit." Juan's tutor, used to delivering precepts, treats the "one word" (hardly a word, little lines of sportive writing run wild) scrawled on a bit of uncertain paper as if it were the lightning of the law, blasting choice. Hardly ethical, Pedrillo's response belongs to what Lyotard calls the "idiom of cognition," wherein "either the law is reasonable, and it does not obligate, since it convinces" (think of this as the Humean option); "or else, it is not reasonable, and it does not obligate, since it constrains" (Hobbes's version).[51] In the case of Pedrillo, doomed by chance, the law both convinces and constrains; he perishes not from a contradiction but from an intolerable redundancy. The naked letter of romance does not, finally, refer to the talismanic quality of words—as though words were magical objects—but to the radical rhetorical force of talismans, which move as drops of ink do, imperatively.

In defending the concept of what he calls "educational power"—a form of "divine violence," which "in its perfected form stands outside the law"—from the charge that it "confers [on us] even lethal power against one another," Walter Benjamin observes: "The question 'May I kill?' meets its irreducible answer in the commandment 'Thou shalt not kill.' This commandment precedes the deed, just as [if?] God was 'preventing' the deed. But just as it may not be fear of punishment that enforces obedience, the injunction becomes inapplicable, incommensurable once the deed is accomplished. No judgment of the deed can be derived from the commandment."[52] It is Pedrillo's fate to be taken in by the disguise in which the Old Testament commandment appears refurbished as a "New" solicitation to mimesis. The historical destiny and the circumstantially specific function of this maneuver is the relegitimation of the law for the modern age: a commensurability between the Old Testament commandments and the New Testament deed, between the law and the way, as between Christ's sacrifice and mine, as between my obedience and my salvation. We can only imagine Pedrillo escaping his fate if he were to recognize his lot as nothing other than a command that can be no law for his actions.

Pedrillo's fate is, of course, the fate of a character invented by the poet. And in that respect the lots are cast with a telling bias: the scapegoating of Pedrillo is, as they say, no accident. It aligns with an antipedagogical bias that has already been expressed in the characterization of Donna Inez and that can be tracked back to the satire of Pomposus in *Hours of Idleness*. The animus, shared by Coleridge ("Frost at Midnight" and *Biographia Literaria*), De Quincey (*Confessions*), Lamb ("Christ's Hospital"), Shelley (*The Necessity of Atheism*), and even Wordsworth (arguably, book 11 of *The Prelude*), might better be called antipreceptorial, for in each case it is not the pedagogic situation as such that is under assault but the dictatorial issuance of precepts that are narrowly formulaic and, as experience shows, unavailing. Unlike Coleridge and Wordsworth, however, whose teachers stand in for a stern, patriarchal Milton, Byron does not dialectically propose an antithetical source of value, be it nature or the Bible.

One effect of that abstention is to heighten the arbitrariness of the selection of Pedrillo to exemplify social suicide. Another is to make downright trivial the criteria by which Juan decides not to partake of the feast. If decision it is. All the narrator says is that

> Juan, who before
> Refusing his own spaniel, hardly could
> Feel now his appetite increased much more;
> 'T was not to be expected that he should,
> Even in extremity of their disaster,
> Dine with them on his pastor and his master.
> (2:78)

It is not clear where the force of the expectation lodges: with Juan, with the group, or with the readership of the poem as some odd combination of both. It is clear that there is no inside to Juan's refusal, which is, importantly, speechless. Because eating Pedrillo is unthinkable for Juan, the refusal to eat him has no ethical resonance. It may be unarguable that Juan's decision is a good one, but it remains difficult to determine what makes it good. Consequences do not count here—at least Juan does not take them into account in the same way the mystified Pedrillo and the cynical narrator do (see 2:79). Juan's abstention seems to be nothing more than an instance of good manners—manners that were not taught him by Pedrillo but bred in him as the all but instinctual *habitus* of his class.

By assigning Juan's abstention to an ambiguously floating expectation, the poet implicitly attributes it to the very Humean social determination (determination by "effects," such as expectations or readers, rather than by "causes," such as intentions or authors) that has been so deftly deconstructed in the case of Pedrillo. And because that determination *has* been deconstructed this passage incurs a notional debt that will have to be repaid later on—repaid both by the narrator who kills off his character and by the hero who is unaccountably advanced a credit that is the moral equivalent of the bankable letters of credit donated by Donna Inez ([2:9] and which, of course, Juan loses in the shipwreck). As we shall see in chapter 9, redeeming that debt will not mean settling on an ethical justification—finding a precept—but ethically asserting a basis for making the right decision.

The basis must be asserted because the modern knows (what Cain, first modern and first aristocrat knew) that even the Old Testament was never founded in the law but, outrageously enough, only in commandments. In the modern age man, for better or worse, gives to himself what God supposedly gave to the Israelite: "Longinus o'er a Bottle, / Or, Every Poet his *own* Aristotle" (1:204).[53] The command precedes the deed, but the command attains its circumstantial force *as* our deed, tactically posited in order that we (always later, always in apposition) may answer to it. "Longinus o'er a Bottle, / Or, Every Poet his *own* Aristotle" epitomizes Byron's unholy alliance with liberalism, the lord lying down with the cockneys. It is a title that commands its readers to obey no commands besides their own, and it is therefore as patently groundless and outrageously effective as *Crede Byron*, the motto of our anonymous poet.

The groundlessness of that speech act marks its difference from the solemnity of the categorical imperative. It is the sublime imperative that Byron directs to every modern poet who is one only because he sublimely gives rules to himself. In Lyotard's terms the "adventitious admixture" of Longinus and Aristotle, fiat and rule, constitutes, like the aristocrat's admixture of merit and blood, a "differend": two heterogeneous phrases in a dispute that cannot be settled by litigation or a higher law but can only be engaged by the "entity's mobility among the instances of phrase universes, upon its resistance to this mobility, and upon its memory of the pre-encounter during the post-encounter" (as untroubled sobriety is recalled during the hangover).[54] Longinus and Aristotle cannot meet in the same court of law, although they might run into each other amid the smoke of cigars and the fumes of Malaga in a posada near Seville. The discrepancy between *a* reader (call him or her conventional, ideal, polite, or general) and *the* reader, *you* or *I*, is solved as the ellipsis linking Longinus and Aristotle. The solvent is drink: not blood or those commercial equivalents that preserve the commercial system by ritually inducing the tonically death-dealing convulsions euphemized as the market cycle, but oceanic intoxication herself, immersion in the dizzying vicissitudes of the world. Lyotard cites Emmanuel Levinas's "exigency": that "one can only phrase ethics ethically, that is, as someone obligated, and not as a scholar, be he or she a critical one."[55] "As someone obligated" translates to "as someone intoxicated" in the phrasing peculiar to *Juan*, which works itself up to the "highest pitch" of "precept" with commands that, though heartfelt, are made to be broken: "Thou shalt believe in Milton, Dryden, Pope; / Thou shalt not set up Wordsworth, Coleridge, Southey" (1:205).

Hobhouse gets Byron exactly wrong when, trying to be his brother's Aristotle, he advises, "If the world shall imagine that taking advantage of your great command of all readers you are resolved to make them admire a style intolerable in less powerful writers, you will find that in a short time a rebellion will be excited, and with some pretext, against your supremacy: and though you may recover yourself it will be only with another effort in your original manner."[56] This cannot last! The decidedly non-Longinian Hobhouse conveniently synthesizes the conventional wisdom on Byron's prominence: he echoes Murray's entreaty that the poet return to the good old *Beppo* style; he repackages Byron's own strictures against Napoleonic scorn in *Childe Harold III*; he imagines an audience of Lady Byrons who will abandon Byron en masse the moment he oversteps that bound where a fear of being exploited overcomes pleasure. Hobhouse may be right; but he has no good reason for being right. From a worldly perspective, Hobhouse sounds foolishly alarmist. The British have not rebelled against the tyranny of Castlereagh; why should they do more than murmur against *Juan*? Moreover, an "original manner" is a contradiction. There is no Byronic style that is not what it is by virtue of its assertion (however inadvertent and spasmodic) of its difference from another style. No style is an object with its own intrinsic, unwavering attractions to which the poet might fix, even were he, impenitently perverse, so inclined. The strength of a style has nothing to do with its status as a pretty piece of writing that might be exhibited in Aitkin's *Cabinet*; the strength inhabits its performance—and then not as a promise, always unfaithful, of gender or genre, but as an imperative that commands belief (first of all the belief in the right to command), thereby opening the text to an always contingent choice:

> "Stop!" cried Philosophy, with air so Grecian,
> (Though she was masqued then as a fair Venetian;)
>
> "Stop!" so I stopp'd.
>
> (2:210–11)

Although some masks have more circumstantial gravity than others, the shipwreck episode, the stanzas on "the British," and Julia's seduction all argue that in a storm of styles most people will seize any pretext for consent, readily forgetting the discrepant "as if" that renders the pretext liable for ethical use in the willful cognition of a law. In the ordinary course of things, consent (and advantage) will follow upon any command that calls upon the reader in the period style. And Castlereagh's cosmos goes on spinning. But if the style hobbles or if it is its lot to limp, its impropriety, the nakedness of its letter, raises the experience of the founding fiction to the highest pitch of precept—and it is any man's guess and every man's decision by what rule the Longinian reader will direct her strength. If she resists *Juan* it is, as the *British* proved, not according to some supposedly categorical standard of decorum and not by some swooning *imitatio* but in response to *Juan*'s circumstantial gravity, which demands an answer. The requisite strength is always there, for, as Lord Byron knows, even though men may have been induced to believe that they once agreed to trade strength for pleasure, no such agreement could have any force. Not only are pleasure and strength incommensurable; strength is no property that can be transferred (we trade in the illusion of power). Strength, like poetry, exists in its assertion. *Crede Byron* asserts the aristocratic basis of what Claude Lefort calls "modern democracy," which is "the only regime to indicate the gap between the symbolic and the real by using the notion of a power which no one—no prince and no minority—can seize. It has the virtue of relating society to the experience of its institution."[57] *Juan* commands its reader to reoccupy the institution of a society in turbulent passage to a democracy that is more than nominal.

The Hueing of *Juan*'s Lot

The passage from Julia's letter to the convulsions of the crew is a self-fulfilling and self-undoing prophecy. Ovidian through and through, the Julia episode hybridizes the *Heroides*, the *Ars amatoria*, and the *Metamorphoses*. And it is as metamorphosis that Julia's story matters, not as history. No one in the longboat would be affected by the sentimental knowledge that the "uncertain paper" had its source in Julia's writing cabinet. No foreknowledge of consequences (were that possible) would deter Julia or Byron from casting their letters upon the waters. That it imagines its own undoing is the strength of the Byronic text. The poem that *Blackwood's* describes as the "very suicide of genius" (*RR* B:1:148)—as if Pedrillo's lot had become (sad fall) the Byronic—is nothing more than the adventure of writing in the world and therefore is radically democratic because, for good or ill, it is potentially anyone's writing and anyone's adventure.

I have said the poem *imagines* rather than *predicts* its undoing because the future of the poem lies hidden in it as the always occulted hieroglyph that is the abbreviated allegory of its turbulent passage through the world. And in that respect it follows upon the knowledge of Julia—who, despite her fetishism of letter and lover, states the doctrine that rules the world of *Don Juan:*

> Man's love is of man's life a thing apart,
>   'Tis woman's whole existence; man may range
> The court, camp, church, the vessel, and the mart;
>   Sword, gown, gain, glory, offer in exchange
> Pride, fame, ambition, to fill up his heart,
>   And few there are whom these cannot estrange;
> Men have all these resources, we but one,
> To love again, and be again undone.
>
> (1:194)

For Julia love is not a thing apart, whether sign or commodity; it is the thing given, which compels woman's repeated doing and undoing. Men's loves, like books, like history, are full of adventures. Sagas of courts, camps, churches, vessels, and marts engage our interest for a time—until it becomes clear that adventures are repetitious and our interest perverse, and finally until even our perversions become routine.

Truman Guy Steffan has written well on this feature of *Don Juan,* correcting those "admirers" who have praised "the 'form of his formlessness,'" and who "have applauded the range of his mock-epic and its bounty of experience, almost as if Byron's talkative verse were a cornucopia of universal satire, and harlequin, by grim contortion, could be Faust, or as if" (and here I interrupt Steffan's flow) the poem led Julia's version of a man's life. Steffan dissipates the "artful illusion" of comprehensiveness and demonstrates that Byron had command of only "a limited number of forces continuously repeated. . . . If we read the poem with backward glance and ear, we begin to notice in canto after canto a recurrence of themes and types, the repetition of the objects of satire, the continuance of familiar autobiographical preoccupations, the basic sameness of the patterns and the tricks."[58] Steffan qualifies Byron's mastery by enjoining an act of critical will to break the illusion and master Byron's manner.

Lord Byron's contemporaries achieved the same insight. J. W. Croker was especially direct: "What sublimity! what levity! what boldness! what tenderness! what majesty! what trifling! what variety! what *tediousness!* . . . The Protean style of 'Don Juan,' instead of checking (as the fetters of rhythm generally do) his natural activity, not only gives him wider limits to range in, but even generates a more roving disposition."[59] Like Julia, Croker is impressed by Juan's "range." But to a critic who prefers fetters to freedom, range only contributes to the tedium. *Don Juan* is not just "tedious," however; the charge soon modulates into "tedious and even obscure"—the latter despite the fact that Croker has just expressed his feeling that for Byron's poetry as for Henry Brougham's oratory, "an impediment in his speech would make him a perfect Demosthenes." Clearly those obscurities are impediments to the flow of *Don Juan*, but not the kind that produce Demosthenic oratory or the "perfection of ease" that is the aristocratic rather than republican ideal Croker upholds. Yet when Croker gets to specifics he complains of "such passages as those about Southey and Waterloo and the British Government and the head of that Government." These passages are not exactly impediments, nor are they obscure; they have become "blemishes" that Croker hopes can be "wiped away" in the next edition. Croker's attribution of this flaw to Byron's unseemly stooping to party politics appears wishful, not only in light of our knowledge that complaints similar to Croker's were coming from the radical Hobhouse, but especially in consideration of Croker's own circumstantial account of the way in which London gossip attaches political rationalizations to something altogether more difficult to explain.

By the conclusion of his long letter, in which the "tedious" *Don Juan* has swept up Brougham, Leigh Hunt, Mr. Gifford, Southey (some named and some unnamed by *Don Juan*), and the conversation at dinner attended by "people of note," Croker has drifted from specific blemishes to a more wide-ranging prescription: "There is little, very little, of this offensive nature in these cantos; the omission, I think, of five stanzas out of 215, would do all I should ask on this point; but I confess that I think it would be much better for his fame and your profit if the two cantos were thrown into one, and brought to a proper length by the retrenchment of the many careless, obscure, and idle passages which *incuria fudit*."[60] Croker does not name the five stanzas, and it is doubtful that he could. Perhaps that is why he so easily slips into recommending wholesale "retrenchment." His recourse to an economic rationale bespeaks Croker's failure to identify any unified code—political, aesthetic, or social—that comprehends those impediments, obscurities, blemishes, and offenses that disturb the flow of *Don Juan* and paradoxically contribute to a tedium that (paradoxically again) galvanizes dinner conversation many months and miles away from its source.

If Croker's notion of an irresistible "tedium" provides a contemporary analogue to the vision of "sameness" that, according to Steffan, can now be overcome only by an act of will, Steffan furnishes us with an insight that clarifies the effect of Croker's "obscurities": "The highest merits of *Don Juan*," Steffan claims, "appear not from distant perspective, but in particular moments, in what Byron does stanza by stanza, line by line."[61] What Croker, "mystified by distance" (2:12), describes is the difficulty of maintaining the proper perspective when acted on by *Don Juan*'s circumstantial gravity. Its blemishes have a way of bringing faces up too close, of crossing distances (compare Selim's transcendent vision in *The Bride of Abydos* with the "transparent glow" of Julia's face in canto 1: bodies are blemishes on the transparency of soul—things that touch us despite the innocence of our gaze). Croker struggles for words to name those things that make distant perspective impossible. It is not that they are instances of nonreferentiality (Croker is modernist enough to care not at all for reference or "principle," as he calls it), but that they are opacities having an equivocal referential status—they mix what ought to be kept separated—and exerting an inexplicable strength.

Take the last couplet of the Julia episode: "The motto, cut upon a white cornelian; / The wax was superfine, its hue vermilion" (1:198). What a difference it would make if the lines, stone and wax, were reversed! *Cornelian* establishes a sentimental, biographical perspective on Julia's letter by resonating with the theme of the cornelian in Byron's poetry and letters. *Cornelian* renders Juan's departure in terms of the pledge that bound Byron to John Edleston, exploiting the same motif of a fragile but undying love, the "emotional quest" that follows Byron everywhere in his poetry.[62] But why *vermilion*? *Vermilion* suggests those blushes that flare across the transparent glow of Julia's face (more distantly, the blood spot of Gulnare in *The Corsair*, that "hue which haunts" the corpse of Greece in *The Giaour*, as well as the red badges of the Spanish partisans in *Childe Harold I*) and anticipates the blood that will be shed by the man whose lot, fabricated from a relic of this letter, will seal his death. But the immediate context that explains *vermilion* is manufactural. Vermilion was the normal if not the sole pigment used in the production of sealing wax. Hence there's something redundant in its mention as well as cosmetic in its application. What makes vermilion thematically suggestive jars with a contextual determination that makes it merely normal. Is it expressive or inert? Is vermilion the fit form of the sentimental—its natural, passional coloring? Or does the final touch of vermilion embarrass the attempt at sentimentality by demonstrating too palpable a design on the part of both Byron and Julia? *Vermilion*, that is, seems to overdress the promise "*Elle vous suit partout*" into something suspiciously like the dramatization of promising. That infelicity is echoed in the return of *vermilion* in canto 2, well after the scattering of Julia's letter;

rhymed with *chameleon*, it appears there as one hue of the luridly theatrical, rainbow-ridden sky that charms the desperate crew, who take the display as designed, as a "good omen" (2:91–92). With respect to the reader, however, perhaps in both cases *audible* design ought to be preferred to visual. Although the rhymes are the most natural in the world, there is still too much of what Croker disparages as "jingle": here, although *jingle* fails to capture the slightly excessive silkiness in the charming affinity of *cornelian*, *chameleon*, and *vermilion* each for the other.

No rhymes are born equal. Some words matter more than others. And it must be asked which word rules this rhyme, *cornelian* or *vermilion? Vermilion* seems to call attention to itself sufficiently to displace the illusion of innocence that funds the sentimental. The sound qualities that make this couplet unsound come to the fore in the *hue*, which, unlike *tint*, has aural as well as visual associations. *Hue* "calls" our attention to the phrase in which it appears and redresses the reader's inability to see the color that Julia chooses. The equivocalness of *vermilion* is the equivocalness of a pigment or a color that is found in nature (and on which we can acquire a perspective as manufacturers, painters, or letter writers—a pigment that you can buy in shops in London and Cadiz) but that has a hue, an apparition that calls to us. Whether the blush is natural or applied, whether the slash of skyey red is god's covenant or nature's accident, each is still the apparition of passion; each still commands belief by a charm that momentarily closes the distance between the text and its reader, always liable to fall again for the promise that he or she knows can never be fulfilled. The practice of calling attention to the sound of words, especially those that close the couplets of the ottava rima stanza, is habitual in *Don Juan*. But this nuance appears nowhere except in these passages toward which we have gravitated.

8

Two Dramatic Case Studies

Marino Faliero *and* Sardanapalus

Inducements must then be found to rouse them from that idleness; motives to awaken their industry and habituate them to regular labour.

Jane Marcet, Conversations on Political Economy

"Hic murus aheneus esto, Nil conscire sibi" — and **so on** *(as Lord Baltimore said on his trial for a Rape)*

Lord Byron to Henry Drury, January 13, 1808[1]

Do those theorists . . . mean to attaint and disable backwards all the kings that have reigned before the Revolution, and consequently to stain the Throne of England with the blot of a continual usurpation?

Edmund Burke, Reflections on the Revolution in France

Marino Faliero and the Fault of Byron's Satire

Ordinarily, when one thinks of Lord Byron's satire it is *Don Juan* and not *Marino Faliero* that comes to mind. In light of the thesis of chapter 7, however, that *Don Juan* is not to be considered *in* context but *as* a context in which distinctive modes of consideration occur, Lord Byron's historical dramas should be read as falling under the dispensation of *Juan*—as instances, exemplifications, or experimental applications of *Juan's* moral force. In this first section I shall try to demonstrate that *Marino Faliero*, a play written during the composition of *Juan* and situated within its generous precincts, represents a poetics of Byron's satire. In the second part I shall examine *Sardanapalus* as a representation of the political and economic problematic of representation.

As license for this somewhat eccentric procedure I appeal to a line from canto 3 of *Don Juan*, which I take as my subject and text: "If I have any fault, it is digression" (st. 96). The line presents the poet in what may be called his mock-confessional vein. It is hard to decide whether this speaking to the point is a true confession or is, after all, a digression wandering away from the poet's "people," who, he says, are "left to proceed alone," and is therefore no efficacious confession at all—hard to decide, that is, whether the statement purges or instances the fault that it announces. It is as if a penitent were to confess to taking illicit pleasure in the act of confessing. And just who *is* confessing? Is this faulty "I" the "I" of the poet qua poet or the "I" of the notoriously sinful lord of Regency gossip? It might be claimed that digression is a peculiarly literary failing that can be confessed only by a poet. But if *Juan* is about anything it is about the impossibility of such a restriction: the poem habitually exploits the traditional association of wandering with sinning, and surely digression is, if nothing else, a form of wandering. Whether digression refers to poet or man, it seems disingenuous of Byron blandly to condense his dirty laundry list of moral and artistic failings into that sole fault. Are sins only formal lapses, or are formal lapses really sins? Perhaps digression is not the problem; perhaps there is something faulty in the notion of fault that allows us to shift so easily between regions of morality and poetic form, as well as between an intentional subject and a contingent personality. Is there truly a fault? If someone *is* at fault who is it? And what is to be done about it?

Such are the questions that give rise to satire, which stands in a special relation to fault. Fault brings satire into being, and satire punishes the faults that make it possible. Now we know that faults or sins or crimes or illegalities do not grow on trees but are determined along with their punishments by historically specific discursive formations. Or at least such is the claim of Michel Foucault. I shall rely on Foucault's concept of discursive formation as a related group of statements, formed by rules and systematically dispersed in order to prosecute two mutually implicated lines of argument.[2] First, I shall connect the decline in the status of satire and the modification of its practice that occurred in the passage from the eighteenth to the nineteenth century with an epochal transformation of the discourse of punishment. Second, I shall characterize the unparalleled strength of Byron's crucially digressive satire by working through a cantilevered interpretation of his dramatic poem and poetics of satire *Marino Faliero, Doge of Venice*.

In *Discipline and Punish* Foucault identifies three successive punitive regimes: the monarchic, the generalized, and the disciplinary. The monarchic mode of punishment was to stage a spectacle of torture that publicly displayed on the body of the accused a vengeance that both vindicated the absolute power of the sovereign and furnished an opportunity for the mass participation of the populace in the imposition of justice. The eighteenth century eliminated the dangerous excesses attendant on monarchic spectacle by redirecting the end of criminal justice from ceremonial revenge to economical punishment. If the exemplary crime for the monarch was murder to be avenged by torture and execution, the definitive crime for the eighteenth century was fraud (theft of property by false representation) to be punished by bringing the occluded causal agent to light and assigning him his proper penalty through the exercise of the common-law aims of detection and reformation.[3] Punishment, according to Foucault, thus becomes generalized, a matter of adjusting "the two series that follow from the crime: its own effects and those of the penalty." It is designed as an example, "a sign that serves as an obstacle" to a repetition of the crime by the criminal and to emulation of the crime by others. The aim, in sum, is to construct a "punitive city" cemented by an "aesthetic of punishment." Hence if the eighteenth century defines its illegalities as the circulation of fraudulent signs of property, punishment of those crimes is legitimated by an appeal to a duly constituted, completely intelligible, ostensibly natural organization of signs. In other words, like illegality, punishment exploits the circulation of signs: "The publicity of punishment must not have the physical effect of terror; it must open up a book to be read."[4] Underline *book*, which is a literal implement of punishment.

Foucault's analysis seems to me to offer the best explanation of why satire was the most forceful kind of literary discourse in the eighteenth century. If, as Defoe claimed, the "end of satyr is reformation," in the eighteenth century that end is identical with the general aim of the civil judiciary.[5] If reformation can be espoused as a completely reasonable aim within a social field conceived of as a determinate array of representations, the artfully managed representations of the satirist are as effective instruments of punishment as any other. And if the power of generalized punishment is owed to its capacity to deploy an "aesthetic of punishment" in a "punitive city" that is also an "open book," the exemplary satire in that period of English history in which satire enjoyed unique power and authority is Pope's *Dunciad Variorum*.[6]

The Dunciad displaces the precedent of monarchic spectacle by including it as a precinct within its own discursive space. The action that the poem imitates, "the removal of the Imperial seat of Dulness from the City to the polite world," depicts the incapacity of older, ceremonial forms of justice to control literary illegalities such as piracy, pornography, and especially slander.[7] The ability of the Dunces to organize their own procession, to move freely through the capital, and to install their own monarch displays the emasculation of the *ancien régime* and supplies the pretext for Pope's own system of justice, which mounts no spectacle but instead bookishly assigns to "nameless somethings sleeping in their causes" the names they deserve.[8] Pope's satire extends the reach of the law beyond overt and justiciable acts to the furtive intentions and acts of those whose very "obscurity renders them more dangerous, as less thought of. . . . Law can pronounce judgment on open Facts, Morality alone can pass censure on Intentions of mischief; so that for secret calumny or the arrow flying in the dark, there is no publick punishment left, but what a good writer inflicts."[9] The law is incapable of reaching a whole class of illegalities that it would, however, punish if it could.

Such mischief makers can be brought to public punishment because a secret calumny, though its cause be occluded, exists as an expression of faith in the coercive power of publicity. Pope's satire redresses the malign "imposition" on the "honest unwriting subject" by setting "the force that drove the criminal to the crime against itself," giving publicity to those who were willing to slander in order to obtain it.[10] The most transparent, gentle, *natural* punishment of these "authors without names," authors whose anonymity is the condition of their criminality, is to acknowledge and reform them simultaneously by "assigning to each some *proper name* or other, such as [the satirist] cou'd find."[11] To be named in a book is the proper and punitive effect of an anonymous literary crime—a consequence that is an obstacle to any further criminality. Hence what Pat Rogers calls the "feedback effect" of *The Dunciad*, which he illustrates by the tale of the fate of Edward Oldmixon: "Oldmixon was presented as a needy hack, surrounded by dissolute and groveling creatures who were terrorised by their master Curll. The picture took on life; and Oldmixon found his reputation lowered, not only with the reading public, but also among his potential employers, the bookselling trade. . . . He was, so to speak, the victim of Pope's self-fulfilling prophecy."[12] Let us cancel the "so to speak." Indeed, let us cancel the anecdote, for as in the sad case of "my grandmother's review—the British" (*DJ* 1:209) it is no accident that the picture took on life, since the life of Oldmixon, or that generalization of life, his livelihood, consisted wholly in a picture that Pope merely reformed and over which he assumed proprietarial rights and punitive authority.

As we have seen, Byron's stubborn adherence to the observant Pope makes just as good sense as Wordsworth's commitment to the blind Milton.

Pope, *the* strong English poet in the tradition of civic humanism, practiced a poetry of tactical statement deployed within the ongoing business of the world. What empowered Pope was the historically specific symmetry between the generic code of satire and the modality of punishment in the state. Satire, which had been there all along, in the eighteenth century suddenly found itself in a central position, the place of the general, perfectly accommodated to the discourse of power. All of Byron's polemics about Pope's propriety are less important than the insight informing *English Bards and Scotch Reviewers* that Pope was a poet who both judged and *enforced*. Pope was not a poet like Swift, who, having written in the service of the Tory state, found himself after 1714 occupying "no place except as outsider to the Whigs' monolithic machine"; he was a poet who, like a magistrate, continually executed public policy—and was a stronger poet than Swift because he could accomplish his ends in spite of the emergent Whig hegemony.[13] In a century of extraordinary reverence toward the law of genre Pope most powerfully exercised the genre of the law.[14]

Lord Byron's practice could not be Pope's. History had intervened between an Augustan *then* and a postrevolutionary *now*. The shift from what Foucault calls a discourse of generalized punishment to a panoptic disciplinary society destroyed the perfect fit between the satirist and the dominant modality of punishment. What the preface to *Sardanapalus* calls the "law of literature" no longer coincided with the law of the community. The decline in the confidence and force of satire after the eighteenth century is not to be attributed to the absence of any norm that would allow the satirist the moral assurance necessary to his undertaking; on the contrary, normality emerged as the great index of behavior in the nineteenth century. The norm, however, was no longer a general principle of consistent application that could be elucidated in a single book. Normality having become absolute, norms were endlessly diversified and analyzed, allotted to and defined by various institutions and professional groups: penologists, critics, physicians. Satire was displaced from its privileged position by the coalescence of a political technology that acted through concrete institutions directly on the docile bodies of its subjects. Mightier than the sword, the pen of the poet had nothing like the power of the prison, the school, or the hospital.[15]

English Bards and Scotch Reviewers is embarrassing evidence of the new order. The very title announces a polarity that was unknown to Pope—a polarity that was actually a new hierarchy: Lord Byron's feeble attempts to invoke a papal authority against the squabbling critical sectarians of his day attest to the plenary sway of the organs of opinion that he affected to disdain.[16] The establishment of literary norms was the business of the reviews, which were one organ for a discipline that was practiced in a variety of outlets in a variety of ways. The *Edinburgh Review* spoke for and to the Whig opposition headquartered at Holland House. John Murray, publisher of Byron and the *Quarterly Review*, had intimate political and financial connections with the Tory ministry. Lord Byron's dual affiliations (he would spend the afternoon in Murray's upper room at Albemarle Street and the evening with Lord Holland) gave him considerable latitude within a well-tended and tolerant consensus. Juvenile as well as Juvenalian, *English Bards* was the sort of spirited behavior by a young aristocratic poet that might be not only tolerated but indirectly rewarded. Subsequently the reviews kept their collective eye on Byron. The phenomenon of "Byron" dramatically testified to a fundamental British agreement, a language game elastic enough to weather even a volcanic prodigy; Byron's aberrations would serve the socially useful purpose of defining a norm to which there was no opposition, only different measures of adjustment.

The defects of *English Bards* are to be attributed to its status as a poem of Byron's minority, which was, of course, not his fault.[17] The strength of *Don Juan*, however, *is* his fault. In order to specify better the force of the fault within Byron's poetry I would like to extend further my line on digression.

The irregularly digressive character of *Juan* makes it difficult to say what, exactly, is a digression *in* the poem. In a text that consistently refers to the process of its own composition, that perversely profits from the contingency of that composition, and that flaunts its capacity both to bring inside anything imagined as outside and to disorder the hierarchy between central and peripheral—in such a text any of the various interruptions that divert the poet from narrative progress, such as the publicized interdiction supposedly imposed on Byron by the decorous Theresa Guiccioli, can be read as elaborations of the text they ostensibly interrupt. All Byron's interruptions of the "epic" project, such as the sallies into love or politics or commerce, though they are pursued as diversions from *Juan*, appear, from the vantage of the poem, as wanderings within *Juan*. All of Byron's antics, deals, and imbroglios embellish the discourse named "Byron" that continually replenishes the equivocal "I" that wanders through the poem. This Don Juanism of *Don Juan* aggrandizes those other texts that emerge during its composition, including the dramas. Although they have been regarded as distinct intentional entities (Byron's insistence on the unities solicited this kind of attention), they appear within the composition of *Juan* as digressions, interludic moves that show the kinds of things a faulty *Juan* does not or cannot do; although they thematically and rhetorically test the possibility of escaping the elastic matrix of *Juan*, their doings come to signify as items in the catalog of faults that is the parodic conquest of the poem.

Marino Faliero, Doge of Venice, a work wherein Romantic ambition labors in a theater of baroque inconsequence, was the first play to be written under the general dispensation of *Juan*. The action begins in abeyance as Faliero awaits the verdict of the Forty (the patrician ruling elite) on Michael Steno for scrawling on the ducal throne a charge of infidelity against the doge's wife Angiolina. When to the offense of Steno is added the insult of a lenient punishment by his peers, the doge, inflamed with resentment, lends his ear to the seditious plot of the discontented plebians, becomes convinced that they have a common cause, and assumes leadership of the incipient rebellion. The doge persuades his followers to strike quickly, and they agree to converge at St. Mark's on the sunrise signal of the bell. The plot, however, is betrayed, the uprising quelled, and Faliero and his lieutenants apprehended. Faliero is tried and executed within the palace, where there is no possibility that his words or demeanor could incite the volatile populace; after his death his engraved name in the gallery of the doges is covered by a black veil, eternal mark of his treason.

Marino Faliero both represents and enacts Byron's ambivalence about his own social status and about the possibility of effective political action in contemporary England. Faliero's grayheaded uselessness within a society that, secure from foreign threat, is intent on routinizing charisma reflects both the post-Napoleonic dejection of a man who had once aspired to noble deeds and who now is convinced that in Wellington the English have got the hero they deserve, and the post–*Childe Harold* cynicism of a poet who appreciates that the charismatic quality of his previously published poetry was only the trumpery of the marketplace. Faliero's biography also telescopes Byron's own idealization of his family history. In *Hours of Idleness* Byron had exposed himself to Henry Brougham's ridicule by his jejune celebration of his nobility; Brougham mockingly exposed not only the poet's graceless boastfulness but, more tellingly, Byron's insecurity about his aristocratic status, which emerged in the poet's Ossianic exertions to concoct and retail a past that proved his nobility was not only ancient but earned in glamorous Highland skirmishes. The aged bitterness of the doge is not simply another trope of Byronic world-weariness but, as a scene in his ancestral mausoleum makes clear, a vehicle to render the return of the fathers in the son: they are at once addressed and impersonated that they might see and suffer the disgrace administered by time and men (comparable moments occur during the convulsive dream in act 4 of *Sardanapalus* and in canto 16 of *Don Juan*).

Moreover, the plot of *Faliero* shows Byron working out in dramatic form some of the political preoccupations that circulate throughout his correspondence. Having become financially solvent enough to worry about keeping rather than finding money, Byron shifted his financial anxiety from moneylenders to investments. His letters are studded with queries about the current state of "the funds," imperious instructions about the management of his interest in them, and dire predictions of financial collapse (*BLJ* 8:135, 137, 181). Indeed, forecasting catastrophe became something of a hobby for Byron; it allowed him to indulge the fantasy that he might return to England during the ensuing chaos as the man on the horse who would command the rebellious masses and shape a new social and economic order—a fantasy in which it is typically difficult to disentangle the purely personal motive from the more generally political one. Again, however, that tangle imitates the doubleness of the motives of Faliero: he is offended in his person but takes that offense as an insult to the sovereignty of an office that is the only guarantor of the legitimacy of the state; he allies himself with republicans, but only as supervisory mind might condescend to act through the soiled instrument of the body. In that light the plot represents both a skeptical view of the possibility of success for such a mobilization and an opportunity to endow with tragic dimensions what might be a rather messy adventure, thereby substituting vicarious experience for the effort of action.

The vacillations in Byron's exchanges with John Murray about the possible staging of *Marino Faliero* enact the ambivalence he represents. Scholars disagree about Byron's intentions. Some argue that despite his vehement protests he really wanted *Marino Faliero* to be staged and disavowed that aim in full confidence (justified by events) that Murray would go ahead and arrange for its production anyway, thereby enabling Byron to deny his interest in the performance should it fail or, in case of triumph, to receive the plaudits like a champion who conquers offhandedly.[18] I do not intend to enter that dispute. What is important here is to note that in the failure of the funds to fail, and in the absence of any other pretext for Byron's physical return to England (the indefatigably drab Southey could not be provoked into a duel), the theater represented the next best thing: a symbolic return made as good as real by its occurrence in a space where symbols have a virtual life.

It is crucial to realize, however, that the "next best thing" would, in this case, also have been the worst. Such a triumph would be poisoned at its heart, since it would merely replay the ironic relation between sovereignty and theatricality that Byron had already exposed in the Bonaparte stanzas of

Childe Harold III. What triumph Byron could have achieved would have had its transitory reality only in the effervescent admiration of a tyrannous audience, and it would in any case not have been fully *Byron's* triumph: Byron was experienced enough in the practices of Murray and the management of Drury Lane to be certain that in the passage to the stage the text would fall under various hands that would prune his drama to customize its force. "Byron" could appear in London only as a lame monarch, one whose sovereignty was conditioned by its self-evident theatricality, one who was hedged about by a peremptory administrative machinery, and one whose acts would be only dim imitations of the sort of executive actions occurring in a real world elsewhere. Byron's irresolute management of *Marino Faliero* dramatizes the ironic thesis common to that play and to *Sardanapalus*: sovereignty can exert its authority only through a self-imaging, but such staging submits that authority to potential humiliation. Sovereignty cannot survive what Byron called its "cursed attempt at representation" (*BLJ* 8:66).

Nothing I have said about the relations between representation and enactment challenges the conventional reading of *Marino Faliero* as a historical tragedy about a grand risk and a glorious failure. And it is surely the case that it was as a piece of tragic sensationalism à la mode that *Faliero* appealed to Murray and his colleagues. Actually, however, the play is not about failure but about success or, to be precise, about the social machinery for transforming failure into success. Faliero's ascendancy to the dogeship was the direct result of his heroic salvation of the state from its foreign enemies. Far from demonstrating that such heroism is irrelevant in an age of impersonal bureaucratic efficiency, the play dramatizes the ritual advantages the hero-king provides for the modern state: Faliero's action in the play neatly repeats the service by which he was originally exalted.

Crucial to this interpretation is Faliero's acknowledgment prior to his meeting with the plebian conspirators, "I am before the hour" (3.1.1). This indication of prematurity is reinforced by the conspirators' expressions of surprise at Faliero's indignant impatience with any counsel of delay. Whatever Faliero's intentions, the effect of his leadership is to precipitate rebellion prematurely, to practice a kind of political homeopathy, inoculating the state with a discord of such weakness that it could be localized and contained, thus allowing the germs of civil conflict to exhaust their malignancy before they could fester into a mortal illness. In this schematically Girardian reading, the execution of the doge is a scapegoating that does not deny his sovereignty but decisively consummates it. He has rescued the state from civil war, and his service is sealed by his identification as the monstrous double who is beheaded and forever marked as unique by the covering of his engraved name in the gallery of the doges.[19] That black veil puts an end-stop to all the emulous strife that unsettles the established order. It naturalizes order by attributing strife not, say, to an irreconcilable class conflict, but to the anarchic passion of a prodigy of nature. The king who betrays the state saves it—such is the plaguey paradox kept under quarantine by the black veil, so that the deep truth may remain nameless.

If we can agree that the secret stratagem of Faliero's revolt is to induce homeopathically what he calls this "game of mutual homicides" so that his sacrificial death can bring the game to a close, we may have resolved most of the effects of the play, but we are still left without any grasp of the causes. We could, of course, pursue a Girardian reading further and argue that the effect is fundamentally the *same* as the cause: that all the actions of Faliero are governed by the final cause of the preservation of hierarchical stability, that his drama is a ritual enactment of ostensible rivalry and civil war performed in order to provide the scapegoat whose succinct execution defuses a divisiveness (represented by the doublings that propagate throughout the play) that might otherwise explode into anarchy and pro-miscuous bloodshed. In other words, the full-scale Girardian reading would require us to interpret *Marino Faliero* as theatrical all the way down: a play about the essentially dissimulative character of a politics designed to satisfy symbolically the demands of a brute nature that can be imagined only as a chaos of blood and poison.

Concentration on the final cause, whether we find it reassuringly order-ly or tyrannously preemptive, has the tendency to efface the potency of Steno's lampoon. That tendency conforms to an implicit convention ob-served by all parties. Patriarch, patrician, and plebe all deny that the scrawl has any consequences. No cause in itself, Steno's lampoon is merely the pretext for an action proceeding from a source of more gravity. Faliero, who urges his nephew to "think upon the cause" (1.2.272),[20] subsequently offers a diagnosis that turns on Mandeville: "Our private wrongs have sprung from public vices" (3.2.154). He specifies the crisis twice, each time identifying it with his election as doge: "Their own desire, not my ambition made / Them choose me for their prince, and then farewell all social mem-ory. . . . No friends, no kindness, / No privacy of life—all were cut off" (3.2.325–27, 348–49). To be made the doge is to feel the full imposition of the public in the joke of sovereignty; to assume the ducal authority is to submit to the constraint of an absent power that the sovereign can never possess but must always represent. If there is a pleasure in ruling, it is a fully masochistic one. As representation the sovereign is incapacitated—not de-prived of power exactly, for to become doge is to learn that one cannot lose what no one has, but stripped of the watery, bourgeois surrogate for power, privacy. Consequently, the provocation of Steno's gibe, according to Faliero, lay in its final spoliation of the one fragile refuge of privacy that remained to him, his domestic life with Angiolina.

Given the synonymity of *the public* and *the theatrical*, Faliero's account squares with my own, except in its insistence on an opposition between the private and the public and on some dramatic moment in which the former is violated by the latter. But such a theory cannot be credited. Certainly Steno's lampoon does not violate any privacy; for in the dialogue between Faliero and Angiolina in which they recall their betrothal, arranged by Angiolina's dying father, it is evident that nothing that could be called privacy ever subsisted between them, no subjective space in which a theoretical liberty could be exercised. Faliero reminds her, "You had / Freedom from me to choose, and urged in answer / Your father's choice." Angiolina agrees: "My lord, I look'd but to my father's wishes" (2.1.322–24, 342). A choice so given is no choice at all; and the freedom of a virtuous woman is not liberty, since virtue is a fixed source of light:

> Vice cannot fix, and virtue cannot change.
> The once fall'n woman must for ever fall;
> For vice must have variety, while virtue
> Stands like the sun, and all which rolls around
> Drinks life, and light, and glory from her aspect.
>
> (2.1.394–98)

The helos of that sun, which fixes the woman within a solar system of virtue, is the father, whose wishes have the authority of a cosmological given. Thus in its form Faliero's marriage "proposal" to Angiolina, made at the behest of her father, recapitulates the bind in which *he* was placed by his election as doge: in proposing marriage he cuts himself and his wife off from all "social memory." Any proposal made by authority addresses a subject whose choice can only be nominal, since to reject the proposal would be to remove oneself from the line of the father that confers the very possibility of choice. There is no power to choose what is not authorized; but it follows that authority is delegated every power except that of conferring the power to choose freely. Every well-formed statement in Venice is a variant of Angiolina's "My Lord, I look'd but to my father's wishes," even, or rather especially, Faliero's pathetically curtailed self-assertion, "I will be what I should be, or be nothing" (2.1.453). The ironical equivocation of that *should* displays the blind vanity of the will that indulges the fancy of a destiny different from what is designed by the father, who has said and is continually saying the same thing. Embedded in the inexorable conjunction of *will* and *should* is the endless reiteration of the compliance of all subjects with the wish of a father who wishes to identify himself with a father ideal making the same wish—a circuitous submission to an ideal authority that is faulted by its structural incapacity to will anything but what it should, a circuit that, in its dynamic iterability, is the expression of an absent cause.

Not only does the play give us no grounds to think that Angiolina is unfaithful; Byron takes pains to dispel the possibility that anyone in Venice could suspect the virtuous wife of the doge of adultery. Steno's slander, then, is by all accounts impotent: it exposes nothing, nor does it propagate rumor. Indeed, Faliero's irate response, a "fury [that] doth exceed the provocation, / Or any provocation" (2.2.136–37), takes the form not of a repudiation of the incredible charge of spousal infidelity but of a denial of his own passion for his wife:

> 'T was not a foolish dotard's vile caprice,
> Nor the false edge of aged appetite,
> Which made me covetous of girlish beauty,
> And a young bride: for in my fieriest youth
> I sway'd such passions; nor was this my age
> Infected with that leprosy of lust
> Which taints the hoariest years of vicious men,
> Making them ransack to the very last
> The dregs of pleasure for their vanish'd joys;
> Or buy in selfish marriage some young victim,
> Too helpless to refuse a state that's honest,
> Too feeling not to know herself a wretch.
>
> (2.1.310–21)

The lust that Faliero denies is the obverse of the innocent "patriarchal love" he affirms (2.1.363). Steno's scrawl does not discover, let alone cause, any infidelity; it marks the exclusion of any physical passion from the Venetian patriarchy that could be anything other than infidelity or incest by bringing to visibility the incestuous format imposed on all private relations between husband and wife, "father" and "daughter." The determination in the last instance is not the father but a discourse that puts any man, any husband, any sovereign in the position of a father who can have no desire except what is already scripted as incestuous. Steno's mark is a provocation not because it speaks of facts but because it signifies at all levels a proscription of desire.

All relations in Venice, even the most intimate, are statements in a discourse that allows for no digression or, what is the same thing, no unintentional, nonhierarchical, wordless sensuality. The linkage is Milton's, from *Paradise Lost*, book 8: "hee, [Eve] knew would intermix / Grateful digressions, and solve high dispute / With conjugal Caresses, from his lip / Nor Words alone pleas'd her" (ll. 54–57). Milton suggests a connection between digression and prelapsarian sexuality as intimately cohabitating within an unrepresentable zone of human freedom, here specifically dissociated from a discourse only not yet totalitarian (or, in the case of Juan and Haidee, not yet piratized). Of course, that *not yet* is disputable; and Byron's Cain does dispute it. Cain and his wife Adah are congruent with Faliero and Angiolina in the lack of that ability to digress either verbally or sexually that Milton attributes to the first couple. But Cain exceeds Faliero in his bitter demystification of any association of that digressive capacity with choice, which Cain recognizes must have been as much an illusion for his parents as it is for him: choice can be intelligible only within an ordered discourse that specifies the options (or in the case of Juan and Haidee, a financial order that funds the options) and that choice naively elaborates, according to the secret discipline of an algorithmic logic. Edenic digression, like unfallen sexuality, is no legitimate option, as C. S. Lewis uneasily observed, because it occurs on the outside or rather on the margin, the outsiding of the inside, of theological discourse. Byron's *Cain* interprets that most peculiar of all biblical narratives as the reinscription by main force of that margin within the providential economy.

As for Cain so for Faliero: digression, like a nondiscursive sexuality, is impossible. It is only an apparent paradox to assert, however, that from the "point of view" of power everything that occurs in Venice—all actions and words of all parties, the whole discourse of society—is nothing but digression. Digression, like theatrical representation, is empty, purposeless speech. It is ordinarily staged as a respite or recreation (what Coleridge in *The Friend* calls a "Landing Place" or what Kant in *The Critique of Judgment* calls the "aesthetic") within a teleological order of executive decisions and effective actions. The text of *Marino Faliero*, however, extends the digressively theatrical to include *all* social and political speech and behavior, which is not framed by any supervisory purpose, and which is distinguished from theatrical representation proper only in that it is both mystified in its production and afflicted with nostalgia, uttered by actors who believe in their parts.

This conception of power, with its implication of a bifocal view of digression, is strongly thematized in Shelley and is most salient in *Prome-*

theus Unbound, where the "dramatic" crux is the distinction between two kinds of digression, each one the expression of a power that is always elsewhere. The problem, to put it crudely, is to transform a pernicious digression—the discourse of causes and effects, of hierarchy, of fathers—into a benign digression: the masque, the love duet, innocent tales let slip in an unseen cave, unthought melodies gently noting the passage of eternity. For Shelley, unlike Byron, art is not in question—it subsists on both sides of the fault line—but the status of theater as a human art surely is: the vector of the "action" of *Prometheus Unbound* aims at transforming classical drama into Promethean masque, tragedy into Ovidian metamorphosis. The most intense narrative in all of Romantic poetry is surely the first four scenes of act 2, Shelley's strenuous overrepresentation of the fault, where, in spendthrift futility, he endeavors to forge a crossing from Prometheus to Asia, from father to power, from curse to love.

In the decidedly postlapsarian state of Venice there are neither mountains nor chasms (those dazzling fragments of the fall, which could stimulate the excited revery of theodicy or apocalypse). Discourse abides no interruptions but overlays and canalizes all relations; a king can talk to but not touch his wife, whose very virtue consists in her abstraction into a cipher that saves all place in a political order empty of social memory. One has the language of causation, the appearance of causation, but also the feeling (insofar as one can be said to feel) that one is the mechanical instrument rather than the producer of effects. In *Marino Faliero* Byron is not stating a problem in political science, or in any science at all. Venice is not a mixed government in which a grasping and decadent oligarchy dangerously constrains the legitimate power of the sovereign and immorally oppresses its lower class; on the contrary, it is a government totally unified and elaborately articulated under the sign of the father. What constraints apply are not the fault of the patrician, the patriot, or the patriarch; they inhere in the paternal root. The father attains, exercises, and preserves his authority only at the expense of all social memory, the recollection of a feeling that was not merely instituted—a fee extorted from him as the price for social order. There is no choice without the father and no real choice with the father; the father gives all freedom; the father has no freedom to give. That he is the emblem of all authority but only the representation of power is the fault in the father.

The wish for privacy is a wish to have a will, to feel, to have some source of power of which one is in control rather than to be the representative through which a power, which is always elsewhere, flows. This wish for an uncharacterted, authentically affective and effective subjectivity can only be inordinate, since the private has no place in a society where every place has already been overwritten by a reticulative discourse. Or, if the private does have a place—as in some sense it must, since it is named over and over again—that place is posited and deployed as the name of the (in)violable in a metaphorics of shame that motivates the drama of social life. Here is the honorable house of Faliero: his name, his shame.[21] The wish for privacy (to be together with a woman just feeling) and the eclipse of privacy (feeling encoded as incestuous desire) occur in the same moment; they are the same gesture, a metaphor in which the vehicle traduces its tenor. As soon as something inner and secret is defined, it is already imprinted with a scene that coordinates it with a discourse that proscribes the *socius* and prevents all social feeling.

We can agree with Faliero, then, that Steno's ribaldry is not the cause of the civil disturbance in Venice. Yet Faliero wants to go further, to claim that the scrawl is nothing at all. He calls it the "mere ebullition of vice" (3.2.403)—a figure that oddly anticipates the trope T. S. Eliot would later use to characterize Byron's poetry: "We have come to expect poetry to be something very concentrated, something distilled; but if Byron had distilled his verse, there would have been nothing whatever left."[22] Cavalier chemist, Eliot employs a scientific metaphor that both stigmatizes Byron and repudiates the laws of physics: could even a Paracelsus have imagined a distillation that would leave nothing? The suave Eliot seems offhandedly to admit the notorious Byronic nihilist at the back door. In this he is an ally of Faliero, whose contemptuous characterization of Steno keynotes a critique of Venetian corruption and a program for its elimination:

> The whole must be extinguished;—better that
> They ne'er had been, than drag me on to be
> The thing these arch-oppressors fain would make me.
> (1.2.321–23)

Although vice itself, the vile substrate from which poisonous ebullitions like Steno's effervesce, Venice is queerly figured as compounded of the same fantastic element as Steno's scrawl; it is a something that can be reduced to nothing. This view of Venice has been called "organic,"[23] but it is surely a root-and-branch organicism, indistinguishable from the sort of nihilism that shadows a swollen, frustrated, so-called Byronic narcissism. Faliero's "political" program is indistinguishable from the project of the ego to which I have already referred: "I will be what I should be, or be nothing," a zero-sum egoism allowing for no action that is not the doomed extension of a wish, or the wishful extension of a doom. Faliero is thus like Eliot, who flaunts a magical power to extinguish that, however, he graciously restrains. And like, curiously enough, a more efficient practitioner of the art of extinction, Robert Elliston, manager of Drury Lane: in his application for a license for *Faliero*, which he had assiduously cut to eliminate all traces of contemporary political comment, Elliston stressed that "we have so curtailed [the play] that I believe not a single objectionable line can be said to exist."[24] Elliston regarded the political gestures of *Faliero* as a "mere ebullition of vice," a digression from an innocuous Byronic entertainment that might be distilled—one that, he claimed, he *had* distilled into nothing.

When, at the end of the play, unable to get within hearing distance of the exchanges at Faliero's execution, members of the populace "curse . . . the distance" and vent the forlorn wish that they could "But gather a sole sentence" (4.4.811, 814)—as if that sentence would distill and resolve the confusing events that have been acted out in the streets of Venice—they are in the same situation as the Drury Lane spectators who watched the mutilated result of Elliston's censorship (which did not include this final scene).[25] All objectionable sentences have been lopped off and hauled away; nothing salient remains. *This is no loss.* There could be nothing truly objectionable in a sentence spoken by Faliero or any actor who might impersonate him. Indeed, the play demonstrates the homology among gathering, distillation, and extinction: there is no substantive difference between the fetishism of distillation (whether it be the Eliotic notion of a crystalline touchstone or the popular wish to gather a single explanatory sentence) and the murderous ambition to extinguish all, to censor the objectionable out of existence. Essence and nothingness turn on the same idealist pivot. The twin beliefs in a distillation that will return either to an essence or to nothing partake of the same alchemical faith, the same mystery-mongering politics. The very attempt to look for a sentence is to look to one's father's wishes.

What remains is the black veil, neither essence nor nothing. It is the mark beyond the sentence of Faliero and its execution—something added to the sacrificial machinery of the state in order economically to seal once and for all its flawlessly sufficient hegemony. Intended as an *Index Expurgatorius* that would put a stop to all further talk, the black veil was itself censored by Elliston; indeed, it is the sign in the play of that censorship, which the veil anticipates and entails as the type ordains and is (all but) canceled by its antitype. Venetian censorship is expunged by a new censorship, which may disable the play as theater but realizes it as a text that has a strength not under the control of the monopolistic discourse of patriarch, patrician, and patriot. The veil marks and its censorship remarks the necessity of a certain craftsmanship of repression. Despite the compelling sophistication of the panoptic order, which is capable of overseeing all representations and recuperating them into its empire, it must, in a kind of nervous atavism, grasp a text in its hands, work it over, recompose it, surely—but without annihilating the textual trace of manual intervention, the signifier that reinscribes the insistent materiality of the text on which the censor labors and by which he is traduced.

The mark of the veil and the censorship of Elliston attest, however unwittingly, to a textual strength that satirizes theatrical professions of meaning by virtue of an indelibly contingent position. That position is written into the play as something that is not and could not be represented in the play and therefore, of course, could never be censored from the performance of the play: Steno's squib, the text that provokes all the action while causing nothing. Steno's offstage scrawl is the parody of the invisible power that expresses itself in the well-formed statements that in their monotonous reiteration constitute Venetian political life. It is a parody that can be named satiric not only because its position, wholly without authority, is contingent, thus describing a border or margin of the hegemonic, but also because it is strong; its strength is attested to rather than sealed by the institutional reproduction of the mark in both the black veil and the censor's erasure—each of which is a self-inflicted pasquinade that belies the power of the master discourse to discipline all signs to its standard of propriety.[26]

Not a proper cause, the strength of the mark is wholly contingent. The path that connects the black veil and the inky scrawl is no vector of necessity but a digressive association that follows the fault of authority from displace to displace, motivating the turgid metaphorics of blood and contamination desperately imposed by rebel and ruler and exposing the futility of Faliero's hope to purify Venice by sounding the clarion in the tower of St. Mark's—as if a single sound could sublate what is not a contradiction but a fault in diction itself, as if one mark, no matter how ringing, could abolish another. Neither a distillate nor nothing, the offstage pasquinade is a literal (that is, noncodified) *Steno-graph*, an abbreviation, which is itself faulted, which takes discourse to its bottom line (a stroke of the pen in a strategic place), and which inscribes that line as a site of possible interpretations, coincidences, disruptions, and evasions.[27] A scrawl on the throne that is bandied about and dismissed but never fully represented or erased; a play that is appropriated from manuscript, censored, performed, and retired but that insists *on* and persists *in* its strong materiality—this stenograph appears not as the formulaic transcription of a master discourse but as the irreducible material occasion for a theater in which sentences tagged to various authorities try to claim or assign power; *its* strength is to mark all such utterances as inconsequential digressions from an unspeakable fault.

Marino Faliero is a poetics of satire in abbreviated form. Byron's satire, like all satire, finds fault; what distinguishes Byron's satire is that what it finds is what it *is*. The only strength that can be exerted by satire in a disciplinary society ordered by a power that no one can speak is to mark the digressiveness of all authoritative utterance. If the fault of Byron's poetry is its digression, a digression that invokes no authority and prospects no teleology, that fault is also its indubitable strength. Byron's digression is the stenographic signifier that cannot be gathered into one sole sentence, that cannot be disciplined. If, then, Byron participates in what Richard Sennett calls the "fall of public man," he does not reify a compensatory zone of "privatized freedom" as a transcendent refuge of the self from the arena of public expression and display; rather, he dramatizes the yearning for such a refuge and the futility of that yearning, shows that the notion of a secret place of self-expression and unencumbered personal relations, of any sort of transcendence, is an illusion that is constituted by and functional within a pervasive disciplinary discourse.[28] Byron opposes every explanation of the private that is in any way systematic but observes the impossibility of proposing any alternative that would not be subject to "this cursed attempt at representation." His undisciplined practice is to inscribe in public a stenograph, which, be it the text of a play, a mock-confessional "I," a potentially endless series of cantos, or merely his adopted initials *N.B.*, has a strength that matters.

Swaying: *Sardanapalus* and the Triumph of Liberalism

In *The Theory of Moral Sentiments* Adam Smith gives this sketch of the British gentleman:

> He acts upon the most indifferent occasions, with that freedom and elevation which the thought [that he is always noticed] naturally inspires. His air, his manner, his deportment, all mark that elegant and graceful sense of his own superiority, which those who are born to inferior stations can hardly ever arrive at: these are the arts by which he proposes to make mankind more easily submit to his authority, and to govern their inclinations, according to his own pleasure: and in this he is seldom disappointed. These arts, supported by rank and preeminence, are, upon ordinary occasions, sufficient to govern the world.[29]

Smith's gentleman has the negligent grace natural to those born to rule. In the Europe of the 1820s, after the cataclysms of the French Revolution and Napoleon's imperial adventure, however, the category "born to rule" has come to have less self-evident grounding in the order of things. In Lord Byron's time—post-Waterloo, post-Peterloo—at the hour tolled by *Sardanapalus*, the notion of an "indifferent" occasion has become an endangered fiction. This is the hour of rebellion actual and threatened. For those gentlemen whose right to rule has been confected over the abyss of their illegitimacy, the difference between fact and portent has become merely nominal.

Literary rulers are similarly imperiled. Consider the warning that the political reformer John Cam Hobhouse delivered to his friend in response to the publication of the first two cantos of *Don Juan* in 1819: "If the world shall imagine that taking advantage of your great command of all readers you are resolved to make them admire a style intolerable in less powerful writers, you will find in a short time that a rebellion will be excited, and with some pretext, against your supremacy: and though you may recover yourself it will be only with another effort in your original manner."[30] Extrapolating domestic resistance exponentially, Hobhouse warns of a popular rebellion against Byron's imperious ascendancy. Recalling Lady Byron's strikingly similar complaint about Byron's tyrannical imposition of outlandish tastes, Hobhouse sounds a note of emergency that was to become something of a commonplace in responses to Byron, shared by parties all along the political spectrum.[31] In his otherwise laudatory review of *Childe Harold IV* John Wilson, who is to Reaction as Hobhouse is to Reform, takes up the theme and predicts an uprising of the coming generation: "It is even probable, that they may perversely withhold a portion of just admiration and delight from him who was once the undisputed sovereign of the soul, and that they may show their surprise at the subjection of their predecessors beneath the tyrannical despotism of genius, by scorning themselves to bow before its power, or acknowledge its legitimacy (*RR* B:2:896). According to Wilson's analysis, the manifestation of genius is an expression of sovereignty; and the trouble of Byron's genius is the trouble of a sovereignty turned despotic. With the integration of poetry into the "literary lower empire" established in the wake of Napoleon's ruin, criticism has become a kind of political science.

In "The Spirit of Conquest and Usurpation and Their Relation to European Civilization" (1814), one of the founding documents of nineteenth-century liberalism, Benjamin Constant offered an especially influential model for the application of a traditional political vocabulary—largely

Montesquieu's—to the novel circumstances of nineteenth-century Europe. Constant identified modern despotism as the usurpation of civil society by a state that had become the "instrument of a single man."[32] I say *modern* despotism because Constant's liberalism cannot think of itself except in terms of modernity, of a "today" that has triumphed over the mystifications of the past, specifically those illusions that had been cynically revived and hypocritically exploited by Napoleon Bonaparte. Writing in Hanover during the final days of 1813, when, as Constant's editor observes, "Napoleon's power seemed on the point of collapse," Constant could confidently declare that

> any government that wished today to goad a European people to war and conquest would commit a gross and disastrous anachronism. It would labour to impose upon that nation an impulse contrary to nature. Since none of the motives that induced the men of past ages to brave so many dangers and to endure so many exertions remain for the men of our own day, it would have to offer them motives compatible with the present state of civilization. It would have to stimulate them to combat by means of that same desire for pleasure that, left to itself, could only dispose them to peace.[33]

Because Napoleon is a throwback to the days when men were roused by the slogans of a "sterile glory," his ambition never had a future: it was the hope of an inveterate gambler and a ruthless daydreamer—one who imagined himself a king and lived as a king only until "nature" reasserted itself. For Constant "nature" is a historical agent that conducts civilization out of history; its emergence coincides with the triumphant instauration of an enlightened epoch of peaceful commercial exchange that abrogates the need for further revolutionary convulsions and military conflict. At one level of the liberal argument, breaking the Napoleonic grip and restoring the partition between the state and civil society entails little more than inducing the burghers of Europe to reset their clocks with a sober eye to the passage of the sun, and then awaiting nature's restoration of the balance. Thus Constant Orientalizes Napoleon's career, representing it as a regressive detour from the westering progress of enlightenment: "Since he could not bring ignorance and barbarism to the heart of Europe, he took some Europeans to Africa, to see if he could succeed in forming them in barbarism and ignorance; and then, to maintain his authority, he worked to make Europe go backwards."[34] For Constant, who learned from Montesquieu, as for Marx, who learned from both, Asiatic despotism stagnates in the wings of history as the very type of anachronism.[35]

According to Constant's rendering of the modern chronotope, despotism should have vanished from the earth with the confinement of Napoleon on Elba. The evidence is otherwise. There is, of course, the Hundred Days. Like Scott and Byron, Constant underestimated Bonaparte's resilience.[36] But there is, as Hobhouse and John Wilson illustrate, also a remarkable persistence of the *language* of despotism, an Oriental residue that, dissociated from the alibi of the Napoleonic career, remarks on a critical lack of synchrony between liberal theory and liberal practice. The discrepancy is most glaring in the United Kingdom that the Anglophiliac Constant took as his pattern for the European future; it reflects the failure of liberal economics to break with the ossified political forms of the past and the consequent necessity of regarding any vital (that is, *unscripted*) political act as potentially revolutionary, an extreme case requiring extreme measures dictated by the sovereign or his representatives.[37] As we shall see, Lord Byron's baroque recourse to Diodorus Siculus for an Asiatic hero on which to build a classical drama is symptomatic of the widespread reoccupation of a superseded and disreputable political vocabulary by the most advanced economic system in the world.

Lord Byron's preface sets the scene for his maneuver by advertising his contempt for contemporary English dramatic practice and announcing his resolution to return to those "unities" that in a better day were the "law of literature throughout the world." The language is tyrannical: it responds to (or imagines) a state of emergency that justifies the intervention of a dictatorship, whose "utopian goal," in the words of Walter Benjamin, "will always be to replace the unpredictability of historical accident with the iron constitution of the laws of nature."[38]

Characteristically, however, Byron immediately softens his authoritarian manner. "The writer," he modestly remarks, "is far from conceiving that any thing he can adduce by personal precept or example can at all approach his regular, or even irregular predecessors"; the writer is, as he says, "merely giving a reason." This "gift" should be appraised in light of Byron's dedicatory address to the "Illustrious Goethe," who, he adds, "has created the literature of his own country, and illustrated that of Europe." Goethe may genially illustrate the literature of Europe, but Byron is rarely so sunny (recall how Marino Faliero's black-veiled name in the gallery of the doges comes to illustrate the law of Venice). *Sardanapalus* has an altogether more ambiguous design. It is offered as reason, or as precept, or as exemplification of the "law of literature." The preface's vacillation on this point may indicate that Byron knows as well as anyone that there is no longer a universal law of literature; he may adhere to this sterile standard because, in exiled remoteness from the audience that has sustained him (he was holed up in Ravenna at the time), he doubts his continued capacity to persuade others to believe that his poetry has the strength to rule regardless of the variable moods of its audience. Like the character Sardanapalus, who at a crucial juncture of the rebellion against his regime elects to display himself outside his fortified palace, the preface appears outside the drama to persuade that its authority is based on grounds manifestly beyond deliberation or debate. Like the indecisive tyrant of the *trauerspiel*, poet and character "appear in the harsh light of their changing resolve."[39] The exact relations between Goethean "illustration" and Byronic "precept" and "example" are left hanging. Perhaps we might adduce the precept that *Sardanapalus* is meant both to illustrate and to apply the force of examples.

FROM DESPOTIC POLITICS TO ECONOMIC DESPOTISM

The political crisis of *Sardanapalus*—how to preserve the regime—is imagined as a rhetorical problem: how to induce other people to do what you want. Sardanapalus conceives of that problem Romantically: he wishes only to wish for others to want to do something in order to have them do it. A prisoner of the very reflexivity that defines his sovereignty, before he can move others the despot/child/poet must come to imagine how he could be moved to want something from others; therefore, he must be moved to put himself in the position of another. Salamenes, the emperor's martial brother-in-law, bluntly declares his strategy right off: "He must be roused" (1:9). Sardanapalus has been *corrupted* from martial activity into the effeminate enjoyment of luxury. Practical-minded, Hobhousean, the trustworthy brother-in-law aims to recall the degraded Sardanapalus to his "original manner."

Although Salamenes gives his reasons, the prevailing state of emergency subordinates moral reasons *why* to the rhetorical challenge *how*. Salamenes, the Stoic soldier, Myrrha, the Greek concubine, Zarina, the discarded wife—all characters in the play reduce to stratagems for arousing Sardanapalus by methods austere or gentle (indeed, all reasons for arousal are interventions designed to arouse). And if the problem is how to arouse a degraded and sated monarch, the answer, we soon learn, is to do it by means of his Myrrha. Mildly chastised by Sardanapalus for being "too prompt to sacrifice [her] thoughts for others," Myrrha answers, "I have no happiness / Save in beholding thine; yet—" "Yet! what YET?" (1:73–74) Sardanapalus replies. Not stopping for an answer, he hastens to add that Myrrha's "sweet will" is the only barrier between them. Despots are hard to please: criticized for being too prompt to sacrifice, Myrrha is next charged with willfulness when she qualifies her love. Clearly Sardanapalus does not conceive of himself as belonging to that category labeled "others." Myrrha's *yet* remarks on a fault line of contingency threading the relations between master and slave. But the alacrity with which Sardanapalus trumps her qualification shows how the flaw in her happiness (as if she could have a happiness not designed for her by the law of the despot) is instantaneously translated into a flaw in his: an imperial symmetry will inexorably drive out the contingent query or quibble in the name of a more perfect reflection, a higher unity.

Sardanapalus, then, is roused from a state of passivity to action, but for him action is itself reflection, merely mirroring—what Myrrha calls "civic popular love, *self*-love, / Which means that men are kept in awe and law, / Yet not oppress'd" (1:584–86). The "other" for whom Myrrha sacrifices her thought is, it turns out, Sardanapalus after all—not the Sardanapalus of the harem but that *ideal* Sardanapalus who, having become as kingly as his state, would be a self worthy of his own love. Ethical applications to a despot may be futile, but Sardanapalus can be lured to sacrifice his thoughts for that Myrrha-ed image of himself, that example of him offered by his slave. Myrrha's precept that "he who loves another loves himself, / Even for that other's sake" (1:533–34), is the mildest of all possible forms of constraint on Sardanapalus's behavior; it urges him to an action that is nothing more than the improvement of his reflection. In a perversion of the psychological dynamics on which Constant aims to found a liberal comity, Sardanapalus is lured to combat by a self-love that should dispose him to repose. Yet how could Sardanapalus resist? Who would not love himself for the sake of his mirror?

Self-entrapped, Sardanapalus becomes the image of his Myrrha's desire. The key exchange is this, which occurs in act 3, just after Sardanapalus has refused the helm of battle:

> *Sfe.*   Sire, the meanest
> Soldier goes not forth thus exposed to battle.
> All men will recognize you—for the storm
> Has ceased, and the moon breaks forth in her brightness.
> *Sar.* I go forth to be recognised, and thus
> Shall be so sooner. Now—my spear! I'm arm'd.
>   [*In going stops short and turns to SFERO.*]
> Sfero—I had forgotten—bring the mirror.
> *Sfe.* The mirror, sire?

Sar.   Yes, sir, of polish'd brass,
Brought from the spoils of India—but be speedy.
                    [*Exit SFERO*]
Sar. Myrrha retire into a place of safety.
Why went you not forth with the other damsels?
Myr. Because my place is here.
                    (ll. 139–50)

Sfero returns with the mirror. Sardanapalus admires his own reflection and then pivots:

Sar. Myrrha, embrace me;—yet once more—once more—
Love me, whate'er betide. My chiefest glory
Shall be to make me worthier of your love.
                    (ll. 170–72)

Sardanapalus is induced to action in the anticipation of a return to his Myrrha—a figure equal to her image of him.

As Constant warned, to be so induced is also be to traduced. During the first heady days after the fall of the Bastille, Thomas Paine jocularly reported to Edmund Burke a Jacobin street etymology that twinned *Iscariot* and *aristocrat*.[40] In his drama Lord Byron works out the implications of the connection for his king of love, who, in returning to what he takes to be his "original manner"—the manner of the line of Nimrod and Semiramis—is called to be his own Judas and betrays himself by a kiss:

Sar.   My Myrrha: [*He kisses her.*]
Kiss me. Now let them take my realm and life!
                    (4:521–22)

Whatever obscure pleasure the Oriental despot once took offstage, in his pavilion on the brink of the Euphrates, he now finds an Occidental pleasure in the lucid representation of himself. The misrecognition of the other as mirror is part and parcel of the misrecognition of his lordly self as being what corresponds to the image that the other reflects. Like the Bonaparte of *Childe Harold III*, Sardanapalus is swayed by that example of the sovereign self with which he would sway; the condition of defending his sovereignty is to image it and lovingly to subject himself to an always virtual or speculative identity. Entering on the Myrrha-stage of his career, Sardanapalus becomes *Sardanapalus*, a "sort of *ignis fatuus*" to the theater-going public (*DJ* 11:27).

Constant promoted the liberal society he found in place in England as a model for modern Europe. Having overcome the forces of barbarism, the victorious Western sovereignties could claim the right to a future in which commerce would succeed to war. "War and commerce," Constant writes, "are only two different means to achieve the same end, that of possessing what is desired. . . . [Commerce] is an attempt to obtain by mutual agreement what one can no longer hope to obtain through violence."[41] Something approaching Constant's perception is implicit in Sardanapalus's retort to the unfavorable comparison drawn between his reign and the Napoleonic militarism of his predecessor Semiramis: "I sway them," he counters, "she but subdued them" (1:192). Conquering is the easy part. The maintenance of hegemony calls for subtlety of a higher order. Yet if in his professions Sardanapalus plausibly mimics Constant, *Sardanapalus* nonetheless dramatizes the Constantine truth that a despot's liberal professions do not count, for despotism must resort to force in order to retain its power. The transition from symbolic swaying to physical subduing in the play is smooth and evidently inexorable, largely because in its seeming, swaying is already seamed: Sardanapalus is swayed to battle by a mirrored image that subdues him into an identification with his framed likeness.

This swing from swaying to subduing follows a logic of representation that troubles both Sardanapalus the despot and *Sardanapalus* the play. The troubles begin in act 1, when, in response to Salamenes's appeal that he be trusted to stifle the incipient antidynastic conspiracy, the emperor relinquishes to him his royal signet, thereby making what, in a letter objecting to the staging of his plays, Byron called a "cursed attempt at representation" (*BLJ* 8:66). Once Sardanapalus has lent his signet to Salamenes, he has constituted him as a representative and has transformed the basis of power in Assyria: henceforth the possession and display of that stereotype will be more decisive than a claim to birthright or than any other dynastic mystery. Approval of Sardanapalus's impulse lies behind the effort of the sympathetic reviewer for the *Examiner* to save *Sardanapalus* for the cause of reform by denying that Sardanapalus is truly a despot. Instead the reviewer perceives a fledgling liberal monarch who deserves credit for his good intentions: "In a word, the license which he takes he grants to his subjects, and would have them, with himself, glide on with love and revelry to the tomb" (*RR* B:3:1013).

Unfortunately, Sardanapalus was better at communicating his intentions to the *Examiner* than to his own subjects, obstinate in rebellion despite their lord's liberality.[42] The transfer of the signet does not have the effect of universally granting the license of luxury; instead it becomes the sign that license cannot be so universalized. It does so for two reasons. First, to grant a license presumes a sovereign and reserved right to grant. Hence Sardanapalus has every power but the power *fully* to license license. Politically, that qualification is momentous, for at the limit of despotic giving emerges the potential for democratic taking. Second, if the authoritarian ruler is restricted in his ability to grant freedom, so is he constrained in his effort to sway. Although the signet is used to allow the exercise of despotic power at a distance, it is a risibly limited extension of power, little more than a doubling, since there can be one and only one signet. The signet may be a representation of the despot, but its sign value is authorized by its approximation of despotic self-display. Even employing the signet, the despot can only show "himself" at two places at once; he cannot display his authority to each and every subject at one time and in one place. And it is at the boundaries of the scene of self-display (the wall of the city, the outlying provinces) where the unsubdued emerge and conflict ensues. Sardanapalus's reliance on the signet as on his Myrrha-ed image shows the limits of the technology by which despotism aims to sway.

But if license cannot be universalized, neither can authority be reclaimed. When Sardanapalus, having recovered his ring, eventually appears before his people to redeem his power by quelling that murmur he could not prevent, he appears as himself a representative or, in the words of the preface, an *example* of that despotic authority for which every act of exemplification potentially triggers a state of emergency. Self-display anywhere, it would appear, is as threatening to despotic hegemony as is the inability to appear everywhere. In this baroque rendition of the plight of absolute power, any representation, however prudent, that the despot makes irreversibly fractures the foundation of despotic power, which subsists (theoretically? fantastically?) only in the dazzlingly inapparent, scandalously personal body of the despot.

Sardanapalus' rendition of the susceptibility of enlightened self-interest to despotic consolidation suggests an ironic turn on Constant's optimism: the play teaches the lesson learned by Voltaire at the court of Catherine, that every enlightened despot remains a despot at heart. Nevertheless (and here Romantic irony rushes in where philosophes fear to tread), the play turns back on itself by dramatizing the futility of the despot's martial measures. However politic, such a strategy entails a representational gesture. That gesture is cursed because in time (in the time that westering representation introduces into the stagnant prehistory that is Asia) it will destroy the myth of a unique inviolability grounding despotic power. And this is true whether it be the power Sardanapalus, tyrant, exercised over Assyria or the power Lord Byron, author, claimed over his so-called closet dramas—which despite his objections were, one after the other, staged in the West End. The end of the play (the spectacular dissolution by fire of Sardanapalus and all that belongs to him) exploits the metaphorical possibilities of closure to identify the triumph of the despot over all the stuff that has ever represented him with the triumph of the play over all the examples of itself that will ever be staged.

But—and this is where the play breaks with Constant—the play's ironic critique of Asiatic despotism entails only the abandonment of the Oriental technology of swaying and subduing, not the despotic aim. Indeed, the foregrounding of that aim is one of the most prominent features of the cultural phenomenon called Byronism. Reviewing *Childe Harold IV* for the *Edinburgh Review,* John Wilson, for example, remarked that all of Byron's heroes were "stamped with the leaden signet of despotism" (*RR* B:2:896). Wilson's image aptly characterizes the way the scarred brows of the heroes of *The Giaour* and *The Corsair* are imagined irresistibly to sway the fascinated watcher; and Wilson implies that the poet's rendering of such scenes inscribes a certain wish that he might have similarly irresistible power to imprint feeling on his readers.

If pathological, such an ambition is hardly peculiar to Lord Byron. Indeed, it was the predominant trait of the tragic theater that in Burke's account most signally distinguished Great Britain from all other nations.[43] The mark of the primitiveness of the political culture of Assyria in comparison with the United Kingdom is simply that Assyria is a theater state without a theater. Here is Wilson, always sensitive to the social implications of art, remarking on the compelling intimacy of theatrical experience: The "tenderest tones of acted tragedy reach our hearts with a feeling as if that inmost soul which they disclose revealed itself to us alone. The audience of a theatre forms a sublime unity to the actor; but each person sees and feels with the same incommunicated intensity, as if all passed only before his own gifted sight" (*RR* B:2:895). Yet if the ideological protocol of the British theater shows a decided advance on Assyrian methods, the limitations of the theater state in Assyria nonetheless antithetically expose the intrinsic shortcomings of stage representation as an effective instrument of hegemony maintenance. Nineteenth-century Britain no longer has a Globe, no single orb in which the populace can be gathered to be swayed by the despotic image of their subjection. *Sardanapalus'* critique of theatrical representation is hand in glove with political economy's assault on the realm of the political as dangerously contingent: located on the edge of the districts devoted to finance, the theater contributes nothing either practically or symbolically to the grand project of capital formation; although all hearts may by a lucky stroke of genius be gathered into a sublime unity, as Laurence Sterne's

Yorick discovered in Paris, in the theater bodies noble and vulgar rub and jostle; friction occurs and with friction a democratic turbulence that threatens the fluid equilibrium designed by the English Constitution and executed by the commercial economy.

From the perspective of a liberal-minded Englishman in the first decades of the nineteenth century the rebellious populace of Nineveh is a theater audience run amok, recalling the riot over ticket prices at the reopening of Covent Garden in 1809, itself anticipating the rebellion over the price of corn at Peterloo in 1819. Under the sign of technology, which supposedly allows objective discrimination between the efficient and the wasteful, the modern and the anachronistic, the play seeks to proscribe politics "itself," understood as a zone of unprescribed give and take, assertion and resistance, as a domain with frontiers where the future may appear and the past lurks unsubdued, a conflictual practice that is, in truth, never simply "itself."[44]

THE EIGHTEENTH-CENTURY BACKGROUND

The eighteenth-century British discourse of despotism cut across the party spectrum. As J. G. A. Pocock has shown, country ideology associated republican virtue with aristocratic ownership and occupancy of the land, each aristocratic holding separate from every other and each at a bracing distance from the oppressive presence of king and court.[45] Republican politics was a sometime thing: having civic virtue meant exercising it only as the occasion warranted; and the aptness of the occasion was determined by local considerations and personal connections.

From the point of view of the capital, these multiple loci of independent power presented an implicit challenge to the legitimacy of central authority, to the reliable conduct of commerce in the inland market and, indeed, to the great and glorious compromise of 1688 on which the Union itself was based; they represented the constant possibility of local broils or, worse, networks of Jacobite conspirators. The taming of the aristocracy by the centralized apparatus of the monarchical state meant overcoming the local political advantage that the nobility commanded by virtue of its proximity to the populace and its control of the militia. In the eighteenth century the distance between king and subject was closed not by Elizabethan royal progresses or the ceremonial transport of the signet from place to place but by dispersing agents and distributing the signs of central authority (the posting of standing armies, of course, but also Ralph Allen's rationalization of the mail, improvements in roads, dissemination of the fashion doll, broadcasting of periodical essays on manners, regular assizes). Thus the traditional relations between one countryman and another were mediated by means of the currency of the capital, and formerly autonomous citizens were subjected to a control that, to the republican imagination, could only appear despotic if it was to appear in any recognizable shape at all.

This despot was not, however, the absolutist terror of Whig ideology—James II redivivus—but was instead the notional shadow or personification of the compromise formation that was in fact and in theory mixed government under the Hanovers. Specifically, the eighteenth-century variant of the despot responded far less to an actual individual threat (even the incursion of the pretender functioned primarily to allow the ventilation of internal pressure) than to the conspicuously fictional status of the monarch within the commercialist system. We can call that fiction precapitalist insofar as it answered the failure on the part of even such sophisticated theorists as David Hume and Adam Smith to realize fully the place and function of capital within modern society. We can call that fiction pre-Romantic insofar as its volatility would later be mitigated by the Romantic meditation on the necessity of fictions to stabilize national and individual identity that was inaugurated by Burke's *Reflections on the Revolution in France.* The idea of the despot, therefore, articulated the insistence of an equivocal, ungrounded *political* agency that was, like each George I through IV, both the residue of an absolutist past and the place saver for a capitalist future.

The same republican discourse of virtuous resistance to the forces of corruption and arbitrary power that was the ideological resort of aristocrats unable or unwilling to accommodate themselves to regulation by the capital was wielded by emergent professionals and marginal tenants intimidated by locally powerful aristocrats. Although those lords of the land may have considered themselves exemplars of republican virtue resisting Hanoverian exactions, they could be and were portrayed as behaving in their neighborhoods with the license of Oriental despots. Godwin's *Caleb Williams* and Goldsmith's *Vicar of Wakefield* exemplify this gentrified despotism in the depredations of Tyrrell and the caprices of Mr. Thornhill respectively. Godwin and Goldsmith turn republican ideology on its head, exploiting country ideology to mount an attack on its traditional exponents, the country squires themselves. They do so not from a nostalgia for the ancient constitution of things but as part of a revaluation of social being, which drastically discounts the merit of individual political activity in favor of a providential economy that (no surprise here) only the novel can adequately represent. Goldsmith is especially pertinent, because his criticism of republican shibboleths—laid out by the Vicar in his declamation to the masquerading butler (chap. 19)—implicitly offers the novel as a more efficient vehicle for inducement to identify with a remote and impersonal monarchic power than an established clergy (to which the Vicar ever more marginally belonged), genre painting (which the Vicar's improvident family vainly commissioned), or traveling stage companies (in which the Vicar's prodigal son had thriftlessly enlisted). *Caleb* and the *Vicar* herald a new dispensation in which authoritarian sloppiness would be remedied through the elaboration of a sophisticated technology of metaphoric identification. This technology is a kind of book called the realist novel, which persuasively presents an image of the everyday as the modest yet infinitely elastic recuperation of the failed ambitions of earlier representational regimes. And no matter how multivalent and articulated that image becomes, under the dispensation of the political economy of the novel, it will be regarded as if projected from an authorial/monarchical center.

Godwin and Goldsmith would have given quite different and divergent accounts of their interests. Nuances aside, however, Godwin and Goldsmith—professional writers scrambling for a living in an embryonic and unforgiving literary market—contributed to the late-eighteenth-century constitution of interest, rather than either domination or obligation, as the key to explain social behavior. They contributed to a decisive shift from political and ethical to economic modes of explanation, from theatrical and rhetorical to novelistic modes of social control.

THE POLITICAL ECONOMY OF SEX

Sardanapalus, swaying between the closet and the stage, hyperbolically both dramatizes and redescribes the shift from the political to the economic. Thus far we have examined that shift in terms of a fault inherent in the representation of the despot that plunges him into an allegorical enactment of the inevitable futility of political action. But no matter how subjective it is, the play is not a soliloquy. Sardanapalus represents himself in part because representations are made to him. Consider the sovereign not as actor (author or producer) but as one who is acted upon (spectator or consumer). Initially, the play posits as the apparent alternative to decisive political action a thriftless life of sybaritic and secluded revelry. Salamenes and Myrrha, however, conspire to keep Sardanapalus from adjourning to his pavilion of delight and collaborate to extinguish that refuge. In doing so they are acting from impulses that are neither Whig nor Tory but liberal (Myrrha's Greek heritage stamps her with liberalism's pedigree). Although they propose to emancipate Sardanapalus from slavery to his perverse impulses, they methodically bring his uncalculated expense of passion into reciprocal, economic balance with the public world. Salamenes's crucial rhetorical question "Were it less toil / To sway his nations than consume his life?" (1:21–22) presupposes the political economist's postulate that all human activity is labor in order that consuming can be measured against swaying as unproductive toil is measured against productive. Acting on that premise, the conspirators retrieve that habitus of dalliance and delight from its offstage, closeted darkness by captivating luxurious waste in a publicly available image of consumption—thereby embodying the interior world of the despot, bringing it to light, "orbing" it within a system of reflections that makes it available for identification by Sardanapalus as by others (see 3:90–92; 5:62–69). The path of action repeatedly urged on Sardanapalus only appears political: no other end is in view but the economic end of preserving the regime, which is identified with the image of the despot, an image that Sardanapalus is aroused to display. In the economy of the play as of the regime, stimulation is followed by no act except another stimulus. Arousal *is* the dramatic action, which is carried out by reasons, examples, precepts, and illustrations.

The play's rhetorization of politics—the evaporation of both its coercive and its ethical dimensions—enables a thoroughgoing sexualization of its plot. The economy of sex is the play's modern equivalent to unity of action. Gone are beginning, middle, and end; there is only arousal, arousal, arousal, and, finally, consummation. Myrrha's contingent *yet* lures Sardanapalus on to the apocalyptic *now*, where happiness and sacrifice are fused beyond separation in act or thought by a consummate phrase stated without qualification: "I come" (5:498). The phrase announces a *modern* despotism, one that powerfully condenses the manifold articulations that traverse social life. Beginning, middle, and end are republican, Greek, classical—those distinctions belong to the world of deliberation, politics, and tragedy. The engine of arousal and consummation is despotic, Assyrian, baroque, and British—the systematic breakdown of distinctions announces the triumph of political economy and thus of liberalism, whose legitimating social doctrine it is. The baroque exceeds the rules and conventions that articulate the classicizing law of literature, just as the post-Napoleonic despot dreamily trumps the penitential protocol by which a constitutional monarchy maintains its merely historical balance. It is not clear, however, that Constant could take any comfort from a drama that may ultimately point the right moral—the individual despot falls—but that in getting to its point exploits the despot's catastrophe in order to reinvest the despotic aim with a modern pathos.

Constant's downright opposition between a commercialized West and a despotic East looks somewhat quaint when tested by the baroque twists of the Byronic dialectic. Recently, however, Colin Campbell, in *The Romantic Ethic and the Spirit of Modern Consumerism*, has reclaimed Romanticism for liberalism by refurbishing Weberian sociological types in order to advance a hedonistic conception of pleasure, a conception that descends less from the bourgeois Constant than from the baroque *Sardanapalus* (although the play is, strangely, unmentioned). Far more sanguine about the residual effect of anachronistic modes of thought than Constant or Francis Jeffrey, Campbell reinscribes romance (Freudianized as the hallucinatory system of infantile satisfaction) dead center in the liberal mind. For Campbell the triumph of liberalism is not a function of people's eagerness for a deathlike repose (which he calls "satisfaction") but depends on their readiness to respond to continually renewed stimulation. In modern commercial society, according to Campbell, such experience occurs in anticipation of, and as an illusory substitute for, a gratification that could only be inadequate to its advertisement. Consumerist society is sustained by the continual failure of the reality test to quell either the individual or the social production of illusions. The consumerist system acquires its formidable reproductive power by recasting the reality test (the moment of consumption) as just another stimulus to further daydreams of pleasure. For Campbell the modern, Romantic consumer does not resist the lures of "glory" because they are sterile (a positive attraction to a Malthusian) but because, though closeted, he can have in daydream all the pleasure that glory might bring and with less toil than on the battlefield. "The individual," Campbell affirms, "is both actor and audience in his own drama, 'his own' in the sense that he constructed it, stars in it, and constitutes the sum total of the audience."[46] Consumer society is the projection of the principles informing Romantic drama, what Byron called "mental theatre."

Constant's bogey is the commission of anachronism. Campbell envisions a global "mental theatre" where such fears are themselves anachronistic. "Traditional hedonism," as he calls it, the elect individual's endeavor to maximize pleasurable sensations, has "an inherent tendency toward despotism . . . toward acquiring greater and greater control over all that surrounds him." "Modern hedonism," on the other hand,

> presents all individuals with the possibility of being their own despot, exercising total control over the stimuli they experience, and hence the pleasure they receive. . . . In addition, the modern hedonist possesses the very special power to conjure up stimuli in the absence of any externally generated sensations. . . . This derives not merely from the fact that there are virtually no restrictions upon the faculty of imagination, but also from the fact that it is completely within the hedonist's own control.[47]

Childe Harold III narrates the progress of Campbell's types: the poem moves from the world of real despots to a modern world represented by the portentous career of Napoleon, who anachronistically attempts to realize what is only a daydream. Bonaparte fails because he lacks what Campbell calls "the distinctively modern faculty, the ability to create an illusion which is known to be false but felt to be true"—he fails, that is, because he is no poet.[48] Modern hedonism begins in earnest with the Byronic representation of traditional despotism as an Oriental daydream available to all readers/purchasers of Byron's poems. Napoleon's career both illustrates the despotism to which all aspire and exemplifies the consequences of madly refusing to accept that such power is only a fantasy. Campbell joins with Addison in the serious enterprise of narrowing the moment of consumption to a theoretical point, as if the "disillusionment" with a "so-called 'new' product," though "largely irrelevant," were nonetheless intolerable. The strategists of consumption aim to control the rhythm of daydream and consumption (its seasons or its meter) and to exile all that is irrelevant to the "moment." Consequently, both the daydream and its disillusion will be stereotyped, transformed into pictures that pornographically induce the wish to which they "respond" as in *Sardanapalus*, where all "reasons" for arousing Sardanapalus are stimuli designed to arouse him.[49]

To say that such stereotyping is pornographic entails a tactical alignment with Lady Byron. It was Lady Byron who famously called the author of *Childe Harold III* the "absolute monarch of words, [who] uses them, as Bonaparte did lives, for conquest." However bloodless, Byron's conquests are conquests just the same. For Lady Byron there is little to choose between using military violence to get people to do what one wants and using symbolic violence, little difference between subduing and swaying. To the aggrieved woman who has learned her philosophy in Byron's bedroom, the difference supposed between a swaying that impels wives and readers into "mutual agreement" and a subduing that compels them to accept what they cannot hope to change is made merely rhetorical by the identity of ends. Lady Byron stands as a strong critic of Byronism by reminding the liberal that an economy sexualized is an economy that has transformed the very impulses of pleasure into a systematic violence.

Lady Byron might have added that in the consumerist society heralded by Byronism triumphant, daydreaming loses its effortless charm by being assigned a *value* as a kind of forced labor. Campbell helps us see that the lively debate among political economists over the usefulness of Adam Smith's category of unproductive labor responded to just this transformation. What could the opposition of productive/unproductive mean in a society where daydreaming has become a form of labor, which, like sex, must be made to pay off? It means nothing, argued J. R. McCulloch, who urged the abandonment of the distinction in his entry on political economy in the *Encyclopaedia Britannica*. McCulloch's heresy roused Thomas Malthus to a defense of the continued merit of Smith's distinction on the grounds that productivity must involve the increase "of the quantity or value of material products"; therefore, the labor of servants (to use the classic example) is unproductive. Malthus nonetheless insists that *unproductive* is a technical term employed without the intention of "stigmatizing" the kinds of labor to which it was applied. In his attempt to preserve Smith's definition, the conciliatory Malthus seems to dissolve the distinction between production and consumption. He concludes that "one of the most powerful causes of wealth must be the general prevalence of such a taste for material products as will occasion the employment of a great and increasing quantity of that kind of labour which produces them."[50] Servants are unproductive and the higher classes' desire for servants equally so. But the taste for ornate furniture is productive because it entails the increase of labor.

Under Malthus's dispensation, then, wanting, desiring, and longing are unified under the sign of consumption and given value as productive labor; it is just a matter of desiring things rather than persons. This maneuver adumbrates the breakdown of the opposition between production and consumption on which political economy implicitly rests.[51] Such a "deconstructive" move is made progressive, *economic*, by Malthus's earlier unexamined commission of the anachronism that violates both Constant's optimistic vision of repose and Campbell's seamless subjectivism: he claims that "the labour which commodities will *command* may be considered as a standard measure of their natural and exchangeable value."[52] Labor measures value; but commodities command labor. To imagine a consumer society (a society where consumption is productive and taste directed toward proper ends) is to require a command economy—an economy, that is, in which fashionable commodities (as opposed to invisible servants or plain-Jane governesses) can command the labor of daydreaming that gives them value in a market where the legitimacy of a price is determined by its ability to command a purchase. Every market transaction is thus an act of conquest, every act of swaying a kind of subduing.[53] No consumer has his pleasure completely under his control; every despot dreams as he is bid.

Because the moment of consumption is imaginary, it can be repeated indefinitely: each moment of arousal leads to another and then another. The final scene of the play, which ends with the suicide of the vanquished Sardanapalus and Myrrha on a grand funeral pyre, metaphorically consummates this sequence of arousals. That is, the funeral pyre condenses the whole play into a single emblematic moment that, however poetically just, seems not so much to conclude dramatically but to annihilate lyrically all that has gone before. The final solution of *Sardanapalus'* rhetorical problem, "He must be roused," ruins the play. The reviewer for *Blackwood's* complains, "There is a great deal of power in Sardanapalus . . . but as a play, it is an utter failure; and in God's name, why call a thing a tragedy, unless it be meant to be a play?" (*RR* B:1:177). The reviewer is answered in the next issue: "Tragedies are made to be acted," it is declared; "if not, they . . . resemble the razors recorded by the facetious Peter Pindar,—not made to shave, but to sell" (*RR* B:1:182).

Not to shave but to sell: *Blackwood's* shrewdly remarks on the complicity of Romantic drama's repudiation of the hurly-burly of stage representation with a certain homeostasis characteristic of the commodity, which, unlike the advertising for the commodity, owes its marketable charm to its recessive self-closure. In its purity the commodity lacks any purpose except to be sold; unsold, it is incomplete and temptingly vulnerable to any false use that could damage its appeal. Considered in its purity the commodity will be sold only if buying befalls it as a fulfillment of it, as a rapt apprehension that owns the right to bring forth this vulnerable thing from its closet for the brief moment of its consumption. It is the participation of *Sardanapalus* in the equivocal status and destiny of the commodity that elevates it above the stagecraft of previous generations and allows the drama to reabsorb its own vulnerability to representation as an element serving the extension of its sway.

To the traditional questions asked of *Sardanapalus*, "What good is a tragedy not made for acting? What good is a king not made for governing?" might be added "What good is a slave not exploited for sexual pleasure?" The slave is good for burning. Ritual cremation has long fascinated the Western imperial imagination.[54] Its canonical locale was India, where, under the Western eyes of J. G. E. Herder, the cult of the suttee served the political end of insuring the allegiance of wives to their despotic husbands. With no hope of surviving her lord, Herder writes, a wife could have no motive for plotting his overthrow: "The men [of Hindustan] were incapable of securing from sparks the inflammable tinder, which their voluptuousness had [gathered in the harem]; and too weak and indolent, to unravel the immense web of female capacities and contrivances, and turn them to better purposes: accordingly, as weak and voluptuous barbarians, they sought their own quiet in a barbarous manner; and subjected by force those, whose artfulness their understanding was unable to sway."[55] Myrrha, however, is not an Oriental wife but a freed Greek concubine. And her death is not coerced but consensual. She goes "freely and fearlessly" to the pyre (5:465). Indeed, her self-sacrifice climactically vindicates Sardanapalus's ability to sway the one subject whose consent counts, because she is the one subject who sees with Western eyes, who can buy (who can *credit*) rather than merely obey. The play triumphs in its imagination of its ability to command a purchase as if it were freely willed. Fully specular, the play reinforces its rule by imagining the consumption of its own consumer—an effect epitomized by Myrrha's last equivocal utterance, "I come," which, by simultaneously *promising* her leap into the consuming fire and *declaring* an orgasmic consummation, finely suspends all finalities. The moment of consumption displays both expectation and fulfillment, a fulfillment enriched by the expectation of more to come.[56]

Myrrha's equivocation is as overdetermined as is Sardanapalus's swaying, which may be a means of exercising social control, but which also expresses an effeminate style that is itself the symptom of some vacillation about the appropriate sexual object of choice.[57] The consummation thus at once raises the question of Myrrha's gender (Does the tyrant construct her as male or female? Does the playwright intend for her to be played by a woman or a boy?) by suspending it. She is either male or female depending on whether the play is adjudged destined for closet or stage. Insofar as she is the *visible* vehicle of a final identification, Myrrha must be female, so that the sexual declaration "I come" may be as empirically unfalsifiable as the rhetorical promise "I come." If an actress says she comes, no gaze can confute her. Indeed, the appearance of a woman mitigates the pun, allows assertion to fade into promise. The woman is the public image of the perfect consumer, fully responsive to the dictates of the market. Insofar as the play is interred in the closet and read in a book, where the claim to come is not subject to visual verification, Myrrha can be and is as male as Salamenes. Her masculinization is the precondition of her capacity to consent. In a book the indecorous pun on *come* becomes legible as the reason for keeping the drama from the stage.

Gender, then, does not make any difference except as a nuance that invigorates the appeal of Myrrha as our (readers and spectators, subjects and objects, guys and gals) equivocal stand-in, an appeal that Delacroix deftly illustrates by depicting Myrrha from behind. Gender equivocation is the open secret of the closet lurking suggestively in every performance on the British stage, just as the possibility of stage representation deliciously enlivens every closeted reading. As for producer and consumer, master and slave, one option inverts the other: the female can be understood as consenting to the consummatory moment insofar as she can be imagined in some closeted region to be really male; the masculine prerogative to grant or withhold consent can be effectively overridden insofar as a man can be effeminized as the object of an imperious and public desire. The pun on *come* decisively proves the play's ability to swing both ways, between closet and stage, private and public, homo and hetero—to swing between poles, to subdue difference, and thereby to *sway*. The play both flaunts and fulfills the ambitions of global comprehensiveness that political economy could countenance only in its dreams.[58] *Sardanapalus* is *The Wealth of Nations* in drag.

Ernesto Laclau and Chantal Mouffe have defined the onset of totalitarianism as that moment when "the state raises itself to the status of the sole possessor of the truth of the social order . . . and seeks to control all the networks of sociability. In the face of the radical indeterminacy which democracy opens up, this involves an attempt to reimpose an absolute centre, and to re-establish the closure which will thus restore unity."[59] *Sardanapalus* efficiently *contains* the leeway that endangers old-fashioned authoritarian regimes by a centering trope of equivocation that sutures action and reflection in the same fashion that genders fortuitously come together, that Myrrha and mirror are apparently seamed, that consumption and labor are economically combined, and that lyric and drama are Romantically hybridized. That equivocation makes possible the rendition of all ostensible fractures in the "network of sociability" as mere nuances and enables the deployment of all nuances as the means to sway; it establishes a volatile center that wavers from side to side on the breezes of a public opinion it reflexively frames. The theatrical technology by which the despot represents his right to rule fails because no despot can go everywhere. Sardanapalus ultimately wins by making everyone come to him. He succeeds in exemplifying a sovereignty that, unlike the laborious and wasteful conquest of his ancestors, has become nothing other than the sheer power of exemplification. This "light / To lesson ages" illuminates the end of history (5:440–41). By this light we can appreciate commercial society's triumphant troping of conquest as repetition compulsion and can liberally endorse repetition compulsion as the economical consumption of commodities in serial moments of choice.

In more traditional terms, the climactic suspension of the sexual and the rhetorical represents the overcoming of what Benjamin calls the "discrepancy between tragic word and situation" that is the empty triumph of the belated *trauerspiel*, which, like a piece of baroque architecture, "repeats itself infinitely, and reduces to immeasurability the circle which it encloses."[60] In more contemporaneous terms, *Sardanapalus* exemplifies

Schlegel's notion of Romantic poetry: "It alone can become, like the epic, a mirror of the whole circumambient world, an image of the age. And it can also—more than any other form—hover at the midpoint between the portrayed and the portrayer, free of all real and ideal self-interest, on the wings of poetic reflection, and can raise that reflection again and again to a higher power, can multiply it in an endless succession of mirrors."[61]

This is the moment that "I come" tries to grasp—the raising of the Myrrha-stage to a higher power. *Sardanapalus* instantiates Romantic poetry as the perfection of the commodity form by rendering the aestheticizing of politics as fulfilled in an act of consumption. It is immaterial whether one chooses Delacroix's trenchant *Death of Sardanapalus* or John Martin's grandiloquent *Fall of Nineveh* as the best pictorial illustration of the closing consummation.[62] The play concludes by offering itself as a thing subject to perfect illustration, as a work of art that can see itself becoming a picture and that authorizes the pictorial part to stand for an imaginary whole. *Sardanapalus'* suspended consummation does, then, illustrate the "law of literature" as promised in the preface; but it is a new law for a modern literature, an edict that what is unified is what, like the realistic novel, continually promises its susceptibility to perfect illustration, a world-view. In that respect Sardanapalus's kingdom and James Tilly Matthews's air loom are of the same order of being.

As fully objectified as his play (and thus reciprocally occupying both the position of himself *and* his mirror, of master and slave, actor and audience), Sardanapalus need never die and nevermore must exert himself in the harem or the throne room. His "sovereignty" is exempt from challenge because it is grounded in the consent not of the governed but of the consumer, whose consent to be ceaselessly aroused is signaled by her/his absorption in a social imaginary anchored by the idea of him-/herself as an Oriental despot. *Sardanapalus* imagines the transformation of a baroque state of emergency into a modern *culture* of emergency where every man is her own despot, and every despot is continuously roused to the moment of consumption. As Constant eloquently warned, "There is no limit to the tyranny that seeks to exact the signs of consent." What Constant did not see is that the "counterfeiting of liberty" he ascribed to the despotism of the "Grand Turk" inheres in every act of consumption by which liberal society maintains its sway.[63]

COMMITTING ANACHRONISM

What could be more felicitous than this triumph of economics over politics and aesthetics over ethics? Approval by the reviewers of *Sar-*

danapalus was, however, fitful and faint. Some of the objections were generic, such as Francis Jeffrey's complaint in the *Edinburgh Review* that "instead of the warm and native and ever-varying graces of a spontaneous effusion, the work acquires the false and feeble brilliancy of a prize essay in a foreign tongue" (*RR* B:2:920). In the *Quarterly*'s response to the play, however, Byron's foreign tongue gets a new twist. Reginald Heber denounces the prefatory attempt to impose the unities as a "law of literature" and urges that

> when . . . these usurpations find an advocate in one who is himself among the most illustrious living ornaments of English poetry, it is time to make up our minds, either to defend the national laws, or to submit to the "Code of Napoleon;" and to examine whether there be really, in favour of this last, so much extrinsic authority or so much intrinsic excellence, as to call on us to adopt it, in place of that ancient licence of pleasing and being pleased in the manner most effectual and most natural, which the poets and audiences of England have, till now, considered as their birthright. (*RR* B:5:2059)

Sardanapalus may hoodwink his Grecian, but, as Hobhouse foresaw, Lord Byron breeds resistance. Here the Tory reviewer resorts to the Whiggish ideology of ancient licenses, updating the Norman yoke as a Napoleonic invasion. Lord Byron's attempt at authoritarian legislation is met with the rousing cries of "Nature and country." Nature (or Shakespeare), not abstract codes, it is urged, is the law for English drama. Paradoxically, the clearest threat to the integrity of English literature is mounted by that speaker who is among English poetry's "most illustrious living ornaments." It is as if the reviewer sickened at the preface as a *surplus* of exemplification that destabilizes the perfectly balanced apparatus of reflection and displaces the example, precept, or illustration from subordination to any law that could give it reason. The unequivocal registration of this displacement by the *Quarterly* reviewer indicates a flaw in the play's economy. It marks the resurgence of the political as a style of assertion that exceeds the closure of the commodity.

Although the *Quarterly* reviewer responds to the preface, the displacement is not confined there. Reviewers' objections to Lord Byron's Napoleonic usurpation were matched by complaints about his various anachronisms: the reference in the Assyrian court to the so-called practices of "Oriental" rulers, the portrayal of a Greek slave before the time enslavement of the Greeks had begun, and Sardanapalus's speculations regarding the contents of pyramids about which he could know nothing. The complaints about anachronism might seem especially odd, for in a certain sense they align Lord Byron with a fine old Shakespearean foible—one of those most ridiculed by his French detractors. Those and other faults might be eliminated with ease, and would be eliminated by a writer who took care over his compositions. Lord Byron's neglect is rendered more troublesome by the linkage between such vicious details and Sardanapalus's own perverse addendum to the cities he founded, the verse that, as he says, contains the "history of all things human":

> Sardanapalus
> The king, and son of Anacyndaraxes,
> In one day built Anchialus and Tarsus.
> Eat, drink, and love; the rest's not worth a fillip.
> (1:296–99)

The *Quarterly* observes that

> the strange story variously told, and without further explanation scarcely intelligible, which represents him as building (or fortifying) two cities in a single day, and then deforming his exploits with an indecent image and inscription, would seem to imply a mixture of energy with his folly not impossible, perhaps, to the madness of absolute power, and which may lead us to impute his fall less to weakness than to an injudicious and ostentatious contempt of the opinions and prejudices of mankind. (*RR* B:5:2066)

By contemptuously defacing his own best work, Sardanapalus combines the characters of Marino Faliero and Michael Steno. It is a deformation we have seen before: a deformation characteristic, as it were, of a poet out of step with the times. The *London Magazine* notices the pattern and, yoking the poet and Sardanapalus, indicts Lord Byron as a " 'chartered libertine,' who has made humanity a jest":

> "Once a jacobin, always a jacobin," was formerly a paradox; "but now the time gives it proof." "Once an aristocrat, always an aristocrat" might pass, with as little question, into a proverb. Lord Byron, who has sometimes sought to wrap himself in impenetrable mystery, who has worn the fantastic disguises of corsairs, giaours, and motley jesters, now comes out in all the dignity of his birth, arrayed in a court suit of the old French fashion, with the star glittering on his breast, and the coronet overtopping his laurels. The costume only has been changed, the man has been the same from the first. (*RR* B:4:1611)

The man who has stayed the same in the face of changes of taste is a man who shows contempt for what Emerson would later call the "voice of humanity."[64] He limps out of the closet onto the stage in a costume that cannot hide that he remains hidden, secretly degrading humanity as he deforms his own best works. "Once an aristocrat, always an aristocrat" identifies that one who troubles the self-identity of humanity by persisting as a chronic disturbance to its synchronism. "Once an aristocrat, always an aristocrat" marks out the noble poet—as it once had marked the scurrilous Jacobin—for inveterate antagonism and eventual sacrifice. But if self-identity does belong to humanity, it cannot belong to the aristocrat, whose charter has no legitimacy, whose contempt has no grounds, and whose anachronistic existence has no historical being. Who, then, is this scapegoat? Or, paraphrasing Keats, who exactly *is* this coming to the sacrifice?

Sardanapalus raises the question himself in the passage that immediately precedes the firing of the pyre and that has offended both critics and directors of the play (it was struck, for good dramatic reasons, from the excellent 1990 performance at Yale University):

> In this blazing palace,
> And its enormous walls of reeking ruin,
> We leave a nobler monument than Egypt
> Hath piled in her brick mountains, o'er dead kings,
> Or *kine*, for none know whether those proud piles
> Be for their monarch, or their ox-god Apis;
> So much for monuments that have forgotten
> Their very record!
>
> (5:480–87)

Profoundly anachronistic and profoundly unnecessary, this is a meditation that could not have been over something that did happen but has been forgotten.[65] What has been forgotten is whether the pyramid memorialized the actual sacrifice of the scapegoat or instead the sacrifice of a scapegoat (scapebull, in this case) for the scapegoat. Humanity has forgotten what it could not help forgetting: what is encrypted in and by the pyramid in its very construction. The solemn encryption is, in effect, a deforming inscription that punningly scatters what it monumentally centers. It is as if Sardanapalus has not only (impossibly) read Herodotus but as if he has read *Childe Harold I*, which links the death of the bull to the death of the aristocrat; and it is as if he has read Coleridge's *Biographia Literaria*, which uses the pyramid to illustrate the brick-bound, canonical unity of a Shakespeare or a Milton. "I was wont boldly to affirm," Coleridge reminisces, "that it would be scarcely more difficult to push a stone out from the pyramids with the bare hand than to alter a word, or the position of a word, in Milton or

Shakespeare, (in their most important works at least) without making the author say something else, or something worse, than he does say."[66] *Sardanapalus* goes beyond the *Biographia* to engage the sacrificial investment that endows such authorities with value—an aboriginal violence that Coleridge was unable to face, whether in this version of Milton and Shakespeare or in his treatment of Wordsworth's "Thorn." But *Sardanapalus* also goes beyond skeptically undermining Coleridge's nervous idealization; it "remembers" the pyramids not as memorials of either the real or the symbolic death of kings or kine, but precisely as the "memorial" of the primordial alteration of the sacerdotal word that names what is encrypted in order to motivate the architectural construction.

Sardanapalus could be imagined to have read Coleridge because he seems to read English: the dramatic fiction that the Assyrian speaks his own language is violated not by a slippage between things (the kind of empirical problem that could be settled by archaeologists or historicists, who might dismantle the pyramid to remove the bones to determine the facts to deliver a lecture) but by a slippage between *letters* that could only occur in English untranslated. Sardanapalus wanders into English as the *g* of *king* wanders into the *e* of *kine*, transgressing kind. We have seen a similar effect in Freud's story of Bain and Abel in chapter 4 above, which hangs the progress from the primal to the civilized on the shift of a letter. *Sardanapalus* comes out in a world all but completely civilized and, therefore, according to Lord Byron, never to be completely civilized because (to our good fortune) never completely subject to unification under the sign of humanity. Neither king nor kine, Lord Byron's strength is demotic and democratic: it "does not reside in his full positivity as a subject, [therefore] any attempt, no matter how refined, to enslave (including his own) him will fail because there is within him something that escapes objectification."[67] English *appears* in *Sardanapalus* as if encrypted within itself as an inextirpable wandering or deformation that cannot be resolved by sacrifice.[68] It appears as that Romantic strength that cannot be captured by a picture and therefore cannot be consumed.

9

Annals of a Line Undone

What Matters in the
English Cantos of Don Juan

We are moved not merely by the actual issue of the trial, but by all
that the orator himself has at stake.

Quintilian, Institutes

But "laissez aller" — knights and dames I sing.

Don Juan, *canto 15*

In the eleventh canto of *Don Juan* "Lord Byron" returns to "England."
Scare quotes capture the spirit of the occasion on which a revenant lord
returns to a home from which substance has been spirited away. *Substance*,
not matter:

> When Bishop Berkeley said "there was no matter,"
>   And proved it—'t was no matter what he said:
> They say his system 't is in vain to batter,
>   Too subtle for the airiest human head;
> And yet who can believe it! I would shatter
>   Gladly all matters down to stone or lead,
> Or adamant, to find the World a spirit,
> And wear my head, denying that I wear it.
>
> What a sublime discovery 't was to make the
>   Universe universal Egotism!

That all's ideal—*all ourselves:* I'll stake the
  World (be it what you will) that *that's* no Schism.
Oh Doubt!—if thou be'st Doubt, for which some take thee,
  But which I doubt extremely—thou sole prism
Of the Truth's rays, spoil not my draught of spirit!
Heaven's brandy,—though our brain can hardly bear it.

(11:1–2)

Leaving off "metaphysical / Discussion," the narrator elaborates his answer to Berkeley in terms of what might be called the physiological argument:

The truth is, I've grown lately rather pthisical:
  I don't know what the reason is—the air
Perhaps; but as I suffer from the shocks
Of illness, I grow much more orthodox.

(11:5)

The physiological argument does not prove the existence of God; it proves orthodoxy on the pulse that, shocked, unsettles idealism's suave self-assurance.

The orthodox reflex is telling, even if orthodoxy should finally prove to be anodyne rather than cure. *Juan*'s rejoinder to "Berkeley" anticipates the critique of the Lowthian model of secularization as the global transposition of explanatory protocols that Hans Blumenberg mounts under the concept of "reoccupation":

> The reoccupation that is the reality underlying the appearance of seculari-zation is driven by the neediness of a consciousness that has been overex-tended and then disappointed in regard to the great questions and hopes. The decisions that were once made outside this world in the absolute acts of divinity and are now supposed to be accomplished in and through man, as moral, social, and political actions, did not, as it turned out, permit a suc-cessful transition to self-disposition. But even apart from its significance for historical explanation, the persistence in language of a stratum of expres-sions also has the consequence that what had already become metaphorical can again be taken literally. Such misunderstandings have their own kind of historical productivity.[1]

In *Juan*'s scheme the orthodoxy that in an earlier and more civil age had lapsed into allegory returns as the black-letter symptom of a diseased skep-ticism.[2] The shocks of illness destroy Berkeley's overextended speculation by detonating the complacent secularizer's claim to have successfully engi-neered a transition from tutelage to self-disposition, whether for the indi-vidual or social body, for citizen or metaphysician.

In one sense Lord Byron's narrator can, like a mimic Bonaparte or Semiramis, profess to stake the world against Berkeley's skepticism because he knows that once the universe has been reduced to "universal Egotism" there is nothing material at stake, nothing like, say, money. *Juan's* jest is echoed by Michel Serres's complaint respecting Descartes's prior and equally pusillanimous doubt. "Money," Serres writes, "is integrally my being. The real doubt is poverty. Radical doubt to the extreme is misery. . . . Descartes cheated; he didn't throw his ducats into the stream. He never lost the world since he kept his money. . . . Descartes never risked losing his 'I,' since he never risked his money. He never played his *malin génie* for high stakes—for the shirt off his back. . . . I have always doubted this doubt that does not go to the zero level of possession."[3] Money is integrally the being of the England to which *Don Juan* returns, a country where, it would seem, only cash matters. And because skeptical idealism indemnifies the Cartesian equation of "I" with propriety, property, and money, what is doubted remains immaterial unless the bank account is put at risk. Thus Berkeley cheats because his supposedly fundamental doubt has the net effect of restoring things to the way they were before. In reducing the universe to universal egotism, the philosopher allows everyone to keep what he has. At the end of the line a universal ego is always *my* ego universalized.

So why not stake the world? "Win or lose, in the long run the end is the same"—such is the political economist's ever-optimistic dictum. Or in *Juan's* phrase, "So the end's gain'd, what signifies the route?" (15:51). Despite appearances, however, that question, which dominates the last six cantos of *Juan*, is not of that kind called "rhetorical." Its divergence marks *Juan's* falling off from the status of what Jacques Derrida in his reading of Jacques Lacan's "Seminar" calls the "full text": a text that "simultaneously gives the questions and the answers"[4]—that is, a text in which the universe is rendered as a universal, if rifted, egotism. *Juan's* question stays for an answer and risks more than Descartes or Berkeley. Repentant, Sardanapalus exclaims,

> To what gulfs
> A single deviation from the track
> Of human duties leads even those who claim
> The homage of mankind as their born due,
> And find it, till they forfeit it themselves!
> (4:432–36)

And despite its mannered insouciance, *Juan* is aware that in the England of its imagination "any deviation from the graces / Might cost both man and master too—their *places*" (16:79). If anything does indeed matter, its route must signify. This is literally true—that is, it is true for letters. As Ralph Allen's career (not to mention the itinerary of Donna Julia's epistle) shows, letters are subject to the fate of all matter: destruction, recycling, theft, scattering, and waste. And something is indubitably at stake in the vicissitudes of the route that *Juan*'s insouciant question travels from manuscript to print, from Italy to England: readers, for example; and the money that gentle readers tender.

If, following Theodor Adorno, we posit that the "ground of modernism is both the absence of a ground and the explicit normative rejection by modernism of a ground, even if there were one,"5 *Juan*'s Berkeley hangs back on the brink of the modernist abyss, refusing to take the plunge. That discretion is replicated by political economy, which skeptically dissolves all that had been fancied substantive (quality, land, spirit, virtue) but stands on the essential propriety of property. Doubt is not doubt if it preserves the privilege—epistemological or economic—of the doubter. Political economy, as Jane Marcet urges in her practical-minded *Conversations on Political Economy* (1817), systematically doubts the existence of any political cause except for the first moment of institution by which property was originally secured.6 Property, as she expounds it, is politically instituted to be put out of political play. What Marcet calls "security" is the functional equivalent of a ground in a commercial society intent on refurbishing privileges and immunities for an age grown skeptical of the traditional language of legitimation.

Economics subtends politics by defining what matters as what can be counted: social being is the effect of enumeration. The doubt of the political economists is not doubting, because it affirms a world where the tides are chartered by the East India Company and where some egos in the universal ego count more than others. Berkeley's reservation of ego to himself and his assignment of immateriality to everything else has its analogue in Malthus's hypocritical indulgence in that "Philo-genitiveness" (*DJ*12:20–22) he proscribes for a people who, because they are propertyless, do not count as he counts, who have reality only as members of a population. *Juan* illustrates the Berkeleyan project by bringing the skeptic face to face with the analogon of his strategic doubt, a world in which there is no *there* there: an England structured like an economy, an economy structured like a dream, a dream structured like a language, and a language in thrall to fashion. In arranging this confrontation, I shall argue, *Juan* puts its property in itself at stake, conducts itself, in Serres's terms, to the "zero level of possession," where it becomes in its "own" words a "*not o'er*grown bulk" (16:123).

Tom As Hero

> *If a highwayman pulls out a pistol from his bosom, shall we wait till he loads and presents it, before we kill and disarm him? Shall we not attack him with like arms, if he displays such weapons. . . . ?*
>
> Edinburgh Review, *January 1803*

Despite being constitutionally healthy and resolutely nonmetaphysical, Juan suffers a shock of his own on his arrival in London. Getting out of his coach on Shooter's Hill, he attempts to attain a strategic perspective on the scene before him—an effort that induces a certain meditative oblivion to the circumstantial world. "Wrapt in contemplation" and "lost in wonder," he apostrophizes the world that he imagines is "here":

> "And here," he cried, "is Freedom's chosen station;
>   Here peals the people's voice nor can entomb it
> Racks, prisons, inquisitions; resurrection
> Awaits it, each new meeting or election.
>
> "Here are chaste wives, pure lives; here people pay
>   But what they please; and if that things be dear,
> 'T is only that they love to throw away
>   Their cash, to show how much they have a-year.
> Here laws are all inviolate; none lay
>   Traps for the traveller; every highway's clear:
> Here"—he was interrupted by a knife,
> With "Damn your eyes! your money or your life!"
>   (11:9–10)

The highwayman's injunction suspends Juan's disquisition. The knife punctures it. Juan does not respond to the assaultive word, for the "freeborn sounds" are shouted in a foreign language, unrecognizable except for the semantically empty "shibboleth" of *damn* (st. 12). Yet Juan "quickly understood" the highwayman's "gesture," and in an impeccably orthodox reply fires his pistol into "one assailant's"—Tom's—"pudding" (st. 13). Having abstracted himself to "Freedom's chosen station," Juan has been suddenly pitched into something like what Mikhail Bakhtin calls the "zone of maximal proximity," where instinct sways.[7]

Juan's welcome convincingly falsifies the Spaniard's preconceptions about English hospitality. No doubt, the notion of "Freedom" choosing a station—which both flatters England as the elected abode of a westering republican virtue and does so in terms of the bourgeois myth of effortless social mobility—is intensely ideological. Nevertheless, it would be a mistake to designate this confrontation as a simple contradiction between a prepackaged ideology and an exigent social reality, not only because "reality" is discursive on both sides (Juan's and Tom's) but also because Juan's own discourse is dramatically inconsistent with itself. Juan does not so much spout ideology as *attempt* to spout it; and his failure to get it right is as telling as Tom's assault. The ideal of individual autonomy that Juan celebrates as peculiarly English was derived from the eighteenth-century variant of civic humanist discourse called country ideology, to which we briefly referred in chapter 8. Country ideology affirmed that the guarantee of political autonomy was landed property, the material foundation for the *zoon politikon*—defined by J. G. A. Pocock as "the individual as an autonomous, morally and politically choosing being."[8] The loss of that land, whether through sale or through ruin, meant the loss of a cognitive ground for virtuous activity in the civic sphere—as demoralizing to the republican ethos as the loss of scriptural certitudes was to the Christian. The commercialization of land undermined its capacity to authorize social action. Here the seepage of concerns for cash and consumption into Juan's apostrophe graphically reflects the corruption of republican discourse that has already occurred in consequence of the loss of its cognitive basis. Juan's speech represents the post-Enlightenment degradation of country ideology into cant.

The mobilization of landed wealth in commerce meant the social elevation of those who, like the stockjobber and the capitalist, understood that what was valuable was that thing susceptible of being reproduced through exchange and, theoretically at least, reproduced without limit. But it remained a real puzzle how that theory—which in the hands of a Malthus led to the demonstration that the progressive reproduction of wealth conflicted with the higgledy-piggledy reproduction of desirous bodies—should be translated into a social practice. Lacking a "commercial ethos," commercial society, according to Pocock, developed a "morality without a material foundation in any way peculiarly its own. The trader was asked to be frugal in just the way the primeval cultivator (who had needed no asking) had been; he was asked to imitate the natural man in place of his artificial self; and he was asked to do this to limit the negative effects of his own activity. The virtue enjoined on him was not of his own making, and was only contingently peculiar to him."[9] The prescribed morality did not abandon the regulatory concept of a ground; from Charles Davenant (whom Pocock has in mind) to Edmund Burke and Lambro, the trader patched together a morality from the plunder of an outmoded ethos. Commercial morality, that is, "freely" took its "station" on the "ground" of a morality whose very ground had been undermined by commerce.

There was no ready redress of this corruption for those who hewed to the civic humanist line, since virtue, like honor, owed its urgency to its fragility. Pocock continues: Since the ethics of eighteenth-century country ideology "were reducible to an ideal of the wholly self-sustaining personality, [that ideology] found it terribly easy to see corruption as irreversible by merely human means; and since its economics tended to ground that personality on a form of property held to have existed in a precommercial past, it tended to see history as a movement away from value which only heroic, not social, action could reverse."[10] After the first fall from republican virtue there is no other. In their different ways *Marino Faliero* and *Sardanapalus* dramatize the impossibility of heroically reversing the change of change into exchange. Tom, the highwayman, is Byron's last hero. He takes the curtain call for heroic action, whether as outlawry or as satire.

The confrontation between Juan and Tom may be taken as an illustration of the aphorism forged in Ismail's fire: "Short speeches pass between two men who speak / No common language" (8:58)—with the proviso that Juan's incomprehension is only partially a function of nationality. Few of Byron's contemporaries (except connoisseurs of the "fancy") could have conversed with Tom, who speaks the cant of his outlaw trade. Tom, we may speculate, entered into his profession for the same reasons that John Edleston once took up his milder but equally fatal occupation: he did not inherit money or the social credit to obtain it. Tom compensates as Charles Skinner Matthews had done before him: by adopting a jargon that would intimately associate knowing fellows and ipso facto confer on them a prepossessing corporate identity. To an outsider the result seems outlandish. It is a familiar comic touch to link linguistic peculiarity with social deprivation, normatively registered as hierarchical or geographical distance from the royal court. *Juan* gives a new twist to the convention, however, by linking linguistic abstraction with criminal extraction. Tom's inability to converse is bound up with his endeavor to acquire by force what by the law of this economy can be gained only by exchange.[11]

The inconversable encounter between Tom and Juan has the features of what Jean-François Lyotard calls a "differend." "As distinguished from a litigation, a differend," Lyotard writes, "would be a case of conflict, between (at least) two parties, that cannot be equitably resolved for lack of a rule of judgment applicable to both arguments." He goes to argue that "a universal rule of judgment between heterogeneous genres is lacking in general."[12] As we have seen, the *Edinburgh's* review of *Hours of Idleness*, the wicked Lord Byron's dispute with Mr. Chaworth, and Lady Byron's intercourse with her husband were instances of such conflict. Marcet's *Conversations on Political Economy* and the *Edinburgh Review* were differently scaled contemporary attempts to establish a universal rule of judgment. De Quincey's later wish for a "symposiarch" who would arbitrate the hurlyburly of conversations evinces a similar, if zanier, ambition.[13] With no symposiarch on the scene, Tom and the boys cannot be sure of the right rule to guide them. Falling back, as we all do in a pinch, on a commonplace, they boldly "seized the lucky hour" (11:11). Good topos; wrong place, wrong time. It is the misfortune of the footpads to apply a "common place" to what, by chance, is a *proper* place. They seize the hour at Shooter's Hill just at the time it is occupied by a man who is armed with a pistol and trained to shoot it. Commonplaces arm invention; invention prompts action; but nought guarantees success. Because luck is always a question of odds, one can rarely land evenly on the hour. It is the lot of the archaic hero, adrift in the backwash of destiny, to be before or behind the hour and thus fatally out of his place. Juan is gifted with propriety. The privilege of metaphor (Shooter's Hill, pistol) is conferred on him: like metaphor, the pistol wonderfully closes distances. Tom, laboring with the metonymic knife and ruled by contingency, dies of his impropriety.

That fault is dramatized when at death's door Tom throws himself with vulgar élan into a role scripted by sentimental drama:

> The dying man cried, "Hold! I've got my gruel!
> Oh! for a glass of *max!* We've missed our booty—
>   Let me die where I am!" And as the fuel
> Of life shrunk in his heart, and thick and sooty
>   The drops fell from his death-wound, and he drew ill
> His breath,—he from his swelling throat untied
> A kerchief, crying, "Give Sal that!"—and died.
>
> The cravat stained with bloody drops fell down
>   Before Don Juan's feet: he could not tell
> Exactly why it was before him thrown,
> Nor what the meaning of the man's farewell.
>
> (11:16–17)

Unlike his phthisic better, Tom's orthodoxy is of the theater rather than the catechism; he stages his death in the manner of the melodrama of his day, writing *finis* with a familiar pathos of gesture and word. Tom's crude attitude unwittingly parodies the Chaworth-position in the famous duel at the Star and Garter on Marlborough Street, recasting the claims to moral superiority made by the dying Chaworth as a melodramatic appeal for sympathy that here falls on deaf (that is, Spanish) ears. Neither the gesture nor the command is understood by Juan, who fails to grasp the "meaning of the man's farewell." He is as unmoved as the fifth Lord Byron. And like the Wicked Lord, Juan is duly exonerated once he does his duty to the "circumstances of the case."

Vulgarly or not, the dying Tom does stake his world—and loses it. His farewell charge, "Give Sal that," is as unlucky as his first strike. The prescriptive phrase has no cognitive referent: *give, Sal, that*—all are equally opaque to his auditor. The injunction misfires; the prescription fails to obligate. It is as if Tom had uttered "Stop!—for thy tread is on an Empire's dust" in Greek. His last words are nothing more than another wasted wish of the intestate dying. In the aftermath Juan turns "meditative," and the narrator waxes mock-eulogistic:

> He from the world had cut off a great man,
>   Who in his time had made heroic bustle.
> Who in a row like Tom could lead the van,
>   Booze in the ken, or at the spellken hustle?
> Who queer a flat? Who (spite of Bow-street's ban)
>   On the high toby-spice so flash the muzzle?
> Who on a lark with black-eyed Sal (his blowing),
> So prime, so swell, no nutty, and so knowing?
>
> But Tom's no more—and so no more of Tom.
>   Heroes must die; and by God's blessing 't is
> Not long before the most of them go home.—
>   Hail! Thamis hail! Upon thy verge it is. . . .
>   (11:19–20)

Tom dies from something very like novelization. According to Bakhtin, "the epic and tragic hero is the hero who, by his very nature, must perish," to be succeeded by "heroes of free improvisation and not heroes of tradition, heroes of a life process that is imperishable and forever renewing itself, forever contemporary."[14] The formula fits *Don Juan* like its birthright, which is, in Bakhtin's terms, its novelistic right to be forever aborning. The novel deals its lots as ruthlessly as evolution. Tom is a hero; Tom must die.

Simple forms must give way to complex. Tom and the epic mode in which he mistakenly sees himself combine to become the composite hero of this killing parody. But in Tom's case the "hero of the parody" is in fact only the parody of a hero. That is, Tom is *made* a hero so that Tom can die.

By leading Tom to the sacrifice, the narrator renders Tom's death as exemplary as Sardanapalus's (even though Sal, unlike Myrrha, does not "come"). And equally suspicious. The narrator cleverly accomplishes what Tom does not. His extraction of Tom's characteristic speech (his only property) succeeds, whereas Tom's attempted seizure had failed. *Juan*'s set-piece citation of Tom's language replicates the reviewers' excerption of Byron's published works. As the reviews novelized the Oriental tales, bringing low the Byronic hero by forcing him into polyglossic contact with partisan politics and the banalities of commerce, so *Juan* novelizes its "hero," extracting his language for display and as the pretext for the narrator's preening improvisation. But there is a crucial difference between the two expropriations. The reviewers *pay* Lord Byron, whether in the coin of the realm or in that of futurity. *Juan* would seem to pay no one. *Juan* is written in what is doubtless a speaking style, but, contrary to received opinion, it is not conversational. The condescending narrator of *Juan* is as inconversable as Tom, his hero. He is that outlaw who does not pay off his debts; and by his evasion he acts out at the level of the narrative drive of the poem the economy of innovative desire that characterizes the folk hero Don Juan: the refusal to enter into exchange.

Bakhtin celebrates the novel for its "authentic folkloric roots."[15] Tom is an example of the folk already uprooted, of those urban dispossessed who will later be named the proletariat. Novelization does not combat the uprooting of the folkloric but abets it. However one judges this expropriation, Lord Byron must feel it in a singular way, for in turning against the past in favor of contemporaneity *Juan* turns against Lord Byron himself, who as poet (fighting off the challenge of Scott's historically momentous historical novels) and as aristocrat (claiming notability on no cognitive grounds) has common cause with other endangered species of Englishman. Byron's linkage with the folk, first forged in his maiden speech in the House of Lords, designates a mutual degradation by a contemporaneity that leaves them equally unfit to face the future grasped by the novel and by political economy.

The link is stronger yet, for if Tom is a hero, he is a hero of satire. Tom's *damn* should be contrasted with the speech act that the narrator identifies with the authenticity of "present life": the "Interjection, / An 'Oh!' or 'Ah!' of joy or misery," which is the "grand Antithesis to great Ennui, / Wherewith we break our bubbles on the ocean" (15:1, 2). By that standard Juan's apostrophe, not Tom's curse, is an interjection. Juan's spontaneous overflow of prescribed feeling breaks like a bubble on the ocean (called scum) of London's "Ennui" (called misery by those who have not reached Juan's station); Tom's *damn* exposes it as just another overextended speculation; the point of his knife bursts it. For this latter act of forcible correction Tom pays with his life. His fate admonishes the satirist, who likewise attacks the canting English reader in order to extract his or her money. Although *damn* is one thing and a knife another, the distinction is difficult to preserve even for native speakers of English, such as the editor of the *British Review* who, as we have seen, misprized satiric speech as the leading edge of character assassination. *Juan*'s most thoroughgoing reflection on its art indirectly meditates the lesson of Tom:

> If I sneer sometimes,
>   It is because I cannot well do less,
>   And now and then it also suits my rhymes.
>   I should be very willing to redress
>   Men's wrongs, and rather check than punish crimes,
>   Had not Cervantes, in that too true tale
>   Of Quixote, shown how all such efforts fail.
>
> Of all tales 't is the saddest—and more sad,
>   Because it makes us smile: his hero's right,
> And still pursues the right;—to curb the bad
>   His only object, and 'gainst odds to fight,
> His guerdon: 't is his virtue makes him mad!
>   But his adventures form a sorry sight;—
> A sorrier still is the great moral taught
> By that real Epic unto all who have thought.
>
> Redressing injury, revenging wrong,
>   To aid the damsel and destroy the caitiff;
> Opposing singly the united strong,
>   From foreign yoke to free the helpless native:—
> Alas! Must noblest views, like an old song,
>   Be for mere Fancy's sport a theme creative?
> A jest, a riddle, Fame through thin and thick sought?
> And Socrates himself but Wisdom's Quixote?
>
> Cervantes smiled Spain's Chivalry away;
>   A single laugh demolished the right arm

Of his own country;—seldom since that day
  Has Spain had heroes. While Romance could charm,
The World gave ground before her bright array;
And therefore have his volumes done such harm,
That all their glory, as a composition,
Was dearly purchased by his land's perdition.

(13:8–11)

Satire's one strength is to kill that culture by which strength is nourished. The hero of satire pays for his access of power with his death. Of course, Cervantes's historical moment is not *Juan*'s, which represents a degraded version of that great disenchantment. Cervantes acquired his glory at the price of his land's perdition. *Juan* faces no such temptation. The English Cantos are the perfect *un*ending for a poem whose textual drift demands that any ending be contingent because the Don Juan myth is *already* completed; arriving in England, as the poet notifies us, Juan has been bodily transported to hell (or in its relativized variant, "Hells" [11:29]).[16]

For eighteenth-century ideologists of civic humanism, according to Pocock, "the subversion of real by mobile property had entered a phase in which reality was seen as endangered by fiction and fantasy."[17] After the first flush of enlightenment the patriot anxiously realizes that the demolition of chivalric fancies in the name of "realism" is in truth the instauration of a greater fiction. But the English Cantos have passed beyond that phase in the rise of the novel and commercial society. The English hell is safe from such subversion. In the orthodox hell, Milton's hell, the damned decorously observed the genre of forensic discourse: devils debated and a winner was declared according to rule. Contemporary England (and *Juan* stretches the contemporary from the 1790s until tomorrow) is all the more hellish in that it presents a Boschian "confusion of the sorts and sexes" (11:3). Familiarized, hell may look like a "game" (12:58), but it is a peculiar one in which the rules not only regulate but constitute its players. The game of *Juan*'s hell (anticipating Lewis Carroll's Wonderland) obeys the primary process operations of the dream, of the language that speaks its speaker according to the logic of condensation and displacement.

William Hazlitt's description of the dream process exactly fits *Juan*'s England: "Any idea that presents itself in this anarchy of the mind is lord of the ascendant for the moment, and is driven out by the next straggling notion that comes across it. The bundles of thought are, as it were, untied, loosened from a common centre, and drift along the stream of fancy as it happens."[18] Juan is just such a fashionable idea for Georgian society. But so is everyone else. Now that the aristocracy has traded its birthright and alienated the ground that moralized its authority, aristocratic status can be redescribed as "quantity . . . but condensed to quality" (13:49)—a mechanical effect of the same prevailing weather that inflated the South Sea Bubble and that condensed England out of the "Sinking Fund's unfathomable sea" (16:99). Even Adeline, whom the narrator rouses himself to individualize with the figure of concentrated nectar in the "very centre" of a bottle of champagne "Frozen into a very vinous ice" (13:37–38), is made rare by virtue of a mechanical condensation that has the half-life of a dream on a summer's eve.

To be an individual in the English hell is to be a half looking to be doubled into a whole: "All matchless creatures, . . . yet bent on matches" (12:53). "Poets of arithmetic" (16:99) run the Exchequer, and dynasts calculating with actuarial precision match maiden with bachelor, seller with purchaser. Both aim to avoid unreproductive oddness. "Here" no one stands alone or stands anywhere for long. An individual is an uncompleted contract in an open market. Each person is a character that can be entered into a ledger or actuarial table. Each character, whether the personification of a Malthusian statistic or the embodiment of a family fortune ("turning marriage into arithmetic" [15:38]), briefly occupies his or her place only to be displaced. Each name is credentialed by his or her profession of a language game, a fantastic but temporarily habitable description of a reality, accredited by "proper placemen" whose proper placement is itself, however, merely nominal, the momentary articulation of an indefinite circulation of characters in a constant displacement. "It is the place and power we bow to, and not the man," writes Hazlitt[19]—a dictum that applies to *all* characters, from the "Countesses of Blank" (13:80) to Lord Henry. The public feast of the Amundevilles, where once upon a time the reconciliation of classes was symbolically achieved by the lord's bounteous expenditure, has been transformed into a commodity exchange, the Gothic temple become a marketplace for the purchase of votes.[20] The heir of the Norman Amundevilles prospers because he has "exactly the just medium hit / 'Twixt place and patriotism" (16:72).

As Pocock tells the story, "Once land and commerce were placed in historical sequence, civic man found himself existing in a historical contradiction."[21] And so the hero became extinct. New, hardier species have arisen in a brave new world:

> 'T is strange,—but true; for Truth is always strange—
>   Stranger than Fiction: if it could be told,

How much would novels gain by the exchange!
　　How differently the world would men behold!
How oft would vice and virtue places change!
　　The new world would be nothing to the old,
If some Columbus of the normal seas
Would show mankind their souls' Antipodes.
　　　　　　　　　　　　　　　(14:101)

Thus *Juan* foretells the project it fulfills. The English hell is not exactly a universal egotism; it is the general *belief* that the world is a universal egotism. England is not so much a world in which private vice is public virtue but one in which private and public have become as interchangeable as virtue and vice. Because that belief is extraordinarily resilient, Columbus's revelations do not much matter; oceanic bubbles and sulphuric bubbles have it in common that "as the old burst, new emerge" (15:99).

Juan's ambivalence about Cervantes registers what is at stake in Tom's fate. Although Tom is called a hero, he is rudely denied the hero's guerdon, that "beautiful death" by which, according to Lyotard, "one escapes death by the only means known—the perpetuation of the proper name."[22] Lord Byron imagined that fate for himself as early as the "Fragment" of *Hours of Idleness*. But although the propagation of the name *Byron* and all that to which it was attached (whether by author or reviewer, publisher or pirate) was the condition for the poet's success, it also exposed the breaking bubble of the name to the vicissitudes of fashion. Under the dispensation of the market *Byron* has no ontology different from that of *Tom*. Tom's run, no doubt, is shorter. Tom lives on in the memory of no one who inhabits the world where he makes his brief appearance. Nor is Tom's death truly sacrificial. His blood neither restores nor advances. Nothing does in *Don Juan*, where each "new one" follows another for no good reason.[23] Among the various misfortunes in the poem, Tom's case is perhaps the most terrible, however, for his end would seem to befall him solely to suit the poet's rhymes. If it is one far-flung consequence of Cervantes's smile that "manners now make men" (15:26), *Juan* countenances the appalling corollary that "men," nothing more than characters under this disenchanted regime, can be erased for the sake of a manner that has the force of law.

That Tom can die to suit the poet's rhyme is the condition of possibility for the condition that Lyotard calls Auschwitz. The Nazi says, "My law kills them who have no relevance to it." The Jew says, "My death is due to their law, to which I owe nothing." The Nazi speaks of the non-Aryan as if he were an aristocrat referring to a "smudge" (or, in *Juan*, to "scum"). For Lyotard's aristocrat "goodwill is hereditary and is proven by one's genealogical tree. Aristocracy (blood and soil, soldier and 'laborer') recognizes no addressee other than itself for the legitimating phrase."[24] The poet's nonchalant appeal to "my rhymes" lays claim to a self-legitimating style that supersedes bourgeois egotism and the transient fashion of the "Great World." Within the world of the poet that style rules with the annihilatory finality of the gas chambers: for Tom, for Pedrillo, for Haidee—for every character, each and all, on whom the poet's rhyme doth fall.[25] Such is Dark Romanticism. The possibility must be confronted that the Romantic recovery of strength entails the capacity to deal death casually yet with unwavering conviction, blithe fascism.

If, then, we devote so much time to Tom, it is because so much is at stake. If anything matters in *Juan*, Tom's death does. And it is because *Juan* not only can bear but demands such inquiry that the poem (which, recall, accords an ethical disposition to a mere "drop of ink") merits our attention. Cervantes launched a project of deadly enlightenment. *Juan* has no project. It has only an ethic: to "speak out" (11:88). The significance of that distinction emerges against the background of the poem's confrontation with the glamour of fascism in cantos 7 and 8. *Juan*'s ethical address becomes audible in the aftermath of the din stirred by the succinct declaration delivered to Suwarrow, commander of the Russian troops before Ismail,

> which said, all in a trice,
> "You will take Ismail at whatever price."
>
> "Let there be light! said god, and there was light!"
> "Let there be blood!" says man, and there's a sea!
>
> (7:40–41)

The sublime word of the prince communicates to the shining Suwarrow its uncreating power, harnessing Longinus to the task of disciplining armies and constructing the apparatus of death.

The siege of Ismail perfects the Orientalist vision of the Westerner as one who comes into his own—who becomes the guarantor of a new world order—as an imaginary relation between an Occidental self and an Oriental other. The episode unsettlingly concludes Byron's long romance with Orientalism by depicting the Turkish foe as a mere resistance that must be annihilated by the Westerner's sublime technology:

> There was enthusiasm and much applause,
> The fleet and camp saluted with great grace,
>   And all presaged good fortune to their cause.
> Within a cannon-shot length of the place
>   They drew, constructed ladders, repair'd flaws

In former works made new, prepared fascines,
And all kinds of benevolent machines.

'T is thus the spirit of a single mind
  Makes that of multitudes take one direction,
As roll the waters to the breathing wind.

(7:47–48)

As the preparation of "fascines" at the merest murmur of the commanding genius' awful soul represents the summit of enlightenment, so is the wastage of the sons of Islam its primordial and ever-returning aim.

No doubt these cantos effect a thematic break with Orientalism. The superiority of the Westerner is exposed as merely technical, not moral: with victory the "crimson cross glared o'er the field, / But red with no *redeeming gore*" (8:122). During the battle the Turks are humanized: faced with imminent death, they display amazing bravery and fidelity. But what makes these cantos unsettling is that attaining a liberalized perspective provides no vision of a kinder, gentler world. Cursed with Western eyes, the poet cannot imagine a world that would put Orientalism behind it. In the deficit of that vision, the Ismail episode veers wildly between the sentimentality of Juan's encounter with the blood-streaked Leila (8:95–96), which revises the Corsair's precedent confrontation with Gulnare in Seyd's prison, and the nihilistic portrayal of the "widows of forty" as wondering "Wherefore the ravishing did not begin!" (8:132), which is a darkly comic reprise of the bullfight scene in *Childe Harold I*.

To show that Western superiority is technical, not moral, entails no moral position. The sentimental attribution of power to the West and virtue to the East does not dissolve Orientalism but historicizes it as a necessary, if disagreeable, stage in the dialectic of enlightenment. Indeed, *Juan*'s moral skepticism exposes the poem to its great temptation, the lure of the Russian general Suwarrow, whose genial spirit mobilizes the attackers, as "waters" taking their direction from the "breathing wind." Suwarrow is as close as *Juan* gets to Napoleon, the greatest infirmity of Byron's noble mind. He is described as a "thing to wonder at beyond most wondering; / Hero, buffoon, half-demon, and half-dirt, . . . Harlequin in uniform" (7:55). Suwarrow is the very monster of modernity. His character hybridizes Joseph Conrad's Kurtz and his crazy Russian servitor. As a "great conqueror [who] play'd the corporal," he is a prototype for the corporal who would play the conqueror, say, as parodied in Charlie Chaplin's *Great Dictator*. Suwarrow is a Sardanapalus in shirt-sleeves, a despot of practical reason. He sways, but deliberately; he condescends to his inferiors, but in order to teach the use of the bayonet, not to revel. Unlike the eroticized Sardanapalus, Suwarrow's very equivocalness is a technical means to a strategic end: when "he dress'd up" it was to clothe "fascines / Like men with turbans, scimitars, and dirks" so that his men could "charge with bayonet these machines, / By way of lesson against actual Turks" (7:53). It would be a fatal mistake to see this use of the fascine to bind men into a killing machine as implying that Suwarrow is subject to some unspeakable fascination. He trains his men with fascines to foreclose the power of any Gorgon to stop their arms. Like the Russian army he commands, Suwarrow has no sex. Suwarrow is coincident with his power. His every word is a command. Anyone to whom he directs his attention is merely a means to getting the thing done.

The characterization of Suwarrow as "Hero, buffoon, half-demon, and half-dirt" echoes the way Byron himself had repeatedly been described in the reviews; and it anticipates the antithetical formation that criticism, more naive than the poem it engages, has thought *Juan* to embody: the mating of the egotistical sublime to Romantic irony. As the synthesis of Coleridge's commanding genius and Schlegel's transcendental buffoon, Suwarrow surpasses the Napoleon of *Childe Harold III* as much as Byron could be said to surpass Wordsworth. This new description of man can deliver the divine fiat but also attend to microdisciplinary bricolage. No amount of buffoonery can diminish the commander's glory, because in the world that Suwarrow is bent on engineering only results count. Results, not product, for Suwarrow is the apotheosis of unproductive labor. He embodies a politics that ruthlessly overrides the calculations of the market and shames the hypocrisies of commercial society. I contend that this vision would be the savage truth of *Juan* (the savage truth of this world in which I now read and write) if its rhyme were indeed capable of killing off Tom with the comic finality it pretends. Such an act would manifest the functional solipsism that the idiom of sublime sovereignty presupposes: a speaking that tolerates no auditor who is not part of the machinery working toward the system's greater glory, an addressor who can dispense with any addressee on the self-legitimating grounds that it is unfit or that it has exhausted its usefulness.

The idiom of sublime sovereignty is part and parcel of the idiom of the spectacle by which domination is exercised both abroad, where the allies attempt to overwhelm the Ottomans with a display of firepower, and at home:

> "Great joy to London now!" says some great fool,
>   When London had a grand illumination,

Which to that bottle-conjuror, John Bull,
   Is of all dreams the first hallucination;
So that the streets of colour'd lamps are full,
   That Sage (*said* John) surrenders at discretion
His purse, his soul, his sense, and even his nonsense,
To gratify, like a huge moth, this *one* sense.

(7:44)

The analysis of the society of the spectacle has been sharpened and broad-ened since first broached in *Childe Harold I*. Indeed, it has been sharpened so keenly that the poet leaves no doubt that his verse makes no break with that spectacular system. The Romantic irony that is so conspicuous a rhetorical feature of the Ismail cantos signals the poet's complicity. Canto 7 begins with the admission that

               my present tale is,
   A non-descript and ever-varying rhyme,
A versified Aurora Borealis,
   Which flashes o'er a waste and icy clime.
When we know what all are, we must bewail us,
   But ne'ertheless I hope it is no crime
To laugh at *all* things—for I wish to know
What, after *all*, are *all* things—but a *show?*

(7:2)

How nicely is the Wordsworthian rainbow, mocked as pledge or covenant in canto 2, metamorphosed into the beautifully metamorphic meteor of the aurora borealis! How ingeniously does the rhetorical question allow the poet to assume a posture of spectator/impresario before the transitory show of things and claim the same kind of strategic distance that is the ultimate preserve of Suwarrow! To laugh is no crime, but it is no critique either. Because the poet's denigration of the world as show cannot be extricated from his appeasement of his mothlike reader's hunger for a "vo-luptuous blaze" (8:115), this justification of his "polar melody" may stir but does not move:

   For I will teach, if possible, the stones
To rise against earth's tyrants. Never let it
   Be said that we still truckle unto thrones;—
But ye—our children's children! think how we
Show'd *what things were* before the world was free!

(8:135)

Byron's show does not obligate anyone to think. It absolves anyone who might continue to live in a world unfree and for whom unfreedom is exactly the privilege to occupy a station where he or she can watch the spectacular aurora borealis of bombs bursting in the chill desert night, to be entertained by a war almost bloodless (if we except only the red spread from the veins of the countless Oriental dead).

There is in cantos 7 and 8 of *Don Juan* nothing that passeth show. Yet the question "*What*, after *all*, are *all* things—but a *show?*" will be answered in the verse that follows from the invocation of Berkeley. The English Cantos are that region of the poem in which no question is merely rhetorical because all questions call for an answer, where rhetoric always touches on the ethical. *Juan*'s rhyme, we know, cannot be reduced to the chilly meteor of the aurora borealis—its preference for the beautiful Aurora will later be both indulged and placed. But that comes later. More important is the evidence that *Juan*'s rhyme is not an instrument for engineering the indiscriminate death of men imagined as characters or of characters imagined as men.

Even as Tom dies the rule of *Juan*'s rhyme responds to Tom's speaking— the poem listens to itself as to an other. If a sneer happens to suit Juan's rhyme, it is not deadly, no more than the "awful footsteps" of the ghost "regular as rhyme" (16:113) are the real steps of a real ghost heralding some real doom. Rhyme happens not for strategic reasons but because something must happen, now and then. In Lyotard's words, "Linkage must happen 'now'; another phrase cannot not happen. It's a necessity; time, that is. There is no non-phrase."[26] Juan's off-rhyme sounds the necessity for that time to fail to be quite *on* time: it deviates, slants, limps. Rhyme does not in truth terminate Tom, whose solution is no more final than Shylock's.

> But Tom's no more—and so no more of Tom.
> Heroes must die; and by God's blessing 't is
> Not long before the most of them go home.—
> Hail! Thamis, hail!

"Tom" may go "home" to suit *Juan*'s off-rhyme, but in almost no time *Juan*'s rhyme revives him, in a manner of speaking. Tom is not redeemed by gore. He does not receive his "resurrection" either by the sublime summons of some beneficent God or on the occasion of a "new meeting or election" (11:9). Finding his home, Tom returns with a new familiarity, internalized, punned into a kind of life, as Thamis, the ghost of what he once was. Tom's one talent is not lodged useless with rocks, and stones, and trees; he is sited as one who overflows his cite. Call this return, which answers to no fiat, the performance of the literal sublime: Tom returns as the spirit of the place, the spirit, to be precise, of the "common place": not one that flows through all things but the inveterate wording that overflows that private and proper place, the infernal island of the grave. "Tom" today, "Thamis" tomorrow, "multifarious 'damme's' " (11:24) in the future.[27] The "shibboleth," sprung from the mouths of the English to entrap the wisest foreign tongue, flows— inexorably—into an ocean of speech, where it passes beyond all citation. Before rhyme is rule it is English; and what inspirits English is the "very soul of swearing," the harsh music and "Attic" force of the commonplace. It is the glory of English that good English—common to Spenser, Byron, and Tom—can never be pure. "Hail Thamis" is *Juan*'s answer to the rough greeting lost on Juan. It is the narrator's reply to a more than Roman commander who has crossed into the language.

In *The Differend* Lyotard puts to himself the question that we have been putting to *Juan* regarding its intralocution:

> Would you say that interlocutors are victims of the science and politics of language understood as communication to the same extent that the worker is transformed into a victim through the assimilation of his or her labor- power to a commodity? Must it be imagined that there exists a "phrase- power," analogous to labor-power, and which cannot find a way to express itself in the idiom of this science and this politics?—Whatever this power might be, the parallel must be broken right away. It can be conceived that work is something other than the exchange of a commodity, and an idiom other than that of the labor arbitrator must be found in order to express it. . . . This is where the parallel ends: in the case of language, recourse is made to another family of phrases; but in the case of work, recourse is not made to another family of work, recourse is still made to another family of phrases. The same goes for every differend buried in litigation, no matter what the subject matter. To give the differend its due is to institute new addressees, new addressors, new significations, and new referents in order for the wrong to find an expression and for the plaintiff to cease being a victim. . . . A new competence (or "prudence") must be found.[28]

Proving that there is honor among thieves, *Juan* gives Tom his due. "Hail Thamis" aborts the parallel between the social explanation of "Toms" and the poetic citation of *Tom*. As we shall unfold, Tom speaks out *within* the poem; he does not labor *for* the poem. In the reverberation of "damme's," Tom speaks out against a political economy that recognizes no idiom in which he can formally make his complaint. The underworld has no genre of discourse in which to make its grievance, because the manorless poor have only a statistical reality with no standing before the law. Tom can either silently submit to his Malthusian lot—a Pedrillo of the streets, a Sardanapalus of the lower depths—or reject his victimage and erupt in inarticulate but imperative speech.

Each case is different. Juan, one of those "whom favour or whom fortune swells" (11:31), gets what he needs before he wants it, and almost always without talking.[29] The narrator, on the other hand, claims to "speak out." And when he does he speaks as a plaintiff. This "plaintiffness" is attuned to the note of human sadness brought into the English Cantos by the thought of change and the prospect of death. In Byron's narratives the posture of complaint is gendered as female. Recall Medora's song and Donna Julia's letter. Although they fail, the complaints of Medora and Donna Julia are at least "sensible," in all the period richness of the word: it makes sense to address a pirate or a lover, not only because pirate and lover have ears to hear and hearts to feel, but because there are genres of discourse in which to utter love's woe. In *Juan* the angelic Aurora Raby is introduced as one who, speechless, "look'd as if she sat by Eden's door, / And grieved for those who could return no more" (15:45). The auroran angel's speechless grief for sin's exiles would seem to oppugn the narrator's griefless speech for time's casualties. To whom should one complain? To God? Bootless to complain to one who, as Cain learned, has the absolute right to decree the death of all his creatures. To Death? How to complain to a creditor to whom we owe everything?

The Spectral Plaintiff

> *Now for a common-place!*
> Lord Byron, Don Juan *(canto 13)*

At one time Lord Byron had been hellbent on severing every connection with the land of his birth. In 1821 he wrote to John Murray of his morbid satisfaction with his immurement in Italy, exile's chosen station:

> If any thing occurs so violently gross or personal as to require notice, Mr. D[ouglas] Kinnaird will let me *know*—but of *praise* I desire to hear *nothing*— You will say—to what tends all this?—I will answer THAT—to keep my mind *free and* unbiased—by all paltry and personal irritabilities of praise or censure;—To let my Genius take it's natural direction,—while my feelings are like the dead—who know nothing and feel nothing of all or aught that is said or done in their regard. (*BLJ* 8:220–21)

Perhaps Catholicized by Italy, perhaps altered by his purgatorial isolation from England, by the time of canto 11 the poet has a different feeling for the dead, as if he were a participant in a community of the estranged:

> "Where is the world?" cries Young, "at *eighty?* Where
>   The world in which a man was born?" Alas!
> Where is the world of *eight* years past? 'T *was there*—
>   I look for it—'t is gone, a Globe of Glass!
> Cracked, shivered, vanished, scarcely gazed on, ere
>   A silent change dissolves the glittering mass.
> Statesmen, chiefs, orators, queens, patriots, kings,
> And dandies, all are gone on the wind's wings.
>
> Where is Napoleon the Grand? God knows:
>   Where little Castlereagh? The devil can tell:
> Where Grattan, Curran, Sheridan, all those
>   Who bound the bar or senate in their spell?
>   (11:76–77)

Even Castlereagh's tyranny now seems a somewhat quaint remnant of a more vigorous age. In the world's fade "England" has become effectively postpolitical, that is, political-economic. The solvent "Silent change" is the silence of the 'Change: "Cash rules the grove, and fells it too besides" (12:14); cash dissolves social blockages and ostensibly bridges social divisions by turning confrontations, addresses, encounters, pleas, demands, ripostes, declarations, and manifestoes each into a "transaction" (12:11). What feeling there is for the unlamented Castlereagh is the sympathy one plaintiff feels for another.

Narrator and minister share the predicament of being "past it." There is no idiom for litigating with death, whose defense goes without saying. Nor is there an idiom for the differend of past and present: all that belongs to the past that has not been successfully translated into the present suffers extinction. So Benjamin Constant, in defense of liberalism, imagines the fate of Napoleon; so Cervantes, in defense of reality, imagines chivalry; so William Godwin's Falkland, in defense of propriety, imagines Caleb; so the novel, in defense of contemporaneity, imagines epic and romance; and so political economy, in defense of the free market, imagines both the folk and the aristocrat. As everyone knows, none can appeal the verdict of history. After the flood of money has dissolved and dissipated the "goodliest soil of Body and of Mind" (13:2), the man of virtue has no more standing at the bar of reason than the madman—as men of "Intense intentions" (14:88), both are equally dangerous to know. Surveying the dissolution of all that had sustained the moral autonomy of the civic man, Pocock advances the paradox that was to test the invention of Montesquieu and, later, Byron: to be virtuous, landlost men had somehow "to be better than their circumstances."[30] Rather like being virtuous in hell.

Don Juan presents cases in which, unpredictably, such virtue happens. There is the example of Juan refusing to eat his preceptor. And there is Juan again, committing that "one good action in the midst of crimes" (8:90) when he rescues Leila. A less agreeable instance is the praise of the miser in canto 12. For post-Humean liberalism the miser is that emblematic man who subverts the subversion of the distinction between fantasy and reality by fetishizing the tokens of commerce and blocking exchange.[31] In one sense the question "Why call we misers miserable?" answers itself, like "Why call we John Johnson?" But *Juan* has learned from *Marino* that the predominance of the paternal root may be specious. *Juan* vindicates the suffix by showing that the miser is "able" for pleasure with a constant intensity unknown to the lover, reveler, or warrior. He possesses the stuff of others' dreams:

> His very cellars might be king's abodes;
> While he, despising every sensual call,
> Commands—the intellectual lord of all.
>
> (12:9)

The miser has the capacity to command what he wants past all wanting. In the discourse of political economy, the miser corresponds point for point with the figure of the Oriental despot: an object of desire and fantastic identification for the middle-class reader. And why not? Once virtue has lost its substantive foundation, any image is liable to be fetishized as the foundation of virtue: one simulacrum is as good as another. The miser is the commercialized deformation of the virtuous man.

As an example of the peculiar competence that the miser enjoys, consider this outburst of indignation that Lord Byron visited on Murray in 1819:

> I know the precise worth of popular applause—for few Scribblers have had more of it—and if I chose to swerve into their paths—I could retain it or resume it—or increase it—but I neither love ye—nor fear ye—and though I buy with ye—and sell with ye—and talk with ye—I will neither eat with ye—drink with ye—nor pray with ye. They made me without my search a species of popular Idol—they—without reason or judgement beyond the caprice of their Good pleasure—threw down the Image from its pedestal—

It was not broken with the fall—and they would it seems again replace it—
but they shall not. (*BLJ* 6:106)

With *Don Juan* under way Lord Byron stands apposed to Byronic speculation, its routine oscillation between idolatry and iconoclasm. This is a
different character with a different diction from the one under contract to
Murray: not a Murray/Byron but, as the series of phrases taken from *The
Merchant of Venice* apprise us, a Byron/Shylock, one who is neither icon nor
iconoclast.[32] As a youthful lord poaching on his prospects, Byron lived off
the parasitism of the London usurers. As a lapsed hero, Lord Byron returns
to that parasitism, or rather refines it into a mutual empowerment of himself and the usurious other. Lord Byron does not identify himself with the
figure of Shylock (he did not dress as Shylock dressed, nor did he hang
the Jew's portrait over his desk as a prod to poetic inspiration); he seizes the
Jew's language (there are no quotation marks setting this off as a citation) in
order to conjure a new phrase. That phrase has no precedent in traditional
moral discourse (or in Shakespeare criticism); it has no civil standing. By
aligning himself with the words of Shylock, landless Jew and friendless
miser, Lord Byron tactically invents an ethical stance out of a cultural
commonplace and enacts the refusal to speculate that is the Israelite's fixed
rebuff to the Gentile's trade in images.

By this abstraction—which is contrasted not with the concrete but with
the simulacrum that in the dream world of commercial culture has taken the
place of the concrete—the poet grounds himself textually, in an impossible,
anachronistic, *psychotic* space, where the scapegoat survives all persecution
to demand obstreperously a debt still owed him. His voice shames the cant
of the enlightened but idolatrous Gentile, Antonio/Murray, who has made
what Serres identified as the Cartesian gamble: a fraudulent risk because
secured by the full force of the state, the theater of the law, and authorial
providence. Byron/Shylock's voice stalls death. Death may be that "dunnest
of duns," the closing grayness in a world where, increasingly, all things tend
to "that very ancient grey, / The sober sad antithesis to glowing" (14:28);
but one way to put off that dun is to insist past all reason (by becoming a
character in a text) that you are the abused creditor who must be satisfied
before death can be paid off. Although satisfaction may be illusory for the
consumer of turbot, the connoisseur of Titians, and the purchaser of votes,
it is as practical a concept for Byron/Shylock as it is for the duelist. Satisfaction simply means demanding that others honor their debts to the letter—
an impossibility for the credit economy, which is nothing more than the
continued refiguration of its debt. Byron/Shylock powerfully insists on an

obligation that only its compounded strength can legitimate, and in doing so expressly confirms the perdurability of the position of the anachronism as a place where the excluded and extinct can make common cause, eternally renewing their claims in effective apposition to the verdicts rendered by history and achieving thereby a plaintiff immortality.

In the context of hell Tom's robbery looks like the desperate recourse of a man attempting to be better than his circumstances. As for the civic man who, fighting off corruption, has no idiom in which to appeal to the stock-jobber, so for "scum" fighting off misery. Tom is not ethical when brandishing his knife, which is force acting as persuasion, but he indubitably is when he speaks out, "Damn your eyes! your money or your life," which is forceful persuasion. The difference, always ambiguous, between persuasion and force is significant enough to cost Tom his life. In *Juan* and for Juan the difference is a matter of timing. An act of persuasion, even the bluntest injunction—"Stop!"—is not merely a trope (and therefore translatable into another vocabulary) but a phrase with a distinct universe of reference; and because it is *phrased* the injunction allows its addressee time to consider the matter as a cause, to weigh how the matter bears on him. What makes orthodoxy orthodox is the immediacy with which, upon the provocation of a shock, dogma snaps back into place—obviating the necessity of a decision. The difference between one knife and a host of knives is of the order of a difference between one odd shock and a systematic series of shocks aimed at overriding what Adorno called the "jolt" of decision (see chap. 2 above). The addressee of an ethical phrase decides whether the phrase is common to him and to the addressor and whether the commonplace fits (always more or less) the occasion.

In *Juan* and for Juan, the difference between persuasion and force is not that the knife is steel and the *damn* is not, but that the knife has a point and the phrase does not. That point, like the shock of illness or the empiricist's sacred fact, is unmistakable; it leaves no time for conjecture. The use of the knife misses the point of the rhetorical occasion, which is to *carry* the point, not stab with it. Once the knife is thrust, the orthodox laws of physics come into play as force is met with force. Point overpoweringly counterpointed, neither highwayman nor satirist can justly complain of his fate. *Juan*'s equivalent to *Childe Harold*'s wish for "one word" of lightning is the Archimedean dream of the "point *d'appui*" or "jot of sense" that would allow one to "prove beyond a single doubt"—a dream of rhetoric as physics that *Juan* avows then abandons as an immaterial abstraction (14:84).[33] As Quintilian instructed, for rhetoric to matter it must be a more or less messy "combination of persons, circumstances of place and time, motives, means, incidents, acts, instruments, speeches, the letter and the spirit of the law."[34] "Or (to the point with Horace and with Pulci) / '*Omne tulit punctum*, quae *miscuit utile dulci*'" (13:81). To be better than his circumstances ("the court, camp, church, the vessel, and the mart" [2:194]) the good rhetorician must construct his own basis, institute new phrases, "build up common things with common places" (14:7).

The *Quixote* "demolished" the world of chivalry and proved the social world to be grounded only in belief. *Juan* takes seriously the possibility of a revolutionary text that would "shatter," "shock," or "demolish" the world according to political economy, which has displaced the traditional discourses of religion and politics by its powerful assertion of an authority to determine what matters. We have seen that hegemony exercised in the judicial verdict on the supposed seditiousness of the first two cantos of *Don Juan*, which dispelled the confusion of sexual sorts and religious kinds by touching the unfailing stone of property right. To its credit *Juan* never professes itself to be the revolutionary text of its dreams. Of course, this swerve away from its proper (that is, *Byronic*) destiny has its prudent side. The reflex to the shock of demolition imperils the noble satirist as surely as the vulgar highwayman. Beyond calculations of prudence, however, the strategy of posing "bare blade and a brazen front" (11:15) would serve only the interest of contradiction. Because Byronic contradiction assails political economy in the name of an identity just as imaginary as the one it opposes, a revolution on such terms would be futile. There is, after all, nought to attack. Property is not a castle, an abbey, or even a windmill. The simulacra in which political economy deals are not substances. Political economy will readily relinquish any position for a new one, in the confidence both that nothing will have changed and that the propertied will have profited from the exchange. The strength of commercial society has always been its ability to capitalize on its substantive weakness. Political economy is the first hegemonic system that knows it is grounded in nothing but belief and has faith that though particular beliefs can be shattered, belief itself— *credit*—remains as the ever-reconstitutable cement binding the commercial ego.

Only rhetoric can challenge political economy's aspiration to be that supreme "discursive art" for which, as Quintilian says, "all is grist for its mill."[35] Political economy, advocate of what Hazlitt calls "'the grinding law of necessity' suspended *in terrorem* over the poor,"[36] assesses all things in terms of their exchange value; anything is a good that can be exchanged. Rhetoric does not challenge political economy at the level of theory; it contests its claim that there is a level of generality capable of comprehending every particular. Rhetoric challenges political economy on a case-by-case basis. The good rhetorician interrupts the smooth exchange between the general and the particular by forming new matters out of unseen and unheard-of collections of circumstances. For political economy the particular pin factory serves merely as an illustration of a more general law. Since every particular is a flawed instance of the general, conflict is inevitable. But because the hierarchy of general and particular, norm and example, population and person, economy and transaction, prevails, conflict can be rendered not only as provisional but as propaedeutic. Political economy has the confidence that it can eventually sublime away the heterogeneity it hypothesizes—by force, if necessary. The aim of the "Police-Philosophy" of political economy (as Hazlitt called it)[37] is control: the cognition of those laws that unimpeded social exchange would naturally follow in order to arrange for the progressive dissolution of all obstructions to mobile, efficient, and predictable commerce.

Rhetoric acts without a norm. And although there is an inconsistency in the uses to which rhetoric is put, the conflict such inconsistency entails is, in Quintilian's words, "between case and case, not between rhetoric and itself." Such conflict can be settled only by another case, which must be linked to a precedent (in this Burke was right) but *whose very mode of linkage is subject to dispute.* A case is a commonplace that is not a *cite* of simple repetition but a *site* of invention. The commonplace impells through discourse the gravity that makes circumstances matter. "The art of rhetoric," according to Quintilian, "is realised in action, not in the result obtained." That action is simply "speaking well."[38] The art of rhetoric is not dialogical. No reciprocity obtains between good rhetoricians, because ethical arguments are not interchangeable. Speaking is well spoken insofar as it brings a community into being by obliging the addressee to honor the addressor as a good man. Liberalism subscribes to the developmental myth in which oratorical communities give way to written and the written gives way to the published, as the published in turn will give way to the facsimiled. That myth invests in a logocentric model of the oratorical in order to draw strong partitions between the present age of a general economy and the past age of a local community, between the quick and the dead. Because for the rhetorician, as for the aristocrat, only action confers value, the "world upon the whole is worth the assertion" (13:41) and *only* the assertion. There is, in truth, no world without the assertion that things matter; and the world is exactly what is at stake in every assertion. At certain times speaking well is simply a matter of speaking out. But it is hard to know what is the right time or idiom for speaking out against property, for example. Or against death.

Fortunately, there is always a maxim at hand. Canto 11's ubi sunt (sts. 76–86), that long complaint for the vanishment of all the proper names by which the poet peopled his world, ends precipitately with no generic bridge to something else. The shade of Plato, canto 1's patron philosopher of transit, is nowhere in sight. Nonetheless, it is imperative that linkage occur, now:

> I have seen malt liquors
> Exchanged for "thin potations" by John Bull—
> I have seen John half detect himself a fool.—
>
> But "Carpe diem," Juan, "carpe, carpe!"
> To-morrow sees another race as gay.
>
> (11:85–86)

The link is made, fitfully, by a citation of the maxim on which Tom unluckily acted. "Carpe diem" is a prescription for all occasions. Classical.

Still, one does not commonly *cite* classical maxims. The quotation marks suggest an anxiety of address, an anticipation that the phrase would not obligate its addressee without the boost of authoritative marks. The quotation marks are what Hazlitt calls an "infliction of the present" on the incorporated maxim, the sign of a time when the existence of the "common place" is itself at stake.[39] *Juan*'s citation compulsion is the symptom of a bookish existence unattached to a community of ethical phrases. "The man of the book has no land," in Lyotard's words,[40] and without land verbal prescriptions seem abstract, derivative; they require the backing of typographical conventions. The citation attempts to generate for the maxim a normative transcendence of the moment of audition. And in fact "Carpe diem" rules the English Cantos, which, like the annals of the United Kingdom, are a tissue of seizures, failed and successful, past and present, literal and figurative. Depending on the occasion, the norm translates as seize the hour; seize the day; seize the language; seize the purse; seize the monastery; seize the monk; or (and this is a literal citation) "seize the last word" (13:98). Citation of the maxim extracted from its ancient circumstances gives the seizure a kind of cosmetic legality, like that conferred on the confiscated monasteries, seized as foreign communities and reoccupied as real estate, in which the religious past persists as properties displayed, cited, and dramatized or like that conferred on the Elgin Marbles, cleaned, mounted, and labeled for exhibit in the British Museum. Quotation marks stake out the boundaries of the contemporary as what encloses the "common place" and turns it into private property.

Although Juan does not seem to hear the narrator any better than he had heard Tom, it doesn't much matter. The citation of the maxim presupposes the lapse of its idiomatic status and thus of the differend between the direct speech of the ancients and those who write "at this time." There is no guarantee that the modernized norm "Carpe diem" will bind the future any more successfully than Sheridan's oratory or Castlereagh's chains, however. We might consider this quotation of the commonplace as a compulsive, "Coleridgean" defense against charges of plagiarism. But considered as the desperate attempt to institute a law or norm in the absence of any circumstantial connection to that culture where the law might be applied, the imperative more closely resembles Coleridge's wish to post an *Index Expurgatorius* in the halls of Parliament or Byron's own Decalogue in canto 1: and thus not a neurotic defense but an act of psychotic aggression.[41]

In *Juan* the narrator's command performs its vocal ministry; it negates, like a rock tossed in the stream, the primary processes' "mobility of cathexis." No phrase has the force of lightning, however, and this one breaks through to nothing new, not even to Juan, who, agog in the spindrift of objects and images, seems oblivious to admonitions. To Juan the narrator's speech, in Lyotard's words, "remains outside, and it remains there in two forms; as an unreal reality, the ghost, and as inaudible speech, the paternal command."[42] Juan not only lives off the financial and political credit of Donna Inez and Catherine the Great, he has all along been providentially favored. Recall, for example, the promise of the rainbow, following the shipwreck in canto 2. Chosen, but knowing not by whom, Juan wanders the face of the earth like the landless Jew-one, looking for the promised land. Granted, "providence," "chosen," and "promised" must, like "God" and "author" and "Carpe diem," be put between quotation marks; the modernity of *Juan*'s dispensation is that neither the narrator nor anyone else can claim on cognitively reliable grounds to be its father. The narrator must forcibly institute the grounds of his own authority, summoning as he does so the maddening aporia of self-legitimating authority.

There is, then, a double misprision here in this failure to hear or be heard. Neither Juan nor the narrator can discover a father in the poem. The difference between the world of the English quality and the world of the narrator is represented as an absolute difference between a mirror-world of images circulating without negation and a world of "discourse without things,"[43] between a tissue of compromises and an uncompromising imperative, between what is seen and what is spoken. This split is psychotic. And because that psychosis spins its wandering in the desert of its saying out of an overestimation of the father so severe that oedipal struggle must be averted at all costs ("I'm not Oedipus," the poet insists [13:12]; recall also the sentimentalizing of the relations between father and son in the longboat of canto 2), the text will, for better or worse, never overcome its incapacity to hear the paternal command and achieve thereby symbolic reconciliation. The psychotic text, *Juan*, can end with no commandatore (and no guillotine), cannot end at all.

Peter Manning and, more recently, Ronald Paulson have commented on the odd turn that *Juan* takes as it nears its (in)conclusion. Although the stage is set for the drama of Oedipus to be enacted among Adeline, Juan, and Lord Henry, those expectations do not "materialize."[44] It suits *Juan*'s rhymes to have Lady Fitz-Fulke step between Juan and the others in this triangle. There is no evident obstacle between Juan and the complaisant Fitz-Fulke, whose husband is already alienated and is anyway laid up with the gout. No figure of the father presents himself as a rival against whom Juan might have to draw his sword. We have seen this swerve from oedipalization before in *The Corsair*, where Conrad's refusal to find in Gulnare an object of desire is the counterpart to a foreclosure of aggressive feelings toward Seyd. "Foreclosure," as Lyotard asserts, "knows nothing of castration."[45] Conrad knows nothing of castration; his petrification in the face of Gulnare's return from the supposed murder of Seyd repudiates the possibility and with it the capacity both for meaningful speech (cf. Lara's convulsion in the gallery of his ancestors) and for effective action (Kaled will stand in as Gulnare stood). When Juan first meets the Friar, he too is "petrified" (16:22), becoming what he couldn't see as he comes face to facelessness with an "unreal reality":

> Once, twice, thrice passed, repassed the thing of air,
> Or earth beneath, or Heaven, or t'other place;
> And Juan gazed upon it with a stare,
> Yet could not speak or move; but, on its base
> As stands a statue, stood: he felt his hair
> Twine like a knot of snakes around his face;
> He taxed his tongue for words, which were not granted,
> To ask the reverend person what he wanted.
>
> (16:23)

Juan becomes the nought he fears to behold. Making visible what the eye will not see, Juan's hair metamorphoses into a Gorgon's nest of writhing snakes. By repudiating castration Juan, like Don Alfonso and the *British* before him, proves "himself the thing he most abhorr'd." He fails to see what is clearly missing. That is, he fails to see nothing. He sees what is not there: a ghost.

It is not difficult to explain the appearance of the ghost within the walls of Norman Abbey. The Amundevilles have their own account of the forefather, who "came in his might, with King Henry's right, / To turn church lands to lay" (16:40). King Henry's right becomes a father's might, which in time becomes Lord Henry's right. The seizure by the forefather's might is doubly "canonized": by monarchical authorization and by the naturalizing passage of years through which the estate has been uneventfully handed down. As in Burke's exemplary *Reflections on the Revolution in France*, the initial usurpation is bracketed in order to quell the potential for dynastic struggle and to preempt challenges to the sanctity of ancient deeds. Adeline's lyrical ballad attempts to master the deviation from rule executed by the Protestant devil of the father by giving the Catholic devil (also a "father") his due.[46]

In doing so Adeline demonstrates the capacity of the sentimental to face modernity's guilty past and to conquer by artful division:

> But beware! beware! of the Black Friar,
>   He still retains his sway,
> For he is yet the church's heir,
>   Who ever may be the lay.
> Amundeville is lord by day,
>   But the monk is lord by night.
> Not wine nor wassail could raise a vassal
>   To question that friar's right.
>   (16:40:1)

The ballad weaves the social "circle" (16:41) around the nightly appearance of the monk. Since everybody in this enlightened age knows that monks present no real threat to social harmony or the security of property, we might speculate that the ghost of a "father" takes the place of the ghost of *my* father—that the mighty ancestor does double duty as both usurping son and castrating father. The ballad represents a past usurpation as doubly legitimated by monarchic decree and by the passage of time. It expresses not so much a reconciliation as an untroubled continuity with the father.

That continuity is in fact mythic, since the seized land has long since been transformed into real estate and the ancestral manor into a market. The insistence on the fluid transmission of land (not a claim likely to be made by the bloody ancestor) exhibits not aristocratic strength (dead and gone forever) but a new and more powerful thing: aristocratic class consciousness as a function of the rulers' strategic adaptation to a bourgeois ideology that is everywhere interested in continuity and eager to enlist even aristocratic claims of privilege in its service. In the world of Norman Abbey Adeline performs what might be called the Coleridge function: her translation of folk ballads into lyrical ballads provides the ideological support for the prevailing property relations and therefore for the preservation of the aristocracy, despite its loss of strength, as a force within nineteenth-century class society. Sentimental art preserves the past it has overcome in order to exemplify the synthetic powers of a secular society and to demonstrate the right of the sentimentalist (now Lord Henry, later Benjamin Disraeli) to rule.

As the trade in the Gothic proved, such a story could be staged anywhere and at any time; it could be about everywhere and nowhere. The difference here is that a ghost *has* actually appeared. The appearance of the ghost (it is immaterial whether it is a real ghost or an aristocrat in drag) demonstrates the failure of such artful *mise en scène* to fuse past and present. The apparition is the mark of repression, the "thing-presentation" within the walls of what dialectic had hoped to contain through artistic representation. The ghost is not so much a return of the repressed father, whom the children can never fully compensate for his deed (though it is that); it is a reminder that the past lives in every exchange, that every commercial transaction (between buyer and seller, author and reader) contains, however encrypted by the language of contract, an unspoken seizure.

Why, then, does the thing appear only to Juan? Lord Henry provides the shadow of an explanation in his comments on the "odd story" that "Fame" tells, when he mentions "that our sires had a more gifted eye / For such sights" (16:36). As John Wilson mused in his review of *Childe Harold IV*, the "gifted sight" of the moderns is in fact leased with the purchase of a theater ticket (*RR* B:2:895). That may be, but until Juan touches the bosom of Fitz-Fulke beneath the cowl, no transaction takes place. There is no other explanation for why Juan sees the ghost except his gift.[47] In a world where people have more than a little unreality (even Juan, tolerant to a fault, comes to doubt "how much of Adeline was *real*" [16:96]), the ghost is a sight for sore, or in this case damned, eyes. For Juan is gifted by Tom: his sight distantly fulfills the curse "Damn your eyes." Although the childlike Juan has failed to hear Tom's spell, the phrase nonetheless has its genealogical way with him. In canto 7, during the Siege of Ismail, the narrator commented on the redundancy of the idiomatic oath for the contemporary John Bull:

'T is strange that he should farther "damn his eyes,"
   For they are damned; that once all-famous death
Is to the devil now no farther prize,
   Since John has lately lost the use of both.
Debt he calls wealth, and taxes paradise;
   And Famine, with her gaunt and bony growth,
Which stare him in the face, he won't examine,
Or swears that Ceres hath begotten Famine.

                (7:45)

Hell is a kind of Newspeak, a blindness to things in their true aspect, a failure to call things by their proper names. By the time the poet comes to reoccupy this hell in canto 11, it has become clear that redemption will not follow upon a new precision of denomination, however, for such self-serving blindness is the symptom of British propriety, which cants that the rightness of a thing can be confirmed or disconfirmed by its correspondence to a proper name. The loss of the satirist's mooring in propriety dishes all prospects of redemption. No Orphic muse, *Juan* does not rouse its readers with the hope of an escape from the hell of their language, perhaps by the advent of some new vocabulary; it implicates them in its navigation of a path through that hell.

Forging the path means recovering the efficaciousness of the curse. As the poem continues past its proper length (a package either the "size of *Rokeby*" or of *Childe Harold III*), continuance itself becomes a kind of virtue—not because it is upheld by the "ontological security" of a routine, but because continuance of the curse after it has served its proper function (whether as exemplary sign of the closure of providential history against the eruption of the contingent, as in the stigmatizing of Cain, or as the hollow admonition uttered by the personification of a wrecked epos, as in the curse of Minerva) suggests a strength in the speaking that is more than functional. I have argued in chapter 5 that routine offered Lord Byron what passed for ontological security because his habit of composition was itself maintained by the speculative grammar of the literary system of Byronism; the virtue of continuance is the virtue of publication without reference and without the support of that literary system. Publication beyond the hope of "fame and profit at once" (10:126)—the basis on which the last cantos of *Juan* proceed—forges a pathway through the pit of modernity. As Juan is John bulled (turned topsy-turvy in the camera obscura of Byron's satire), so is the ethic of republication Byron's version of republican virtue. Byron's gift to the republican tradition is to turn publication into a kind of material foundation and to demonstrate the possibility of civic virtue in hell.[48] The lesson of *Juan*'s continued publication applies the lesson of Tom's utterance of the curse: what seems compulsive when referred to oneself (John Bull damns his own eyes) may be compelling if addressed to another.

Compelling captures the residue of vengefulness that clings to the poet's ambition, which, even in March 1823, is associated generally with repayment of prior wrongs and specifically with the aim of returning to England in order to "bring affairs to a crisis with Henry Brougham" (*BLJ* 10:126), as if Byron were in fact the Black Friar and the Black Friar were indeed capable of taking vengeance on the usurpers of his estate. In a matter of days, however, Byron drops the "direct" aim of revenge for aims ever more ulterior. Jettisoning his anxiety about the preservation of copyright, he writes to Douglas Kinnaird: "I expect that those [proofs] corrected already are to be published immediately. I care nothing for what may be the consequence—critical or otherwise—all the bullies on earth shall not prevent me from writing what I like—& publishing what I write—'coute qui coute'" (*BLJ* 10:132). To compel is to care for consequences. And *compelling* thus misses the way language moves in *Juan*, which is not by literal imposition but by figural apposition.[49] Tom's phrase does not father. It comes to matter by virtue of the prefigural linkage that occurs between one phrase and another: from the "damn" of Tom to the "multifarious 'damme's'" that extend his song and raise its tone, and to the "gentle sound of Thamis" (11:24); from Thamis to the double-jointed "damme" (damn me/Damn ye)—endorsed by the poet as "Platonic blasphemy, the very soul of swearing"—and to any one of the multifarious "dames" ("heroic and chaste too" [16:17]) who pass through the Abbey like spirits, erecting "palisades" and making suit (14:61; 12:42). The embodiment of the ghost that is condemned to haunt the walls and threatens to literalize Juan's descent into "Hell" (16:116) is accomplished by the most formidable "dame" of all, "her gracious, graceful, graceless Grace, / The full-grown Hebe of Fitz-Fulke" (16:49).

The Psychotic Text and the Problem of a Double Figure

Believing in Tom's "phrase-power" obliges you to believe in the Sandman—to credit, that is, popular superstition's belief in the power of magical, unfathered speech to affect the way children see. Moreover, you should hold that belief not despite its impossibility but, as the narrator says, "*quia impossible.*" This is the way the strong Romantic poet links up with the cognitive phrase of empiricism: Hume says all truth is the result of belief; the poet commands, "Believe: if 't is improbable you must / And if it is impossible, you *shall*" (16:6). It is a fact beyond contradiction that if believed the impossible will, by belief, be brought about.

The implications of this injunction appear during the account of the daily business conducted at Norman Abbey. Justice encounters a mystery:

> There were two poachers caught in a steel trap
>   Ready for jail, their place of convalescence;
> There was a country girl in a close cap
>   And scarlet cloak (I hate the sight to see, since—
> Since—since—in youth, I had the sad mishap—
>   But luckily I have paid few parish fees since)
> That scarlet cloak, alas! unclosed with Rigour,
> Presents the problem of a double figure.
>
> A reel within a bottle is a mystery,
>   One can't tell how it e'er got in or out;
> Therefore the present piece of natural history,
>   I leave to those who are fond of solving doubt;
> And merely state, though not for the consistory,
>   Lord Henry was a justice, and that Scout
> The constable, beneath a warrant's banner,
> Had bagged this poacher upon Nature's manor.
>
> Now Justices of Peace must judge all pieces
>   Of mischief of all kinds, and keep the game
> And morals of the country from caprices
>   Of those who have not a licence for the same;
> And of all things, excepting tithes and leases,
>   Perhaps these are most difficult to tame:
> Preserving partridges and pretty wenches
> Are puzzles to the most precautious benches.
>
> The present culprit was extremely pale,
>   Pale as if painted so; her cheek being red
> By nature, as in higher dames less hale
>   'T is white, at least when they just rise from bed.
> Perhaps she was ashamed of seeming frail,
>   Poor soul! for she was country born and bred,
> And knew no better in her immorality
> Than to wax white—for blushes are for quality.
>
> Her black, bright, downcast, yet espiègle eye,
>   Had gathered a large tear into its corner,

Which the poor thing at times essayed to dry,
    For she was not a sentimental mourner,
Parading all her sensibility,
    Nor insolent enough to scorn the scorner,
But stood in trembling, patient tribulation,
To be called up for her examination.

Of course these groups were scattered here and there,
    Not nigh the gay saloon of ladies gent.
The lawyers in the study; and in air
    The prize pig, ploughman, poachers; the men sent
From Town, viz. architect and dealer, were
    Both busy (as a general in his tent
Writing dispatches) in their several stations,
Exulting in their brilliant lucubrations.

But this poor girl was left in the great hall,
    While Scout, the parish guardian of the frail,
Discussed (he hated beer yclept the "small")
    A mighty mug of *moral* double ale.
She waited until Justice could recall
    Its kind attentions to their proper pale,
To name a thing in nomenclature rather
Perplexing for most virgins—a child's father.

(16:61–67)

Faced with an amassing body, justice in its "Rigour" uncloses the scarlet cloak to present the "problem of a double figure." Justice follows the same analytical rule that Freud resorts to when, on his journey through "The Uncanny," he confronts "the mass of themes to which [he] is tempted to ascribe the uncanny effect" of E. T. A. Hoffmann's *Elixiere des Teufels* (1816); Freud brings the disparate phenomena under control by comprising them under what he calls the "idea of the 'double.'" The analytical rule, then (for Freud, as for Locke), that makes judgment possible: When in doubt, double.[50] Doubling stabilizes sudden, "multifarious" growth by attributing identity, which is always a matter of correspondence: here the figure refers not merely to the doubling in size of a "nonpregnant" body but to the double of the father who, justice presumes, must have *caused* this change. The official diagnosis of pregnancy attributes what Coleridge would call "personeity" to the thing by establishing it in a relation of correspondence to some other person who is capable of having property in it. Once the problem of the double figure has been superimposed on the body of the country girl, justice can follow the normative English protocol of match-making.

At one level the problem of a double figure is the moral problem of preventing unsanctified liaisons among the unmarried. But morality as such has just the importance of ale as such. As in the precincts of Bedlam, so within the "proper pale" of "Nature's manor," Norman Abbey: what is actually at stake is the application of "moral management," which in its rustic version closely resembles animal husbandry. Justice is charged with "preserving partridges and pretty wenches"—saving them from poaching surely, but, more broadly, preserving them from the idiomatic, *carpe diem* mentality that contributes not only to thievery and rape but to the promiscuous breeding that the Malthusian knows would eventually destroy the health of the population.

Of course, as the fifth Lord Byron had proved in his fracas with Mr. Chaworth, the right means of managing game was subject to dispute. Unlike Chaworth's monitorial regime, the Wicked Lord's libertine policy (Let them breed! Let them poach!) had no moral basis. In Lyotard's terms, the duel between Chaworth and the fifth Lord Byron marked the absence of a genre of discourse capable of settling the differend between aristocratic license and gentrified licensing. There was no available calculus for turning animals into double figures—that is, into things both themselves and numerals in a statistical survey that accounted for them as a population governed by rules of procreation and subject to actuarial odds. Hence the greater need for management of game to be "precautious." Once precautions fail and the game has been poached, morals give way to finance and guidance to interrogation. Justice asks, "Who is going to pay?" The father/poacher must pay the parish fees, as the narrator of *Juan* once paid his. Otherwise, the financial burden would fall on a community ill prepared to assume it. British justice occurs in a world that is in the process of transforming itself into a commercial society where the obligation to take care is fast becoming an unintelligible notion.

Justice, then, has an interest in a solution. And though no one can tell at a glance how the reel got into the bottle, the double figure assumes that what is within the girl can be doubled as information and itemized as a name of which she can be delivered by its obstetric intervention. Whatever information the girl should give, it will necessarily be a defense of property; for to name the father is by definition to acknowledge the property of the father in the infant. Immaculately empirical, justice's task is also purely ideological. It need not deliver the name of the actual father (an emissary from the Real), but only the name of *a* father, because to name any father is to give the name of *the* father. Justice asks the kind of question that Ralph Allen during his crusade (conducted in the name of the king) against "promiscuous mixing" of letters asked time and time again: What male got into the wrong pouch?[51]

Jacques Lacan phrased the problem differently: "It is in the *name of the father* that we must recognize the support of the symbolic function which, from the dawn of history, has identified his person with the function of the law."[52] There is no way to make sense without uttering the name of the father. No way for a maiden to speak without acknowledging a man's property in her. No way for a Tom to speak without having his words subject to extraction. No way for an aristocrat to speak out without identifying himself as a double figure: his honor upheld by the duel, his land of value only in market terms, his superiority a function of his class. Justice bleaches the country woman of her natural color to make her an image, substituting a scarlet cloak that can theatrically be drawn to reveal a social problem. As the law of fashion forbids her to blush, so the law of the magistrate turns her into a blank on which the nomenclature of paternity can then be stamped.

If to speak would be to defend property, muteness can be read, under the license of the double figure, as the complaint of the silent woman—psychotic, hysteric, witch, gypsy. The law states (and here I am licentiously applying the lessons of *Heart of Midlothian* and "The Thorn" to a situation answerable to their precedent) that the maiden's complaint could be heard only under the sign of castration and thus heard ironically: as a defense of that by which she is injured. Such is the irony that entraps Donna Julia, who, whether complaining of her husband's suspicions ("Was it for this?") or of her lover's range, indemnifies the patriarchal regime that gives her the words to make her plea. The condition of her finding "at length a voice" (1:142) is her sacrifice to the service of the father—whether as represented by the lawyer before whom she pleads or by the convent altar before which she prays.

The overgrown maiden of canto 16 does not find her voice; she is in the predicament of a specter or monster, of that woman who has lost her spell and thus can no longer bind the bar that is authorized to condemn her to elect marriage, extinction, or the kind of psychotic speech adopted by Martha Ray and Madge Wildfire. But in *Juan* the double figure, as applied by justice, performs as a hinge that swings the maiden *toward* a marital doom unreached, and it therefore indulges our strong wish to interpret the suspension of her registration in the symbolic order as a prefigural resistance to that symbolization. Calling something "uncanny" or "double" is a strategy for giving order to a bewildering, unmeaning "feminine contrivance"; the heap of body becomes a symbolic pyre on which the female is sacrificed in the name of the father. The British judicial interrogation of the maiden who has contrived to become pregnant serves the social purpose that, as we have seen, J. G. E. Herder fantasized for the Hindu or Assyrian suttee (see chap. 8 above). Here, however, the sacrifice is conducted not by spendthrift fire but by economical enlightenment: the examination of the country girl quashes ambiguity by exacting the signs of consent. At least it *would* if it were not the case that the case remains suspended on an eternal eve of examination. That disposition is right, if not just. In *Juan* before problems are solved contradictions must be endured, such as an event that supposedly occurs within "natural history" but is indicted as a trespass against "Nature's manor," such as a pregnant woman who is called, with as little irony as the poem can muster, a "virgin."

Nature's manor is Lord Henry's property, seized and enclosed; nature's manner is imaginable only in terms of the customary law that the manor sustains. There can be no appeal to a natural history that is not subject to the Malthusian curriculum or to one that ignores the proprieties of nature's manor. The only appeal with any strength is one launched from that impossible place common to the country girl, the narrator, and the reader, where we assemble groundlessly to hail an immaculate (not emasculate) conception.[53] The country girl is not just an abstracted space, a pale page to be imprinted with justice's pure signifier. She is a place that amasses; like the amazing walls of Norman Abbey, her body swells as with rumor,

> the rumour which such spots unfold,
> Coined from surviving superstition's mint,
>   Which passes ghosts in currency like gold,
> But rarely seen, like gold compared with paper.
>   (16:22)

Juan's Knotical Existence

> *They speak an unnatural dialect, and are constrained by a masquerade habit.*
>
> Francis Jeffrey, review of Byron's tragedies, *in* Edinburgh Review,
> February 1822

> Glo. *Upon what cause?*
> Clar.   *Because my name is George.*
> Shakespeare, Richard III

We could spend forever spreading ever more finely the rumor of the ghost or untying the social, political, and cultural implications of the country girl with swollen girth and *espiègle* eye, braiding them back into this hospitable text. Like Wordsworth's "dismantled warrior," we could endlessly spin interpretive gold "Out of the bowels of those very schemes / In which [the poem] did first extravagate" (*Prelude* 5:501–3). But to what profit? Wealth out of all proportion to a producer or a product may be the very soul of wealth, but what does it matter? Besides, *eventually* the child must be referred to its father, text to context, wealth to economy. It is for all conjurers as it is for the pregnant woman. As Lacan dourly observes, "If the symbolic context requires it, paternity will nonetheless be attributed to the fact that the woman met the spirit at some fountain or some rock in which he is supposed to live."[54]

On occasion *Juan* moralizes in a Lacanian vein:

A something all-sufficient for the *heart*
　Is that for which the Sex are always seeking;
But how to fill up that same vacant part?
　There lies the rub—and this they are but weak in.
Frail mariners afloat without a chart,
　They run before the wind through high seas breaking;
And when they have made the shore through ev'ry shock,
'T is odd, or odds, it may turn out a rock.

(14:74)

Or it may turn out to be nought. Here as elsewhere "the Sex" ought to be read as "the Female," for in *Juan* to be sexualized is to experience a vacancy in need of filling. Here is Juan awaiting the return of the ghost:

Were his eyes open? Yes! and his mouth too.
　Surprise has this effect—to make one dumb,
Yet leave the gate which Eloquence slips through
　As wide as if a long speech were to come.
Nigh and more nigh the awful echoes drew,
　Tremendous to a mortal tympanum:
His eyes were open, and (as was before
Stated) his mouth. What opened next?—the door.

It opened with a most infernal creak,
　Like that of Hell. "Lasciate ogni speranza
Voich' entrate!" The hinge seemed to speak,
　Dreadful as Dante's rhima, or this stanza;

> Or—but all words upon such themes are weak;
>   A single shade's sufficient to entrance a
> Hero—for what is substance to a Spirit?
> Or how is 't *matter* trembles to come near it?
> (16:115–16)

Eyes, mouth, door—a series of cavities to be filled by infernal sights unseen. Abandon all hope ye heroes who are entranced here! The hinge's creak almost makes us forget that we are already in hell (and thus Gothically epitomizes the social function of the Gothic genre). It seems to announce a world that inverts the everyday world point for point—but also, consolingly, a world that bottoms out on what Blake called the "limit of opacity." What will come through the door? Odds are (tradition is a banker) it will be the father or a rock or the rock of the father.

Or so might the plot unfold under the hand of Lacan, who winds up "The Freudian Thing" with a morose admonition that acquires its pathos from the story of Don Giovanni: "Will our action go as far, then, as to repress the very truth that it bears in its exercise? Will it send this truth back to sleep . . . : namely, that it is out of the forfeits and vain oaths, lapses in speech and unconsidered words, the constellation of which presided at the putting into the world of a man, that is moulded the stone guest who comes, in symptoms, to disturb the banquet of one's desire?"[55] *Juan* and Lacan agree that no oath is vain and that no banquet of desire will go undisturbed, but the masquerade of truth each imagines is dramatically different.

When the sable Friar appears in the doorway "he" awakens the correspondent breeze of Juan's own "internal ghost":

> And then his dread grew wrath, and his wrath fierce,
>   And he arose, advanced—the shade retreated;
> But Juan, eager now the truth to pierce,
>   Followed, his veins no longer cold, but heated,
> Resolved to thrust the mystery carte and tierce,
>   At whatsoever risk of being defeated:
> The ghost stopped, menaced, then retired, until
> He reached the ancient wall, then stood stone still.
> (16:119)

Heroes are easy—easy to entrance, easy to arouse. Odds are this hero, like all others in Byron, will be defeated. And what does it matter? Like Chaworth in the closet with the Wicked Lord, Juan fights according to the code by which his body has been disciplined; he knows that the risk of defeat is only death. The risk of *not* being defeated is to discover that there is something other than death that crowns human action.

Odds are the hero, like "the Sex," will not pierce to the shore of truth but will crash into the rock: "Juan put forth one arm—Eternal powers! / It touched no soul, no body, but the wall" (16:120). *Hic murus*. Wall for stone, a human construction instead of an unconscious projection. That Chaworthian thrust resolves nothing, however:

> But still the Shade remained: the blue eyes glared,
>   And rather variably for stony death;
> Yet one thing rather good the grave had spared,
>   The ghost had a remarkably sweet breath;
> A straggling curl showed he had been fair-haired;
>   A red lip, with two rows of pearls beneath,
> Gleamed forth, as through the casement's ivy shroud
> The moon peeped, just escaped from a grey cloud.
>
> And Juan, puzzled, but still curious, thrust
>   His other arm forth—Wonder upon wonder!
> It pressed upon a hard but glowing bust,
>   Which beat as if there was a warm heart under.
> He found, as people on most trials must,
>   That he had made at first a silly blunder,
> And that in his confusion he had caught
> Only the wall, instead of what he sought.
>
> The ghost, if ghost it were, seemed a sweet soul
>   As ever lurked beneath a holy hood:
> A dimpled chin, a neck of ivory, stole
>   Forth into something much like flesh and blood;
> Back fell the sable frock and dreary cowl,
>   And they revealed—alas! that e'er they should!
> In full, voluptuous, but *not o'er*grown bulk,
> The phantom of her frolic Grace—Fitz-Fulke!
>
> (16:121–23)

The climactic exclamation comes as a surprise, not only because we might have expected almost anyone to appear from beneath the cowl in this cryptic place, but because even at the climax it is not clear who is exclaiming or exactly what is being said. If instead of "Fitz-Fulke!" it were "the name of the father!" things would fall into their proper place. The exclamation is not, however, a signifier pure and simple but a messy compound. Moreover, it brings to an ambiguous finale what is a short-lived Gothic drama in free indirect style. In stanza 112 there is this: "And not in vain he listened;—

Hush! what's that? / I see—I see—ah no!–'t is not—yet 't is— / Ye powers! it is the—the—the—Pooh! the cat!" Who is speaking, narrator or character? More of the same in stanza 113, and again in the exclamation of stanza 120: "Eternal powers!" Who is speaking? If the "whole matter" were in truth to rest "upon eyesight" (12:71), this compounding of speech by narrator and character would have to be sorted out, for to say "I see" is to determine who is that one who by his sight has earned the right to cite himself as "I" ("I, Freud," "I, the law," "I, Byron"). In this text, however, the evidence of the visible remains precariously propped on the tangible; here the truth, like the liaison with Donna Julia, like close combat, is one of those "matters [that] must be carried by the touch" (8:78), and in this case a double touch: both the grasp of the hand of him who has found "what he sought" and the touch of him who calls the name linked to the material bust. Narrator and character share a "common place" in the narrative flow, a phrase that binds them just as (now!) the hyphen compounds the *Fitz* and the *Fulke* into a dynastic knot.

The lie of the Friar may be the "truth in masquerade," but when the cloak is unclosed (with a notable lack of rigor) the truth does not appear as the problem of the double figure. One of those Byronic corruptions of the language that is "neither English nor poetry" (*BLJ* 7:182), the phrase "Fitz-Fulke" *describes* a certain "full, voluptuous, but *not o'er*grown bulk," while it coincidentally *prescribes* a form of sexual behavior that deviates from a sexuality properly placed. Spoken out on an English tongue the Norman "Fitz-Fulke!" sounds as the Saxon shibboleth "Fist-fuck!"—an imperative that tangibly deviates from normative heterosexuality, apparently toward a place made familiar by the deductions of Louis Crompton and Cecil Lang (see chap. 3 above). A homelier, declassed variant of the "Carpe diem!" topos, "Fist-fuck!" invites the decipherment of the more lurid Gothic motifs in terms of the kind of pictorial homoerotic code familiarized by the eponymous Monk Lewis: it is not a woman but a "he," with a "straggling curl," a "red lip," and pearly teeth, who appears under the moonlight. Circumstanced by those adjectives and pronouns, the object of "the Sex" seems same-sexual; and the creaking hinge threatens to swing Juan into an under- or nether world that is as much Beckfordian as Dantean: the dark backward and abysm of the body. Entranced by that open hole through which no articulate speech comes (*to fist* can mean to break wind, according to the *OED*), Juan is poised on the threshold of an object choice that would pitch him into a dark and hopeless future.[56] Yet the gate never quite swings shut. Contrary to the Lady Byron school of Byron criticism, the punctual moment in which the destiny of a character or a poet or a nation or a sexual partner is fatally *rhymed* never quite arrives in *Juan*. Moreover, this admonition to a hands-on form of sexuality is not gender-specific in the giver or the receiver (does not, in fact, indicate that there is a difference between giver and receiver, since the act of fist-fucking could very well be masturbatory). It answers to the confusion of sorts and sexes, but without appeal to justice or to normative rigor. Whether through negligence or through design, the poet's exclamation instances for the last time (oddly enough) that "old luck" by which he is "always *near* something serious, & generally escaping as now with a *slight* accident" (*BLJ* 2:237).

Lord Byron's revelation handily eludes Radcliffean rationalization. Just because the Friar is exclaimed to be Fitz-Fulke does not make it any less a "phantom." If it is true, according to John Locke, that "no man in civil society can be exempted from the laws of it," and if it is true, according to Thomas Hobbes, that justice is justice the world over,[57] those truths are the vehicles of an anti-aristocratic policy, decrees that lawfully erase the local, the virtuous, the ethical, and the obligatory—dispel anything that could stay the verdict of reason. And if those truths are true, to claim a privilege of speaking out (regardless of the cant of the law) means that one speaks from an impossible place outside of civil society, beyond the sweep of Broughham. *Juan* does so in this encounter with "Fitz-Fulke," who in Blackstone's reading of the law fully earns the designation "phantom" because "she" has suffered something like a "civil death":

> The civil death commences if any man be banished the realm by the process of the common law, or enter into religion; that is, goes into a monastery, and becomes there a monk professed. . . . For . . . such a monk, upon his profession, renounces solemnly all secular concerns: and besides, as the popish clergy claimed an exemption from the duties of civil life, and the commands of the temporal magistrate, the genius of the English law would not suffer those persons to enjoy the benefits of society, who secluded themselves from it, and refused to submit to its regulations. A monk is therefore accounted *civiliter mortuus.*[58]

This is not the first instance in Byron of someone taking on monkish habits. There is Donna Julia, of course; there is also the Giaour's removal to a monastery after slaying Hassan; there are Lord Byron's visits to the Armenian monastery outside of Venice in 1816–17 to pursue his lexicographical interests; there is the Capuchin convent in Athens where the playful lord indulged himself with Nicolo in 1810. The civil death that in Britain's vindictively Protestant society is visited on those who choose to be regulated by rules that are not the state's is the same fate suffered by a man, like

William Beckford, who has sexual relations with boys, or a person, like James Tilly Matthews, who receives intelligence from unseen assailers speaking in compounds unrecognized by Johnson. Fitz-Fulke's imposture is serious play: by reoccupying the habits, by embodying a vanished caste once exempt from the rule of monarch and Parliament, "she" dramatizes the civil death that is the exorbitant price for claiming lordly exemption from social regulation. Fitz-Fulke acts out the phantomization of the aristocracy; a spectre whom (in the words of *Childe Harold IV*) "no exorcism can bind" (st. 24), "she" speaks with the special posthumous strength of the strong poet.

Once again Juan cannot be swung into Dante's or Mozart's or Beckford's hell because *Juan* already *is* a fitting hell: "Why need we talk of a fiery Hell?" Coleridge asks. "If the will, which is the law of our nature, were withdrawn from our memory, fancy, understanding, and reason, no other Hell could equal, for a spiritual being, what it would then feel, for the anarchy of our powers. It would be conscious madness—a horrid thought!"[59] Coleridge's "horrid thought" is not a bad paraphrase for the primary process world of England, an immoral world where the will is just another cant expression, a bourgeois culture where every value is the "phantom of aristocratic values."[60] Lord Byron's separation, which we have Freudianized as a repudiation of castration, preempts the recession of the will and the eclipse of moral strength by withdrawing meaning from what he perceives. The question "Where is the world?" discombobulates the hierarchy of generic identities that sustains Coleridge's theology and his poetics. By foreclosing the "name of the father" from the memory, fancy, understanding, and reason, *Juan* represents a hell in apposition to the proper British hell, a hell of *virtuous* madness.

Juan's spectral existence has its basis in its manner of speaking out. In his commentary on Schreber's psychosis Lacan refers to the "voices that use the *Grundsprache*," which he translates as "'basic language' (*langue-de-fond*), and which Schreber describes as 'a somewhat archaic, but always rigorous German that is particularly marked by its great wealth of euphemisms.' Elsewhere," Lacan adds, "he refers regretfully to 'its form, which is authentic on account of its characteristics of noble distinction and simplicity.'" The phenomena of the psychotic code are "specified in expressions that are neological in form (new compound words—the process of compounding being governed here by the rules of the patient's language, *langue*) and usage."[61] Lacan's commentary brings Schreber in touch with cultural discourse in England during the first quarter of the nineteenth century, where the "form and usage" of compounds was a subject of considerable debate.

Coleridge launches his self-criticism in the *Biographia* by seconding the objections made by the critics of his first volume of poetry to a "profusion of new-coined double epithets." He recounts how in the "after editions [he] pruned the double epithets with no sparing hand." And in a footnote he cites the authority of Milton and Shakespeare, whose early work was equally culpable. Coleridge adds that the

> rule for the admission of double epithets seems to be this: either that they should be already denizens of our language, such as *blood-stained, terror-stricken, self-applauding;* or when a new epithet, or one found in books only is hazarded, that it at least be one word, not two words made one by virtue of the printer's hyphen. A language which, like the English, is almost without cases, is indeed in its very genius unfitted for compounds. If a writer, every time a compounded word suggests itself to him, would seek for some other mode of expressing the same sense, the chances are always greatly in favour of his finding a better word.[62]

The writer will succeed in finding a better word by excluding the deviations from good breeding that the compound (like Donna Julia's blood-staining of the pure hidalgo line) inflicts on the developmental line of language.

It matters whether this twist of diction is called a compound or a double epithet. Coleridge's choice of *double* anticipates Freud's rigor. But things can always be seen differently. Whereas Coleridge sees almost no cases in English, William Cobbett sees a profusion. For Cobbett every illustration of a grammatical principle is a case, and every case is political. Cobbett calls aggregated words "compounds" and associates their form and usage with the renewable strength of the language:

> Sometimes the sign of the possessive case is left out, and a *hyphen* is used in its stead: as, "Edwards, the *government-spy.*" That is to say, "the government's spy;" or "the spy of the government." These two words, joined in this manner, are called a *compound* noun; and to this compounding of nouns our language is very prone. . . .
>
> This is an advantage peculiar to our language. It enables us to say much in few words, which always gives strength to language; and, after *clearness,* strength is the most valuable quality that writing or speaking can possess.[63]

Although Cobbett is perhaps too optimistic about harmonizing clarity and strength, his comments distinguish him poetically and politically from Coleridge, who evaluates diction according to its "fitness," the requirement that there be a "reason assignable, not only for every word, but for the position of every word."[64] What Cobbett would call "strength" (a nounlike, inherent competence) Coleridge would call "method" (a principle of arrangement—hence epithetic—and economy).[65]

For Coleridge the unfitness of the double epithet is of same order as the unfitness of the commonplace on which the undisciplined Coleridge intemperately relied in his student compositions: the "example of Alexander and Clytus." That topos was, Coleridge recalls,

> equally good and apt whatever might be the theme. Was it ambition? Alexander and Clytus! Flattery? Alexander and Clytus! Anger? Drunkenness? Pride? Friendship? Ingratitude? Late repentance? Still, still Alexander and Clytus! At length the praises of agriculture having been exemplified in the sagacious observation that, had Alexander been holding the plough, he would not have run his friend Clytus through with a spear, this tried and serviceable old friend was banished by public edict *in secula seculorum*.[66]

Coleridge equates the "example" of Alexander and Clytus with the "simile" of the similarly proscribed manchineel fruit. By giving them the traits of doubles rather than commonplaces, Coleridge can invoke the principle of economy and cancel them as a waste of speech. The *Biographia* campaigns for the elimination of what Cobbett calls those advantages "peculiar to our language" as the precondition for the globalization of the language under the banner of English literature. Coleridge's wish to interdict examples, similes, and double epithets targets just those qualities of profusion and unregulated or counterfeit growth that he censors in Wordsworth's "Thorn" and that *Juan*, coming in touch with Wordsworth under cover of a scarlet cloak, exuberantly endorses under the name of superstition and by the usage of the commonplace. This sub rosa complicity between Wordsworth and Byron instantiates a strong Romanticism that can be classed neither as High nor Low but as the quickening compound of both.

Although Coleridge would hold himself no friend to political economy (no more than he would consider himself a foe to Wordsworth), his imperial rhetoric seconds Malthus's own seconding of what Adam Smith "has very justly observed[,] that nations as well as individuals grow rich by parsimony and poor by profusion, and that therefore every frugal man was a friend and every spendthrift an enemy to his country."[67] As political economy projects the extension of the category of "civil death" to every man possessed by the degrading urge to spend without object, so Coleridge's barely facetious notion of "an index expurgatorius of certain well known and ever returning phrases . . . hung up in our law courts and both Houses of Parliament" projects the codification of the usage of commonplaces in order to classify them as crimes against society.[68]

In *Beginnings* Edward Said aligned Piaget's conception of "*structure* as (1) a system of transformations, (2) a totality, (3) something capable of self-regulation" with Coleridge's notion of method as presupposing a "principle of unity with progression."[69] The resemblance also applies to Coleridge's model of the evolution of the language as a process of "desynonimization."[70] Like Piaget's structure, Coleridge's method or language is a political economy. And political economy is a historically specific system in which the historicity of politics is "once and for all" superseded by the mechanical or organical (the difference is mere nuance) development of the whole, which harmonizes with the interest of each part. Coleridge's notorious proscription of allegorical representation is of a piece with his objection to a diction of compounds, a rhetoric of commonplaces, and a genealogy of morals. This post-1815 discourse may be ideology, but it is wildly inapt to call it "the Romantic ideology," for it is constructed to interdict the strong phrasings by which Romanticism materializes then and now. The performative affirmation of the historicity of politics is coextensive with strong Romanticism, which we can now define as the continually unforeseen and unregulated compounding of prescriptions that obligate without cognitive propriety.

Juan's profuse compounding joins with its anti-Malthusian celebration of the miser in a perverse misalliance that deconstructs the fragile antithesis that Malthus strenuously endeavors to preserve between frugality and waste and that Coleridge anxiously seeks to preserve between meaning and nonsense.[71] For Byron there is no morality that is not a genealogy of morals, one that performs the contingent historicity it affirms, that obligates as it speaks. The compounding of *Juan* may be "archaic," but it is not "rigorous." Whether that makes it more or less psychotic, more or less authentic than Schreber's world, I am not prepared to say. It certainly makes it less German. *Juan* genealogizes the English language as a continuing and contingent history of "cases," of odd things that befall "Nature's manor." The notion of a *Grundsprache*—let us Anglicize it as "landspeech"—is particularly pertinent here; the Haroldian entwinement of the "hopes of being remembered" with the "land's language" is in *Juan* a twining with a language that grounds the land in the same way that the ocean grounds the island with which as "Thamis" it resoundingly twines. The basis of *Juan*'s rhetoric is neither Horace nor some conversational reciprocity, but this textual weave of a residual past with a possible future, this knot o'ergrown—

a talisman that, in Adorno's phrase, "disenchants the disenchanted world."[72] Let Alexander twine with Clytus! Love there may be though nought comes of it.

We have lent an ear to the landspeech of Tom/Thamis, whose "gentle sound" mixes with the murmurous *damns/dammes/dames* as *Juan* sings its song. That primal curse gifts Juan's sight and saves his eyes by diverting him from his mastering sight to the tactical touch. The finale of canto 16 discloses the "*not o'ergrown bulk*" of "Fitz-Fulke," which, dismantled, compounds with other parts. Recall the "knot of snakes" that Juan's hair becomes as his (*damn*ed, *damm*ed, *dam*ed) eye confronts the Friar. Recall the "Gordian knot" of his slightly askew necktie the morning after. Recall the description of Lord Henry's defense of his country from the "perdition" threatened by those parricidal demagogues who would

> with a butcher's knife
> Cut through and through (oh! damnable incision!)
> The Gordian or the Ge*ord*-ian knot, whose strings
> Have tied together Commons, Lords, and Kings.
>
> (16:74)

(Gorgon) knot → Gordian knot → Gordian or Geordian knot: by compounding, the "*not o'ergrown*" becomes a Gorgon/Gordian/Geordian and (it speaks its unspokenness) a *Gordon* knot. Which of the tempting leads do we follow? If we tug one strand, what looks like a snake has the feel of an umbilical cord: the destination that cannot be avowed is not strictly samesexual but more richly incestual.

In canto 11 the narrator asks,

> What after all can signify the site
> Of ladies' lucubrations? So they lead
> In safety to the place for which you start,
> What matters if the road be head or heart?
>
> (11:34)

Juan answers: It matters if it's mater. To reach this "place" neither Juan nor his narrator can know that this is the place for which he starts; to countenance it as a goal would entail the oedipal drama that would interdict it. In *Juan* it is the condition of being at the goal that one mistakes it (in this sense the poem is a demotic version of the grandly underreaching *Prelude*). Both narrator and character are getting what they have sought, because, gifted by the *Juan* effect, their indirection makes possible an arrival at a destination that can *be* the desired conclusion just because it is not the *recognized* conclusion or object of desire. The *Juan* effect makes all the difference between the fully material encounter with the robust "Fitz-Fulke" and the "loveless eye" that the self-policing poet cast on Ianthe, or the prosopopoeia by which the poet summoned up the twilight shape of Minerva—or, more sensationally apposite, the Giaour's Gothic vision of the Gorgon-braided hero at the "half-illumined wall" (*Giaour*, ll. 890–908). This place, though maternal, is not Coleridge's "reversionary wealth of the mother tongue" but the vulgar strength of the mother *fist*, which, as the *OED* indicates, captures the meaning of the "hand that one writes." And that "one" who writes, as one archaic meaning of *Fulke* has it, is the folk. The French-English compound discloses the hand that claims the aristocrat as the son of the folk. Facing the Gordon is to discover an encrypted genealogy of the mother hand by which the aristocrat grasps the vulgar wording in place before the imposition of the name of the father, when the knot is cut.

We have found something. A man who compounds with his mother, or an author who is not a father. Consider another possibility: that this is neither the narrator nor Juan speaking, but Fitz-Fulke announcing "herself" by commanding Juan's response—an assertion of authority whose only precedent is Tom's cursed greeting. Who is Fitz-Fulke to Juan or Juan to Fitz-Fulke? Recall the knot: Gorgon → Gordian → Geordian → Gordon. What distinguishes canto 16 from all of Lord Byron's other works is that it betrays not a "contagion of Byronism" but a contagion of *Gordonism*. And the difference is tangible, for if, in the landspeech of canto 16, we hear Geordian Gordon, we see in the robes of the Friar the figure of what matters in and for the poem: not the demoralized "wreck" of "Minerva's self . . . weak and shaftless e'en to mortal glance" but the potent figure of the commonplace that invents and commands belief (*Curse of Minerva*, ll. 75, 82). Geordian Gordon is the knotted signature of the writer before he is entitled to be an author, before he enters on the social and symbolic gradient of minor to major, while he is still his mother's child.[73] It is also the fisted signature that knots together the differend of the poet's given name with the period and the genre in which *Juan* appears: the Georgian era and the Georgic mode compounded in the "likeness of a Georgian page" (*Giaour*, l. 456) and with that demotic "Geordy" who slangs through the dingier neighborhoods of Newcastle-on-Tyne.[74] Geordian Gordon prescribes the failure of any patriarchal name to claim property in this text as its cause or context.

Impossibly heeding the unheard authorial command, "Carpe diem," Juan luckily seizes what matters and grasps his maker: the poet as mother, the poet dragged, degraded to the status of George Gordon, who is a pre-oedipal figure with no title to what he makes, and who truthfully appears in the poem masquerading as what Lyotard calls a "monster of originary invention."[75] For the maker to embody himself in this talismanically mimetic moment is to compound with the maternal figure. "Detached from the object," Adorno aphorizes Romantically, "autonomy is fictitious."[76] The apparition fulfills the exiled lord's promise to his countrymen that he will "come" and fulfills it not as Myrrha-ed spectacle but in the spirit with which it was made: "Recollect—that I shall come (if at all) as strictly *incog.* as is possible in an age of tittle tattle and newspapers" (*BLJ* 10:89). In materializing for his character "he" performs the genealogy of "his" Romantic strength, renewing an incognito autonomy that antedates republican virtue and is safe from corruption because clenched to, twined with, the object more inextricably even than man is with his land. Byron's strength is Geordian Gordon's strength: what cuts through the cords may be the swordlike "one word," but what invents the knot that is the world is the *first* word, which is not a single word—be it divine fiat, paternal ejaculation, or childish cry—but a compound, which is the "common place" of multifarious voices, a matrix for the profusion of new phrases as of new families.

Fitz-Fulke does not describe what Juan sees. Nor does it fracture the object of fascination. In a remarkable tour de force the hand reaches out to manhandle a bust (the head-and-shoulders icon of conqueror and poet) and feels a bust (the breast of a breathing figure): the image is of a Galatea who writes her own transformation from "hard" stone to "glowing" flesh as a response to an intimate touch (recall Donna Julia's "glowing arm" in canto 1). This is not iconoclasm but a metamorphosis all the more credible for its unrepresentability. Unrepresentability is at the farthest remove from the unspeakable; there is nought that cannot be spoken. A similar ineffability affects *Fitz-Fulke*. Both fist and name are each (k)not there in this impossible idiom that successfully performs what Coleridge (commenting on Milton's depiction of Death) called the substitution of "a grand feeling of the unimaginable for a mere image."[77] We may call this writing act "equivocation," in order to render the multifariousness of its voicings ("Fitz-Fulke!" knots narrator, Juan, French, English, man, woman, exclamatory, imperative) but not at the cost of suggesting that the phrase *avoids* solving some problem, such as the problem of a double figure. *Fitz-Fulke* quite literally compounds, whether as a mind-forged pun or as a word conjured forth by what the text neologizes as a "*not o'ergrown.*"

Juan knows what Cain could by definition (it is the condition of being named) learn only too late: the strong word is not the thing that cuts but the speaking out that compounds with an auditor who is obligated to reply.

"Fitz-Fulke!"—the materialization of Geordian Gordon—is the nightmare of enlightenment: the figure of the ever-undead, the pale Gordonian who has conquered the grave and who, against all reason, continues to obligate the present to answer to an inextirpably anachronistic "past." The specter that materializes on the ramparts of modernity is, in Claude Lefort's moving words, a "sense of immortality" that

> proves to be bound up with the conquest of a place *which cannot be taken,* which is invulnerable, because it is the place of someone—who is neither an individual in the contemporary sense of the word nor a subject in the philosophical sense of the word—who, by accepting all that is most singular in his life, refuses to submit to the coordinates of space and time and who is so disproportionate that he sets free breaks and relations which no one before him has experienced and which we now experience through him.[78]

The Revolutionary Text

> *[Byron] admits that it amuses him to* hoax *people, as he calls it, and that when each person, at some future day, will give their different statements of him, they will be so contradictory, that* all *will be doubted, — an idea that gratifies him exceedingly!*
>
> *Lady Blessington,* Conversations with Lord Byron

I have spoken of *Juan* rather than Lord Byron, because although Byron could certainly grasp this reading of the English Cantos, he could not confirm it. The landspeech of the psychotic text breaks with the biographical model of explanation. Recently, Marjorie Levinson has succinctly updated a commonplace of Byron criticism. "Byronic irony," she writes, "no matter how inclusive, is always recuperated by the biographical subject-form coded in all the poems."[79] 'T is against *that* that I am writing. Levinson's categorical proposition of Byron's shortcoming is the kind of tautological move that our reading of Byron's reviews has made familiar. It confirms the recuperative effect of the biographical code by performing its own recuperation, the distillation of the Byronic text into a stereotype—reducing a picture of the text into the schema that was *posited* in order for the picture to be formed. Thus description yields to another description valorized as more abbreviated, economical, and formal. But if one reads Lord Byron's writing rather than descriptions of it and of him (which, as critics from the *British* to Jerome McGann show, do come to the same thing) and answers the prescriptives it phrases, it is unnecessary, even

(Hume would compound with Lyotard here) impossible, to translate that writing into some cognitive phrase, like the "biographical subject-form" of Byron.

Levinson's formulation might be aligned with Raymond Williams's distinction between cynicism and opposition. "It was impossible not to be cynical about it," Williams writes "while the game was being played, but equally this cynicism never reached the point of renouncing the advantages which were being played for; that is why it is cynicism, rather than real opposition."[80] Williams does not have Byron in mind, but he might as well have. His definition of cynicism shares with Levinson's version of Byron the criterion that something is kept in reserve, whether a "biographical subject-form" or "advantages"; indeed, in Byron they come to the same thing, for the biographical subject-form is the basis for the advantages of money and fame that the copyrighted Byron acquires, despite his claim to be "born for opposition."[81] The difference between Williams's account and Levinson's is that whereas Levinson totalizes a mode of Romantic irony in which she mimetically participates, Williams's standard is not an a priori judgment but an ethical standard. To the ironist Williams's ethic looks naive, for the ironist knows that there is no renunciation (even the renunciation of determinacy) that cannot be cynically redescribed as working to the advantage of that one who is cited as the "I" who renounces.

Psychosis is the last refuge against irony. *Juan* fails to renounce for the same reason it fails to oppose—because there is no position on which to take a stand independent of the phenomenon it would satirize. The conventional Carlylean question of what standards of moral behavior *Juan* affirms looks facetious in light of the absence of any "here and now" (as distinct from the contemporary, of which there is a surplus) in the world of the poem. Moreover, the absence of the "here and now" cannot in good faith be the subject of authorial complaint, for Lord Byron was the willing accomplice in its passing. Landless, he did not lose or renounce his patrimony; with greater and lesser degrees of sentimentality he sold off Rochdale and Newstead, thereby exchanging the real supports of his entitlement to privilege *or* renunciation for the ready cash that he (cynically?) proclaimed, "is Virtue" (*BLJ* 9:113). I mean to say not that the "here and now" has become emptied in relation to some earlier historical moment of full self-presence and autonomy, but that the rhetorical nature of the reality in which stands must be taken has become intensely clear. The insistence of that rhetoricity is as fatal to the moral system of civic humanism as the commodification of land is fatal to the aristocracy. But the end of a moral system is not the end of ethics, nor is the end of the aristocracy the end of an ethos of excellence. If it is psychotic to insist on giving ethical prescriptions without any ground except that of the landspeech in which the prescriptions are made, it is also democratic. Anyone can be a psychotic. Anyone can speak out. And anyone speaking well (that is, obligingly) links with the phrase of another, a Tom or a Fitz-Fulke. Democratic politics makes strange fist-fellows.

The contagion of Gordonism has no standing in the copyrighted biographical subject named Byron. Hence *Juan* satisfies the law's criterion (the only one that counts) for a revolutionary text as enunciated by Mr. Shadwell, who found that the objectionable "passages [of *Juan*] are not of such a nature as to overturn the property of it."[82] The punning implications of *Fitz-Fulke* have no nature that is not unnatural, and the knot of this passage is signed for by a George Gordon, who, having suffered a civil death (twice over—see below), has no standing before the law. Geordian Gordon overturns Lord Byron's or anyone else's right to property in the text. In August 1823 the courts could read no more: "The copyright of *Don Juan* was ruled invalid by Sir John Leach, the Vice-Chancellor, after a piratical printer named William Dugdale asked to publish a work, which, upon reconsideration, was declared licentious if not libelous."[83] The text had become revolutionary by having overturned the rights to property in it—by publishing, as Lord Byron promised, "past fame and profit" (*BLJ* 10:126). Because renunciation always cites some privilege, it can never take one to what Serres called the "zero level of possession"; *Juan*'s landspeech, however, unknowingly goes to the level of "nought," which is not nothing or nihilism but a compounding before property is assigned and classes are denominated. This, then, is not *Byron's* revolution. It has no empirical referent—no proper place or hour of its occurrence. No kingdoms fell in consequence: no petticoats were raised or kept down.[84] The revolutionary text haunts the enclosure of the contemporary, the voice of the unextinguished past heralding the impossible idiom of the future.

Beyond Biography

In an essay on Locke's "intellectual akrasia," his ability to hold and pursue ostensibly incompatible lines of thought, John Dunn offers this apology for his biographical approach:

> If the range of individual plasticity characteristically increased throughout the human lifetime, instead of decreasing, a biographical approach to the constitution of the self would be merely perverse. But since in most (if not in all) cases, it very definitely does not do so . . . there is . . . real merit in

seeing the earlier stages in the constitution of social identity as setting relatively firm constraints on the range of credal and affective potentiality for an individual.[85]

Lord Byron inhabits the parenthesis in Dunn's formulation of what I take to be a liberal version of the way social identity is formed. *Juan* is the most striking evidence of an increased and increasing plasticity in the career of any English writer of the nineteenth century. It is a plasticity beyond Lord Byron, who heroizes himself as the emancipator of the Greeks and ventures off to an admirable death in an admirable cause. Because of this plasticity (or psychosis, if you will), a biographical account, even a biographical account attuned to the social projection or coding of the individual life as career or product line, would be a perverse constraint on a social existence that is no identity, and that matters just so far as it challenges the kinds of constraints presupposed by the liberal version of social development.

What is the referent for the biographical subject-form of the writer of *Juan?* How would it be identified except tautologically? Perhaps by those empirical objects and canonical icons associated with the bodily form that gives Byron integrity as a thing? That integrity was in some sense a matter of public record. Busts of Byron were advertised by William Hone on the same page as those of Napoleon. His portrait was often taken, bought, sold, stolen, and exchanged—usually at the instigation of Murray (Colonel Parker to Byron's Elvis), who had the most considerable investment in the integrity of a certain biographical subject-form. As Murray frankly acknowledged, his "name" was "attached" to Byron's "fame."[86] But as *Juan* came to exceed the bounds of what Murray could tolerate even for the sake of profit, so, coincidentally, Byron's body came to exceed the iconographic code by which all perversity was ironically to be recuperated.

Byron had always been subject to wild fluctuations of weight and shape, partly as a result of his attempt to fit himself to the dandiacal pattern. His early letters avidly calibrate a weight loss that carries him to the verge of unrecognizability: "Since *we* met they tell me I am grown taller, & so much thinner from Illness and violent Exercise, that many who had lived with me in habits of Intimacy, even old *Schoolfellows* found great difficulty in acknowledging me to be the *same person (BLJ* 1:133).[87] He describes how, slave to the "Fashion," he controls his weight "by means of hard exercise, abstinence." Those techniques were abetted by an "occasional complaint which attacks me on every excursion to town" (*BLJ* 1:145). The bulimic cycle of binge and purge continued for most of Byron's life, but the fluctuations became more extreme during his last years in Venice. Even while disputing the account that he had fattened to a "stupendous" degree, Byron conceded in 1819 that his "size [was] certainly increased considerably" (*BLJ* 6:174); and Newton Hanson described a Byron who "had grown very fat, his shoulders broad and round, and the knuckles of his hands . . . lost in fat" (*BLJ* 6:78n). By 1823, at any rate, when an evident decline in his popularity ("the run against me") led him to contemplate setting up "a printing office of my own" in order to publish the remaining cantos of *Don Juan* in "my own way" (*BLJ* 10:108, 70), he had thinned drastically, as if registering public disfavor on his body. He joked about his attenuation to Augusta, and to Richard Belgrave Hoppner he described himself as being "as thin as a Skeleton" (*BLJ* 10:111–12). One may be tempted to apply Bakhtin's concept of the "grotesque body [that] outgrows its own self, transgressing its own body, in which it conceives a new, second body."[88] But like the Freudian concepts of the uncanny and the primally antithetical word, the grotesque body too readily subjects excessive phenomena to the "problem of a double figure." Byron's swings more accurately reproduced the fluctuations of Addison's figure of Credit as a hysterical female, whose shape was preternaturally sensitive to the swings of the market (*Spectator*, no. 3). Like Addison's Credit or J. M. Barrie's Tinkerbell, Byron's physique was the public's bubble. If people believed Byron, he swelled; if not, he thinned to almost nothing.

To the reader of Byron's texts, however, the strongest impression is not of two bodies, fat and thin, but of a way of writing about the body that makes it matter by separating it from the iconographic codes in which it had been entrapped. Here is one of the most peculiar of the many strange commentaries of Byron on an appearance without any natural form:

> I am glad that you like her picture.—Mr. West is not in fault about mine— for I was *then*—what it appears—but since that time—and indeed since you saw me—I am very much reduced—partly by uncertain health in the winter and partly by the rigorous abstinence necessary to preserve it.—But it is so far better—that it made me more like what I used to be ten years ago—in part at least.—Kinnaird—who had not seen me for two years and a half— was as much struck with the *re-alteration* at present—as he had been with the *former* alteration in the fourth or fifth year since I left England." (*BLJ* 10:198; to Lady Hardy, June 10, 1823)

Whatever Byron's body actually *is*, representing it has become a matter of cross-referencing among various sightings and depictions. Lord Byron has lost property in a body that is recognizable as the body of Byron not by the application of some abstract code but only by virtue of the most careful assemblage of disparate bits of information from the accumulated pile of Byroniana. Because the body of the writer of the English Cantos has been fully textualized, it can give no metaphorical coherence to the metaphysical concept of a biographical subject-form.

This apparently paradoxical notion can be circumstantially grounded in John Cam Hobhouse's remarkable eyewitness account of his visit to the body of the dead Lord Byron as it lay in state in London in July 1824. The body had been shipped back from Greece in a cask of spirits, fully intact except for a piece here and a piece there. Hobhouse, who in rosier days had written to his friend, "I pant for a sight of you as the hart after the water brooks,"[89] manages, on the occasion of this observation, to be both matter-of-fact and Gothic. "Hanson [Byron's family attorney] had just been looking at Lord Byron," he records:

> He told me he should not have known him except he had looked at his ear and his foot—Kinnaird went into the room to look at him—I followed—& drawn by an irresistible inclination—though I expected to be overcome by it—approached the coffin—I drew nearer by degrees—till I caught a view of the face—it did not bear the slightest resemblance to my dear friend— the mouth was distorted & half open showing those teeth in which poor fellow he once so prided himself quite discoloured by spirits—his upper lip was shaded with red mustachios which gave a totally new character to his face—his cheeks were long and bagged over the jaw—his nose was quite prominent at the bridge & sank in between the eyes—perhaps from the extraction of the brain—his eye brows shaggy & lowering—his forehead marked with hack marks probably—his eyelids closed & sunken—I presume the eyeballs having been removed when he was embalmed—his skin was like dull yellow parchment—So complete was the change that I was not affected as I thought I should be—It did not seem to be Byron—I was not moved so much scarcely as at the sight of his hand writing or any thing that I knew to be his—I did not remark what Hanson told me he had observed in his life time that his left eye was much larger than his right.[90]

Even the body as what it actually *is* resists Byronic encoding. Hobhouse's blazon of the unhaloed corpse—so different from the decaying body of Greece at the beginning of *The Giaour*—aims to dissociate Lord Byron as friend, author, and biographical subject from the mere dead thing that lies embalmed before him. The body has returned from the symbolic to the real—there is nothing to be made out of the mutilation of the face, done not by the Sandman for the sake of punishment but by the embalmer for the sake of expediency. Hobhouse (who never faltered in his service to the

Byronic biographical subject-form) refuses to recognize this as Lord Byron (and if Hobhouse denies it, if Hanson accepts it only on ocular evidence that Hobhouse finds novel and unreliable, whose confirmation is to be preferred?). On one level this refusal is in complete accord with Hobhouse's zeal to burn the *Memoirs:* any fact that could violate the picture of the Lord Byron he wanted preserved in public memory was to be denied or destroyed. Superficially, the *Memoirs* present a harder case, since they are something that Hobhouse "knew to be his." But it is just because Hobhouse knew them to be "his" that he wanted them destroyed in the name of the book of Byron that Hobhouse would save from contamination by the "hand writing" that authorized their publication.

This repudiation of Lord Byron's authorization, however, is not simply a matter of Hobhouse's denial of the problem of a double figure and his dogged commitment to whatever scriptural truths favor the myth. The hierarchy of recognition between "hand writing" and face was consistently promoted by those poems from Byron's hand that render the face as ground for an indelible and unmistakable signature. Yet that hierarchy, which the orthodox Hobhouse violates to Lord Byron's greater glory, is itself undermined by the Byronic text. The Byronic text does not enfranchise Hobhouse's *particular* license; it could not. But it does assure that such misrecognition will be commonplace by authorizing, as it were, the misrecognition of the biographical subject through a radical abbreviation and ineradicable deformation of the "hand writing" that could sign Lord Byron's will and lay claim to property in his works.

We have already examined the political implications of the stenograph in the discussions of *Childe Harold IV* and *Marino Faliero.* The topic is engaged with characteristic panache by Cobbett in the chapter "Points and Marks" of his *Grammar of the English Language:*

> As a mark of *Abbreviation*, the full point is used: as, "Mr. Mrs." But, I know of hardly any other words that ought to be abbreviated; and if these were not, it would be all the better. People may indulge themselves in this practice, until at last, they come to write the greater part of their words in single letters. The frequent use of abbreviations is always a mark of slovenliness and of vulgarity. I have known Lords abbreviate almost the half of their words: it was, very likely, because they did not know how to spell them to the end.[91]

Whether or not aristocrats were indeed literate, it was part of the spell they once cast that they did not need to spell things out. The scrawling abbreviation of words had become a kind of signature of lordship, which asserted its inalienable sovereignty by a privileged neglect of the orthographical conventions that constrained bourgeois property transactions.[92] As the fair hand had been introduced into the British aristocracy by humanist clerks in an earlier age to register and stabilize the invisible passage of blood, so the adoption of a scrawl attested to the security that could neglect such clerkish concerns as perspicuity. The degradation of the hand to "slovenliness" and "vulgarity" indicates the decisive divergence between aristocratic abbreviation and the refinements of stenography, which were designed to avoid illegibility. In Cobbett's eyes the historical decline of the master to the level of the rustic—that figure whom it is Cobbett's aim to tutor into deliberate autonomy—corresponded to the degradation of his signature.

Lord Byron's hand was difficult to read (he applauded those who could make out his manuscripts), his tendency to abbreviation pronounced (cf. the coded messages to Charles Skinner Matthews), and his signature conspicuously variable: not only did he occasionally alter the spelling of his name from Byron to Burun, but the form of his signature metamorphosed from conventional English orthography to Greek to a scrawl that Marchand reproduces like so:

Such practiced negligence[93] was suspended in January 1822 by the long-awaited death of Lady Noel, Byron's mother-in-law, which according to the separation agreement brought Byron a life interest in a portion of the Wentworth estates. Marchand reports that Byron's "moiety," roughly twenty-five hundred pounds, doubled his income. But the supplement came with a condition: by the terms of the will Byron was required to take the Noel arms and thenceforth to sign himself, legibly, *Noel Byron*.[94] In order to derive any benefit from his mother-in-law's estate he had to consent to surrender his birthright and subject himself to what was in effect a copyright: thenceforth any use of his own name by Noel Byron would be, like plagiarism, a technical violation of the law that governed the sign by which he could authorize his writings.

There is nothing sanguinary about this change. Unlike the young Byron's accession to the title, this name change does not appear like a gift and makes no reference to a natural succession. Moreover, Noel Byron obediently fulfilled the will of the law to the letter. As we have already had occasion to observe, however, there is no letter, no matter how nakedly literal, without the spirit of romance. Because only Byron's subjection to the law (to the will, right, and fate of property) matters, it is part of the logic of the law (as the history of stenography in the courtroom proves) to permit abbreviation of the law's dictates. Hence it is in the spirit of the law and part of the fate he assumes for Lord Byron customarily to abbreviate *Noel Byron* as *N.B.*, for it is only as a citation of the dictate of the law that the signature counts. The intention of the law is achieved more efficiently, more unmistakably, more literally, by abbreviation of the name than by spelling it out.

This narrowing of the name to a citation produced a coincidence. Byron, according to Leigh Hunt, "delighted, when he took the additional name of Noel . . . to sign himself N.B.,' 'because,' said he, 'Bonaparte and I are the only public persons whose initials are the same'" (*BLJ* 9:171n). Marchand rightly calls this delight "childish," for the coincidence achieved the kind of sweet fit that appealed to the poet when in the mood and manner of Childe Harold.[95] One might also call it Byronic, because the coincidence designates a "holy new alliance" between public figures attained Byronically rather than Napoleonically—attained, that is, inadvertently, without the exercise of arms or the expense of men. Lord Byron had expressed a similar delight in a journal entry of 1821: "Murray, the magnificent (the illustrious publisher of that name) has just sent me a Java gazette—I know not why, or wherefore. Pulling it out, by way of curiosity, we found it to contain a dispute (the said Java gazette) on Moore's merits and mine. . . . There is *fame* for you at six and twenty! Alexander had conquered India at the same age; but I doubt if he was disputed about, or his conquests compared with those of the Indian Bacchus, at Java" (*BLJ* 8:27). Byron's fame is not, like Alexander's and Semiramis's, the result of his imperial conquests. *N.B.* claims for Byron all due credit for the insight that "great names are nothing more than nominal" (*DJ* 1:1). Lord Byron's fame *is* his achievement, his empire the report of his name around the world.

Or almost Byron's achievement: it is Murray who sends Byron the newspaper, and it is Murray, owner of the copyright, who profits from the fame. The conjunction of Byron with Moore, like the alliance with Napoleon in *N.B.*, remarks once again on the transience of a celebrity that is linked to imperial gesture or empirical conquest and wedded to the regime of a proper and propertied name. As Hobhouse reports from Paris in 1814,

> The present uppermost are taking every pain, pitiful enough as I must think them, to efface every positive memorial of the last reign. There is however some excuse to be made for blotting out the insignia of the dethroned Emperor, as by a vanity not to be pardoned, that fallen Star took care to insert his imperial initial in every ovolo and cavetto of sculpture, every medallion or other ornament of glazing or painting & every tissue of embroidery or palace furniture. Marbles & stuccoes, temples and chambers,

insides and outsides, ceilings & floors, domes and chair bottoms all bear the redoubtable N or did bear them, for I can assure you that the enemies of tyranny have made a very laudable progress in eradicating these signs of subjection.[96]

As the Napoleonic will make its farcical return in the Eighteenth Brumaire, so Byron will parody this imperial appropriation by having the name *Don Juan* painted on the sail of P. B. Shelley's new boat, named, at William Trelawny's suggestion, after the poem. Edward Williams recorded Shelley's chagrin and the attempts to undo the damage: "Unbent the main sail and took it to Magliana to see if the letter could be erased which Lord B[yron] in his contemptible vanity or for some other purpose begged Roberts to inscribe on the boat's main sail—all efforts useless." According to Mary Shelley, the evidence of tyrannical imposition was finally removed: "At length the piece has been taken out and the reefs put, so that the sail does not look worse. I do not know what Lord Byron will say, but Lord and Poet as he is, he could not be allowed to make a coal barge of our boat."[97] Byron's Napoleonic "vanity" led him to an imperial gesture that degraded its object, stimulated resistance, and ended in the piecemeal eradication of the magical name *Don Juan* (Mary Shelley is at one with the outraged reviewer of the *Courier*, who had described *Juan*'s author as an "unsexed Circe")[98] that could metamorphose a trim sailboat into a coal barge. The excision of the letter recalls the "gelding" of *Juan* itself insisted on by Murray, Gifford, and Hobhouse—and had quite the same success as the expurgation of Martial by learned men recounted in canto 1 of the poem: in that volume the repressed returns in an appendix; in Shelley's story the repressed returns as a shipwreck. All things considered, a coal barge might have been a more prudent vehicle for an Ariel unsuited to a nautical existence.

But Byron's vanity was subject to its own undoing. Another coincidence unsettled his delighted identification with Napoleon. Byron's comment to Leigh Hunt is not his only expression of delight in the character that the law had inadvertently bestowed. He concludes a letter to Moore, "P.S.—You see the great advantage of my new signature; it may either stand for 'Nota Bene' or 'Noel Byron,' and, as such, will save much repetition, in writing either books or letters" (*BLJ* 9:171). There is nothing childish about this pleasure: it is the hardheaded perception of a poet who, knowing that there is "nothing but time" and that time is money, can justly conclude that "Cash is Virtue" (*BLJ* 9:113). *N.B.* is a good abbreviation because it saves time and thus money. Thus Byron eagerly summons his lawyer to "send me a Seal with the new arms—& a smaller one with the Coronet and initials of *N B* upon it for notes &c &c" and concludes with the salutation:

> Believe me
> yours ever & truly
> NOEL BYRON.

> (*BLJ* 9:115)

We must believe him true (or "sincere," in Matthew Arnold's vocabulary) because we must believe him; and that obligation is no longer grounded in the dynastic prestige of "the" family motto; it is here commanded from a position of newly compounded strength. Similarly, the citation of *nota bene* is not just another Hobhousean economy—no more than the commitment to publish past "fame and profit" was driven by economic motives. Lord Byron exploits the contingency of the way letters fall to compound a motto that is a "new one" of extraordinary tactical versatility and trenchant ethical import. Whenever Lord Byron signs *N.B.* he not only identifies himself with the Wentworth property, aligns himself with Napoleon's destiny, and adopts the stenographer's transcriptive economy, he also commands: Mark well! The adverb *well* presupposes a value in excess of the economy that the adjective *good* designs; that is, *N.B.* not only commands "pay attention to" but commands "attention" by a "good" (virtuous? ethical? colorful? strong?) marking. To read Byron's signature in(to) his text is to mark well. To mark well is to answer in kind the wholly illegitimate ethical imperative that is the proper citation of Byron's legal name. Every time someone admonishes (anytime it is admonished) to mark well, it will be a citation of that Byron whose right to that acknowledgment, and to all the royalties appertaining to it, has been fantastically assigned to him by law, a right sealed by the lord's own notable performance of an extralegal, well-placed imperative each time he signs his name.

N.B. is a citation but also a site—indeed, a parasite. Imperially confident in its displacement of indigenous populations and its appropriation of the European past, *Childe Harold IV* subscribes to the proposition that "power is nothing but the occupation of space."[99] But the poem also represents the fragility of occupation, the fictionality of physical space. The compound abbreviation *N.B.* is the mark of an alternate, neologistic power not accrued but performed by the tactical occupation of a marginal space—a strength not subject to ruin or annihilation.

N.B. might be apposite to an indefinite number of sites/cites, interpolated anywhere along the line that twines from George Gordon to Lord Byron to Noel Byron, from the Elgin Marbles to the Jungfrau. The fate of the law and the name of the father are undone by the comedy of a contingent character, what Hobhouse calls the "anagram of [his] ineffable name."[100] That character perverts the law or, rather, as in the case of Cain, whom Byron represents as God's first and inevitably errant publication, *marks* the law's perversion by foreign characters that aboriginally compound with it. As the fifth Lord Byron had shortened his sword in the dark in order to turn on his foe and mark him with fatal strength, so the sixth Lord Byron shortens his hand to turn on the language of his land and entwine his character. *N.B.* renders the aberration in the law that returns as an ethical injunction ever entwined with the language of the Roman West, haunting its every margin, remarking on its every word.

I shall conclude with this knottily Byronic commonplace: The hand that marks may be remarked. "I am truly sorry," Lord Byron wrote to Lord Blessington in April 1823,

> that I cannot accompany you in your ride this morning, owing to a violent pain in my face, arising from a wart to which I by medical advice applied a caustic. Whether I put too much, I do not know; but the consequence is, that not only I have been put to some pain, but the peccant part and its immediate environ are as black as if the printer's devil had marked me for an author. As I do not wish to frighten your horses or their riders, I shall postpone waiting upon you until six o' clock, when I hope to have subsided into a more christianlike resemblance to my fellow-creatures. My infliction has partially extended even to my fingers; for on trying to get the black from off my upper lip at least, I have only transfused a portion thereof to my right hand, and neither lemon-juice nor eau de Cologne, nor any other eau have been able as yet to redeem it also from a more inky appearance than is either proper or pleasant. But "out, damn'd spot"—you may have perceived something of the kind yesterday; for on my return, I saw that during my visit it had increased, was increasing, and ought to be diminished; and I could not help laughing at the figure I must have cut before you. (*BLJ* 10:148)

Lord Byron suffers a contagion of writing disfiguring his face and increasing past all reckoning. In the event, the spot was to be stopped only by undertaking a biographically satisfying regression to the humanist mythos of emancipation and the beautiful death. In Greece, of course. Hobhouse was the first of many faithful executors of that biography. Because he was sworn to that faith, Hobhouse cannot be blamed for refusing to recognize the decidedly unbeautiful body steeping in spirit, whose "parchment" skin and "forehead marked with *hack* marks" register the unsparing application of the caustic of satire to the incurable itch of scribbling. Hobhouse cannot be blamed for looking for a corpse rather than reading the text of his notable friend. Yet if Hobhouse had listened as well as looked, he might have heard the lordly hack laughing at the ghastly figure he has cut before us.

Notes

Chapter 1: Theorizing Byron's Practice

· 1. David Hume, *A Treatise of Human Nature*, ed. L. A. Selby-Bigge, 2d ed., rev. P. H. Nidditch (Oxford: Clarendon Press, 1978), p. 363.

2. See Charles Levin, "Art and the Sociological Ego: Value from a Psychoanalytic Perspective," in *Life after Postmodernism: Essays on Value and Culture*, ed. John Fekete (New York: St. Martin's, 1987), pp. 23–24.

3. Michel Foucault, *Power/Knowledge: Selected Interviews and Other Writings*, ed. Colin Gordon, trans. Gordon et al. (New York: Pantheon, 1980), pp. 88–89.

4. *Burkean* might also be appropriate here as the name for the project of reference that adapts Hume's epistemological argument to changed political circumstances. Edmund Burke identifies the "learned and reflecting part of this kingdom" as those "persuaded that all things ought to be done with reference, and referring all to the point of reference to which all should be directed" (*Reflections on the Revolution in France* [1790; rpt. Harmondsworth: Penguin, 1968], pp. 195–96).

5. "The discovery of Newton was not the discovery of a fact, but the generalization of a particular fact" (*Edinburgh Review* [January 1803], p. 474). See also *Memoirs and*

Correspondence of Francis Horner, M.P., ed. Leonard Horner, 2 vols. (Boston: Little, Brown, 1853), for Horner's detailed account of his systematic study of law, which, as he says, involved "arranging it in my head under general principles" in order to "secure the assistance of an artificial memory" (1:93–94).

6. Michel Serres, *The Parasite*, trans. Lawrence R. Schehr (Baltimore: Johns Hopkins Univ. Press, 1982), p. 215.

7. For an account of the attack on substance (which he associates with Locke), see Levin, "Art and the Sociological Ego," p. 24.

8. Hume, *Treatise*, p. 139.

9. Jerome J. McGann, *"Don Juan" in Context* (Chicago: Univ. of Chicago Press, 1976), passim.

10. For a good recent account of Addison's rhetorical strategies, see Michael Ketcham, *Transparent Designs: Reading, Performance, and Form in the "Spectator" Papers* (Athens: Univ. of Georgia Press, 1985), pp. 11–26.

11. The best account of the proliferation of these regularities in the eighteenth century is Neil McKendrick's "Commercialization and the Economy," in *The Birth of a Consumer Society*, ed. Neil McKendrick, J. H. Plumb, and John Brewer (Bloomington: Univ. of Indiana Press, 1982), pp. 9–33. Addison's strategic exploitation of the commercial and political advantages of this proliferation argues that Jon P. Klancher severely foreshortens the historical narrative when he ascribes to such late-eighteenth-century journals as James Anderson's *Bee* (1790) the policy of "colonizing social groups previously excluded from [the reading public]" (*The Making of English Reading Audiences, 1790–1832* [Madison: Univ. of Wisconsin Press, 1987], pp. 24–26).

12. On the founding of the British Museum, see Richard D. Altick, *The Shows of London* (Cambridge, Mass.: Harvard Univ. Press, 1978), p. 25.

13. Benjamin Boyce, *The Benevolent Man: A Life of Ralph Allen of Bath* (Cambridge, Mass.: Harvard Univ. Press, 1967), p. 52.

14. Ibid., p. 18.

15. *Ralph Allen's Own Narrative, 1720–1761*, ed. Adrian E. Hopkins, Postal History Society Special Series no. 8 (Bath, 1960), p. 25.

16. Ibid., p. 17.

17. Ibid., p. 25.

18. See Howard Anderson and Irvin Ehrenpreis, "The Familiar Letter in the Eighteenth Century: Some Generalizations," in *The Familiar Letter in the Eighteenth Century*, ed. Howard Anderson, Philip B. Daghlian, and Irvin Ehrenpreis (Lawrence: Univ. of Kansas Press, 1966), pp. 269–70.

19. See Horner's discussion of the central banking system in his anonymous review of Henry Thornton's *An Inquiry into the Nature and Effects of the Paper Credit of Great Britain*, in the inaugural issue of the *Edinburgh Review* (October 1802), pp. 186–90.

20. Hume, *Treatise*, p. 146.

21. Julia Kristeva, "The Ethics of Linguistics," in *Desire and Language: A Semiotic Approach in Literature and Art*, ed. Leon S. Roudiez, trans. Thomas Gora, Alice Jardine, and Leon S. Roudiez (New York: Columbia Univ. Press, 1980), p. 25.

22. Karl Marx, "The Eighteenth Brumaire of Louis Bonaparte," in *Karl Marx and Frederick Engels: Selected Works* (New York: International Publishers, 1968), p. 99.

23. Harold Perkin, *Origins of Modern English Society* (London: Routledge, 1969); Lawrence and Jeanne C. Fawtier Stone, *An Open Elite? England 1540–1880* (Oxford:

Clarendon Press, 1984); J. C. D. Clark, *English Society 1688–1832* (Cambridge: Cambridge Univ. Press, 1985); J. V. Beckett, *The Aristocracy in England 1660–1914* (Oxford: Basil Blackwell, 1986); John Cannon, *Aristocratic Century: The Peerage of Eighteenth-Century England* (Cambridge: Cambridge Univ. Press, 1984); Immanuel Wallerstein, *The Modern World System III: The Second Era of Great Expansion of the Capitalist World Economy, 1730–1840* (San Diego: Academic Press, 1989).

24. Beckett, *Aristocracy*, pp. 43 and 13.

25. J. G. A. Pocock, *Virtue, Commerce, and History: Essays on Political Thought and History, Chiefly in the Eighteenth Century* (Cambridge: Cambridge Univ. Press, 1985), p. 195.

26. A. V. Dicey, quoted in Clark, *English Society*, p. 7.

27. David Castronovo, *The English Gentleman: Images and Ideals in Literature and Society* (New York: Ungar, 1987), p. 7. Although Castronovo quotes Bailey's Dictionary to make this distinction, he also notes that since the fifteenth century *gentleman* had been a "designation of rank" for the gentry and had thus become desynonymized from *noble* (p. 9). J. Lawrence observes in *On the Nobility of the British Gentry*, "It is only since the gentry permitted the plebians to encroach on them that the peers began to disdain the title of gentleman, a title which the first peers, nay, the princes of the blood, would not have disdained" (quoted in Beckett, *Aristocracy*, p. 10).

28. See Pierre Bourdieu, *Distinction: A Social Critique of the Judgment of Taste*, trans. Richard Nice (Cambridge, Mass.: Harvard Univ. Press, 1984), pp. 23–24.

29. Michael McKeon, *The Origins of the English Novel, 1600–1740* (Baltimore: Johns Hopkins University Press, 1987), p. 155.

30. Here is Charles James Fox, during the parliamentary debate on the Quebec Government Bill (May 11, 1791): "Nor could any government be a fit one for British subjects to live under, which did not contain its due weight of aristocracy, because that he considered to be the proper poise of the constitution, the balance that equalized and meliorated the powers of the other two extreme branches, and gave stability and firmness to the whole" (paraphrased in Cannon, *Aristocratic Century*, p. 64). Fox's "economic" explanation of the aristocracy—its importance as a weight—is the British version of the evacuation of specificity attached to the word *aristocrat* in revolutionary France, as attested by Thomas Paine in a 1790 letter to Edmund Burke: "The Term Aristocrat is used here, similar to the Word Tory in America;—it in general means an Enemy to the Revolution, and is used without that peculiar meaning formerly affixed to Aristocracy" (quoted in *The Correspondence of Edmund Burke*, ed. Alfred Cobban and Robert A. Smith [Chicago: Univ. of Chicago Press, 1967], 7:68). Both Burke's career and Byron's occur in the wake of this emptying of the meaning of *aristocracy:* the former by giving it a transcendental and corporate identity, the latter by reoccupying the term and reinfusing it with its disturbing peculiarity.

For a searching discussion of the history of the "gentry controversy," which attends to the ideological implications of the classification of gentry and peerage, to the conflict between class and status as principles of social categorization, and to the destabilization of categories that occurred in seventeenth- and eighteenth-century Great Britain, see McKeon, *Origins of the English Novel*, pp. 159–66. It will be seen that the argument prosecuted here, like that of J. H. Hexter and J. G. A. Pocock, favors what McKeon calls "a strict identification of the middle class with a commercial bourgeoisie" and an insistence on the anachronism of "class-based categories" to explain social change (p. 168). Yet this reading of Byron shares McKeon's suspicion of investments in "aristocratic ideology," which, he says, "names the impulse . . . to conceal the perennial alterations in ruling elites as a static unity of status and virtue, the ongoing 'rule of the best.'" And it accepts the ratio by which "the vigor of the aristocratic rationale" comes to bear "something like an inverse relation to the efficacy of its ideology." If, however, it is true that aristocratic social relations "undergo the more elaborate sort of 'theatricalization' that is likely to occur whenever social convention is raised to the level of self-conscious practice" (p. 169), that truth applies to the commercial phenomenon of "Byron," which is a coherent set of aristocratic social relations collaboratively theatricalized so that they could be merchandised to the reading public. It does not apply to the Byronic text, which *rhetoricizes* aristocratic values in the course of a resistance to economistic categorization and in a manner that compounds aristocratic style with an ethos of democratic self-assertion.

31. M. L. Bush observes that "for the peerage and the baronetcy, landownership was not so important as a means of aristocratic identity since the privileges of both remained immune to commoner adoption and clear indicators of noble status" (*The English Aristocracy: A Comparative Synthesis* [Manchester: University Press, 1984], p. 5). According to the Stones, in "a few special areas, it can be argued that by the eighteenth century the conflation of landed and monied interests was so complete that in purely economic terms—though not in status ones—the distinction between the two had lost all meaning" (*Open Elite?* p. 285).

32. Robert Lacey, quoted in Beckett, *Aristocracy*, p. 13.

33. Responding to Leigh Hunt's published query on why he "did not speak oftener" in the House of Lords, Lord Byron vented his oppositional temperament: "When a proper spirit is manifested 'without doors' I will endeavour not to be idle within— . . . my forefathers were of the other side of the question in Charles's days—& the fruit of it was a title & the loss of an enormous property.—If the old struggle comes on—I shall lose the one & shall never regain the other—but—no matter" (*BLJ* 5:19).

34. Friedrich Nietzsche, *On the Genealogy of Morals*, trans. Walter Kaufmann (New York: Random House, 1969), p. 45. The best correspondent to Nietzsche's notion of a "neutral substratum" in Byron criticism is McGann's claim that "Byron has built into *Don Juan* a stylistic base beyond which it is impossible for him to fall" (*"Don Juan" in Context*, pp. 97–99). As we shall see in our discussion of the Oriental tales in chap. 3 below, the so-called base is an indefinitely reproducible code.

35. Ralph Waldo Emerson, "Heroism," in *Essays, First Series*, vol. 1 of *Emerson's Works*, 5 vols. (New York: Bigelow and Brown, n.d.), p. 161.

36. Leslie A. Marchand, *Byron: A Biography*, 3 vols. (New York: Knopf, 1957), 2:722.

37. Castronovo, *English Gentleman*, p. 5.

38. Thomas Moore, *The Life of Lord Byron*, 2 vols. in 1 (Philadelphia, 1854), p. 16.

39. As the Stones inform us, the dream of suddenly being made noble was a common one, fostered by the hazards common to noble life: "Since almost everyone was sick so much of the time, since death even among adults of all ages was still so common that it was taken for granted, since the ministrations of doctors were so often positively lethal, everyone could plausibly dream of the possibilities that might come his way by the hazards of biological chance" (*Open Elite?* p. 195).

40. Paul de Man, *Allegories of Reading* (New Haven: Yale Univ. Press, 1979), pp. 268–69.

41. Arguments that this incompatibility is structural appear in the grammatical

projects of Horne Tooke, William Cobbett, and Samuel Taylor Coleridge, who in prosecution of radically different aims attempted to render genealogocial *aporiae* in terms of etymological evolution. See, for example, Coleridge's discussion of "desynonimization" in the first chapter of the *Biographia Literaria*.

42. De Man, *Allegories*, p. 269.

43. Pierre Bourdieu, *Outline of a Theory of Practice*, trans. Richard Nice (Cambridge: Cambridge Univ. Press, 1977), p. 236, n. 42.

44. Doris Langley Moore, *Lord Byron: Accounts Rendered* (London: John Murray, 1974), p. 50.

45. Perkin, *Origin*, pp. 237ff.

46. The Stones, for example, write of the "virtual abdication of responsibility for local government by the elite in Northamptonshire, and to a lesser degree in Hertfordshire in the eighteenth century" (*Open Elite?* p. 274).

47. E. P. Thompson, "Patrician Society, Plebeian Culture," *Journal of Social History* 7 (Summer 1974): 382–405.

48. Catherine Clément, "The Guilty One," in Hélène Cixous and Catherine Clément, *The Newly Born Woman*, trans. Betsy Wing (Minneapolis: Univ. of Minnesota Press, 1986), p. 7.

49. Marcel Mauss, *The Gift: Forms and Functions of Exchange in Archaic Societies*, trans. Ian Cunnison (New York: Norton, 1974), p. 7. Cf. also Louis Hyde, who ends the introduction to *The Gift: Imagination and the Erotic Life of Property* (New York: Random House, 1983) by describing his concern as "the gift we long for, the gift that, when it comes, speaks commandingly to the soul and irresistibly moves us" (p. xvii).

50. The supreme representation in Lord Byron's poetry of the dynamics of the "thing given" (misnamed "sexual attraction") is *Don Juan* (1:111–12):

> The hand which still held Juan's, by degrees
> Gently, but palpably confirm'd its grasp,
> As if it said, "Detain me, if you please;"
> Yet there's no doubt she only meant to clasp
> His fingers with a pure Platonic squeeze:
> She would have shrunk as from a toad, or asp,
> Had she imagined such a thing could rouse
> A feeling dangerous to a prudent spouse.

> I cannot know what Juan thought of this,
> But what he did, is much what you would do
> His young lip thank'd it with a grateful kiss,
> And then, abash'd at its own joy, withdrew.

51. *Hours of Idleness* was the title of the third volume of Lord Byron's poems, published by John Ridge of Newark, to whom Byron donated the copyright. The first two volumes, *Fugitive Pieces* and *Poems on Various Occasions*, were published privately. *Hours of Idleness* represented the careful revision of the earlier works with an eye to public consumption. Despite his air of nonchalance and his disdain of financial profit, Byron paid keen attention to the merchandising and sales (see the letter of July 13, 1807, to Elizabeth Pigott in *BLJ* 1:126). For the details of the transformation of the manuscripts, see *CPW* 1:360–63.

52. Addison's precept is quoted from the anonymous attack on the code of honor entitled *The Duelist* (London, 1824), p. 110.

53. For a different view, see Kurt Heinzelman's stimulating essay on Byron's career, "Byron's Poetry of Politics: The Economic Basis of the 'Poetical Character,'" *Texas Studies in Literature and Language* 23 (Fall 1981): 361–88. Other useful studies of *Hours of Idleness* are those by Jerome J. McGann, *Fiery Dust* (Chicago: Univ. of Chicago Press, 1968), pp. 3–28; Robert F. Gleckner, *Byron and the Ruins of the Terrestrial Paradise* (Baltimore: Johns Hopkins Press, 1967), pp. 1–26; and Frederick W. Shilstone, *Byron and the Myth of Tradition* (Lincoln: Univ. of Nebraska Press, 1988), pp. 1–15.

54. Brougham's notion of originality is actually a policing of the terrain established for the orderly appearance of recognizable novelty called a "period style." "A period style," according to Rosalind Kraus, "is a special form of coherence that cannot be fraudulently breached. The authenticity folded into the concept *style* is a product of the way style is conceived as having been generated: that is, collectively and unconsciously. Thus an individual could not, by definition, consciously will a style" ("The Originality of the Avant-Garde: A Postmodernist Repetition," in *Art after Modernism: Rethinking Representation*, ed. Brian Wallis [Boston: Godine, 1984], p. 17). And thus Brougham's injunction "Have a style" is a double bind: Lord Byron cannot be a poet unless he has a style and cannot have a style if he wills it.

55. Byron had been forewarned that, as he writes to the Rev. John Becher, "a most violent attack is preparing for me in the next number of the Edinburgh Review," but he regarded this as part of their "System" of "universal attack" and "indiscriminate abuse" (*BLJ* 1:157). He was not prepared for Brougham's personal, discriminate abuse.

56. William Hazlitt's version of Lord Byron reads like applied Brougham. Lord Byron, he complains, "chiefly thinks how he shall display his own power, or vent his spleen, or astonish the reader either by starting new subjects and strains of speculation, or by expressing old ones in a more striking and emphatic manner than they have been expressed before. He cares little what it says, so that he can say it differently from others" ("Lord Byron," in *The Spirit of the Age; or, Contemporary Portraits*, ed. W. Carew Hazlitt, 4th ed. [London: George Bell and sons, 1906], p. 121).

57. Moore, *Life*, p. 17.

58. The entry continues: "It is said . . . that the title of lord was first given to deformed persons in the reign of Richard III from several persons labouring under that misfortune being created peers by him" (1811 *Dictionary of the Vulgar Tongue: A Dictionary of British Slang*). My thanks to Jared Carter for the reference.

59. McGann, *"Don Juan" in Context*, p. 95.

60. See the discussion of the trial of William Hone in chap. 4 below.

61. Jean Baudrillard, *For a Critique of the Political Economy of the Sign*, trans. Mark Poster (St. Louis: Telos, 1981), p. 119.

62. Samuel Taylor Coleridge, *Biographia Literaria*, ed. James Engell and Walter Jackson Bate, 2 vols., vol. 7 of *Collected Works*, gen. ed. Kathleen Coburn (Princeton: Princeton Univ. Press, 1983), chap. 21, 2;107–14.

63. Benjamin Heath Malkin, *Essays on Subjects Connected with Civilization* (London, 1795), p. 208.

64. John Haslam, *Observations on Madness and Melancholy* (1809; rpt. New York: Arno, 1976), p. 293.

65. The encyclopedia of these linkages and the place where the "moral physiology"

of authorship is sketched is Isaac Disraeli's *The Calamities and Quarrels of Authors* (1812–14).

66. Shakespeare served as both the frame of reference and the medium of exchange for reviewers of literature, reformers of society, political partisans, and diagnosticians of the insane, including Haslam (see, e.g., his citations from *Henry IV, Part I*, and *Hamlet* in *Observations*, pp. 36 and 61). Note also Lord Byron's remark, "I see all the papers in a sad commotion with these eight lines ["To a Lady Weeping"]—and the M[orning] Post in particular has found out that I am a sort of R[ichard] 3d.—deformed in mind and *body*—the last piece of information is not very new to a man who passed five years at public school" (*BLJ* 4:49). The Richard III whom both Byron and his assailants have in mind is Shakespeare's, not the ruler to whom the *Dictionary of the Vulgar Tongue* refers.

67. Andrew Abbott, *The System of Professions: An Essay on the Division of Expert Labor* (Chicago: Univ. of Chicago Press, 1988), p. 8.

68. Jane Marcet, *Conversations on Political Economy; in Which the Elements of That Science Are Familiarly Explained* (Philadelphia, 1817), p. 15.

69. Even the notorious failures of Gifford to publish the *Quarterly* punctually ought to be understood as a gesture of traditionality—cf. the discussion of the *Spectator* above.

70. Abbott, *System*, p. 98.

71. Ibid., p. 92. See the discussion of Adam Smith, chap. 4 below.

Chapter 2: A Genealogy of Morals

1. Ralph Waldo Emerson, "Heroism," in *Essays, First Series*, vol. 1 of *Emerson's Works*, 5 vols. (New York: Bigelow and Brown, n.d.), p. 161.

2. See David Hume, *A Treatise of Human Nature*, ed. L. A. Selby-Bigge, 2d ed., rev. P. H. Nidditch (Oxford: Clarendon Press, 1978), p. 74.

3. My reading of the encryption of the secret impulse in Byron has been strongly influenced throughout by Nicholas Abraham, "The Phantom of Hamlet or the Sixth Act: Preceded by the Intermission of 'Truth,'" trans. Nicholas Rand, *Diacritics* 18 (Winter 1988): 2–19, and Nicholas Rand, "Family Romance or Family History? Psychoanalysis and Dramatic Invention in Nicholas Abraham's 'The Phantom of Hamlet,'" *Diacritics* (Winter 1988): 20–30.

4. For a discussion of the publication history and the characterization of the two satirical moods as Juvenalian and Horatian, see McGann's commentary in *CPW* 1:397–99. The "paper bullets of the brain" boast, quoted from *Much Ado about Nothing* (2.3.220), is adapted from a letter to the Rev. John Becher in March 1808, where Lord Byron claims, with considerable metaphorical license, that they have taught him "to stand fire" (*BLJ* 1:162). He made the same Shakespearean allusion in a letter to Francis Hodgson at the time of the publication of the first edition of *English Bards and Scotch Reviewers* a year later (*BLJ* 1:198), this time deleting, as he did in the paper, the boast about standing fire.

5. Leslie A. Marchand, *Byron: A Biography*, 3 vols. (New York: Knopf, 1957), 1:145–49. In a particularly telling exchange with Hobhouse Byron disowned a so-called "attack" against the "Body" of the Whig club—provoked by the review in the *Edinburgh*—with the self-pitying bluff that represents the extremity of Byron's mortification: "I am most willing to grant any species of satisfaction to any, or all the society, and he who shall avenge them successfully will do me a favour, for I am at present as miserable in mind and Body, as Literary abuse, pecuniary embarrassment, and total enervation can make me" (*BLJ* 1:160).

6. See Thomas Moore, *The Life of Lord Byron*, 2 vols. in 1 (Philadelphia, 1854), p. 23.

7. *Annual Register for the Year 1765*, p. 208.

8. Ibid., p. 209.

9. Ibid., pp. 209–210.

10. Ibid., pp. 210–11.

11. Ibid., p. 212.

12. Here, as throughout my discussion of dueling, I have relied heavily on Donna T. Andrew's excellent essay "The Code of Honour and Its Critics: The Opposition to Duelling in England, 1700–1850," *Social History* 5 (October 1980): 409–34. Andrew distinguishes among judicial dueling, trial by combat, and the "modern code of honour" imported from the Continent in the late sixteenth century. "Like the judicial duel, the introduction of the modern duel served to limit violence and regulate its expression." She goes on to stress the formality of the duel, comparing it to the minuet (pp. 410–11). For a more recent, commendably comprehensive, extremely lively, and highly partisan history of the duel, see G. V. Kiernan, *The Duel in European History: Honour and the Reign* (Oxford: Oxford Univ. Press, 1989).

13. Julian Pitt-Rivers, "Honour and Social Status," in *Honour and Shame: The Values of Mediterranean Society*, ed. John G. Peristiany (Chicago: Univ. of Chicago Press, 1974), pp. 25–26.

14. Immanuel Kant, *Foundations of the Metaphysics of Morals*, trans. Lewis White Beck (Indianapolis: Bobbs-Merrill, 1959), p. 74.

15. Theodor W. Adorno, *Negative Dialectics*, trans. E. B. Ashton (New York: Seabury, 1979), pp. 212–13. Cf. Lord Byron to Lady Blessington: "The events in life that have most pained me . . . have not depended on the persons who tortured me,—as I admit that the causes were inadequate to the effects:—it was my own nature, prompt to receive painful impressions, and to retain them with a painful tenacity, that supplied the arms against my peace" (*Lady Blessington's "Conversations of Lord Byron,"* ed. Ernest J. Lovell, Jr. [Princeton: Princeton Univ. Press, 1969], p. 179).

16. The classic version of this aggression in English literature is the fate of Harley in *Man of Feeling*, whose agonized death nearly murders the object of his love.

17. Kant, *Morals*, p. 17, n. 2.

18. Adorno, *Negative Dialectics*, p. 220.

19. Moore, *Life*, p. 4.

20. Adorno, *Negative Dialectics*, p. 269.

21. Ibid., pp. 221–23.

22. Hans Blumenberg, *The Legitimacy of the Modern Age*, trans. Robert M. Wallace (Cambridge, Mass.: MIT Press, 1983), p. 75.

23. Moore, *Life*, p. 11.

24. Kant, *Morals*, pp. 34 and 31.

25. The family's account of the origin of the motto is respectfully if skeptically retold by Violet W. Walker in *The House of Byron: A History of the Family from the Norman Conquest, 1066–1988* (London: Quiller, 1988), pp. 16–17. Traditionally, the inscription was monarchic, Henry IV's commemoration of the faithfulness of John Byron in the service of Sir Gervase Clifton at the Battle of Bosworth Field in 1485. As Walker shows, that account—versified by Sir John Beaumont in a narrative that ironically anticipates the Chaworth episode—does not gibe with all the facts. What was attributed to the monarch may have been the invention of Byron, who clearly seized what opportunities were

available and who was burdened by a debt that, as Walker informs us (p. 4), had been as continuous in the long history of the family as their good name.

26. Kant, *Morals*, p. 17, n. 1.

27. Adorno, *Negative Dialectics*, pp. 228–29. Adorno's addendum speaks to Claude Lefort's concept of "difference" (*Democracy and Political Theory*, trans. David Macey [Minneapolis: Univ. of Minnesota Press, 1988], p. 91):

> What philosophical thought strives to preserve is the experience of a difference which goes beyond differences of opinion . . . ; the experience of a difference which is not at the disposal of human beings, whose advent does not take place *within* human history, and which cannot be abolished therein; the experience of a difference which relates human beings to their humanity, and which means that their humanity cannot be self-contained, that it cannot set its own limits, and that it cannot absorb its origins and ends into those limits.

28. Adorno, *Negative Dialectics*, pp. 226–27.

29. Walker, *House of Byron*, p. 5.

30. Charles Moore, *Treatise on the Duel*, 2 vols. (London, 1790), 2:255.

31. William Godwin, *Caleb Williams*, ed. David McCracken (New York: Norton, 1977), p. 98.

Chapter 3: Sex, Class, and the Naked Letter of Romance

1. Mary Wollstonecraft, *A Vindication of the Rights of Woman* (London: Dent, 1929), p. 44.

2. Friedrich Nietzsche, *On the Genealogy of Morals*, trans. Walter Kaufmann (New York: Random House, 1969), p. 80.

3. Wollstonecraft, *Vindication*, pp. 42, 97, 47–50, and passim. Wollstonecraft's usage of *exercise* shows her conformity with the Enlightenment project of transforming the notion of exercise as deployment into exercise as training. This project (which ought to be considered a variant of the Foucauldian theme of disciplinary administration—see Michel Foucault, *Discipline and Punish: The Birth of the Prison*, trans. Alan Sheridan [New York: Vintage, 1979]) ranges over mental and physical culture. Its literary historical origin lies with the Renaissance shift from *legere* to *exercere*—a shift, made possible by the invention of the printing press, which means that instead of "an elegy we have an exhortation to revive the ancient splendors, the glories of Rome" (Chenu, *Nature, Man, and Society*; quoted in Elizabeth Eisenstein, *The Printing Press As an Agent of Change*, 2 vols. in 1 [Cambridge: Cambridge Univ. Press, 1979], p. 184). Its modern British itinerary starts with Dr. Fuller's "Medicina Gymnastica, or, a treatise concerning the power of Exercise, with respect to the Animal OEconomy" (5th ed., 1718) and Cheyne's treatise *The English Malady*, published some twenty years after Fuller's. (See Isaac Disraeli, *The Calamities and Quarrels of Authors* [1812–14], ed. Benjamin Disraeli [London, 1860], pp. 71–72n, for an interesting application of these texts to the "maladies of authors.") The path might be tracked from *Spectator*, no. 94, where Addison endeavors "to show how those parts of life which are exercised in study, reading, and the pursuits of life are long but not tedious," through Lord B's self-congratulation for the "innocent exercises" he has given Pamela's wit, to Thomas Reid, the philosopher of common sense. In a particularly Wollstonecraftian moment, Reid exclaimed that the "extent of human power is perfectly suited to the state of man, as a state of improvement and discipline. By the proper exercise

of this gift of God, human nature, in individuals and societies, may be exalted to a high degree of dignity and felicity, and the earth become a paradise" (*Philosophical Works*, 2 vols.[Hildesheim: Georg Olms Verlagsbuchhandlung, 1967], 2:530). In his great sports romance "The Fight," William Hazlitt endorses a regimen similar to Reid's: "The whole art of training . . . consists in two things, exercise and abstinence, abstinence and exercise, repeated alternately and without end" (*Selected Writings*, ed. Ronald Blythe [Harmondsworth: Penguin, 1970], p. 82). Hazlitt's celebration might be compared with William Cobbett's earlier defense of boxing against attempts to regulate it out of existence (*Political Register* [August 1805], in *Selections from Cobbett's Political Works*, ed. John M. and James P. Cobbett, 4 vols. [London, n.d.], 2:11–17. Writing and prizefighting tend to converge at the beginning of the nineteenth century. Byron had a keen, "scientific" interest in pugilistic training as well as fencing (see *HVSV*, pp. 87 and 79). In the 1830 introduction to *Lady of the Lake* Walter Scott conspicuously lamented that during his early poetic prominence he had been more the "champion of pugilism" than the "champion of chivalry." The most thorough and complex historiographic meditation on the virtue of exercise appears in Edward Gibbon's deeply ambivalent description, "The State of Germany Till the Invasion of the Barbarians," chap. 9 of *The Decline and Fall of the Roman Empire*.

4. Wollstonecraft, *Vindication*, p. 152.

5. In this instance Wollstonecraft was following the lead of Thomas Paine, who in *The Rights of Man* observed that "when compared with the active world [aristocrats] are the drones, a seraglio of males, who neither collect the honey nor form the hive, but exist only for lazy enjoyment" ([Penguin: Harmondsworth, 1984], p. 249).

6. Harold Bloom, *A Map of Misreading* (New York: Oxford Univ. Press, 1975), p. 37.

7. Edmund Burke, *Reflections on the Revolution in France* (1790; rpt. Harmondsworth: Penguin, 1968), p. 169.

8. Ibid., p. 165.

9. Another example that falls in the line of Crazy Kate and Margaret is the anecdote that Scott tells in the introduction to *Guy Mannering* of his "solemn remembrance of a woman *of more than female* height, dressed in a long red cloak," who became the prototype for Meg Merrilees (emphasis added). As a group such scenes fall within Geoffrey H. Hartman's category "eastering," a regressive countermovement back along the path of westering enlightenment. See "Blake and the Progress of Poesy," in *Beyond Formalism: Literary Essays, 1958–1970* (New Haven: Yale Univ. Press, 1970), pp. 199–200. The phenomenon might be extended beyond the confines of literature—or, rather, its extension to exiled tourist attractions like Lady Emma Hamilton and Lady Hester Stanhope Romantically equivocates the boundaries between literature and life. On the notorious Lady Hamilton, mistress of Naples and Nelson, whose appearance prefigured both the fallen Beau Brummell and the Venetian Lord Byron (in one of his phases): "She is the most extraordinary compound I ever beheld. Her person is nothing short of monstrous for its enormity, and is growing every day. She tries hard to think size advantageous to her beauty, but is not easy about it. Her face is beautiful" (November 6, 1796; *The Life and Letters of Sir Gilbert Elliott, First Earl of Minto*, ed. the Countess of Minto, 3 vols. [London, 1874], 2:366). The woman clearly needed exercise.

10. Michel Foucault, *The History of Sexuality: Volume 1, An Introduction*, trans. Robert Hurley (New York: Pantheon, 1978), p. 121.

11. David Hume, "Of Refinement in the Arts," in *Essays Moral, Political, and Literary*,

ed. Eugene F. Miller (1777; rpt. Indianapolis: Liberty*Classics*, 1985), p. 268. For a useful history of the Western concept of luxury, see Alan J. Sekora, *Luxury: The Concept in Western Thought, Eden to Smollett* (Baltimore: Johns Hopkins Univ. Press, 1977), pp. 23–131.

12. Wollstonecraft, *Vindication*, p. 44. For another, more spectacular example of this classificatory strategy—the attempt by David Hume, in the name of enlightenment, to contain Rousseau by labeling him a chimerical "imaginary being"—see Jerome Christensen, *Practicing Enlightenment: Hume and the Formation of a Literary Career* (Madison: Univ. of Wisconsin Press, 1987), pp. 251–55.

13. A classical move. In *Greek Homosexuality* (New York: Random House, 1978), K. J. Dover quotes from the peroration of Aiskhine's *Prosecution of Timarkhos* (346 B.C.): "Tell those who are hunters of such young men as are easily caught to turn to foreign visitors or resident foreigners, so that they may not be denied the pursuit of their inclinations and you (*sc.* the people of Athens) may come to no harm" (p. 31). In the eighteenth century this regulated, if not calculated, displacement of perverse desire is parasitic on the hysterical language of taint and contagion. As we have seen, Wollstonecraft ably synthesized a variety of motifs. Catherine Clément's account of the dynamics of this systematic strategy is compelling (Hélène Cixous and Catherine Clément, *The Newly Born Woman*, trans. Betsy Wing [Minneapolis: Univ. of Minnesota Press, 1986], pp. 8–9):

> The imaginary groups thus defined have only a fictive independence. . . . [As Levi-Strauss says,] "Their peripheral position in relation to a local system does not prevent their being an integral part of the total system in the same way that this local system is." They provide, somehow, the guarantee that locks the symbolic systems in, taking up the slack that can exist between them, carrying out, in the Imaginary, roles of extras, figures that are *impossible at the present time.*

Compare Freud's account of the three stages of cultural development in "Sexual Morality and Modern Nervousness": "First, the stage in which the sexual impulse may be fully exercised in regard to aims which do not lead to procreation; a second stage, in which the whole of the sexual impulse is suppressed except that portion which subserves procreation; and a third stage, in which only legitimate procreation is allowed as a sexual aim" (*Sexuality and the Psychology of Love*, trans. James Strachey [New York: Collier Books, 1963], p. 27).

Wollstonecraft's precedent allows us to see the ambiguity in Freud's idea that in the first stage of development nonprocreative sexual activity is being "freely exercised." In this passage we can certainly hear the accent of the enlightened, muscular, nineteenth-century reformers of Eton and Harrow. But it should also be observed that what Freud stages developmentally in terms of the individual Wollstonecraft has already synchronized in a global system. To the late-eighteenth-century Englishman, the world presents a multiplication of realms—some, like England, where only procreative activity is acceptable, some, like Greece, Portugal, and Italy, where other impulses can be freely exercised. The greatest threat to the enjoyment of this pluralistic vision was, of course, Napoleonic expansion—imperialism in an altogether different style.

14. Jean Baudrillard, *For a Critique of the Political Economy of the Sign*, trans. Mark Poster (St. Louis: Telos, 1981), p. 67.

15. Theodor W. Adorno, *Prisms*, trans. Samuel and Shierry Weber (Cambridge, Mass.: MIT Press, 1981), p. 21.

16. Romantic classicism was not, of course, Byron's invention; it has a long and varied pedigree. One path extends backward to the Jacobins and refracts through Napoleon. The Napoleonic career was always before Byron, whose own politico-sexual itinerary could be described as a mock-Bonapartism. See, for example, Byron's attempt to resolve disputes among his tenants upon his return from the East: "But I shall not interfere further (than like Buonaparte) by diminishing Mr. B's *kingdom*, and erecting part of it into a *principality* for Field Marshal Fletcher!" (*BLJ* 2:52).

17. In denying that Lord Byron was initiated into homosexuality before departing from England, I am rejecting Louis Crompton's revisionary reading of the texts surrounding the supposed advances made to Lord Byron by Lord Grey de Ruthyn, tenant of Newstead Abbey, during Byron's visit with Grey in 1804. Differing from Lord Byron's biographers Leslie A. Marchand and Doris Langley Moore, Crompton argues that the available evidence supports the inference that some sexual contact occurred (*Byron and Greek Love: Homophobia in Nineteenth-Century England* [Berkeley: Univ. of California Press, 1985], pp. 81–85). The strong evidence of repulsion disables Crompton's case, though it is not, I would argue, repulsion toward homoerotic contact. Byron was disgusted not by the sexual nature of Grey's advances but by the advancing nature of Grey's sexuality. In the same letter to his mother in which Byron mysteriously refers to Grey as his "inveterate enemy," he boasts, "But however the way to *riches* to *Greatness* lies before me, I can, I will cut myself a path through the world or perish in the attempt. Others have begun life with nothing and ended Greatly. And shall I who have a competent if not a large fortune, remain idle, No, I will carve myself the passage to Grandeur, but never with Dishonour" (*BLJ* 1:49). All other evidence of Byron's relations with boys shows him in the active role. To imagine him in the pathic with the tenant of his ancestral home is to promote an incredible aberration—particularly in one strongly afflicted with status anxiety and who takes his erotic patterns from the Greeks. My reservations are much the same, though much less strenuous, in regard to Cecil Y. Lang's ingenious but strained claim that there was a sexual liaison between Byron and the Ali Pacha on Byron's trip East. (See "Narcissus Jilted: Byron, *Don Juan*, and the Biographical Imperative," in *Historical Studies and Literary Criticism*, ed. Jerome J. McGann [Madison: Univ. of Wisconsin Press, 1985], pp. 143–79).

18. Besides Foucault, my analysis depends heavily on Baudrillard, especially "Fetishism and Ideology," chap. 3 of *Critique*.

19. Jerome J. McGann, *The Beauty of Inflections: Literary Investigations in Historical Method and Theory* (Oxford: Clarendon Press, 1985), p. 260. Cf. Maurice Godelier's comment that "the image of Asia stagnating for millennia in an unfinished transition from classless to class society, from barbarism to civilisation, has not stood up to the finding of archaeology and history in the East and the New World. . . . What was born in Greece was not civilisation but the West, a particular form of civilisation which was finally to dominate it while all the while pretending to be its symbol" ("The Concept of the 'Asiatic Mode of Production' and Marxist Models of Social Evolution," quoted in Anthony Giddens, *A Contemporary Critique of Historical Materialism* [Berkeley: Univ. of California Press, 1981], p. 87). Cf. the review of *Childe Harold's Pilgrimage* in the *Monthly Review* of May 1812, which after quoting Byron's patronizing remarks about the Greeks' need for interposition, observes that "perhaps [Lord Byron] rather under-rates the value of the co-operation of the natives, which would certainly be essential on such an occasion" (*RR* B:4:1734). As William St. Clair argues, this underrating of the natives was at

the conceptual center of philhellenism as an emancipatory movement in the second two decades of the nineteenth century, which sought to "regenerate" the modern Greeks from Turkish corruption by "restoring" a Hellenism that was a construction of European classicism (*That Greece Might Still Be Free: The Philhellenes in the War of Independence* [London: Oxford Univ. Press, 1972], pp. 13–22).

20. Sexualized, Byron's notion of the "interposition" of himself between the aggressor Turk and victimized Greek, giving and receiving, would be diagnosed as bivalently sadomasochistic, a structure capacious enough to fit the aggression of the Ali Pacha as well as of all the oppressors of the Greeks in the Oriental tales.

21. Byron's liberation of Eustathius amounted to a substitution of a "green shade" for "that effeminate parasol"—a change in inflection but no reconstitution of the boy's sign value (*BLJ* 2:7). Not that the change in inflection, accent, or color is insignificant. In his prose account of their travels Hobhouse commented that while traveling in the Greek provinces of the Turkish empire, it was necessary to hire only "Franks" (those who wear European dress) as dragomen, because only they avoided the "submissive cringing tone" with which it is "the nature of things for a man in the Greek habit to talk" to a Turk. "The Greek," he says, "appears to feel himself free the moment he places the hat upon his head, and throws away the cap, which, in our own times, and in another country, was the badge of liberty" (Lord Broughton [John Cam Hobhouse], *Travels in Albania and Other Provinces of Turkey in 1809 & 1810* (1813), new ed., 2 vols. [London: Murray, 1855], 1:19–20). Changing headgear makes one "feel" free. The action simulates liberation, which may be useful for the tourist who requires a guide with "relative autonomy," but which increases rather than reverses the degradation by institutionalizing a discrepancy between social signs and political reality that correlates with the neurotic adaptation requisite to success in the market economy.

Hobhouse's ironic reference to France (it is evidently a Phrygian cap the Greek discards) suggests the ideological significance of these distinctions. Neil Hertz addresses the phenomenon of often hysterical reaction to the size and shape of headgear in his subtle discussion of the history of the debates regarding the proper shape of the ideologically charged Phrygian cap of the Jacobins, which veered between a drooping, emasculated/ing, Asiatic, Medusa-like model and the more than Roman cone shape ("Medusa's Head: Male Hysteria under Political Pressure," *The End of the Line* [New York: Columbia Univ. Press, 1985], pp. 179–91). Although there is, I think, a fair analogy between parasol/shade and droopy cap/cone cap, it would be too far-fetched to mention were it not that the two articles of clothing are linked in one of the most influential colonialist fantasies in the English language, *Robinson Crusoe*. A brilliant account of the political, economic, racial, and sexual themes invested in Crusoe's goatskin parasol and cap is given in Derek Walcott's stage play *Pantomime*.

22. Hobhouse approved of the theory of a Mr. De Pauw that the Turkish male's sexual practices are compensations for the lack of beauty among Turkish females: "I am inclined . . . to attribute the astonishing influence of the Greek courtezans, and what he calls a depravation of instinct, partly to the same cause. Had the women generally been beautiful, the whole of Greece, young and old, soldiers, orators, and philosophers, would not have been prostrate at the feet of Aspasia or Lars, Pryyne or Pythonice, nor have fallen so entirely, perhaps, into the prevailing enormity" (*Travels* 1:445–46).

23. Not always so moralizing. The parliamentary defeat of Burke's consuming crusade against Warren Hastings could be interpreted as the forced recognition of the

linkage between regulation and repression—that is, the linkage between the extension of British rule (the rule of law) and the quickening of rapacious sexual desire.

24. See Doris Langley Moore, *Lord Byron: Accounts Rendered* (London: John Murray, 1974), p. 89, and Crompton, *Byron and Greek Love*, p. 152.

25. Doris Langley Moore, *Lord Byron*, pp. 88–90.

26. T. A. J. Burnett, *The Rise and Fall of a Regency Dandy: The Life and Times of Scrope Berdmore Davies* (London: John Murray, 1981), p. 36.

27. Ibid., p. 14.

28. Edward C. Mack refers to "the virtual conquest of the public schools by those who attended them" in his *Public Schools and British Opinion 1780 to 1860;* quoted in J. C. D. Clark, *English Society 1688–1832* (Cambridge: Cambridge Univ. Press, 1985), p. 103.

29. Burnett, *Rise and Fall*, p. 14. Because the "face unglimpsed" is no face at all, perhaps it would be slightly more accurate to note that in *Northanger Abbey*, for example, Austen gives a face to the other side of the eighteenth century and "Romantically" names it Gothic.

30. St. Clair, *Greece*, p. 21.

31. Mark Girouard, *The Return to Camelot: Chivalry and the English Gentleman* (New Haven: Yale Univ. Press, 1981), pp. 163–76. Girouard's history could be read as an extended commentary on Scott's recollection in the general preface to the Waverley novels of the schoolboy "bicker" in which neighborhood brawled with neighborhood and class fought class in a brutal melee on the streets of Edinburgh, until, magically, "a lady of distinction presented a handsome set of colours," eradicating peculiar devices by chivalrizing one and all. Scott's recollection, offered with an aplomb that almost disarms criticism, not only craftily deploys all the motifs and devices we have been addressing, but is characteristically self-conscious about the social and political implications of their deployment.

32. Maurice Keen, *Chivalry* (New Haven: Yale Univ. Press, 1984), pp. 86–90, 125–34.

33. Cf. Girouard's account of the humiliating failure of the Eglinton Tournament in 1839 (*Return to Camelot*, pp. 87–110).

34. Crompton, *Byron and Greek Love*, p. 129. In his usage Crompton does not clearly distinguish between the terms *homosexual* and *gay*. John Boswell incisively frames the terminological issue in his *Christianity, Social Tolerance, and Homosexuality* (Chicago: Univ. of Chicago Press, 1980), p. 44. For an admirable, historically nuanced discussion of the variations in homosexual identity that were constructed in the nineteenth century, see Jeffrey Weeks, *Sex, Politics, and Society: The Regulation of Sexuality since 1800* (London: Longman, 1981), pp. 108–17.

35. Crompton, *Byron and Greek Love*, pp. 127–29.

36. Crompton mentions that the code was first deciphered by Gilbert Highet in 1957 at the request of Leslie A. Marchand (ibid., p. 128). That it remained mysterious for so long has more to say about the decline of classical education than it does about the inherent difficulty of the code.

37. But not the only fruit. In a later letter Byron jokingly promised a treatise on sodomy (*BLJ* 1:208). During the journey the friends hatched the project of launching a literary journal to be called the *Bagatelle* (allowing glimpses of the cat in the bag?). The

Wollstonecraftian characterization of Childe Harold appears in George Ellis's review for the *Quarterly* in March 1812 (*RR* B:5:1991).

38. Eve Kosofsky Sedgwick, *Between Men: English Literature and Male Homosocial Desire* (New York: Columbia Univ. Press, 1985), p. 95.

39. For Defoe on jargon, see *The Complete English Tradesman in Familiar Letters*, 2 vols. (1727; rpt. New York: Augustus Kelley, 1969), 1:26–34; for Swift, see the *Examiner* (November 2, 1710), in *The Works of Jonathan Swift*, ed. Thomas Roscoe, 6 vols. (New York: O'Shea, 1865), 3:454; for Coleridge, see *Biographia Literaria*, ed. James Engell and Walter Jackson Bate, 2 vols., vol. 7 of *Collected Works*, gen. ed. Kathleen Coburn (Princeton: Princeton Univ. Press, 1983), 1:60–67 and 2:109–10. Here is a frustrated Lord Byron addressing his publisher John Murray: "Indeed you are altogether so abstruse and undecided lately—that I suppose you mean me to write—'John Murray Esqre. a *Mystery*' a composition which would not displease the Clergy nor the trade" (*BLJ* 9:168).

40. Jacques Lacan, "Aggressivity in Psychoanalysis," in *Ecrits: A Selection*, ed. and trans. Alan Sheridan (New York: Norton, 1977), p. 17.

41. St. Clair, *Greece*, pp. 9–10.

42. Dover, *Greek Homosexuality*, p. 47.

43. Hobhouse, who generally advised travelers for the sake of convenience to substitute "hard money" for commodities as gifts to the natives, is explicit about the 2–3 piasters suitable as hire for a dragoman (*Travels* 1:30 and 185).

44. Cf. Foucault: "Homosexuality appeared as one of the forms of sexuality when it was transposed from the practice of sodomy onto a kind of interior androgyny, a hermaphrodism of the soul. The sodomite had been a temporary aberration; the homosexual was now a species" (*History of Sexuality*, p. 43).

45. Hobhouse financed his trip with a loan from Byron, who subsidized them both by borrowing against the future sale of his estate. See Leslie A. Marchand, *Byron: A Biography*, 3 vols. (New York: Knopf, 1957), 1:178.

46. Wollstonecraft, *Vindication*, p. 21.

47. Richard Hurd, *Letters on Chivalry and Romance* (1762), ed. Hoyt Trowbridge (Los Angeles: Augustan Reprint Society, 1963), p. 113. Jacques Derrida, "Differance," in *Speech and Phenomena: And Other Essays on Husserl's Theory of Signs*, trans. David B. Allison (Evanston: Northwestern Univ. Press, 1973), pp. 129–60.

48. On the definition "of a culturally-defined elite" according to a code that "expresses the sense of distance which separated gentlemen from those who were not gentlemen" in eighteenth- and nineteenth-century England, see Clark, *English Society*, pp. 103–5. Anxiety was endemic to the task of defining oneself according to a code while observing the Johnsonian precept that it was "the essence of a gentleman's character to bear the visible mark of no profession whatever" (quoted in Lawrence and Jeanne C. Fawtier Stone, *An Open Elite? England 1540–1880* [Oxford: Clarendon Press, 1984], p. 268). On the varieties of Methodist association with political and religious ferment, which extended from radical revivalism to reactive quietism to what Cobbett described as the corporatism of a "new bureaucracy, composed of 'the most busy and perservering set of men on earth,'" see E. P. Thompson, *The Making of the English Working Class* (New York: Vintage, 1963), pp. 350–400. For a definition of Methodism that lumps all "classes of fanatics" into "one general conspiracy against common sense, and rational orthodox christianity," see the *Edinburgh Review* (January 1808), p. 342. For another example of the

use of neologism as a homosocial device, see Coleridge's promotion of his coinage *aspheterized* to his pantisocratic comrade Robert Southey in 1794 (*The Letters of Samuel Taylor Coleridge*, ed. Earl Leslie Griggs, 6 vols. [Oxford: Clarendon Press, 1956–71], 1:84). Scott makes the connection among slang, Methodism, prurience, and a corruptiveness that hovers between the political and the sexual in his contemptuous dismissal of Thomas Moore's early, pseudonymous erotic poetry: "In fact, it is not passages of ludicrous indelicacy that corrupt the manners of a people—it is the sonnets which a prurient genius like Master Little sings *virginibus puerisque*—it is the sentimental slang, half lewd, half methodistic, that debauches the understanding, inflames the sleeping Passions, and prepares the reader to give way as soon as the tempter appears" (John Gibson Lockhart, *Memoirs of Sir Walter Scott*, 5 vols. [London: Macmillan, 1900], 1:431). It is not possible to disentangle these various connotations and alliances here, but it is worth noting that not only can Matthews's fate be read (see below) as a judgment on such debauchery, Byron depicts just such a victim of "sentimental slang, half lewd, half methodistic" in the tragicomic figure of Tom the highwayman, who is fatally wounded by Juan at the beginning of canto 11 of *Don Juan*. Tom, not the poet, fulfilled the prediction "of those who," Lord Byron mentioned to Scott, "prophesy I will turn Methodist" (*HVSV*, p. 114).

49. Theodor W. Adorno, *Negative Dialectics*, trans. E. B. Ashton (New York: Seabury, 1979), p. 146; trans. amended by David Held, *Introduction to Critical Theory: Horkheimer to Habermas* (Berkeley: Univ. of California Press, 1980), p. 220.

50. "I think they must own that I have more *styles* than one" (*BLJ* 8:155).

51. Applied to the Jacobins by Burke, *Reflections*, p. 128. Note that Matthews, who perversely substituted French verbal formulas and legalistic prescriptions for the good old English method of experience, who was a homosexual (and therefore only theoretically a man), and who was a homosexual only in theory (he apparently did not practice what he professed), was nicknamed *citoyen* Matthews by Byron and Hobhouse. If the illustration is uncanny, it is because it releases something hidden in Burke's own text: the homoerotic subtext and pretext of *Reflections*: entitled *A Philosophical Enquiry into Our Ideas of the Sublime and the Beautiful*, it stands in the unnatural relation to its successor of a theory that dictates ensuing practice.

52. For a similar moral applied to another friend, Edward Noel Long, who died of drowning, see *BLJ* 8:23–24.

53. See, for example, the discussion of rust and embarrassment that begins the narrative in Henry Mackenzie's *Man of Feeling*.

54. In the Miltonic iconography of the postrevolutionary period the giant is identifiable as Moloch. The image was a favorite of Coleridge's. See, for example, *The Friend* (1809), ed. Barbara Rooke, 2 vols., vol. 4 of *Collected Works*, gen. ed. Kathleen Coburn (Princeton: Princeton Univ. Press, 1969), 1:47.

55. J. M. W. Turner, Lecture 6 (1812); reproduced in John Gage, *Colour in Turner: Poetry and Truth* (London: Studion Vista, 1969), p. 199.

56. Gage, *Colour in Turner*, pp. 61–62.

57. For a subtle and persuasive reading of a similar scene and accessories, see Hertz, "Medusa's Head," pp. 162–68.

58. On Byron's readiness to "assemble the elements of conventional Whig discourse," see Malcolm Kelsall, *Byron's Politics* (Totowa, N.J.: Barnes and Noble, 1987), p. 38 and passim.

59. Michel de Certeau, *The Practice of Everyday Life*, trans. Steven F. Rendall (Berkeley: Univ. of California Press, 1984), p. xix.

60. Hobhouse, *Travels* 1:154. In context Hobhouse is assessing the indecent puppet shows of the Turks.

61. A highly vexed historical issue; see chap. 1 above.

62. Peter J. Manning, "*Don Juan* and Byron's Imperceptiveness to the English Word," *Studies in Romanticism* 18 (Summer 1979): 207–33.

63. Cf. the disruption of this scene of fascination with Wordsworth's *Ruined Cottage*, where the pedlar must await the stilling of the hand of Margaret before her battered wall (foiling him no matter how distracted its movements) before he can take possession of her "plot."

64. The *Antijacobin Review* on *Childe Harold's Pilgrimage: A Romaunt:* "That such a child should never attain to manhood is devoutly to be wished. How the noble bard could have had the patience to pourtray this froward object of his own creation, or even how his mind could have engendered so monstrous a being, we profess ourselves unable to comprehend" (*RR* B:1:11).

65. My ideas on Wordsworth's corporatism have been shaped by "'Transferred Language': Authorizing *The Convention of Cintra*," an unpublished essay by Margaret Russett.

66. Quoted in Crompton, *Byron and Greek Love*, pp. 215–16.

67. Ibid., p. 216.

68. Wollstonecraft: "Unless [women's] morals be fixed on the same immutable principles as man . . . " (*Vindication*, p. 11). Cf. Hobhouse: "It is not fair to appreciate the merits of any man without a reference to the character and customs of the people amongst whom he is born and educated. In Turkey the life of man is held exceedingly cheap, more so than any one who has not been in the country would believe; and murders which would fill all Christendom with horror excite no sentiments of surprise or apparent disgust, either at Constantinople or in the provinces; so that what might, at first sight, appear a singular depravity in an individual, would in the end be found nothing but a conformity with general practice and habits" (*Travels* 1:110). And Byron: "I see not much difference between ourselves & the Turks, save that we have foreskins and they none, that they have long dresses and we short, and that we talk much and they little.—In England the vices in fashion are whoring & drinking, in Turkey, Sodomy & smoking, we prefer a girl and bottle, they a pipe and pathic.—They are a sensible people" (*BLJ* 1:238).

69. Lady Byron to Mrs. Clermont, in Malcolm Elwin, *Lord Byron's Wife* (New York: Harcourt, Brace and World, 1962), p. 393.

70. On Lord Byron's economizing in the East, see his letter to his mother of November 12, 1809, where, commenting on the wish of the Albanians to receive love rather than sequins as compensation for their hospitality, he exclaims, "It is astonishing how far money goes in this country" (*BLJ* 1:230; see also the postscript on p. 231). Crompton's enlightened endorsement of Lord Byron's bisexuality involves some fudging of sexual power relationships. In the case of Byron's homosexual liaisons, this entails a certain amount of sentimentality about boy-love, which takes the form of the pathos of the pederast (and, of course, the Orientalist): "In our day and age we speak of the sexual exploitation of the young. This may occur, but in such affairs it is often the emotional vulnerability of the older male that makes him most open to exploitation, as Byron's later attachment to Lukas Chalandrutsanos was to demonstrate" (*Byron and Greek Love*, p. 238).

71. Baudrillard, *Critique*, p. 135.

72. Cf. John Galt's report of his conversation with his Greek interpreter in *Letters from the Levant* (London, 1813): "'His father commands a hundred soldiers in Buonaparte's service, but he likes the English better.' 'Why does he like the English better?' said I. 'Because,' replied Jacomo, 'they are richer, and pay better'" (p. 13).

73. Doris Langley Moore, *Lord Byron*, p. 444.

74. Unsigned review from the *Quarterly Review*, issued in September 1818; quoted in *Byron: The Critical Heritage*, ed. Andrew Rutherford (New York: Barnes and Noble, 1970), p. 140. Cf. the *Antijacobin* on *The Giaour*, which is perhaps even closer to Annabella's predicament: "When, however, Lord Byron advances any paradoxical position, he clothes it in such pleasing strains, that we are almost seduced to admit the justice of his reasoning by the fascination of his language" (*RR* B:1:33).

75. Quoted in G. Wilson Knight, *Lord Byron's Marriage: The Evidence of Asterisks* (New York: Macmillan, 1957), p. 209. In the view of Hobhouse (as expressed in his diary at the time), Byron's vice is merely the coloring of sentiments: "He was in the habit of communicating all his passing notions, paradoxical or not, to her; and the more she expressed her surprise the more highly did he colour his sentiments, and to clench his doctrine sometimes represented his principles as being deduced from his own practice" (*HVSV*, p. 160).

76. Even the exceptions are literary and are to be traced back to Byron's own promptings. In his very useful reconstruction of Lady Byron's narrative self-vindication, Malcolm Elwin stresses the literariness of her account, particularly her collaboration with Byron in dramatizing their relationship in terms of Radcliffe's *The Italian* and of the struggle between Caleb and Falkland in Godwin's *Caleb Williams* (Elwin, *Lord Byron's Wife*, pp. 297 and 258).

77. Elwin, *Lord Byron's Wife*, p. 418.

78. *Eclectic Review*, reviewing *The Giaour* (November 1813; *RR* B:2:715). In its review of *The Giaour* the *Christian Observer*, also nervous, "beseeched" Lord Byron "not to add himself to the infamous catalogue of those who have endeavoured to make vice reputable, who have ruined their country by overthrowing its altars and expelling its gods" (November 1813; *RR* B:2:574).

79. Elwin, *Lord Byron's Wife*, pp. 446–47n.

80. See Peter Paret's discussion of the way Napoleonic "institutional and tactical modernization spread to armies far beyond France," contributing to the decline of Napoleon's absolute superiority ("Napoleon and the Revolution in War," in *Makers of Modern Strategy from Machiavelli to the Nuclear Age*, ed. Peter Paret [Princeton: Princeton Univ. Press, 1986], pp. 134–36).

81. March 1816 review of *The Siege of Corinth* and *Parisina* (*RR* B:2:733).

82. Wollstonecraft, *Vindication*, p. 22.

83. *The Knight Errant*, 1817 review of *Manfred* (*RR* B:3:1223). Once again, Hobhouse's partisan version, that the bad Byron is "some imaginary monster created by the envy and malice of mankind," preserves the same terms as Byron's adversaries while reversing their value (*HVSV*, p. 165).

84. Pamela had her Mr. B; Annabella, adjusting for class and intimacy, calls her adversary "B," never, as Augusta did, "George."

85. Elwin, *Lord Byron's Wife*, p. 426.

86. According to one source of professional advice, Henry Brougham, Byron could

have succeeded in court. This was advice that Annabella received, not Byron, however. As Elwin notes, it is not clear whether Byron rejected the strategy of litigation or whether his attorney John Hanson failed either to foresee or to communicate the advantages (Elwin, *Lord Byron's Wife*, p. 458). Except in the case of Hobhouse (and in the drama of the *Memoirs* even there), Byron was always unlucky in his seconds.

87. Doris Langley Moore, *Lord Byron*, pp. 444–45.

88. Knight, *Lord Byron's Marriage*, p. 247. The most solid documentary evidence is Hobhouse's marginal note in Thomas Moore's *Life* next to the speculation about imposture: "Something of this sort, certainly, unless, as Lord Holland told me, he tried to———her" (Elwin, *Lord Byron's Wife*, p. 446n).

89. Doris Langley Moore, *Lord Byron*, p. 447. A conversation with Annabel Patterson helped me think through the relative merits of Moore's objections, which echo Hobhouse's: "Wilmot [an intermediary between lord and lady], it appeared, has been partially told Lady Byron's charge which seems to fill him with so much horror. He told me it was no enormity—indeed I told him it never could be, or she would have quitted the house at once" (Elwin, *Lord Byron's Wife*, p. 431).

90. Byron prescribed a Romantic regimen of oblivion: "It seems strange; a true voluptuary will never abandon his mind to the grossness of reality. It is by exalting the earthly, the material, the *physique* of our pleasures, by veiling those ideas, by forgetting them altogether, or at least, never naming them hardly to one's self, that we can prevent them from disgusting" (*BLJ* 3:239). Lady Byron's fall from the voluptuary's special grace shows how fragile such exaltation can be.

91. Elwin, *Lord Byron's Wife*, p. 457.

92. Edward Young, "Conjectures on Original Composition" (1759), in *The Great Critics*, ed. James Harry Smith and Edd Winfield Parks (New York: Norton, 1932), p. 419.

93. The former is Gillian Rose's description of the project of Gilles Deleuze's *Dialectic of Nihilism: Post-Structuralism and the Law* (Oxford: Basil Blackwell, 1984), p. 2. The latter is Julia Kristeva's description of the rejection that reaches "what lies beneath the paranoid homosexuality laid bare by signifying production" (*Revolution in Poetic Language*, trans. Margaret Weller [New York: Columbia Univ. Press, 1984], p. 156), a "polymorphism" that in the terms Byron uses to Matthews corresponds not to "ports of Falmouth" but to "parts adjacent," whatever they may be. Cf. George Bataille's exaltation of "the image of terrestrial love without condition, erection without escape and without rule, scandal, and terror" ("The Solar Anus," *Visions of Excess: Selected Writings, 1927–1939*, trans. Allan Stoekl et al. [Minneapolis: Univ. of Minnesota Press, 1985], pp. 8–9).

Chapter 4: Perversion, Parody, and Cultural Hegemony

1. Cf. Lady Byron's charge that in Byron's case "transgression was desired as such" (*HVSV*, p. 105).

2. The most thoroughgoing prosecution of Byron for complicity with the perceived social changes in the reading public is Philip W. Martin's *Byron: A Poet before His Public* (Cambridge: Cambridge Univ. Press, 1982). Martin's chapter on the Turkish tales is very informative on those social changes, alert to the significance of nuances of diction, and shrewd in its analysis of the way Byronism was employed by the reviews to mold the middle-class reader. But Martin's essay, as condescending toward his subject as he accuses the reviews of being toward theirs (p. 34), cannot master the contradiction it produces between a Byron who was able to "delude himself about the real nature of his

relationship to his audience" and who "recognized himself as a producer, a poet providing a commodity in demand" (p. 62). The pressure of the contradiction is relieved if one abandons (as the vicissitudes of both Scott's and Byron's careers insistently urge us to do) the crudely empiricist notion that the relation of poet to audience has a "real nature" that either party could manfully face. For a defense of the Oriental tales as projections "of the complex network of relations that defines and ultimately controls social reality" in the Regency era, see Daniel P. Watkins, *Social Relations in Byron's Eastern Tales* (Cranbury, N.J.: Associated Univ. Presses, 1987). For an interesting discussion of Byron's Oriental tales, which engages an earlier version of this chapter, see Eric Meyer, " 'I Know Thee Not, I Loathe Thy Race': Romantic Orientalism in the Eye of the Other," *ELH* 58 (Fall 1991): 657–99.

3. See, for example, the *Quarterly*'s review of *The Corsair*, which objects that "Conrad is a personage so eccentric, so oddly compounded of discordant qualities, and so remote from common nature, that it is difficult to sympathize in his feelings, at the same time that the affinity of his character to those of the Giaour and Childe Harold is so marked, as to do away the merit, whatever it may be, of singularity, and to give him the appearance of a mere copy from a capricious original" (*RR* B:5:2026).

4. For examples of similar reactions to *Lara* and *Parisina*, see the *Champion* and the *Eclectic Review* (*RR* B:2:523–25, 727–30, 732–36).

5. Sigmund Freud, *Three Essays on the Theory of Sexuality*, trans. James Strachey (New York: Basic Books, 1962), p. 1.

6. A sexuality very much like marriage. Thomas Moore recollects Byron's deliberations about the latter step: "A person, who had for some time stood high in [Byron's] affection and confidence, observing how cheerless and unsettled was the state both of his mind and prospects, advised him strenuously to marry; and, after much discussion, he consented. The next point for consideration was—who was to be the object of his choice" (*Life of Lord Byron*; quoted in *HVSV*, p. 89).

7. Freud, *Three Essays*, p. 14.

8. Arnold I. Davidson, "How to Do the History of Psychoanalysis: A Reading of Freud's *Three Essays on the Theory of Sexuality*," *Critical Inquiry* 14 (Winter 1987): 265.

9. Leo Bersani, *The Freudian Body* (New York: Columbia Univ. Press, 1986), pp. 83 and 100.

10. Jean Baudrillard, "The Structural Law of Value and the Order of Simulacra," trans. Charles Levin, in *The Structural Allegory: Reconstructive Encounters with the New French Thought*, ed. John Fekete (Minneapolis: Univ. of Minnesota Press, 1984), p. 63.

11. See Walter Benn Michaels, "Fictitious Dealings: A Reply to Leo Bersani," *Critical Inquiry* 8 (Fall 1981): 165–71.

12. Bersani, *Freudian Body*, p. 32.

13. Fredric Jameson, *The Political Unconscious: Narrative As a Socially Symbolic Act* (Ithaca: Cornell Univ. Press, 1981), p. 148.

14. Not for the first time. Byron publicly introduced the topic of perversion in his 1813 preface to *Childe Harold*, where he observed that "early perversion of mind and morals leads to satiety of past pleasures and disappointment in new ones."

15. Leo Bersani, *A Future for Astyanax: Character and Desire in Literature* (New York: Columbia Univ. Press, 1969), p. 97. Martin argues that in the verse tales Byron "is more concerned with manufacturing something which has the appearance of verse than with creating a narrative" (*Byron: A Poet before His Public*, pp. 45–46).

16. *RR* B:1:429. The *Champion* refers to Colley Cibber's *She Wo'd and She Wo'd Not*. Hobhouse mentions the play in an 1813 letter to Lord Byron. See *Byron's Bulldog: The Letters of John Cam Hobhouse to Lord Byron*, ed. Peter W. Graham (Columbus: Ohio State Univ. Press, 1984), p. 110.

17. Adam Smith, *Essays on Philosophical Subjects*, ed. W. P. D. Wightman and J. C. Bryce (Indianapolis: Liberty *Classics*, 1980), pp. 33–66.

18. Cf. the *Dublin Examiner*'s review of *Childe Harold III*: "The fickleness of women has been, in all ages, such a favorite topic with most authors, that it is in the present day become proverbial. This charge, however, when made exclusively against the fair sex, shall no longer bear the authority of our sanction; for every day's experience clearly proves to us, that the *Lords* of the creation are, for the most part, as subject to this infirmity as their weaker companions" (*RR* B:2:688). For the comparison of Byron's waning popularity to a dying meteor, see the *British Critic*'s review of *Childe Harold III* (*RR* B:1:266).

19. Mary Wollstonecraft, *A Vindication of the Rights of Woman* (London: Dent, 1929), p. 44.

20. Sigmund Freud, "The Antithetical Sense of Primal Words," trans. M. N. Searl, in *Character and Culture*, ed. Philip Rieff (New York: Collier Books, 1963), p. 44–46.

21. Samuel Taylor Coleridge, *Biographia Literaria*, ed. James Engell and Walter Jackson Bate, 2 vols., vol. 7 of *Collected Works*, gen. ed. Kathleen Coburn (Princeton: Princeton Univ. Press, 1983), 1:82–84 and n.

22. *The Three Trials of William Hone for Publishing Three Parodies; viz. The Late John Wilkes's Catechism, The Political Litany, and The Sinecurist's Creed; on Three Ex-Officio Informations, at Guildhall, London, During Three Successive Days, December 18, 19, & 20, 1817; Before Three Special Juries, and Mr. Justice Abbott, on the First Day, and Lord Chief Justice Ellenborough, on the Last Two Days* (London: Hone, 1818) 1:4.

23. See Peter Manning, "The Hone-ing of Byron's *Corsair*," in *Textual Criticism and Literary Interpretation*, ed. Jerome J. McGann (Chicago: Univ. of Chicago Press, 1985), pp. 107–26, for an excellent account of Hone's piracy.

24. For an admirable discussion of Hone's career that situates him in a transitional moment between two modes of production and interprets his trial for blasphemy as a struggle against discursive hegemony, see Olivia Smith, *The Politics of Language: 1791– 1819* (New York: Oxford Univ. Press, 1984), pp. 154–201.

25. *Three Trials* 1:45.

26. Edmund Burke, *Reflections on the Revolution in France* (1790; rpt. Harmondsworth: Penguin, 1968), p. 211.

27. The challenge is forcefully put by Eve Kosofsky Sedgwick in her essay "The Character in the Veil: Imagery of the Surface in the Gothic Novel," *PMLA* 96 (1981): 255–70. On the importance of Byron's superficiality, see Jean Hall's wide-ranging essay, "The Evolution of the Surface Self: Byron's Poetic Career," *Keats-Shelley Journal* 36 (1987): 134–57.

28. Jean Baudrillard, *For a Critique of the Political Economy of the Sign*, trans. Mark Poster (St. Louis: Telos, 1981), p. 96.

29. William Hazlitt, "Lord Byron," in *The Spirit of the Age; or, Contemporary Portraits*, ed. W. Carew Hazlitt, 4th ed. (London: George Bell and Sons, 1906), p. 126.

30. Cf. Gulnare in *The Corsair*, whose angry question "What, am I then a toy for

dotard's play, / To wear but till the gilding frets away?" (3:342–43) is a denial that she is a book or a corpse.

31. Cf. Benjamin Haydon responding to Payne Knight's depreciation of the Elgin Marbles (quoted in the *Quarterly Review* [January 1816], p. 541):

> At last Mr. Knight hints that they *may* be original, but are too much broken to be of any value! Far be it from Mr. Knight to know, that in the most broken fragment the same great principle of life can be proved to exist as in the most perfect figure. Is not life as palpable in the last joint of your forefinger, as in the centre of your heart?— Thus break off a toe from any fragment of the Elgin Marbles, and *there* I will prove the great consequences of vitality, as it acts externally, to exist.

Superficially, this is antithetical to the kind of morbidity of which Hazlitt complained in Byron, but in fact the equation of a principle of art with a principle of life leads to the conclusion, brutal and bizarre, that the toe broken off from the body has as much life as the toe connected to the perfect figure (not to mention to the heart). The Marbles' augmentation of life comes at the deficit of man's—just the economy that Byron is exploring in *The Giaour* with rather more self-awareness than either Hazlitt or Haydon displays.

32. Walter Benjamin, "The Work of Art in the Age of Mechanical Reproduction," in *Illuminations*, ed. Hannah Arendt, trans. Harry Zohn (New York: Schocken, 1969), p. 223.

33. Here is the advice of John Murray, Byron's publisher: "Now, I do think that you should *fragmentize* the first hundred, and condense the last thirty, of 'Corinth,' and then you have, in words of the highest compliment, two poems . . . as good as any you have written" (Samuel Smiles, *A Publisher and His Friends: Memoir and Correspondence of the Late John Murray*, 2 vols. [London: Murray, 1891], 1:354). Cf. Hobhouse's advice to his friends regarding *Don Juan:* "Tom Moore read it in my room the other day and perfectly coincided with us about the impossibility of entire publication—I suggested extracts fragments &c, of course including the stanzas to his TM's honor and glory" (*Byron's Bulldog*, p. 263). For an analysis of *The Giaour* as a fragment, see Marjorie Levinson, *The Romantic Fragment Poem* (Chapel Hill: Univ. of North Carolina Press, 1986), pp. 115–28.

34. Smiles, *A Publisher and His Friends* 1:219n.

35. For a markedly less confident perspective, see Samuel Johnson's "Preface to Shakespeare," where the critic repudiates an Addisonian notion of absorption on the grounds that "delusion, if delusion be admitted, has no certain limitation; if the spectator can be once persuaded, that his old acquaintance are *Alexander* and *Caesar*, . . . he is in a state of elevation above the reach of reason, or of truth, and from the heights of empyrean poetry, may despise the circumscriptions of terrestrial nature" (*The Great Critics*, ed. James Harry Smith and Edd Winfield Parks [New York: Norton, 1932], p. 456).

36. On the Romantic aesthetic of the "effect," see Martin Meisel, *Realizations: Narrative, Pictorial, and Theatrical Arts in Nineteenth-Century England* (Princeton: Princeton Univ. Press, 1983), pp. 69–87.

37. So rapid was Lord Byron's style that it presented reviewers with the delightful paradox that the verse was more succinct than any prose summary. As the *Christian Observer* notes, "It is somewhat singular that it should be possible to express sentiments more briefly and strongly in verse, artificially constructed, than in prose: and yet such is

the fact" (*RR* B:2:573). The more one padded one's review with verse extracts, the shorter and more impressive the review became.

38. My approach to Byron's Orientalism is deeply indebted to the discussion of that discursive formation in Edward W. Said's landmark study *Orientalism* (New York: Pantheon, 1978).

39. *To Lord Byron: Feminine Profiles*, ed. George Paston and Peter Quennell (New York: Scribner's, 1939), pp. 100–101.

40. Smiles, *A Publisher and His Friends* 1:224.

41. Letter from Elizabeth Pigott, 1807, in *To Lord Byron*, p. 5. Cf. Byron's letter to Hobhouse from Patras in 1810:

> Odious! in boards, twould any Bard provoke,
> (Were the last words that dying Byron spoke)
> No let some charming cuts and frontispiece
> Adorn my volume, and the sale increase,
> One would not be unpublished when one's dead
> And, Hobhouse, let my works be found in *Red*.
>
> (*BLJ* 2:15)

42. Apart from the format and bindings of the volumes, a good indicator of expense was the size of the margins, a topic much discussed between Murray and Byron and noted by the *Satirist*, which, in complaining of the expense of *The Giaour*, applied to it Sheridan's description, "a rivulet of text flowing through a meadow of margin" (*RR* B:5:2134).

43. See Charles Levin, "Art and the Sociological Ego: Value from a Psychoanalytic Perspective," in *Life after Postmodernism: Essays on Value and Culture*, ed. John Fekete (New York: St. Martin's, 1987), pp. 22–63.

44. Martin, *Byron: A Poet before His Public*, p. 62.

45. See Baudrillard, *Critique*, chap. 4, "Gesture and Signature," pp. 103–11.

46. On genre as "social contract," see Jameson, *Political Unconscious* pp. 106–7.

47. Thomas De Quincey, "Style," in *The Collected Writings of Thomas De Quincey*, ed. David Masson, 14 vols. (London, 1897), 10:202.

48. Jacques Derrida, "Declarations of Independence," trans. Tom Keenan and Tom Pepper, *New Political Science* (Summer 1986), p. 10.

49. William Hazlitt, "On Reason and Imagination," in *The Plain Speaker: Opinions on Books, Men, and Things* ed. William Carew Hazlitt (London: George Bell and Sons, 1903), p. 72.

50. Cf. the warning of the *British Review* in its review of *The Bride of Abydos*: "We have still, however, a general objection to those Turkish habiliments with which he delights to encumber himself. All the glittering oriental names of dress, caparisons and arms have lost their fascination by becoming familiar, and we begin to feel, that in his haram, her kiosk, or his serai, the Turk exhibits an inferior specimen of his kind" (*RR* B:1:417).

51. See the discussion of the "shock" in the first part of chap. 9 below.

52. John Gibson Lockhart, *Memoirs of Sir Walter Scott*, 5 vols. (London: Macmillan, 1900), 2:332.

53. This becomes increasingly clear in the progressively more elaborate prefaces to the novels. See Kathryn Sutherland, "Fictional Economies: Adam Smith, Walter Scott, and the Nineteenth-Century Novel," *ELH* 54 (Spring 1987): 97–128.

54. The assignment of property is not merely to a man but to an author, however,

and that assignment carries with it the presumption of cause. Such a presumption invariably involves some mystification, for the display of the relations of production is incomplete—not that it abridges the full man who could be shown (say, by a bigger window) but that it occludes the place of capital, as it is occluded in Scott's novels and career. A later, Balzacian realism of bankruptcy and ruin will teach Scott that the artifice of law is no defense against the exigencies of economics.

55. Baudrillard, *Critique of Political Economy*, p. 106.

56. The transactions with Caroline Lamb that bear on the *Giaour* are complicated. The key letters that replay the themes and imagery of the tales are to Lady Melbourne, April 5 and 7, 1813. Lord Byron was in the process of trying to extricate himself from the relationship. Lady Caroline had asked for a lock of his hair in return for a portrait of him she had appropriated. Byron's faithless response was to send her a "double," in fact a lock of the hair of his new lover, Lady Oxford. The trick parodies the fetishism of the referent that allies Lady Caroline with biographical criticism of an empiricist bent and justifies Lady Caroline's amendment of Byron's motto to *Ne Crede Byron*.

57. Theodor W. Adorno, *Prisms*, trans. Samuel and Shierry Weber (Cambridge, Mass.: MIT Press, 1981), p. 21.

58. Said, *Orientalism*, p. 32.

59. Selim as breaker: 2:45, 65, 125, 255, 482, 565. Giaffir as piercer: 1:104, 108, 224, 325; 2:570. Zuleika as binder: 1:180–85, 282, 325, 350.

60. William Hazlitt, "The Literary Character," in *The Complete Works of William Hazlitt*, ed. P. P. Howe, 21 vols. (London: J. M. Dent, 1930–34), 4:135.

61. Adam Smith, *The Wealth of Nations*, quoted by Stephen A. Marglin, "What Do the Bosses Do? The Origins and Functions of Hierarchy in Capitalist Production," in *Classes, Power, and Conflict*, ed. Anthony Giddens and David Held (Berkeley: Univ. of California Press, 1982), p. 291.

62. Marglin, "Bosses," p. 293.

63. As John Wilson notes in *Blackwood's* (May 1818), sameness is no obstacle to appreciation of Byron at his best: "His is indeed a mind under the dominion of its passions, and which cannot escape from them even in imagination. This may, indeed must, make a sameness in his writings. But in proportion to their sameness is their variety. It is almost incredible, that a man producing continually the same passions and the same feelings, should produce them, as he has done, in such continual change of shape, that we never complain of repetition" (*RR* B:1:129).

64. As this comment from the *Dublin Examiner* (reviewing *The Siege of Corinth*) shows, Lord Byron was fast approaching that self-parodic point of being famous for wanting to be famous: "We cannot bring ourselves to suppose that Lord Byron writes with a view to any pecuniary advantage, which might tempt him to hurry his poems, prematurely, into the world; the only motive that we can believe urges him on in his poetical career, is the love of fame so universally inherent in the constitution of his genius" (*RR* B:2:683). Fame is the natural object of desire hypothesized for geniuses to save them from perversity.

65. Julia Kristeva, *Revolution in Poetic Language*, trans. Margaret Waller (New York: Columbia Univ. Press, 1984), pp. 14, 10.

66. Theodor W. Adorno, *Negative Dialectics*, trans. E. B. Ashton (New York: Seabury, 1979), p. 270.

67. That castration could itself effectively parody masculinity is the burden of some anthropological comments of Byron's on sexual practices in Italy, where

> the women prefer the *"Musici"* for two reasons—first they do not spend—they go on "in eterno" and serve an elderly lady at all times—being constantly in line of battle, or ready to [per?]form—without exhausting themselves.—To my own knowledge— Velati the Capon carried off Aglietti's adopted daughter from an *entire* man—and Chevalier—and Soldier of twenty nine who would *have married* her—so the said discarded Cavalier with the testicles told me himself—lamenting to be cut out by a codless [Hermogesser?]. (*BLJ* 7:153)

For Byron the castrated lover represents the possibility that the desire to keep going can overpower the desire for any object.

68. Adorno, *Negative Dialectics*, p. 222.

69. Ibid., p. 227; *Quarterly Review* (January 1817), p. 510.

70. Lockhart, *Memoirs of Scott* 2:323–24.

71. Jacques Lacan, "Desire and the Interpretation of Desire in *Hamlet*," trans. James Hulbert, in *Literature and Psychoanalysis: The Question of Reading: Otherwise, Yale French Studies* 55/56 (1977): 38. My use of Lacan is indebted to Jonathan Crewe's unpublished essay "'Naught So Damned As Melancholy': *Hamlet* and the Future of Psychoanalytic Criticism."

72. Lacan, "Desire," p. 12.

73. Ibid., p. 38.

74. Lockhart, *Memoirs of Scott* 2:321–22.

75. For a discussion of the bearing of Napoleon's career on the construction of the Romantic subject, see Alan Liu, "Wordsworth: The History in Imagination," *ELH* 51 (Fall 1984): 505–48. My inspiration for this line of argument was the title of David V. Erdman's essay "The Man Who Was Not Napoleon," *Wordsworth Circle* 12 (Winter 1981): 92–96.

76. Coleridge, *Biographia Literaria* 1:30–31.

77. Frederick William Hackwood, *William Hone: His Life and Times* (London: T. Fisher Unwin, 1912), p. 167.

78. "The appeal to arms is indeed the last resource of sovereign princes, because they have no superior on earth to determine their differences. Every duellist therefore makes himself as it were an independent sovereign, when he appeals only to his sword" (Charles Moore, *A Full Inquiry into the Subject of Suicide with Two Treatises on Duelling and Gaming* (1790), p. 267n; quoted in Donna T. Andrew, "The Code of Honour and Its Critics: The Opposition to Duelling in England, 1700–1850," *Social History* 5 (October 1980): 423n.

79. Linda Hutcheon, *A Theory of Parody: The Teachings of Twentieth-Century Art Forms* (New York: Methuen, 1985), pp. 69–83.

80. Hélène Cixous and Catherine Clément, *The Newly Born Woman*, trans. Betsy Wing (Minneapolis: Univ. of Minnesota Press, 1986), p. 37.

81. The best contemporary statement of the former tendency appears in the *Critical Review*'s remarks on *The Corsair*: "We know of no one, to whom scenery, dress, and decoration, are less necessary, and who is therefore likely to lose more, by being locally attached. These adjuncts are body and soul to many writers; and, having spent half their life in the acquirement of a costume, they must make the most of it. A painter of the passions may practice anywhere" (*RR* B:2:636). The line is inadvertently continued in

Georg Lukács's critique of the Enlightenment view of history, which leads him to a similar derogation of costume: "The greatest obstacle to an understanding of history lay in the Enlightenment's conception of man's unalterable nature. Thus, any change in the course of history had meant, in extreme cases, *merely* a change of costume and, in general, merely the moral ups and downs of the same man" (*The Historical Novel*, trans. Hannah and Stanley Mitchell [Harmondsworth: Penguin, 1962], p. 27; emphasis added). For a sophisticated rendering of the problem of costume in Byron, see Susan Wolfson, "'Their She Condition': Cross-Dressing and the Politics of Gender in *Don Juan*," *ELH* 54 (Fall 1987): 585–617.

82. Smiles, *A Publisher and His Friends* 1:221; *RR* B:5:2245; *RR* B:5:2141; *To Lord Byron*, p. 57; *Henry Crabb Robinson on Books and Their Writers*, ed. Edith J. Morley, 3 vols. (London: J. M. Dent, 1938), 1:85. For a recent echo of this chorus, see Martin, *Byron: A Poet before His Public*, pp. 49–50.

83. Adam Smith, *Essays on Rhetoric and Belles Lettres*, ed. J. C. Bryce (1983; rpt. Indianapolis: Liberty*Classics*, 1985), p. 3.

84. On the issue of the imperspicuousness of Lord Byron's language, see Peter J. Manning's superb essay, "*Don Juan* and Byron's Imperceptiveness to the English Word," *Studies in Romanticism* 18 (Summer 1979): 207–33. A circumstantial and insightful account of the lameness of Byron's lines appears in Truman Guy Steffan, *Lord Byron's Cain* (Austin: Univ. of Texas Press, 1968), pp. 109–31.

85. *To Lord Byron*, p. 68.

86. Doris Langley Moore, *Lord Byron: Accounts Rendered* (London: John Murray, 1974), p. 61.

87. E. H. Coleridge, ed., *Complete Poetical Works of Samuel Taylor Coleridge* (Oxford: Oxford Univ. Press, 1969), p. 453.

88. Jean-François Lyotard, "Rules and Paradoxes and Svelte Appendix," trans. Brian Massumi, *Cultural Critique*, no. 2 (Winter 1986–87), p. 213.

89. Hazlitt, "Lord Byron," p. 124.

90. The unpronounceability of Byronic names was a theme of the reviews that Byron delighted in. See, for example, the *British Review*'s remarks that the "sphynx"-like "word Giaour might have been too much for OEdipus himself, as it walks either on one, two, or three feet, or in other words, is composed of one, two, or three syllables, as it may be convenient to pronounce it" (*RR* B:1:409). This was not an effect over which Byron was always in control. See his account to Sir William Knighton of his introduction to his future father-in-law, Ralph Milbanke: "I had an amicable reception. The only personal question put to me was when I was mounting my horse: Sir Ralph called after me, 'Pray, my Lord, how do you pronounce your name? Birron or By-ron?' I replied, 'B Y, sir, spells *by*, all the world over" (*HVSV*, p. 96).

91. Compare this Byronic confoundment with Michael Fried's account of the suspension of Thomas Eakins's signature on his canvases between the planes of what Fried calls the "pictorial" and the "graphic" (*Realism, Writing, Disfiguration: On Thomas Eakins and Stephen Crane* [Chicago: Univ. of Chicago Press, 1986], pp. 53–55). In *Redgauntlet* Walter Scott renders the Byronic signature in the story that Mr. Herries of Birrenswork ("Byron's work") tells to the imprisoned Darsie Latimer to explain the maidservant's startled reaction to Latimer's "brent broo"—which should be translated, as the *Critical*'s decoding of the Giaour's countenance instructed both us and Scott, "Byroned brow."

Chapter 5: The Speculative Stage

1. Leslie A. Marchand, *Byron: A Biography*, 3 vols. (New York: Knopf, 1957), 2:563.

2. Although Lady Byron is the writer here, it might have been Hobhouse or Shelley, both of whom objected to the degrading characters with whom Byron associated. "Abominable trade" invokes the homoerotic motif latent in all of Lady Byron's insinuations about Byron's extradomestic habits; as we have seen in chap. 2, however, the trade in bodies and in books produces interchangeable sites of the perverse.

3. Discussing the history of wrangling over literary property, Isaac Disraeli (a friend and adviser of Murray's) takes exception to Samuel Johnson's flattering designation of booksellers as the "patrons of literature." He insists that they are always "commercial men." On the other hand, he distances contemporary practices from the ignorant venality of a Tonson, claiming that "in these times such a mere trader in literature has disappeared" (*The Calamities and Quarrels of Authors* [1812–14], ed. Benjamin Disraeli (London, 1860), pp. 15–17 and n.). "Mere traders" have become sophisticated speculators.

4. Pierre Bourdieu, *Distinction: A Social Critique of the Judgment of Taste*, trans. Richard Nice (Cambridge, Mass.: Harvard Univ. Press, 1984), p. 56.

5. For a discussion of the monopolistic practices of eighteenth-century booksellers, see Jerome Christensen, *Practicing Enlightenment: Hume and the Formation of a Literary Career* (Madison: Univ. of Wisconsin Press, 1987), pp. 184–96, and Mark Rose, "The Author As Proprietor: *Donaldson* v. *Becket* and the Genealogy of Modern Authorship," *Representations* 23 (Summer 1988): 51–85.

6. "In the economic genre, the rule is that what happens can happen only if it has already been paid back, and therefore has already happened. Exchange presupposes that the cession is canceled in advance by a countercession, the circulation of the book being canceled by its sales. And the sooner this is done, the better the book is" (Jean-François Lyotard, *The Differend: Phrases in Dispute*, trans. Georges Van Den Abbeele [Minneapolis: Univ. of Minnesota Press, 1988], p. xvi).

7. *Letters of Thomas Moore*, ed. Wilfred Dowden, 2 vols. (Oxford: Clarendon Press, 1964), 1:321n.

8. On the reasons for *Rokeby*'s relative failure, see John Gibson Lockhart, *Memoirs of Sir Walter Scott*, 5 vols. (London: Macmillan, 1900), 2:256, 269; on the betting between "enthusiastic academics" on the "issue of the struggle" between the "elder favourite" and *Childe Harold*—a variant of the publishers' speculation in copyrights—see 2:249.

9. Jean Baudrillard, *For a Critique of the Political Economy of the Sign*, trans. Mark Poster (St. Louis: Telos, 1981), p. 119. Over the mantel in the large, handsome first-story room in the publishing house on Albemarle Street where Byron, Murray, and their colleagues frequently met there still hangs the portrait of the group that Murray commissioned. Murray's salon is distinguished fundamentally from the club of Matthews or from the salon of the prerevolutionary French philosophes by a capacity of self-representation metaphorized by the painting but realized by Murray's publication.

10. Although Lord Byron protested against Murray's shifts, he was no innocent in the game of self-promotion. As Marchand notes, Byron was aware that his bookseller Crosby arranged a review of *Hours of Idleness* in a "periodical which he published and controlled" (*BLJ* 1:130, n. 1). See Kurt Heinzelman, "Byron's Poetry of Politics: The Economic Basis of the 'Poetical Character,'" *Texas Studies in Literature and Language* 23 (Fall 1981): 361–72.

11. The most notorious eighteenth-century attempt to manipulate copyright in order to establish what Isaac Disraeli called a "new government in the literary world" was William Warburton's employment of the "immortal works of Pope" to divide the world "into two parts, the *Warburtonians* and the *Anti*." What Disraeli calls the "machine" for this "revolution" was put together when Warburton "obtained a royal patent to secure to himself the sole property of Pope's words [so that] the public were compelled, under the disguise of a Commentary on the most classical of our Poets, to be concerned with all his literary quarrels, and have his libels and lampoons perpetually before them" (*Calamities*, pp. 270–71). Disraeli was one of Murray's most trusted advisers, but it seems to have been Lord Byron who learned most from reading him. In 1814 the Warburtonian breakthrough occurred: "Some pious person has written & is about to publish a long poem— an 'Anti-Byron' which he sent to *Murray*—who (not very fairly) sent it to me—and I advised him to print it—but some strange sort of book-selling delicacy won't let him— however some one else will" (*BLJ* 4:82). Murray's "delicacy" also later kept him from taking Lord Byron's advice that he outflank literary pirates by preemptively pirating his own editions of Byron. Murray's scruples, which prevented the consolidation of the "machine" and contributed to Byron's decision to secede from the circle and join with the Hunts and Shelley in the project of forming a new "literary government" under the rubric of the *Liberal*, are to be attributed to his desire not to appear a mechanic: for Murray, publishing was a speculation in social prestige as well as in money. The acquisition of social capital, such as the house at Albemarle Street he obtained with the profits from *Childe Harold*, and of political influence, such as he obtained through the editorial policy of the *Quarterly*, was as important to him as financial accumulation.

12. Michel de Certeau, *The Practice of Everyday Life*, trans. Steven F. Rendall (Berkeley: Univ. of California Press, 1984), p. xix.

13. Samuel Smiles, *A Publisher and His Friends: Memoir and Correspondence of the Late John Murray*, 2 vols. (London: Murray, 1891), 1:93.

14. See ibid., pp. 192, 106, 107, 114.

15. Ibid., p. 223.

16. Lockhart, *Memoir of Scott* 3:417.

17. Ibid., p. 203. And, of course, that grasp was none too strong: both Czar Archibald and John Ballantyne, the "Dey of Aljeers," were brought to ruin and Scott with them.

18. On the *Edinburgh Review*'s practice of instructing its readers "on French events through an endless display of historical analogies," see Biancamaria Fontana, *Rethinking the Politics of Commercial Society: The "Edinburgh Review" 1802–1832* (Cambridge: Cambridge Univ. Press, 1985), pp. 12–13.

19. Shelley to Thomas Love Peacock in 1819 discussing his plans for the *Liberal* (William H. Marshall, *Byron, Shelley, Hunt, and "The Liberal"* [Philadelphia: Univ. of Pennsylvania Press, 1960], p. 23.

20. "I sought no homage from the Race that write; / I kept, like *Asian* Monarchs, from their sight" (Alexander Pope, *Epistle to Dr. Arbuthnot*, ll. 219–20).

21. Malcolm Elwin, *Lord Byron's Wife* (New York: Harcourt, Brace and World, 1962), p. 349. Cf. Lord Byron's reported account in *Lady Blessington's "Conversations of Lord Byron,"* ed. Ernest J. Lovell, Jr. (Princeton: Princeton Univ. Press, 1969), pp. 226–27.

22. In his close and circumstantial reading of the symbolic force of this poem, W. Paul Elledge insightfully remarks that the persuasiveness of Byron's language, which

"goes a long way toward redeeming the banality of Byron's Petrarchan conventions," is "recognition that the 'blow' so brutally delivered and stingingly felt here serves as metaphor for the composition and signing of the separation document" ("Talented Equivocation: Byron's 'Fare Thee Well,'" *Keats-Shelley Journal* 35 (1986): 51.

23. For a discussion of "resumption" in the context of professionalization and critical appropriation, see William H. Epstein, "Counter-Intelligence: Cold War Criticism and Eighteenth-Century Studies," *ELH* 57 (Spring 1990): 66.

24. See Edward W. Said, *Beginnings: Intention and Method* (Baltimore: Johns Hopkins Univ. Press, 1975), pp. 191–275. The influence of Said's work on my conception of Lord Byron's career has been formative.

25. Anthony Giddens, *The Constitution of Society: Outline of the Theory of Structuration* (Berkeley: Univ. of California Press, 1984), pp. xix, xxiii.

26. Pierre Bourdieu, *Outline of a Theory of Practice*, trans. Richard Nice (Cambridge: Cambridge Univ. Press, 1977), pp. 164–71.

27. For a subtle account of Hume's rhetorical strategies in this section of the *Treatise*, see John Richetti, *Philosophical Writing* (Cambridge, Mass.: Harvard Univ. Press, 1983), pp. 200–209.

28. See Nancy Armstrong, *Domesticity and Desire in the Novel* (New York: Oxford Univ. Press, 1987), pp. 59–95, and the discussion of Addison in chap. 1 above.

29. *Quarterly Review*, no. 27 (1815–16). Extracted in *Sir Walter Scott on Novelists and Fiction*, ed. Ioan Williams (New York: Barnes and Noble, 1968), pp. 225–36.

30. Cf. the later comment to Hobhouse: "Surely you agree with me about the real *vacuum* of human pursuits, but one must force an object of attainment—not to rust in the scabbard altogether." On "pursuits" see James Field Stanfield's 1813 *Essay on the Study and Composition of Biography*, where he invokes the "doctrine of PURSUITS . . . Pursuits, directed to certain ends, adjusted by precise regulations and specified means of advancement" (pp. 311–12). Stanfield is quoted and contextualized in relation to the determination of a "life-course" in William H. Epstein's *Recognizing Biography* (Philadelphia: Univ. of Pennsylvania Press, 1987), pp. 143–44.

31. The antecedent here is in Addison: "A gay old woman, says the fable, seeing all her wrinkles represented in a large looking-glass, threw it upon the ground in a passion, and broke it into a thousand pieces; but as she was afterwards surveying the fragments, with a spiteful kind of pleasure, she could not forbear uttering herself in the following soliloquy: 'What have I got by this revengeful blow of mine? I have multiplied my deformity, and see an hundred ugly faces where before I saw but one'" (*Spectator*, no. 451).

32. Ross Chambers defines the "specular text" in *Story and Situation: Narrative Seduction and the Power of Fiction* (Minneapolis: Univ. of Minnesota Press, 1984), p. 29.

33. See Sheila Emerson's searching essay "Byron's 'One Word': The Language of Self-Expression in *Childe Harold III*," *Studies in Romanticism* 20 (Fall 1981): 363–82, which meditates on "the analogy between the figure Byron cuts as he regards himself in the world, and the configuration of his reflexive language—language that often is, or is used to explore, the maneuver of an imagination that reflects on itself" (p. 364). For a discussion of "self-making" and "text-making" in *Childe Harold* as "parallel acts," see Frederick Garber, *Self, Text, and Romantic Irony: The Example of Byron* (Princeton: Princeton Univ. Press, 1988), pp. 7–31.

34. Guy Debord, *Society of the Spectacle* (Detroit: Black and Red Books, 1977), no. 4.

35. Samuel Taylor Coleridge, *Biographia Literaria*, ed. James Engell and Walter

Jackson Bate, 2 vols., vol. 7 of *Collected Works*, gen. ed. Kathleen Coburn (Princeton: Princeton Univ. Press, 1983), 1:205.

36. Ibid., pp. 304–5.

37. Cf. Lyotard: "Reality is not what is 'given' to this or that 'subject,' it is a state of the referent . . . which results from the effectuation of establishment procedures defined by a unanimously agreed-upon protocol, and from the possibility offered to anyone to recommence this effectuation as often as he or she wants. The publishing industry would be one of these protocols, historical inquiry another" (*Differend*, p. 4).

38. Barbey D'Aurevilly, *The Anatomy of Dandyism, with Some Observations on Beau Brummel* (1844), trans. D. B. Wyndham Lewis (London: Peter Davies, 1928), p. 6.

39. David Hume, "The Rise and Progress of the Arts and Sciences," in *Essays, Moral, Political, and Literary*, ed. Eugene F. Miller (1777; rpt. Indianapolis: Liberty Classics, 1985), p. 120.

40. While Colin Campbell seems basically right in seeing the dandy as an adaptation of the aristocratic ethos, particularly in his reliance on a coterie for recognition, his assertion that "refinement in conversation led to a premium being placed upon wit" does not square with Brummelliana—refined in dress, sarcastic in speech (*The Romantic Ethic and the Spirit of Modern Consumerism* [Oxford: Basil Blackwell, 1987], p. 168). The "fat friend" anecdote is retailed in Captain Jesse's *Life of George Brummell, Esq., Commonly Called Beau Brummell*, 2 vols. (London, 1844), 1:258. Jesse attributes the break between the prince regent and Brummell to the latter's sarcastic remarks about the prince's mistress, Mrs. Fitzherbert.

41. Jesse, *Life of Brummell* 2:358.

42. D'Aurevilly, *Anatomy*, pp. 12–13.

43. Jesse, *Life of Brummell* 1:59. Cf. Bourdieu, *Distinction*, p. 68, on the ideology of natural taste. D'Aurevilly remarks that "independence makes the Dandy. Otherwise there would be a Dandiacal code, which there certainly is not" (*Anatomy*, p. 27).

44. On the "grotesque body," see Mikhail M. Bakhtin, *Rabelais and His World*, trans. Helene Iswolsky (Bloomington: Indiana Univ. Press, 1984). For a suggestive application of the Bakhtinian concept to the modern conception of authorship, see Peter Stallybrass and Allon White, *The Politics and Poetics of Transgression* (Ithaca: Cornell Univ. Press, 1986), pp. 100–125; see also their interesting discussion of manners and what they call the eighteenth century's "will to refinement," pp. 89–94.

45. D'Aurevilly, *Anatomy*, p. 46n. Lord Byron claimed that he was the "only literary man" whom the dandies tolerated (*BLJ* 9:22). But as the narrator's self-dramatization in *Beppo* indicates, there was a discontinuity between the dandy and the writer (as there was between the dandiacal body and the sexual body). The poet is the dandy "unraveled":

> But I am but a nameless sort of person
>   (A broken Dandy lately on my travels),
> And take for rhyme, to hook my rambling verse on,
>   The first that Walker's Lexicon unravels,
> And when I can't find that, I put a worse on,
>   Not caring as I ought for critics' cavils;
> I've half a mind to tumble down to prose,
> But verse is more in fashion—so here goes.
>
>   (*Beppo*, st. 52)

However full of "pith" the wisdom of the dandies (see Leigh Hunt's preface to the *Liberal*), it was programmatically oral. Brummell wrote little and that little was deliberately ephemeral. No book was allowed to vie with the authentic image. Brummell hazarded much and often, but he never risked ink stains on the immaculate glove that epitomized his social being by insulating him from human contact and physical labor.

46. The two names most closely associated with this debate were John Abernathy and William Lawrence. Coleridge defended Abernathy and the vitalist position in his unpublished tract *Theory of Life*.

47. Disraeli, *Calamities*, pp. 19 and 13. The sacrificial model was culturally pervasive, especially in reviews that attempted to portray Lord Byron as the desecrator of the tribal altars. For a generalized rendition of sacrifice in relation to authorial anxiety, see Coleridge's citation of Milton's image of "Moloch, horrid king, besmeared with blood / Of human sacrifice and parent's tears," in *The Friend* (1809), appendix A, p. 45. Lord Byron, whose antisacrificial stance was consistent throughout his career (see below, chap. 6; see also Michael Foot on Byron's abhorrence of Molochism in *The Politics of Paradise: A Vindication of Byron* [New York: Harper and Row, 1988], pp. 111–12), defended the Nottingham framebreakers to Lord Holland according to the bloody consequences of mechanical progress (*BLJ* 2:165).

48. *Quarterly Review* (July 1816), p. 345. If visualized, the reviewer's imaginary author might resemble William Hone's new description of man (see chap. 4 above). Cf. Alexander Welsh, "Writing and Copying in the Age of Steam," in *Victorian Literature and Society: Essays Presented to Richard D. Altick*, ed. James R. Kincaid and Albert J. Kuhn (Columbus: Ohio State Univ. Press, 1984), pp. 30–34.

49. John Haslam, *Illustrations of Madness: Exhibiting a Singular Case of Insanity, and a No Less Remarkable Difference in Medical Opinion: Developing the Nature of Assailment, and the Manner of Working Events* (London, 1810), pp. 2, 10.

50. Ibid., pp. 19–20.

51. In his account of the separation, Marchand tells how the frightened and suspicious Lady Byron consulted Dr. Baillie (the same doctor "who had been brought into consultation on Byron's foot when the poet was a boy") about Byron's sanity. Failing to get a satisfactory answer, the Caleb-like Lady Byron (at least according to Hobhouse) pried open the trunks and letter cases of her Falkland for secret evidence to explain his strange moods. She found laudanum and, apparently, Sade's *Justine*—the equivalent of Matthews's machinery for stimulation and punishment. Hobhouse also reports, "Her Ladyship had provided herself with a volume of the *Medical Journal* in which she thought a case described of *hydrocephalus* designated the peculiar malady so exactly, that she marked the most prominent and apposite features on the margin with a pencil" (Marchand, *Byron*, pp. 558–59). Diagnosing her husband means marking his place in a codified series of cases like those rehearsed by Haslam in his *Observations on Madness and Melancholy* (1809). Although Lady Byron seems au courant in her recourse to contemporary medical discourse, in fact she gets stuck in what might be called the Gothic or physiognomic stage of medical development. As commentator after commentator on the relationship has duly observed, Lady Byron never progressed beyond the thrill of discovery to the deliberate business of what Haslam calls "moral management."

52. Haslam, *Illustrations*, p. 19.

53. Or, possibly, a Romantic epistemology. With the help of Bloom's ratios (see *The Anxiety of Influence* [Oxford: Oxford Univ. Press, 1973]) a "psychotic" reading of the fitted

and fitting quality of the Wordsworthian interchange in "Tintern Abbey" could be constructed. Some such reading seems to be the inevitable extension of the Abramsian understanding of Wordsworth's project as a secularized theodicy (see M. H. Abrams, *Natural Supernaturalism* [New York: Norton, 1971], passim).

54. Matthews explains that the gang had him committed to Bedlam in order to prevent his exposure of their plans (for they are French spies) to disorganize the British navy.

55. Roy Porter, *A Social History of Madness* (New York: E. P. Dutton, 1987), pp. 58–59.

56. J. Ann Hone, *For the Cause of Truth: Radicalism in London, 1796–1821* (Oxford: Clarendon Press, 1982), p. 50.

57. Kim Wheatley, "Shelley's Poetry and the Paranoid Style" (Ph.D. diss., Johns Hopkins University, 1992).

58. François Furet, *Interpreting the French Revolution*, trans. Elborg Forster (Cambridge: Cambridge Univ. Press, 1981), p. 25.

59. *Lady Blessington's "Conversations of Lord Byron,"* pp. 226–27.

60. Walter Benjamin, *The Origin of German Tragic Drama*, trans. John Osborne (London: NLB, 1977), p. 178.

61. Lockhart, *Memoirs of Scott* 3:11.

62. See Francis Jeffrey's judgment in his unsigned review of *Childe Harold III* in the *Edinburgh Review* of December 1816 (*RR* B:2:873).

63. Bourdieu, *Distinction*, pp. 55–56.

64. The procedure will be parodied in the catalog of stereotypical heroes in the first two stanzas of *Don Juan*.

65. Hume, "Rise and Progress of the Arts and Sciences," p. 79. Benjamin Constant, "The Spirit of Conquest and Usurpation and Their Relation to European Civilization," in *Political Writings*, trans. and ed. Biancamaria Fontana (Cambridge: Cambridge Univ. Press, 1988), p. 90.

66. Even Hazlitt, who never recanted his admiration for Napoleon, could in "On the Spirit of Monarchy" find no better way to distinguish between a ruler like George III and Napoleon than to contrast two kinds of acting styles: the pompous strutting of Young and the radical, heartfelt realism of Kean (*The Complete Works of William Hazlitt*, ed. P. P. Howe, 21 vols. [London: J. M. Dent, 1930–34]), 19:256–57. One wonders whether Hazlitt is being willfully naive or abysmally ironic when, to indicate Kean's superiority, he remarks that he "has that within which passes shew," thereby endorsing Kean's authenticity with one of the more theatrical utterances of one of the more famous characters Kean portrayed. We cannot, of course, know the truth about Hazlitt (or Kean) when all the truth lies in the show of passing show. Hobhouse compares Napoleon and Kean, who share the "same habit of *chewing*," in a letter to Byron from Paris in 1815 (*Byron's Bulldog: The Letters of John Cam Hobhouse to Lord Byron*, ed. Peter W. Graham [Columbus: Ohio State Univ. Press, 1984], p. 197).

67. Constant, "Spirit of Conquest," p. 366.

68. Ibid., p. 80.

69. See Bourdieu's interesting conjunction of H. Kantorovich's analysis of the king's two bodies with Durkheimian theories of social reproduction in *Distinction*, p. 72.

70. John B. Thompson, *Studies in the Theory of Ideology* (Cambridge: Polity, 1987), p. 56.

71. Ibid., pp. 58–59.

72. Quoted in Stallybrass and White, *Transgression*, p. 83.

73. Haslam, *Observations on Madness and Melancholy* (1809; rpt. New York: Arno, 1976), pp. 304–5.

74. Donald Davidson, "Paradoxes of Irrationality," in *Philosophical Essays on Freud*, ed. Richard Wollheim and James Hopkins (Cambridge: Cambridge Univ. Press, 1982), p. 305; quoted in Richard Rorty, *Contingency, Irony, and Solidarity* (Cambridge: Cambridge Univ. Press, 1989), p. 49.

75. Rorty, *Contingency*, p. 7.

76. Constant, "Spirit of Conquest," p. 59.

77. See Mary Douglas, *Purity and Danger: An Analysis of the Concepts of Pollution and Taboo* (London: Routledge and Kegan Paul, 1966), chaps. 1 and 2.

78. Haslam, *Illustrations*, p. 68.

79. Constant makes much the same criticism of Napoleon, who failed to live up to his cynical maxim that "one must give the French something new every three months" ("Spirit of Conquest," p. 89). The *Observer* anticipates the principle in the sociology of taste advanced by Colin Campbell: "A given stimulus, if unchanging, rapidly ceases to be a stimulus" (*Romantic Ethic*, p. 63). The question that follows and that Lord Byron's text (like, say, John Cage's) continually and forcefully poses is, "Just exactly when does a stimulus become 'unchanging'?"

80. Porter, *Madness*, pp. 58–59.

81. The idea behind Porter's *Social History of Madness*, to see the "world through the eyes of the insane" (his subtitle) by taking their narratives seriously, is authorized by Matthews's signature.

82. On aposiopesis as a device of eighteenth-century stagecraft, see Oliver Goldsmith, *Citizen of the World*, no. 21.

83. Jacques Derrida, "Force of Law: The Mystical Foundation of Authority" (unpublished), p. 33.

84. Laurence S. Lockridge, *The Ethics of Romanticism* (Cambridge: Cambridge Univ. Press, 1989), p. 418.

Chapter 6: The Shaping Spirit of Ruin

1. On the general phenomenon of spectralization, which she defines as the "absorption of ghosts into thought," see Terry Castle, "Phantasmagoria: Spectral Technology and the Metaphorics of Modern Reverie," *Critical Inquiry* 14 (Fall 1988): 26–61. Castle refers to Byron's description of George III in *The Vision of Judgment* on p. 44.

2. John Cam Hobhouse, *Historical Illustrations of the Fourth Canto of "Childe Harold"* (London, 1818), pp. 256–57 (emphasis added).

3. Malcolm Kelsall, *Byron's Politics* (Totowa, N.J.: Barnes and Noble, 1987), p. 77.

4. Cf. Hobhouse's *A Defence of the People in Reply to Lord Erskine's "Two Defences of the Whigs"* (London, 1809), where he attacks the apostate champion of the people's cause for a cynical and futile adherence to the "name of Whig" (p. 12). In the difference between a desperate clinging to the "token" of a name and a deliberate reiteration of potent maxims is the difference between a bankrupt Whiggism and a banknoted radicalism.

5. Cf. *Lara:* "A word's enough to raise mankind to kill" (2:223). In a de facto division of labor, Hobhouse had long served as Lord Byron's man of maxims. Byron writes to his friend in 1808, "I do not write often, but I like to receive letters, when therefore you are

disposed to philosophize, no one standeth more in need of precepts of all sorts than Yours very truly BYRON" (*BLJ* 1:159).

6. For contemporary praise of the platitudinous, see Richard Rorty, *Contingency, Irony, and Solidarity* (Cambridge: Cambridge Univ. Press, 1989), pp. 76–78.

7. Barbey D'Aurevilly, *The Anatomy of Dandyism, with Some Observations on Beau Brummell* (1844), trans. D. B. Wyndham Lewis (London: Peter Davies, 1928), p. 6 (see chap. 5 above). It should be noted that although Hobhouse strikes a Brummellian chord in his contempt for the "fopperies of royalty," the phrase in fact points to a significant difference between Brummell and Bonaparte. The latter dressed himself in the costume of the monarch. The former became the pattern for his prince's dress: the prince regent copied the fopperies of Brummell.

8. As Hobhouse remarks in another place, where his Byronism sounds most Burkean, "Had it been possible to establish the popular government which was the aim of Rienzi, during the absence of the popes, the Romans, whose love of liberty was to be kept alive by a constant reference to the institutions of their ancestors, would have been taught to venerate, *although blindly*, the *trophies* of their former glory" (*Illustrations*, pp. 140–41; emphasis added). As we have seen in our analysis of the Venice passage above, it is exactly the task of Byron to teach this veneration to the members of the English middle classes who are the reformist readers of his text.

9. Hobhouse, *Illustrations*, p. 136.

10. Ibid.

11. Ibid., pp. 316–17.

12. The passage competes on favorable terms with Shelley's more notorious description of Byron's Venetian surroundings. Byron, Shelley writes, "associates with wretches who seem almost to have lost the gait and physiognomy of man, and who do not scruple to avow practices which are not only not named, but I believe seldom even conceived in England" (*HVSV*, p. 219)—the point not being that Shelley is right or wrong, more or less homophobic than Hobhouse, but that his assertion of an English perspective allows for the sickening possibility that the Venetians have names for every perversion of gait, physiognomy, and object choice—and, of course, an absolution to fit the name and the crime. Cf. Hester Thrale's earlier association of Italy, homosexuality, and Catholicism: "Our *Beckfords & Bickerstaffs* too run away at least from the original Theatre of their Crimes, & do not keep their Male Mistresses in Triumph like the Roman Priests & Princes. This Italy is indeed a Sink of Sin; and however lives long in it, *must* be a little tainted. . . . External Rites of Worship here are supposed a complete compensation for the utter Absence of all Moral Virtue, & all Sense of honor" (quoted in Louis Crompton, *Byron and Greek Love: Homophobia in Nineteenth-Century England* [Berkeley: Univ. of California Press, 1985], p. 56).

13. Hobhouse, *Illustrations*, p. 321.

14. Ibid., p. 322.

15. Conspicuous Romantic examples of this misrecognition are Wordsworth's encounter with the Leech Gatherer in "Resolution and Independence" and De Quincey's recreational, opiated visits to the haunts of the working class in *Confessions of an English Opium Eater* (the meditation on the Piranesi print in the same volume systematically misrecognizes industrial as Gothic darkness). For a recent and glittering representation of this cultural trope, see the episode in David Lodge's 1988 novel *Nice Work*, where the

enlightened "heroine" visits the floor of the foundry managed by a businessman she has been assigned to "shadow."

16. Hobhouse, *Illustrations*, p. 316.

17. Hobhouse, *Essay on the Origin and Intention of Sacrifices* (Cambridge, 1809), p. 3.

18. Ibid., pp. 8–9, 40–41. Cf. Robertson Smith's later representation of Israel's "religious life [as] fundamentally more ethical than that of any of the surrounding peoples" (Mary Douglas, *Purity and Danger: An Analysis of the Concepts of Pollution and Taboo* [London: Routledge and Kegan Paul, 1966], pp. 16–17).

19. Hobhouse, *Illustrations*, pp. 327–44. I am grateful to Mark Canuel for bringing this passage to my attention.

20. On redescription, see Rorty, *Contingency*, pp. 3–9.

21. Jean-François Lyotard, "Complexity and the Sublime," *ICA Documents 4: Postmodernism* (1985): 10.

22. Sir Isaac Pitman, *A History of Shorthand*, 4th ed. (London: Pitman and Sons, 1917), p. 4.

23. Francis Horner, October 1802 review of Henry Thornton's "An Inquiry into the Nature and Effects of the Paper Credit of Great Britain," in the *Edinburgh Review*; rpt. in *The Economic Writings of Francis Horner in the "Edinburgh Review," 1802–1806* (London: London School of Economics, 1957), p. 33.

24. There was an element of secrecy attached to the practice of shorthand, but it was a secrecy overcome by anyone willing to pay the price of a shorthand manual and submit to the discipline of its method. The fastest writer of shorthand in the world cannot be as successful as one who is able to propagate his system widely. Thus although the history of shorthand records few innovations, there were scores of handbooks offering to instruct in the mastery of a technique for making money. Pitman observes that from the time of Edmund Willis's perfectly titled "An Abbreviation of Writing by Character" (1618) "to the present day [and Pitman's own innovation] the history of shorthand is little more than the repetition of the titles of the various systems that have appeared" (*History of Shorthand*, p. 6). Printed and circulated, a shorthand system made easy itself becomes a stereotype that acquires tremendous representative power.

25. Pitman, *History of Shorthand*, pp. 30–31.

26. See Joseph Anthony Wittreich, Jr., *Visionary Poetics: Milton's Tradition and His Legacy* (San Marino, Calif.: Huntington Library, 1979), pp. 22–24. On transition in this sense, see the discussion of Freud's "Antithetical Sense of Primal Words" in chap. 4 above.

27. Pitman, *History of Shorthand*, p. 30.

28. See Coleridge, *The Statesman's Manual, On the Constitution of Church and State, Aids to Reflection*, passim. Coleridge's adherence to the seventeenth-century style can in part be understood in terms of a model that resists reduction into shorthand. When practiced by a Launcelot Andrewes, it is a form of oral speech that cannot be rapidly understood, that is, as it were, delivered as if it were already written—a kind of longhand speech. Coleridge, who was himself a parliamentary reporter for the *Morning Post*, lectured in a style that, whether by contrivance or compulsion, baffled stenographers. According to H. N. Coleridge (quoted in *Lectures 1808–1819 on Literature*, ed. R. A. Foakes, 2 vols., vol. 5 of *Collected Works*, gen. ed. Kathleen Coburn [Princeton: Princeton Univ. Press, 1987], 1:lxxxiii):

a very experienced short-hand writer was employed to take down Mr. Coleridge's lectures on Shakspeare, but the manuscript was almost entirely unintelligible. Yet the lecturer was, as he always is, slow and measured. The writer—we have some notion it was no worse an artist than Mr. Gurney himself—gave this account of the difficulty: that with regard to every other speaker whom he had ever heard, however rapid or involved, he could almost always, by long experience in his art, guess the form of the latter part, or apodosis of the sentence by the form of the beginning; but that the conclusion of every one of Coleridge's sentences was a *surprize* upon him. He was obligated to listen to the last word.

29. Quoted in Pitman, *History of Shorthand*, pp. 69–70.

30. *Quarterly Review* (October 1816), p. 252. Contemporaries recognized the change in parliamentary rhetoric under way in the eighteenth century as parliamentarians adapted themselves to the media of shorthand and newspapers that gave them access to an increasingly attentive, clamorous, and dispersed public. The change had already been applauded by Hume in "Of Eloquence." Much of it involved arming oneself for improvisation with maxims borrowed from the inventor—who might have been oneself, remembered in a printed form mediated by stenographic transcription. Burke was especially notorious for such repetition.

31. De Quincey, *Style*, in *The Collected Writings of Thomas De Quincey*, ed. David Masson, 14 vols. (London, 1897), 10:192.

32. Leslie A. Marchand, *Byron: A Biography*, 3 vols. (New York: Knopf, 1957), 2:612.

33. The moral is the same one that Pitt allegedly applied to the elephantine and expensive *Political Justice* (see Isaac Kramnick's introduction to his edition of William Godwin's *Enquiry Concerning Political Justice* [Harmondsworth: Pelican, 1976], p. 12).

34. Edmund Burke, *Reflections on the Revolution in France* (1790; rpt. Harmondsworth: Penguin, 1968), p. 143.

35. Isaac Disraeli, *The Calamities and Quarrels of Authors* (1812–14), ed. Benjamin Disraeli (London, 1860), p. 231.

36. See McGann's notes to *Childe Harold III*, vol. 2 of *CPW*, pp. 298, 308, and 311.

37. J. C. D. Clark, *English Society 1688–1832* (Cambridge: Cambridge Univ. Press, 1985), p. 109.

38. Hazlitt's objection, made in a review of the poem in the *Yellow Dwarf*, is apt: "As to his vow of revenge, which is to end in forgiveness, it is unconscious, constitutional caprice and contradiction: it is self-will exerting itself in straining at a violent conclusion; and then, by another exertion, defeating itself by doing nothing" (*RR* B:5:2338).

39. Textbook sublimity. Cf. Alexander Gerard's *Essay on Taste* (1759): "When a large object is presented, the mind expands itself to the extent of that object, and is filled with one grand sensation. . . . It finds such a difficulty in spreading itself to the dimensions of its object, as enlivens and invigorates its frame: and having overcome the opposition which this occasions, it sometimes imagines itself present in every part of the scene which it contemplates; and from the sense of this immensity, feels a noble pride, and entertains a lofty conception of its own capacity" (p. 12; quoted in Sheila Emerson, "Byron's 'One Word': The Language of Self-Expression in *Childe Harold III*," *Studies in Romanticism* 20 [Fall 1981]: 367n.).

40. Quoted in Zachary Leader, *Reading Blake's "Songs"* (London: Routledge and Kegan Paul, 1981), p. 71.

41. And a goal that in principle can be reached repeatedly, routinely, as a kind of inadvertent style. Here is Thomas Moore, one who did not count among his merits the ability to forget himself, from his journal of January 28, 1819 (*Journal of Thomas Moore,* ed. Wilfred S. Dowden, 2 vols. [Newark: Univ. of Delaware Press, 1983], 1:137):

> Called upon Shee, the Painter, who told me Lord Holland was so much pleased with his picture of me . . . that he said he must have it—"must have my friend Moore's picture"—"This shows (said Shee) how you stand in that {noble} House"—& it is certainly flattering—Went to Murray—Rogers had told me that Murray said he would himself, whether Wilkie came into it or not, run all risks in publishing my Life of Sheridan and give me a thousand pounds for it—I now found this was the case— talked of {the} Don Juan—but too true that it is not fit for publication—he seems, by living so long out of London to have forgotten that standard of decorum in society, to which every one must refer his *words* at least, who hopes to be either listened to or read by the world.

Moore's hard-won fit with the standard of decorum is emblematized not so much in the value of his portrait as ornament as in his own Byronic mobility between the house of the Whig grandee and the salon of the Tory publisher. The social indeterminacy of Lord Byron's words, their lack of reference to a standard of decorum (the effect of a continual forgetting), is expressed as an inability to acquire the social credit required for the author to engage in the kind of exchange that will keep him solvent.

42. In the event, as we shall see below, it was not the body of Byron that was burned but his memoirs. Nonetheless, the disfiguration of this body assured that he could not be fully re-membered, even by Hobhouse.

43. See Peter J. Manning: "It is precisely in proportion to his refusal to exalt the individual word that Byron is able to display the multiple functions of language itself" (*Don Juan* and Byron's Imperceptiveness to the English Word," *Studies in Romanticism* 18 [Summer 1979]: 208).

44. Captain Jesse, *Life of George Brummell, Esq., Commonly Called Beau Brummell,* 2 vols. (London, 1844), 2:358.

45. John Galt, *The Life of Lord Byron,* 3d ed. (London, 1830), p. vii. Had Lady Caroline Lamb been possessed of Galt's genealogical information it would have spared her some trouble, for, Byron ruefully remarks, "one of her amusements by her own account has been engraving on the said [livery] 'buttons' *Ne* 'crede Byron' an interesting addition to the motto of my family which thus atones for it's degradation in my acquaintance with her" (*BLJ* 3:9).

46. Stendhal was no doubt correct in his supercilious comment that "the great poet esteemed himself much more as a descendant of the Byrons of Normandy, who followed William, later the conqueror of England, than as the author of *Parisina* or *Lara*" (*HVSV,* p. 197): Byron never felt that his greatness was tied to either of those poems. But with the entry onto the terrain of *Don Juan,* the poet's self-esteem, no longer the simple reflection on himself that Stendhal and *Childe Harold III* register, became a matter of his own conquest (in "line of [his] cut-throat ancestors") of England from Italy—a longer crossing than from Normandy.

47. Johann Peter Eckermann, *Words of Goethe* (New York: Classic Publishing, 1933), p. 75.

48. The possibility that lines could register color values as well as forms—a practical

issue for heralds and engravers—was a subject of theoretical interest for J. M. W. Turner—see John Gage, *Colour in Turner: Poetry and Truth* (London: Studion Vista, 1969), pp. 50–51.

Chapter 7: Circumstantial Gravity

1. Jerome J. McGann, *"Don Juan" in Context* (Chicago: Univ. of Chicago Press, 1976), p. 83. Other works of criticism on *Don Juan* that have been broadly useful in the formation of my approach to the poem are Frederick L. Beaty, *Byron the Satirist* (Dekalb: Northern Illinois Univ. Press, 1985); Leslie Brisman, *Romantic Origins* (Ithaca: Cornell Univ. Press, 1978); Michael Cooke, *Acts of Inclusion* (New Haven: Yale Univ. Press, 1979); Frederick Garber, *Self, Text, and Romantic Irony: The Example of Byron* (Princeton: Princeton Univ. Press, 1988); Robert F. Gleckner, "From Selfish Spleen to Equanimity: Byron's Satires," *Studies in Romanticism* 18 (Summer 1979): 173–206; M. K. Joseph, *Byron the Poet* (London: Gollancz, 1964); and George M. Ridenour, *The Style of Don Juan*, Yale Studies in English no. 144 (New Haven: Yale Univ. Press, 1960).

2. *Byron's Bulldog: The Letters of John Cam Hobhouse to Lord Byron*, ed. Peter W. Graham (Columbus: Ohio State Univ. Press, 1984), July 15, 1819, p. 275; also n. 4, p. 277.

3. See the opening paragraph of the anonymous *"Don John," or "Don Juan" Unmasked; Being the Key to the Mystery, Attending That Remarkable Publication; with a Descriptive Review of the Poem and Extracts* (London: William Hone, 1819): "'In a few days, DON JUAN.' These words *alone*, neither preceded or followed by explanation, appearing in the advertising columns of our newspapers, were more novel in their form than the first appearance of the new comet; and in their import, certainly not less mysterious. The curiosity of the town was raised to the highest pitch to know the meaning of the enigmatical line" (p. 6).

4. *Byron's Bulldog*, p. 275.

5. For a systematic assault on Castlereagh's twisted discourse, made in the name of right politics and good grammar, see William Cobbett, *A Grammar of the English Language* (1819; rpt. Oxford: Oxford Univ. Press, 1984), pp. 159–63, 167–70.

6. Cf. Wordsworth's portrayal of the limits of political economy in "The Old Cumberland Beggar":

> He sat, and ate his food in solitude:
> And ever, scattered from his palsied hand,
> That, still attempting to prevent the waste,
> Was baffled still, the crumbs in little showers
> Fell on the ground; and the small mountain birds,
> Not venturing yet to peck their destined meal,
> Approached within the length of half his staff.
>
> (ll. 15–21)

As the Wordsworth illustrates Castlereagian futility, so it resonates with the fate of Julia's letter in canto 2.

7. Jerome J. McGann suggestively discusses Southey as Byron's "dark double" with somewhat different reflections on the similarity between their "apostasies" in "The Book of Byron and the Book of a World," in *Beauty of Inflections: Literary Investigations in Historical Method and Theory* (Oxford: Clarendon Press, 1985), pp. 277–83. See also Peter W. Graham's exploration of the relations between Byron's *Juan* and Southey's *Letters*

from England in *"Don Juan" and Regency England* (Charlottesville: Univ. of Virginia Press, 1990), pp. 34–61. On *Don Juan* as the formal embodiment of the way the world goes, see Gleckner, "Byron's Satires," pp. 200–205.

8. For Coleridge's defense of Southey against the charge of apostasy, see *Essays on His Times*, ed. David V. Erdman, 3 vols., vol. 3 of *Collected Works*, gen. ed. Kathleen Coburn (Princeton: Princeton Univ. Press, 1978), 2:449–60, 466–78. On Coleridge's philosophical analysis of apostasy, see Jerome Christensen, "'Like a Guilty Thing Surprised': Coleridge, Deconstruction, and the Apostasy of Criticism," in *Coleridge's "Biographia Literaria": Text and Meaning*, ed. Frederick Burwick (Columbus: Ohio State Univ. Press, 1989), pp. 175–76.

9. Michel Serres, *The Parasite*, trans. Lawrence R. Schehr (Baltimore: Johns Hopkins Univ. Press, 1982), p. 38.

10. On colors and party disputes, see David Hume, "Of Parties in General," in *The Philosophical Works of David Hume*, ed. T. H. Green and T. H. Grose, 4 vols. (London, 1874–75), 3:130.

11. For a fuller condemnation of Southey's apostasy, see Byron's letter of May 9, 1817, to Murray (*BLJ* 5:220–21).

12. The pedigree of apposition as a trope of world formation is Epicurean. For a fascinating rendition of the Lucretian position, including a discussion of "negative entropy," see Michel Serres, "Lucretius: Science and Religion," in *Hermes: Literature, Science, Philosophy*, ed. Josue V. Harari and David F. Bell (Baltimore: Johns Hopkins Univ. Press, 1982), pp. 98–124. In *The Legitimacy of the Modern Age* (trans. Robert M. Wallace [Cambridge, Mass.: MIT Press, 1983], p. 169) Hans Blumenberg provides a concise formulation of the Epicurean model:

> The initial conditions of all the processes in the universe are defined by the fact that all the atoms are traveling in parallel straight lines through infinite empty space. This basic state of affairs is characterized by an extremely rational order and at the same time by sterile unproductiveness. Only on the assumption that individual atoms can break this "order," that by minor deviations from their parallel paths they can encounter the atoms and thus initiate the formation of a vortex of atoms, do the elementary bodies even come into contact, in accordance with their affinities, and finally realize a world. The "sufficient" reason for the fact that anything at all comes into existence and everything does not remain in the eternal fruitfulness of the atoms' parallel paths is as trivial as it could conceivably be.

13. On this feature of the picaresque, see Frank Wadleigh Chandler, *The Literature of Roguery*, 2 vols. in 1 (1907; rpt. New York: Burt Franklin, 1974), 1:4.

14. *Courier* (October 26, 1822), pp. 2–3; quoted in William H. Marshall, *Byron, Shelley, Hunt, and "The Liberal"* (Philadelphia: Univ. of Pennsylvania Press, 1960), pp. 103–4.

15. Marchand notes that in early 1814 a "long solemn satire called *Anti-Byron*" had been sent to Byron's publisher, Murray, who in turn sent it to Byron. Byron encouraged Murray to overcome his "strange sort of book-selling delicacy" and publish it (*BLJ* 4:81–82).

16. The existential problem put to Caleb Williams—hero, narrator, and machine—in William Godwin's novel.

17. Ross Chambers, *Story and Situation: Narrative Seduction and the Power of Fiction* (Minneapolis: Univ. of Minnesota Press, 1984), p. 4.

18. Martin Meisel, *Realizations: Narrative, Pictorial, and Theatrical Arts in Nineteenth-Century England* (Princeton: Princeton Univ. Press, 1983), pp. 8–10.

19. On period style, see Rosalind Kraus, "The Originality of the Avant-Garde: A Postmodernist Repetition," in *Art after Modernism: Rethinking Representation*, ed. Brian Wallis (Boston: Godine, 1984), p. 17.

20. The difference between a pirate and an epic hero is that the former must imagine himself as ungrounded by a mimetic tradition that he naively imitates. A pirate must continue to invent his own story for the entertainment of a gang who are not only warriors but readers.

21. See Jean Laplanche, *Life and Death in Psychoanalysis*, trans. Jeffrey Mehlman (Baltimore: Johns Hopkins Univ. Press, 1976), pp. 15–18.

22. Wortley Clutterbuck [Lord Byron], "A letter to the Editor of 'My Grand-mother's Review,'" *Liberal*, no. 1 (1822), p. 43.

23. In *The Romantic Ethic and the Spirit of Modern Consumerism* (Oxford: Basil Blackwell, 1987), Colin Campbell argues that the "distinctive modern faculty" is the "ability to create an illusion which is known to be false but felt to be true" (p. 78).

24. For a classic statement of the importance of the price's ability to command, see Thomas Malthus, "The Measure of Value" (1823), in *The Works of Thomas Robert Malthus*, ed. E. A. Wrigley and David Souden, 8 vols. (London: William Pickering, 1986), 7:180. For a recent version of the conventional claim that the special historical distinction of democratic capitalism is its break with the command economy, see Michael Novak, *The Spirit of Democratic Capitalism* (New York: Simon and Schuster, 1982), pp. 68–70.

25. In *Happy Slaves: A Critique of Consent Theory* (Chicago: Univ. of Chicago Press, 1989), Don Herzog observes, "I don't want a host of sadistic possibilities, possibilities I leave the grisly reader to conjure up for herself, to occur to me as I walk down the street. If they did, and I carefully deliberated on each one before rejecting it, I wouldn't congratulate myself on having choices and exercising autonomy" (p. 191). Life in liberal society as just such an outrageous series of degrading possibilities is the vision that *Juan* conjures up for its reader.

26. Or according to de Tocqueville, in Claude Lefort's paraphrase, what it means to be American (*Democracy and Political Theory*, trans. David Macey [Minneapolis: Univ. of Minnesota Press, 1988], p. 173):

> Subjection in minor affairs breaks out every day and is felt by the whole community indiscriminately. It does not drive men to resistance, but it crosses them at every turn, till they are led to surrender the exercise of their own will. . . . It is in vain to summon a people who have been rendered so dependent on the central power to choose from time to time the representatives of that power; this rare and brief exercise of their free choice, however important it may be, will not prevent them from gradually losing the faculties of thinking, feeling, and acting for themselves, and thus gradually falling below the level of humanity.

27. Clutterbuck, "Letter," p. 41.

28. See the discussion of Selim's penetrating gaze in chap. 4 above.

29. On the concept of "worldliness" see Edward W. Said, *The World, the Text, and the Critic* (Cambridge, Mass.: Harvard Univ. Press, 1983), pp. 31–53.

30. By failing to quote, the *British Review* can be intelligible only to a readership that has bought *Don Juan*—William Roberts, reviewer and editor, links the fate of his journal to what has libeled it. In its panic the *British* abandoned the implicit claim that it could virtuously *substitute* the review for the poem—as it had, for example, in its review of *The Giaour*, which pursued the commercially prudent and culturally acceptable procedure of wholesale extraction from the subject poem. The *British*'s paralysis—the paranoia of the culture police—answers a text that cannot be expurgated and marks its own circumstantiation in the text.

31. *Byron's Bulldog*, p. 260.

32. Quoted in Said, *World*, p. 184.

33. Serres, *Hermes*, p. 111.

34. For a contemporary version of this denial, see McGann, "The Book of Byron and the Book of a World," pp. 256–93.

35. Or *cherchez le sodomite*. In a lecture entitled "Cannibalism, the Grand Tour, and Literary History" delivered at Johns Hopkins University in September 1991, George S. Rousseau elaborated the affiliations in the eighteenth century between two discourses of the unspeakable, cannibalism and sodomy. Although Rousseau did not refer to *Don Juan*, clearly the connection he delineated contributed to the sense of outrage of those men who, reading the shipwreck scene of canto 2, could not help believing that the horrible picture of men consuming parts of men accurately represented their social practice as the deformed expression of repressed desire. For another moral, see Andrew Cooper's discussion of this passage in *Doubt and Identity in Romantic Poetry* (New Haven: Yale Univ. Press, 1988), pp. 130–49.

36. In the best commentary on Donna Julia's letter, Lawrence Lipking analyzes the identification of Lord Byron with Donna Julia (*Abandoned Women and Poetic Tradition* [Chicago: Univ. of Chicago Press, 1988], pp. 41–47).

37. Advising Murray of his decision to publish anonymously, he wrote, "Now I prefer my child to a poem at any time—and so should you as having half a dozen" (*BLJ* 7:196).

38. Leslie A. Marchand, *Byron: A Biography*, 3 vols. (New York: Knopf, 1957), 2:830.

39. Samuel Smiles, *A Publisher and His Friends: Memoir and Correspondence of the Late John Murray*, 2 vols. (London: Murray, 1891), 1:405–6.

40. Ibid., pp. 407–9.

41. Michel de Certeau, "The Arts of Dying: Celibatory Machines," in *Heterologies: Discourse on the Other*, trans. Brian Mussumi (Minneapolis: Univ. of Minnesota Press, 1986), p. 161. In some places and in some times this fade is more pronounced than others. It is, of course, most particularly advanced in England's commercialist society and most dramatic at the end of the Napoleonic Wars when the greatest land army the world had ever known was defeated by an island empire.

42. Marchand, *Byron* 2:770.

43. For a discussion of the Humean theme and strategy of social composition, see Jerome Christensen, *Practicing Enlightenment: Hume and the Formation of a Literary Career* (Madison: Univ. of Wisconsin Press, 1987), pp. 21–44.

44. *Journal of Thomas Moore*, ed. Wilfred S. Dawden, 2 vols. (Newark: Univ. of Delaware Press, 1983), 1:137.

45. *Cain* tells this story by dramatizing the discrepant biblical account of the remembering of this forgetting.

46. Cf. Kant: "Taste that requires an added element of charm and emotion for its delight, not to speak of adopting this as the measure of its approval, has not yet emerged from barbarism" (*Critique of Judgment*, quoted in Pierre Bourdieu, *Distinction: A Social Critique of the Judgment of Taste*, trans. Richard Nice [Cambridge, Mass.: Harvard Univ. Press, 1984], p. 43).

47. See Terry Eagleton's discussion of the transformation of the proportions between coercion and consent that accompanied the "growth of early bourgeois society" in *The Ideology of the Aesthetic* (Oxford: Basil Blackwell, 1990), p. 23. For another critical look at the question of consent in liberal theory, see Carole Pateman, *The Problem of Political Obligation: A Critique of Liberal Theory* (1979; rpt. Cambridge: Polity, 1985).

48. Blumenberg, *Legitimacy*, p. 189.

49. William Hazlitt, "On the Conversation of Lords," in *Sketches and Essays and Winterslow*, ed. W. Carew Hazlitt (1872; rpt. London: George Bell and Sons, 1902), p. 199.

50. Jean-François Lyotard, *The Differend: Phrases in Dispute*, trans. Georges Van Den Abbeele (Minneapolis: Univ. of Minnesota Press, 1988), p. 107.

51. Ibid., p. 117.

52. Walter Benjamin, "Critique of Violence," in *Reflections*, ed. Peter Demetz, trans. Edmund Jephcott (New York: Harcourt Brace Jovanovich, 1978), pp. 297–98.

53. See Richard Rorty's adaptation of Harold Bloom's anxiety-filled notion of the strong poet to a redescription of democratic liberalism in *Contingency, Irony, and Solidarity* (Cambridge: Cambridge Univ. Press, 1989), pp. 28–37. Rorty's version is less turbulent than Byron's.

54. Lyotard, *Differend*, p. 112.

55. Ibid., p. 125.

56. *Byron's Bulldog*, p. 259. Cf. Hobhouse's slightly later comment to Byron that he has had the "wicked will of your friends" (p. 276). In this as in other instances, Hobhouse proved himself Byron's friend by tolerating what Lady Byron could not.

57. Lefort, *Democracy*, p. 228.

58. Truman Guy Steffan, *Byron's "Don Juan": The Making of a Masterpiece*, 4 vols. (Austin: Univ. of Texas Press, 1957), 1:130–31.

59. Smiles, *Memoir*, pp. 413–14.

60. Ibid., p. 416.

61. Steffan, *Byron's "Don Juan"* 1:131.

62. Chandler, *Rogue*, p. 347.

Chapter 8: Two Dramatic Case Studies

1. Byron quotes Horace's *Epistolae* (1.1.60). Marchand's translation: "Be this your wall of brass, to have no guilty secrets, no wrong-doing that makes you turn pale" (*BLJ* 1:145).

2. Michel Foucault, *The Archaeology of Knowledge*, trans. A. M. Sheridan Smith (New York: Harper Colophon, 1976), pp. 31–39.

3. Cf. Pat Rogers, *Grub Street: Studies in a Subculture* (London: Methuen, 1972), p. 295.

4. Michel Foucault, *Discipline and Punish: The Birth of the Prison*, trans. Alan Sheridan (New York: Vintage, 1979), pp. 93, 94, 113, 106, 111.

5. Quoted in Rogers, p. 341, n. 42.

6. In applying Defoe's definition to Pope's satire, I am deliberately disregarding Pope's more pessimistic and regressive notion of satire avowed in a letter to Dr. Arbuthnot (August 2, 1734): "But General Satire in Times of General Vice has no force, & is no Punishment: People have ceas'd to be ashamed of it when so many are joind with them; and tis only by hunting One or two from the Herd that any Examples can be made. If a man writ all his Life against the Collective Body of the Banditti, or against Lawyers, would it do the least Good, or lesson the Body? But if some are hung up, or pilloryed, it may prevent others. And in any low station with no other Power than this, I hope to deter, if not to reform" (quoted in Vincent Carretta, *The Snarling Muse: Verbal and Visual Political Satire from Pope to Churchill* [Philadelphia: Univ. of Pennsylvania Press, 1983], p. 133). I might plead that Pope is wiser (and more forceful) in his practice than in his precepts. But I think Pope's claim is most useful as a confirmation of his strict and singularly appropriate choice of dunces: writers and booksellers, who could be reformed, rather than lawyers and banditti, who could not. Moreover, Pope's comment seems more appropriate to the Horatian ethos of the verse epistles than to the hypermimetic *Dunciad*, which in its continuing revision attests to ambitions of a different order. Carretta gives a good account of the modification of those ambitions from the literary satire of the 1729 *Variorum* to the more global and political *New Dunciad* of 1743 in *Snarling Muse*, pp. 140–42.

7. *The Dunciad Variorum*, in *The Poems of Alexander Pope*, ed. John Butt (New Haven: Yale Univ. Press, 1963), p. 345.

8. Ibid., 1:54, p. 354.

9. Ibid., p. 320.

10. Ibid., p. 322; Foucault, *Discipline and Punish*, p. 106.

11. Pope, *Dunciad Variorum*, p. 346.

12. Rogers, *Grub Street*, p. 196.

13. Edward W. Said, *The World, the Text, and the Critic* (Cambridge, Mass.: Harvard Univ. Press, 1983), p. 62.

14. Terry Eagleton comments that "there are texts which establish a less 'fraught' relation to ideology, without thereby merely 'reproducing' it. Pope's *Essay on Man* is a highly 'produced' version of an ideology which is not thereby thrown into conflict with itself—where acceptable contradictions ('paradoxes') inherent in the ideology can be negotiated without notable self-mutilation" (*Criticism and Ideology* [London: NLB, 1978], p. 93). My view of *The Dunciad* is not remote from Eagleton's characterization of *The Essay on Man*, although I would eschew the whole problematics of ideology in favor of an understanding of *The Dunciad* as the literal apparatus through which power can be exerted.

15. Carretta associates the decline in satire's potency with the fall of Walpole and the general perception that there were no differences in principles between Walpole's successors and their opponents, which created the impression that there were "only personalities . . . left to attack. Namier's thesis that personalities were more important than principles in mid-eighteenth-century English politics is," he observes, "lent considerable support by literary and artistic evidence" (*Snarling Muse*, p. 177). Normalization or, to employ the favored term in post-Humean British discourse, naturalization was the corollary of the triumph and consolidation of the Venetian oligarchy. Satire either was marginalized or it became one of the state's instruments of punishment against those outside the consensus. The most effective positive satire of the Napoleonic years was the

government-financed *Antijacobin Review*. Not only part of what Louis Althusser calls the "ideological-State apparatus," it was also a wing of the "(Repressive) State Apparatus"—that is, to be satirized in the *Antijacobin* meant that the poet could soon be sent to prison ("Ideology and Ideological State Apparatuses [Notes towards an Investigation]," in *Lenin and Philosophy and Other Essays*, trans. Ben Brewster [London: NLB, 1971], pp. 127–86).

16. In fact, the conceit of papal authority that Byron adopts is exactly that employed by the *Edinburgh Review* in its famous attack on the Lake School (review of Robert Southey's *Thalaba* in inaugural issue of 1802).

17. *Minority* unifies both Byron's aristocratic status and his adolescence. These are not the same, though it has historically been the case that critics and scholars from Henry Brougham to Lawrence Stone have identified them (for the latter's characterization of aristocratic childishness, see *The Crisis of the Aristocracy, 1558–1641* [Oxford: Oxford Univ. Press, 1965], p. 223). One difference between Pope and Byron as satirists is that Pope is always partisan: given his principles, it is possible to state what, in theory at least, would satisfy him. Byron is not partisan: there is no change in policy or personalities that would satisfy him.

18. The classic statement of Byron's ambivalence is David Erdman's essay "Byron's Stage Fright: The History of His Ambition and Fear of Writing for the Stage," *ELH* 6 (September 1939): 219–43. See "Lord Byron," in *Shelley and His Circle* (Cambridge, Mass.: Harvard Univ. Press, 1961–70) 3:321 for a summary of Erdman's four essays on Byron's politics.

19. René Girard, *Violence and the Sacred*, trans. Patrick Gregory (Baltimore: Johns Hopkins Univ. Press, 1977), passim. See also Jerome J. McGann's fine reading of *Marino Faliero* in *Fiery Dust* (Chicago: Univ. of Chicago Press, 1968), which is attentive to the doublings and ironic reversals in the play. McGann concludes, however, that despite the general wreckage the values of consciousness and of expressing "vital passion" are upheld—a "human redemption" that is, in my view, an idealization of Byron's more radical critique (pp. 205–15, esp. pp. 214–15).

20. Cf. Byron's defense of his characterization to John Murray: "The Doge *repeats; true*—but it is from engrossing passion—and because he sees *different* persons—and is always obliged to recur to the *cause* uppermost in his mind" (*BLJ* 7:195).

21. The affiliations of Byron's Faliero and Angiolina with Lear and Cordelia as Stanley Cavell presents them are several and strong. See Cavell's rich essay "The Avoidance of Love: A Reading of *King Lear*," in *Must We Mean What We Say?* (New York: Scribner's, 1969), esp. pp. 286–89 and 299–301.

22. T. S. Eliot, "Byron," in *On Poetry and Poets* (New York: Farrar, Straus and Cudahy, 1957), p. 224.

23. McGann, *Fiery Dust*, p. 209.

24. Thomas L. Ashton, "The Censorship of Byron's *Marino Faliero*," *HLQ* 26 (November 1962), 28. The contemporary political events that *Marino* most closely touched upon were the divorce proceedings initiated against Queen Caroline by her royal husband and the discovery and quashing of the Cato Street Conspiracy. Closer to home, as a pattern for Steno's political prank Byron surely had in mind the recent (December 1819) arrest and imprisonment of his longtime friend John Cam Hobhouse for "scandalous libel in contempt of the privileges and constitutional authority of Parliament." Hobhouse's actions are discussed in Robert E. Zegger, *John Cam Hobhouse: A Political Life, 1819–1852* (Columbia: Univ. of Missouri Press, 1973), pp. 78–79.

25. See Ashton, "Censorship," pp. 34–38, for the details of Elliston's handiwork. *Gather* has the same piously conservative connotation at the opening of *Cain*, where Adam instructs his wife and children to "gather . . . again" the fruit of the forbidden tree (1.1.31).

26. Steno's graffito veers between two traditions: the "audacious and treasonable" papers that in the late eighteenth century were plastered on walls (including those of St. James's Palace), which John Brewer describes as "expressions of a rather rudimentary demotic political consciousness"; and the divine writing on the wall monumentalized in John Martin's enormous painting *Belshazzer's Feast*, which was displayed at the British Institute in 1820 and expresses a rather sophisticated reactionary political consciousness. Byron's "To Belshazzer" (1815; first published 1831) anticipated Martin's treatment of the subject. See Brewer, *Party Ideology and Popular Politics At the Accession of George III* (Cambridge: Cambridge Univ. Press, 1976), pp. 152–53, and Martin Meisel, *Realizations: Narrative, Pictorial, and Theatrical Arts in Nineteenth-Century England* (Princeton: Princeton Univ. Press, 1983), pp. 21–22.

27. Cf. the altogether different notion of the Baudelairean stenograph (mentioned in his criticism of Constantin Guys) as interpreted by Paul de Man: "The *stenos* in the word stenography, meaning narrow, could be used to designate the confinement of literature within its own boundaries. . . . But the fact that the word designates a form of writing indicates the compulsion to return to a literary mode of being, as a form of language that knows itself to be mere repetition, mere fiction and allegory, forever unable to participate in the spontaneity of action or modernity" ("Literary History and Literary Modernity," in *Blindness and Insight: Essays in the Rhetoric of Contemporary Criticism* [New York: Oxford Univ. Press, 1971], pp. 160–61). De Man reifies the "literary" in order to force an ironic reading on Baudelaire; in my view the stenographic *is* Byronic strength, without irony.

28. Richard Sennett, *The Fall of Public Man: On the Social Psychology of Capitalism* (1977; rpt. New York: Vintage Books, 1978), p. 217.

29. Adam Smith, *Theory of Moral Sentiments*, quoted in J. C. D. Clark, *English Society 1688–1832* (Cambridge: Cambridge Univ. Press, 1985), p. 102.

30. *Byron's Bulldog: The Letters of John Cam Hobhouse to Lord Byron*, ed. Peter W. Graham (Columbus: Ohio State Univ. Press, 1984), pp. 258–59.

31. See, for example, the plea of John Murray, Lord Byron's publisher, that the poet abandon the indecencies of *Don Juan* and return to the "tone of Beppo" (Leslie A. Marchand, *Byron: A Biography*, 3 vols. [New York: Knopf, 1957], 3:1040).

32. Benjamin Constant, "The Spirit of Conquest and Usurpation and Their Relation to European Civilization" (1814), in *Political Writings*, trans. and ed. Biancamaria Fontana (Cambridge: Cambridge Univ. Press, 1988), p. 93.

33. Ibid., p. 55.

34. Ibid., p. 100. Constant has specifically in mind Napoleon's expedition in Egypt during 1798–99. But as his accompanying reference to the contemporary attempt "to revive a style fallen into desuetude since Cambyses and Xerxes" makes clear, his political mythography recognized no significant distinction between Africa and the Levant, both of which fall under the rubric of Asia.

35. For a critique of Marx's employment of the category of "Asiatic mode of production," see Anthony Giddens, *A Contemporary Critique of Historical Materialism* (Berkeley: Univ. of California Press, 1981), pp. 81–88.

36. See chap. 3 above.

37. According to Claude Lefort, there is an "essential difference" between "political liberalism, as formulated by Tocqueville, and economic liberalism." The latter "may ally itself with despotism; the view that free institutions and respect for the rights of individuals are indissociable is part of his critique of omnipotent power" (*Democracy and Political Theory*, trans. David Macey [Minneapolis: Univ. of Minnesota Press, 1988], p. 166).

38. Walter Benjamin, *The Origin of German Tragic Drama*, trans. John Osborne (London: NLB, 1977), p. 74.

39. Ibid., p. 71.

40. *The Correspondence of Edmund Burke*, ed. Alfred Cobban and Robert A. Smith (Chicago: Univ. of Chicago Press, 1967), 6:72–73.

41. Constant, "Spirit of Conquest," p. 53.

42. For the case that Byron can be identified as a "Romantic liberal" see Peter Thorslev, "Post-Waterloo Liberalism: The Second Generation," *Studies in Romanticism* 28 (Fall 1989): 437–61.

43. See Edmund Burke, *Reflections on the Revolution in France* (1790; rpt. Harmondsworth: Penguin, 1968), pp. 175–76.

44. On the use of technological justifications to mystify the political motivation for retaining hierarchical structures of authority in the supposedly rationalized industrial workplace, see Stephen A. Marglin, "What Do the Bosses Do? The Origins and Functions of Hierarchy in Capitalist Production," in *Classes, Power, and Conflict*, ed. Anthony Giddens and David Held (Berkeley: Univ. of California Press, 1982), pp. 285–98.

45. See J. G. A. Pocock, *The Machiavellian Moment: Florentine Political Thought and the Atlantic Republican Tradition* (Princeton: Princeton Univ. Press, 1975), chaps. 13 and 14. For a fuller discussion, see chap. 9 below.

46. Colin Campbell, *The Romantic Ethic and the Spirit of Modern Consumerism* (Oxford: Basil Blackwell, 1987), p. 78.

47. Ibid., p. 76.

48. Ibid., p. 78. For a similar argument in defense of liberalism, see Richard Rorty, *Contingency, Irony, and Solidarity* (Cambridge: Cambridge Univ. Press, 1989), esp. chaps. 1 and 2.

49. Ibid., p. 89. See also Jean Baudrillard on sex and productivity in *Seduction*, trans. Brian Singer (New York: St. Martin's, 1990), pp. 37–49.

50. Thomas Robert Malthus, "On Political Economy," *Quarterly Review* (1824), rpt. in *The Works of Thomas Robert Malthus*, ed. E. A. Wrigley and David Souden, 8 vols. (London: William Pickering, 1986), 7:261, 263.

51. See Thomas De Quincey's attempt to overcome this opposition in the first chapter of his treatise *The Logic of Political Economy* (1844), in *The Collected Writings of Thomas De Quincey*, ed. David Masson, 14 vols. (London, 1897), 9:122–200.

52. Malthus, "The Measure of Value" (1823), in *Works* 7:180 (emphasis added).

53. Lord Byron to Douglas Kinnaird: "Do not all men try to abate the price of all they buy?—I contend that a bargain even between brethren—is a declaration of war" (*BLJ* 8:153).

54. Deirdre David, "Grilled Alive in Calcutta," lecture delivered at the Johns Hopkins University, December 1988.

55. Johann Gottfried Herder, *Outlines of a Philosophy of the History of Man* (1784), trans. T. Churchill (New York: Berbman, 1966), p. 213.

56. Cf. Marjorie Levinson's interesting allegorization of John Keats as representative of the "eternally coming" middle class in her *Keats's Life of Allegory: The Origins of a Style* (Oxford: Basil Blackwell, 1988), p. 24. The difference here, and it is considerable, is that the orgasmic vocabulary is not merely descriptive, such as it is in Keats's "coming musk rose," but performative as well. Moreover, Byron's play dramatizes that equivocation as the "middle class's" hovering reflection on itself: that is, Byron's scene includes the "Levinson" position as well as the "Keats" position.

57. Susan J. Wolfson shrewdly investigates the implications of Sardanapalus's effeminacy in "'A Problem Few Dare Imitate': *Sardanapalus* and 'Effeminate Character,'" *ELH* 58 (Winter 1991): 867–902.

58. For a discussion of the despotic dreams of political economy as they play out in the exemplary *agon* between David Hume and Jean Jacques Rousseau, see Jerome Christensen, *Practicing Enlightenment: Hume and the Formation of a Literary Career* (Madison: Univ. of Wisconsin Press, 1987), pp. 243–73.

59. Ernesto Laclau and Chantal Mouffe, *Hegemony and Socialist Strategy: Towards a Radical Democratic Politics* (London: Verso, 1985), p. 188.

60. Benjamin, *Origins*, pp. 109 and 83.

61. *Friedrich Schlegel's "Lucinde" and the Fragments*, trans. Peter Firchow (Minneapolis: Univ. of Minnesota Press, 1971), p. 174.

62. On the pairing with Martin, see Meisel, *Realizations*, p. 174.

63. Constant, "Spirit of Conquest," p. 95.

64. Ralph Waldo Emerson, "Heroism," in *Essays, First Series*, vol. 1 of *Emerson's Works*, 5 vols. (New York: Bigelow and Brown, n.d.), p. 161.

65. For a Hegelian vindication of the "necessary anachronism" in the novels of Walter Scott, which "consists . . . simply in allowing his characters to express feelings and thoughts about real, historical relationships in a much clearer way than the actual men and women of the time could have done," see Georg Lukács, *The Historical Novel*, trans. Hannah and Stanley Mitchell (Harmondsworth: Penguin, 1962), pp. 67–69.

66. Samuel Taylor Coleridge, *Biographia Literaria*, ed. James Engell and Walter Jackson Bate, 2 vols., vol. 7 of *Collected Works*, gen. ed. Kathleen Coburn (Princeton: Princeton Univ. Press, 1983), 1:23.

67. Lefort, *Democracy*, p. 181.

68. The point could be pursued by attending to the linguistic scattering that exceeds the sacrificial centering, particularly in terms of the way the doubling of Myrrha into the visual order of mirror is supplemented and destabilized by the olfactory sense of her as "myrrh" ("Bring frankincense and myrrh" [5:280]).

Chapter 9: Annals of a Line Undone

1. Hans Blumenberg, *The Legitimacy of the Modern Age*, trans. Robert M. Wallace (Cambridge, Mass.: MIT Press, 1983), p. 89.

2. A conspicuous example of this allegorization of orthodoxy appears in Bishop Richard Hurd's reading of Spenser's *Faerie Queene*. According to Hurd, Spenser responded to the disbelief of his audience in romantic wonders by "giving an air of mystery to his subject, and pretend[ing] that his stories of knights and giants were but the cover to abundance of profound wisdom" (*Letters on Chivalry and Romance*, ed. Hoyt Trowbridge [1762; rpt. Los Angeles: Augustan Reprint Society, 1963]), letter 12, p. 114.

3. Michel Serres, *The Parasite*, trans. Lawrence R. Schehr (Baltimore: Johns Hopkins Univ. Press, 1982), p. 229.

4. Jacques Derrida, *The Post Card: From Socrates to Freud and Beyond*, trans. Alan Bass (Chicago: Univ. of Chicago Press, 1987), p. 473.

5. Theodor W. Adorno, *Aesthetic Theory*, trans. C. Lenhardt (London: Routledge and Kegan Paul, 1984), p. 34.

6. Jane Marcet, *Conversations on Political Economy; in Which the Elements of That Science Are Familiarly Explained* (Philadelphia, 1817), pp. 28–30.

7. M. M. Bakhtin, "Epic and Novel," in *The Dialogic Imagination*, ed. Michael Holquist, trans. Caryl Emerson and Michael Holquist (Austin: Univ. of Texas Press, 1981), p. 23.

8. J. G. A. Pocock, *The Machiavellian Moment: Florentine Political Thought and the Atlantic Tradition* (Princeton: Princeton Univ. Press, 1975), p. 501.

9. Ibid., p. 446.

10. Ibid., p. 486. For a good account of the "civic discourse of art" in the eighteenth and nineteenth centuries, see John Barrell, *The Political Theory of Painting from Reynolds to Hazlitt: "The Body of the Public"* (New Haven: Yale Univ. Press, 1986), introd., pp. 1–68.

11. The symmetry between the ability to enter into economic exchange and the ability to converse was a prominent theme of eighteenth-century handbooks on the social graces (see Leland E. Warren, "Turning Reality Round Together: Guides to Conversation in Eighteenth-Century England," *Eighteenth-Century Life* 8 [May 1983]: 65–85); it was later a determining feature of the plot of Jane Austen's *Emma*, where on Strawberry Hill an ill-tempered Emma insultingly apportions Mrs. Bates's words to her poverty. The connection is screwed up a notch by Marcet, who argued that not only the ownership of property but the *knowledge* of political economy was indispensable cultural capital. Marcet goes so far as to have her instructor in the "science" gently chide her interlocutor for an "incapacity to enter on most topics of general conversation whilst you remain in ignorance of it" (*Conversations*, p. 7). Without the ability to converse on "topics of general conversation" one simply does not count—or counts only as "singular," counts as do those evolutionary losers, heroes, among the dead.

12. Jean-François Lyotard, *The Differend: Phrases in Dispute*, trans. Georges Van Den Abbeele (Minneapolis: Univ. of Minnesota Press, 1988), p. xi.

13. Thomas De Quincey, "Conversation," in *The Collected Writings of Thomas De Quincey*, ed. David Masson, 14 vols. (London, 1897), 10:264–65. Alternatively, Lyotard's differend evokes Mikhail Bakhtin's emancipatory vision of the inauguration of an "actively polyglot world" ("Epic and Novel," p. 12). Like Lyotard's differend, Bakhtin's polyglot world is not so much a historical moment (when this "irreversible change" occurred is as hard to pin down as the first moment that the polis suffered corruption) as a constant and contingent possibility, threatening all monologues as corruption threatens autonomy.

14. Bakhtin, "Epic and Novel," p. 37.

15. Bakhtin, "Epic and Novel," p. 21.

16. Compare the account of Molière's hero by Michel Serres in "The Apparition of Hermes: Dom Juan" in *Hermes: Literature, Science, Philosophy*, ed. Josue V. Harari and David F. Bell (Baltimore: Johns Hopkins Univ. Press, 1982), pp. 3–14.

17. Pocock, *Machiavellian Moment*, p. 451.

18. William Hazlitt, "Dreams," in *The Plain Speaker: Opinions on Books, Men, and*

Things, ed. William Carew Hazlitt (London: George Bell and Sons, 1903), p. 23.

19. William Hazlitt, "On the Spirit of Monarchy," *Liberal*, no. 2 (1823), p. 235.

20. On the transformation of the feast, see Raymond Williams, *The Country and the City* (New York: Oxford Univ. Press, 1973), p. 31.

21. Pocock, *Machiavellian Moment*, p. 499.

22. Lyotard, *Differend*, p. 100.

23. For an excellent discussion of this aspect of *Juan*, see Jerome J. McGann, *"Don Juan" in Context* (Chicago: Univ. of Chicago Press, 1976), pp. 116–23.

24. Lyotard, *Differend*, pp. 101 and 104.

25. See Paul West, *Byron and the Spoiler's Art* (London: Chatto and Windus, 1960), on Byron as a poet of "elimination" (p. 16).

26. Lyotard, *Differend*, p. xii.

27. This is the time to acknowledge the crucial stimulus to this argument provided by a seminar paper written at John Hopkins University by Jody Mikalachki, which first called my attention to the importance of Tom's *damn* and the auditory puns on his name in the poem. Mikalachki's association of these phenomena with a pursuit of the etymon and of linguistic purity on the part of Byron, though suggestive, diverges from the path followed here, which emphasizes the dependence of Tom's speech for its performative power on its "impurity."

28. Lyotard, *Differend*, pp. 12–13.

29. See Peter J. Manning, *"Don Juan* and Byron's Imperceptiveness to the English Word," *Studies in Romanticism* 18 (Summer 1979): 208–16.

30. Pocock, *Machiavellian Moment*, p. 485. Being better than one's circumstances, which is the aspiration of a few, must be distinguished from appearing better than one's condition, which, as Benjamin Constant writes, is the "obsession of almost all men" ("The Spirit of Conquest and Usurpation and Their Relation to European Civilization" (1814), in *Political Writings*, trans. and ed. Biancamaria Fontana [Cambridge: Cambridge Univ. Press, 1988], p. 137).

31. David Hume, *A Treatise of Human Nature*, ed. L. A. Selby-Bigge, 2d ed., rev. P. H. Nidditch (Oxford: Clarendon Press, 1978), p. 313. For Byron in praise of avarice, see *Lady Blessington's "Conversations of Lord Byron,"* ed. Ernest J. Lovell, Jr. (Princeton: Princeton Univ. Press, 1969), pp. 182–83.

32. For a forcefully argued view of Byron's relation to icons that differs from my own, see Ronald Paulson, *Breaking and Remaking: Aesthetic Practice in England, 1700–1820* (New Brunswick: Rutgers Univ. Press, 1989), pp. 114–34. According to Paulson, "What begins (or was formerly) a process of breaking and remaking becomes an act of mourning for, seeking a memory of, the breakage or loss—as well as, in some ultimate aristocratic nostalgia, the wholeness before the breakage and loss" (p. 123).

33. On the distinction between "what the law is and what the gunman does," see Stanley Fish's essay "Force," in *Doing What Comes Naturally* (Durham: Duke University Press, 1989), p. 502. *Juan*'s practical demonstration of the circumstantial difference between words and knives may be opposed to Fish's theory that "force is simply a (pejorative) name for the thrust or assertion of some point of view" (p. 521). Not in some formal distinction between force and persuasion or in opposition to interpretation but in Fish's parenthetical discounting of the force of the pejorative lies the difference between the two "points of view."

34. Quintilian, *Institutio oratoria*, trans. H. E. Butler, 4 vols. (London: William Heinemann, 1920), 3.5.18 (1:407).

35. Ibid., 2.21.7–8 (1:359).

36. Hazlitt, "The New School of Reform," in *Plain Speaker*, p. 270.

37. Ibid., p. 254.

38. Quintilian, *Institutio*, 2.15.1 (1:319) and 2.17.25–26 (1:337).

39. The best testimony to the ill repute of commonplaces occurs in an essay by perhaps their greatest Romantic user, Hazlitt's "On Paradox and Common-place," in *Table Talk: Essays on Men and Manners*, ed. William Carew Hazlitt (London, 1891), pp. 199–213. The quoted phrase appears on p. 212.

40. Jean-François Lyotard, "Figure Foreclosed," in *The Lyotard Reader*, ed. Andrew Benjamin (Oxford: Basil Blackwell, 1989), p. 84. This searching essay has strongly influenced my interpretation of canto 16 throughout.

41. Samuel Taylor Coleridge, *Biographia Literaria*, ed. James Engell and Walter Jackson Bate, 2 vols., vol. 7 of *Collected Works*, gen. ed. Kathleen Coburn (Princeton: Princeton Univ. Press, 1983), 1:11. For a discussion of the relation of Byronic aggression to his "value pluralism," see Laurence S. Lockridge, *The Ethics of Romanticism* (Cambridge: Cambridge Univ. Press, 1989), pp. 443–49.

42. Lyotard, "Figure Foreclosed," p. 74.

43. Ibid., p. 82.

44. Peter Manning, *Byron and His Fictions* (Detroit: Wayne State University Press, 1978), p. 225; Paulson, *Breaking*, p. 116.

45. Lyotard, "Figure Foreclosed," p. 91.

46. W. Paul Elledge calls attention to the "anachronistic and residual" status of "this monkish ambassador of a spiritual reality" in his excellent, as yet unpublished essay, "Immaterialistic Matters: Byron, Bogles, and Bluebloods."

47. And even then the fact that Juan finds Fitz-Fulke the second time—after his demeanor has made it clear to almost all that he has seen something strange—that grasp does nothing to cancel the apparition of the spirit the *first* time.

48. My thinking on these matters was sharpened by Meredith McGill, who in her discussion of the difference between the ideology of copyright in eighteenth-century Great Britain and nineteenth-century America remarks, "The notion that an individual author had a *natural* right to his printed text—a private or personal right which was prior to and in excess of the protection granted by the state—was fundamentally incompatible with a political philosophy that associated the depersonalization of print with a kind of selfless publicity, the exercise of civic virtue" ("Poe, Literary Property, and the Technology of Print," draft Ph.D. diss., Johns Hopkins Univ.).

49. John Hollander, *Melodious Guile: Fictive Pattern in Poetic Language* (New Haven: Yale Univ. Press, 1988), pp. 1–2. See also the discussion of poetic cursing on pp. 83–84.

50. Sigmund Freud, "The Uncanny," in *Studies in Parapsychology*, ed. Philip Rieff (New York: Macmillan, 1963), p. 32. This doubling is also the labor of judgment according to John Locke in *Essay Concerning Human Understanding*, bk. 2, chap. 2.

51. This procedure is graphically exemplified in Scott's *Heart of Midlothian*. Effie's fate hangs on the English law that requires the public testimony "I am pregnant," which identifies the Scottish woman and her child as British subjects—subject to the law of the king, which, *a fortiori*, is the law of the British queen. Scott's twist on the postal theme occurs in *Waverley* with the crucial misdirection of the letters between Edward Waverley

and his commander during his long absence without leave during his enchanted stay with the Jacobite Bradwardines and McIvors.

52. Jacques Lacan, "Function and Field of Speech and Language," in *Ecrits: A Selection*, ed. and trans. Alan Sheridan (New York: Norton, 1977), p. 67.

53. In "The Thorn" Martha Ray's "Oh misery! oh misery! / Oh woe is me! oh misery!" is by repetition rendered as such a standing place, common to wind, woman, narrator, and (as Coleridge complains) Wordsworth. For a discussion of the intersection of subjectivities in this complaint, see Jerome Christensen, "Wordsworth's Misery, Coleridge's Woe: Reading 'The Thorn,'" *Papers on Literature and Language* 16 (September 1980): 268–86.

54. Lacan, "On the Possible Treatment of Psychosis," in *Ecrits*, p. 199.

55. Lacan, "The Freudian Thing," in *Ecrits*, p. 143.

56. Juan is not the only person with something to fear at the hands of the plotting Byron: "It is to be hoped that no such person as *Percy Bysshe Shelley*, the author, exists, and that the atrocious poetry committed in his name is but the well-intentioned device of some fiery moralist, who employs the name of Lord Byron's friend and pupil to show, by a species of *reductio ad absurdum*, the infernal portal to which his Lordship's system pushed to its limit will necessarily lead" (*RR* C:1:39).

57. John Locke, *The Second Treatise of Government* (1690; rpt. Indianapolis: Library of Liberal Arts, 1952), p. 54; Thomas Hobbes: "Even if actions which are just in one state are unjust in another, justice, which is the obedience of the law, is the same everywhere," quoted in Jürgen Habermas, *Theory and Practice*, trans. John Viertel (Boston: Beacon Press, 1973), p. 62.

58. Sir William Blackstone, *Commentaries*, 2 vols. (London, 1765), 1:128.

59. Coleridge, *Specimens of the Table-Talk of Samuel Taylor Coleridge*, ed. H. N. Coleridge, 2 vols. (Oxford, 1835), 1:113.

60. Jean Baudrillard, *For a Critique of the Political Economy of the Sign*, trans. Mark Poster (St. Louis: Telos, 1986), p. 119.

61. Lacan, "Psychosis," in *Ecrits*, p. 184.

62. Coleridge, *Biographia Literaria* 1:6.

63. William Cobbett, *A Grammar of the English Language* (1819; rpt. Oxford: Oxford Univ. Press, 1984), p. 68.

64. Coleridge, *Biographia Literaria* 1:9. It is worth remembering that Coleridge's theory was rarely consistent with a practice that enriched it beyond summary paraphrase. Note, for example, the way Coleridge attempts to unravel his political and philosophical past by reference to the way *Spinoza* is compounded as *Spy nozy* (1:193–94).

65. Although in his criticism of Wordsworth's "equivocation in the word 'real'" Coleridge counters with a Dantean version of the vernacular, the alternative of the *lingua communis* is proposed tactically as an expedient way to correct Wordsworth rather than as a model for poetry (ibid., 2:56 and 99).

66. Ibid., 1:10–11. For a fuller discussion of this passage, see Jerome Christensen, *Coleridge's Blessed Machine of Language* (Ithaca: Cornell Univ. Press, 1981), pp. 175–77.

67. Thomas Malthus, *An Essay on the Principle of Population* (1798), ed. Philip Appleman (New York: Norton, 1976), p. 97.

68. Coleridge, *Biographia Literaria* 1:10.

69. Edward W. Said, *Beginnings: Intention and Method* (Baltimore: Johns Hopkins Univ. Press, 1975), pp. 191–93.

70. Coleridge, *Biographia Literaria* 1:82–83.

71. For Malthus's retort to William Godwin's valorization of miserliness as a condign form of economic independence, see *Principles*, pp. 96–100.

72. Adorno, *Aesthetics*, p. 86.

73. Identification of the corpse of this ghostly figure would begin with the "pearly teeth" of which the poet was so proud—see Hobhouse quotation below.

74. Thanks to Jonathan Kramnick for the Newcastle slang.

75. Lyotard, *Differend*, p. 123.

76. Theodor W. Adorno, *Negative Dialectics*, trans. E. B. Ashton (New York: Seabury, 1979), p. 223.

77. Samuel Taylor Coleridge, *Lectures 1808–19 on Literature*, ed. R. A. Foakes, 2 vols., vol. 5 of *Collected Works*, gen. ed. Kathleen Coburn (Princeton: Princeton Univ. Press, 1987), 1:303–16.

78. Claude Lefort, *Democracy and Political Theory*, trans. David Macey (Minneapolis: Univ. of Minnesota Press, 1988), p. 279.

79. Marjorie Levinson, *Keats' Life of Allegory: The Origins of a Style* (Oxford: Basil Blackwell, 1988), p. 17.

80. Williams, *The Country and the City*, p. 52.

81. For a sophisticated treatment of the problems involved in "recognizing the biographical subject," see William H. Epstein, *Recognizing Biography* (Philadelphia: Univ. of Pennsylvania Press, 1987), pp. 71–89.

82. Samuel Smiles, *A Publisher and His Friends: Memoir and Correspondence of the Late John Murray*, 2 vols. (London: Murray, 1891), 1:407.

83. Frederick L. Beaty, *Byron the Satirist* (Dekalb: Northern Illinois Univ. Press, 1985), p. 121.

84. "For the reading or non-reading a book—will never keep down a single petticoat" (to Richard Belgrave Hoppner, October 29, 1819; *BLJ* 6:237).

85. John Dunn, "Individuality and Clientage in the Formation of Locke's Social Imagination," in *Rethinking Modern Political Theory* (Cambridge: Cambridge Univ. Press, 1985), pp. 20–21.

86. Leslie A. Marchand, *Byron: A Biography*, 3 vols. (New York: Knopf, 1957), 3:1040.

87. Note the odd comment by James R. Thompson that "Byron's *Don Juan* and his group of eight plays differ so much that were either anonymous, it would be difficult to assign them to the same author"—odd because *Don Juan*, of course, *was* anonymous ("Byron's Plans and *Don Juan*," in *Byron's Poetry*, ed. Frank D. McConnell [New York: Norton, 1978], p. 405).

88. Mikhail M. Bakhtin, *Rabelais and His World*, trans. Hélène Iswolsky (Bloomington: Indiana Univ. Press, 1984), p. 317.

89. *Byron's Bulldog: The Letters of John Cam Hobhouse to Lord Byron*, ed. Peter W. Graham (Columbus: Ohio State Univ. Press, 1957), p. 178.

90. Marchand, *Byron* 3:1256–57.

91. Cobbett, *Grammar*, pp. 63–64.

92. For a detailed account of the genealogy of the English signature, see Jonathan Goldberg, *Writing Matter: From the Hands of the English Renaissance* (Stanford: Stanford Univ. Press, 1990), pp. 233–78.

93. Hobhouse, who in his letters to Byron exhibits an extraordinary interest in

matters orthographical (autographs, abbreviations, etc.), complained of Byron's scrawl by imitating it and asking for "the Byron at full length"—a request that is the graphic equivalent of the dream of *Don Juan* brought to a fitting conclusion (*Byron's Bulldog*, p. 154).

94. Marchand, *Byron* 3:970–71.

95. Ibid., p. 971.

96. *Byron's Bulldog*, p. 125.

97. Marchand, *Byron* 3:1003.

98. *Courier* (October 26, 1822), pp. 2–3. Quoted in William H. Marshall, *Byron, Shelley, Hunt, and "The Liberal"* (Philadelphia: Univ. of Pennsylvania Press, 1960), pp. 103–4.

99. Serres, *Parasite*, p. 142.

100. *Byron's Bulldog*, p. 154.

Index

Abbott, Andrew, 29, 30
Abel, K., 94–95, 96
Abernathy, John, 395 n.46
Abraham, Nicholas, 371 n.3
Abrams, M. H., 212
Addendum, Adorno's conception of, 44–45
Addison, Joseph, 6, 9, 20, 44, 46–47, 102–3, 104, 135, 178, 290, 355, 366 n.11, 373 n.3, 393 n.31
Adorno, Theodor, 40, 42, 48, 124, 221, 303, 348, 350, 373 n.27; conception of addendum, 44–45; on degeneration of difference, 52–53
Allen, Ralph, 7–9, 44, 285
Althusser, Louis, 407 n.14
Anachronism, 171, 181, 277, 289, 295, 324, 351
Andrew, Donna T., 372 n.12

Andrews, Launcelot, 399 n.28
Annual Register, 41–42
Anxiety of Influence (Bloom), xxii
Apposition, 215–20
Arendt, Hannah, xvi
Aristocracy, xvii, 124–25, 192, 225, 248, 330–31, 352, 367 n.27, 367–68 n.30, 368 n.31; definitions of, 10–14; Romantic conception of, 12–13
Arnold, Matthew: on Byron's poetry, xiv–xv; on concept of sincerity, xiii–xiv, 361
Ausonius, 202
Austen, Jane, 58, 155, 216, 378 n.29, 412 n.11

Bain, A., 94–95
Bakhtin, Mikhail, xix, 305, 308, 309, 355, 394 n.44, 412 n.13

Ballantyne, John, 149

Bataille, George, 383 n.93

Baudrillard, Jean, 27, 80, 90, 98, 108, 114, 146, 177

Beaumont, Sir John, 372 n.25

Beckford, William, 51, 52, 66, 67, 344

Beginnings: Intention and Method (Said), 347

Benjamin, Walter, 101, 167, 249, 278, 294

Bersani, Leo, 90–91, 92

Biographia Literaria (Coleridge), xxv, 28, 131, 158, 179, 298–99, 345, 346, 369 n.41, 415 n.64

Blackwood's, 231, 253, 292, 388 n.63

Blessington, Lady, 166–67, 372 n.15

Blessington, Lord, 362

Bloom, Harold, xxii–xxiii, 50, 406 n.53

Blumenberg, Hans, 42, 247, 301, 403 n.12

Bourdieu, Pierre, 17, 144, 154, 155, 169, 396 n.69

Boyce, Benjamin, 7

Brewer, John, 409 n.26

Bride of Abydos, The (Byron), 102, 115–18, 139–40, 256, 387 n.50

British Critic, The: review of *Don Juan*, 216, 217, 220–26, 229

British Review, The, 83, 310; review of *Don Juan*, 226–33, 234, 405 n.30; review of *The Bride of Abydos*, 387 n.50

Brougham, Henry, 84, 137, 139, 239, 333, 370 nn.54, 55, 382 n.86; review of *Hours of Idleness*, 19, 20–22, 26–27, 28–29, 30–31, 264

Brummel, George (Beau), 159, 160–61, 395 n.45, 398 n.7

Burke, Edmund, 50, 96, 104, 205–6, 286, 330, 365 n.4, 367 n.30, 377–78 n.23, 380 n.51

Bush, M. L., 368 n.31

Byron, George Gordon, sixth Lord: accession to title of *Lord*, 22–23; as allegory of ruin, 191–92; on aristocracy, 14–15; bisexuality of, 79–80, 381 n.70; and Brougham's review of *Hours of Idleness*, 19, 20–22, 26–27, 28–29, 30–31, 35, 45–46; as dandy, 159–61; death of, 356–57; and *English Bards and Scotch Reviewers*, 32–35, 41, 45–46, 47–48, 262–63; family motto of, 43–44; hero in poetry of, 114–25; homosexuality of, 54–65, 376 n.17; impact of uncle's duel on, 36–43, 48; Jeffrey's criticism of, 172–81, 182–83,

296; literary identity of, 53–65; name change of, 358–60; Napoleon depicted by, 168–72; oppositional writing of, 88–89; Oriental tales of, 97–106, 107–13, 130, 135–41, 165; perversion and parody in poetry of, 89–96; reaction of, to Napoleon's abdication, 128; seriality and, 5–6, 89–90; strength in poetry of, xvii–xviii, xxiv–xxv, 3–5, 63–65, 214–15, 299, 350; Venice as depicted by, 185–94; wife seeks separation from, 78–87, 142–43, 149–51, 382 n.86. *See also* Byronism; *Childe Harold's Pilgrimage: A Romaunt; Don Juan*

Byron, John (Jack), 18

Byron, Lady (Annabella Milbanke), 276, 290, 382 n.76, 391 n.2, 395 n.51, 401 n.42; seeks separation from Byron, 78–87, 142–43, 149–51, 382 n.86, 383 nn.88, 89, 90

Byron, Sophia, 83

Byron, William, fifth Lord, duel with Mr. Chaworth, 35–43, 308, 336

Byron, William John, 18

Byron and Greek Love: Homophobia in Nineteenth-Century England (Crompton), 59, 376 n.17

Byronic hero, 16, 115

Byronism (Byron as literary system), xx, 5, 15–16, 53, 77, 82, 130, 147–48, 153–54, 172–84, 187–88, 190, 263, 284, 332, 383 n.2, 398 n.8; and *Don Juan*, 215–20, 221

Caleb Williams (Godwin), 46, 286–87

Campbell, Colin, 289–91, 394 n.40, 397 n.79

Canning, George, 147

Carlisle, Lord, 19

Carlisle, Richard, 144

Carlyle, Thomas, 18

Carretta, Vincent, 407 n.15

Castlereagh, Robert Stewart, Viscount, 217–18, 402 n.5

Castronovo, David, 14, 367 n.27

Categorical imperative, 39–40, 44

Cavell, Stanley, 408 n.21

Cervantes, Miguel de, 310–11, 314, 321

Chambers, Ross, 223

Champion, 92, 93, 119

Chaworth, Mary, 37

Chaworth, William, fifth Lord Byron's duel with, 35–43, 336

Childe Harold's Pilgrimage: A Romaunt (Byron), xviii, xx, 13, 58, 65–78, 125, 131, 151, 361, 376 n.19, 381 n.64, 384 n.14; conclusion of, 175–76, 207–13; Ellis's review of, 137–38; "fit" in, 181–84; Hobhouse's defense of, 194–201; liberation in, 56; metaphors of ruin in, 185–94; Napoleon depicted in, 168–72, 290; reviews of, 385 n.18; role of, in Byron's development, 142–49, 152–54; significance of *e* in, 138–39; as speculation, 156–59; Wilson's review of, 276, 284, 331

Christabel (Coleridge), 179

Christian Observer, The, 97, 100, 102–3, 105, 107, 141, 176, 180, 382 n.78, 386 n.37, 397 n.79

Cintra, Convention of, 76

Circumstantial gravity, 229–31, 246

Clarke, Hewson, 35

Clément, Catherine, 19, 135, 375 n.13

Cobbett, William, 345–46, 357, 374 n.3

Coleridge, Samuel Taylor, xxv, 28, 94, 131–32, 140, 158, 161, 179, 298–99, 328, 335, 344, 350, 369 n.41, 399 n.28, 415 nn.64, 65; on double epithets, 345–47

Commands, 39–40, 44, 182–84, 228, 252–53, 291, 308, 314–16, 333–34, 349–50

Commodification, 158–59, 179–80, 191–92, 292–99

Commonplace, xviii, xxiv–xxv, 44, 101, 301, 324–25, 327, 342, 346

Constable, Archibald, 148, 149

Constant, Benjamin, 170–71, 276–78, 281–82, 283, 284, 288–89, 295, 321, 397 n.79, 409 n.34, 413 n.30

Constitution of Society, The (Giddens), xxii

Consumerist society, 289–92

Contingency, Irony, and Solidarity (Rorty), xxiii

Convention, 76–78, 79, 87, 208

Conversations on Political Economy (Marcet), 303, 307

Convulsiveness, 23, 95, 181, 242

Copyright, 17, 143–46, 192, 237–40, 353

Corsair, The (Byron), 24–26, 59, 91–92, 118–25, 126, 129, 136, 140–41, 147–48, 151, 384 n.3, 389 n.81

Courier, 221

Cowper, William, 21, 50–51

Critical Review, The, 47, 82, 116, 124, 140–41, 389 n.81

Croker, J. W., 254–56

Crompton, Louis, 59–60, 79, 161, 342, 376 n.17, 378 n.34, 381 n.70

Cruikshank, George, 134

"Curse of Minerva, The" (Byron), 73

Dallas, Charles, 143, 146, 169

Dandies, 159–61, 394 nn.40, 43, 394 n.45

D'Aurevilly, Barbey, 159, 161

Davidson, Donald, 174, 183

Davies, Scrope Berdmore, 57–58, 64, 160

Death, in *The Giaour*, 109–11

Death of Sardanapalus (Delacroix), 295

Debord, Guy, 158

de Certeau, Michel, 70, 72, 147, 241

Defoe, Daniel, 260, 407 n.6

Delacroix, Eugène, 295

de Man, Paul, 15, 233, 409 n.27

Democratization, 203–6

De Quincey, Thomas, 109, 204, 307

Derrida, Jacques, 62–63, 109, 183, 231–32, 302

Descartes, René, 302

Despotism, 277–78; in *Sardanapalus*, 278–85

de Tocqueville, Alexis. *See* Tocqueville, Alexis de

Dickens, Charles, 202

Didot, M., 162

"Differend," 306–7

Differend: Phrases in Dispute, The (Lyotard), 245, 319

Discipline and Punish (Foucault), 259–60

Disraeli, Isaac, 161–62, 206, 391 n.3, 392 n.11

Dobbs, Maurice, xv

Don Juan (Byron), xv, xix, xx–xxi, xxiv–xxv, 23, 25, 39, 59, 173, 188, 210–11, 401 n.46, 402 n.3; *British Critic's* review of, 216, 217, 220–26, 229, 233; *British Review's* review of, 226–33, 405 n.30; as context, 215, 259–60; Croker's critique of, 254–57; double figure in, 333–38; English cantos of, 300–304, 320–33; "Fitz-Fulke" in, 341–43, 353; interpretations of, 338–53; and *Juan* effect, 214–15; Julia's letter in, 234–37, 241, 242, 253–54, 320, 405 n.36; legal issues sur-

Don Juan (Byron) — *con't.*
  rounding, 237–42; as parody, 96–97;
  Pedrillo's fate in, 242–47, 249–51; re-
  views of, 215–20; "situation" in, 223–25;
  social contract in, 242–43; strength of
  style in, 252–53; Tom as hero in, 304–
  20; "vermilion" in, 256–57
"Don Juan" in Context (McGann), 214
Douglas, Mary, 179
Dover, K. J., 61, 375 n.13
Dowden, Wilfred, 145
Dublin Examiner, The, 388 n.64; review of
  Childe Harold, 385 n.18
Duelling, 33–48, 83–84, 132–33
Dugdale, William, 353
Dunciad, The (Pope), 260–61, 407 n.14
Dunn, John, xxiv, 353–54

Eagleton, Terry, 406 n.47, 407 n.14
Eakins, Thomas, 390 n.91
Eclectic Review, The, 81, 82
Edinburgh Review, The, xv, 4, 9, 28, 29, 32,
  45–46, 102, 147, 148, 179, 263, 284, 296,
  392 n.18, 408 n.16. *See also* Brougham,
  Henry
Edleston, John, 16, 55, 57, 256
Elgin, Lord, 62, 73, 77
Elgin Marbles, 327, 386 n.31
Eliot, T. S., 272
Elixiere des Teufels (Hoffmann), 335
Elledge, Paul, 392 n.22, 414 n.46
Ellenborough, Lord, 132–35
Ellis, George, 100, 102, 137–38, 147, 181,
  212
Elliston, Robert, 273–74
Elwin, Malcolm, 83, 382 n.76
Emerson, Ralph Waldo, 14, 33
Emma (Austen), 155, 412 n.11
English Bards and Scotch Reviewers (Byron),
  32–35, 41, 45–46, 47–48, 106, 143, 262,
  263
"Epistle to Augusta" (Byron), 151
Erdman, David, 408 n.18
Essay on Man (Pope), 407 n.14
Essay on Taste (Gerard), 400 n.39
Eustathius, 54, 55–56, 377 n.21

Faerie Queene, The (Spenser), 75–76,
  411 n.2
Fall of Nineveh (Martin), 295
"Fare Thee Well" (Byron), 150

Fascination, scene of, 50–52, 53, 69, 74–75,
  82, 98, 111–12
Fish, Stanley, 79, 413 n.33
Foucault, Michel, 4, 51, 54, 55, 259–60,
  379 n.44
Fox, Charles James, 165, 367 n.30
Frere, John Hookham, 136
Freud, Sigmund, 90, 91, 94, 225, 335,
  375 n.13
Fried, Michael, 390 n.91
Friendly Society, 61
Fugitive Pieces (Byron), 106
Furet, François, 165, 167

Galt, John, 113, 212, 382 n.72, 401 n.45
Gentry. *See* Aristocracy
Gerard, Alexander, 400 n.39
Giaour, The (Byron), 89, 107–13, 114–16,
  136, 141, 151, 190, 349, 382 n.78,
  386 n.33, 387 n.42, 390 n.90; death in,
  110–11; objects of desire in, 97–106
Gibbon, Edward, 169, 374 n.3
Giddens, Anthony, xxii, xxv, 154
Gifford, William, 29, 105, 146, 147,
  371 n.69
Gift, 19–20, 142, 169, 278
Girard, René, 266–67
Giraud, Nicolo, 59, 61
Girouard, Mark, 58, 378 n.31
Godelier, Maurice, 376 n.19
Godwin, William, 46, 47, 52, 286–87, 321
Goethe, Johann Wolfgang von, 212, 278, 279
Goldberg, Jonathan, 416 n.92
Goldsmith, Oliver, 286–87, 397 n.82
Graham, Peter W., 215
Grammar of the English Language, A (Cob-
  bett), 357
Gray, Thomas, 21
Grey de Ruthyn, Lord, 376 n.17

Hall, Jean, 385 n.27
Hamilton, Lady Emma, 374 n.9
Hanson, John, 383 n.86
Hanson, Newton, 355
Hartman, Geoffrey H., 374 n.9
Haslam, John, 28, 163–65, 166, 173, 180,
  182, 198, 395 n.51
Haydon, Benjamin, 386 n.31
Hazlitt, William, 110, 120, 141, 247–49,
  311–12, 325, 326, 327, 370 n.56,
  374 n.3, 396 n.66, 400 n.38

Heart of Midlothian, The (Scott), 414 n.51
Heber, Reginald, 296
Hebrew Melodies (Byron), 82
Hegel, Georg Wilhelm Friedrich, 158
Herder, J.G.E., 292, 338
Hertz, Neil, 377 n.21
Herzog, Don, 404 n.25
Hexter, J. H., 367 n.30
Highet, Gilbert, 378 n.36
History of Sexuality, The (Foucault), 54
History of Shorthand, A (Pitman), 201
Hobbes, Thomas, 243, 249, 415 n.57
Hobhouse, John Cam, 54, 59–60, 64, 72,
    87, 205, 206, 252, 359–60, 362–63,
    371 n.5, 377 n.21, 379 nn.43, 45,
    381 n.68, 382 nn.75, 83, 383 n.88,
    395 n.51, 396 n.66, 397 n.4, 397 n.5,
    398 nn.7, 8, 406 n.56, 408 n.24,
    416 n.93; on Byron's death, 356–57,
    401 n.42; on *Childe Harold's Pilgrimage*,
    194–201, 209; on *Don Juan*, 215–16,
    234, 276, 386 n.33
Hodgson, Francis, 61, 206, 371 n.4
Hoffmann, E.T.A., 335
Hohendahl, Peter, 172
Homosexuality, 378 n.34, 379 n.44; Byron's
    experience of, 376 n.17; Byron's notion
    of, 54–65; jargon of, 60–61
Hone, J. Ann, 165
Hone, William, 95–96, 132–35, 144,
    385 nn.23, 24
Honor, 11, 20, 41, 46, 72
Hoppner, Richard Belgrave, 355
Horkheimer, Max, 221
Horner, Francis, xv, 201, 366 nn.5, 19
Hours of Idleness (Byron), 14, 58, 66, 178,
    187, 191, 369 n.51, 391 n.10; Brougham's
    review of, 19, 20–22, 26–27, 28–29, 30–
    31, 35, 45–46, 264
Hume, David, 5, 33, 102, 154, 159–60,
    243–44, 333, 365 n.4, 375 n.12,
    393 n.27, 400 n.30; on causes, 113; on
    historical truth, 9; on luxury, 51; on
    power versus strength, 4; on social com-
    position, 243
Hunt, Leigh, 359, 360, 368 n.33
Hurd, Richard, 62, 220, 411 n.2
Hutcheon, Linda, 134
Hyde, Louis, 369 n.49
Hypothetical imperative, 44

Identification, 16–17, 60, 63, 244, 282, 293
Illustrations of Madness (Haslam), 163, 182
Imperatives. *See* Commands
Imperialism, 57, 61, 77, 186–90

Jacqueline (Rogers), 126
Jameson, Fredric, 91
Jeffrey, Francis, xv, xx, 41, 48, 102, 147,
    158, 168, 188; criticism of Byron, 172–
    81, 182–83, 296, 396 n.62
Johnson, Joseph, 144
Johnson, Samuel, 386 n.35, 391 n.3
Juan effect, 214–15, 348–49

Kant, Immanuel, 39–40, 42, 44, 406 n.46
Keats, John, xvii, 66, 411 n.56
Keats's Life of Allegory: The Origins of a Style
    (Levinson), 411 n.56
Kelsall, Malcolm, 194, 351 n.58
Kinnaird, Douglas, 146, 320, 333, 355, 356
Knight, G. Wilson, 84, 85
Knight, Payne, 386 n.31
Kraus, Rosalind, 370 n.54
Kristeva, Julia, 9–10, 122, 383 n.93

Lacan, Jacques, 61, 129, 131, 132, 302, 337,
    339, 340, 344
Laclau, Ernesto, 294
Lady of the Lake, The (Scott), 145, 374 n.3
Lalla Rookh (Moore), 145
Lamb, Lady Caroline, 136, 140, 388 n.56,
    401 n.45
Land, 10, 12, 241, 305–6, 312, 347, 352–53
Lang, Cecil, 342, 376 n.17
Laplanche, Jean, 225
Lara (Byron), 26, 89, 108; Byronic hero in,
    125–31, 136, 139, 141
Lavater, Johann Kaspar, 210
Law, 38–41, 84–88, 95–96, 132–35, 227–
    28, 237–42, 249, 251–52, 260–61, 313–
    14, 319–20, 334–38, 343–49
Lawrence, J., 367 n.27
Lawrence, William, 395 n.46
Leach, Sir John, 353
Lefort, Claude, 253, 351, 373 n.27,
    404 n.26, 410 n.37
Levin, Charles, 5, 107
Levinas, Emmanuel, 251
Levinson, Marjorie, 351, 352, 411 n.56
Lewis, C. S., 270
Lewis, James Henry, 203

Linebaugh, Peter, xii
Lipking, Lawrence, 405 n.36
Locke, John, 343, 353
Lockhart, John Gibson, 111–12, 145, 148, 391 n.8
Lockridge, Laurence, 183–84
Lodge, David, 398 n.15
Longman (publisher), 145
Lukàcs, Georg, 390 n.81
Lushington, Stephen, 83, 85, 86–87
Lyotard, Jean-François, 141, 201, 245, 248–49, 251, 306–7, 313–14, 318, 319, 327, 328, 329, 336, 350, 391 n.6, 394 n.37, 412 n.13

McCulloch, J. R., 291
McGann, Jerome J., xiii, xiv, 5, 23, 56, 214, 215, 351–52, 368 n.34, 371 n.4, 402 n.7, 408 n.19
McGill, Meredith, 414 n.48
McIntyre, Alasdair, xix
McKendrick, Neil, 366 n.11
McKeon, Michael, xix, 11, 367 n.30
Making of the English Working Class, The (Thompson), 32
Malkin, Benjamin Heath, 28
Malthus, Thomas, 291, 305, 346, 347, 404 n.24
Manfred (Byron), 156, 194, 382 n.83
Manning, Peter J., 72, 329, 381 n.62
Marcet, Jane, 303, 307, 412 n.11
Marchand, Leslie A., 35, 358, 391 n.10, 395 n.51, 406 n.1
Marglin, Stephen A., 121
Marino Faliero, Doge of Venice (Byron), 306; as a poetics of Byron's satire, 258–75
Marking, 41–42, 73, 109–10, 113, 189, 199–201, 210, 244, 248, 269, 273–74, 362–63
Marmion (Scott), 147
Marshall, William, 11
Martin, John, 295, 409 n.26
Martin, Philip W., 383 n.2, 384 n.15
Marx, Karl, 10
Matthews, Charles Skinner, 59–60, 62–64, 65, 70, 138–39, 358, 380 nn.48, 51
Matthews, James Tilly, 163–67, 174, 180, 182, 295, 344, 396 n.54
Mauss, Marcel, 5, 19
Maxims, 39–40, 43–44, 117, 194–95, 213, 327–28. *See also* Commands; Commonplace

Meisel, Martin, 223, 224
Memoirs of Sir Walter Scott (Lockhart), 111, 145, 391 n.8
Merchant of Venice, The (Shakespeare), 323–24
Methodism, 379 n.48
Mikalachki, Jody, 413 n.27
Milbanke, Annabella. *See* Byron, Lady
Milbanke, Ralph, 390 n.90
Millar, Andrew, 148
Milton, John, 270
Monastery, The (Scott), 124–25
Montesquieu, Baron de La Brède et de, 277
Moore, Charles, 46, 47
Moore, Doris Langley, 18, 80, 84–85, 140
Moore, Thomas, 15, 17, 22–23, 35, 41, 43, 81, 91, 145–46, 221, 244, 380 n.48, 384 n.6, 386 n.33, 401 n.41
Mouffe, Chantal, 294
Murray, John, xix, 5, 24, 95, 105–6, 130, 136, 143–45, 146, 147–48, 149, 170, 172, 173, 192, 216, 248, 252, 263, 265, 266, 320, 322–23, 359, 379 n.39, 386 n.33, 387 n.42, 391 nn.9, 10, 392 n.11, 403 n.15, 408 n.20; Murray circle, 146–47; as publisher of *Don Juan*, 238–39, 240, 354
Mysteries of Udolpho, The (Radcliffe), 155

Napoleon: abdication of, 127–30; Byron's depiction of, 168–72; Constant on, 397 n.79; as despot, 277–78; as hero, 396 n.66; as metaphor, 148, 376 n.16
Newton, Isaac, 365 n.5
Nice Work (Lodge), 398 n.15
Nietzsche, Friedrich, xvii, 13–14, 49, 368 n.34
Nobility. *See* Aristocracy
Noel, Lady, 358
Northanger Abbey (Austen), 155, 216, 378 n.29

Objectification, resistance to, xxii, xxv, 13, 215
Observations on Madness and Melancholy (Haslam), 28, 395 n.51
Oldmixon, Edward, 261
"On the Conversation of Lords" (Hazlitt), 247
On the Origin and Intention of Sacrifices (Hobhouse), 199
On Violence (Arendt), xvi

Oriental tales, 165, 230–31; Byronic hero in, 114–25; function of, for poets, 97–106; as representative of Otherness, 108–13
Origins of the English Novel, 1600–1740, The (McKeon), xix, 367 n.30

Paine, Thomas, 367 n.30, 374 n.5
Paradise Lost (Milton), 270
Paranoia, xxii, 61, 70, 82, 98, 163–67, 174
Parisina (Byron), 92
Parody, 94–96, 132–35, 138, 188
Patterson, Annabel, 383 n.89
Paulson, Ronald, 329, 413 n.32
Perkin, Harold, 18
Perkins, David, xiv
Phantoms, 26–27, 42, 107–9, 127, 194, 210–11, 320–21, 329–33, 339–45, 363
Piaget, Jean, 347
Pigott, Elizabeth, 57
Pitman, Sir Isaac, 201, 202, 203, 399 n.24
Pitt-Rivers, Julian, 38
Pocock, J.G.A., xvi, 11, 285, 305–6, 311, 312, 367 n.30
Polidori, John, 172
Political economy, xv–xvii, 4, 51–52, 303–4, 325–26, 347, 402 n.6, 411 n.58
Pope, Alexander, 260–62, 407 n.6
Porter, Roy, 165, 180
Practical Observations on Insanity (Cox), 173
Professionalism, 28–31, 103–4, 180, 203, 286–87
Prometheus Unbound (Shelley), 270–71
Psychoanalysis, 17–19, 90–91
Pursuits, doctrine of, 393 n.30

Quarterly Review, The, 29, 100, 102, 125, 146, 149, 162, 167, 203–4, 263, 296–97, 384 n.3
Quintilian, xxiv, 325, 326

Radcliffe, Ann, 155
Rand, Nicholas, 371 n.3
Randall, Mary Ann, 204–5
Reflections on the Revolution in France (Burke), 50, 205–6, 286, 330
Regulative hypothesis, 6–9, 203
Reid, Thomas, 373 n.3
Republicanism, 101, 195, 285–87, 305–6, 311, 332
Rethinking Modern Political Theory (Dunn), xxiv

Return to Camelot, The (Girouard), 58
Rhetoric as discursive art, 325–26
Ridge, John, 369 n.51
Rights of Man, The (Paine), 374 n.5
Roberts, William, 405 n.30
Robinson, Henry Crabb, 136–37
Rogers, Pat, 261
Rogers, Samuel, 101, 126
Rokeby (Scott), 145, 149
Romance, 24–27, 62–63, 85–86, 91
Romantic Ethic and the Spirit of Modern Consumerism, The (Campbell), 289
Romanticism, xxi, xxii, 120, 130–31, 294–95, 314, 346–47
Romantic poetry, perceptions of, xiii–xiv
Rorty, Richard, xxiii–xxiv, 177, 406 n.53
Rousseau, George S., 405 n.35
Rousseau, Jean Jacques, 15, 169, 375 n.12
"Ruined Cottage, The" (Wordsworth), 51
Russett, Margaret, 381 n.65

Sacrifice, xxi, 266–67, 279, 292–93, 298–99
Said, Edward, 108, 153, 347, 387 n.38, 393 n.24
St. Clair, William, 61, 376 n.19
Sardanapalus (Byron), 266, 306; anachronism in, 295–99; despotism in, 278–85; eighteenth-century background for, 285–87; political economy of sex in, 287–95; reviews of, 295–98
Satire, 407 n.6, 408 n.17; in *Don Juan*, 309–11. See also *Marino Faliero, Doge of Venice*
Satirist, The, 35, 136, 387 n.42
Schlegel, Friedrich, 295
Scott, Sir Walter, xv, xix, 80, 145–46, 147, 148, 155, 201–2, 374 n.3, 374 n.9, 378 n.31, 380 n.48, 390 n.91, 411 n.65, 414 n.51; reaction of, to Napoleon's abdication, 127–28, 129–30; realism of, 111–13, 124–25; on Waterloo, 167–68
Sedgwick, Eve Kosofsky, 60, 385 n.27
Sedley, Sir Charles, 36, 37
Sennett, Richard, 275
Seriality in Byron's poetry and career, 5–6, 89–90
Serres, Michel, 5, 219, 302, 304, 353
Shadwell, Mr., 239, 240, 353
Shakespeare, William, 131, 132, 371 n.66
Shelley, Mary, 360
Shelley, Percy Bysshe, 64–65, 270–71, 360, 398 n.12, 415 n.56

Shorthand, 201–7, 357, 399 n.24, 399 n.28, 400 n.30
Siege of Corinth, The (Byron), 93
Signature, 113, 115–16, 141, 182, 358–63
Sincerity and Authenticity (Trilling), xiii
Sincerity as criterion for excellence, xiii–xiv
"Sketch, A" (Byron), 152
Sleep and Poetry (Keats), xvii
Smiles, Samuel, 103
Smith, Adam, 29, 93, 120, 131, 137, 275–76, 290, 346
Smith, Robertson, 399 n.18
Social Contract (Rousseau), 15
Southey, Robert, 97, 161, 218, 238, 241, 265, 402 n.7
Spectator, The, 6–7, 104, 132, 373 n.3
Spenser, Edmund, 65, 137–38, 411 n.2
Spenserian stanza, 75–76, 181, 188
"Spirit of Conquest and Usurpation and Their Relation to European Civilization, The" (Constant), 276–77
Stanfield, James Field, 393 n.30
Steffan, Truman Guy, 254, 255–56
Stendhal, 159, 161, 401 n.46
Stenograph, 274. *See also* Shorthand
Stewart, Dugald, 29
Strength: in Byron's poetry, xvii–xviii, 3–5, 63–65, 214–15, 299; as criterion for excellence, xiii, xiv; definitions of, xv–xvi; as distinguished from power, 4–5; ethical dimension of, 215; and sexual difference, 49–50, 69
Swift, Jonathan, 262
Swinburne, Algernon, xiii, xiv
Symbolic Illustrations of the History of England (Randall), 204–5
System of Professions, The (Abbott), 29

Task, The (Cowper), 51
Textuality, 231–33, 302
Thalaba, the Destroyer (Southey), 97
Theatrical Inquisitor, 136, 139–40
Theory of Moral Sentiments, The (Smith), 275
Thompson, E. P., 19, 32
Thompson, James R., 416 n.87
Thompson, John B., 171, 172

Thornton, Henry, 366 n.19
Thrale, Hester, 398 n.12
Tiro, 201
Tocqueville, Alexis de, 404 n.26
"To Ianthe" (Byron), 73, 78
"To Romance" (Byron), 24, 27, 152
Treatise of Human Nature (Hume), 154
Trelawny, William, 360
Trilling, Lionel, xiii, xiv
Turner, Sharon, 238–39, 240
Two Foscari, The (Byron), 189

Value, market, 61–62, 145–46, 158, 199–200
Vampire (Polidori), 172
Venice, Italy, as depicted by Byron, 185–94. See also *Marino Faliero, Doge of Venice*
Vicar of Wakefield, The (Goldsmith), 286–87
Vindication of the Rights of Woman (Wollstonecraft), 49–50
Voltaire, 169

Walker, Violet W., 372 n.25
Warburton, William, 392 n.11
Waterloo. *See* Napoleon
Waterloo (Webster), 162
Wat Tyler (Southey), 238
Waverley (Scott), 131, 414 n.51
Weber, Max, xvii
Webster, J. Wedderburn, 162–63, 167
Webster, Lady Frances Wedderburn, 105, 106, 107, 167
Wheatley, Kim, 165
Williams, Edward, 360
Williams, Raymond, 352
Willis, Edmund, 399 n.24
Wilson, John, 157, 165, 188, 276, 284, 331, 388 n.63
Wolfson, Susan J., 411 n.57
Wollstonecraft, Mary, 160–61, 373 n.3, 374 n.5, 375 n.13, 381 n.68; on male dominance, 49–52, 69, 82, 93
Wordsworth, William, 51, 76, 177, 246, 346, 402 n.6

Young, Edward, 86